Handbook of Research on Current Trends in Cybersecurity and Educational Technology

Remberto Jimenez
New Jersey City University, USA

Veronica E. O'Neill
New Jersey City University, USA

IGI Global
PUBLISHER of TIMELY KNOWLEDGE

A volume in the Advances in Educational Technologies and Instructional Design (AETID) Book Series

Published in the United States of America by
IGI Global
Information Science Reference (an imprint of IGI Global)
701 E. Chocolate Avenue
Hershey PA, USA 17033
Tel: 717-533-8845
Fax: 717-533-8661
E-mail: cust@igi-global.com
Web site: http://www.igi-global.com

Library of Congress Cataloging-in-Publication Data

Names: Jimenez, Remberto, 1974- editor. | O'Neill, Veronica, 1958- editor.
Title: Handbook of research on current trends in cybersecurity and educational technology / Remberto Jimenez and Veronica O'Neill, editors.
Description: Hershey, PA : Information Science Reference, [2023] | Includes bibliographical references and index. | Summary: "With educational technology constantly changing, this is a good resource to help showcase some of the most recent trends and ideas that could play a major role in supporting both current and future learners, especially highlighting the importance of vigilance with respect to cybersecurity"-- Provided by publisher.
Identifiers: LCCN 2022035932 (print) | LCCN 2022035933 (ebook) | ISBN 9781668460924 (h/c) | ISBN 9781668460948 (ebook)
Subjects: LCSH: Educational innovations. | Distance education. | Web-based instruction--Security measures. | Computer conferencing in education--Security measures. | Internet and children--Security measures. | Computer security.
Classification: LCC LB1027 .H3351 2023 (print) | LCC LB1027 (ebook) | DDC 371.33/4--dc23/eng/20220824
LC record available at https://lccn.loc.gov/2022035932
LC ebook record available at https://lccn.loc.gov/2022035933

This book is published in the IGI Global book series Advances in Educational Technologies and Instructional Design (AE-TID) (ISSN: 2326-8905; eISSN: 2326-8913)

British Cataloguing in Publication Data
A Cataloguing in Publication record for this book is available from the British Library.

For electronic access to this publication, please contact: eresources@igi-global.com.

Advances in Educational Technologies and Instructional Design (AETID) Book Series

Lawrence A. Tomei
Robert Morris University, USA

ISSN:2326-8905
EISSN:2326-8913

Mission

Education has undergone, and continues to undergo, immense changes in the way it is enacted and distributed to both child and adult learners. In modern education, the traditional classroom learning experience has evolved to include technological resources and to provide online classroom opportunities to students of all ages regardless of their geographical locations. From distance education, Massive-Open-Online-Courses (MOOCs), and electronic tablets in the classroom, technology is now an integral part of learning and is also affecting the way educators communicate information to students.

The **Advances in Educational Technologies & Instructional Design (AETID) Book Series** explores new research and theories for facilitating learning and improving educational performance utilizing technological processes and resources. The series examines technologies that can be integrated into K-12 classrooms to improve skills and learning abilities in all subjects including STEM education and language learning. Additionally, it studies the emergence of fully online classrooms for young and adult learners alike, and the communication and accountability challenges that can arise. Trending topics that are covered include adaptive learning, game-based learning, virtual school environments, and social media effects. School administrators, educators, academicians, researchers, and students will find this series to be an excellent resource for the effective design and implementation of learning technologies in their classes.

Coverage

- Instructional Design
- Virtual School Environments
- Social Media Effects on Education
- Web 2.0 and Education
- K-12 Educational Technologies
- Collaboration Tools
- Online Media in Classrooms
- Digital Divide in Education
- Higher Education Technologies
- Adaptive Learning

IGI Global is currently accepting manuscripts for publication within this series. To submit a proposal for a volume in this series, please contact our Acquisition Editors at Acquisitions@igi-global.com or visit: http://www.igi-global.com/publish/.

The Advances in Educational Technologies and Instructional Design (AETID) Book Series (ISSN 2326-8905) is published by IGI Global, 701 E. Chocolate Avenue, Hershey, PA 17033-1240, USA, www.igi-global.com. This series is composed of titles available for purchase individually; each title is edited to be contextually exclusive from any other title within the series. For pricing and ordering information please visit http://www.igi-global.com/book-series/advances-educational-technologies-instructional-design/73678. Postmaster: Send all address changes to above address.

Titles in this Series

For a list of additional titles in this series, please visit: http://www.igi-global.com/book-series/advances-educational-technologies-instructional-design/73678

Promoting Diversity, Equity, and Inclusion in Language Learning Environments
Karina Becerra-Murillo (Jurupa Unified School District, USA & American College of Education, USA) and Josefina F. Gámez (Jurupa Unified School District, USA)
Information Science Reference • © 2023 • 300pp • H/C (ISBN: 9781668436325) • US $215.00

Engaging Students With Disabilities in Remote Learning Environments
Manina Urgolo Huckvale (William Paterson University, USA) and Kelly McNeal (William Paterson University, USA)
Information Science Reference • © 2023 • 305pp • H/C (ISBN: 9781668455036) • US $215.00

Using Assistive Technology for Inclusive Learning in K-12 Classrooms
Jeremy Bell (University of Louisiana at Monroe, USA) and Timothy Gifford (Movia Robotics Inc, USA)
Information Science Reference • © 2023 • 300pp • H/C (ISBN: 9781668464243) • US $215.00

Handbook of Research on Interdisciplinarity Between Science and Mathematics in Education
Bento Cavadas (Lusófona University, Portugal & Polytechnic Institute of Santarém, Portugal) and Neusa Branco (Polytechnic Institute of Santarém, Portugal & CIAC, Algarve University, Portugal)
Information Science Reference • © 2023 • 418pp • H/C (ISBN: 9781668457658) • US $270.00

Handbook of Research on Perspectives in Foreign Language Assessment
Dinçay Köksal (Çanakkale 18 Mart University, Turkey) Nurdan Kavaklı (Izmir Demokrasi University, Turkey) and Sezen Arslan (Van Yuzuncu Yil University, Turkey)
Information Science Reference • © 2023 • 400pp • H/C (ISBN: 9781668456606) • US $270.00

Practices That Promote Innovation for Talented Students
Julia Nyberg (Purdue University Global, USA) and Jessica Manzone (University of Southern California, USA)
Information Science Reference • © 2023 • 300pp • H/C (ISBN: 9781668458068) • US $215.00

Strategies for Promoting Independence and Literacy for Deaf Learners With Disabilities
Nena Raschelle Neild (Ball State University, USA) and Patrick Joseph Graham (Rochester Institute of Technology, USA)
Information Science Reference • © 2023 • 320pp • H/C (ISBN: 9781668458396) • US $215.00

IGI Global
PUBLISHER of TIMELY KNOWLEDGE

701 East Chocolate Avenue, Hershey, PA 17033, USA
Tel: 717-533-8845 x100 • Fax: 717-533-8661
E-Mail: cust@igi-global.com • www.igi-global.com

List of Contributors

Table of Contents

Detailed Table of Contents

Cybersecurity has become increasingly important in all industries. Universities are developing academic programs in cybersecurity education in response to the demand for professionals with expertise in application areas of cybersecurity. Education should help students to deal with complex cybersecurity problems. We must ensure that cybersecurity education has a balance between breadth and depth, which integrates science, technology, management, and culture. When looking at cybersecurity education from a breadth perspective, it should provide the students with an understanding of the foundations of various components. Nevertheless, the debate can go further when taking into consideration the legal restrictions imposed on the subject. Law advocates to regulate and give a sense of order and peace for avoiding plausible controversies. Consequently, it seeks to regulate human behaviors for ensuring order, and in this case, it does so by stablishing regulations towards privacy and cybersecurity.

The software-defined network (SDN) has recently developed as a network paradigm due to its high network programmability and flexibility, which can overcome the difficulty in traditional networks by detaching the control plane from the data plane. Following the controller's decision in the control plane, the data plane will transfer the packets. This unified administration will make it possible to see the network architecture as a whole in an abstract way. The controller is exposed to a significant threat if control is lost due to its centralised structure. Data plane resources are attacked by the attacker by focusing on switches that support OpenFlow. DDoS attacks damage network performance by overloading the SDN

In the fast-changing global environment, educational apps are widely used with hybrid and multi-cloud environments and intelligent devices. They offer various society services such as quality data for monitoring and prediction skills with protection and reliability. Smart learning systems pose a unique security risk because many people access and operate different techniques simultaneously over multiple networks. As a result, cybercrime has been brought about by the internet and the availability of intelligent devices. The security of online learning systems has received significant consideration. Because today's creative learning is open, distributed, and networked, ensuring that authorized users only have access to the appropriate data at the right time is a considerable challenge. The current security practices are outdated; hence, this chapter examines cyber-attacks on smart learning systems from their standard architecture and security requirements and proposes a cyber security model for educational operations from a multi/hybrid cloud-based learning environment.

The chapter aims to discuss how people interested in incorporating different aspects of cyber security into the curriculum in higher education, corporate learning, and non-traditional learning environments can do so. Due to the COVID-19 outbreak, more businesses are switching to online platforms, which has resulted in a dramatic spike in the need for cybersecurity controls. The objective is to share how the immense impact of educational technology (ED Tech) in the age of COVID-19 lockdown is digitally focused on educational content and the basic need to be flexible and adaptable for students. Overall, this chapter proposes that the need for cyber security is becoming a more crucial facet of life. So, the report by intelligence system can examine threats and the platforms/applications for processing data can be examined. Cyber ED Tech protects against a variety of attacks, including cloud security breaches, denial of service (DoS), malware, zoombombing, password policy violations, and so on.

Our society exists in a 21st century digital world, reliant on technology to function. Daily lives are reliant on the technological functions of the modern world, and often leave us vulnerable to evolving cyber attacks globally. Staying ahead of cyber criminals is a difficult task, but one of the most important defenses we have in maintaining online safety. It is essential to develop students to not only be aware of how to keep themselves safe in a digital world, but also to be creative innovators to help thwart criminal attempts online. Through the implementation of STEAM education, students can be exposed to developing new collaborative and creative skills that can help inspire future computer scientists and policymakers tasked with battling the frontier of cybersecurity.

Smart classrooms are created by using smart environments equipped with various software and hardware devices and applications. The smart classroom is the integration of advanced teaching technologies into the classroom environment beyond the traditional classroom environment in order to contribute to the development of the student's learning ability and participation in the lesson. In general, the concept of the smart classroom will be discussed in this chapter from two aspects: (1) physical and (2) instructional. These two aspects are important in terms of showing how learning processes are affected in terms of educational technologies. This chapter also includes the outputs and experiences of the ongoing technology-enriched smart classroom project supported by a scientific research fund of Ege University.

Today, smartphones have become a very popular learning tool. More specifically, educators have been using smartphones to enhance their teaching and students' learning. Using smartphones, educators can ensure flexible course delivery and provide learners access to online learning resources. In this study, the author examines how smartphones can be used as an effective learning tool for distance education. This study utilized a survey of university students in Karachi, Pakistan to find the effects of using smartphones in their learning activities and what factors inhibit their use of smartphones in their learning.

Safe use of media sources is a part of curriculums for all students, including those with intellectual disabilities. Educators are promoting cyber-wellness through social emotional learning (SEL) incorporated with digital and media literacy skills. When students are prepared to face risky online interactions, they are more equipped to safely navigate dangers encountered online. Students with intellectual disabilities may interact safely in virtual settings either for social activities, learning, or employment when prepared with appropriate functional skills and provided accessible methods and tools. Educators utilizing proven instructional strategies can support students with intellectual disabilities as they access the internet. Students' awareness of potential online dangers along with the development of digital literacy skills can motivate them to be positive online risk takers.

The placement of students with disabilities in the inclusion setting alongside their peers has increased in recent years due to a variety of federal mandates. Technology has become an important component of this learning experience since digital tools and resources can provide students with support while accessing the grade-level curriculum. This chapter addresses the various ways that technology can be utilized in the inclusion classroom, including assistive technology, mainstream educational technologies, and accessible digital resources. The existing research tends to focus on how specific tools can be integrated, but this chapter synthesizes this information to show educators how technology can be leveraged to support all learners in the classroom. The intent of this chapter is to share research-supported strategies for making classrooms more inclusive using available technologies.

Asynchronous and synchronous modes of online communication utilizing a variety of technology applications provide students with opportunities to engage in both student-to-student and team discourse. Through experiential and project-based learning, students develop skills in digital literacy, virtual teamwork, empathy, and cross-cultural communication—all requisite 21st century skills for employment. The authors will showcase their virtual exchange collaborations utilizing the latest educational tech tools. Challenges, considerations, and opportunities inherent in developing and delivering virtual exchange projects plus student reflections will be shared. Teaching strategies that embrace a diversity, inclusion, equity, and social justice learning environment will be discussed.

This chapter provides an overview of a relative newcomer to education at all levels, esports. Esports has become very popular in recent years, and it is important for educators to understand the issues surrounding this activity, as well as the benefits to student participants with respect to the experience itself and to potential careers in the field. A brief history is provided and the issues surrounding esports in education are examined. Resources are provided relevant to starting an esports program at all levels: collegiate, secondary school, and middle school.

This chapter provides context for teacher preparation programs to adjust their approach based on the lessons learned from emergency remote and hybrid instruction necessitated by the COVID-19 pandemic. This research makes reference to the TPACK framework and its impact on educator training and is framed on Bandura's theory of self-efficacy. A list of post-pandemic skills that teachers need is discussed,

Preface

INTRODUCTION

Technology is everywhere. The ubiquitous nature of technology has changed the way we learn, work, and conduct our personal lives. Technology has impacted various social, ideological, political, educational/academic, and work-related systems around the world (The Emirates Center for Strategic Studies and Research, 2015). Technology affords different avenues to complete a task, make money, or even connect with family. One such technology that has revolutionized the way we work and connect with others is the internet.

The advent of the internet has broadened our access to ideas and information from across the globe, regardless of time or location. Through a plethora of devices, access to the internet has enabled various digital technologies to emerge over the last three decades that have become ubiquitous. Whether it's the use of social media platforms, Google products, or even online gaming, the internet has played a role in making these resources commonplace and easily accessible. We also can't forget about the plethora of devices where we can access information. We can check our emails through our smart phones, receive SMS text messages from a smart watch, and even record our heartbeat and steps taken through variety of devices that make up the "internet of things."

We can use these devices to gain insights, learn, communicate, and keep in contact with family and friends. We can use these devices for work purposes, for school, or personal goals and endeavors. Yet, like anything else, there are considerations and precautions that must be considered in terms of the safety and privacy of one's data. The websites that are visited, the passwords to bank accounts, and even one's own medical information could easily fall into the wrong hands if these devices and systems are not properly secured from an information technology perspective. However, that is one side of the problem. The other side of the problem is on the end user who connects to unknown Wi-Fi-networks, enters their information on a phishing site, or responds to email and text scams.

That is why educating oneself on acceptable technology use and cyber security prevention is key to navigating our current world. Whether you are the information technologist in an organization, a school administrator, or anyone that wants to understand the privacy and security risks that come with technology and internet use, learning about cybersecurity is everyone's business.

For those looking to grow their knowledge and skills for a career change, for the student that needs accommodations to help in their learning, or for the life-long leaner who wants to expand their knowledge on a topic, understanding what educational technologies are available is key. For teachers, professors, instructional designers, corporate learning leaders, and human resource leaders, understanding what educational technology is available for learner and employee development is important to address organizational learning needs and requirements. Beyond learning the technology, and how to use it safely and educating oneself on how to best mitigate privacy or security concerns.

This is the reason that we proposed the creation of this book. We wanted to educate people on current cyber security and educational technology trends. We want to empower scholars, technicians, to the most laymen of individuals on the ideas of cybersecurity, educational technology, and in the areas where these topics intersect. As we approach the end of the first quarter of the twenty-first century, we must find new ways to better ourselves by learning new ideas and new ways of thinking. We need to learn how to create better experiences and safer online environments for all. Finally, we need to teach as many people as possible the ways to manage and conduct themselves online to further support safer online spaces and environments. Although we can't solve every single issue or problem, we hope that the ideas found in this book will give readers a new set of perspectives on the topics of cyber security and educational technology.

OVERARCHING CONCEPTS

One area that has benefitted from the proliferation of technology and internet ubiquity is the learning profession. Specifically, the use of educational technologies to support learning in schools, for individual and life-long learning, or any workplace that looks to upskill their employee base. Educational technology involves the disciplined application of knowledge for the purpose of improving learning, instruction and/or performance (Spector, 2015, p. 10). Another way of looking at educational technology is to think of it as the myriad tools, resources, and processes that support learners in their knowledge-creating and skill-enhancing endeavors.

Educational technology goes beyond the use of a computer, app, or the manipulation of a piece of code. It is the conduit through which learners engage in meaningful knowledge and skill building activities, either on their own, in-person, or collaboratively through any number of computer-mediated environments. It is the medium that enables both active engagement, collaboration, and exploration of a topic at any time or any place. Educational technology can be found everywhere. Yet, it is only as useful as the instructional and pedagogical strategies that are being supported through the available technology. Technology by itself is neither empowering nor useful. It is the intention of what we do with it and how we use it that can make a difference.

The use of such educational technologies in the learning profession allows for near instant access to valuable resources such as e-books, podcasts, simulations, and apps. These educational technologies allow for learners to engage with content in different ways, while also supporting the learning goals and objectives provided by a teacher, institution, or corporate learning professional. The COVID-19 pandemic saw many schools around the world move to hybrid and online learning models to support their students. Both local and global corporations pushed many formerly face-to-face learning activities to online webinars or e-learning modules. While different organizations and institutional bodies benefitted, so did the individual life-long learner thanks in part to the creation of podcasts, webinars, and e-books. In short, education as an industry, and as an organizational function, has benefited from the ever-evolving tools and resources that technological advances can provide.

For every benefit that internet access affords us, there are also risks that are part of any ubiquitous resource. With this increased access to resources across the internet, the risk of encountering bad actors who are attempting to access user personal data, or organizational information increases. In the United

States, cyber security has been emerged as one of the top national security issues for the 21st century. Cyber security can be seen as a transboundary phenomenon that occurs across multiple sectors, both private and public, in complex and highly politicized ways (Carr & Lesniewska, 2020). Cyber security efforts evolve as the technology of the day is used for personal or organizational purposes.

However, just because a certain technology is new and perceived to be more secure, it doesn't make the technology immune to attack by bad actors. Cyber criminals push the boundaries to see what new ways they can attack and target their victims. For example, although cyber-attacks decreased in 2021, ransomware attacks increased year over year by 15.4% for US K-12 public schools (Wells, 2022). Sutton (2017) describes how many of the services and applications that that use may be far less secure than we think. Credit card information, email addresses, and other critical information can be in the hands of hackers, or other dark agents that are using such personal information for more nefarious actions. Even current countermeasures against cybersecurity attacks have their limitations and may be vulnerable to waves of attacks (El-Alfy et al., 2019). Issues of privacy and security emerge as well as potential financial and credibility losses that can come from such attacks.

Cybersecurity and educational technology are inextricably linked as more individuals and organizations create digital footprints across the world-wide-web. We all need to consider the tools that we are using and apply sound digital citizenship practices to mitigate the damage that can occur from bad actors on the world stage. Twenty-first century skills, such as digital citizenship offer us the strategies to consider and hopefully minimize what information we are disclosing every time we log on to the internet, browse a website, or check our social media accounts. Organizations large and small need to consider new ways of strengthening their efforts to stop malicious attacks, including DDoS attacks and phishing attempts.

Therefore, cybersecurity is an area of study that is not just in the purview of information technology experts or government agencies, but it is an area that anyone with internet access, or digital personas, needs to understand as we move further in the 21st century. As the cybersecurity profession develops new methodologies to enhance networks and limit attacks, so must the individual be versed in taking the preventative actions to control their information and use sound digital citizenship strategies. As we look to the future, the use of educational technologies will only continue to grow over time. At the same time, we must also realize that the challenges and complexity of cybersecurity will also increase over time as well. Therefore, educating anyone that uses the internet to understand how to be safe online is a priority across all sectors. In addition, informing learners of all ages on the educational technologies available, and how they can be used in a safe and secure way, is also needed as well. Technology use will only continue as more tools are introduced into the landscape of our world. As these new tools emerge, so too will the potential for new forms of malicious attacks. Education is the best weapon to help us prepare for what is coming and how we can best address cybersecurity and educational technology needs for our society.

This book will explore the spectrum of challenges and opportunities that exist in the areas of both cybersecurity and educational technology respectively. This can include anyone teaching and or learning in K-12, to higher education, to professional development, and lifelong learning. It also includes the businessperson in China, the economist in India, the student in Brazil, or the engineer in Germany. We all must understand the current trends and issues that exist in the world that makes up cyber security and educational technology. As the world continues to evolve and deal with the current events of the day, protecting our cyber footprint, and educating ourselves on the tools and resources available to further our own learning, will also continue as well.

This book was written for any instructor, researcher, student, or any lifelong learner interested in where the fields of educational technology and cybersecurity are going. It is appropriate for K-12, higher education, corporate learning, or non-traditional learning environments. This book is for anyone who is interested in how they could drive learning through the mediated use of technology. It is also for anyone who is interested in understanding more about current cybersecurity strategies and tactics. This book is also for those who are at the intersection of educational technology and cybersecurity and want to understand the implications when a new technology is introduced to support the learning function.

ORGANIZATION OF THE BOOK

The book is organized into 21 chapters that cover various issues and trends across the cybersecurity and educational technology disciplines. Each of the authors shared their research and perspectives that hopefully will give the reader some new ideas to consider as the fields of cybersecurity and educational technology continue their evolution. A brief description of each of the chapters is listed below.

Chapter 1 is "Reimaging Cybersecurity in Educational Practices: An International Case Study." Authors Nicole Simon, of SUNY Nassau Community College in the United States, and José Luis Jiménez and Daniel Strocchia, of Universidad Cathólica Andres Béllo in Venezuela, discuss the importance of cybersecurity studies in higher education. All industries are susceptible to attacks, which have grown in complexity and prevalence in recent years. The authors examine the requirements for university study in this discipline, and the need for balance between cybersecurity and personal privacy.

In Chapter 2, "Detection of DDoS Attack Using Machine Learning Techniques in Software-Defined Networking," authors K. Muthamil Sudar, Ruba Soundar Kathavarayan and P. Vinoth of Mepco Schlenk Engineering College in India, and P. Nagaraj and V. Muneeswarah of Kalasalingam Academy of Research and Education, also in India, discuss a new way of controlling networks not within individual devices, but centralized within the network. When the control is in individual devices, the network is vulnerable to attack on any one of the devices, which can effectively shut down the entire operation. The authors propose a method of detecting these attacks so they can be thwarted.

Chapter 3, "Incidence Response, Disaster Recovery, and Business Continuity Planning: Their Role in an Institution's Risk Management Plan," was authored by Peter J. McAliney and Guy J. Albertini, of Rutgers University – Camden, and Shannon D. Ramsaywak, of Nathaniel Rand, Inc. As advances are made in educational technology, institutions are increasing their reliance on third-party products, such as learning management systems and open educational resources. While these products can broaden access to quality educational resources, they can also increase the institution's vulnerability to outside attack. Therefore, it is essential that institutions develop robust Incidence Response and Disaster Recovery procedures.

In Chapter 4, "New Identification of Political Conflict and the Asymmetric Threat Phenomenon on the Example of Cyber Warfare," author Nika Chitadze of International Black Sea University in Georgia discusses the impact of the new security challenges that threaten today's computer systems. The impacts of these non-traditional security threats on human, national, and environmental security are examined.

In Chapter 5, "The Relationship Between Cybersecurity and Public Health," Rita Komalasari of YARSI University in Jakarta, Indonesia examines the factors which influence public health programs with respect to cybersecurity. A particular focus was protection against malware, and the need for international government involvement to secure public health systems. A recommendation to form a World Cyber Health Organization is promoted to enhance protection of public health systems worldwide.

In Chapter 6, "Unified Cybersecurity Data Analytical Model for Smart Learning Operations", authors Palanivel Kuppusamy and Suresh Joseph K, of Pondicherry University in India, discuss the need to secure educational applications from the threat of cybercriminals. They argue that the current security of educational systems is outdated and leaves the systems vulnerable to attack. They provide recommendations for improving security across educational applications.

In Chapter 7, "Integrating Ed Tech into the Curriculum Cybersecurity," V. Deepa, B. Sivakumar, G.L. Swathi Mirthika and K. Abinaya, of SRM Institute of Science and Technology in Chennai, India, examine how cybersecurity can be integrated into the curriculum in higher education, corporate learning, and non-traditional learning environments. The COVID-19 pandemic brought the need for cybersecurity to the forefront, as remote learning became ubiquitous. The authors discuss the importance of defending educational systems against various cyber-attacks

In Chapter 8, Dana Smerda-Mason, of New Jersey City University in the United States, discusses the importance of a strong STEAM (Science, Technology, Engineering, the Arts, and Mathematics) education in "Integration of STEAM Education Supports the Future of Cybersecurity." A strong STEAM education makes students more aware of how to protect themselves from cyberattacks, and also prepares the next generation of cybersecurity professionals to be effective in the evolving world of cybercrime.

In Chapter 9, "The Importance of the Use of Technology in the Education of Refugee Populations in Sub-Saharan Africa in the Digital Age," author Sedar Pougaza, of Stockton State College and New Jersey City University, brings a global perspective to his research. He has lived and worked in the Ivory Coast, China, and several universities in the United States. His current research revolves around the use of technology to support the education of refugee populations in Sub-Saharan Africa, especially in the Central African Republic. His personal experiences in the area, including multiple trips to the area to support this research, lead to many insights on the importance to technology to these student populations.

In Chapter 10, author Carol Munn of New Jersey City University explores "Computational Thinking, 21st Century Skills, and Robotics." This topic combines children's love of playing with robots with the advanced thinking and mathematical skills needed to program a robot. Students are actively learning in a fun and engaging environment.

In Chapter 11, "Using Hybrid Gamification to Build Community and Self-Efficacy Among Diverse University STEM Students," is authored by Karen J. Cotter of New Jersey City University. There are many opportunities for careers in STEM fields as technology evolves and becomes more ubiquitous. However, many of these jobs are vacant. In higher education, there is a lack of diversity in students studying STEM subjects. Many institutions have attempted to correct this imbalance by hosting STEM Bridge programs, which prepare incoming students for STEM studies, and provides a support system throughout their college years. This chapter focuses on an innovative program at one university which utilizes a hybrid gamification strategy to increase a sense of community in these students and create support systems to assist in persistence throughout their university years.

In Chapter 12, authors Firat Sarsar, Özge Andiç Çakir, Gülben Çaliş, Beril Ceylan, Alev Ateş-Çobanoğlu, Orhan Dağdeviren, and Mehmet Emin Kaval, of Ege University in Turkey, explore "The Effects of a Technology-Enriched Classroom on Students' Learning: The Smart Classroom Model." This model entails the integration of teaching technology into the classroom, with the goal of enhancing student learning and engagement. The chapter incorporates actual experiences from the Smart Classroom initiative at Ege University to support its findings.

In Chapter 13, Amin Manzoor, of the Karachi Institute of Business and Leadership in Karachi, Pakistan, brings us "Using Smart Phones as Educational Technology to Promote Effective Learning."

Smartphones have become a ubiquitous part of everyday life, and educators have discovered that they can be used effectively to enhance teaching and learning. A study of students in Pakistan is utilized to illustrate their perspectives about learning enhanced with smartphones.

In Chapter 14, Patricia Holzman and Wendy Thompson, both of A. Harry Moore School, New Jersey City University, authored "Digital Literacy for Students With Intellectual Disabilities." The authors describe the philosophy of the school with regard to using the Internet to enable students with intellectual disabilities safely. These skills can help students interact socially and prepare them for future employment.

Chapter 15, "Making Learning Environments More Inclusive for All Students With Educational Technology," was authored by Kathryn Nieves Licwinko of Wayne Township Public Schools. Many students with disabilities are now placed in inclusion settings due to recent federal regulations. Technology can be an important tool to allow these students to fully engage in the curriculum. The use of this technology benefits all students in these classrooms, not just the students with disabilities.

In Chapter 16, authors Patricia Szobonya and Catherine Roche, both of SUNY Rockland Community College in New York, describe an innovative virtual exchange experience. Their students interact with a partner class in another country, to devise solutions for problems that are common to both groups. This allows them to develop real relationships, and a deeper appreciation of culture and social justice.

In Chapter 17, author Veronica O'Neill of New Jersey City University in the United States wrote "Esports in Education: An Overview." In this chapter the author provides an overview of the esports industry, as it gains importance in the education sector. While once pioneered in colleges and universities, the activity is now found in high schools and middle schools. The chapter details the history of the esports movement, as well as some of the advantages and challenges involved in playing esports at all levels. Suggestions and resources are included to help educators who are considering establishing an esports program for their students.

Chapter 18, "What's Next for Teacher Preparation Programs?" was contributed by author Joanna Antoniou, from Passaic Public Schools, in New Jersey. In this work, the changes in preservice teacher education programs that were brought into focus during the COVID-19 pandemic are examined. It is not enough to teach how to use technology; the technology must be used in a way that enhances student understanding and engagement. The TPACK framework is utilized throughout the chapter as a framework for analysis.

Chapter 19, "Case Studies in Remote Living and Remote Learning," was authored by Cari Marks, an educator in Virginia, and Christopher Shamburg, New Jersey City University. The chapter explores the impact of the COVID-19 pandemic on families living in remote areas of Appalachia. The case study method is used to explore the lives of four families as they the challenges of living and learning during the pandemic.

In Chapter 20, the topic of "Blended Learning in Higher Education" is examined; the chapter was authored by İbrahim Halil Özdemir and Firat Sarsar of Ege University and Steve W. Harmon, of Georgia Institute of Technology. While blended learning has been used in higher education for several years, the advent of COVID-19 brought the technique to the forefront of educational approaches. Blended learning is embraced by learners, teachers and educational institutions as an effective technique for higher education.

In Chapter 21, "Workplace Learning and Learning Knowledge and Content Strategy," the authors, Remberto Jimenez, and Veronica O'Neill, from New Jersey City University, present the notion of a learning knowledge and content strategy to support workplace learning and employee retention. Although this is seen as an outgrowth of the impact felt by the "great resignation," it is considered a strategy that will help shift the learning function to the next level. The authors offer a framework to support organizational needs through a holistic learning and development content strategy. The authors suggest how such a framework can be implemented using a variety of content resources that can be internally made, purchased, or obtained through "free" platforms on the internet.

CONCLUSION

The preceding chapters provide key insights and concepts that are universal to anyone who accesses the internet to perform even the most minute of functions. Regardless of whether you are a student, a lifelong learner, a corporate analyst, or prime minister, learning safe cyber security-based practices and concepts are integral to current and future internet use. For those looking to drive their own learning, or to support the learning function for others, understanding the various ways that technology can be used, safely and securely is of great importance. Together, the topics of cybersecurity and educational technology are, and will continue to be topics of interest for anyone that has an internet connected device. The chapters in this book will add to the body of literature across these two dynamic fields and offer insights and new pathways to finding solutions.

Remberto Jimenez
New Jersey City University, USA

Veronica E. O'Neill
New Jersey City University, USA

REFERENCES

Carr, M., & Lesniewska, F. (2020). Internet of Things, cybersecurity and governing wicked problems: Learning from climate change governance. *International Relations*, *34*(3), 391–412. doi:10.1177/0047117820948247

Cavelty, M. D., & Wenger, A. (2022). Cyber Security Politics: Socio-Technological Transformations and Political Fragmentation (vol. 1). Routledge.

El-Alfy, E., Eltoweissy, M., Fulp, E. W., & Mazurczyk, W. (2019). *Nature-Inspired Cyber Security and Resiliency : Fundamentals, Techniques and Applications*. The Institution of Engineering and Technology.

Spector, J. M. (2015). *Foundations of educational technology: Integrative approaches and interdisciplinary perspectives*. Routledge. doi:10.4324/9781315764269

Sutton, D. (2017). *Cyber Security: A Practitioner's Guide. BCS*. The Chartered Institute for IT.

The Emirates Center for Strategic Studies and Research. (2015). *Technology: Impacts, Challenges and the Future*. The Emirates Center for Strategic Studies and Research.

Wells, A. (2022). Schools and Underwriters Do Their Cyber Security Homework. *Insurance Journal.* https://draweb.njcu.edu/login?url=https://www.proquest.com/trade-journals/schools-underwriters-do-their-cyber-security/docview/2673364071/se-2

Acknowledgment

Editing a book can be a daunting task, and many people along the way helped us in this effort. First, we must thank all our authors, from around the globe and from the United States. These diverse professionals brought a wealth of perspectives to this volume. We could not have completed this project without each of you.

Next, we would like to thank everyone at the New Jersey City University Educational Technology Department. We especially want to thank Dr. Laura Zieger and Dr. Chris Shamburg, for their enthusiastic support of this project. Our fellow alumni of the Educational Technology Leadership Program were supportive and encouraging as well, even when they were not able to contribute a chapter. We also must acknowledge Dr. Dana Mason, who was always available to lend a hand throughout the process.

Finally, we would also like to thank Elizabeth Barrantes, Assistant Development Editor for IGI Global, for her support during the creation of this book. We also thank IGI Global for the opportunity to edit this project from beginning to end. We are happy to contribute to the fields of educational technology and cybersecurity through the creation of this book.

Dr. Jimenez: I would like to offer a special thank you to my family Jose, Maria, Aisha, Derek, Divina, Devin, and Betty for their continued support during this project. Their continued support brought me the strength and clarity needed through the creation and editing of this book. Thank you for supporting me in all my academic research endeavors.

Dr. O'Neill: A special thank you to my family. My husband Kevin and daughter Sarah had to make sacrifices throughout this project. Their support and enthusiasm carried me through this process.

Chapter 1
Reimaging Cybersecurity in Educational Practices:
An International Case Study

Nicole Simon
SUNY Nassau Community College, USA

José Luis Jiménez
https://orcid.org/0000-0001-6640-0515
Andrés Bello Catholic University, Venezuela

Daniel Strocchia
Universidad Católica Andrés Bello, Venezuela

ABSTRACT

Cybersecurity has become increasingly important in all industries. Universities are developing academic programs in cybersecurity education in response to the demand for professionals with expertise in application areas of cybersecurity. Education should help students to deal with complex cybersecurity problems. We must ensure that cybersecurity education has a balance between breadth and depth, which integrates science, technology, management, and culture. When looking at cybersecurity education from a breadth perspective, it should provide the students with an understanding of the foundations of various components. Nevertheless, the debate can go further when taking into consideration the legal restrictions imposed on the subject. Law advocates to regulate and give a sense of order and peace for avoiding plausible controversies. Consequently, it seeks to regulate human behaviors for ensuring order, and in this case, it does so by stablishing regulations towards privacy and cybersecurity.

DOI: 10.4018/978-1-6684-6092-4.ch001

THE DAWN OF CYBERSECURITY

Background and Current Trends

Cyber security has been an ongoing discussion in Higher Education as well as in the K-12 sector. Recently, P-20+ educators and technologists have found themselves at cross-roads to better understand both the needs of institutions as well as those individual needs of students, while complying with national and international standards in a borderless environment. Internet usage has positively affected people's lives, but it has also led to negative consequences. Internet users are not aware of the mechanisms for protecting themselves against cyberbullying, online fraud, racial abuse, pornography and gambling, which has led to an increase in incidents of cyberbullying, online fraud, racial abuse, pornography, and gambling.

Previous research (Zhang-Kennedy & Chiasson, 2020) has indicated that Internet users are still unaware or only moderately aware of this ongoing issue of cyber awareness and cybersecurity. Young children must be taught knowledge and awareness of the Internet from a very early age, as one of the vital measures. There is a need to educate young children about cyberspace safety and how to protect themselves. Using a systematic review approach, this paper examines why it is crucial to educate learners about the risks of living in cyberspace and strategies that stakeholders can use to mitigate those risks, cyber security education can be promoted in schools and, even, higher education using this tool.

Parents are concerned about cybercrime against children and adolescents, since they sometimes don't realize their child has been victimized. Parents are often unaware of what their children do online. Commenting and insulting may be used by bullies to hurt some children; moreover, they may also suffer from intimidation, harassment, abuse, or sexual exploitation. With search engines such as Google and Yahoo, and video sharing sites such as YouTube, all information is now available at people's fingertips. However, with the advent of the internet, humans can enjoy both their real life and their virtual world (Mountrouidou, Li, & Burke, 2018). With video sharing sites such as YouTube and Google, as well as search engines such as Google and Yahoo, information sharing has become non-stop and significantly unregulated.

An education that stimulates critical discernment processes in the individual to act with freedom, autonomy and reflective sense is essential to prepare our students to be competent in the challenging times that characterize our current global reality (Mountrouidou, Li, & Burke, 2018). These ethical concerns, together with scientific and technological skills at the service of justice and sustainable development, are the primary objectives of the pedagogy of virtual awareness (Aldawood & Skinner, 2018; Khalid, 2017).

To achieve these goals and find creative ways to foster depth of thought and imagination in our students, it is necessary to study the emerging cross-cultural worlds in which they live and the technology they use. In addition to understanding the cultural elements that are transformative of their own person and their social relationships. This is particularly important in a popular cross-cultural context marked by superficial media outlets that often convey a stereotyped mass culture. It is necessary that students in this era of globalization dominated by a strong trend towards consumerism, exercise empathy, and develop skills and abilities with a high level of emotional and spiritual maturity to become agents of change or, at least, be aware of their digital fingerprint.

Social media is often used as a platform to express feelings, to generate discussion, or to become known. Consequently, many people want to be the first to share an issue, they sometimes ignore whether the information presented is authentic or not. Using the internet is not only for adults, but children should also have a basic understanding of cybersecurity in this day and age of technology and multimedia (Khalid, 2017; Annasingh & Veli, 2016). Despite the vast potential and benefits of the Internet, excessive use may cause cyber risks, such as cyber addiction, gaming and gambling addiction, cybersex, pornography, and exposure of personal information (Aldawood & Skinner, 2018; Ratten, 2015).

Cybersecurity is also defined as the process, ability, or state of ensuring the security of information and communications. Among students, Facebook, Instagram, LinkedIn, YouTube, and Twitter are the most popular social media platforms (Annasingh & Veli, 2016). As a result of this explosion of information, there are various risks associated with privacy and security. In this virtual space, information's authenticity and accuracy can also be questioned. In the event of cyber threats, children must be prepared to defend themselves and take responsibility for their actions. In addition to ensuring teachers are adequately trained and up-to-date, there is a need to guide students and parents in their use of the internet at home while promoting critical understanding rather than restrictive approaches to cybersafety.

Lack of expertise, funding, and resources are the major challenges schools face when implementing cybersecurity education. There is a lack of knowledge and expertise among teachers regarding cyberspace. It may be difficult for schools and government agencies to implement cybersecurity education due to a lack of resources and facilities. New risks arise with the rapid pace of technological change, requiring new solutions. It may be difficult for teachers to keep up with the latest technology and ensure students' safety. Having access to learning materials and being aware of technological advancements is a major obstacle for teachers. Symposiums on cybersecurity should be promoted at schools to provide early exposure and training to students. The world's future cyber defense will come from people who are exposed to and trained in cybersecurity.

Learners can actively engage in online learning experiences using digital technologies. Despite rapid technological advancements, teachers may find it challenging to keep up with the changes and evaluate the efficiency of new technologies in online learning environments (Mountrouidou, Li, and Burke, 2018). Student-to-student, student-to-content, student-to-teacher, and teacher-to-content are all examples of learning interactions. All of these activities will provide you with detailed and insightful feedback. This should help us gain a better understanding of the field and respond accordingly. Emerging technologies are frequently used to address the same issues and problems that motivated educators and researchers to engage with older technologies, which were once emerging technologies. Because we use a presentation of view that focuses on theory and practice, our discourse and special visualization are easily accessible to learners. The reality of education in today's world demands a change of paradigm for adapting to a constantly changing environment.

Presently, it is possible to add another new type of interaction in the learning environment thanks to breakthroughs and democratization of AI technologies: content-to-student. Software packages and systems are offering newer forms of interaction that extend to almost every aspect of our daily lives, and education is not exempt. Yes, any interaction must start with an active subject, a simple software or machine cannot trigger a learning process, nevertheless, the balance shifts with the development of the methodology. The human is not the active part of the relationship anymore, but rather the software, evolving into a content-to-student relationship.

For instance, when a student enrolls in a self-learning system or methodology, such as an app for learning a new language, it is an expression of his will towards a content (student-to-content); but as the process develops, it is now the software who dictates the pace of learning: constant notifications, due dates, rewards and punishment, etc. Content now redefines itself as a teacher, albeit, a «fake» one in the *stricto sensu* interpretation of what a «teacher» is; alas, the student now interacts with it as it would with a regular teacher, but content does not (and cannot) comply with the duties that its human counterpart normally would, nor behaves in the same way. In essence, it cannot be expected to behave in the same way or to produce the same kind of interactions, so it has to be a new kind of relationship: content-to-student.

IMPLICATIONS OF CYBERSECURITY

Reimagining Education

As per Mayer (2001), studies of brain activity and our growing understanding of how we process ideas have inspired much of this work. Constructivism or epistemic engagement, which has been the most recent educational vision guiding educational technology engagement, is most reminiscent of constructivist learning theories. Among both researchers and educators, guidance is currently the most popular approach to learning. Scholars and educators must appreciate that the promise of developing technologies is not limited to the technology itself, but also includes the tools. It is the way in which new technologies are constructed for use in education that has an impact on online teaching and learning. We must reimagine online learning in terms of design, curriculum, and pedagogy. Experiential and inquiry-based learning are rooted in fundamental theoretical approaches to learning, as per Kolb (1984).

Indeed, technology is very dynamic, with innovations appearing almost in a matter of days in terms of software and hardware, and we must adapt promptly. Emerging technologies cluster most of the technological breakthroughs, and play an essential role in education. So why shouldn't education also be dynamic, if what it is based on changes so often? Either we disgrace it or not, it is already changing, not because we forced it to, but because the center of its nature (humans) inevitably evolve.

Emerging technologies facilitate and promote the free exchange of knowledge becoming the ideal platforms for learning and civic engagement. Transmedia narratives are characterized by telling stories complemented through a media ecosystem, involving the participation of the audiences. Transmedia literacy has positioned itself in virtual education as a fundamental strategy for transformative learning. The creative component of this pedagogy opens up new spaces of engagement favoring the construction of, even, democracies. Dynamics generated between students and the audiences promote an active community that interacts through social networks establishing the basis of collective intelligence.

Learners must permanently get updated on information and communication technologies, and on the security and protection measures of these systems, learn to coexist, to serve, and to put knowledge into action. The student recognizes the problems society faces today, appreciates and cultivates in a reflective, ethical, responsible, and committed way, her/his relationship with others and with the physical, sociocultural, local, and global environment, to contribute to the collective welfare through learning to learn (metacognition). Through the use of cognitive strategies and processes that promote autonomous learning, the participant engages in: observation, investigation, comparison, understanding, analysis, synthesis, discussion, evaluation, and creation.

There is considerable interest and investment in security training and research from both the public and private sectors. As a result, the majority of efforts have been focused on physical security, while cyber security and digital security have received less attention. Recent high-profile cyber-attacks have exposed the need for cyber security training. Security is an industry that is complex and highly valued. Research and training in this subject have attracted lots of government and private sector investment in recent years due to rapid changes in the security landscape. Physical security has been the focus of most training interventions to date. The security of computer infrastructure has received less attention. Unlike physical security, computer networks and infrastructure are responsible for controlling many vital functions in society, such as banking and air travel.

Cyber security is a serious problem in all businesses, but it is especially so for higher education executives. Colleges and universities are vulnerable to cyber-attacks because they store important biographical and financial data, as well as data linked to research and development of new technologies. Cyber security coordination, implementation, and direction has become a key problem on college campuses, with the campus leader or president often having final control over the cyber security strategy.

Cybersecurity has become increasingly important in all industries, including banking, finance, homeland security, insurance, and medicine. Universities and institutions are developing academic programs in cybersecurity education in response to the demand for professionals with expertise in application areas of cybersecurity (Aldawood & Skinner, 2018; Ratten, 2015). Hence, the education on this matter should help students to deal with complex cybersecurity problems, as it would "require a learning methodology that produces a deeper level of understanding and critical thinking in order to defend against increasingly complex cyber-attacks" (Dasgupta, Ferebee and Michalewicz, 2013, p. 20). We must ensure that cybersecurity education has a balance between breadth and depth, which integrates science, technology, management, and culture. When looking at cybersecurity education from a breadth perspective, it should provide the students with an understanding of the foundations of various components, such as computer science, information technology, social organizations, law, culture, ethics, mathematics, behavior and psychology, and writing skills, among others. By contrast, when focusing on depth, it should substitute for some of the breadth for additional training, practice, and information specific to a particular area of information security (Burley & Spafford, 2014, p. 43).

The term "data analytics" has a broad and somewhat nebulous definition. In its purest sense, it merely refers to examining data sets in order to draw conclusions. In general usage, however, the assumption is that the data sets are large, semi-structured, and that computer technology is used to find hidden patterns and connections. In practice, visual representation is typically the vehicle used to denote these patterns and associations. When these visual representations, along with standard numerical information, are combined into a compact representation, or "dashboard", it allows decision makers to gain valuable insights into the operation and status of an enterprise.

SUNY (State University of New York) Exploring Emerging Technologies for Lifelong Learning and Success Project (#EmTechMOOC; (http://suny.edu/emtech) is a voluntary online learning opportunity that has been embraced by participants from around the world. #EmTechMOOC is targeted at college students, faculty, current and career-seeking professionals, and anyone from across the globe who is interested in keeping pace with the constant evolution of digital technology. The MOOC enables participants to build lifelong learning skills and develop their mastery of the 4Cs of 21st-century learners: Communication, Collaboration, Creativity, and Critical Thinking. Participants learn about the value and implications of using freely available emerging technologies for both personal and professional growth.

The EmTech project has been focused on keeping pace with the constant evolution of digital technology. The project includes a socially curated WIKI that encompasses within its platform emerging technology tool records that have been assessed in terms of privacy and accessibility. As part of the early research and investigations, it is clear that formation in cybersecurity is key for both students and educators, but is especially so for educators, who are enforced (in many cases by the law) to keep in mind and asses the privacy and accessibility issues of the platforms they would be using in their courses.

Nevertheless, the debate can go further when taking into consideration the legal restrictions imposed on the subject. Law advocates to regulate and give a sense of order and peace for avoiding plausible controversies. Consequently, it seeks to regulate human behaviors for ensuring order, and in this case it does so by establishing regulations towards privacy and cybersecurity. In a closed legal ecosystem this makes perfect sense, however reality is not so kind due to the digital environment being practically borderless; with the simple press of a button your IP address may change from your current position, to wherever you wish it to be. Conflicts come when different regulations come into conflict due to the subjective reality of the legislator who enacted it. Furthermore, it poses a difficult barrier for intercultural exchanges, a phenomenon more and more common thanks to online exchanges (Sadykova & Meskill; 2019).

PRIVACY RIGHTS AND REGULATIONS

In recent years, many countries have developed privacy guidelines, especially when it comes to online information. Family Educational Rights and Privacy Act [FERPA], which was enacted pre-Internet and is specific to higher education in the U.S., and the General Data Protection Regulation [GDPR], which is a broader European privacy standard, are the two most prevalent privacy regulations affecting higher education and Virtual Exchanges. It is important to note that the latter has been replicated in many countries outside the E.U., making it the lead example worldwide of privacy regulation (Thales, 2021).

In order to protect the privacy of students, FERPA was enacted. Students have been protected by this law when using traditional and virtual learning tools. Although not all educational tools comply with FERPA regulations, U.S. educators and their colleagues should be aware of FERPA, which prevents a third party from sharing student data without the student's explicit consent or their parents/legal tutor (in the case of K12 and others). In accordance with the website of the United States Department of Education (United States Department of Education, 2021), "*FERPA is the federal law that protects the privacy of personally identifiable information (PII) in students' education records*". FERPA provides students and their parents the right to access and amend the student's educational records, and the right to protect the student's PII. A student who qualifies as an 'eligible student' will have the following information: the student's name, address, phone number, date and place of birth, honors and awards, and dates of attendance (FERPA, § 99.3).

Educational technology companies must take responsible actions with respect to student data as higher education institutions implement new technology platforms. Businesses strive to maintain a trusting relationship with students, schools, and parents in order to comply with both federal and state FERPA laws. While FERPA does not address specific application software, online educational companies have increasingly collected large amounts of 'metadata' or operational information through transactions or keystroke identifiers while students navigate websites. The metadata refers to the information that gives context to the overall data that is being collected. There are also many educational software companies that have committed to following the Student Privacy Pledge, which is accountable to the Federal Trade Commission and supports student privacy, which strengthens outside relationships with educational stakeholders and students to inform the public of transparency.

In the case of GPDP, as it is a more novel regulation, it goes further in the regulations of online interactions and the construction of educational relations inside the digital environment, as well as outside of it. GDPR recognizes several key structures along the process of collecting, handling, and processing data; and imposes regulations on all of these figures. Although GDPR advocates for personal data in an understanding similar to what FERPA defines as PPI (GDPR, art. 4 §1), that is to say: "any information relating to an identified or identifiable natural person"; it has very important repercussions for educators. One of the main differences when compared to U.S. regulations is that data subjects (the ones who the information belongs to) have the right to request the withdrawal of all their data if they request so at any given time. GDPR imposes a harsh obligation in favor of European citizens to data handlers and, specially, to cloud based technologies, since it overextends the jurisdiction of the EU to, practically, anywhere in the world as long as they handle data form EU citizens (Tsiptse, 2021).

With both FERPA and GDPR, Educational Technologists suggest viewing privacy rights on a technology tool website prior to using the tool and/or recommending it for student use. Privacy policies can be found in most technology tool sites and should be read for student's protection. There are many sites that are transparent about these, and we recommend checking them against campus policies and requesting, if necessary, support from respective scholars or campus authority.

GENERAL DATA PROTECTION REGULATION (GDPR) PRIVACY RIGHTS

General Data Protection Regulation (GDPR) Privacy Rights provides certain protective rights to citizens of the European Economic Area (EEA) with respect to using services that collect and process personal data. GDPR provides the following rights for individuals (Official Journal of the European Union, 2018):

- the right to be informed;
- the right of access;
- the right to rectification;
- the right to erasure/right to be forgotten, the right to restrict processing;
- the right to data portability;
- the right to object;
- and rights in relation to automated decision making and profiling.

Since GDPR specifically refers to personal data (GDPR, art. 4 §1), using a third-party tool such as Emerging Technologies [EmTech], which does not require students to share personal details such as their email addresses, should be acceptable. In accordance with GDPR and Data Protection Acts, a data controller is responsible for determining how personal data is used and processed:

- "Obtain and process personal data lawfully, fairly and in a transparent manner;
- Keep it only for one or more specified and explicit lawful purpose(s);
- Process it only in ways compatible with the purpose of which it was given initially;
- Keep data accurate, relevant, and not excessive;
- Retain it no longer than is necessary for the specified purpose or purposes;
- Keep personal data safe and secure." (Data Protection Commission, n.d.).

Individuals have the right to have their personal information protected, used in a fair and legal manner, and made available upon request. Any information presented in an erroneous manner may also be corrected by individuals. For this protection, the GDPR Data Protection Commission has outlined the six lawful reasons for the processing of personal data: (1) consent; (2) to carry out a contract; (3) in order for an organization to meet a legal obligation; (4) where processing the personal data is necessary to protect the vital interests of a person; (5) where processing the personal data is necessary for the performance of a task carried out in the public interest; and (6) in the legitimate interests of a company/organization (except where those interests contradict or harm the interests or rights and freedoms of the individual) (Official Journal of the European Union, 2018).

Student's rights and privacy were not intended to be protected by GDPR, as it was originally developed for the protection of consumers. Considering the amount of personal data stored within educational institutions across Europe, GDPR has had a significant impact on how these institutions manage student data. Due to the complexity of the regulation, and the fact that it was only recently enacted (May 2018), each European educator engaging in Virtual Exchanges should identify the person at their institution who may provide them with the support they need to ensure that GDPR is followed. For example, educators may be required to use their own LMS if their partner's LMS does not meet GDPR requirements or if the partnering teachers decide to use Google Classroom but cannot guarantee that the servers are in Europe.

Some of the practical privacy needs that teachers should consider are:

- Unless all students agree and this information is distributed securely, do not share phone numbers or email addresses within a class.
- The use of technology tools in a course(s) must be informed to campus IT policy-makers to ensure privacy needs are met.
- All student partners should be informed about campus policies regarding technology tools.
- Encourage students to use only the tools outlined in the project plans - or any other tools they may have in mind.
- Make sure instructors are aware of such alternative tools before using them.

Privacy, then, becomes a subjective matter: what some consider "private", others may not; this is what happens between the US and the EU in this subject and it has being a long sticking point in U.S.-EU economic and security relations (Fefer and Archick, 2020).This contrast has derived in the appearance of new barriers for privacy and cybersecurity compliance for both privates and public organizations, and specially for the education sector, since international collaborations now require further compliance aside from the national context of the institution. The education sector not only has to ensure the physical, digital, and electronic security of their students, but also comply with the legal restrictions and different laws just to guarantee a minimum standard of security and privacy, a reality that has gotten more complex with the digital migration resulting from the Covid-19 pandemic.

A QUICK MENTION TO COVID-19 TRENDS ON THE SUBJECT

Thousands of companies in all economic sectors have been forced to transform from on-board work to remote work due to the Covid-19 pandemic. The probability that a company would be hacked has increased significantly recently. Anft (2020) reported that "more than 500 educational institutions, including colleges and K-12 schools, suffered ransom attacks in 2019". It is necessary to shed light on the aforementioned subject, based on secondary literature reports on the topic and to identify weaknesses and barriers in cybersecurity in, particularly, education organizations as well as best practices for combating these breaches.

The outcomes serve as an eye opener for security officers in charge of the safety of organizational intellectual properties and stimulate organizations to adopt protection systems and safety practices.

Cybersecurity has undoubtedly gained importance and has become a priority matter of both private and public concerns. The year 2020 witnessed an increase in cyberattacks and an increment of ransomware incidents that Marr (2020) asserts the critical role that cybersecurity plays in protecting the individual's privacy, rights, freedoms, and practices up to and including his/her physical safety. Moreover, with the advent of COVID-19 pandemic, there is an increased movement of global transformation of physical and vital infrastructure to online. The transformation to online is therefore more vulnerable and open to digital attacks, to data breaches (leak of personal information and ransomware) and up to cyberwar between countries and terrorism.

SUBJECTIVENESS IN DEFINITIONS

We have already seen how data and personal information is regulated in a very different manner in Europe compared to the U.S. Subjectiveness is not limited to data or PPI, but is present in almost every aspect of what cybersecurity should cover, starting with the question: *what information has to be protected?* The question goes beyond the EU and the U.S., it relies on who (individually) you pose the question to. From a legal standpoint, the discussion of what is public (concern of the State or related to it when acting with *ius imperium*) and what is private (concerning the relationships between individuals) is very controversial, with authors even denying such division (Rosenfeld, 2013). We have already seen how for FERPA purposes it is fine for students just to have access to their information, nevertheless, for GDPR this is insufficient and people have the right to freely dispose of their information, being able to erase it on demand.

Going back to the question: "*what is private?*", both FERPA and GDPR agree that private information is any kind of data that can be directly used to identify a person; this is a definition totally opposite to the traditional legal definition of "private", because it is completely unrelated to what the role of the State is on the juridical relation. Nevertheless, it still leaves some uncertainties, like: what can be used to directly identify a person? Is metadata sufficient or it only refers to the data being actively shared by the user? For instance, it is not the same if I, as a user, voluntarily give an educational institution my email address; compared to if the educational institution passively records my IP address through the use of cookies. This is the issue that needs to properly be addressed in a global manner, since there is uniformity in regulations.

To further complicate things, what happens when we add social aspects to the question? For example, if a teen posts a *TikTok* giving PPI, is that *TikTok* subject to compliance of GDPR or FERPA? Can that be considered «private» data since it is being openly shared to the public in a social network? Regardless of how it was shared, from a legal standpoint that can be considered as a PPI and has to be subjected to FERPA or GDPR, accordingly. This consideration is of special importance for teachers when evaluating educational platforms and environments for class interactions. Yes, social media can be an interesting and, perhaps, useful exchange platform, but is it well suited for complying with the legal demands? No, social media is not in compliance with legal demands needed to protect the rights of students.

Transmedia Literacy, Global Citizens, and the Benefits and Challenges of Emerging Technologies: A Case Study in Venezuela

Emerging technologies facilitate and promote the free exchange of knowledge becoming the ideal platforms for learning and civic engagement. Transmedia narratives are characterized by telling stories complemented through a media ecosystem, involving the participation of the audiences. Transmedia literacy has positioned itself in virtual education as a fundamental strategy for transformative learning. The creative component of this pedagogy opens up new spaces of engagement favoring the construction of democracies. Dynamics generated between students and the audiences promote an active community that interacts through social networks establishing the basis of collective intelligence.

According to Robledo and Atarama in their article "Transmedia Political Journalism; Strategies for the Development of the Profession in the Current Media Ecosystem", transmedia narratives have become the best journalists' ally for the dissemination of news that affect society as a whole (Robledo & Atarama 2016). They state that the fundamental motto of the journalism profession today is social service. To illustrate this point, the authors quote on Casero-Ripollés work who establishes three essential characteristics of the journalism profession: (1) Journalism is the guardian monitoring public life. (2) The journalist provides information to a community of citizens about their common interests, the collective problems, and alternatives to solve them. (3) The responsibility of the journalist is to provide platforms for discussion on matters that affect society as a whole (Sánchez, Mallorquí, Briones, Zaballos, & Corral 2020).

Amid the challenges that Venezuela faces today, it is of pivotal importance to integrate comprehensive educational models into higher education institutions with the goal to train citizens that positively impact their communities, schools, and public and private organizations. Universities must develop mechanisms that go beyond the acquisition of knowledge in traditional disciplines, find solutions to the collective social problems, and contribute to the reconstruction of democracy.

The living conditions of most Venezuelan students do not meet the minimum levels of consumption for basic needs such as food, water, clothing, shelter, sanitation, security, and healthcare. Education cannot rely on traditional approaches to face this reality. It is necessary to understand the deteriorating conditions of life of the students in order to design instructional strategies that can help to create an environment for a depth of thought and creation that is transformative for individuals and society. Data from the Institute for Economic and Social Research (IIES), in its National Survey of Living Conditions (ENCOVI) report points out that of the 7 million 863 thousand individuals between the ages of 3 and 17 who are in the educational system, 40% miss classes "sometimes" due to water service (23%), blackouts (17%), lack food at home (16%), transportation (7%), teachers missing (18%). Educational coverage has fallen more strongly in the population aged between 18 and 24 years. School attendance among individuals of these ages went from 48% in 2016 to 25% in 2019. Of the group between 18 and 24 years (3 million 136 thousand), about 2 million 282 thousand young people are not educated (ENCOVI 2019-20).

Journalism students face other pressures such as lack of employment and persecution. As Michelle Bachelet manifests, there are multiple signs that the civic space is shrinking in the country. "Since September, my Office has documented at least 66 cases of intimidation, harassment, disqualification, and criminalization of journalists, media outlets, human rights defenders, humanitarian workers, union leaders, and members or supporters of the opposition" (Bachelet, 2021). In January alone, Bachelet stated that at least three search and seizures operations were conducted at the premises of media outlets. During those operations, equipment was seized, offices sealed, staff intimidated and broadcast suspended (Bachelet,

2021). The impact of this violence, as Guido Villamizar describes, produces long term traumas on the press workers:

2017 was an initiation year on a personal level, now I jokingly refer to it as the year of the first apocalypse. The lengthy protests that shaped it were followed by a year marked by nationwide blackouts that lasted for weeks, and then, a global pandemic. That year I was studying my second semester in the specialty of journalism at the university, the protests interrupted the free mobility of citizens and the classes were seen virtually. Most of the classes were converted into weekly or biweekly readings and deliveries. I was working as a producer in an opposition digital journalism medium, in Venezuela polarization dominates even in the press. When the riots began, I went from studying, to reporting the day-to-day life on the streets. The prevailing reality was violence between both sides, my life became a 12-hour shift work. The time between adrenaline injections passed with unstoppable vertigo until one night, while at work, they arrested me and my team. I was released unharmed that same morning, but the boys, my team, were jailed for thirty days… My press team was imprisoned in the worst conditions. The basement of a residential building, where the boiler was working, served as the compound. They were crowded with twenty other prisoners, each in worse conditions than the other, they ate only what their families managed to bring them, when they were allowed to visit. The room had such poor sanitation that one of them contracted scabies. In an attempt to embolden myself, a few days after the arrest, I stood in front of the cameras and filed a complaint at the Public Ministry alone with the Press Workers Union; it did not have much impact (Guido Villamizar, 2021). Student of Transmedia Journalism in 2017.

The complexity of violence experienced by Venezuelan students on a daily basis has serious effects on their well-being, not every individual deal with it the same way, some handle it better, but some others contribute to its reproduction by behaving aggressively against their peers. Aguamiel Mendoza in her following testimony shows lights on how learners have to navigate in a multiplicity of rough situations such as lack of food, aggression from their own friends and brutality from the government forces:

At the university I overcame many obstacles despite the most serious situations, a destroyed economy manifested in peers without breakfast or lunch, which is difficult to study without having food. Colleagues who do not have values and harm others, as well as supportive and professional ones. The situation at the time period in which I studied communications was very complicated and critical, as one of the heaviest moments of repression began in the country. The students decide to go out to the streets to protest, to hold marches, to fight for a decent future. Several peers went out to protest and never made it home (Aguamiel Mendoza, 2021). Student of Documentary in 2017.

Repression by government forces in Venezuela occurs daily and it is recognized by international organizations, the United Nations High Commissioner for Human Rights reported in March 2021 that extrajudicial executions are frequent in the context of security operations.

The primary goal of the Transmedia pedagogical strategy implemented at the Andres Bello Catholic University in Venezuela since 2016, is to train citizens and professionals capable of performing adequately in the field of digital journalism through the design and implementation of high-impact projects that encourage critical thinking, professional ethics, collaborative work, and citizen participation. Using a wide range of technologies of communication and information, the students become protagonists and content creators of their own learning. Learners permanently get updated on information and communication technologies, and on the security and protection measures of these systems.

The model consists of four fields of action integrated in several journalism and communications courses. These fields of action are: (1) High Impact Projects: Transmedia Journalism and Human Rights; (2) Reframing Reality: Documentary and Visual Anthropology; (3) Multicultural Collaboration: Collaborative Online International Learning; and (4) The Healing Power of Nature: Ecotourism and Sustainable Living.

The strategy has been focused on the production, by the students, of high impact projects that provide solutions for the 17 Sustainable Development Goals from the UN's Agenda 2030: (1) No Poverty, (2) Zero Hunger, (3) Good Health and Well-being, (4) Quality Education, (5) Gender Equality, (6) Clean Water and Sanitation, (7) Affordable and Clean Energy, (8) Decent Work and Economic Growth, (9) Industry, Innovation and Infrastructure, (10) Reducing Inequality, (11) Sustainable Cities and Communities, (12) Responsible Consumption and Production, (13) Climate Action, (14) Life Below Water, (15) Life On Land, (16) Peace, Justice, and Strong Institutions, (17) Partnerships for the Goals.

To comply with the responsibilities of the profession today, the courses on Transmedia Journalism emphasize on the development of three important skills: (1) Learn to interact in the global context. This objective aims to train journalists with managerial competencies within the process of media convergence. The student understands the importance of audiences in the production of complex informational content, and knows how to handle the tools of transmediality: she/he skillfully uses communication and information technology equipment and applications to interact with others in the global context. Learners must permanently get updated on information and communication technologies, and on the security and protection measures of these systems. (2) Learn to coexist, to serve, and to put knowledge into action. The student recognizes the problems society faces today, appreciates and cultivates in a reflective, ethical, responsible, and committed way, her/his relationship with others and with the physical, sociocultural, local, and global environment, to contribute to the collective welfare. (3) Learn to learn (metacognition). Using cognitive strategies and processes that promote autonomous learning, the participant engages in observation, investigation, comparison, understanding, analysis, synthesis, discussion, evaluation, and creation.

The high impact projects assigned to the students during the course are guided by a series of learning objectives organized into levels of complexity and specificity according to the revised Bloom's Taxonomy of Educational Objectives (Anderson et al. 2000). They are carried out in the following order: (1) Remember, (2) Understand, (3) Apply, (4) Analyze, (5) Evaluate and (6) Create. For the purpose of this curriculum, two additional learning goals have been integrated into the taxonomy: (7) Design and (8) Engage with the audience. To accomplish these objectives, a global challenge is introduced at the beginning of the semester. During the first class, the assignment is presented to the students. The project will have a series of phases or sub challenges that will be completed (individually and as groups) throughout the semester. Learners will investigate, discuss, argue and design models and strategies of communication and share them to a live audience.

The assignment is to develop an informative Transmedia Narrative Universe (a communication strategy) based on a specific article from the UN's Universal Declaration of Human Rights to provide solutions to one or more UN's Sustainable Development Goals (SDG's). In the process, individuals act, with human and ethical sense, to improve their socio-cultural environment. Students select the topic according to their interest and motivations; learners identify and assume as their own the problems of their community.

Based on the selected human rights' article and SDGs, students must find and investigate the current situation in their communities to develop a communication strategy. Throughout the process, learners will interview citizens and professionals associated with the subject of investigation. This way, they recognize the problem, appreciate and cultivate in a reflective, ethical, responsible and committed way, their relationship with other people and with the physical and socio-cultural environment.

After the investigation, students distribute their results in a system of social networks and digital channels (they use internet resources as a communication tool and adequately manage apps, programs and applications) to inform and interact with real audiences. They must generate a public discussion aimed to promote a social change (students propose solutions from their disciplinary field to solve problems in their communities and share with others their commitment). In this exercise, learners understand and assume the reality and allow themselves to be questioned by it, connecting knowledge with their sociocultural reality to propose and execute, with a human and ethical sense, solutions that promote the common welfare.

During the past seven years, course participants have developed team leadership skills such as collaboration, shared purposes, respect for diversity, assignment of responsibilities, and group learning. Through the activities and challenges, participants have engaged in effective communication processes. They have developed common agendas and formed groups with people of diverse backgrounds to work cooperatively. In addition, learners have proposed new, unconventional solutions to institutional, community, and social situations.

Confronting the country's socio-political reality, participants have fostered a sense of civic responsibility and self-reflection on their values and principles. They have acquired skills to evaluate, self-evaluate, and knowledge about leadership approaches. And finally, participants have skillfully interacted in working groups using information and communication technology equipment, and applications to interact with others in the global context. They permanently got updated on information and communication technologies, and on the security and protection measures of these systems.

Students have made significant contributions to research and discovery basing their projects on the Sustainable Development Goals formulated by UN's Agenda 2030. Some topics explored are: peace, justice, and strong institutions; decent work and economic growth; reducing poverty; zero hunger; good health and well-being; quality education; clean water and sanitation; gender equality; and climate action.

The following testimonials manifest how, during the process, learners move beyond the savior/victim state of mind and engage with others in civic responsibilities and self-reflection:

Student Testimonial 1. High impact project: Article 19 of the Universal Declaration of Human Rights, 1948 (UDHR) states: Everyone has the right to freedom of opinion and expression. SDG, 2015: (8) Decent Work and Economic Growth. This student participated in the course during the spring of 2017:

We decided to make a documentary, after some debate, we agreed to make a compilation of attacks on media workers during the coverage of the protests: 100 DÍAS DE CENSURA. Deep down I hoped to hear the scant testimonies full of vocation that define journalists and that this temperance would calm my nerves. The day I first went back to work after being arrested I was scared; standing around where I have always lived with my press ID, terrified me. I saved the contacts of those journalists involved in the most recognized cases of abuse and Abi (my partner) would call them to be interviewed... I wanted the testimony of my colleagues facing violence to restore my strength, but my hypothesis could not fall further from reality. With the first glance I did at the hours of video material that Abigail had collected I could see how the cold gaze of the press workers was broken into a brutally honest way, remembering the aggressions they had experienced. Fear and frustration prevailed in these testimonies, but above them, there was a firm condition that I thought so much debacle had taken away from us: humanity (Guido Villamizar, 2021).

Student Testimonial 2. High impact project: Article 25 of the Universal Declaration of Human Rights, 1948 (UDHR) states: Everyone has the right to health and an adequate standard of living. SDG, 2015: (3) Good Health and Well-being. This student participated in the course during the spring of 2020:

I got together with three of my friends to create a transmedia narrative universe called "Medicando" to show the status of Venezuela's health system during the coronavirus pandemic. We dedicated six months to investigating the circumstances and realized that the majority of hospitals located in Caracas are operating at a fraction of their capacity and without proper conditions to do it. The experience of enrolling in this course was very enriching. We place the bases of a project we want to continue in the future to get the attention of the global community about Venezuela's collapsing health care system, which according to the United Nations became a regional threat too. Also, we understood the importance of being able to connect with people using all the resources possible (Albany Diaz, 2021).

Multicultural Cooperation and Emerging Technologies: Collaborative Online International Learning (COIL)

How do we convey to our students the benefit of understanding the worldviews of others building an emerging participatory culture with a human sense that promotes solutions for socio-environmental well-being and at the same time promote awareness about benefits and risks of engaging with emerging technologies? The educator as a citizen committed to the formation of people, must be aware of his responsibility as an agent of social change through the encounter with his students and the transformation of knowledge into action. To do this, our pedagogical strategies must activate a climate of mutual support, strengthen our students' listening skills and develop a shared sense of empathy, honesty and integrity to grow inside and outside the classroom.

In the chapter entitled "Building empathy through a comparative study on popular cultures between the cities of Caracas, Venezuela and Albany, United States" within the book Virtual Exchange: Towards Digital Equity in Internationalization, researchers Ilka Kressner from the University of Albany (State University of New York) and José Luis Jiménez, professor and Coordinator of COIL projects at the Andrés Bello Catholic University, establish that the International Collaborative Online Learning pedagogy fosters the formation of a participatory culture that involves the responsible management of the different individuals in global contexts. The authors indicate that after participating in virtual exchange pedagogical experiences, students go beyond an individualistic state of mind to interact in a context in which they engage with other individuals in a process of shared responsibilities and self-reflection (Jiménez and Kressner, 2021). https://research-publishing.net/manuscript?10.14705/rpnet.2021.53.1294

Emerging technologies facilitate free exchange of knowledge, becoming ideal platforms for high impact experiential learning in a virtual exchange experience. The SUNY Center for Collaborative Online International Learning (COIL) has existed since 2004. Its early mission was to develop more online courses with an international dimension and to "explore ways to bring international students into their classrooms using technology" (http://coil.suny.edu/index.php/page/brief-history-suny-coil-center). This pedagogy of virtual exchange, also called Global Network Learning or Telecollaboration, offers authentic opportunities for students under intercultural and transnational learning within the curricula in the classrooms of universities around the planet. Through co-developed and co-taught modules, this virtual exchange encourages students to develop skills to enter the 21st century workforce and provides opportunities for applied learning experiences.

In Venezuela, Virtual Exchange collaborations have been implemented since 2019. The following case study describes the first of 60, at the time, COIL experiences conducted at the Andres Bello Catholic university. During a six-week period, two classes adopted the COIL methodology and engaged in a shared module titled Popular Culture and Contemporary Media. From October to November 2019, 58 students, 26 from UAlbany (SUNY) and 32 from the Andrés Bello Catholic University of Venezuela jointly developed task-based projects on expressions of popular culture in teams of seven to eight participants. Following a challenging learning curriculum, transformative learning, formulated by Mezirow (1997), goes beyond memorization of information and has both individual and social dimensions and implications. Rennick argues that this pedagogic method emphasizes high impact learning; it is experiential, collaborative, active, and engaging. While applied consciously, students become an active part of world citizenship and are committed to the great purposes of humanity (Rennick, 2015).

Learners from both countries explored practices and reflected on variations of popular culture through descriptive and critical assignments and tasks, the drafting of a joint video script, and the creation of a ten-minute video that focused on popular expressions in both cities. Students choose their topics among their teams. Among the choices selected were practices of Indie music, graffiti and other street art, inclusive performance spaces, the creation of community sites among others, and media of contemporary social interaction that particularly communicated popular cultural content. The methodology of the collaborative virtual module was concentrated on intensive weekly group activities and a learning challenge across the two institutions. Both professors chose the activities, they included readings, the watching of videos, and lectures in Spanish and English by cultural and media theorists and practitioners. The readings were between 2,000 and 7,000 words long and were dedicated to the topics of the impact of new media (processes of democratization, hypermediations, ecosystems) and cultural contrasts and comparisons (essays by Roland Barthes, Noam Chomsky, Stuart Hall, and Edward Said).

Testimonials from students who have participated in these virtual exchange experiences confirm that the activities developed within their collaborative projects have a positive and long-term impact on their lives. In this sense, students from a university in the United States and a Venezuelan university, working as a single group, state that they have overcome basic communication barriers and cultural disparities. "All the experience showed us that despite apparently adverse circumstances, shared academic goals can be achieved, when working with a clear course of action and a range of alternatives" (Ruiz et al., 2021). The students argue that the main motivations that helped them carry out the project were responsibility, commitment, the desire to learn from other cultures, and resilience. "Our professors played a fundamental role offering the orientation that fostered the leadership and proactivity of the participants" (Ruiz et al., 2021). This experience was proof that the typical and obvious limitations can be handled by the students themselves with due preparation. "We show that a 100% virtual international collaboration is perfectly possible" (Ruiz et al., 2021) https://doi.org/10.14705/rpnet.2021.53.1295.

Teams were tasked to summarize and explain key theoretical terms and were invited to contextualize them using examples of their own life-worlds and cultural experiences. Providing purpose and agency, students were challenged to develop a ten-minute documentary comparing popular culture of two cities, Albany and Caracas. During this process, we discussed with our teams and classes what it means to act with an ethical sense and to understand their own and their teammates' socio-cultural environments.

Participants selected the topic according to their interest and motivations. They identified and assumed as their own the problems of their socio-cultural context. In this exercise, students observed their realities anew and allowed themselves to be challenged by them, and they connected knowledge with their multicultural reality.

Among the examples discussed were the notion of the popular – is an activity popular if it is performed by many, if it is free of charge, or can an activity performed by a small group also become popular? Another discussion centered on the presence or absence of the state to define and make space for a cultural activity such as a concert or dance as popular. Students compared the benefits of large cultural organizations offering concerts free of charge to large audiences with grassroots events that bring together artists and listeners in smaller and more improvisational fora. During this process of action-oriented re-framing, the students developed new frames of reference. In her feedback, one student describes how she was able to track the development of her own awareness, identify new competencies, acknowledge cognitive challenges from the experience abroad, and identify competencies that facilitated active responses to the new perspectives developed in the learning process.

This is illustrated from the quote below from a student who participated in the collaboration held in 2019. "Making a recount, having an experience of collaboration with students from a different area, culture and reality was only the beginning, because while we lived this exchange, I think that we hardly realized all the tools that we managed to apply as a group, in terms of our audiovisual training. We were completely immersed in the project and this is proven in the richness of the final documentary which, for me, is made up of all that learning" (Sofia Ruiz, 2021, student of class on 'Documentary', Venezuela, 2019).

According to Jiménez and Kressner, COIL projects promote activities that require individuals to participate in effective communication processes, the development of common agendas, and the formation of groups with people from diverse cultures to work cooperatively. These experiences stimulate students to propose new solutions for global socio-environmental well-being. "The virtual exchange modules encourage civic responsibility, self-reflection on the values and principles that guide the participants, the acquisition of skills to evaluate, self-assess, and acquire knowledge with leadership approaches and theories" (Jiménez and Kressner, 2021).

REFERENCES

Aldawood, H., & Skinner, G. (2018, December). Educating and raising awareness on cyber security social engineering: A literature review. In *2018 IEEE International Conference on Teaching, Assessment, and Learning for Engineering (TALE)* (pp. 62-68). IEEE. 10.1109/TALE.2018.8615162

Alotaibi, F., Furnell, S., Stengel, I., & Papadaki, M. (2016). A review of using gaming technology for cyber-security awareness. *International Journal of Information Security Resources.*, *6*(2), 660–666. doi:10.20533/ijisr.2042.4639.2016.0076

Anft, M. (2020). An Emerging Threat: Ransomware. *The Chronicle of Higher Education.* https://bit.ly/3z1j1sx

Annasingh, F., & Veli, T. (2016). An investigation into risks awareness and e-safety needs of children on the internet. *Interactive Technology and Smart Education, 13*(2), 147–165. doi:10.1108/ITSE-09-2015-0029

Bachelet, M. (2021). *Statement by the United Nations High Commissioner for Human Rights on Venezuela. 46th session of the Human Rights Council.* https://www.ohchr.org/EN/NewsEvents/Pages/DisplayNews.aspx?NewsID=26874&LangID=E

Casero-Ripollés, A. (2012). El periodismo político en España: algunas características definitorias. In A. Casero-Ripollés (Ed.), *Periodismo político en España: concepciones, tensiones y elecciones* (pp. 19–46). Sociedad Latina de Comunicación Social.

DHS. (2014). *A glossary of common cybersecurity terminology*. National Initiative for Cybersecurity Careers and Studies: Department of Homeland Security. http://niccs.uscert.gov/glossary

Fefer, R., & Archick, K. (2020). *EU Data Protection Rules and U.S. Implications*. Congressional Research Service (CRS). https://bit.ly/3Pwcddp

General Data Protection Regulation. (2016). *European Parliament*. https://bit.ly/2Ln3kBr

Hendrix, M., Al-Sherbaz, A., & Victoria, B. (2016). Game based cyber security training: Are serious games suitable for cyber security training? *International Journal of Serious Games, 3*(1), 53–61. doi:10.17083/ijsg.v3i1.107

Jiménez, J. L., & Kressner, Ia. (2021). Building empathy through a comparative study of popular cultures in Caracas, Venezuela, and Albany, United States. In Virtual exchange: towards digital equity in internationalisation (pp. 113-127). Research-publishing.net. doi:10.14705/rpnet.2021.53.1294

Khalid, F. (2017). Understanding university students' use of Facebook for collaborative learning. *International Journal of Information and Education Technology (IJIET), 7*(8), 595–600. doi:10.18178/ijiet.2017.7.8.938

Kolb, D. A. (1984). *Experiential Learning: Experience as the Source of Learning and Development*. Prentice Hall. http://academic.regis.edu/ed205/Kolb.pdf

Krotidou, D., Teokleous, N., & Zahariadou, A. (2012). Exploring parents' and children's awareness on internet threats in relation to internet safety. *Campus-Wide Information Systems, 29*(3), 133–143. doi:10.1108/10650741211243157

Marr, B. (2020). *The 5 biggest cybersecurity trends in 2020 everyone should know about*. Forbes. https://bit.ly/3b5w8kq

Mayer, R. (2001). Multimedia learning and games. *Computer Games and Instruction., 41*, 281–305. doi:10.1017/CBO9781139164603

Mezirow, J. (1978). Perspective transformation. *Adult Education, 28*(2), 100–110. doi:10.1177/074171367802800202

Mezirow, J. (1991). *Transformative dimensions of adult learning*. Jossey Bass.

Mezirow, J. (1997). Transformative Learning: Theory to Practice. *New Directions for Adult and Continuing Education, 1997*(74), 5–12. doi:10.1002/ace.7401

Mezirow, J., & ... (Eds.). (2000). *Learning as transformation*. Jossey Bass.

Mosalanejas, L., Dehghani, A., & Abdolahofard, K. (2014). The students' experiences of ethics in online systems: A phenomenological study. *Turkish Online Journal of Distance Education, 15*(4), 205–216.

Mountrouidou, Li, & Burke. (2018). *Cybersecurity in liberal arts general education curriculum*. . doi:10.1145/3197091.3197110

Ratten, V. (2015). A cross-cultural comparison of online behavioral advertising knowledge, online privacy concerns and social networking using the technology acceptance model and social cognitive theory,||. *Journal of Science & Technology Policy Management, 6*(1), 25–36. doi:10.1108/JSTPM-06-2014-0029

Rennick, J. (2015). Learning that Makes a Difference: Pedagogy and Practice for Learning Abroad. *Teaching & Learning Inquiry: The ISSOTL Journal, 3*(2), 71–88. doi:10.20343/teachlearninqu.3.2.71

Robledo, K., & Atarama, T. (2016). Periodismo político transmedia. Estrategias para el desarrollo de la profesión en el actual ecosistema mediático. *Correspondencias & Análisis*, (6), 31–45. doi:10.24265/cian.2016.n6.02

Rosenfeld, M. (2013). Rethinking the boundaries between public law and private law for the twenty-first century: An introduction. *International Journal of Constitutional Law, 11*(1), 125–128. https://bit.ly/3RXOB2Z. doi:10.1093/icon/mos053

Sadykova, G., & Meskill, C. (2019). Interculturality in online learning: Instructor and student accommodations. *Online Learning, 23*(1), 5-21. https://bit.ly/3zsa5xK doi:10.24059/olj.v23i1.1418

Sánchez, J., Mallorquí, A., Briones, A., Zaballos, A., & Corral, G. (2020). An integral pedagogical strategy for teaching and learning IoT cybersecurity. *Sensors (Basel), 20*(14), 3970. doi:10.339020143970 PMID:32708876

Thales Group. (2021, May). *Beyond GDPR: Data Protection Around The World*. Thales Group. Retrieved July 1, 2022, from https://bit.ly/3BeU6o7

Tsiptse, O. (2021). *Protection of Personal Data in the Era of COVID-19*. http://hdl.handle.net/11544/29755

Zhang-Kennedy, L., & Chiasson, S. (2020) A Systematic Review of Multimedia Tools for Cybersecurity Awareness and Education. *ACM Comput. Surv., 54*(1). doi:10.1145/3427920

Chapter 2
Detection of DDoS Attack Using Machine Learning Techniques in Software Defined Networking

Muthamil Sudar K.
https://orcid.org/0000-0001-9640-3477
Mepco Schlenk Engineering College, Sivakasi, India

Ruba Soundar K.
https://orcid.org/0000-0003-1300-6519
Mepco Schlenk Engineering College, Sivakasi, India

Vinoth P.
Mepco Schlenk Engineering College, Sivakasi, India

Nagaraj P.
Kalasalingam Academy of Research and Education, India

Muneeswaran V.
Kalasalingam Academy of Research and Education, India

ABSTRACT

The software-defined network (SDN) has recently developed as a network paradigm due to its high network programmability and flexibility, which can overcome the difficulty in traditional networks by detaching the control plane from the data plane. Following the controller's decision in the control plane, the data plane will transfer the packets. This unified administration will make it possible to see the network architecture as a whole in an abstract way. The controller is exposed to a significant threat if control is lost due to its centralised structure. Data plane resources are attacked by the attacker by focusing on switches that support OpenFlow. DDoS attacks damage network performance by overloading the SDN controller and network links, depleting the victim's bandwidth, and flooding the server with massive amounts of data. To address this issue, the authors employ statistical-based and machine learning-based techniques in SDN controller to inspect the new incoming flows.

DOI: 10.4018/978-1-6684-6092-4.ch002

INTRODUCTION

Traditional networks are challenging to operate due of their vertical integration. The data plane and control plane functions in modern networks are incorporated into the networking components. This limits the networking infrastructure's ability to adapt and innovate. Each network device needs to be individually configured using vendor-specific instructions in order to enforce security policies. This makes configuration more difficult and limits the ability to change the network dynamically. Software-Defined Network, a potent model that will foster more creativity in networking development and research, has recently been developed as a solution to these issues (Muthamil et al., 2020). Decoupling the control plane from the data plane is the fundamental tenet of SDN. The network administrator can take control of the complete network infrastructure using this approach. The core premise of SDN is to introduce dynamic programming ideas into data plane switching hardware via a southbound interface. The controller can have a global perspective of the network since it is logically centralised.

Distributed Denial of Service is one of the frequent and serious threats to the SDN because of its centralised structure (Muthamil et al., 2021). A DDoS attack's main goal is to reduce the network's performance by overtaxing the SDN controller and network links, using up all of the victim's bandwidth, and inundating the server with a tonne of data. Due to the high volume of malicious traffic, this causes the target system to lag, crash, or even shut down. The attacker can then impose the necessary tools on the compromised system in order to attack the server. A bot is a term used to describe this infected machine, while a botnet is a term used to describe a collection of compromised systems. In recent research, there has been a strong emphasis on providing a security solution against DDoS attacks in SDN systems.

In this paper, utilising statistical and machine learning techniques, we present a detection mechanism against DDoS attacks. Flow information is collected from incoming incoming flows and the essential features necessary to detect the DDoS attack are extracted. In order to train the machine learning classifier, we intend to employ NSL KDD Dataset. Finally, we employ a hybrid machine learning classifier to more effectively and accurately detect the attack with a low percentage of false alarms.

BACKGROUND AND RELATED WORKS

Software Defined Networking

An eminent technology, software defined networking uses advancements in networking research and development to overcome the issues in traditional network. Data, control, and application planes make up the three layers of software defined networking (SDN) architecture. By establishing an application programming interface between the three layers, it is possible to separate the data and control planes in the SDN. Network devices in the data plane forward traffic in accordance with the decisions made by the controller in the control plane, who determines the optimal way to manage network traffic (Sudar et al., 2022, Deepa et al., 2018). In addition to enabling the network administrator to make dynamic changes to the network, the separation offers a high degree of flexibility and scalability. Since, the controller is the SDN's central node, it requires the highest level of security. The network switching components in the data plane have no control functionality and forward traffic in line with the controller's commands. An interface known as a southbound interface (SBI) or control-data plane interface allows network components to communicate with the controller. Security and business applications, as well as virtual network and memory management features, are all included in the application plane. A northbound interface (NBI) is used by the controller to communicate with application plane apps.

A common application programming interface (API) in research and academia is the OpenFlow protocol (OF) (Sudar et al., 2020). Similar to an Ethernet switch that has one or more flow tables, an OpenFlow switch also has one or more flow tables. In the SDN, a switch typically looks for a matching flow in its TCAM (ternary constant addressable memory) table when it gets a new packet to determine the output port. Every entry in the flow table is divided into three sections: match, action, and stats. In the event of a match, the appropriate action is carried out, and the counter updates its statistics for matching packets. The switch sends the specific packet_in message to the controller and requests a new flow rule if the packet does not match an existing entry in the table. The controller chooses a routing path based on the request and tells all associated switches to process the new flow. Each flow entry might have its own time-out, after which the switch would delete it. Software programmes running on the application plane can be used to programme the control logic in addition to programmes for load balancing, firewalls, QoS (quality of service), and network monitoring. NOX, POX, RYU, Floodlight, and OpenDaylight are just a few examples of the SDN controller software that has been created by open-source communities. The controller and forwarding devices are logically separated from one another, allowing for the deployment of dynamic features and maximum network flexibility. Figure 1 depicts the SDN architecture.

Figure 1. SDN Architecture

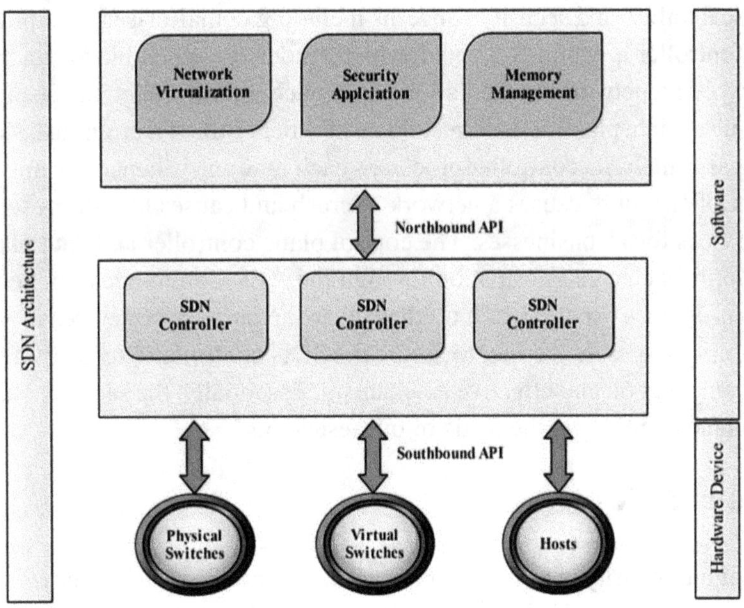

Benefits of SDN

Big data, the cloud, and virtualization are developing technologies that have put strain on traditional networks, which are often characterised by a lack of innovation, sluggish development, and production delays. The SDN is effective in a networking environment that is optimised and automated for dynamic changes, which promotes quick innovation in production and development. By combining the centralised controller and data plane switches into a single, unified platform, the SDN addresses issues in traditional networks. Through a centralised user interface, the SDN enables network managers to update policies, alter traffic flows, and universally make changes to all network devices. The SDN's ability to swiftly execute complete requests coming from many devices utilising a programming interface is a definite advantage. With an abstract view of the network, the software-based controller enables users and administrators to efficiently regulate traffic flow.

When necessary, network managers increase bandwidth and other resources while spending little on new physical equipment. The SDN's centralised intelligence converts networking into a powerful and dynamic function. Low operational expenses, an abstract view of the complete network infrastructure, management of virtual and physical devices from the centralised controller, and interaction with the public cloud are all features of the SDN. By centralising and automating the administrative process, the SDN lowers total operational expenses. The SDN's effective traffic management, which automatically improves the quality of service (QoS) for multimedia transmissions and Voice over IP, is an additional benefit.

Challenges in SDN

Powerful and dynamic networking is made possible by the SDN for IT businesses and communication service providers. However, there are issues that need to be resolved in terms of controller location, availability, reliability, scalability, and security concerns including denial-of-service and man-in-the-middle attacks. The SDN controller is centrally located, which renders it vulnerable to attacks, and single-point failures. Attacks involving network manipulation begin once the controller has been compromised. Additionally, compromised data plane devices result in a number of traffic reroutings, side-channel attacks, and traffic-sniffing assaults. The controller processes each new entry, hence disruption is the main goal of the attacks. Controller failure causes a network to crash and causes long-term service interruptions, which degrades services for IT businesses. The control plane controller and data plane devices operate independently and only exchange information through the API. Communication between a single controller and numerous devices experiences a bottleneck as the number of devices in the data plane rises, which causes scalability issues. It is easier to assure the SDN controller's security, availability, stability, and scalability by using a good and effective mechanism. Essentially, the security challenges in the data plane and control plane of SDN are the focus of our research.

Security Issues in SDN

Providing and managing security in a computer network is complex, with the network administrator having to provide security to safeguard it from internal and external intruders. A 2019 survey of cyberattacks revealed that more than 64%, 62%, 59% and 51% of all companies faced web-based, phishing, botnet and DDoS attacks, respectively. Network intrusion is intended to disrupt the target's system resources by stealing confidential information, disabling its functionalities and launching miscellaneous attacks. The threat looms large for large-scale organizations just as much as it does for medium and small-scale ones, because the latter are often unable to afford high-level security measures. Often, it results in attackers focusing on vulnerable medium and small-scale organizations. The most common threats to networks are from malware, SQL injection, phishing, botnet, cross-site scripting, DoS and DDoS attacks.

Malware attacks occur across devices and operating systems. They are fairly common attacks where malicious software is developed and installed to gain access to a victim's system without their knowledge. The attacks seek access to the victim's personal information in the form of credentials and confidential information; damage the system's resources and gain complete access for financial gain. Major malware attacks include spyware, viruses and ransomware.

A structured query language (SQL) injection uses SQL statements to attack databases by identifying their vulnerabilities. It gives an attacker access to data that cannot be retrieved by unauthorized users. Using the access thus gained, the attacker modifies or deletes confidential records from databases, irreversibly damaging the application. An attacker can also create a backdoor to pave the way for attacks in the near future, without the knowledge of the target user.

Phishing attacks target confidential login credentials and financial information by sending a potential victim deceptive mails. The aim is to trap the victim by sending mails that appear to be legitimate. Alternatively, attackers clone a legitimate website and alter the login page to steal login credentials. Further, they cause legitimate sites to be redirected to phishing sites using pop-up malicious dialogue boxes.

In botnet attacks, attackers called botmasters compromise several computers by installing malware and taking control of a victim's system. Using the control so obtained, malicious activity aimed at the target system is generated without the victim's knowledge. Botnet attacks disrupt regular business processes and financial transactions and the access gained enables attackers to impersonate root users.

In cross-site scripting attacks, attackers run malicious code in a victim's web browser by embedding it in web applications. A kind of client-side attack, it is triggered when the victim tries to access the malicious code-injected web application. Once the script is executed, the malicious code accesses the session information stored in the victim's browser.

In denial of service (DoS) and distributed denial of service (DDoS) attacks, authorized or intended users are restricted access to the resources available by the attackers generating more fake requests than the server can process. Both attacks aim to slow down or disrupt the process of handling legitimate requests. While DoS attacks are generated from a single source, DDoS attacks are generated from a large number of unknown and unsuspected sources. Botnets are generally used to launch DDoS attacks. DoS / DDoS attacks are categorized into two, buffer overflow attacks and flood attacks. In the former, the attacker consumes the physical resources available, such as memory and hard disk space. In the latter, the attacker floods the targeted server with such a massive volume of requests that the server is simply unable to process legitimate requests.

Utilizing firewalls in the application layer restricts unauthorized access within the network. Firewalls, however, help protect the network only when predefined security policies are applied. Despite the effective mechanisms put in place to handle security issues, the presence of the centralized controller poses security threats to SDN architecture. The controller in the control plane gives applications an abstract view so resources in the data plane may be used. If the controller is compromised, attackers modify the network controller's rules and stop legitimate users from accessing available resources. Major security issues caused by attackers in the controller are denial of service, data modification, data leakage and illegitimate network access. With unauthorized access and data modification, an attacker pretends to be the controller, manipulating and modifying network operations so as to take complete control of the entire network.

Each OpenFlow switch in the data plane has its own forwarding table with rules for packet handling. It is possible for an intruder to detect the action applied for each packet, using packet processing time analysis. For instance, the time taken by a single packet to be processed from one port to another is shorter than for it to be processed from a port to the controller. After identifying the nature of the packet, an attacker procures additional information about the network. Applying these techniques, the attacker generates a number of fake requests and dispatches them to the controller. The process, which stops legitimate users from accessing network resources, is termed a data leakage attack.

Given that any third-party application can be integrated into the application layer in the application plane, the imposition of a malicious application helps attackers exert control over the controller. Further, poorly designed or buggy applications could cripple the SDN architecture. Common security issues in the SDN can be effectively handled by incorporating an IDS into the SDN architecture.

High-Rate DDoS Attacks

The SDN controller and network links are overloaded by high-rate DDoS attacks, which also exhaust the victim's bandwidth and inundate the server with a massive amount of traffic. Due to the huge amount of malicious traffic generated, these elements lead the target system to slow down, crash, or completely shut down. An attacker can then combine the tools needed to attack the server using the compromised system. A bot is a compromised system, and a botnet is a collection of compromised systems. Before flooding the SDN controller with attack packets, it is essential to identify the attacks as soon as feasible. These attacks primary goal is to degrade the performance of services by using up all available system resources, including memory, processing power, and network bandwidth. The development of security measures to defend SDNs from DDoS attacks has received significant research attention. Several methods have recently been adopted to enhance SDN security in order to increase the system's detection accuracy with a low false alarm rate.

RELATED WORKS

According to Sudar, 2020, machine learning techniques for DDoS detection perform better than other statistical methods. Deepa (2018) claims that ensemble approaches perform more effectively than single level classifiers. In SDN control plane, machine classifiers offer superior accuracy with less complexity, according to comparative research of Sudar 2020. The Intelligent Flow-Based IDS by Sudar 2021 demonstrates how crucial feature identification is to machine learning-based detection.

To identify DDoS attacks in SDNs, Barki et al., 2016 employed a variety of machine learning algorithms, including Naive Bayes, K-nearest Neighbor, K-means, and K-medoids. A method for reducing overload in the controller and forwarding tables in the switches without compromising detection accuracy was developed by Dridi and Zhani, 2016. Furthermore, sampling techniques were used to determine the best site for the detector module to be installed. The findings of their experiment demonstrate that smart detector module placement enhances controller efficiency and lowers traffic overhead without compromising detection accuracy. The support vector machine (SVM) and neural network (NN) are two machine learning algorithms that Meti et al., 2017 presented as a method for increasing detection accuracy . With a real-time time dataset, they tested with the aforementioned methodologies on a Ryu controller. The detection accuracy of the SVM and NN algorithms was evaluated, along with controller functionality, and the experimental results demonstrate that the SVM technique performs better in the SDN environment.

Giotis et al., 2014 proposed a modular architecture that enforces the imposition of sFlow monitoring data to divide the SDN control plane from the data gathering procedure. Mehdi et al., 2011 looked at three alternative detection techniques in the context of SDN, including rate restriction, NETAD (Rule-based), and an entropy-based method. The findings indicate that using sFlow decreases traffic transmitted to the controller more effectively than using native OpenFlow. By combining the capabilities of SDN and flow approaches, Lu and Wang 2016 proposed a source-based detection mechanism to identify botnet-based DDoS flooding attacks. By using information distance (ID) as a metric in SDN controllers, Sahoo et al[16] .'s proposal for an effective detection strategy against DDoS flooding attacks. According to their experimental findings, the proposed mechanism outperformed Shannon entropy and other statistical-based methods in terms of accuracy. Entropy-based detection techniques for high rate DDoS flooding assaults in SDN-cloud environments were investigated by Mishra et al., 2018. By comparing the difference in entropy between the regular and attack traffic, they can identify the DDoS attack. A strategy to effectively fight against DDoS flooding attacks was developed by Cui et al., 2019 employing computing that was cognitively inspired. Deep learning DDoS defender was created by Li et al., 2018 using a variety of deep learning techniques, including convolutional neural networks (CNN) and long short-term memories (LSTM). They asserted that statistical and machine learning techniques aid in the earlier and more accurate detection of attacks as well as the development of effective countermeasures.

Low-rate DDoS attack is another important networking environment. It is very hard to detect low rate attacks because the nature of such attack traffic is very similar to normal traffic. In fact, the impact of low-rate DDoS attack is similar to high-rate DDoS flooding attack and it leads to degradation in performance and service unavailability to legitimate users. Here, we analyze some of the related works which addressed low rate DDoS attacks.

Pérez-Díaz et al., 2020 attempted to identify L-DDoS attacks using machine learning models like SVM, J48, Multi-layer Perceptron, REP tree, Random forest and Random tree in SDN environments. Zhijun et al., 2020 used factorization machine (FM) technique to detect low-rate DDoS attacks in SDN data planes by analyzing four essential features from flow information such as time duration, number of packets, match bytes and packet intervals. But, their experimental result shows that it failed to achieve good detection accuracy in case of huge network traffic.

Cheng et al., 2020 used machine learning mechanisms namely SVM, Naïve Bayes, K-Nearest Neighbour (KNN) and Random forest (RF) to detect low-rate DDoS attacks in SDN enabled IoT networks. Xinghsu et al., 2019 proposed a machine learning-based framework to defend against low-rate DDoS attacks in SDN cloud environments. Their experimental result claims that the proposed framework effectively detects low-rate DDoS attackswith 19 improved accuracy of 99.3%. However, processing time and resource utilization is not assessed in different network scenarios, when machine learning techniques are adapted.

Bhuyan et al., 2015 examined several information metrics to detect both high-rate and low-rate DDoS attacks in traditional environments. Ain et al., 2016 analyzed two rank correlation techniques like partial rank correlation and spearman rank correlation to detect low-rate DDoS attacks in traditional environments. Similarly, Hoque et al., 2016 proposed a framework called Feature feature score (FFSc) to defend against both low and high-rate DDoS attacks. They consider only three essential features such as source IP, destination IP and protocol type to train and test the proposed framework. Their experimental results claimed that the spearman rank correlation provides better accuracy with low false alarm rate. Their experimental result achieves high false alarm rate under average network traffic rate. The reason is they considered only limited random features for model development. This made clear that analyzing IP addresses alone will not be helpful for detection of high-rate DDoS attacks.

Toklu et al., 2018 designed architecture to filter both high-rate and low-rate DDoS attacks from legitimate flows. They used a decision with average filter (DAF) module to identify the high-rate attack and a decision with Discrete Fourier Transform (DDFT) to identify the low-rate attack by analyzing the arrival time. They claimed that the proposed architecture helps to efficiently classify the high and low-rate DDoS from normal traffic with low false alarm rate but at the cost of a high computation overload. Proposed work is suitable only for small and medium-sized network traffic. Early detection of attack is also not addressed in this work.

From the existing works, we have identified the following issues such as (i) The requirement for early attack detection, (ii) a fixed threshold value results in a high percentage of false alarms. (iii) accuracy is poor when random feature selection is used. By taking into account these problems, we have proposed our methodology, which involves identifying the key features from the SDN flow data and detect DDoS attacks using machine learning techniques.

PROPOSED WORK

Our proposed methodology is based on two methods that both employ flow-based data to detect high-rate DDoS attacks: statistics and machine learning. A group of subsequent packets that share the same characteristics and travel via the same network at the same time are referred to as a flow. By examining the quantity of incoming packets from the same or various IP addresses, entropy-based algorithms assist in the detection of attacks. Variations in the IP address range of packets cause an increase in false alarm rates. For the purpose of identifying frequent DDoS attacks, IP address analysis is not sufficient. By examining extra information in the arriving packets, machine learning techniques can identify threats. However, when there are a large number of arriving packets, the process becomes complicated. Therefore, this raises the requirement for an effective technique to both detect attacks earlier and deal with a large volume of incoming packets. Taking this into account, we use entropy- and machine-learning-based approaches to identify DDoS attacks. The gathered traffic flows are used to derive SDN-based traffic features. Using that, DDoS attacks in traffic samples will be recognised by statistical and machine learning models. In order to train the machine learning models, NSL-KDD dataset is utilised. Figure 2 illustrated the architecture of proposed work.

Figure 2. Architecture of proposed work

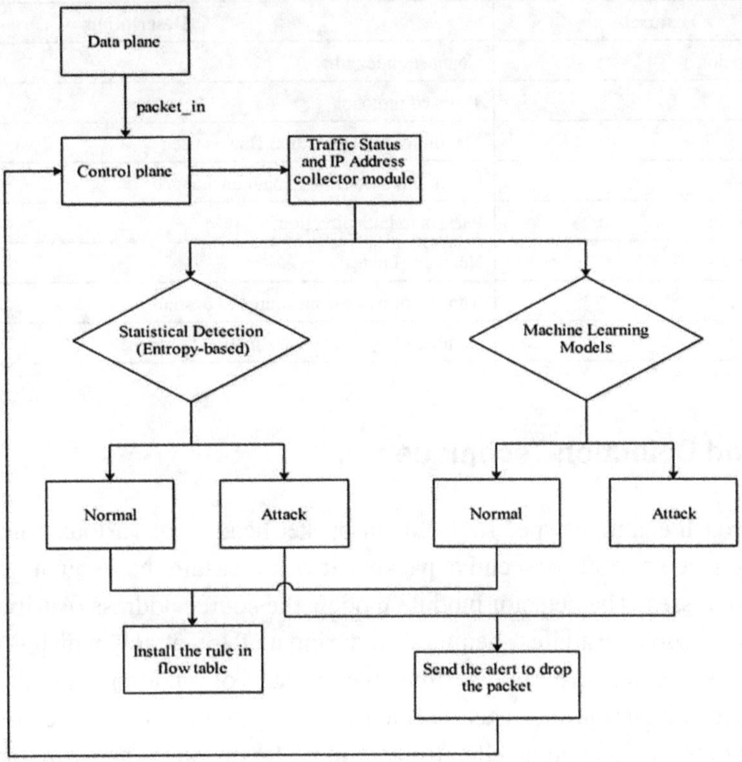

SDN-based Feature Extraction

We selected 8 essential features for further processing from the gathered incoming flows. We chose these 8 constrained characteristics from the 48 available features because they substantially correlate with the features in the NSL KDD dataset. The duration of the connection and the volume of data transferred are key factors in detecting DDoS attacks. The list of features extracted from the SDN flow is tabulated in table 1. We extract this set of features from the collected traffic samples and send them to machine learning models for DDoS attack detection. The NSL-KDD dataset is used for training the machine learning model, and the 8 key features are used for testing. This recognition of important features aids in reducing the complexity of identifying DDoS attacks.

Table 1. Features extracted from SDN flow

No.	Feature	Description
1	Flow_Duration	Connection length
2	Protocol	Types of protocol
3	use_Flow	Maximum time particular flow is used
4	idle_flow	Maximum time flow remain unchanged
5	bi_packets	Packets in both direction
6	count_packets	Number of bytes
7	packets_Tx	Number of bytes from source to destination
8	packets_Rx	Number of bytes from destination to source

Statistical-based Detection Technique

The statistical approach examines specific fields in packet headers at various points. For instance, if the detector module receives 500 consecutive packets, it will measure the frequency of the 500 packets' unique source IP addresses. The detector module models the source address distribution process based solely on the victim's source IP address being faked during a DDoS attack, which is the only reason the source IP address was selected. We can determine the measure of randomness with this distribution by performing extensive calculation. For each defined packet attribute, the suspicious activity detection module periodically reports the computed entropy value. The threshold and window size variables are selected in order to identify the attack. The entropy value will be low if each packet for a specific time window is specifically intended for one host. The entropy value will be low, however, if every packet sent within a certain time interval is headed for a different host. On the basis of the entropy attribute, randomness is estimated. Entropy can be used to analyse the value drop that occurs when a large number of packets attack a single host or group of hosts.

When a single host is the target of an attack, more packets will help the attack. The packets will exhaust the window's maximum size, devalue the maximum number of distinct IP addresses, and end up with a poor entropy value. Every IP address will only be revealed once, increasing the entropy value. Additionally, if a botnet is the target of an assault, its IP addresses will be regularly revealed over a period of time. An ideal threshold value must be determined in order to recognise the attack.

Information entropy is calculated using the following equation 1. Where, p_i is the periodicity of IP address and n indicates numbers of IP address in particular time window.

$$Entropy = -\sum_{i=1}^{n} p_i \log_2 p_i \tag{1}$$

Machine Learning-based Detection Technique

A dynamic strategy is needed to identify and stop network attacks due to the dynamic changes in attack patterns. The machine learning technology is used to achieve this criterion. The data that is readily available in the environment is used by machine learning techniques to learn. Statistical-based techniques can be used without any prior information of an attack or the behaviour of the attacker, but they have a significant potential for false alarms. As a result, machine learning techniques perform far better than statistical methods while having a lower percentage of false alarms. For proposed work, we used C4.5 Decision tree, Support Vector Machine (SVM), Naïve Bayes classifier and K-Means Clustering. For proposed work, we plan to implement with both single level and hybrid level classifier.

1. C4.5 Decision Tree

Unseen sample data can be accurately classified using decision trees, a well-known supervised machine learning model that correctly classifies training data. From a collection of sample data, decision trees use the divide-and-conquer strategy. The output, which takes the shape of a tree with each leaf node representing a decision for the tree, is created using a set of classified data as input. Pruning the initial tree solves the problem of complicated trees that are produced as a result of misclassification and are typically triggered by real data. When working with a lot of data or when numerous trees need to be constructed, the decision tree model's effectiveness is essential.

The C4.5 decision tree algorithm model, created by Ross Quinlan, is the most well-known. The information gain ratio serves as a splitting factor in the C4.5 algorithm. In order to divide the original dataset into subgroups, the algorithm chooses the best attributes. For data splitting, the attribute with the highest information gain value is chosen. Recursively, this procedure is applied to its subtree. The decision of any one class is represented by the leaf node. When the number of instances that need to be divided is below a predetermined threshold, the splitting procedure is terminated.

2. Support Vector Machine (SVM)

A supervised machine learning model called the SVM is primarily employed for classification and regression problems. In order to categorise upcoming instances, it maps training instances into an n-dimensional feature space and determines the best hyperplane between normal and attack instances. In the n-dimensional feature space, each data point in the SVM is a vector. The data points that are closest to the hyperplane serve as support vectors and constitute the classifier. The margin is affected by modifications to the support vectors but is unaffected by the addition or deletion of non-support vectors.

3. Naive Bayes

A popular classification method built on the idea of Bayes' theorem is the Naive Bayes classifier. It is a probabilistic model that, under the premise of interdependence between predictors, determines probabilities of class membership. This model is simple to construct and useful with huge datasets. Equation 2 indicates the naïve bayes calculation by strong assumption that there is no dependence between A and B.

$$P(A|B) = \frac{P(B|A)P(A)}{P(B)} \tag{2}$$

4. K-Means Clustering

One of the well-known machine learning strategies has been the usage of clustering techniques. The fundamental goal of clustering is to create clusters based on the data members maximum uniformity within a cluster and their minimum uniformity within different clusters. K-Means clustering has been used more frequently in this circumstance due to its simplicity, minimal complexity, and potential for success in clustering huge datasets. K- means clustering primary goal is to divide and organise the data into normal and attack instances. Based on their feature values, it divides the input dataset into k-disjoint clusters, where k is the preset positive parameter. Then, for each cluster, the centroid value will be calculated by computing the average value of the statistical information. By calculating the squared distance between centroids and the input data points, each input data point will be assigned to the nearest centroid. After then, a new centroid value for each cluster will be utilized to calculate the input data points assigned to each cluster.

4. Hybrid Machine Learning Classifier

A hybrid classifier combines different machine learning (ML) methods to improve the efficiency of the classifier (Sudar et al., 2022). A hybrid approach is divided into two functional stages. In the first step, gathered information is used as input to produce interim findings. The second phase, which generates the ultimate outcomes, then incorporates the intermediate results as input. Clustering methods are commonly employed in this situation to remove inconsistent data from in the incoming data. The output of several clustering algorithms is utilised as training data to build the classifier. A hybrid machine learning methodology combines two machine learning methods, with the first one emphasising parameter optimization to improve performance in the second phase.

In hybrid classifier, we combined K-means clustering with C4.5, SVM and Naïve Bayes classier. To separate the input dataset into k distinct clusters, the K-Means technique is used. We next train the collected data in each cluster using the C4.5 decision tree, Naive Bayes, and SVM. The K-Means technique ensures that each piece of training data is only present in one cluster. We determine the nearest cluster during the cluster selection phase by calculating the Euclidean distance for each input data point. The decision tree for the found cluster is then built. During the classification step, we deploy the test items to the nearest cluster that the C4.5 decision tree has found. Finally, we designate each data point in the test dataset as an attack or a normal data point.

EXPERIMENTAL SETUP

In our proposed work, we employed Mininet, a common network emulation tool for SDN. A huge number of virtual hosts, network switches, connections, and controllers can be added to an SDN-based environment. The functionalities of the controller in the control plane are simulated using the Python-based POX controller. The OpenFlow Virtual Switch (OVS) is employed for network switching. We have built a network structure with a single controller, three switches, and 12 hosts using Mininet. Figure 3 depicts the experimental network topology. We have produced numerous types of traffic using the Scapy tool for both normal and attack purposes. We utilised the NSL-KDD dataset to train the machine learning model. Only DoS attack samples were used in that.

NSL KDD Dataset

As a sample training set for our machine learning module, we selected the NSL-KDD dataset. The redundant data issue in the KDD'99 dataset is resolved in the NSL-KDD dataset, which is an upgraded version of the KDD Cup 1999 dataset. There are a total of 41 features with attack and normal patterns in the NSL-KDD dataset. User-to-root (U2R), remote-to-local (R2L), probing attacks, and denial-of-service (DoS) assaults are the four categories into which the attack patterns in the dataset are divided. The training dataset has 125,973 occurrences, whereas the testing dataset has 22,554 samples of network traffic. DoS attacks account for 53% of attack cases. We intend to train the machine learning module using that.

Figure 3. Experimental network topology

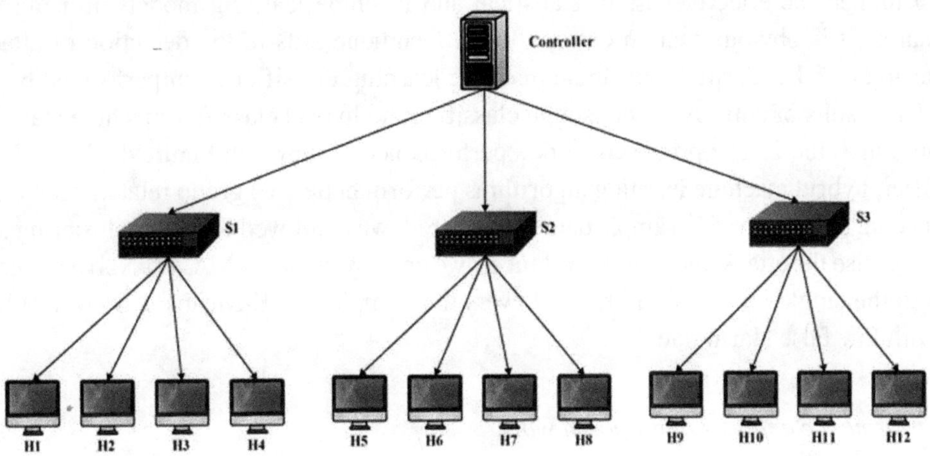

EVALUATION METRICS

Performance of proposed work is measured in terms of accuracy, precision, recall and F-score. Over all the classified data, accuracy (AC) determines the attack and normal data that is correctly classified. Over all of the positive categorised data, precision (P) identifies correctly identified positive data. How accurately the model recognises true positive is measured by recall (R). The F-score represents the average of recall and precision. Both the correctly categorised normal and attack flows are denoted by TP and TN, respectively. Indicators FP and FN denote incorrectly classified normal and attack flows, respectively. Equation 2,3,4,5 computes the accuracy, precision, recall and F-score respectively.

$$Accuracy = \frac{TP + TN}{TP + FP + TN + FN} \tag{2}$$

$$Precision = \frac{TP}{TP + FP} \tag{3}$$

$$Recall = \frac{TP}{TP + FN} \tag{4}$$

$$F\text{-}Score = 2 * \frac{Precision * Recall}{Precision + Recall} \tag{5}$$

RESULTS AND DISCUSSION

We have examined the effectiveness of statistical and machine learning models utilising the assessment measures. It is obvious that an entropy-based technique aids in the detection of attacks with a high proportion of false alarms. The single machine learning classifier is outperformed by the hybrid classifier. The results of entropy-based, single classifier and hybrid classifier machine learning models are compared in Table 2. The proposed work's performance is shown in Figure 4. Compared to single level classifier, hybrid machine learning algorithms perform better. To group related data and get rid of inconsistent data from the traffic sample data we gathered, we employed K-means clustering techniques. Then, to categorise the attack and regular instances, we employed the SVM/C4.5/Naive Bayes approach. Compared to the single level classifier, this lowers the complexity. K-Means + SVM results in better accuracy with low false alarm rate.

Table 2. Performance analysis of proposed work

Models	Accuracy	Precision	Recall	F-Score
Entropy	90.42	88.3	93.5	90.8
C4.5 Decision Tree	93.31	94.2	93.4	93.8
SVM	92.12	89.9	95.1	92.4
Naïve Bayes	93.12	94.2	93.1	93.6
K-Means Clustering	91.94	95.63	92.92	94.26
KMC+c4.5	96.73	96.97	98.41	97.68
KMC+ SVM	**98.66**	**98.66**	**99.04**	**97.34**
KMC+Naïve Bayes	91.36	92.7	91.3	92

Figure 4. Performance analysis of proposed work

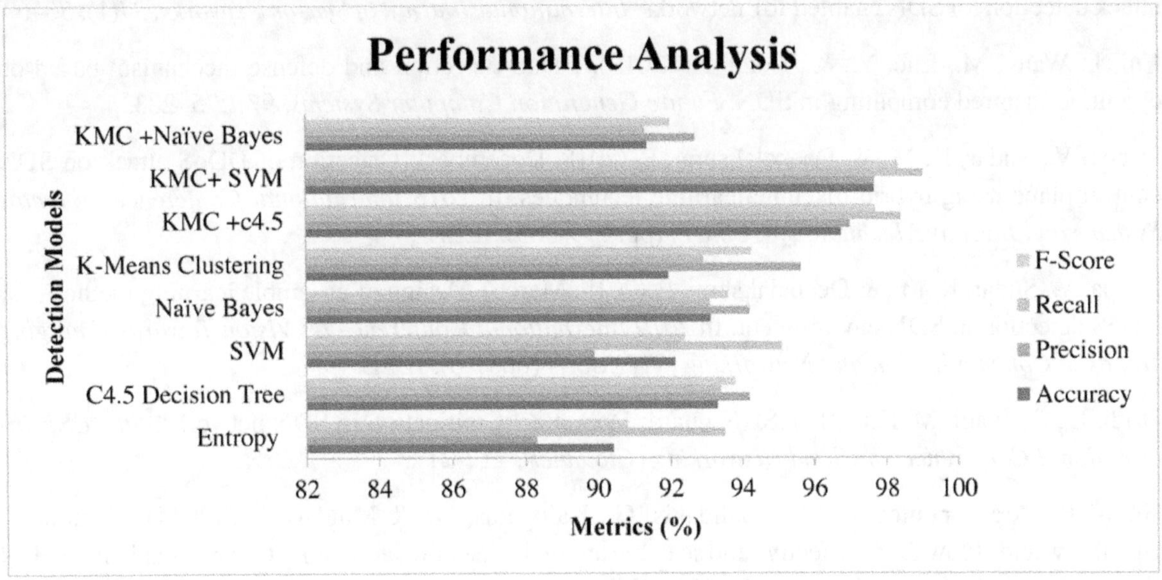

CONCLUSION

The main goal of the work is to defend network resources in the SDN control plane and data plane against network threats. It is essential to quickly and accurately identify attacks. One of the most dangerous threats to a networking environment is a DDoS flooding attack. A strong attack detection system must also have a low false alarm rate in order to be effective. From the traffic that the SDN controller collected, we derived the eight most important features. We used our learned machine learning models on that in order to detect DDoS attacks. The hybrid machine learning classifier (K-means Clustering and SVM) achieves superior accuracy with a reduced false alarm rate, according to the findings of our experiments. This research's advancement might involve the use of efficient attack mitigation techniques.

REFERENCES

Ain, A., Bhuyan, M. H., Bhattacharyya, D. K., & Kalita, J. K. (2016). Rank Correlation for Low-Rate DDoS Attack Detection: An Empirical Evaluation. *International Journal of Network Security*, *18*(3), 474–480.

Barki, L., Shidling, A., Meti, N., Narayan, D. G., & Mulla, M. M. (2016). Detection of distributed denial of service attacks in software defined networks. *IEEE International Conference on Advances in Computing, Communications and Informatics (ICACCI)*, 2576-2581.

Bhuyan, M. H., Bhattacharyya, D. K., & Kalita, J. K. (2015). An empirical evaluation of information metrics for low-rate and high-rate DDoS attack detection. *Pattern Recognition Letters*, *51*, 1–7.

Cheng, H., Liu, J., Xu, T., Ren, B., Mao, J., & Zhang, W. (2020). Machine learning based low-rate DDoS attack detection for SDN enabled IoT networks. *International Journal of Sensor Networks*, *34*(1), 56–69.

Cui, J., Wang, M., Luo, Y., & Zhong, H. (2019). DDoS detection and defense mechanism based on cognitive-inspired computing in SDN. *Future Generation Computer Systems*, *97*, 275–283.

Deepa, V., Sudar, K. M., & Deepalakshmi, P. (2018, December). Detection of DDoS attack on SDN control plane using hybrid machine learning techniques. In *2018 International Conference on Smart Systems and Inventive Technology (ICSSIT)* (pp. 299-303). IEEE.

Deepa, V., Sudar, K. M., & Deepalakshmi, P. (2019, March). Design of ensemble learning methods for DDoS detection in SDN environment. In *2019 International Conference on Vision Towards Emerging Trends in Communication and Networking (ViTECoN)* (pp. 1-6). IEEE.

Dridi, L., & Zhani, M. F. (2016). SDN-guard: DoS attacks mitigation in SDN networks. *5th IEEE International Conference on Cloud Networking (Cloudnet),* 212-217.

Giotis, K., Argyropoulos, C., Androulidakis, G., Kalogeras, D., & Maglaris, V. (2014). Combining OpenFlow and sFlow for an effective and scalable anomaly detection and mitigation mechanism on SDN environments. *Computer Networks*, *62*, 122–136.

Hoque, N., Bhattacharyya, D. K., & Kalita, J. K. (2016). FFSc: A novel measure for low-rate and high-rate DDoS attack detection using multivariate data analysis. *Security and Communication Networks*, *9*(13), 2032–2041.

Li, C., Wu, Y., Yuan, X., Sun, Z., Wang, W., Li, X., & Gong, L. (2018). Detection and defense of DDoS attack–based on deep learning in OpenFlow-based SDN. *International Journal of Communication Systems*, *31*(5), 1–14.

Lu, Y., & Wang, M. (2016). An easy defense mechanism against botnet-based DDoS flooding attacks originating in a SDN environment using sFlow. *Proceedings of the 11th International Conference on Future Internet Technologies*, 14-20.

Mehdi, S. A., Khalid, J., & Khayam, S. A. (2011). Revisiting traffic anomaly detection using software defined networking. *International Workshop on Recent Advances in Intrusion Detection*, 161-180.

Meti, N., Narayan, D. G., & Baligar, V. P. (2017). Detection of distributed denial of service attacks using machine learning algorithms in software defined networks. *International Conference on Advances in Computing, Communications and Informatics (ICACCI)*, 1366-1371.

Mishra, A., Gupta, N., & Gupta, B. B. (2021). Defense mechanisms against DDoS attack based on entropy in SDN-cloud using POX controller. *Telecommunication Systems*, 1–16.

Muthamil Sudar, K., & Deepalakshmi, P. (2020). A two level security mechanism to detect a DDoS flooding attack in software-defined networks using entropy-based and C4. 5 technique. *Journal of High Speed Networks*, *26*(1), 55–76. doi:10.3233/JHS-200630

Muthamil Sudar, K., & Deepalakshmi, P. (2021). An intelligent flow-based and signature-based IDS for SDNs using ensemble feature selection and a multi-layer machine learning-based classifier. *Journal of Intelligent & Fuzzy Systems*, *40*(3), 4237–4256.

Pérez-Díaz, J. A., Valdovinos, I. A., Choo, K. K. R., & Zhu, D. (2020). A flexible SDN-based architecture for identifying and mitigating low-rate DDoS attacks using machine learning. *IEEE Access: Practical Innovations, Open Solutions, 8*, 155859–155872.

Sahoo, K. S., Puthal, D., Tiwary, M., Rodrigues, J. J., Sahoo, B., & Dash, R. (2018). An early detection of low rate DDoS attack to SDN based data center networks using information distance metrics. *Future Generation Computer Systems, 89*, 685–697.

Sudar, K. M., Beulah, M., Deepalakshmi, P., Nagaraj, P., & Chinnasamy, P. (2021, January). Detection of Distributed Denial of Service Attacks in SDN using Machine learning techniques. In *2021 International Conference on Computer Communication and Informatics (ICCCI)* (pp. 1-5). IEEE.

Sudar, K. M., & Deepalakshmi, P. (2020). Comparative study on IDS using machine learning approaches for software defined networks. *International Journal of Intelligent Enterprise, 7*(1-3), 15–27.

Sudar, K. M., & Deepalakshmi, P. (2022). Flow-Based Detection and Mitigation of Low-Rate DDOS Attack in SDN Environment Using Machine Learning Techniques. In *IoT and Analytics for Sensor Networks* (pp. 193–205). Springer. doi:10.1007/978-981-16-2919-8_18

Sudar, K. M., Deepalakshmi, P., Nagaraj, P., & Muneeswaran, V. (2020, November). Analysis of Cyberattacks and its Detection Mechanisms. In *2020 Fifth International Conference on Research in Computational Intelligence and Communication Networks (ICRCICN)* (pp. 12-16). IEEE.

Sudar, K. M., Deepalakshmi, P., Ponmozhi, K., & Nagaraj, P. (2019, December). Analysis of Security Threats and Countermeasures for various Biometric Techniques. In *2019 IEEE International Conference on Clean Energy and Energy Efficient Electronics Circuit for Sustainable Development (INCCES)* (pp. 1-6). IEEE. 10.1109/INCCES47820.2019.9167745

Sudar, K. M., Deepalakshmi, P., & Singh, A. (2022). TFAD: TCP flooding attack detection in software-defined networking using proxy-based and machine learning-based mechanisms. *Cluster Comput.* doi:10.1007/s10586-022-03666-4

Toklu, S. İ. N. A. N., & Şimşek, M. (2018). Two-layer approach for mixed high-rate and low-rate distributed denial of service (DDoS) attack detection and filtering. *Arabian Journal for Science and Engineering, 43*(12), 7923–793.

Xingshu, C., Qiang, H., Yitong, W., Long, G., & Yi, Z. (2019). Research on low-rate DDoS attack of SDN network in cloud environment. *Journal of Communication, 40*(6), 210.

Zhijun, W., Qing, X., Jingjie, W., Meng, Y., & Liang, L. (2020). Low-rate DDoS attack detection based on factorization machine in software defined network. *IEEE Access: Practical Innovations, Open Solutions, 8*, 7404–17418.

KEY TERMS AND DEFINITIONS

DDoS: Distributed denial of service attack is a deliberate attempt to flood the target or its surrounding infrastructure with Internet traffic in order to maliciously disrupt the regular traffic of a targeted server, service, or network. By using numerous compromised computer systems as sources of attack traffic, DDoS attacks are made effective.

ML: Artificial intelligence (AI) in the form of machine learning (ML) enables computer programmes to forecast outcomes more accurately without having been expressly taught to do so. Machine learning algorithms forecast new output values using historical data as input.

SDN: Software-defined networking is dynamic, manageable, affordable, and adaptive, making it perfect for the high-bandwidth, dynamic nature of today's applications. With this architecture, network control and forwarding operations are separated.

Chapter 3
Incidence Response, Disaster Recovery, and Business Continuity Planning:
Their Role in an Institution's Risk Management Plan

Peter J. McAliney
Rutgers University, Camden, USA

Guy J. Albertini
Rutgers University, USA

Shannon D. Ramsaywak
Nathanial Rand, Inc., USA

ABSTRACT

Between advances in educational technology and learner expectations, higher education institutions are becoming increasingly dependent on third-party educational technologies such as learning management systems, metaverse-related technologies, open educational resources, and eportfolios to support learning. While this permits these institutions to deliver more engaging learner experiences, it also brings increased exposure to cyber-attacks. This chapter addresses the hierarchy that is implied by the threat of cyber-attack and the importance of developing the front-line incidence response (IR) and disaster recovery (DR) plans within the context of the business continuity plan (BCP), recognizing that the BCP must also be consciously integrated as part of the institution's overall risk management plan. This chapter walks through the key steps of building an IR program and DR plan, illustrating how they support the key cyber security components of the BCP that are incorporated into the institution's overall risk management plan. The vital role that communication plays will be addressed.

DOI: 10.4018/978-1-6684-6092-4.ch003

INTRODUCTION

Between advances in educational technology and learner expectations, higher education institutions are becoming increasingly dependent on third-party applications to support learning. While this permits these institutions to deliver more engaging learner experiences, it also brings with it increased exposure to cyber-attack. According to an Educause-Arctic EWS joint research report, many universities have excessively penetrable firewalls and, further, do not have clearly articulated firewall management rules to deal with the cyber risks that may be associated with this (Educause, 2021). Many universities have recognized the exposure that this implies, and as such, have taken action in three areas. They have: developed incident response (IR) and disaster recovery (DR) plans as part of their Business Continuity Plan (BCP); taken out insurance policies to address possible breaches; and, in some cases, have chartered the role of a Chief Information Security Officer (CISO). However, while both the IR and DR need to be created in alignment with the BCP, they must also be developed within the context of their role in the university's overall risk management plan. Failure to do so may result in a sub-optimal risk management plan.

Risk Management

Risk is an event that negatively impacts tangible and intangible assets associated with an individual, business or institution (Pallavi, 2019). Pallavi further describes risk as an energy that cannot be created or destroyed but only passed on or managed. Whether you are an individual, business, or higher education institution, the management of risk needs to play an integral role in decision-making. Marieke Liem, PhD, in her course titled, "Risk in Modern Society" proposes that risk is one of the defining features of modern society (Liem, 2022).

In higher education and other industries, the management of risk is addressed by the development of a risk management process that consists of five components (KirkpatrickPrice, 2022):

- Risk identification;
- Risk analysis;
- Response planning;
- Risk mitigation; and,
- Risk monitoring.

Risk Identification

As the name implies, this is the practice of identifying risk. Depending on the industry and type of business, the identification of risk can vary. Risks associated with retail brick-and-mortar businesses – such as Walmart – differ from risks associated with service industries, such as higher education institutions. This can be observed, for example, in the area of credit risk. Retail brick-and-mortar businesses customers tend to have a shorter time frame associated with payment horizons. In higher education institutions, however, payment horizons are longer. These are manifest as risks associated with student accounts, which can have both a longer payment horizon as well the potential for risk associated with third-party funders.

During this phase, risk is also documented and categorized. Risk categories are established to classify the risk relevant to the organization, which will help those responsible for managing risk to develop the context associated with the risk and to quickly understand its impact (Thakur, 2022). Like many organizations, higher education institutions may experience one or more of the following risk categories: operational risk; budget risk; supplier risk; regulatory compliance risk; infrastructure risk; health risk; and, of course, information security and technology risk (Thakur, 2022). Many institutions, for example, were recently faced with managing health risks associated with the COVID-19 pandemic.

Risk Analysis

Once risks have been identified, documented, and categorized, analysis of each risk follows. Depending on the objectives, institutions may elect to use a quantitative method, a qualitative method, or a combination of both.

A quantitative risk analysis is an evidence-based method that uses numbers or measurable data points to identify weaknesses or vulnerabilities (Guthrie, 2020). Given its numerical use, this type of analysis is typically favorable with boards and institution leaders (Meir, 2020).

Alternatively, a qualitative risk analysis uses a method that predicts the likelihood and impact of a risk associated with an asset (Guthrie, 2020). An analyst will typically conduct a qualitative risk analysis by interviewing stakeholders to determine the potential impact of any asset resulting from the exploitation of a vulnerability. Depending on the potential impact from the risk, a rating of high, medium, or low will be assigned to the risk. Although this method is not as accurate as a quantitative risk analysis, it is used more often due to its ease of use, cost, and speed.

On some occasions, institutions may opt to use both methods.

Response Planning

The next step in the risk management process consists of the response planning phase. In this phase, an analyst would typically explore what steps should be taken to address the identified risk (KirkpatrickPrice, 2022). Institutional leaders should fully understand the risk during this stage to develop an appropriate risk mitigation plan. For example, a Chief Information Security Officer (CISO) may develop specific security awareness training plans for users that opened or responded to a simulated phishing campaign. For more information on the role of a CISO and a list of resources intended for CISOs and other security professionals new to their role in higher education, visit Educause's "Toolkit for New CISOs" (Educause, 2017).

It's important to also note that during this phase, the institution's leadership team has the option to accept, transfer, mitigate, or avoid risk (Verry, 2016). The options selected to address the risk rely on the overall risk tolerance of the institution. Factors that can influence the risk tolerance of an institution include, but are not limited to compliance, cost, and culture.

- Compliance: Most higher education institutions are required to comply with federal laws such as the Family Educational Rights and Privacy Act (FERPA) and the Gramm-Leach-Bliley Act (GLBA). Ignoring a risk associated with either of these laws could result in unwanted consequences for an institution. Among the options to address risk, ignoring risk is not an option when addressing compliance-related operating factors.
- Cost: The cost associated with addressing a risk may be one of the biggest factors. Leadership has to weigh the cost of addressing a risk versus avoiding it (Verry, 2016). In many instances, avoiding

a risk may be the most cost-effective option. Institutions may simply opt to do without a service or product. Another option is to transfer it (Verry, 2016). Most, if not all, institutions now transfer portions of their overall risk to a third-party. Many industries, including higher education, transfer portions of their cybersecurity risk to insurance companies. This option particularly benefits institutions that may not have the talent or skills to effectively mitigate cybersecurity risk.

- Culture: The culture of an institution also plays a role in how risk is handled (Statman, 2010). It is often said, "culture is the glue that binds organizations together" (Rosowsky & Hallman, 2020). One of the attributes that distinguishes higher education from other industries is the practice of shared governance – the distribution of leadership among the board, faculty, and administration (Jackson, 2020). The decision-making process in a shared governance model often involves one or all of the governing members. Accordingly, risk-based decisions in such a model can also be influenced by one or all members. Given the impact risk-based decisions have on institutions, it is important for governing bodies to collaborate and combine their skills and talents to collectively manage institutional risk.

In this phase, institutions may also develop a risk register to record known risk and stay abreast of potential issues that can derail intended outcomes (Ray, 2021). Risk Managers may create or purchase a solution to keep track of the risks. Depending on the organization, a risk register may include the following elements: risk identification number; risk description; risk categories; risk analysis; risk probability; risk priority; risk response; and, risk ownership (Ray, 2021). One of the most important elements in the register is the risk owner. Every institutional risk should have an assigned owner to ensure adequate resources are available to mitigate the risk. Many institutions today have a risk office where a senior executive serves as the owner of institutional risk.

Risk Mitigation

Risk mitigation is the set of activities that define how the response plan is executed and by whom. Authorized generally by management, the response plan identifies the actions to be taken by the institution to reduce the effects of the risk (KirkpatrickPrice, 2022). Following the previous example, the institution may opt to establish mandatory security awareness training for all employees and acquire training materials that specifically focus and address the weaknesses detected during the test campaign. During the risk mitigation phase, institutional leaders may also test the effectiveness of the controls used to mitigate each risk. For instance, the CISO could launch another simulated phishing campaign to see if fewer users respond.

Risk Monitoring

The final step in the risk management process is risk monitoring (KirkpatrickPrice, 2022). It is important to understand that risk management is not a destination, it's a journey. Controls implemented today may no longer be effective in the future. As the ever-changing climate of cyber-attacks continue, it is imperative that institutions establish appropriate protocols to continuously monitor for indicators or change in controls used to mitigate past risk. Monitoring for potential future risk is also applicable. Accordingly, institutions should begin to assess potential risks associated with the use of the next iteration of the web – Web 3.0.

Risks typically increase as new technology is introduced, and Web 3.0 does not disappoint. The Web 3.0 system consists of a "Metaverse" – a virtual reality environment where users can explore, shop, play, socialize, attend events, conduct business, and learn (Monzon, 2022). In addition to all of the wonderful innovations that will be offered by Web 3.0, security experts believe it will also provide new opportunities for threat actors (Monzon, 2022). Those concerns stem from Web 3.0's use of cryptocurrency, blockchain technology, the decentralization of applications and file storage (Monzon, 2022). Institutions that begin to review the use and risks associated with Web 3.0 will be ahead of the curve in mitigating related risks prior to its ubiquitous use.

It is helpful for institutional leaders to manage the overall risk of the organization by establishing a risk management policy. Such a policy would include the institution's philosophy, high level objectives for the management of institutional risk, strategic goals, acceptance criteria, roles and responsibilities, and conditions to determine performance (Talbot, 2021). To support the policy, institutions could choose to also implement related standards that outline requirements to meet objectives in the policy. A standard, for example, could include the use of an industry standard risk management framework such as ISO, NIST, or RISK IT (Wright, 2020). As the institution matures and the climate of risk changes, objectives outlined in the policy should also evolve to reflect current conditions.

Managing risk is not a trivial task – there are many facets to consider. It involves a lot of hard work from various stakeholders. All levels of management must work together to address institutional risk. To mitigate cybersecurity risks, for example, a CISO may work primarily with the chief information officer (CIO), the General Counsel, and the chief operating officer (COO) of an organization. Their analysis would be further enhanced with input from associated internal personnel in risk management, communications and media, law enforcement, the institution's President, and the board. All areas must function as one to effectively manage the risk. Institutions clearly benefit when risk management plans are established. In fact, well thought out plans will invariably save institutions money (Egencia, 2022). For instance, risks associated with cybersecurity could be extremely costly. Employing risk management tactics could potentially reduce the cost of such eventualities by proactively assessing the risk and deploying adequate controls to mitigate any identified risk (Egencia, 2022). Additional benefits of risk monitoring include the avoidance of regulatory issues, reduced litigation and liability problems, and improved employee relationships (Egencia, 2022).

Between advances in educational technology and learner expectations, higher education institutions are becoming increasingly dependent on third-party applications to support learning. This trend must be factored into a university's risk management plan. While this permits these institutions to deliver more engaging learner experiences, it also brings with it increased exposure to cyber-attack. According to an Educause-Arctic EWS joint research report, many universities have excessively penetrable firewalls and, further, do not have clearly articulated firewall management rules to deal with the cyber risks that may be associated with this (Arctic Wolf-Educause, 2021).

CYBERSECURITY THREATS IN HIGHER EDUCATION

The 2022 Educause Horizon Report (Ebner, 2022) explicitly calls out cybersecurity as a trend for higher education institutions to monitor. Of the five major trends identified – Social, Technological, Economics, Environmental, and Political – cybersecurity is addressed explicitly in the Technological trend and indirectly in the Economic trend, where it is folded into considerations associated with the digital economy.

The education industry is one that bad actors see as vulnerable and, as such, is one of the industries most impacted by cybersecurity threats. In 2020, thousands of students have had their data compromised due to cybersecurity breaches (Schwartz, 2020). In 2021, 88 educational institutions or school systems were impacted by ransomware, including 26 colleges and universities (Ebner, 2022). This has become an area of increasing concern due to the increase of data emanating from a variety of sovereign nations around the globe, increased online utilization resulting from COVID-19, and increased use of third-party tools and new mechanisms for collecting personal data (e.g., vaccination status).

Cybersecurity in higher education must be treated with a holistic approach to improve data privacy, to implement measures against unauthorized access to data, and to protect users from various forms of data surveillance (Fouad, 2022). It also relates to managing risks associated with data availability (i.e., ensuring users can access data when needed) and data integrity (i.e., protecting data against unauthorized modifications). The security of systems and networks in which data is stored also needs to be addressed, which is why the development and implementation of a Business Continuity Plan (BCP)is so important.

CATEGORIZING CYBER-ATTACKS

Learners have expanded the array of devices that they use for accessing learning assets from the institutions that they attend. With the different types of educational technologies that learners employ, their personal data is stored in a variety of locations. As such, storage on this array of remote servers, laptops, and cellphones makes it easier for cyber attackers to find an entry point into a network through a personal device (University of North Dakota, n.d.).

While there are many specific types of attacks that can occur, these threats can be organized into seven categories:

1. Malware: This category contains "malicious" software such as spyware, ransomware, viruses and worms. It engages when a learner clicks on a malicious link or attachment. This will then activate the installation of software that can block access to key network components (ransomware), install additional harmful software, unsuspectingly access information by transmitting data from the hard drive (spyware), or corrupt individual parts of the system that can take down the entire system.
2. Denial of Service: A denial of service (DoS) attack overwhelms a computer or network so it can't respond to requests. A more serious DoS is the distributed DoS (DDoS), which is where the attack originates from a computer network. One specific kind of DDoS is the botnet (or zombie systems), which overwhelms a target's processing capabilities by installing hacker-controlled malware that can infect multiple systems. These types of attacks are used to disrupt the "handshake" process to gain entry. Often, cyber attackers will embed other attacks in the series of overwhelming requests to the system during a DoS or DDoS.
3. Man in the Middle: Just as it sounds, a man-in-the-middle (MITM) attack is when a hacker places themself between two parties in a two-party transaction. From this position, they have visibility to all traffic and can filter and steal data. These types of attacks often occur when a learner visits an unsecured public Wi-Fi network.
4. Phishing: These kinds of attacks employ disingenuous communications, such as a text or an email, to dupe the recipient into opening it and carrying out the instructions inside.

5. SQL Injection: A Structured Query Language (SQL) injection inserts malicious code into a SQL server. When compromised, the server disperses sensitive information.
6. Password Attacks: When an attacker has access to a learner's password, they can gain access to all the information associated with the system to which the password is attached. When a cyber attacker obtains a learner's password on one system – either through an algorithm, educated guess, or outright guessing – it is easier for them to attack other systems that the learner might be associated with. This is why it is so important to have secure and varied passwords.
7. Emotet: An Emotet, as described by the Cybersecurity and Infrastructure Security Agency (CISA), is "an advanced, modular banking Trojan that primarily functions as a downloader or dropper of other banking Trojans." According to CISA, these tend to be among the most costly and destructive types of malwares.

A relatively recent type of cyber-attack that has appeared in higher education in particular is a phenomenon called "zoombombing" (Gunnell, 2020). This is where online video conferencing platforms are interrupted by unwanted participants. These intruders will disrupt learning by entering an online classroom to inject hate speech against students during online classrooms or expose learners to unwanted and harmful media during online class sessions. This can impede learning and create fear of using technology.

TYPES OF EDUCATIONAL TECHNOLOGIES

Educational technology is multi-contextual and, as such, has a variety of definitions. One of the earliest definitions was one-dimensional and summarized educational technology as the application of physical sciences and engineering technology to provide mechanical instruments or "hardware" to be used for instructional purposes (Finn, 1960). The concept of educational technology has grown to absorb additional facets and now is most often considered to include pedagogy/andragogy and ethical components. For example, the Association for Educational Communications and Technology (AECT) defines educational technology as "the study and ethical practice of facilitating learning and improving performance by creating, using, and managing appropriate technological processes and resources" (Richey et al., 2008). In Spector's (2015) oft-cited textbook entitled "Foundations of educational technology: Integrative approaches and interdisciplinary perspectives," he identifies educational technology as the disciplined application of knowledge for the purpose of improving learning, instruction, and/or performance.

The focus of this chapter is the hardware, software, and telecommunications facets associated with educational technology.

There are many types of educational technologies that higher education institutions are employing to support learners. The goal of institutional information technology departments is to seamlessly integrate these third-party technologies into the institution's information technology infrastructure.

Some of the systems and technologies that are part of an institution's information technology infrastructure include:

- Learning Management Systems (LMS) – These are applications for the "administration, documentation, tracking, reporting, automation, and delivery of educational courses, training programs, or learning and development programs" (Wikipedia, n.d.).

- Online Program Managers (OPMs) – OPMs are third-party partners that can take on a variety of learning support roles for an institution. Their services can include program design and delivery, learner recruitment and retention, or some combination of services to support an institution.
- Learning Analytics – These are applications for the "measurement, collection, analysis and reporting of data about learners and their contexts, for purposes of understanding and optimizing learning and the environments in which it occurs" (Wikipedia, n.d.).
- Open Educational Resources (OERs) – OERs are educational resources found in the public domain. A cataloging system and licensing system called Creative Commons define how these materials can be used.
- Teaching Bots – These are virtual teaching assistants that can support an instructor in an online classroom. They can answer simple logistics questions such as assignment due dates as well as further definitions of course module content and assignment composition.
- Metaverse Related Technologies – The metaverse is an integrated network of 3D worlds that emulate real life activities (Terminalfour, n.d.). It is a blanket term that includes artificial intelligence (AI), augmented reality (AR), virtual reality (VR), and extended reality (XR). It can be further enhanced with the use of wearables – physical devices such as headsets – that a learner deploys to shape their 3D experience.
- ePortfolios – ePortfolios are an organized catalog of a learner's work that can be accessed to support learner self-sovereignty of artifacts they create in their learning journey. They have emerged as a way for learners to meet the increased demand by the workplace for examples of learner capabilities that help hiring managers make more informed hiring decisions.

BUSINESS CONTINUITY PLANNING

Many universities have recognized the exposure that third party applications – and their underlying infrastructures – can bring to their security, and have enhanced their Business Continuity Plans (BCP) to incorporate incident response (IR) and disaster recovery (DR) plans that specifically address cybersecurity risks (Figure 1). Many have taken out insurance policies to address possible breaches, and in some cases, have chartered the role of Chief Information Security Officer (CISO). However, while it is clear that both IR and DR need to be created in alignment with the BCP, they must also be developed within the context of their role in the overall risk management plan. Failure to do so may result in a sub-optimal risk management plan for the university.

Figure 1. Risk management hierarchy

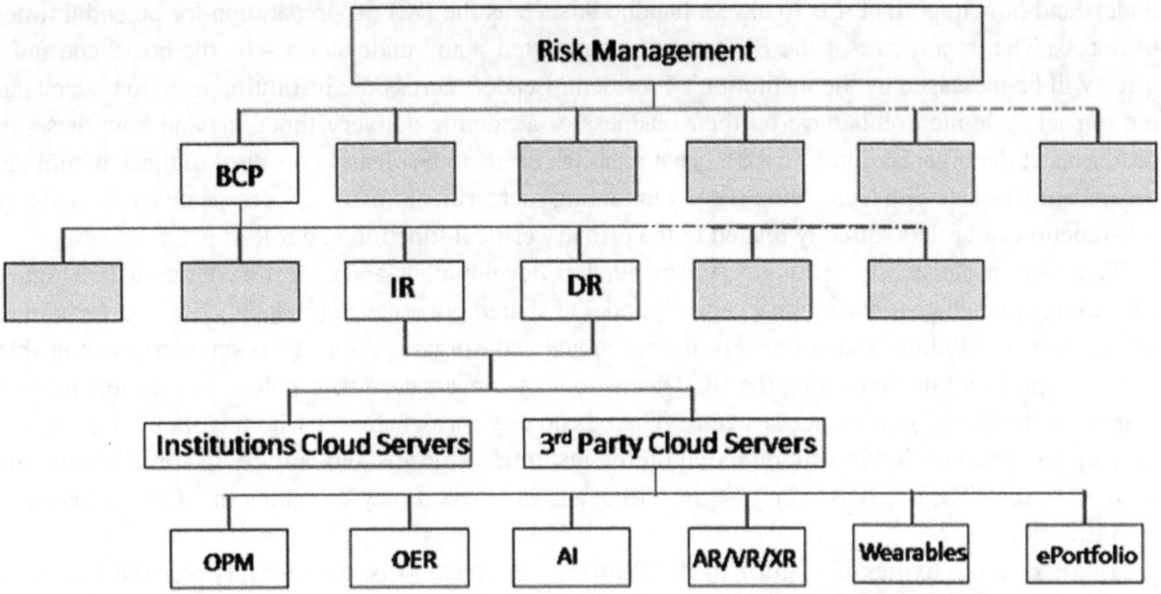

Understanding the role of a BCP, with its corresponding IR and DR components, and how to ensure it properly accounts for this new ecosystem of educational technologies, is paramount for protecting against potential cybersecurity breaches.

Business Continuity Planning – or Business Continuity Management – is an integral component of a comprehensive Risk Management Plan. It addresses the criticality of "availability" in what is called the CIA Triade (i.e., Confidentiality, Integrity and Availability) to ensure information technology systems are fully available for access by all stakeholder after problematic conditions unfold (Van der Ham, 2021). In higher education, these stakeholders include staff, faculty, administrators, and students.

Business Continuity Planning is the process that is followed to create a comprehensive system of prevention and recovery from potential threats to a company. The document that is produced –the BCP – addresses those actions that are required to ensure that personnel and assets are protected and can function quickly in the event of a disaster (Hiles, 2010). A comprehensive Business Continuity Planning strategy in higher education should consider the 4 P's: people (i.e., staff, faculty, administrators, and students), processes (i.e., the technology and processes required), premises (i.e., on-site and remote locations) and providers (i.e., suppliers and partners). This methodology enables leadership to take a holistic view of business continuity across the entire institution (Kenton, 2022).

A cybersecurity attack that causes damage, loss, or corruption of information technology – including voice and data communications, servers, computers, operating systems, applications, and data – is but one disruptive scenario that a BCP needs to address (Ready, n.d.; Leigh, 2015). The BCP also must contain contingencies for business functions, roles, facilities, assets, human resources and third parties. It ensures that all key stakeholders of each critical business function within the organization have a specific/unique handbook to execute their respective critical business functions during and after any business interruption event.

Executive sponsorship is critical in ensuring that the varied academic and administrative departments understand how important it is to have a handbook such as the BCP in preparation for potential times of duress. The importance of the BCP must be supported – and understood – by the board and most often will be messaged by the institution's President. Leaders across the institution need to understand the impact systemic events have on their business or academic delivery functions and how these, in turn, impact the organization's mission. That message needs to be clearly conveyed to those within the organization tasked with identifying and documenting each critical function, its respective role, and any sub-function and role(s) directly related to the primary critical function and role.

There are special considerations around ownership, development, and execution of the BCP in higher education. Given higher education's general model of shared governance (Jackson, 2021), determining roles and responsibilities and, ultimately, the individual in the organization who is singularly responsible for developing and implementing the BCP needs to be a conversation that includes all those who participate in the shared governance structure. There is no one correct answer who this should be – it will vary by higher education institution based on the institution's norms and culture. In some institutions it might be the CIO, in others it may be the CISO, and in others it may be yet another C-level leader at the institution.

Two essential activities that inform the BCP are the creation of a disaster recovery plan (DRP) and an incident response plan (IRP). The DRP focuses on the whole enterprise; the IRP focuses on an incident. A DRP addresses the questions about how the organization can resume normal operations after a disaster disrupts your business activities. An IRP increases the probability that your institution is prepared for possible information security incidents such as a data breach, a system outage, or a security breach. These risks can cause lasting damage to both operations and the student experience.

Another way to think about it is that the DRP addresses *types* of *disruption* (e.g. equipment outage, weather disruption, cyber-attack) and are intended for anyone in the organization to use, so his or her team can contribute to resuming normal operations An IRP, on the other hand, is drawn up to address *specific issues that cause a disruption* (e.g., data breach, ransomware attack, phishing attack) and are intended for incident response teams trained in addressing and mitigating known cybersecurity risks. Both plans are needed as they outline pre-approved steps that have been clearly communicated across the organization so that employees know what to do to recover as quickly as possible from a disruption. Developing both plans that are clearly articulated and communicated before a disruption occurs positions your organization to act, not waste time with prioritization or decision-making when a disruption occurs (Reciprocity, 2021).

Disaster Recovery Plan (DRP)

A Disaster Recovery Plan (DRP) captures the elements of a systems-oriented mitigation strategy. The DRP is a documented, structured approach describing how an organization can quickly resume work after an unplanned incident (Brush, n.d.). Disaster recovery planning specifically involves identifying the information technology systems associated with critical functions and documenting a recovery plan for each affected system in the event of a major system failure of hardware, software, and/or connectivity.

Some components of a DRP as outlined in NIST Special Publication 800-82 (Stoufer et.al, 2015) include:

- Required response to events or conditions of varying duration and severity that would activate the recovery plan.
- Roles and responsibilities of responders.
- Processes and procedures for the backup and secure storage of information.
- A complete and up-to-date logical network diagram.
- Personnel list for authorized physical and cyber access to facilities and technology infrastructure.
- Communication procedure and list of personnel to contact in the case of an emergency including vendors, network administrators, information technology system support personnel, etc.
- Current configuration information for all components.
- Schedule for exercising the DRP.

The plan should also indicate requirements for the timely replacement of components in the case of an emergency. If possible, replacements for hard-to-obtain critical components should be kept in inventory.

Putting together a DRP (see Figure 2) can be considered using the seven-phase approach (Cybase,n.d.; Dosal, 2020; Educause, n.d.).

Figure 2. The Disaster Recovery (DR) seven-phase approach

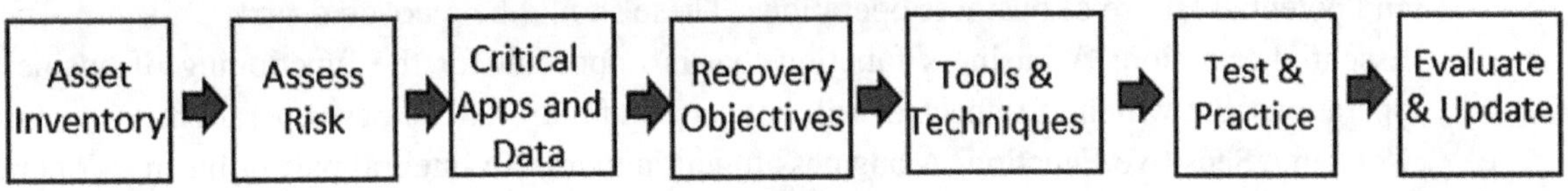

Figure 3. Develop an asset inventory

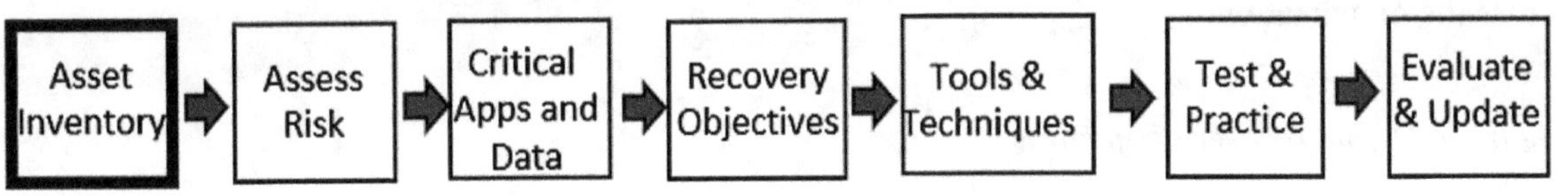

1. Develop an asset inventory (see Figure 3) – The first phase in developing a DRP is to catalog an inventory of all your IT assets to develop a macro picture of your institution's environment, including IaaS, IDaas, Saas. This list should include all the information technology assets under management, including all servers, storage devices, applications, data, network switches, access points, and network appliances. Physical locations, network affiliations, and dependencies must then be identified.

Figure 4. Conduct a risk assessment

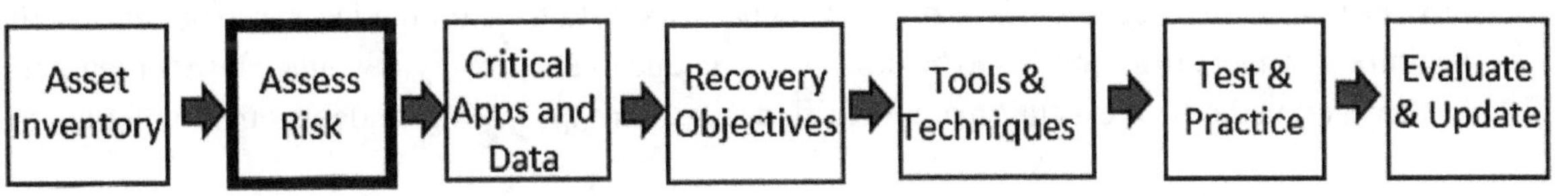

2. Conduct a risk assessment (see Figure 4) – For all assets and interrelationships identified in the asset inventory, list the internal and external threats. Develop scenarios for low probability events (e.g., massive cyber security attack), most likely events (e.g., power outages), and high probability events (e.g., IT hardware failure) with their corresponding negative impacts. It is important in this phase to include a wide variety of perspectives from stakeholders across the organization.

Figure 5. Define criticality of applications and data

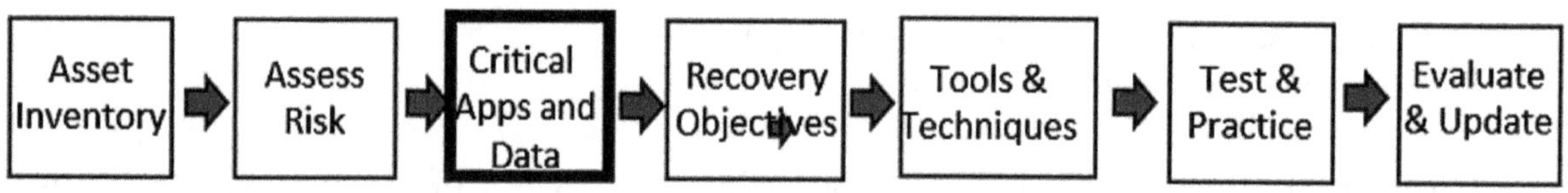

3. Define criticality of applications and data (see Figure 5) – Prioritize data and applications according to their criticality. Three categories are usually identified:

    a. Mission-Critical Function: A business function whose failure will cause serious ramifications, and potential failure of business operations. These should be recovered first.
    b. Essential Function: A business function that is important for the functioning of business operations, but which, if impacted, will not cause a failure of business operations.
    c. Not Time Sensitive Function: A business function that is an integral part of business operations, but which is not immediately necessary for the longevity of the business.

Look for commonalities and group them according to the criticality to your business continuity, frequency of change, and retention policy. This will allow you to implement a less complex strategy to recover. Similar to the risk assessment phase, include a wide variety of perspectives from stakeholders across the organization.

Figure 6. Define recovery objectives

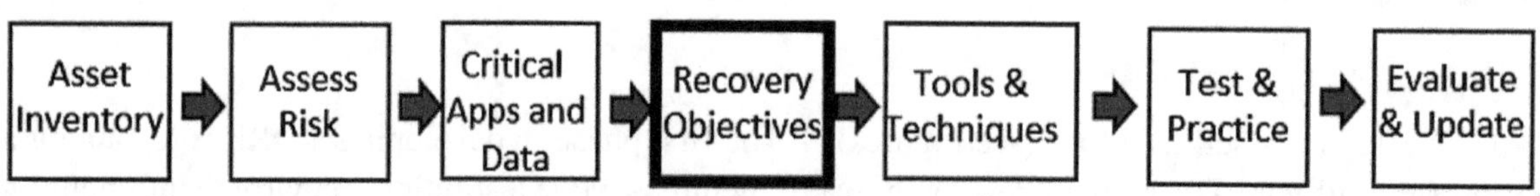

4. Define recovery objectives (see Figure 6) – Different categories have different recovery objectives. While a function cannot be readily replaced, the process of identifying alternate methods of execution is vital. For instance, a cyber-attack on an LMS at the end of a term where several courses rely on internally developed exams would be critical to recover and have very aggressive recovery objectives because of the negative impact it would have on the learner experience – the institution cannot afford for this to be down for long due to the anxiety it would cause for learners. If alternate methods of execution are identified (e.g., perhaps having students email assignments

to an instructor if the learning management system (LMS) has been the target of a cybersecurity attack), less stringent recovery objectives can be set. Two concepts inform the development of your institution's recovery objectives:

a. Recovery time objective (RTO) — This is the acceptable time any of your data, administrative, and educational delivery systems can be unavailable.
b. Recovery point objective (RPO) — This is the acceptable amount of data your organization can afford to lose, which can vary from hours to minutes to seconds.

Of note, in this phase, setting recovery objectives without consulting all relevant stakeholders is the number one cause for misalignment. It's imperative that you involve them in this process to ensure your institution can recover with minimal interruption to the learner experience.

Figure 7. Determine the right tools and techniques

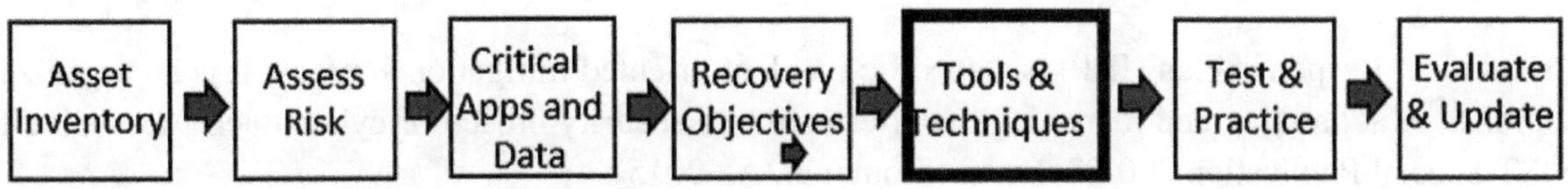

5. Determine the right tools and techniques (see Figure 7) – There is a wide selection of solutions to choose from that will afford you the appropriate level of protection. There is a balance between over-protection (which can cost needless expenditures and introduce unnecessary complexity) and under-protection (which can put your business continuity at risk). A critical component of your backup and disaster recovery plan is offsite protection. The method – be it tape vaulting service or replication to the cloud – should be in line with your recovery objectives. To the extent possible, in this phase you will want to consider how best to automate the recovery process, as key IT staff may be unavailable. Additionally, automation minimizes the risk of human error.

Figure 8. Test and practice your DR plan

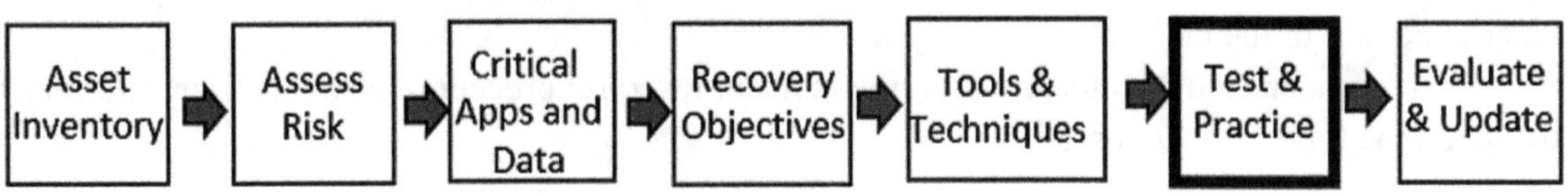

6. Test and practice your DRP (see Figure 8) – Conducting dry runs of your disaster recovery plan will help identify weaknesses in it and give participants experience with its execution firsthand. Not only will it help you find and rectify correct problems in your plan, but it will also enable you to execute it faster and more accurately. Everyone – everyone – who has a role to play needs to participate. It is not necessary to conduct a test of the entire plan in one session; it can be tested in logical segments.

Figure 9. Evaluate and update your plan

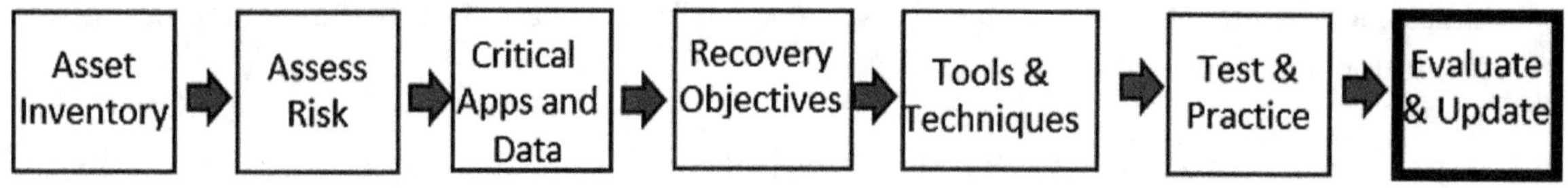

7. Evaluate and update your plan (see Figure 9) – Your disaster recovery plan is a living document. To that end, it needs to be reviewed on a scheduled basis as many of the underlying assumptions, institutional priorities, technologies, and threats are constantly changing. Think, for example, of how the need for higher education to address the concept of "bring your own device" has now grown to more complex issues associated with the multiplicative increase in third party educational technology applications and soon-to-be realized issues associated with Web 3.0 and the Metaverse.

Incident Response Plan (IRP)

An Incident Response Plan (IRP) is a specific incident-oriented mitigation strategy. It is an organized approach to addressing and managing the aftermath of a security breach or cyberattack. According to NIST Special Publication 800-82, Rev.2 (Stoufer et. Al, 2015):

"An incident response plan is documentation of a predetermined set of instructions or procedures to detect, respond to, and limit consequences of incidents against an organization's information systems. Response should be measured first and foremost against the "service being provided," not just the system that was compromised. If an incident is discovered, there should be a quick risk assessment performed to evaluate the effect of both the attack and the options to respond. For example, one possible response option is to physically isolate the system under attack. However, this may have such a dire impact on the service that it is dismissed as not viable."

During or after an "incident" that has been detected, the priority is to assess the risk the incident poses to the information technology systems and the overall organization. Sometimes the first instinct is to stop the effects of the incident; and in some circumstances, that is the preferred action. However, the goal is to prevent the attack, or similar attack from happening again so understanding the source ("attack vector") of the incident is very important.

In order to understand the attack vector, the incident response procedure would call for forensics to execute on the following strategies:

1. Analyze the nature of the incident (what's the purpose of this attack? Is it to disrupt the organization; is it for monetary gain; is it Hacktivism; is it Nation-State sponsored; is it a non-attack, which was an unintentional, internal mistake made by someone, etc.)?
2. Understand the signature of the attack/incident (unique behavior and characteristics).
3. Discover the attack vector (a system, person or credentials).
4. Remediate or mitigate future attacks from the same and/or similar attack vectors.

Putting together the IRP could be considered using the following four-phase approach (Educause, n.d.; Kime, 2021; Zhao, 2022).

Figure 10. Preparation

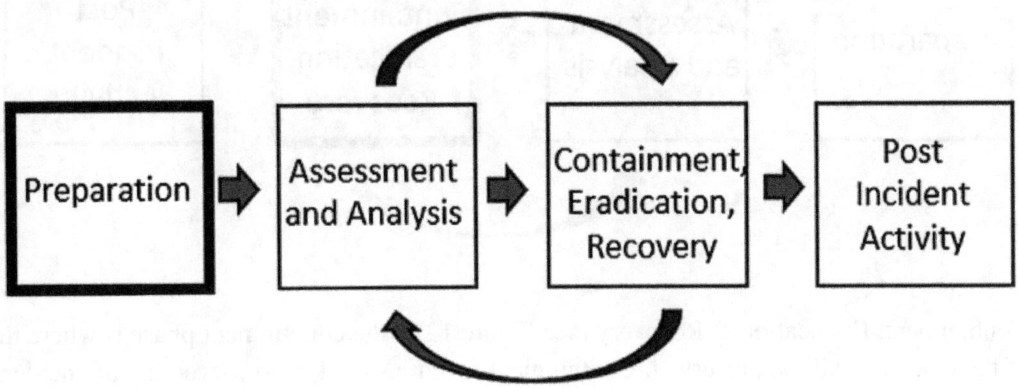

1. Preparation (see Figure 10) – the Preparation Phase establishes the controls, processes, and materials that should be acquired, implemented, and made available to handle incidents in an effective, efficient, and timely manner. This phase is a "living document," as each incident will allow you to continuously evolve and ensure the incident response process is rapid, agile and meets the needs of your environment.

Figure 11. Detection & analysis

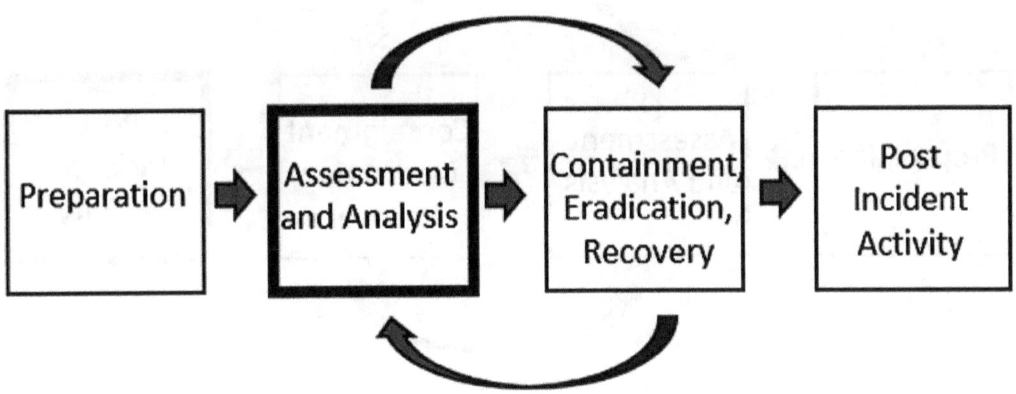

2. Detection & Analysis (see Figure11) – the Detection and Analysis phase involves receiving warning of a possible cybersecurity incident (which may come from several sources) and working quickly to analyze and validate each event following a pre-defined process and documenting each step.

Figure 12. Containment, eradication & recovery

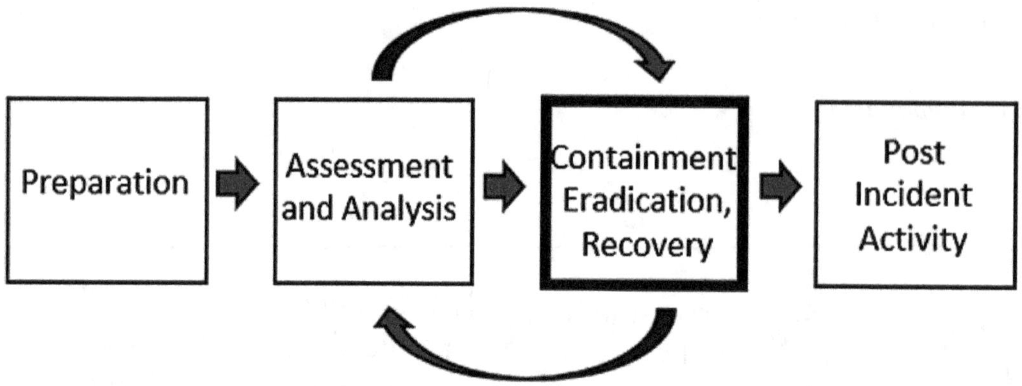

3. Containment, Eradication & Recovery (see Figure 12) – the containment phase is where the bulk of the evidence will be preserved. Containment activities are key to preventing an incident from overwhelming your organization's resources or increasing damage. After an incident has been contained, eradication activities may be necessary to eliminate components of the incident, such as deleting malware and disabling breached user accounts, as well as identifying and mitigating all vulnerabilities that were exploited. Lastly, recovery activities ensure your Critical Incident Response Team (CIRT) restores systems to normal operation, confirms that the systems are functioning normally, and (if applicable) remediates vulnerabilities to prevent similar incidents.

Figure 13. Post-incident activity

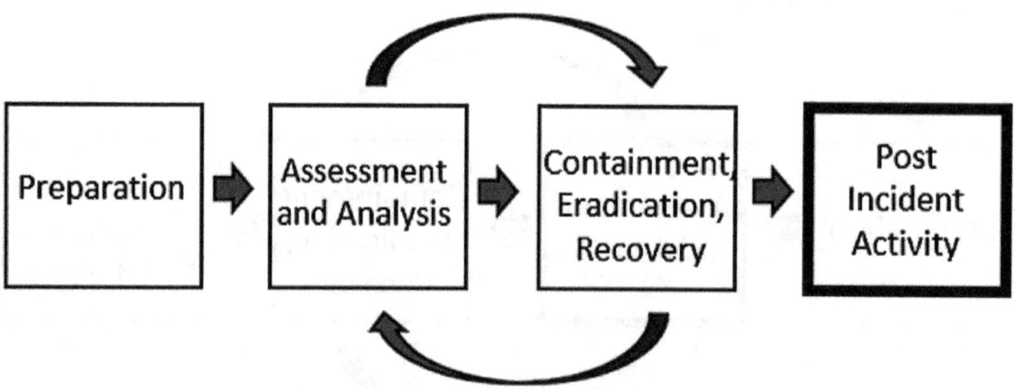

4. Post-Incident Activity (see Figure 13) – the fourth phase of the incident response process focuses on Post-Incident Activity such as, incident closure, process improvement, investigations, and metrics.

No organization is completely self-sustained and isolated. Having a component of your organization's functions built upon technologies provided by third parties leverages the ability to serve learners and build economies of scale. Everything from billing and collections to learning management systems to integration of artificial intelligence associated with the Metaverse provides for an attack vector, each of which carries increased security challenges (Renz & Hilbig, 2020). The security of an organization is only as good as the weakest link in its information technology ecosystem.

Having a third party adhere to the same or even greater risk management framework than your institution is crucial in ensuring points of an incident are reduced (Joint task force, 2018). Given the wide range of applications that institutions are currently employing – Learning Management Systems (LMSs), AI, Open Educational Resources (OERs), AR/VR/XR, wearables, and eportfolios – a major element of an institution's BCP must consider the integrity of third-party risk management plans. In today's interconnected world, a malicious actor no longer needs to attack an organization directly to disrupt its information technology systems and its institutional mission. Many successful attacks and incidents originate from less-secured, third parties to the target organization, such as vendors and other supply-chain actors, regulatory agencies, partners, and sometimes rogue students. Essentially, these third-party interfaces are an extension of your higher education institution and need to be treated with at least the same controls.

The IRP, then, also needs to consider the interfaces with myriad third parties and must address their level of protection against cyber threat with the same diligence as that of the institution's IR program. The institution must review all third-party agreements, define each vendor's compliance requirements, and document all acceptable (compensation) controls. The documentation of these conversations should be housed in the IRP in a well-constructed Third-Party Risk Management plan (Educause, n.d.; Leigh, 2015; PWC, n.d.).

A valuable tool that your team can employ in validating the IRP is a Tabletop exercise (Cybersecurity & Infrastructure Security Agency, n.d.). A tabletop exercise is a discussion-based session where team members meet in an informal, classroom setting to discuss their roles during an emergency and their responses to a particular emergency situation. A facilitator guides participants through a discussion of one or more scenarios. This exercise of taking participants through the process of dealing with a simulated incident scenario provides hands-on training for participants that can then highlight flaws in incident response planning. Some of the specific questions that would be addressed include:

- What happens when you encounter a breach?
- Who does what, when, how, and why?
- What roles will legal, IT, law enforcement, marketing, and company officers play?
- Who is spearheading the effort and what authority do they have?

THE ROLE OF COMMUNICATIONS IN DEVELOPING THE BCP

Once you have consulted all of the key stakeholders, you will want to enlist an executive-level sponsor who will get behind you and the project. The importance of collaboration, consensus and executive support to your BCP's success cannot be emphasized enough.

Developing the two components of your BCP – both your DRP and IRP – requires an extensive commitment to communications. You must go well beyond the information technology department and involve key stakeholders across the institution. Impacted stakeholders need to be involved from the inception in the planning phase and need to come to agreement on the organization's priorities. Their expectations need to be managed through defined service level agreements (SLAs) that are mutually developed.

Clarifying roles and responsibilities are an important facet of the BCP. A useful tool to incorporate in the conversations that lead to the development of your IRP and DRP is the RASCI chart (Friedman,

2008). A RASCI chart is a tool that is used to help identify all the roles and responsibilities of individual stakeholders in performing an activity or a set of integrated activities. This tool can be used to frame the conversation of the key stakeholders as to who assumes the different levels of participation.

Roles are defined as follows:

1. **Responsible –** the one responsible for performing the task, i.e., who must lead the effort to plan, do, and complete the task.
2. **Accountable –** the one who is responsible for the *deliverable* associated with the task, has the power to delegate the task to be done to the person responsible, and has control over the resources to do the task. Responsible and accountable can be the same person. It is also true that a best practice dictated that there is no more than one accountable individual per task.
3. **Support –** the ones or teams that work together and under the coordination of the responsible person for performing the task.
4. **Consulted –** the ones or teams who do not participate in the task execution but who need to be consulted before or while the task is being performed, as they can provide relevant inputs to its execution.
5. **Informed –** the ones or teams who do not participate in the task execution, nor need to be consulted before or while the task is being performed, but who need to be informed when the task is completed.

Table 1. RASCI chart

Phase	Trustees	President	Chief Academic Officer	Chief Information Officer	Chief Information Security Officer	Legal/ Compliance	Third Party Providers	Others …
Plan Definition								
Plan Activation (BCP Team)								
Business Recovery								
Return to Business as Usual								
Continual Improvement								
R – Responsible I A – Accountable I S – Support I C – Consulted I I – Informed								

The following RASCI chart depicts the roles involved in putting together the DRP and IRP (Table 1).

One final note, be sure to store your BCP strategy where it can be accessed during a disaster. Ideally, it should be printed, posted, and stored in multiple locations.

CONCLUSION

The potential for an institutional cybersecurity attack is – or should be – high in the institution's overall risk management matrix. Older systems still operating at many institutions were not designed with robust security features and new cybersecurity attack vectors are on the rise – this scenario results in increased risk exposure. The pandemic has increased the vulnerability of organizations by permeating the confines of the campus and creating borderless networks. As security breaches at higher education institutions are publicized in the media, the trust that students and other stakeholders have in their institutions is waning. Having a robust BCP is a necessary component of the institution's risk management plan.

REFERENCES

Arctic Wolf-Educause. (2021) *Arctic EWS research paper: A strong case for the utility of cybersecurity monitoring in higher education.* Educause. https://library.educause.edu/-/media/files/library/2021/11/arcticsecurityeducause.pdf

Brush, K. (n.d.). *Disaster recovery plan.* TechTarget. https://www.techtarget.com/searchdisasterrecovery/definition/disaster-recovery-plan

Cybase. (n.d.). *9 steps to putting together a disaster recovery plan.* https://cybasetech.com/site/9-steps-building-disaster-recovery-plan/

Cybersecurity and Infrastructure Security Agency. (n.d.). *Guide to Industrial Control Systems (ICS) Security.* https://www.cisa.gov/cisa-tabletop-exercises-packages

Dosal, A. (2020, April 7). *How to create an effective disaster recovery plan.* Compuquip. https://www.compuquip.com/blog/disaster-recovery-plan

Ebner, M. (2022, Apr 18). *2022 EDUCAUSE Horizon Report | Teaching and Learning Edition.* https://library.educause.edu/-/media/files/library/2022/4/2022hrteachinglearning.pdf

Educause. (2017). *Toolkit for New CISOs.* Educause. https://www.educause.edu/focus-areas-and-initiatives/policy-and-security/cybersecurity-program/resources/information-security-guide/career-and-workforce-development/toolkit-for-new-cisos

Educause. (n.d.a). *Business continuity and disaster recovery.* https://www.educause.edu/focus-areas-and-initiatives/policy-and-security/cybersecurity-program/resources/information-security-guide/business-continuity-and-disaster-recovery

Educause. (n.d.b). *Incidence management and response.* https://www.educause.edu/focus-areas-and-initiatives/policy-and-security/cybersecurity-program/resources/information-security-guide/incident-management-and-response

Educause. (n.d.c). *Vendor and third-party management.* https://www.educause.edu/focus-areas-and-initiatives/policy-and-security/cybersecurity-program/resources/information-security-guide/vendor-and-thirdparty-management

Egencia. (2021, Nov 22). *What is risk management and why is it important?* https://www.egencia.com/en/business-traveler-risk-management-process-importance

Finn, J. D. (1960). A new theory for instructional technology. *Audio Visual Communication Review, 8*(5), 84-94. https://www.jstor.org/stable/30216956

Fouad, N. S. (2021). Securing higher education against cyberthreats: From an institutional risk to a national policy challenge. *Journal of Cyber Policy, 6*(2), 137–154. doi:10.1080/23738871.2021.1973526

Friedman, S. (2008). *Roles, responsibilities, and resources: best practices in managing people.* Paper presented at PMI® Global Congress 2008—North America, Denver, CO. Newtown Square, PA: Project Management Institute.

Gunnell, M. (2020, Apr 10). *What is Zoombombing, and how can you stop it?* https://www.howtogeek.com/667183/what-is-zoombombing-and-how-can-you-stop-it/

Guthrie, G. (2020, Nov 3). *Qualitative risk analysis vs quantitative risk analysis: What's the difference?* https://backlog.com/blog/qualitative-risk-analysis-vs-quantitative-risk-analysis-whats-difference/

Hiles, A. (2007). *The Definitive Handbook of Business Continuity Management*. John Wiley and Sons Ltd.

Jackson, T. (2021, Dec 15). *Examining the shared governance model in higher education*. Convene. https://www.azeusconvene.com/articles/examining-the-shared-governance-model-in-higher-education

Joint Task Force. (2018). *SP 800-37 Rev. 2: Risk Management Framework for Information Systems and Organizations: A System Life Cycle Approach for Security and Privacy*. U.S. Department of Commerce. https://csrc.nist.gov/publications/detail/sp/800-37/rev-2/final

Kenton, W. (2022, June 28). *Business Continuity Planning*. Investopedia. https://www.investopedia.com/terms/b/business-continuity-pla
nning.asp

Kime, C. (2021, Dec 9). *How to create an incident response plan*. https://www.esecurityplanet.com/networks/incident-response-how-to-prepare-for-attacks-and-breaches/

KirkpatrickPrice. (2021, Mar 15). *The 5 components of risk management*. https://kirkpatrickprice.com/blog/5-components-risk-management/

Leigh, D. (2015, Oct 29). *Cybersecurity risk management*. Educause. https://er.educause.edu/blogs/2015/10/cybersecurity-risk-management

Liem, M. (n.d.). *Risk in modern society*. Coursera. https://www.coursera.org/learn/risk-in-modern-society

Meir, M. (2020, June 15). *The 2 types of risk assessment methodology*. Security Scorecard. https://securityscorecard.com/blog/types-of-risk-assessment-methodology#:~:text=There%20are%20two%20main%20types,assessment%20methodologies%3A%20quantitative%20and%20qualitative

Monzon, L. (2022, April 16). *The 5 most common security concerns for the Web 3.0 world*. https://www.itnewsafrica.com/2022/04/the-5-most-common-security-concerns-for-the-web-3-0-world/

Pallavi, K. (n.d.). *Risk: Meaning, concept and characteristics*. https://www.yourarticlelibrary.com/business/risk-management/risk-meaningconcept-and-characteristics/89506

Pallavi, K. (n.d.). *The history of risk*. https://www.youtube.com/watch?v=96_I4wEoTjM

PWC. (n.d.). *Mapping and managing cyber risks from third parties and beyond*. https://www.pwc.com/us/en/services/consulting/cybersecurity-risk-regulatory/library/third-party-risks.html

Ray, S. 2021. *What is a risk register & how to create one*. ProjectManager. https://www.projectmanager.com/blog/guide-using-risk-register

Ready. (n.d.). *Business impact analysis*. https://www.ready.gov/business-impact-analysis

Reciprocity. (2021, Oct 25). *Incident response -vs- disaster recovery.* https://reciprocity.com/blog/incident-response-plan-vs-disaster-recovery-plan/

Renz, A., & Hilbig, R. (2020). Prerequisites for artificial intelligence in further education: Identification of drivers, barriers, and business models of educational technology companies. *International Journal of Educational Technology in Higher Education, 17*(1), 14. doi:10.118641239-020-00193-3

Richey, R. C., Silber, K. H., & Ely, D. P. (2008). Reflections on the 2008 AECT definitions of the field. *TechTrends, 52*(1), 24–25. doi:10.100711528-008-0108-2

Rosowsky, D., & Hallman, K. (2020, May 26). *Communicating culture in a distributed world.* Inside Higher Ed. https://www.insidehighered.com/views/2020/05/26/importance-culture-binding-higher-ed-institution-together-during-crises-pandemic

Schwartz, J. (2020). *The cyber-security problem schools and ed. tech need to face.* Education Week. https://www.edweek.org/technology/opinion-the-cyber-security-problem-schools-and-ed-tech-need-to-face/2020/01

Spector, J. M. (2015). *Foundations of educational technology: Integrative approaches and interdisciplinary perspectives.* Routledge. doi:10.4324/9781315764269

Statman, M. (2010). *The cultures of risk tolerance.* SSRN Electronic Journal. https://papers.ssrn.com/sol3/papers.cfm?abstract_id=1647086 doi:10.2139/ssrn.1647086

Stouffer, K., Lightman, S., Pillitteri, V., Abrams, M., & Hahn, A. (2015). *SP 800-82 Rev. 2: Guide to Industrial Control Systems.* U.S. Department of Commerce, Washington, D.C. NIST Series SP 800-82 Rev. 2. Supersedes: SP 800-82 Rev. 1 (05/14/2013). https://csrc.nist.gov/publications/detail/sp/800-82/rev-2/final

Talbot, J. (2021, Feb 14). *Example of a risk management policy.* https://www.juliantalbot.com/post/example-of-a-risk-management-policy

Terminalfour. (n.d.). *The Metaverse – The future of higher education.* https://www.terminalfour.com/blog/posts/the-metaverse---the-future-of-higher-education.html

Thakur, M. (2022). *Risk categories.* Wallstreet Mojo. https://www.wallstreetmojo.com/risk-categories/

University of North Dakota. (n.d.). *7 types of cybersecurity threats.* https://onlinedegrees.und.edu/blog/types-of-cyber-security-threats/

Van der Ham, J. (2021). Toward a better understanding of "cybersecurity". *Digital Threats., 2*(3), 1–3. doi:10.1145/3442445

Verry, J. (2016, Dec 22). *Risk tolerance: To avoid, transfer, mitigate or accept — that is the question!* https://www.pivotpointsecurity.com/blog/risk-tolerance-in-business/

Wainganker, R., & Vaidya, D. (n.d.). *Risk transfer.* Wallstreet Mojo. https://www.wallstreetmojo.com/risk-transfer/

Wikipedia. (n.d.a). *Learning Analytics.* https://en.wikipedia.org/wiki/Learning_analytics

Wikipedia. (n.d.b). *Learning Management Systems.* https://en.wikipedia.org/wiki/Learning_management_system

Wright, D. (2020, Nov 24). *Selecting a risk management framework for your organization.* https://www.pluralsight.com/guides/selecting-a-risk-management-framework-for-your-organization

Zhao, J. (2022, Mar 31). *How to create a cybersecurity incident response plan.* https://hyperproof.io/resource/cybersecurity-incident-response-plan/

Chapter 4
New Identification of Political Conflict and the Asymmetric Threat Phenomenon on the Example of Cyber Warfare

Nika Chitadze
International Black Sea University, Georgia

ABSTRACT

The end of the Cold War has given rise to a fresh set of security challenges that today pose a threat to the stability of any state. The focus is now as much on threats arising due to inter-state rivalries based on balance of power as on intra-national and transnational security threats that cannot be classified into the traditional security studies framework. Covering a wide range of situations, these non-traditional security threats have real consequences towards human, national, and environmental security. This chapter seeks to understand some of the most critical non-traditional security threats faced by international community on the example of cyber warfare.

INTRODUCTION

The socioeconomic well-being, health, and life of every citizen largely depend on the security of information systems and electronic services. Cyber-attacks have a great impact on all sectors of the economy, hinder the normal functioning of the economic space, reduce public confidence in electronic services and threaten the development of the economy through the use of information and communication technologies. Against the backdrop of global cyber threats, when cyber attacks, cyber espionage, cyber terrorism, and disinformation are carried out daily, the development, implementation, and development of new protection mechanisms is an important issue. It is noteworthy that NATO – together with other appropriate international institutions, such as EU etc. plays an important role in cyber security issues. This Euro-Atlantic Institution itself is a kind of security umbrella for both member countries and partner countries.

DOI: 10.4018/978-1-6684-6092-4.ch004

Every age comes with its problems. Cybercrime has become one of the most dangerous phenomena of the 21st century, with many people, private companies, and government agencies suffering every day. Billions of dollars are already being spent on defense.

Discussing again NATO, it should be pointed out, that all NATO concepts and doctrines emphasize that, based on basic principles, no member state should be forced to rely solely on its forces. The Alliance's strategy allows each member state to pursue national security goals by collective means.

Every leading country in the world has a national cybersecurity strategy that is a defining factor in public policy. The national security strategy aims to identify, prevent, reduce and eliminate existing threats. Cooperation with partner countries and organizations is of great importance for many countries in the world.

In the face of existing threats and challenges, many countries have effective protection systems, such as the functioning of the Cyber Security Bureau and the Data Exchange Agency, and other relevant structures. As stated in the national security strategies of various countries, the goal of a particular country is to become a regional provider of cybersecurity services and develop the necessary infrastructure to operate the communication systems of other countries located on its territory. This is impossible without the development of cooperation with partner countries.

For example, taking as an example the former soviet republic – of Georgia, reports from the Georgian Security Service (which was the victim of Russian aggression in 2008) indicate that hacking by foreign intelligence agencies, cyberattacks on government infrastructure, and cyber-surveillance operations pose a significant security risk to the country (Jiadze, 2022).

Threats cannot be avoided without modern technologies, professional personnel, and cooperation with leading states. Therefore, the only way is international cooperation. For same Georgia, in terms of security, cooperation with NATO and the intelligence services of leading countries should be strengthened to take timely preventive measures. Closer cooperation with the security services of neighboring states is also necessary (Jiadze, 2022).

Why it is important for Georgia to cooperate with NATO on Cyber security issues, its should be underlined that, NATO is the organization with the technical, financial, or human resources to counter cyber threats. Therefore, it is important to study, analyze, and explore the current situation and plans for the future from a practical point of view. The researchers argue that if the scientific approach is correct, the results of cyberbullying will not be as devastating as in previous years.

The Theory of Behaviorism and Its Relation to Cybersecurity

The development of technology is always reflected and has an impact on society. We cannot deal with technological challenges without taking human nature into account, and the experts in human nature are behaviorists or behaviorists. The emergence of the theory of behaviorism is associated (1913) with the declarations of John Watson, which were collected in his article "Psychology from the Perspective of the Behaviorist" (Wiley Online Library, 2019).

Behaviorists study the individual and social behavior of a person. We discuss this theory in the context of cybersecurity. The methodology has been established in various leading countries. It might be weird on a technical side like the cyber world, how should behaviorism treat it? Cybersecurity expert Bruce Schneier explains the problem this way: "Only amateurs attack machines, professionals attack people" (MDS, 2017).

Take, for example, the technique of one of the hacker attacks called "phishing". In a phishing attack, an attacker attempting to break into a computer system primarily targets the user rather than an automated defense mechanism. The attacker sends an email message to users on a fake website, even though it looks like the original. For example, it could be a bank message that masquerades as a guarantee of authenticity, but if the recipient opens a fake link, this may inadvertently prevent an attacker from gaining access to personal information.

A system designed to protect consumers requires the use of a behavioral methodology. Scientists can help cybersecurity experts in two ways: first, improve system security, and educate users about how human nature can make consumers vulnerable; Second, they can use knowledge of human nature to develop educational campaigns that warn users about cyberattacks.

The United States Army is actively using the theory of behaviorism to combat cyber attacks. Cyber Behavior Model Analysis, or the modern commercial method, emerged after an event held by the US Army (Cyber Quest 2017) as one of the responses to the cyber threat. According to Colonel Stephen Wren, the key to normal monitoring of traffic and user behavior in cybernetics may be to identify situations and actions that indicate that a hacker has compromised the system (Caputo, 2020).

According to commercial developers, cyberspace consists of four layers: physical, networked, social, and personal. Threat monitoring involves collecting behavioral data at each level and then correlating and combining that data. According to the American military colonel Wren, the theory of behaviorism does not see the rules, but through this theory, we look at the way of life in cybernetics. This system works like this: during monitoring, for example, one server always establishes a connection with another server, but after a while, it enters a connection with a router or another server. In this case, detailed observation and analysis take place. When using services in internal networks, the method of behavioral analysis will become an important tool for reducing the risks of cyber attacks and security breaches (Caputo, 2012).

Not surprisingly, the use of this methodology poses a broad data problem. However, General Morrison stated: "The solution lies in the creation of artificial intelligence and machine learning technology. Artificial intelligence will allow us to react much faster to events in cyberspace. Often in the network, and then a situation is created that everything is checked "(Caputo, 2012).

The theory of behaviorism should be studied, deciphered, analyzed, and mastered by programmers working in the private sector, as well as government employees. We receive a lot of letters from different countries or organizations almost every day by email, at this time we do not know what is fake and what is true. If we want to get rid of serious threats, hackers do not have access to our personal information, there are no effective cyber-attacks, then we must understand and learn how to effectively resist.

Here it is important to determine what has changed and what can Covid-19 change in the world, what will it change from the point of view of cybers? The virus has changed the agenda, endangering both human health and the economy. The danger is multifaceted - borders are closed, flights are banned, quarantines have been declared in many countries, and a state of emergency, curfews, and travel restrictions have been introduced. Nobody expected such a dramatic turn of events. Everyone agrees that the virus will pass, and someday it will disappear, but life will not be the same as it used to be. The real world has moved into the virtual space in large doses, and many companies and government agencies have switched to remote work. Against this background, hackers, spammers, scammers, and people who use the Internet and social networks for personal gain are very useful (Kuprashvili, 2022).

For example, fraud (phishing) has been active since the spread of the virus. Malware is trying to instill more fear and confusion in Internet users. Hacker attacks on medical clinics in exchange for a ransom have become more frequent. The attacks halted operations and caused delays. Such attacks pose the greatest threat to the health of patients.

Following the events, the Washington Post published an article titled: "Hackers Use Coronavirus Fears to Steal Identity." This article discusses the rising tide of hacker attacks in the wake of the coronavirus. Israeli cybersecurity organization Check Point has published a report that reveals the campaign launched by the most effective hacker group called Vicious Panda. The report states that "Vicious Panda", or a hacking organization, used forged documents and spread false information on behalf of the Mongolian Minister of Health. He seemed to be announcing a terrible situation to the world. The goal of the hackers was to convey as much information as possible to as many people as possible, after which they would gain access to users' data. It will be through smartphones or computers. The report also cited Latte Finklintin, head of defense intelligence at Check Point, who warned the public sector and telcos: "Covid-19 poses not only a physical threat but also a cyber threat. With documentation and websites" (Craig, Tony, 2020).

According to Lukas Oleinik, an independent cybersecurity expert, today the world is completely vulnerable to this massive global crisis and the situation could worsen (Newman, 2020).

In this case, we can consider the example of the post-Soviet republic - Georgia, where in a smaller dose, but still, similar attacks occur, both at the hacker level and the information level. For example, hackers published the personal information of 4,934,863 citizens of Georgia (including the deceased). The American edition of ZDNet devoted an extensive article to this issue (Catalin, 2020). What was necessary to obtain and disseminate personal data? It serves to induce vulnerability syndrome in people and sow panic. Especially when the country is dominated by disinformation agencies and TV channels that supply the population with this material more intensively than it is. Links to these databases indicated that the source of the information was the system of the Central Electoral Commission. However, this information has not been confirmed. The Central Electoral Commission (CEC) released a statement emphasizing that the database is fundamentally different from what is stored on their system. There is no personal data in this database that could endanger our population, but the dissemination of this data is still a crime. For people who are not tech-savvy, there is a feeling of fear and insecurity, which was the goal.

During the state of emergency, messages were sent to the population of Georgia containing disinformation: "UCKEBA", the content of which was: "You are fined for violating the curfew, the amount of the fine is 3,000 GEL (Ministry of Internal Affairs of Georgia, 2021).

This further strengthens the suspicion that panic among the population was deliberately sown. The Ministry of Internal Affairs said that short text messages are not true and were not sent by them. Numerous sites and statistics that go beyond reality have appeared on the Internet, where hackers have manipulated coronavirus statistics through various sites. The numbers game caused panic in society. Internet users unintentionally become victims of Internet viruses and, upon finding information, are automatically redirected to websites where the infected program is loaded. Hackers gain unauthorized access through various manipulations. Such examples have already been published and are being actively studied. One such video was published by GEORGIAN HACKERS COMMUNITY - GHC. The video shows the Coronavirus-map.com.exe file containing the AZORult malware, which was created many years ago to steal information. AZORult steals data from your browser's cookies, everything that even the browser has stored on your computer - passwords, identification numbers, etc. Allows hackers to access your data, which poses a very serious threat to the protection of personal data and its unauthorized use (SECLAB, 2020).

DIGITAL CURRENCY AND CYBERSECURITY

Cryptocurrency. In recent years, the banking and financial sector has developed strongly. This is what concerns the creation of electronic currency. What is digital money? How is it different from a standard or traditional currency?

Take for example one of the first and most popular cryptocurrencies, bitcoin, which appeared on the network in 2008. Its creation is associated with a programmer known as Sato Nakamoto. Cryptocurrency is not printed, unlike the standard currency. It is generated, stored, and consumed electronically. It is not controlled by either the state or the bank. Bitcoin originated from complex mathematical processing through computer networks. Traditional currency is based on the value of gold, while digital currency is based on mathematics. The process of creating bitcoins is called mining (Satoshi, 2020).

A system of computers and servers is needed to mine digital currency. Recently, special applications have been actively appearing that allow you to generate digital currency from a smartphone. As for Bitcoin, its number worldwide cannot exceed 21,000,000. In general, a lot of information and misinformation is spread about digital currency, but it is almost impossible to fake a transaction made directly with Bitcoins. It is known that transaction data is stored in fragments, and not on a single server. It is important to note that bitcoin payments have long been allowed in online stores such as eBay, Amazon, etc. (PAXFUL, 2020).

Given the current reality, it can be assumed that the successful use of digital currency on a global scale and its popularization can lead to a complete replacement of the printed, traditional currency. The most trusted digital currency today is Bitcoin (BTC).

Electronic money is built on P2P technology, it is a completely independent and decentralized network. This is what allows any customer to pay or transfer directly. The transfer in this case is confirmed by other network users, called miners. Confirmation is carried out by a cryptographic signature and after each signature, the user receives a certain commission. The disadvantage of electronic currency is volatility, its market value depends on demand. Also, the transaction is not insured, it is impossible to return the transferred currency. Online trading exchanges are created for buying and trading electronic money, the most relevant exchanges are bit panda and binance. Through these exchanges, you have the opportunity to buy and sell cryptocurrencies with your card (Goguadze, 2017). Of course, it's not just bitcoin, there are many similar currencies today.

Digital currency is not very popular in many countries – especially in the Global South. However, we can also indicate the countries where bitcoin trading is officially allowed - in the US, bitcoin trading is allowed. However, there are many more countries in the world where that are trying to legally limit and even ban e-currency because virtual money is not supported by either the economic system or physical values. It is also noteworthy that in 2015 the European Supreme Court ruled that Bitcoin can be bought for physical money without VAT (Chkoidze, Tomaradze, 2014).

Given all this, the future of cryptocurrency is still uncertain. However, it looks quite attractive, both for large companies and for individuals. It should also be noted that hackers are also very good at using cryptocurrencies for fraud, hackers encrypt your data into a computer at the request of ransomware or a ransom, and then demand a large reward for restoring access to the data. However, access to your data will not be restored even if you pay. This type of scam has a lot to do with anonymous cryptocurrencies like bitcoin (Bueger, Liebetrau, 2021).

DISCUSSING THE CASE OF THE ISLAMIC REPUBLIC OF IRAN

On January 3, 2020, in Iraq, near Baghdad airport, as a result of a US missile attack, General Qasem Suleiman, commander of the Al-Quds special unit of the Iranian Islamic Revolutionary Guard Corps, was killed. The Pentagon later released the following information:

"By the direction of US President Donald Trump, our military took effective defensive measures to protect Americans abroad and killed General Qassim Suleiman. Al-Quds, the group he led, has been designated as a terrorist organization in the United States. General Suleiman planned attacks on American diplomats in Iraq and on troops throughout the region. "Al-Quds is responsible for the deaths of hundreds of US and coalition troops" (Imedinews, 2021).

What caused the Middle East to become so volatile and cause the Islamic Republic of Iran to declare jihad with the call "Death to America"? On December 31, 2019, protesters in Baghdad attacked the US embassy to protest the US invasion of Iraq. Earlier, the Ministry of Foreign Affairs of Iraq condemned the US actions, and Iran, which supports Hezbollah, from its turn, called the attack "a clear example of terrorism." On December 29, the US Air Force carried out strikes against Kataib Hezbollah targets in Syria and Iraq.

The day after Suleiman's death, the U.S. Department of Homeland Security released a statement saying that Iran could launch a cyberattack on the United States:

"The Islamic Republic of Iran has a very strong cyber program and Tehran is known for its politically motivated cyber attacks" (1tv, 2020).

As you can see, even the White House admits that Iran has a pretty strong cyber program. Here, one very remarkable fact should be noted: after the neutralization of the Iranian general, President Trump himself and other dignitaries actively used social networks, in particular Twitter, to express their views and spread statements. The same method was used by Iranian officials. The military confrontation between the Islamic Republic of Iran and the USA is taking place against the backdrop of an information war. The fact is that Donald Trump has repeatedly threatened on social networks that if the Islamic Republic of Iran launches attacks on our country, we will bomb 52 Iranian targets, and the strike will be fast and strong. In its turn, Iranian President Hassan Rouhani sent the following message to US President: "Never threaten the Iranian people" (imedinews, 2020).

The Islamic Republic of Iran did not fail to "insult" Suleiman and fired 35 ballistic missiles at US military bases in Iraq. It was later reported that the Iraqi government had alerted the Americans and that the military managed to infiltrate the bunkers (CNN, 2020).

The whole world was waiting for a retaliatory strike from the United States, but President Trump chose a reasonable path - no war, only tough sanctions. I do not rule out that this may be a temporary peace, the Islamic Republic of Iran may use other means - terrorist acts, cyber attacks, and so on. It is clear that in the event of a fading military confrontation, all attention will be switched to cyber attacks and information warfare.

The reputation of Iran also suffered due to the crash of a Ukrainian plane at Tehran airport, which killed 178 passengers and nine crew members. The Americans claim that the Iranians blew up the passenger plane with a Russian missile. The Islamic Republic of Iran accuses the United States of lying. Government spokesman Ali Rabi said no one would take responsibility for such a big lie. According to him, this is a psychological special operation against the Islamic Republic of Iran. Although the information war on this issue did not last long, on January 11, the authorities of the Islamic Republic of Iran admitted that the plane was shot down by mistake, calling it a "human error" (Kupreishvili, 2020).

It should be recognized that the Islamic Republic of Iran has suffered a complete defeat in this military confrontation and information war. However, what this unpredictable republic will do next is difficult to predict, yes and no - as a rule, the war against the United States and the rest of the world should move into cyberspace. It should not be forgotten that Iran has already declared the US military a "terrorist organization". The bill was unanimously approved by the parliament of the Islamic Republic of Iran, and "it applies to all US military personnel, Pentagon employees and those responsible for the assassination of Iranian General Suleiman." The Parliament of the Islamic Republic of Iran also supported an increase of 200 million euros in funding for Al-Quds, an elite unit of the Islamic Revolutionary Guard Corps. This unit is responsible for conducting special operations outside the Islamic Republic of Iran (Georgian Public Television, 2021).

CYBER SECURITY CAPABILITIES AND SYSTEMS OF THE ISLAMIC REPUBLIC OF IRAN

The United States is not going to give up. Dissatisfied Donald Trump once again noted that the United States is making the main contribution to NATO, which is unfair. Previously, he said that the US spends billions to protect Europe when the US itself does not receive adequate support at critical moments. According to media reports, Trump told NATO Secretary General Stoltenberg that NATO should expand into the Middle East:

"I think that NATO needs to expand, we need to include the Middle East. Stoltenberg is delighted with this point of view. We can call the new alliance NATO + Middle East." What a wonderful name. I know the names well" (Trump, 2020).

And against this background, when NATO plans to expand into the Middle East, what opportunities do its main target, the Islamic Republic of Iran, have to counter even in terms of cybersecurity the European-American military alliance? Where is Georgia at this time, which is a reliable partner of the United States? The Cybersecurity Bureau of the Ministry of Defense of Georgia developed a strategy in 2015 that (Chapter 35) considers the cyber capabilities of the Islamic Republic of Iran and the interests of this state. Today, all experts note that there are normal relations between Georgia and Iran in terms of economic and cultural relations, but it is still considered a threat because together with Russia it is a strong cyber player not only in the region but also in the world. . Hundreds of cyber organizations have been established in the Islamic Republic of Iran to work on various issues, including political, cultural and religious ones. The most powerful of these is the IQA, created by the Islamic Revolutionary Guard Corps in 2005 and associated with the country's armed forces. This organization carries out cyber attacks on the borders of Iran from outside, the UK, China, Pakistan, and Saudi Arabia (Kegley, Raymond, 2021).

In September 2019, Foreign Minister of the Islamic Republic of Iran Javad Zarif reported on the Stuxnet computer virus and also denied allegations of interference in the 2020 US presidential election. He said that Tehran did not support any of the parties in the elections and did not interfere in the internal affairs of other states (Pernik, 2022).

Relations between the Islamic Republic of Iran and the United States deteriorated after September 14, when two oil terminals in Saudi Arabia were attacked. Although the Yemeni Husseins claimed responsibility for the incident, the United States and Saudi Arabia placed the blame for the incident on Iran. Tehran denies the allegations, but Washington still imposed new sanctions on Iran on September 20.

Furthermore, relations between the two countries more deteriorated after Washington announced its withdrawal from the nuclear deal with Tehran. In May 2018, despite criticism from European partners, the United States unilaterally abandoned the nuclear deal with the Islamic Republic of Iran. In November, Washington reimposed sanctions on Tehran and demanded that allied governments stop buying oil from Iran. Otherwise, the US threatened to impose sanctions against the companies concerned. By the way, the US intelligence agencies knew from the very beginning that Iran was preparing for an attack on Syria and Iraq. The information obtained by intelligence was justified, but in the sense that it was carried out by Iran after the neutralization of Suleiman (Sosanya, 2022).

When we talk about Iran, we must also remember that since 2012 this country has had a cyber conflict with neighboring Azerbaijan, followed by a "bombing" of hundreds of websites. In January 2012, a group of Azerbaijani hackers calling themselves the "Real Azerbaijani Cyber Army" attacked Iranian websites in response to previous attacks. Up to a dozen official websites in Azerbaijan, including those of President Aliyev, the ruling party, the Constitutional Court, the Ministry of Internal Affairs, and the Ministry of Communications, have become inaccessible. If anyone tries to go to these sites, then on the front page there will be information that the Azerbaijani cyber army is responsible for this and that Baku "serves the Jews." On the same day, Israeli websites were attacked. Among them were the sites of the airline "El Ali" and the Tel Aviv Stock Exchange. Relations between Iran and Azerbaijan at that time were strained because Tehran accused Baku of collaborating with Israel. Israel receives a significant portion of its oil from Azerbaijan. In December of the same year, the Azerbaijani Foreign Minister delivered a speech in Washington, DC, exposing Iran's cooperation with Armenia, helping that country in the occupation of Nagorno-Karabakh. In short, from time to time one gets the impression that there are warm relations between Iran and Azerbaijan (even because of their monotheism), but in reality, the situation is different - Iran is the enemy of anyone who deals with the US and Israel, even economically (Salomon, 2022).

All the concepts of the North Atlantic Alliance strategy address cyber defense issues and cost billions of dollars every year. Moreover, more will be needed if the North Atlantic Alliance is to be established in the Middle East and then begin to expand. Naturally, all this can not be done without creating cyber defense systems and strengthening existing systems.

Asymmetric Threats and Jihadist Cyberwars

We are talking about cyber warfare, cyber attacks, information wars, propaganda, disinformation, fake news, and hybrid wars in general, and the pros and cons of technology. We need to find out in whose hands technological progress is a weapon and a threat. We are talking not only about aggressor countries but also about non-state actors well-versed in new technologies. Terrorism has a long history and many definitions, just like cyberterrorism, and this definition is more plausible: cyberterrorism means the use of computer and telecommunications technologies, including the Internet, to commit acts of violence that threaten life or cause death. Cyber terrorist acts are aimed at achieving political or ideological advantages through intimidation and threats. The term "cyberterrorism" was first used in the 1980s. Cyberterrorism is sometimes viewed as the deliberate damage to computer networks by various means, such as viruses, phishing, and other malicious software.

A 2018 report published by the Georgian State Security Service details what a jihadist cyber company is and what dangers we may face.

For Georgia, as well as for many countries of the world, the main challenge is the Islamic Caliphate (DAISH) terrorist organization and groups associated with it. Daesh continued to operate with a new strategy developed after weakening and territorial losses. In this context, the mobilization of supporters in Syria and Iraq has ceased to be a priority for ISIS. Carrying out terrorist acts outside the conflict zone has become the main tool of the terrorist organization. Daesh called on radicalized people living in different countries of the world to carry out terrorist attacks by any means. This organization, using modern technologies, including the Internet and social networks, is still actively spreading its ideology and recruiting people. As we read in the report:

Al-Qaeda operates primarily through regional groups operating in the Middle East and Africa. "The Taliban continue to attack Afghan government forces and international troops in the country" (Georgian Security Service Report, 2019).

A thorough study of this topic was conducted by a group of researchers in Georgia. They particularly mentioned, that

"These are terrorist organizations inspired by the idea of creating a single 'Islamic Caliphate' in the Middle East" (Georgian Times, 2020).

Jihadist networks appear on the Internet every day in various forms. In this regard, selective work is being carried out to educate a new generation of jihadists. As Vakhtang Maisaia points out, these are second-and third-generation jihadists who must work "behind the enemy's back."

Today, there are over 10,000 websites in cyberspace that spread jihadist ideology and terrorist practices. If we add more than 10 thousand sites to various social networks, we will get a very big threat, which also needs to be countered with more force. One of the main challenges for the modern world is such a type of asymmetric threat as international terrorism and transnational organized crime.

What is jihad and what could be a threat to Georgia? The word "jihad" is of Arabic origin and means striving and effort. It is used in classical texts mainly to refer to battle and war. The phrase "fight in the way of God" is often quoted from the Qur'an, which has been interpreted in many ways, from moral aspirations to armed struggle. According to Muslim law, war is justified against 4 types of enemies: infidels, apostates, rebels, and robbers. All four types of fighting are indeed legal, but only the first two are considered jihad. Thus, jihad is a religious obligation. Discussing the phenomenon of holy war, Muslim jurists distinguish between offensive and defensive jihad. Jihad during an attack is the responsibility of the Muslim community as a whole and is carried out by volunteers and professionals. In a defensive war, this becomes the duty of every Muslim. Bin Laden promoted exactly this principle in his declaration of war on the United States. According to Muslim tradition, the world is divided into two parts: the House of Islam (Dar al-Islam), where Muslim rule exists, and the House of War (Dar al-Harb) - the rest of the world, where non-believers live. Jihad must continue until the whole world either accepts Islamic laws or submits to Muslim laws. Whoever commits jihad will be rewarded in both lives. He will have possessions in the earthly life and paradise in the Hereafter. Jihad is sometimes considered a Muslim synonym for a crusade, and the two are perceived as more or less the same (TDI, 2018).

On June 6, 2013, a shocking video titled "Jihad Against Georgian Forces in Afghanistan" (Georgian Public Television, 2013) was posted on YouTube containing threats against the Georgian Armed Forces participating in the Afghan mission. The publication of the threatening video was followed by the victim. Before the death of Georgian soldiers became known, this video was not taken seriously by the Georgian authorities. The Department of Defense has also launched an investigation into its origins. The general text was as follows:

"We know your names, addresses, relatives and will soon arrive in Georgia! We want revenge!" (Zaman, 2013).

Jihadists also threatened terrorist attacks in Georgia at the time. According to military expert Giorgi Tavdgiridze, when we send a mission to Afghanistan, it's not just that we have soldiers there, and therefore we are left alone. The country should also take certain security measures:

"The Georgian budget allocates significant funds for such activities, border and airport control, so the relevant services should act as they do in the event of such a threat" (For. Ge, 2013).

Yes, France, Western Europe in general, and the United States, in general, are considered the main targets of terrorists, but this does not mean that Georgia is completely protected and there is no threat. Caucasus, Georgia, as a transit carrier, is a lucrative route for drug traffickers.

The decisive word here belongs to the State Security Service, intelligence, one of the main priorities of which is the fight against terrorism. Since November 2015, access to sites promoting radical ideology and groups registered on social networks has been restricted in Georgia. However, the number of people from the Pankisi Gorge to the "Islamic Caliphate" (up to 200 young people at that time) clearly showed that restricting access to websites and blocking terrorist groups on social networks is not enough - in particular, ideological and propaganda work in the Pankisi Gorge. According to the information provided by the State Security Service, for prevention, measures are constantly taken - between the relevant authorities of the partner states, there is a constant exchange of information about persons who are members or accomplices of a terrorist organization, as well as about persons who wish to move in transit:

"To prevent exit and entry for terrorist activities, in cooperation with the Ministry of Internal Affairs, proper control is carried out (the border strip, as well as border crossings). Visitors are interviewed. All border points are equipped with nuclear material detectors" (Georgian Service, 2020).

It is noteworthy that the fight against the threats posed by terrorism and organized crime required international growth, which led to the creation of a transnational international police system - Interpol. Cooperation is keenly involved in the Internet, thanks to which documents, films, and photographs are instantly distributed around the world.

According to official figures, the number of jihadists varies as follows: 43,600 people in Syria, 27,000 people in Afghanistan, 40,000 people in Pakistan, 15,000 people in Iraq, 10,000 people in Libya, 7,000 people in Nigeria, 7,000 people in Somalia, and 3 people in Yemen. Mali - 3200. About 67 active jihadist groups are active, representing a relative increase of 180% (Jiadze, 2022).

Experts say that the jihadists have lost influence in Iraq and Syria, but are not completely defeated - no one knows their current technologies and when they will act. The goal of the jihadists is unshakable, they "remain a great idea to create an Islamic caliphate. At the moment, they are trying to overthrow the governments of the Middle East and intensify the fight against the United States. However, despite numerous terrorist attacks and attempts to create a state, the idea remains a dream.

A NEW MODEL OF POLITICAL CONFLICT AND THE 2008 RUSSIA-GEORGIA CYBER FACTOR

In August 2008, Russia carried out aggression against Georgia on two fronts - there was a real military attack and it was an unreal or virtual attack on the Internet. Before the real war started, Russian hackers orchestrated the websites of state agencies. According to official information, the cyber attack took place on about 60 websites. Most of them featured propaganda calls and photos of former President Mikheil Saakashvili being equated with Adolf Hitler.

Was this cyber attack unexpected for Georgia and the international community? As further assessments showed, the attack was not unexpected, but no one expected such a strong attack. It was later evaluated as a lesson. Former government officials say that with the help of international partners, state-owned websites have been moved to US servers and the problem has been resolved, but the issue remains open - Russia has reached the crossroads, seizing both the real military training ground and the Internet. The investigation of the Ministry of Defense of Georgia revealed that the attack was prepared two years before the war. Former Deputy Defense Minister Batu Kutelia says there are several facts to prove this:

"Cyber-attacks were carried out from web platforms that had previously served criminals. Specifically, these were scams that were a platform for Russian organized crime. 2 years before the war, it was just launched in 2008 "(On. Ge, 2020).

According to Andria Gotsiridze, a cybersecurity expert, the DDoS cyberattacks against Estonia and Lithuania in 2007-2008 were a punitive operation and a kind of political message aimed at provoking civil unrest and mass unrest. Served as security. As for the Russia-Georgia war, the use of the cyber element here was a process directly accompanied by conventional actions aimed at facilitating the fulfillment of military objectives for the Russian Armed Forces, creating an information vacuum, gaining information advantage, and establishing a Russian narrative on the conflict (Gotsiridze, 2019).

Cyber attacks from Russia do not happen every day. However, the fact that Russian propaganda is constantly growing stronger is also recorded at the official level in the reports of the State Security Service. According to experts, the Kremlin has not only softened the tone but also applied the principle of decentralization - creating small marginal groups that spread radical views. This is like an attack when a lot of information comes together, and the server loads and stops. Pro-Western NGOs also point out in their reports that another important pillar of Kremlin propaganda in Georgia is the recent proliferation of pro-Russian NGOs, including two in particular - the Eurasian Institute and the Eurasian Choice (IDFI, 2016). According to them, these organizations are distinguished by anti-Western rhetoric and rely on Russian sources when publishing analytical papers or articles. According to the public registry, the list of founders and heads of pro-Russian NGOs often includes the same people. The link between the organizations is also indicated on their websites. In addition, a network of pro-Russian NGOs has links to anti-Western rhetorical media. Pro-Western NGOs may not be lying in part, but the organizations they name claim that the opposite is true - the Western course is being thwarted by organizations that are presented with fake pro-Western packaging. If the so-called. Organizations of the "Eurasian" denomination do not hide their orientation and often say that they are doing business, not for Russia, but for Georgians.

Some non-governmental organizations also write that pro-Russian political parties have multiplied in Georgia. Statements are often made as if several political parties and politicians, directly or indirectly, are spreading propaganda useful to the Kremlin. Political parties are divided into two parts: first - they have an openly pro-Russian agenda, meet with Russian politicians and visit Moscow; second, the parties that, at the declaration level, distance themselves from the Russian political elite and instead declare themselves pro-Georgian, pro-neutral parties. Despite the differences, the basic messages of both political parties are the same - their calls for membership in European and Euro-Atlantic structures arouse skepticism. Georgia's aspirations toward Western institutions are presented as fruitless as a dream. Instead, the idea of pro-Russian sentiment and Georgian neutrality is being popularized (Kuprashvili, 2022).

Part of some non-governmental organizations suspects that clergymen are also involved in the anti-Western campaign. They spread the myth that Georgian traditions are incompatible with Western culture. Some clerics in the sermon develop the idea of civilizational unity with Russia and ideological or moral opposition to the West. Indirect or direct dissemination of the Kremlin's propaganda messages is a serious problem, and the clergy enjoys high trust and influence in Georgian society. According to pro-Western NGOs, this can not be accidental, it turns out, that the public likes and recognizes their orientation. If the public is fascinated by such sermons, then the problem is partly with the population.

It is obvious that Russia is the source of many problems for Georgia, but there is another kind of illusion in the society, which is invented by fishermen: many preach that Russia will be disintegrated, emptied, and rescued day by day; Second - a democratic government will come to Russia and we will annex the territories without any problems; Third - Russia will soon run out of oil, go bankrupt and also help us. Maybe someday everything will happen, but with such considerations, we can not go far. What will follow the collapse of Russia for humanity and also what will follow the arrival of a democratic government in Russia, no one knows yet.

Against this background, there is a virtual threat - cyber and information front, which is open in several directions. One is open propaganda, the other is disguised propaganda, that is, pursuing Russia's interests through pro-Western shields. Russia is attacking the United States, the Baltic states, Ukraine, Georgia, Europe, and the rest of the world with cyber-methods, pre-processed hybrid methods, and disinformation. For example, the Russians in Slovakia and the Czech Republic are focused on criticizing US energy policy and trying to portray the US as acting solely in its interests, provoking conflicts in various parts of the world. In Russia, Russian-funded media outlets are trying to misrepresent EU membership and undermine democratic institutions. In Sweden, the government is portrayed as a follower of sexual depravity. Propaganda is being spread in Ukraine about corruption, poverty, disorder, and the "puppet" regime ruled by the West. In Lithuania, Latvia, and Estonia, the propaganda machine works to discriminate against Russians in these countries because of their ethnic or linguistic characteristics (IDFI, 2016).

Despite the Russian aggression, in the name of all post-Soviet countries, it must be said that after the collapse of the Soviet Union, mass persecution of Russians and the Russian-speaking population began nowhere, there was no bloodshed and cruelty. Perhaps the decisive factor, in this case, was the fact that for at least 70 years kinship ties and other cultural or social relations were formed. Instead of warning Russia of these relations, it began to create a space similar to the Soviet Union, where it is constantly carrying out military aggression and waging a hybrid war. It is known that the main driving force of Russian propaganda in the Baltics is the "First Baltic Channel", as well as the online site Regnum.ru, which has been operating for more than 10 years. Recently, the Russians launched the site Baltnews, which anonymously publishes information and news in Estonian, Lithuanian and Latvian (Damoukide-bloba. ge. 2020).

According to the German edition "Bild", according to its sources, if the United States openly intervened in the 2008 Georgian-Russian war, the Russians would decide to attack the Baltic states, and if the Americans would help the Baltic states, then they would consider using nuclear weapons.

According to the publication, as part of the exercise, Russia tested the bombing and capture of the Norwegian city of Spitsbergen. As we have seen, this plan did not materialize, the United States did not succumb to Russian provocation in the events of 2008, but since there is a similar model plan, Russia is still doing its job with hybrid warfare and cyber-attacks, do not rule out the same crisis again. In June 2018, the Pentagon acknowledged that in the event of a Russian invasion, it would not be able to defend the Baltic states and Poland. According to the "Washington Post", this conclusion was reached at the Pentagon as a result of simulating military resistance between EU countries and Russia. According to the publication: "Russia will be able to occupy the Baltic states until the US Army completes 17 forms to move NATO advanced forces from Germany to Poland." The newspaper writes that another major problem for the US military is the narrow streets and unreliable transport infrastructure, even the bridges are so weak that they can not withstand the weight of American equipment. European bureaucracy also creates problems at borders (The Washington Post, 2018). Russia has opened several fronts in the post-Soviet space, involving high-ranking government officials. For example, in September 2019, Foreign Minister Sergei Lavrov noted that the Baltic states are still living on EU subsidies and their assistance will soon cease (Iagorashvili, 2019). Of course, this is deliberate misinformation, through which the Russians are trying to instill nihilism and despair in the people of the Baltic states - Ager, today the EU is helping you, you are satisfied with the West, but tomorrow you will stop helping it. Russia is under constant ideological pressure - for example, the Kremlin has consistently argued that the Sovietization of the Baltic states was following international law and that the term "occupation" could not be used here. The Kremlin hides the fact that the so-called foreign ministers of these countries. They did not want to sign the agreement, they feared that it would violate their neutrality. After the refusal, Molotov addressed the representative of Estonia as follows: "We can not wait long. I advise you to agree with the Soviet Union's wish to avoid worse. Do not force the Soviet Union to use force" (Iagorasvili, 2020). This is the same "invitation" of the Russian troops as the Bolsheviks under the leadership of Sergo Orjonikidze were "invited" to Georgia. Falsifying history - this is another direction of Russia, or part of a larger strategy, which "fits" perfectly in the framework of a hybrid war.

CONCLUSION

Cybersecurity is a relatively new area in today's world. From a global point of view, there is a problem of the lack of a legal framework and international standards in the world, which, in the context of globalization and the modern world order, complicates the process of developing a regional and national cybersecurity strategy. However, cybersecurity mechanisms largely depend on the experience of individual countries, at least the examples of the post-Soviet space and Georgia in this matter show such a picture. As for the countries that are members of NATO and the European Union, as well as individual countries that have and spend large amounts of money in this direction, several facts indicate that none of these zones is fully protected.

Given the above, one might wonder to what extent cyber warfare can be perceived as a new reality of political conflict?

Cyber warfare is indeed a new reality of political conflicts. This is evidenced by the current political events in the world - already interested states interfered in the internal affairs of many states, mainly in the electoral process. Russia actively seeks to gain political influence in cyberspace, both in the countries of Eastern Europe and in the countries of the post-Soviet space, an example of which is Ukraine. Even the Islamic Republic of Iran, which is not a major political player in the world, is trying to interfere in the US presidential election. This has been repeatedly stated in the White House.

It is, therefore, possible that cybercrime could have a devastating impact on the international community, not excluding the disruption of the normal functioning of states and societies. Cybercrime will be catastrophic from unrealistic to real space, business, economy, almost all leading industries will suffer, terrorist organizations will become more active, intelligence operations will be disrupted, the life and health of many people, financial security, and private property rights will be threatened.

Given the existing problems, the question naturally arises, what is the plan of action and the components of the military strategy in cyberspace.

In cyberspace, the plan of action and the components of the military strategy must be carried out according to predetermined details. The implementation of the action plan is carried out by special agencies, in this case, the main agency on the international level is NATO's Cyber Security Centre. Concerning the national levels, in the example of Georgia, it should be mentioned about the State Security Service and the Cyber Security Bureau are under the Ministry of Defense.

Cybercrime, cyberattack, virtual threats, information warfare, cyberespionage, asymmetric threats, cyberterrorism, and cybersecurity are the main research topics and the content of the article. Also, the subject of the study is what serious problems and dangers the civilized world faces, what benefits the development of technology brings, and at the same time what challenges arise daily. Opportunities of different countries in terms of cyber technologies, for example, the USA, Russia, Islamic Caliphate, China, and so on.

REFERENCES

Bild. (2017). *German media: Russians intended to use nuclear weapons in 2008*. Retrieved from: resonancedaily.com: http://www.resonancedaily.com/index.php?id_rub=2&id_artc=42590

Bueger, C., & Liebetrau, T. (2021). *Protecting hidden infrastructure: The security politics of the global submarine data cable network*. Retrieved from: tandfonline.com

Caputo, D. (2012). *Applying behavioral science to the challenges of cybersecurity*. Retrieved from: https://www.mitre.org/careers/working-at-mitre/employee-voices/applying-behavioral-science-to-the-challenges-of-cybersecurity

Catalin, C. (2020). *Personal details for the entire country of Georgia*. Retrieved from: https://www.zdnet.com/article/personal-details-for-the-entire-country-of-georgia-published-online/?fbclid=IwAR0Jp5j_NCrd w9Et4k80WGwhWW3r2l2FV6COSv7MYWTqj6Qd9YpV_50jcA8

CNN. (2020). *Trump says 'Iran appears to be standing down following its retaliatory attacks against Iraqi bases housing US troops'*. Retrieved from: https://edition.cnn.com/2020/01/07/politics/rockets-us-airbase-iraq/index.html

CyberMedia. (2020). *The coronavirus is being manipulated by hackers*. Retrieved from: https://seclab.ge/post/CoronaCovid19

Damoukidebloba. (2020). *Information Warfare*. Retrieved from: http://damoukidebloba.ge/c/news/sainformacio_omi

For.Ge. (2013). *We know your names, addresses, and relatives and we will come to Georgia soon! We are seeking revenge!* Retrieved from: https://for.ge/view/23153/jihadi-Cven-viciT-Tqveni-saxelebi-misamarTebi-naTesavebi-da-male-saqarTveloSi-CamovalT-Cven-Su rs-viZiebT.html- დაწ

Ge, O. (2019). *How We Defeated Cyber Assault and Propaganda in 2008*. Retrieved from: https://on.ge/

Georgian Public Television. (2020a). *Iran has declared the US military as a terrorist organization*. Retrieved from: https://1tv.ge/news/iranma-ashsh-is-samkhedro-dzalebi-teroristul-organizaciad-gamoackhada/

Georgian Public Television. (2020b). *A new confrontation between USA and Iran*. Retrieved from: https://1tv.ge/news/ashsh-is-usafrtkhoebis-uwyeba-iranis-mkhridan-shesadzloa-ashsh-ze-%E2%80%8Bkibertavdaskhma-gankhorci eldes/

Georgian State Security Service. (2019). *The number and potential supporters of Daesh living in Georgia have decreased*. Retrieved from: https://imedinews.ge/ge/samartali/100997/susi-saqartveloshi-mtskhovreb-daeshis-shesadzlo-mkhardamcherta-raodenoba-da-gav lena-shemtsirda

Georgian State Security Service. (2020). *Combating Terrorism*. Retrieved from: https://ssg.gov.ge/page/counter-terrorism

Gotsiridze, A. (2019). *Cyber-Dimension of the 2008 Georgia-Russia War*. Retrieved from: https://www.gfsis.org/ge/blog/view/970

Iagorashvili, I. (2019a). *Russia's 2 Myths About the Baltic States*. Retrieved from https://www.mythdetector.ge/ka/myth/rusetis-2-miti-baltiispiretis-kveqnebis-shesakheb

Iagorashvili, I. (2019b). *Maria Zakharova denies the occupation of Estonia by the USSR*. Retrieved from: https://www.mythdetector.ge/ka/myth/maria-zakharova-ssrk-mier-estonetis-okupatsias-uarqops

IDFI. (2016). *Kremlin Information War Against Georgia: The Necessity of State Policy to Combat Propaganda.* Retrieved from: https://idfi.ge/ge/informational-war-of-kremlin-against-georgia-the-necessity-of-having-state-policy-against-propaganda

Imedi News. (2020a). *American Militaries killed Iranian General.* Retrieved from: https://imedinews.ge/ge/msoflio/124873/amerikelma-samkhedroebma-iraneli-generali-kasem-suleimani-mokles

Imedia News. (2020b). *Rouhani replies to Trump's Announcements.* Retrieved from: https://imedinews.ge/ge/msoflio/125067/rouhani-52-iranuli-obieqtis-shesakheb-trampis-gantskhadebas-pasukhobs

Impact, A. (2017). *Cyber Quest 2017.* Retrieved from: https://www.actionimpact.com/blog/2017/7/25/cyber-quest-2017-inspiring-the-next-generation-of-cyber-warriors-89mgj

Jiadze, N. (2022). *Georgian cybersecurity policy and International challenges.* Georgian Technical University.

Kegley, C., & Raymond, W. (2021). Realism in the Age of Cyber Warfare. *Ethics & International Affairs.*

Kuprashvili, H. (2022). *National Security of Georgia.* Universal.

Kupreishvili, T. (2020). *Everything we know about the Ukrainian plane crash.* Retrieved from: netgazeti.ge: https://netgazeti.ge/news/418935/

Maisaia, V. (2017). *Specifics of Information-Propaganda/Cyber-Virtual War of the Islamic Caliphate - The Concept of "Soft Power".* Retrieved from: http://geotimes.com.ge/blogi/?m=82&post_id=18&lng=geo

Mamuka, G. (2017). *Bitcoin, the future currency – Crypto Currency.* Retrieved from: https://financer.com/ge/kriptovaluta-bitcoin/

MDSNY. (2017). *Human Error, We meet again. Are the employees the weakest link in the fight against cyber vulnerabilities?* Retrieved from: https://www.mdsny.com/human-error-we-meet-again-cyber-security-basics/

Ministry of Internal Affairs of Georgia. (2020). *Citizens received messages on behalf of the Ministry of Internal Affairs - what statement does the Ministry of Internal Affairs make.* Retrieved from: https://www.ambebi.ge/article/243012-shss-s-saxelit-mokalakeebs-mesijebi-miuvidat-ra-g/

Myvideo.ge. (2013). *Al Qaeda threatens Georgian jihad against Georgian troops in Afghanistan.* Retrieved from: https://www.myvideo.ge/v/2058973

Natalia, C., & Tomaradze, G. (2014). *Virtual/cryptocurrency and its features Regulation of virtual currencies (on the example bitcoin).* Retrieved from: https://www.nbg.gov.ge/uploads/journal/2014/2014_3/4.pdf

Newman. (2020). *Coronavirus Sets the Stage for Hacking Mayhem.* Retrieved from: https://www.wired.com/story/coronavirus-cyberattacks-ransomware-phishing/

Paxful. (2020). *What Happens When All the Bitcoin in the World Has Been Mined?* Retrieved from: https://paxful.com/blog/what-happens-when-all-21-million-bit coins-mined/

Pernik, P. (2022). *Drivers of Change Impacting Cyberspace in 2030 Cyberspace Strategic Outlook 2030: Horizon Scanning and Analysis 2022*. NATO CCDCOE Publications.

Salomon, J. M. (2022). *Public-Private Partnerships and Collective Cyber Defence. 2022 NATO CCD-COE Publications*. Tallinn CCDCOE.

Satoshi, N. (2020). *Bitcoin: A Peer-to-Peer Electronic Cash System.* Retrieved from: https://bitcoin.org/ bitcoin.pdf

Sosanya, V. (2022). *Beyond Cyber Security Tools: The Increasing Roles Of Human Factors And Cyber Insurance In The Survival of Social Media Organisations*. https://www.researchgate.net/profile/Olutunji-Sosanya

TDI. (2018). *Violence in the Name of Religion and the Importance of Interpretation*. Retrieved from: https://www.tdi.ge/ge/page/zaladoba-religiis-saxelit-da-inte rpretaciis-mnishvneloba

The Washington Post. (2020). *The Pentagon has acknowledged that in the event of a Russian invasion, it will not be able to defend the Baltic states and Poland*. Retrieved from: https://imedinews.ge/ge/msoflio/67383/pentagonma-agiara-rom-rusetis-shechris-shemtkhvevashi-baltiispiretis-qveknebis-da-polonetis-datsvas-ver-moastsrebs

Timberg & Romm. (2020). *Hackers are seizing on coronavirus fears to steal data, researchers and U.S. regulators warn.* Retrieved from: https://www.washingtonpost.com/technology/2020/03/12/hackers -are-using-coronavirus-fears-target-people-looking-informati on-infection-maps/

Trump, D. (2020). *NATO should also cover the Middle East and call the new alliance "NATO + Middle East" - what a wonderful name, I guess the names well.* Retrieved from: interpressnews.ge: https://www.interpressnews.ge/ka/article/580527-donald-tramp i-nato-m-axlo-agmosavletic-unda-moicvas-da-axal-alianss-dava rkvat-natoaxlo-agmosavleti-ra-mshvenieri-saxelcodebaa-saxele bs-kargad-vigoneb/

Wiley Online Library. (2019). *Reevaluating the initial impact of John Broadus Watson on American psychology: The necessity of comparative parameters*. Retrieved from: https://onlinelibrary.wiley.com/ doi/full/10.1002/jhbs.21962

Zaman, H. (2013). *Is the Taliban threatening Georgia with revenge? A shocking video from YouTube*. Retrieved from: https://www.palitravideo.ge/garthoba/skhvadaskhva/32044-gaiz iare-bedniereba-erthi-qilidan-sayvareli-sasmeli-akhali-shefu thvith.html?start=140&fullComments

KEY TERMS AND DEFINITIONS

Behaviorism: Is a theory of learning based on the idea that all behaviors are acquired through conditioning, and conditioning occurs through interaction with the environment. Behaviorists believe that our actions are shaped by environmental stimuli.

Cyber Attack: An assault launched by cybercriminals using one or more computers against single or multiple computers or networks. A cyber attack can maliciously disable computers, steal data, or use a breached computer as a launch point for other attacks. Cybercriminals use a variety of methods to launch a cyber attack, including malware, phishing, ransomware, and denial of service, among other methods.

Cyber Security: The practice of defending computers, servers, mobile devices, electronic systems, networks, and data from malicious attacks. It's also known as information technology security or electronic information security. The term applies in a variety of contexts, from business to mobile computing, and can be divided into a few common categories.

Cyber Space: A virtual and dynamic environment comprised of electronics and communication devices over various networks to store and utilize electronic data. The cyberspace structure is like the structure of a human brain.

Cyber-Warfare: Is the use of computer technology to disrupt the activities of a state or organization, especially the deliberate attacking of information systems for strategic or military purposes.

Chapter 5
The Relationship Between Cybersecurity and Public Health

Rita Komalasari
https://orcid.org/0000-0001-9963-2363
Yarsi University, Indonesia

ABSTRACT

In this chapter, the authors discuss the relationship between cybersecurity and public health. They consider that open wellbeing logic may offer assistance. They explore the standardizing legitimization for—and moral limitations on—government engagement on the internet, as well as how to put these higher standards into reality through open wellbeing arrangement and education. In this open cyber-health worldview, non-malicious dangers to organize vigor and flexibility are treated genuinely, as is the effect of arranged dangers and activities on wellbeing and health.

INTRODUCTION

The ideas presented in the book "Current Trends in Cybersecurity and Educational Technology" are the foundation for the reviews included in this chapter. This chapter will use the academic community and the public. Take, for instance, a lecturer who works with health regulations and online learning from an educational technology standpoint. This chapter looks at the connection that exists between cyber-security and public health. The following is how the chapter is organized: a literature-based technique was discussed in more detail in the beginning. Second, we present the literature review findings in the "Results." Third, a theory-based approach for fusing fresh evidence is shown in the discussion section. This evidence includes the connection that exists between cybersecurity and public health. In the last portion of the report, titled "Conclusion," we offer a solution, a recommendation, and suggestions for further study.

Cybersecurity and educational technology systems have become more popular (Jimenez & O'Neill, 2022). Recently, a concern has been raised regarding self-interested actions by private marketplaces or national health services that may not deliver adequate public benefits if we leave them to their own devices (Boettke & Powell 2021). The United Nations has a dedicated organization for worldwide public health

DOI: 10.4018/978-1-6684-6092-4.ch005

called the World Health Organization. The greatest degree of health for all people is stated as the WHO's primary goal in its constitution. A growing number of these public goods are now part of WHO's mission, which has flourished. While the WHO monitors disease outbreaks, we also use it as a location for studies and classes on crisis management and for creating standards for readiness and response. Public goods that call for and provide benefits for all nations are known as global public goods. GPGs differ from other public goods in that they call for cooperation across states in a situation where no one state can compel another state to act. The World Health Organization's surveillance of infectious illnesses is a good example. The fact that these public goods are participatory is their second commonality.

In contrast to many others, a participatory public benefit calls on recipients to contribute more than just their tax dollars to its creation. Herd immunity is the poster child for participative public use. Herd immunity in public health necessitates vaccination, but in the context of technology, it necessitates device patching. In both situations, it becomes substantially more difficult for diseases to propagate after a certain proportion of the network is secured. Even if the production of GPGs requires international cooperation, it is essential to remember that individual governments play a necessary part in GPG supply (Brown & Susskind, 2020). Aside from the WHO's logistical support and direct provision of some of these goods, the organization collaborates closely with public health institutions. To keep illnesses at bay, these government health institutions work tirelessly (Nicola et al., 2020). However, the connection between cybersecurity and public health still needs to be explored. In the following section, we look at the method for searching for research relevant to the intertwined between cybersecurity and public health.

This review proposes a literature synthesis of research on the relationship between cybersecurity and public health. The current review's primary emphasis was on qualitative research and reported on the commons-based resources that promote healthy online health. On the one hand, we concentrated much of our focus on malware mitigation and the standardizing legitimization of—and moral limitations on—government engagement on the internet. We may better understand how to make these higher standards reality through open welfare arrangements and education. The purpose of compiling this information is to achieve two goals: (1) to shed light on the interplay between cybersecurity and public health; and (2) to highlight where further international health regulations are required.

RESULT

We present the findings of a literature review as follows. Building an international organization comparable to the WHO could be required for the cyber-health equivalent; this organization might be called the World Cyber Health Organization (Wilner et al., 2021). A significant number of the public goods provided by the WHO are also essential to cyber-health. Some examples are basic research, crisis coordination, reaction and preparation norms, instruction, monitoring programs, and information sharing. Even though we have concentrated on malware throughout this chapter, many of these public goods have the potential to help minimize the adverse impact that environmental hazards or human mistakes have on networks. The World CyberHealth Organization would have ongoing ties with the organizations and enterprises that manage cyber health top-level domains (TLDs) and internet infrastructure (such as routing and transmission equipment, DNS certificates, and transmission lines). A group of security professionals, eventually referred to as the Conficker Working Group (CWG), did recognize that Conficker posed a threat to the whole internet. They started researching the worm and developing strategies to manage it soon after it appeared. Early participants in the all-volunteer CWG included representatives of Microsoft, a nonprofit research institute, and several organizations. This group oversaw TLDs and several independent security researchers and academics. Many of these participants knew one another via conferences and social media. A volunteer group like the CWG cannot get that. A World Cyber Health Organization could also solve many of the CWG's organizational issues since it could distribute responsibilities and hold individuals and organizations responsible for their performance. This responsibility would also extend to the organization itself, given that ultimately—even indirectly—elected officials oversee governmental and intergovernmental organizations (Moon, 2007). The World Health Organization (WHO) has a governing body composed of delegates from each member nation. If the CWG could not complete its task, there would have been no sufficient cause or process to hold them responsible for their performance if they had failed. Meanwhile, the World Organization for Cyber Health may continue to look after many of the CWG's qualities.

Independent and private-sector security specialists might still form specialized working groups if the organization faces a problem beyond its technical capabilities (Tether & Tajar 2008). However, to put their ideas into reality, these organizations would need to have access to institutional resources and lawful power.

A group may also implement preventive measures to which the CWG did not have access. The World Health Organization's (WHO) guidelines on drug abuse and non-communicable disease prevention illustrate this strategy in public health (Lauber & Gilmore 2021). Rather than focusing solely on assisting those who have already gained a dependency on drugs or alcohol, the World Health Organization encourages the implementation of programs that are geared toward Pregnant women, early childhood education, mental health therapy, school enrollment maintenance, mentorship initiatives, and media campaigns all fall within this broad category. For non-communicable illnesses, these organizations advocate monitoring the elimination of premature death. One of the most effective ways to decrease sudden death and disability is to eliminate risk factors and promote health throughout one's life (WHO, 2019).

Regarding Conficker, the CWG reacted rather than taking a proactive approach, which would have been preferable (Mueller et al. 2013). If they were adopted, public education and more robust security standards would have made a half-million-computer botnet less harmful than one with 10 million machines. While asking people to patch their systems may have been an unduly demanding requirement, it may have been an excessively cumbersome requirement.

Even though the discussion has changed, public goods and private-goods preventive actions are inextricably linked for two reasons. Individuals, corporations, and even entire countries tend to under-invest in preventative strategies when confronted with threats such as malware or contagious disease (White & Banda 2016). First, because these strategies generate significant externalities, individuals, corporations, and even entire countries tend to under-invest. There is no guarantee that the positive effects of individual actions will be entirely realized by those actors alone. Private markets can often not implement second preventive tactics to address global dangers since such strategies are only successful with extensive international coordination. This coordination leads to the second point. Because of this, they are often only able to take preventive steps as part of the public's response.

Even though there is not yet a World Cyber Health Organization, it is possible. The National Cybersecurity and Communications Integration Center are already looking at this approach to cybersecurity from a public health perspective at the national level (NCCIC). The NCCIC deals with several of the functions I listed before, including (Examples include monitoring, crisis response, and information exchange.) They found that the United States recognizes the need to provide cyber-health public benefits while being too small to achieve these objectives (Demchak 2021). For instance, the National Cybersecurity and Communications Integration Center (NCCIC) only has seven cybersecurity advisers on staff as of 2016, increasing from one in 2009. These experts were there to educate us on protecting critical infrastructure from the private sector. It should not come as a surprise that the private sector protects vital infrastructure from cyberattacks since the staffing levels are so low, even though private enterprises often have incentives that are in direct competition with one another (e.g., it costs them money to upgrade their systems). At least when seen from an international perspective, the NCCIC presents its inherent conflicts of interest as a component of the security apparatus. For instance, the United States may have a strategic interest in withholding information that might benefit the rest of the world. One such example has weaknesses that intelligence agencies can strategically exploit. Those that operate from a public health perspective are more likely to share this information. In contrast, those who work from a security perspective are more likely to keep it to themselves.

DISCUSSION

The Similarity Between Transportation Industry and Communicable Diseases

The following section presents a discussion on how cybersecurity and public health are related to one another. The author discussed concepts to aspects of the transportation industry. The author compared elements of IT to how biology behaves. Despite the relevance of cyber-health to these core obligations, many nations' United States-based private firms operating vital infrastructure have traditionally been allowed to decide whether investments in robustness and resilience are worthwhile (Gross, 2015). While cyber-health is critical to the state's core duties, this is the situation. In their analysis of the situation in the United States, Nifakos et al. (2021) cite the following quote from the chief executive officer of a cybersecurity company: "Most of the important infrastructure is lagging for cyber security." There has been much emphasis on sectors such as financial water management, the chemical sector, and the ports, all of which pose more relevance and danger but have received much less attention in regulation and investment. For example, research in 2021 revealed that just one of the six main American ports had adequate cybersecurity (Gunes et al. 2021). As a result, they left the ports unregulated and unprotected owing to the lack of authority and knowledge held by the Coast Guard and Department of Transportation authorities. A public health-inspired approach gives the state the power to do its job by providing the normative reason for internet intervention. In contrast to the conventional "feudal" approach to cybersecurity, which is discussed in the introduction, they considered the security and resilience of these networks a personal benefit.

The Similarity Between Malware and Communicable Diseases

In the following paragraph, the author compares the elements of IT to how biology behaves. It seems to be one of those to ensure that critical infrastructure is kept safe, including networks used by the military and the government. The user would hinder the capacity of a state to fight a defensive war if vulnerabilities to such networks existed. Maintaining a solid internet infrastructure and encryption standards should also be included in that list for reasons analogous to the last. It would be essential to do further study to evaluate whether the ability to control malware meets the cut. However, there are grounds to believe that it should. Personal devices should be patched, the user should practice safe surfing practices, and we should install real-time malware protection to engage in malware reduction actively. These measures seem manageable when weighed against the advantages of preventing malware infections and helping to secure vital infrastructure. We may educate individuals, The government can subsidize security software, and standards can Install security upgrades that should be made more accessible and consistent. States can establish regulations to assist people in meeting their participatory commitments. The situation is comparable to that of governments that encourage herd immunity. For instance, to reduce the amount of work required from participants, the government of the United Kingdom pays for most vaccinations. Personal devices should be patched, we should practice safe surfing practices, and we should install real-time malware protection to engage in malware reduction actively.

In avoiding malware infestations and enhancing critical infrastructure security, the benefits outweigh the costs, and these procedures seem manageable. Because maintaining an up-to-date system and engaging in safe browsing practices yield considerable individual benefits, it appears appropriate to place the burden of proof on the person who objects and require them to show that the costs are higher than the benefits. Individuals may have a duty to contribute to creating cyber-health through tax contributions. However, its location is open for debate on where we should draw the boundary. Real-time malware monitoring may significantly reduce expenses, so it appears logical that people have to support cyber-health production via tax contributions. Given the cost to an individual's freedom, automated patching may be desirable, but it is not worthwhile to mandate that people exercise safe surfing habits while using the internet. Our aim here is not to find solutions to these particular problems; instead, we want to show how framing discussions are. Cybersecurity as a public good may help us think about how people's access to the internet might lead to mutually beneficial duties (Canazza 2018).

Because malicious software (malware) and contagious diseases are similar, this is an enticing argument for thinking about corporate responsibility to control malicious software. Similar to the transmission of infectious illnesses across devices, the damage that malware may inflict is not insignificant, and there are ineffectual mitigation techniques. The following is the consequence of adopting Dawson's theory of malware mitigation: Malicious software can inflict significant damage and may be spread to other people via actions that the person did not do intentionally. Suppose the gadget in question has some appropriate safety safeguards. In that case, we can lessen the likelihood that it may cause injury (including, but not limited to, the most recent fixes and strong passwords). Our fundamental moral responsibility is to avoid doing anything that could harm other people because of our acts or inactions. Given the above consideration, companies may lessen the likelihood of unnecessarily inflicting damage on third parties by patching their equipment and including reasonable safety precautions in the products they develop and produce for other companies (if applicable).

Given those mentioned above, one may draw the following consideration: manufacturers have a moral obligation to address security flaws in their products and to provide adequate defenses against them. Those who acknowledge a universal moral need to avoid causing damage to other people should find this argument persuasive. If individuals who were affected were the ones who intentionally purchased items with deficient security features, then the concept of harm to others may not apply. However, people who disagree with being exposed to harm may be harmed by insufficient security procedures. A lack of adequate security rules might imperil even individuals without an internet connection because of critical infrastructure.

Even though this line of reasoning implies that businesses have a legal responsibility to safeguard their products and to guarantee that the products they manufacture have sufficient levels of security, we must make two essential qualifications (Betsch et al. 2017). First, the responsibility ceases to exist when there is a condition of herd immunity since receiving a vaccination would not result in any extra benefits. It may even harm the person receiving the vaccination (negative effects, for example). Second, non-communicable disease vaccinations are unnecessary, such as tetanus, since there is no responsibility to do so. Malware does not adhere to any of these conditions.

To begin with, we may disregard the claim that there is "no extra advantage" since acquiring herd immunity while dealing with malware is considerably more challenging because infected computers may spread infections to other devices or take part in assaults. Local herd immunity is ineffective in limiting the harm posed by a botnet since it might originate from anywhere globally. For instance, in 2017, ten years after the first discovery of Conficker, they reported two million new infections throughout the globe (Çetin et al. 2019). These newly discovered viruses from around the world might come together to form a single botnet capable of assaulting targets in any location. Dawson's claim that there is no extra value to safeguarding one's devices does not hold water, given that we are constantly in a state of immunity to malware at the sub-herd level. We may gain additional benefits by protecting one's equipment.

In contrast to vaccinations, which only guard against a particular illness, the anti-malware tactics described above are effective against various types of malware. Certain particularly focused malware assaults may be comparable to tetanus. However, the officer can stop most malware using the same strategies (patches for general security, good online behaviors, and real-time monitoring) (Tawalbeh et al., 2020). An analogy to this situation would be the existence of a single vaccine that is effective against all illnesses. According to the author's logic, getting this immunization is a moral obligation since it protects the population from potentially deadly infectious diseases. This immunization would be the case because the vaccine prevents the spread of disease. Many methods have been devised by philosophers and politicians working in public health to evaluate the efficacy of an intervention as well as its effects on individual rights. We may violate individual liberties and privacy because of public health measures.

It is possible to stop the spread of disease by ordering everyone to stay inside their homes; however, such a measure is unethical in all but direct circumstances. With digital interventions that benefit the public, they may infringe on individual rights similar to physical ones. Ethical difficulties in these disciplines are different, but it is vital to remember that there are certain commonalities. In the previous part of this article, we discussed that as virtual reality becomes more commonplace, worries about one's physical integrity might arise when medical equipment is updated. Digital quarantining can limit one's freedom of association and mobility. This limitation has the potential to create enormous social and economic damage, particularly for those who have relatively limited access to the internet. This part will discuss how ethics review boards and the Intervention Ladder stem from public health. They may help balance providing efficient answers and safeguarding individuals' rights in a digital setting.

A Cyber-Health Intervention Ladder

The following paragraph discusses the importance of a cyber-health intervention ladder. The intervention ladder serves as a helpful reference point. Based on the risk assessment level, we may perform one of the following interventions, with the amount of intrusiveness rising with each successive intervention: Make no moves. Encourage people to learn about cybersecurity without compromising their liberty (Huang & Pearlson, 2019). Make it possible for the owners of all newly purchased PCs to activate anti-malware software. Make it easier for people to protect themselves by making it the default for new PC users to opt into having anti-malware software and automatic updates installed on their machines. The government should subsidize anti-malware software, and we should establish a comparable fund to compensate the Patching injuries under the Vaccine Injury Compensation Program. Users who need more protection should pay extra to use the internet. Internet service providers (ISPs) can limit access to unprotected personal computers so that they may only visit websites that have been verified as secure. Internet service providers can impose severe restrictions on unprotected computers until the owners install anti-malware software. Even though the provided could also justify a more invasive alternative, one should always consider all available choices and, in most cases, go with the one that requires the least amount of interference to achieve the desired result, as was done with the example of the soda tax.

A cyber-health intervention ladder will other rungs than the one defined by the Nuffield Council are required to meet the needs. For a specific example of the internet, it may be more onerous to charge people who have not been protected a higher fee for internet access rather than limit their access to safe websites (Lemley 2017). Because they restrict a person's capacity to move about and interact with others, quarantines for public health reasons are more demanding than fines. It is still a helpful tool, even in its present condition. Method to consider how to achieve a balance between conflict and peacebuilding in cyberspace among dangers, responses, and individual rights. This approach to public health, which evaluates a broad array of therapies and strives to achieve the correct individuals that employ the Cybersecurity Standards of assurance (LoA), strikes a unique balance between effectiveness and ethical costs (Nifakos et al., 2021). Cybersecurity quality assurance is a claim to a certain identity made during authentication that the person can trust to represent the claimant's "real" identity with a given level of (identification) confidence. Higher degrees of assurance decrease the possibility of identity theft and boost transaction security. Still, they can also be more expensive and inconvenient for identity holders and other parties that rely on them, which might result in exclusion. Therefore, practitioners must consider the various LOA needs of different use cases. For instance, while some transactions—like making a medical appointment online—carry less risk than others, biometric-based verification is probably not acceptable for usage across all use cases. Because people that employ the Cybersecurity LoA view cybersecurity as a private matter, companies choose the activities that are in their competence and power in their self-interest.

Although an ISP can disable a user's internet connection, it cannot automatically enable application security updates. Even if they could, they may have little interest in doing so. According to previous research, just 27 percent of internet service providers monitor outbound assaults (Lin et al., 2019). Of those that watch outbound attacks, only 50 percent take any preventative measures against them. Because of their limited skills and motivations, private firms must be better suited to find and execute the cyber-health solution that best balances efficacy with individual rights. This challenge makes it difficult for private companies to identify and implement the solution. Considering how well-equipped businesses are to offset efficiency and cost, they may play an essential part in bringing the expense of public cyber-health policies under control. For example, suppose policymakers decide internet service providers (ISPs) should block access to specific websites. In that case, the ISP is better positioned to prevent spammers and other malicious software from gaining access to the internet than the policymaker to devise a solution that is both cost-effective and satisfies the requirement that it does so. Most of the time, only private businesses will implement certain cyber-health precautions, such as updating proprietary code.

The Intervention Ladder is only one example of how public health professionals think daily in their work in public health organizations. This intervention is something that needs to be emphasized. This way of thinking, which is this style that explicitly addresses individual rights, non-financial damages, and the impact of externalities in the broader network, is what the Public Cyber health LoA attempts to do.

Public health interventions directly affect people's lives. Hence, there is an increasing tendency to include many stakeholders in discussions about specific projects. As previously mentioned, this is because of the direct impact that most public health measures have. Individually, via informed consent procedures, on a community level, public health specialists interact with patients on an equal playing field and a national level through an organization like the World Health Organization (WHO). It is all because businesses often favor deciding in private rather than engaging in fruitful public discourse, and they regularly hide their intentions on purpose by using terms and conditions that are difficult to understand. Everyday capitalism may have been tolerable and even desirable when technical difficulties seemed more like overlapping issues. It is becoming more common for people to be concerned about these overlapping issues since the internet has become an essential connecting thread in today's contemporary life.

For this reason, it is vital to emphasize these practices, even if they are not directly derived from the Cybersecurity LoA. This practice exemplifies how the public cyber-health concept has broad relevance beyond just network failure. However, the history of public health shows that it is conceivable for a new framing device to replace a well-known LoA like cybersecurity. We directly linked the cholera outbreak in London in 1854 to the city's water supply management privatization (Tulchinsky, 2018). While the cholera outbreak was going on, private companies supplied many water sources with little to no oversight. According to John Snow, the most probable culprit was a particular water pump in the cholera outbreak. The predominant notion ascribed cholera to miasma or polluted air. John Snow discovered this by mapping incidences of the illness. He also found out that the company that supplied the water was getting some of its water from parts of the Thames that sewage had polluted.

As more people noticed the significance of having access to clean water, governments played a more active part in monitoring water quality. Londoners did not just sit around and wait for the water corporations to volunteer their services as advocates for public health who take responsibility for their actions and do the right thing (Caplan et al. 2020). We must reevaluate our conceptions of the private rights of corporations and general duties because modern life increasingly depends on the internet and other digital technology. These technologies are the foundation of both critical infrastructure and social interactions. The alternative is to prioritize safety and security that will take precedence above all else for our digital lives and the crucial infrastructure on which we rely—profit maximization above the flourishing of human beings.

CONCLUSION

In this chapter, we summarize how cybersecurity and public health are related to one another. Our argument in this chapter was to go to the public health field for guidance on how to think about the general benefit of enhancing cyber-health. In particular, we concentrated on one of the more traditional concerns of cybersecurity, namely the elimination of malware. Open welfare logic can help us think about government behavior regarding its moral justifications and limitations on the internet and how to put these higher standards into practice via available welfare arrangements and education. The Open Cyber health worldview considers both the threats, vicious and non-malicious, to the vitality and adaptability of an organization and the impact that threats and activities posed by an organization have on an individual's wellness and health. There are some suggestions in this chapter for future studies. This proposal calls for a greater emphasis to be placed on the establishment of the WHO and the international provisions.

This proposal could show how, over time, we can reach a global agreement on stopping malware from spreading.

REFERENCES

Betsch, C., Böhm, R., Korn, L., & Holtmann, C. (2017). On the benefits of explaining herd immunity in vaccine advocacy. *Nature Human Behaviour*, *1*(3), 1–6. doi:10.103841562-017-0056

Boettke, P., & Powell, B. (2021). The political economy of the COVID-19 pandemic. *Southern Economic Journal*, *87*(4), 1090–1106. doi:10.1002oej.12488 PMID:33821055

Brown, G., & Susskind, D. (2020). International cooperation during the COVID-19 pandemic. *Oxford Review of Economic Policy*, *36*(Supplement_1), S64–S76. doi:10.1093/oxrep/graa025

Canazza, M. R. (2018). The internet as a global public good and the role of governments and multilateral organizations in global internet governance. *Meridiano*, *47*, 19. doi:10.20889/M47e19007

Caplan, J. M., Kennedy, L. W., & Neudecker, C. H. (2020). Cholera deaths in Soho, London, 1854: Risk terrain modeling for epidemiological investigations. *PLoS One*, *15*(3), e0230725. doi:10.1371/journal.pone.0230725 PMID:32226024

Çetin, O., Ganán, C., Altena, L., Kasama, T., Inoue, D., Tamiya, K., . . . Van Eeten, M. (2019, February). Cleaning Up the Internet of Evil Things: Real-World Evidence on ISP and Consumer Efforts to Remove Mirai. NDSS.

Demchak, C. (2021). Achieving Systemic Resilience in a Great Systems Conflict Era. *The Cyber Defense Review*, *6*(2), 51–70.

Gross, O. (2015). Cyber Responsibility to Protect: Legal Obligations of States Directly Affected by Cyber-Incidents. *Cornell Int'l LJ*, *48*, 481.

Gunes, B., Kayisoglu, G., & Bolat, P. (2021). Cyber security risk assessment for seaports: A case study of a container port. *Computers & Security*, *103*, 102196. doi:10.1016/j.cose.2021.102196

Hadarics, K., Leitold, F., & Arrott, A. (2017). Distributed vulnerability assessment applied to measuring citizen cyber-health and securing online public services. *Central and Eastern European eDem and eGov Days*, *325*, 137-144.

Huang, K., & Pearlson, K. (2019, January). For what technology can't fix: Building a model of organizational cybersecurity culture. *Proceedings of the 52nd Hawaii International Conference on System Sciences*. 10.24251/HICSS.2019.769

Jimenez, R., & O'Neill, V. (2022). Strategies to Maximize Asynchronous Learning. In *Handbook of Research on Managing and Designing Online Courses in Synchronous and Asynchronous Environments* (pp. 499–521). IGI Global. doi:10.4018/978-1-7998-8701-0.ch025

Lauber, K., McGee, D., & Gilmore, A. B. (2021). Commercial use of evidence in public health policy: A critical assessment of food industry submissions to global-level consultations on non-communicable disease prevention. *BMJ Global Health*, *6*(8), e006176. doi:10.1136/bmjgh-2021-006176 PMID:34426403

Lemley, M. A. (2017). Rationalizing internet safe harbors. In *Copyright Law* (pp. 291–309). Routledge. doi:10.4324/9781315095400-9

Lin, T., Capecci, D. E., Ellis, D. M., Rocha, H. A., Dommaraju, S., Oliveira, D. S., & Ebner, N. C. (2019). Susceptibility to spear-phishing emails: Effects of internet user demographics and email content. *ACM Transactions on Computer-Human Interaction*, *26*(5), 1–28. doi:10.1145/3336141 PMID:32508486

Moon, J. (2007). The contribution of corporate social responsibility to sustainable development. *Sustainable Development*, *15*(5), 296–306. doi:10.1002d.346

Mueller, M., Schmidt, A., & Kuerbis, B. (2013). Internet security and networked governance in international relations. *International Studies Review*, *15*(1), 86–104. doi:10.1111/misr.12024

Nicola, M., O'Neill, N., Sohrabi, C., Khan, M., Agha, M., & Agha, R. (2020). Evidence based management guideline for the COVID-19 pandemic-Review article. *International Journal of Surgery*, *77*, 206–216. doi:10.1016/j.ijsu.2020.04.001 PMID:32289472

Nifakos, S., Chandramouli, K., Nikolaou, C. K., Papachristou, P., Koch, S., Panaousis, E., & Bonacina, S. (2021). Influence of human factors on cyber security within healthcare organisations: A systematic review. *Sensors (Basel)*, *21*(15), 5119. doi:10.339021155119 PMID:34372354

Tawalbeh, L. A., Muheidat, F., Tawalbeh, M., & Quwaider, M. (2020). IoT Privacy and security: Challenges and solutions. *Applied Sciences (Basel, Switzerland)*, *10*(12), 4102. doi:10.3390/app10124102

Tether, B. S., & Tajar, A. (2008). Beyond industry–university links: Sourcing knowledge for innovation from consultants, private research organisations and the public science base. *Research Policy*, *37*(6-7), 1079–1095. doi:10.1016/j.respol.2008.04.003

Tulchinsky, T. H. (2018). John Snow, Cholera, the broad street pump; waterborne diseases then and now. *Case Studies in Public Health*, 77.

White, K., & Banda, M. (2016). The role of civil society in pandemic preparedness. In *Innovation in Global Health Governance* (pp. 123–146). Routledge.

Wilner, A. S., Luce, H., Ouellet, E., Williams, O., & Costa, N. (2021). From public health to cyber hygiene: Cybersecurity and Canada's healthcare sector. *International Journal (Toronto, Ont.)*, *76*(4), 522–543. doi:10.1177/00207020211067946

World Health Organization. (2019). Department of Noncommunicable Diseases and Mental Health: Our goal is to build a better, healthier future for people in the Region (No. WHO-EM/NMH/001/E). World Health Organization. Regional Office for the Eastern Mediterranean.

ADDITIONAL READING

Komalasari, R. (2022). A Social Ecological Model (SEM) to Manage Methadone Programmes in Prisons. In Handbook of Research on Mathematical Modeling for Smart Healthcare Systems (pp. 374-382). IGI Global.

Komalasari, R. (2022). Pemanfaatan Kecerdasan Buatan (AI) Dalam Telemedicine: Dari Perspektif Profesional Kesehatan. *Jurnal Kedokteran Mulawarman*, *9*(2), 72–81.

Komalasari, R. (2022). Gambaran Sistem Perawatan Kesehatan Untuk Lansia Berbasis Informasi Teknologi (Literature Review). *Jurnal Manajemen Informasi dan Administrasi Kesehatan*, 5(2).

Komalasari, R. (2023). Digital twin elderly healthcare services. In *Digital Twins and Healthcare: Trends, Techniques, and Challenges*. IGI Global.

Komalasari, R. (2023). Telemedicine in Pandemic Times in Indonesia: Healthcare Professional's Perspective. In N. Vajjhala & P. Eappen (Eds.), *Health Informatics and Patient Safety in Times of Crisis* (pp. 138–153). IGI Global.

Komalasari, R. (2023). Designing Health Systems for Better, Faster, and Less Expensive Treatment. In *Exploring the Convergence of Computer and Medical Science Through Cloud Healthcare*. IGI Global.

Komalasari, R. (2023). History and Legislative Changes Governing Medical Cannabis in Indonesia. In *Medical Cannabis and the Effects of Cannabinoids on Fighting Cancer, Multiple Sclerosis, Epilepsy, Parkinson's, and Other Neurodegenerative Diseases*. IGI Global.

Komalasari, R. (in press). The ethical consideration of using Artificial Intelligence (AI) in medicine. In *Advanced Bioinspiration Methods for Healthcare Standards, Policies, and Reform*. IGI Global. doi:10.4018/978-1-6684-5656-9.ch001

Komalasari, R. (in press). Spirituality and health benefits. In *Supporting Children and Youth Through Spiritual Education*. IGI Global.

Komalasari, R. (in press). Postnatal mental distress, exploring the experiences of mothers navigating the health care system. In *Perspectives and Considerations on Navigating the Mental Healthcare System*. IGI Global.

Komalasari, R. (in press). Treatment of menstrual discomfort in young women and a cognitive behavior therapy (CBT) program. In *Perspectives on Coping Strategies for Menstrual and Premenstrual Distress*. IGI Global.

Komalasari, R. (in press). Literature Review: Health Aspects and Legal Protection for Children in Scotland and Indonesia. *Buana Gender: Jurnal Studi Gender dan Anak*.

Komalasari, R. (in press). Manfaat Positif Allium Sativum L. (Bawang Putih) Dalam Kaitannya Dengan Berbagai Penyakit. *Jurnal Farmasimed*.

Komalasari, R. (in press). Pelatihan Kesehatan dan Pengembangan Profesional Berkelanjutan untuk Pendidik Olah Raga. *Jurnal Ilmiah STOK Bina Guna Medan*.

Komalasari, R. (in press). Persepsi Hakim tentang Rehabilitasi Pengguna Narkoba:Tantangan dan Peluang. *Arena Hukum*.

Komalasari, R. (in press). Pariwisata Medis Sebagai Pasar Niche Yang Unik Dalam Konteks Indonesia. In *Journey: Journal of Tourismpreneurship*. Culinary, Hospitality, Convention and Event Management.

Komalasari, R., Ernawati, K., Fadilah, M. R., Rachman, M. A., Nadira, C., Sartika, P. A. J., & Jannah, F. (2022). Implementasi Kebijakan Program Pengendalian Demam Berdarah Dengue di Puskesmas Kresek, Kabupaten Tangerang. *Public Health and Safety International Journal*, *2*(02), 140–145. doi:10.55642/phasij.v2i02.244

Komalasari, R., & Mustafa, C. (2021). Meningkatkan Pelayanan Administrasi Publik di Indonesia. *PaKMas: Jurnal Pengabdian Kepada Masyarakat*, *1*(1), 20–27. doi:10.54259/pakmas.v1i1.29

Komalasari, R., & Mustafa, C. (2021). Pendidikan Profesi dan Pengabdian Masyarakat di Indonesia. *PaKMas: Jurnal Pengabdian Kepada Masyarakat*, *1*(1), 28–36. doi:10.54259/pakmas.v1i1.30

Komalasari, R., & Mustafa, C. (2022). Empowerment of Women with Narcotic Cases. *Buana Gender: Jurnal Studi Gender dan Anak*, *7*(1).

Komalasari, R., Nurhayati, N., & Mustafa, C. (2022). Insider/Outsider Issues: Reflections on Qualitative Research. *Qualitative Report*, *27*(3), 744–751. doi:10.46743/2160-3715/2022.5259

Komalasari, R., Nurhayati, N., & Mustafa, C. (2022). Enhancing the Online Learning Environment for Medical Education: Lessons From COVID-19. In Policies and procedures for the implementation of safe and healthy educational environments: Post-COVID-19 perspectives (pp. 138-154). IGI Global.

Komalasari, R., Nurhayati, N., & Mustafa, C. (2022). Kebijakan Penanganan Penyintas HIV/AIDS Di Lembaga Pemasyarakatan. *Jurnal Kesehatan Kartika*, *17*(1), 19–27.

Komalasari, R., Nurhayati, N., & Mustafa, C. (2022). Professional Education and Training in Indonesia. In *Public Affairs Education and Training in the 21st Century* (pp. 125–138). IGI Global. doi:10.4018/978-1-7998-8243-5.ch008

Komalasari, R., Wilson, S., & Haw, S. (2021). A systematic review of qualitative evidence on barriers to and facilitators of the implementation of opioid agonist treatment (OAT) programmes in prisons. *The International Journal on Drug Policy*, *87*, 102978. doi:10.1016/j.drugpo.2020.102978 PMID:33129135

Komalasari, R., Wilson, S., & Haw, S. (2021). A social ecological model (SEM) to exploring barriers of and facilitators to the implementation of opioid agonist treatment (OAT) programmes in prisons. *International Journal of Prisoner Health*, *17*(4), 477–496. doi:10.1108/IJPH-04-2020-0020

Komalasari, R., Wilson, S., Nasir, S., & Haw, S. (2020). Multiple burdens of stigma for prisoners participating in Opioid Antagonist Treatment (OAT) programmes in Indonesian prisons: A qualitative study. *International Journal of Prisoner Health*.

Mustafa, C. (2021). The Challenges to Improving Public Services and Judicial Operations: A unique balance between pursuing justice and public service in Indonesia. In Handbook of research on global challenges for improving public services and government operations (pp. 117-132). IGI Global. doi:10.4018/978-1-7998-4978-0.ch007

Mustafa, C. (2021). Key finding: result of a qualitative study of judicial perspectives on the sentencing of minor drug offenders in Indonesia: Structural inequality. *Qualitative Report*, *26*(5), 1678–1692. doi:10.46743/2160-3715/2021.4436

Mustafa, C. (2021). The view of judicial activism and public legitimacy. *Crime, Law, and Social Change*, *76*(1), 23–34. doi:10.100710611-021-09955-0

Mustafa, C. (2021). Qualitative method used in researching the judiciary: Quality assurance steps to enhance the validity and reliability of the findings. *Qualitative Report*, *26*(1), 176–186. doi:10.46743/2160-3715/2021.4319

Mustafa, C. (2021). The News Media Representation of Acts of Mass Violence in Indonesia. In *Mitigating Mass Violence and Managing Threats in Contemporary Society* (pp. 127–140). IGI Global. doi:10.4018/978-1-7998-4957-5.ch008

Mustafa, C., Malloch, M., & Hamilton Smith, N. (2020). Judicial perspectives on the sentencing of minor drug offenders in Indonesia: Discretionary practice and compassionate approaches. *Crime, Law, and Social Change*, *74*(3), 297–313. doi:10.100710611-020-09896-0

Suhariyanto, B., & Mustafa, C. (2022). Analysis And Evaluation Of Legal Aid In The Indonesian Court. *Jurnal Hukum dan Peradilan*, *11*(2), 176-194.

KEY TERMS AND DEFINITIONS

CWG: A group of security professionals, eventually referred to as the Conficker Working Group, did recognize that Conficker posed a threat to the whole internet. They started researching the worm and developing strategies to manage it soon after it appeared. Early participants in the all-volunteer CWG included representatives of Microsoft, a nonprofit research institute, and several organizations that oversaw top-level domains, as well as some independent security researchers and academics. Many of these participants knew one another via conferences and social media.

Cyberhealth: The use the internet for telehealth.

Cybersecurity: Protection from electronic assaults such as cyberwarfare.

GPG: Public goods that call for and provide benefits for all nations are known as global public goods. GPG differs from other public goods in that they call for cooperation across states in a situation where no one state can compel another state to act. The World Health Organization's surveillance of infectious illnesses is a good example. The fact that these public goods are participatory is their second thing in common. In contrast to many others, a participatory public benefit calls on recipients to contribute more than just their tax dollars to its creation. Herd immunity is the poster child for a participative general help. Herd immunity in public health necessitates vaccination, but in the context of technology, it necessitates device patching. In both situations, it becomes substantially more difficult for diseases to propagate after a certain proportion of the network is secured.

LoA: Standards of assurance. It is a claim to a certain identity made during authentication that can be trusted to represent the claimant's "real" identity with a given level of (identification) confidence. Higher degrees of assurance decrease the possibility of identity theft and boost transaction security. Still, they can also be more expensive and inconvenient for identity holders and other parties that rely on them, which might result in exclusion. Therefore, practitioners must consider the various LoA needs of different use cases. For instance, while some transactions—like making a medical appointment online—carry less risk than others, biometric-based verification is probably not acceptable for usage across all use cases.

WHO: The United Nations has a dedicated organization for worldwide public health called the World Health Organization. The greatest degree of health for all people is stated as the WHO's primary goal in its constitution.

Chapter 6
Unified Cybersecurity Data Analytical Model for Smart Learning Operations

Palanivel Kuppusamy
https://orcid.org/0000-0003-1313-9522
Pondicherry University, India

Suresh Joseph K.
Pondicherry University, India

ABSTRACT

In the fast-changing global environment, educational apps are widely used with hybrid and multi-cloud environments and intelligent devices. They offer various society services such as quality data for monitoring and prediction skills with protection and reliability. Smart learning systems pose a unique security risk because many people access and operate different techniques simultaneously over multiple networks. As a result, cybercrime has been brought about by the internet and the availability of intelligent devices. The security of online learning systems has received significant consideration. Because today's creative learning is open, distributed, and networked, ensuring that authorized users only have access to the appropriate data at the right time is a considerable challenge. The current security practices are outdated; hence, this chapter examines cyber-attacks on smart learning systems from their standard architecture and security requirements and proposes a cyber security model for educational operations from a multi/hybrid cloud-based learning environment.

I. INTRODUCTION

The education system currently faces various difficulties, including poor quality, high dropout rates, low enthusiasm, health and nutritional needs for students from poorer households, a weak reading environment, and gender inequities (Government of Rwanda, 2020). The other challenge is improving access to education for vulnerable students, especially those with disabilities. To address these challenges, a

DOI: 10.4018/978-1-6684-6092-4.ch006

transition is required to track the education coverage and access to understand education quality and equity across different dimensions. The present education system must be assessed and changed to keep up with modern business trends (Linda Darling-Hammond et al., 2020). To achieve this, the education sector needs data to respond to policy and planning questions and the changing reforms in the education system.

The next-generation digital learning ecosystem (Rob Abel, 2017), shown in Figure 1, can be built on a technological foundation that smoothly integrates established and new digital products. Digital devices and technologies can enable the development of smart and intelligent services in education. Educational sectors use smart technologies such as mobile, unified communications, remote access solutions, educational platforms, and tools in their environment. Smart technologies (Palanivel, 2020) include artificial intelligence (AI), blockchain, big data, cloud computing, edge computing, the Internet of Things (IoT), Machine Learning (ML), Deep Learning (DL), and robotic process automation (RPA), which fundamentally changes how education is conducted through the Internet and prompted the creation of a smart learning environment (SLE).

Figure 1. Next-generation digital learning system

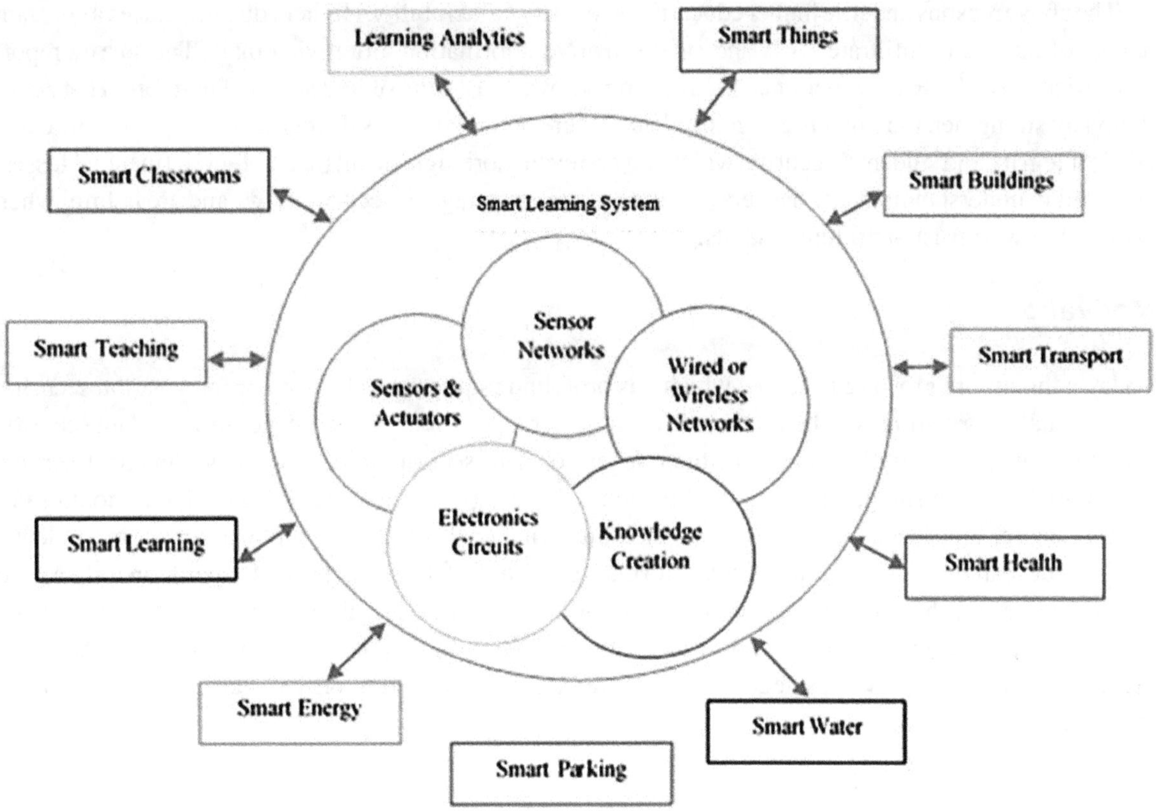

SLE powers data-driven solutions in educational operations (García-Tudela, 2021). This data can be used to manage finances, oversee and enhance instruction, monitor teaching-learning activities, evaluate student learning outcomes, monitor progress, and contain educational materials. Data can highlight differences and allow decision-makers to design policies that ensure equity and resource allocations in the context of Sustainable Development Goals (SDG) (Unesco, 2017).

Educational institutions, including Higher Education Institutions (HEIs), research organizations, and training centers, require an integrated view across the organizations (Sonali 2019) to give strategies to regulate and handle the educational data. With supply chain data and analytics apps, this integrated view combines technical, academic, and operational processes. HEIs store a substantial amount of confidential information, including student identities and priceless intellectual property, which, if stolen, could cause serious harm that extends outside the institution's boundaries. The vast amount of private information kept by HEIs, including student identities and priceless intellectual property, could be seriously damaged if hacked. Topal (2022) states that HEIs are particularly vulnerable for the following reasons.

1. Many HEIs still rely on outdated systems, which are attackable.
2. HEIs, take pride in their lack of openness and transparency.
3. Because HEIs are accessible online, attacks are aware of these shortcomings.
4. Attackers can take advantage of educational institutions that are hopelessly out-of-date and under-resourced by utilizing cutting-edge techniques and technologies.

The above reasons underlie higher education's security vulnerability. Higher education faces a constant deluge of attacks to infiltrate HEIs and steal sensitive information, often via email. The survey report (Joel Alcon, 2016), HEIs experience the most ransomware assaults of any sector. Therefore, HEIs continuously strengthen their defenses against these severe potential losses. Cyberattacks seriously threaten HEI's integrity and students' security, which may be even more significant than potential financial losses. HEIs aid in understanding how hackers attempt to take advantage of security flaws and are helpful when deciding how to frustrate future assaults.

Motivation

Today's threats are growing in scope, which has profound implications for data or information security. Educational information is to be protected from deliberate or accidental damage through data security. Most educational institutions confront the dangers of data security, cloud security, denial of service (DoS), malware, phishing, and unsecured personal devices (Debasis Behura 2021). They should safeguard, secure, and keep the information, including financial assistance applications from students, sensitive research, intellectual property, information on online learning portals, operational data, and more. As a result, they are showing various cyber-threats targeted at gaining sensitive information. As shown in Figure 2, cybersecurity and information security professionals (from inside and outside the organizations) aim to prevent, safeguard against, reduce, react to, and improve a variety of cyber threats to networks and systems.

Figure 2. Motivation example for smart learning

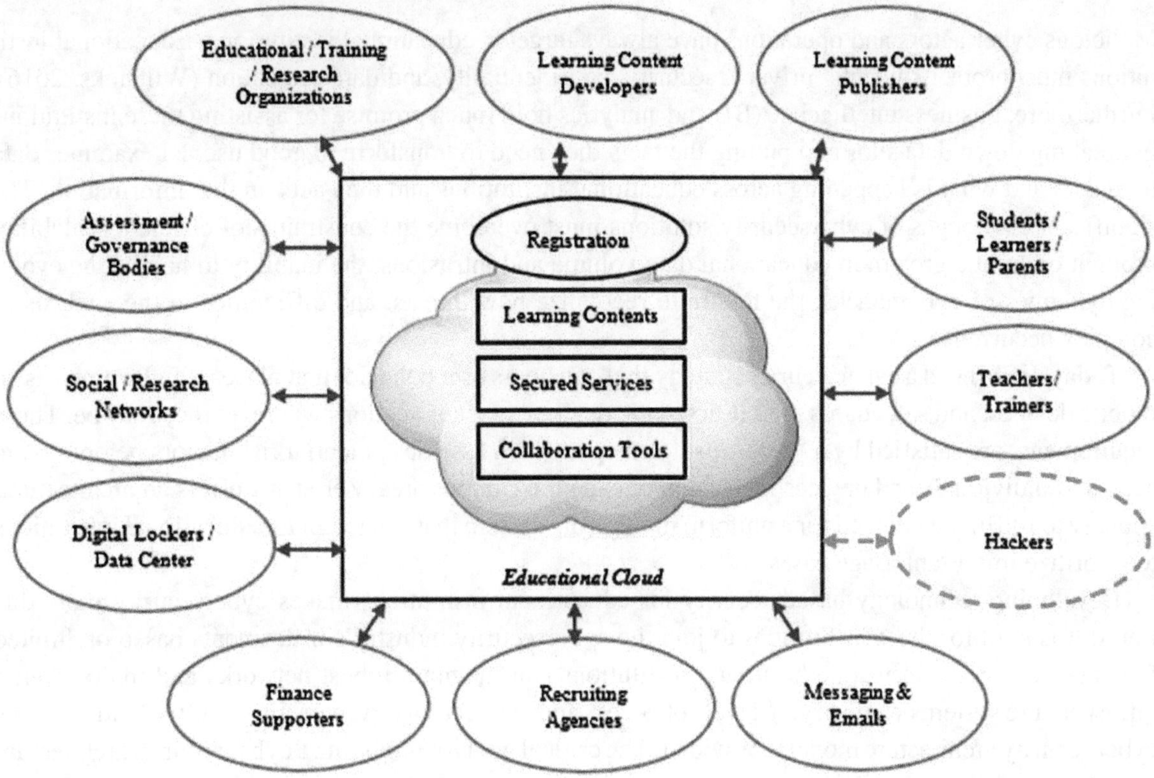

One of the most important races for educational institutions is ensuring the security of the next generation's learning system. They have evolved from transactional systems to a multidimensional, interconnected network that helps the business achieve its mission and goals. Hence, EdTech has become a top target for frequent and intense cyberattacks due to ransomware attacks, malware, and data breaches (Praveen Yeleswarapu, 2021), which are increasing each year quickly.

Cybersecurity techniques include confidentiality, integrity, authentication, availability, non-repudiation, auditing, and digital signature to safeguard systems and networks from malicious and unintentional disruption in cyberspace (Camille Cobb et al., 2018). It is essential to predict the possibility of cyberattacks to combat the rising threat of cyberterrorism. The cyber-attacks include phishing, man-in-the-middle assaults, password attacks, DoS and DDoS, malware and virus-based attacks, drive-by downloads, malvertising, compromising digital privacy, etc. With the aid of cyber security apps, future antivirus, ransomware safety, and protection systems are all being developed. It offers protection data and secure information, increasing antivirus, firewalls, network security, threat hunting, risk and compliance, and incident reaction. It must realize the different approaches to secure educational institutions, devices, applications, communities, or tools.

Solution

Malicious cyber actors and operations have always targeted educational institutions. Educational institutions must protect students' privacy, security, confidentiality, and data protection (Wilbanks, 2016). Furthermore, business intelligence (BI) and analytics hold much promise for assisting these institutions in breaking down data silos and putting the facts they need to transform to good use. BI examines data to understand what is happening across educational institutions and then acts on that information. The significant challenges of cybersecurity solutions must overcome the constraints of efficient scalability brought on by the growth in educational data volume and intrusions, the inability to handle the evolving dynamics of cyberattacks, the failure to recognize new threats, and difficulties in the analysis of complex occurrences.

Today, HEIs need a cybersecurity strategy that considers user behavior that places a high emphasis on mobile devices, and safeguards their users' data, devices, and applications wherever they may be. These requirements are satisfied by a "zero-trust" strategy, which assesses potential risk factors before giving access to individuals and devices inside and outside the campus area. Zero trust offers an architectural strategy to fulfill the demand for a uniform monitoring system that is enough for educational institutions to prioritize important usage cases.

Developing technology-based security for educational institutions makes cybersecurity more difficult. It is hard for these institutions to join the cybersecurity industry's instruments based on limited financial resources. Instead, educational institutions can maintain robust networks and multi-layered infrastructure systems with varying levels of access and connectivity. As a result, a multi-cloud system's cyber security architecture model is provided. The critical goals of providing a cyber security architecture model are as follows:

- To recognize the various cybersecurity attacks and describe how traditional systems address these threats.
- To identify appropriate, realistic situations for multi-cloud environments and to protect information access in an SLE context.
- To achieve Quality of Service (QoS) in multi-cloud real-world environments while ensuring intrusion detection and prevention in SLE.
- To propose a cyber security model with high attack detection, restricted false alarms, and low overhead in hybrid/multi-cloud scenarios with a converged data analysis method.

The integrated data analytics model may be based on a high-level education architecture model that conforms to the smart education framework. As a result, the connected platform brings data from disparate sources and offers various services to stakeholders, including those in other sectors needing education data.

The rest of the chapter is organized as follows. The background section introduced the concepts of Educational Technology, smart learning environment, cybersecurity threats, technology, and security components in section II. The materials and methods are described in section III. The literature review and methodology are presented in Section IV. The results and consequences are presented in section V. The discussions, future enhancements, and concluding observations are specified in section VI.

II. BACKGROUND

This section outlines the Educational Technology or EdTech, smart learning environment, cybersecurity threats, and technological and security components of the architecture used in smart educational systems.

Emerging Technology in Educational Institutions

The education system is one of the mechanisms and objectives of building society and contributes to human capital, well-being, and wealth. Because of the many violent and terrorist acts, security and privacy concerns are often a big deal in educational institutions. Educational institutions need the autonomy to move their applications and workloads to the optimal environment as their requirements change and gain traction in the market (Joe, 2017). Today, advanced technologies are creating game-changing opportunities in the world of education. Growing demand for educational technology has recently resulted in the creation of new advanced degree programmes that aim to enable teachers to adopt an innovator's attitude and become transformative technology leaders in their classrooms and educational institutions.

Educational technology, or EdTech (Serhat Kurt, 2015), is the philosophy and practice of implementing radical educational strategies for learning and student achievement. Moreover, EdTech organizations have grown significantly in the last few years, incorporating all levels of education, from elementary to higher education. Numerous online classes (Venugopal et al., 2020) have been organized using Zoom, Google Classrooms, Microsoft Teams, Cisco Webex, etc., because of the Covid-19 pandemic. Corporate companies conduct their training programmes through online to facilitate remote work. The digital transformation of education leads to many challenges in the present scenario, as shown in Figure 3.

Figure 3. Digital transformation in education

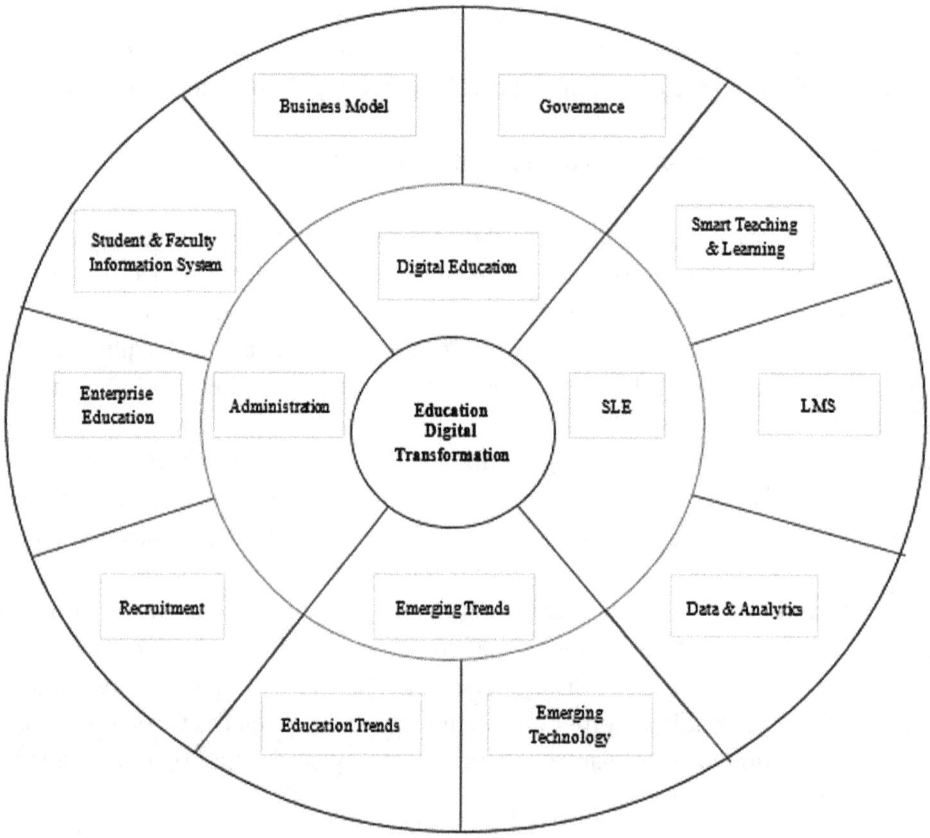

Digital equality and cybersecurity issues still exist in the EdTech space as educational institutions progressively adopt virtual learning, and the adoption of various digital learning platforms and video-conferencing programs continues to gain speed (Reeta Sonawat, 2021). Adopting multiple digital learning platforms and video-conferencing programmes is gaining steam in educational institutions, but concerns about cybersecurity and digital equity still exist.

Smart Learning Environment

The digital transformation in education (i.e., e-Learning or innovative or smart education) supports society effectively and efficiently using technologies. Smart education (Huawei, 2018) is an advanced form of modern education, making pedagogy education merely a conventional theoretical concept in contemporary Information and Communication Technology (ICT) methods. It offers educational system innovation solutions to enhance students' capacity to deal with the difficulties of the 21st century (Kim, 2014). AI-based smart education (Ellis 2019) focused on predicting learning performance in online or blended learning environments, whereas the data sources were divergent. The smart education model is shown in Figure 4.

Figure 4. Smart education model

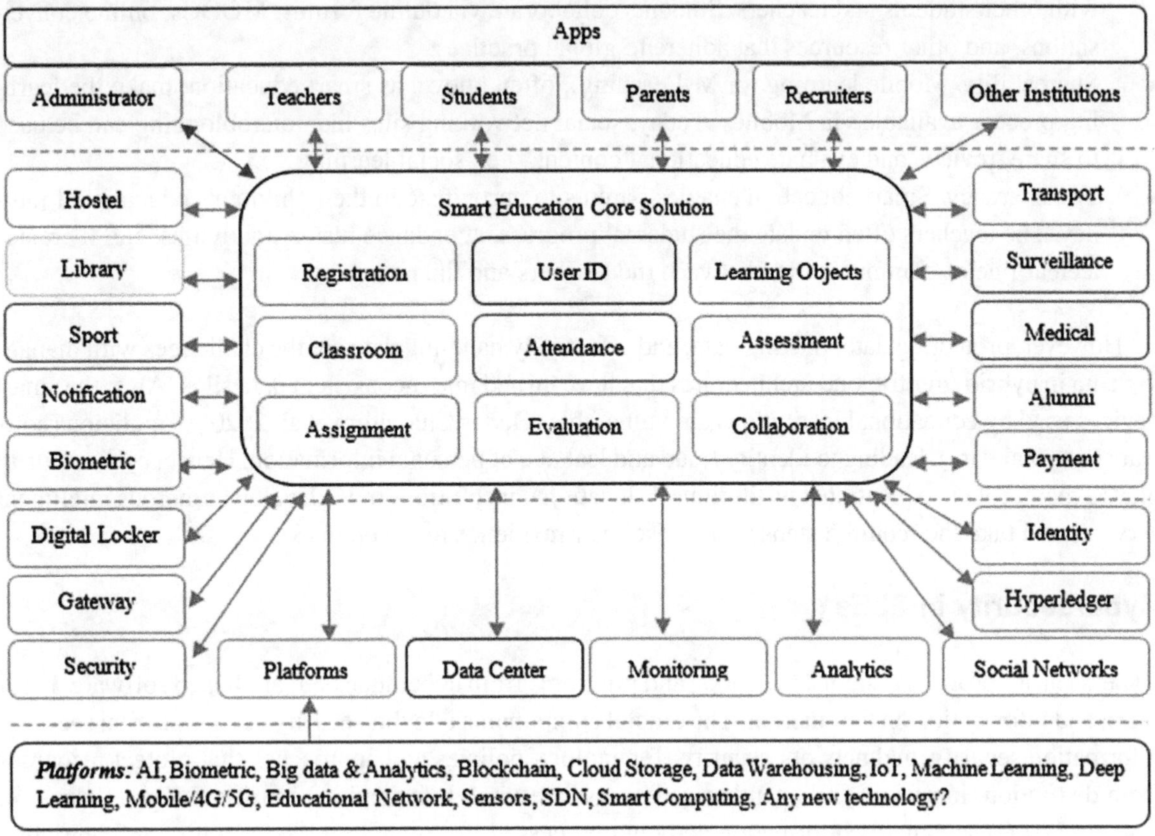

In a smart education system, only authorized users can access a smart education system via Apps, gadgets, browsers, etc. A smart education environment can be designed with innovative methods, such as hybrid and multi-cloud environments for educational institutions (Doug Bonderud, 2021). Educational cloud service providers must ensure exceptional security protection with a growing demand for developments and smart devices. The educational software, digital locker, data center, research network, and social networks data are the data suppliers. The learning infrastructure provides access to many recent technologies needed to implement smart educational solutions. Trubina (2019) discussed information aspects of identifying student educational performance with their learning objectives in the SLE. This gives more comprehensive and objective data on student learning progress.

Smart education, or adaptive learning (Yusep Rosmansyah et al., 2022), promotes incremental improvements than traditional education. SLE is "a hybrid learning system that provides learners and other stakeholders with a joyful learning process while achieving learning outcomes as a result of the employed intelligent tools and techniques." The advantages of SLE are analytics, reachability, shareability, and transparency.

- Analytics. Learning analytics uses data gathered about students' learning preferences, motivation, and comprehension, among other things. By using it, students can develop more effective teaching methods that suit their requirements.

- Reachability. With technology, contemporary teaching methods enable students to communicate with other students and teachers. Students collaborate via online forums, MOOCs, online conversations, and other resources that adhere to global practices.
- Shareability. Mobile learning (or M-Learning), often known as smart education, make the learning process available via Mobiles. Today, social networking sites like microblogging can be used to share, review, and evaluate educational content., i.e., social learning.
- Transparency. Smart education enables parents to participate in their children's educational journey. The teachers often update the students' progress, attendance history, activities, etc. It creates a clear line of communication between the teachers and the parents.

However, protecting data, moving data, and effectively handling data are the challenges with managing data in hybrid /multi-cloud architectures that have turned into inconsistent data silos. Also, the smart devices used by educational institutions are vulnerable (Hadas Chassidim et al. 2020) to malicious software (i.e., malware), leading to identity fraud and leakage of personal information. Hence, cybersecurity plays a major role in educational institutions. Educational institutions must develop numerous intelligent services and take the required steps to increase their resilience to cyberattacks.

Cybersecurity in SLEs

Cybersecurity protects systems, networks, and programs from cyberattacks. It applies to software, hardware, and information on the Internet. The crucial components of cybersecurity are application security, information security, and network security. Technology policies and approaches that protect resources from disruption, intrusion, and unauthorized access are vital. Information security (Burgos Salazar & Campos, 2009) safeguards information and data processed by computer systems with confidentiality, integrity, and accessibility (CIA) aims. Cyber-physical systems (Juliza & Jemmy, 2018) that disrupt real-world scenarios are considered systems security.

EdTech entities are currently engaged in a costly protection race, purchasing the latest security technologies and approaches to combating cybersecurity risks and attacks. These strategies support operational protection and response to future cyber-attacks. The possible types of seizures in cyberspace are physical, network and software.

- Physical attacks are related to the physical activation of equipment, which causes them to malfunction. Physical harm, such as physical shutdown, the introduction of a malicious device, mechanical fatigue of physical buttons or triggers, etc.
- Network attacks are associated with direct actuation via network traffic to create a system failure - IP protocols, device impersonation attacks, sniff communications, battery-draining behavior, etc.
- Software attacks entail attaining access to a network device and altering its software to cause the device or service to malfunction - viruses, worms, malicious scripts, unexpected command injection, etc.

Cyber attackers and hackers aim for the users of cloud services to negotiate their services via the backdoor. The different attacks can be corruption, DoS, disclosure of information, theft of resources, and physical destruction. This is due to the threat landscape increasing in complexity. The numerous risks include sophisticated malware, insider threats, transaction frauds, encrypted attacks, data exfiltration, the exploitation of run-time programs, account takeovers, and lateral displacement. The most common cyberattacks frequently are cloud security breaches, phishing, denial of service (dos), malware, and Zoombombing.

- Cloud Security Breaches: Cloud-based solutions may raise the possibility of data breaches involving the personal, financial, and operational processes of EdTech institutions. These data may be used fraudulently to send payments to accounts under the control of hackers.
- Phishing: EdTech platforms normally face phishing attacks. In phishing, a hacker poses as a reputable company to trick a victim into disclosing personal data like credit card details.
- Denial of Service (DoS): Due to network congestion brought on by the flood of data, genuine users are prohibited from accessing the data/systems they typically utilize. In EdTech, it is forbidden for teachers and students to use virtual learning resources.
- Malware: It can be of different forms, including ransomware, worms, and adware. It is used to steal data and carry out internet crimes like extortion. Blackbaud, a cloud service provider for educational institutions, affected millions of users in the most recent big security breach.
- Zoombombing: Recently, it has become common for intrusions to disrupt video conferences. Incidents like student exposure hamper learning platforms to unwanted and harmful media during online lessons, which imparts a fear of utilizing technology.

These hacks are intended to evaluate, alter, or delete sensitive data, demand money from users, or obstruct regular corporate operations. Numerous market risks (Abdulaziz & Saleh, 2020), memory degradation, gaining privileged access, vulnerabilities, etc., are further cybersecurity issues.

Ensuring rigorous protection against any outside cyberattacks becomes important in educational institutions.

Cybersecurity Frameworks, Architectures, and Models

Many educational institutions are progressively phasing out on-premises results, substituting cheaper, scalable, cloud-based replacements, and migrating how they store and manage data. The cybersecurity tools in educational institutions have led to more complex defenses with device integration. Hence, they must install more than one cyber security tool. Cybersecurity frameworks (Trim & Lee, 2021) follow various phases to reach a matured security management program, including identifying, protecting, detecting, responding, and recovering. They recognize current practices and protect their resources and network to use the management program better.

An effective security model and architecture (Anssi Kärkkäinen, 2013) can decide the level of protection needed for educational institutions. It allows the business to become involved in the decision-making on appropriate security architecture. Today, AI and ML are refining cybersecurity, but at the same time, hackers promise cybercrimes to the extent that they require human intervention from their side. They can help maintain with cybercriminals, automate threat detection, and respond more effectively than traditional software-driven or manual procedures in today's rapidly developing cyberattacks and increasing gadget proliferation.

Several cybersecurity applications included various attack types and malicious domain names used by botnets. As shown in Figure 3, different cyber security and vulnerability expectations models are considered to design a cyber security architecture for enterprise organizations. Feba Babu (2018) studied vulnerability prediction models such as Copula, GARCH, and ARIMA. However, the majority of cyber security characteristics of the quantification model (Asif Khan, 2010) of cyber security. This was a generic model that could be applied in a variety of operational contexts thanks to its adaptability. It included several models: attack, consequence, reliability, risk, threat, and vulnerability.

The attack model anticipates the quantity of attacks that took place at the time 't.' The attack is a subjective thing with a potentially harmful purpose. The consequence model foresees how an attack will turn out at time' t.' The impact of growth is the result. The reliability model determines whether a system is reliable at a time 't.' The quality of reliability is perfection. If the disaster rate is specified as f, the system's dependability at time t will be determined. The risk model determines the hazards one step at a time 't.' Risk is the potential or likelihood that any digital resource will be lost. It is impossible to do accurately and promptly quantify. It assigns relative values to it using special techniques. The Threat Model foresees the threat at the time 't.' A threat is an adversary motivated to exploit system vulnerability and cause damage. The vulnerability model forecasts a system's weakness at a specific time 't.' A system is vulnerable if it has flaws or defects that could harm it.

This cybersecurity model recognizes educational organizations' current procedures to protect their network. It leads them to improve their performance and add the appropriate steps to reach cybersecurity maturity (José & Montealegre, 2016) model.

Emerging Technology in Cybersecurity

Cybersecurity for EdTech is at risk considering the current advancements. While security has been overlooked inside or outside educational institutions, Learning Management Systems (LMSs) (Soegoto & Rinaldy, 2020) have adopted technologies to improve educational experiences. Cybersecurity threats will be much harder to define, discover, and mitigate; hence, cybersecurity specialists, IT divisions, and business executives are highly aware of cyber threats. Emerging technology, industry practices, and processes may be combined to detect and respond to cyberthreats accurately and rapidly.

- **5G Technology:** The 5G network may reform how the IoT (Xingjie & Huaqun 2019) devices connect and communicate in the digital age. The threat from 5G can have even more significant geopolitical consequences, and companies will be used as pawns in politically driven cyber-attacks. Educational institutions can still ensure the security of their own 5G infrastructure by adopting advanced encryption.
- **Artificial Intelligence (AI)**: Merging AI in cyber security has become active. According to (Cube Labs, 2021), AI-powered cyberattacks (e.g., Emotet Trojan) allow hackers to remain hidden and operate remotely, keeping them safe from being caught. AI boosts cybersecurity (Stefanini, 2021), password protection and authentication, phishing detection and prevention control, vulnerability management, network security, and behavioral analytics. AI tools can apply AI and ML to security experts' and researchers' processes, knowledge, and capabilities (Balbix, 2022) to detect hidden attacks,
- **Blockchain Technology:** Blockchain empowers educational institutions to authorize privileges about qualifications promptly and with a high level of certainty. Blockchain technology can readjust education's credentialing system to today's digital world.
- **Cloud Computing**: The stakeholders can use web-based tools to collaborate among themselves. The educational cloud decreases the necessity for in-house investment in resources.

- **Cognitive Computing**: It is an advanced type of AI that leverages various forms of AI, including Machine Learning (ML) and Deep Learning (DL) algorithms, which get more robust and more competent over time.
- **Data Mining**: These techniques identify patterns in large datasets in cybersecurity solutions to discover vulnerabilities and gather baselining indicators (Barabde et al. 2019). Different data mining techniques could be used for malware detection and detecting various types of fraud, from financial scams to telecommunications fraud and computer intrusions (Santhosh & Silambarasan, 2017).
- **Deep Learning:** With technological advancement, DL alters businesses, transforming security into a paradigm of protection (Fargana & Abdullayeva, 2020). The DL Apps (Li et al., 2021) can assist with network monitoring, predictive user analysis, spyware, spamming, social engineering detection, and intrusion detection and prevention systems.
- **Internet of Things (IoT):** Educational institutions are striving to integrate IoT technologies into teaching and learning actions. The IoT remains to arrive in the education sector (Dragan Kreculj et al. 2021), cooperates more closely, and attains relevant insights from the composed, analyzed, and operational data. The IoT allows teachers and students to complete tasks automatically.
- **Learning Analytics:** It promises to connect the authority of advances in data mining, explanation, and modeling to recover an understanding of teaching and learning.
- **Machine Learning:** ML algorithms can support educational organizations in better-analyzing threats and respond to attacks and security occurrences. In addition to enhancing human analysis, ML can block assaults, identify malicious activities, evaluate mobile terminals, simplify tedious security operations, and zero-day patch vulnerabilities.
- **Mobile Technology**: Mobile technology in the classroom diminishes more rational attention about its value. The mobile devices' comparatively low cost and low setup support necessities help spur their adoption as authoritative educational aids.
- **Multimedia Aids**: Educational institutions are progressively integrating moderately reasonable multimedia in the classroom. Educators can use multimedia tools to improve classroom learning understanding and can inspire contribution and student engagement.
- **Personal Learning Environments (PLE):** A PLE is personalized by design, which differs from person to person. Widespread acceptance of PLEs involves changing attitudes toward technology, teaching, and learning.
- **Quantum Computing**: Beyond AI, the progress of quantum computing poses another threat to organizations across the board. A sophisticated quantum computer could decode the complex cryptographic algorithms that retain safe data once adjusted in a hacker's hands.

The above technologies aim to improve and increase instruction delivery quality, accessibility, and cost-efficiency (Murad et al. 2019) in the smart environment. Educational institutions can use these technologies to improve students' teaching and learning involvement.

III. MATERIALS AND METHODS

This chapter is developed within the lines of applied research (Hernández Sampieri & Mendoza Torres 2018) that works with previous knowledge supported by theoretical contributions and activities, allowing us to determine the possible causes of the problem posed and thus demonstrate them. This will allow, together with the research results, to generate a useful document to propose a cybersecurity analytics model that can be adapted in different IES. Therefore, the following general guide is presented, leading to the formulation of the specific security model for HEIs.

Step I: It reviews various cybersecurity models that may be a reference for creating the proposed model and compares them based on the established indicators.
Step II: Then, it defines the contributions and extracts the most important points from the comparison to building a new model.
Step III: After comparing, it builds a cybersecurity analytics model based on certain standards and represents it graphically.
Step IV: Finally, it evaluates the model from a validated tool based on reliability, validity, and objectivity.

IV. LITERATURE REVIEW AND METHODOLOGY

HEIs can generate some problems, which grow over time, and as the probability of being the target of computer attacks increases, the greater the impact of risk. The main objective is to introduce a cybersecurity analytics model that can include all functional areas to evaluate cybersecurity and cybernetic readiness in HEIs.

In an SLE, the security model must protect the data from creating significant conclusions in the hybrid/multi-cloud business education. Hence, the literature review involved smart education/SLE and cyber security. A thorough literature analysis on technology advancement and information security follows the latest ideas. They give the suggested procedure a theoretical foundation. Research of relevant literature on technological innovations and cyber security can be found in this subsection. The core study area of cyberattack identification has already generated many investigations, reviews, and publications. However, very few papers on analyzing application issues in cybersecurity are available. Hence, surveying various models, architectures, and technologies is mandatory to switch strategies to hit their targets.

Step I: Review Various Cybersecurity Models

Asif Khan (2010) proposed a quantification cyber security model, which considered most cyber security parameters. This was a standard model that could be applied in a variety of operational contexts thanks to its adaptability. Anssi Kärkkäinen (2013) developed a five-layer cyber-security architecture for military networks, described as technical functionality consisting of security elements controlled by a cognitive process. In e-Learning and smart education, a method for comprehending, assessing, analyzing, assessing, and managing cyber security concerning e-Learning systems was detailed by Bandara et al. (2014). Tadas Limba et al. (2013) aimed to provide theoretical aspects of the cyber security management model, ensuring critical infrastructure security. Mayieka (2019) examined the methods used to exploit HEIs, the scope of those intrusions, and the measures HEIs might take to protect themselves from malicious actions. Aguilar Quintero et al. (2019) designed an information security model applicable to higher education institutions that effectively controls their processes. Alexei Arina (2021) identified the attacks that significantly impacted the assets and recommended increasing cyber security in e-Learning conditions.

Augusto-Gonzalez et al. (2019) introduced the GHOST security architecture to secure IoT-based smart houses. It aims to overcome the security vulnerabilities raised by various assaults, including network, device, and software-based ones. A DDoS attack is crucial to best use cloud resources and lessens user latency. Sirisha Potluri et al. (2020) researched the subject and provided a detailed analysis of the consequences of DDoS assaults on the cloud platform and the crucial protection measures involved. In the majority of apps, data is kept in the backend databases. The Structured Query Language Injection Attack is one of the flaws (SQLIA). Latchoumi et al. (2020) discussed the shortcomings in several of these countermeasures and used an effective hashing method to foil them. They implemented ML using the Support Vector Machine (SVM) technique to identify and stop SQL injection. Li (2021) examined and highlighted deep learning (DL) issues with cyber security. The results showed how DL enhanced various facets of cyber security.

Many factors, including energy economy, detection accuracy, latency, and false-positive leverage ratio, must be considered while designing intrusion detection and prevention schemes (IDPs) (Islabudeen & Kavitha, 2020) to enhance the MANET environments. Veerendra et al. (2017) talked about many data mining methods that have been effectively used for cyber security.

Daniel et al. (2019) offered an analysis of DL approaches. Yadigar (2020) provided an organized and thorough study of the significant cyberattack detection techniques and examined and presented the new scientific approaches of DL on cybersecurity. Choi et al. (2020) thoroughly evaluated recent studies on applying DL methods to computer security problems. Iqbal et al. (2021) provided a thorough overview of these neural networks and DL methods in response to the variety of needs of today, including intrusion detection, malware or botnet classification, spoofing, and cyberattack prediction, such as denial-of-service threats, fraud prevention, cyber discrepancies, etc.

Security programs can offer crucial security measures by gaining access to vast volumes of private data and guarding against rogue apps, phishing emails, and other risks in mobile operating systems. A flexible and event-adaptable model of artificial social system man-machine cyber security was put up by Ciufudean (2014). It enabled novel artificial social systems with cognition, self-healing capacities, and automated decision-making features. Hadas et al. (2021) examined factors disturbing the readiness to install mobile security applications by considering cyber-security applications. Laković et al. (2021) dealt with cybersecurity in Industry 4.0 to promote novel, adapted methodological frameworks and quantify the assessments of the current level and potential impacts of change within the field. Varona Taborda et al. (2021) signified a dynamic cybersecurity model that could be practiced in diverse establishments and institutions based on ISO/IEC 27032:2012, ISO/IEC: 20000-1, ISO/IEC: 20000, ISO/IEC 27002, ISO/IEC 29119: 2013 and ISO 19770-1 standard. Mohmed Afridhi & Palanivel K (2022) presented a digital forensic model that may be utilized to build an automated digital device categorization tool employed in real-world criminal investigations.

Step II: A Comparison Study of Existing Models

Table 1 shows the comparative study of various cybersecurity models concerning indicators. This can be done based on the technology, attacks, multiple applications, models & architectures.

Table 1. Various Cybersecurity Models: A Comparison

S/N	Proposed Works	Technology	Attacks	Applications	Models/ Architecture
1	Quantification Cyber Security Model (Asif Khan, 2010)	-	Cybersecurity	Operational Contexts Adaptability.	Security
2	Five-Layer Cyber-Security Architecture (Anssi Kärkkäinen, 2013)	cognitive process	Cybersecurity	Military Networks	Architecture
3	Cyber Security Management Model (Tadas Limba et al. 2013)	-	Cybersecurity	Infrastructure Security.	Management
4	GHOST Security Architecture (Augusto-Gonzalez et al. 2019)	IoT-based	Cybersecurity	Smart Home	Security Architecture
5	Information Security Model (Aguilar Quintero et al., 2019)	-	Cybersecurity	HEIs Educational Processes	Information Model
6	Dynamic Cybersecurity Model (Varona Taborda et al. 2021)	-	Cybersecurity Practices	Educational Institutions	Information Model
7	Digital Forensic Model (Mohmed Afridhi & Palanivel, 2022)	ML	Device Categorization	Crime Investigation	Classification Model
8	Cybersecurity Audit Model (Sabillón, 2019)	-	Evaluation	Any Organization	Audit Model
9	Cybersecurity Standards (José & Montealegre, 2016).	-	Cybersecurity Standards	Small & Medium organizations	Cybersecurity Standards
10	Reference Model (Burgos Salazar & Campos, 2009).	-	Cybersecurity Policy & Standards	Any Organization	Reference Model
11	Veerendra et al. (2017)	Data Mining	Security Methods	Attacks Classification	Classification of Attacks
12	Mayieka (2019)	Intrusions and the measures	Cybersecurity	HEIs	Analysis of Attacks
13	Sirisha Potluri et al. (2020)	Cloud	DDoS & Protection Measures	-	Analysis of Attacks
14	SQLIA (Latchoumi et al., 2020)	ML & SVM	Attacks and Protection Measures	Data Management	Data Management
15	Alexei Arina (2021)	Identification of Attacks	Cybersecurity	HEIs	Analysis of Attacks
16	Li (2021)	DL	Security Issues	-	Analysis of Attacks
17	IDPs (Islabudeen & Kavitha, 2020)	-	Enhance the Security	MANET Environments.	Analysis of Attacks

Findings

From the literature, no cyber security model with data analytics was available for the data generated or collected from various security applications in hybrid and multi-cloud environments. The above review requires a cyber security model to resolve generalizability, interpretability, vulnerabilities, and restrictions.

- Generalizability. To evaluate the current modification detection methods, all datasets were used. The published diagnosis accuracy is therefore highly confident.
- Interpretability. Considering DL is a closed system, most detection algorithms are difficult to understand and seldom guarantee identification.
- Vulnerabilities. Disrupting attacks has a significant impact on deep learning-based detection methods. They might be vulnerable to malicious activities with covert incremental faults.
- Restrictions. With such defined approaches, consistent frameworks and technologies for altering production and classification methods can be produced, assessed, configured, and compared.

As shown in Figure 2, it is proposed to design a unified cybersecurity model with integrated data analytics for the multi-cloud/hybrid cloud environment that can fulfill the above requirements. The cyber security model may address various physical attacks by detecting communication patterns among the devices in cyberspace. It deals with network attacks by analyzing variations in the communication templates characterizing respective devices within the system. It is crucial for protecting the physical, network, and software in SLE against various attacks using network monitoring and analyzing tools.

Design Challenges

The data integration and data linking are challenges of a unified cybersecurity analytics model. Data integration focuses on the individualized, rigid, and scalable integration of social networks, devices, and IoT devices. Data linking enables multiple stakeholders in educational institutions to share and utilize the developed data. According to Alexandru (2018), the design principles considered in the design of the unified cybersecurity analytics model ecosystem are below:

- Accessibility. It achieves digital equity and guarantees that teachers are equally competent with technology to improve teaching and prepare students to utilize it.
- Flexibility. It rapidly reformed a wide range of SLE services and features.
- Heterogeneity. The model must consider multiple entities, patterns, standards, and kinds of hardware and software platforms because it is an open system.
- Scalability. It must be flexible to accommodate several connected entities and devices.
- Security. It should have multiple security layers, such as identification, authorization, authentication, and data protection.
- Strong Coupling. It permits the separation of time and space for processing facilities, communication channels, and digital things.

Why Unified Cyber Security Model?

Educational institutions use data analytics to learn from academic data and take appropriate action. They gather a wide variety of data and frequently wish to improve their data and analytics setups to suit cutting-edge use cases, such as creating AI/ML/DL models for recognition, researching IoT data, and putting chatty bots into place. Sophisticated data and analytics advancements have frequently surpassed educational institutions' capacity to manage this data and analytics for business significance. This encourages educational institutions to start integrating the platform with advanced analytics. To stay up with evolving difficulties, a good cyber security analytics system must use various analytical techniques like behavioral models, AI/ML/DL, and the necessary data collection for full visibility. Cybersecurity models and software developers use different methods to increase the number of zero-day attacks recognized and the effectiveness, speed, and quality of intrusion detection systems (Barabde 2019).

To overcome these challenges, educational institutions need a dependable, integrated approach to functioning with apps and data across clouds with the proper security measures. The construction of a model involves the subsequent steps:

1. Investigate the information security protection determined by the organization.
2. Define the importance of the model to socialize with the organization's stakeholders.
3. Establish cybersecurity objectives with clear and quantifiable goals.
4. Choose the reference framework for applying cybersecurity with the standards that can be defined as a model to manage and control an educational institution.

V. SOLUTIONS AND RECOMMENDATIONS

Security solutions give businesses a reasonable, cost-effective method for managing their IT assets and mission-critical data. Customers must be far more vigilant about using secure techniques to store credentials and protect the gadgets they use to connect cloud-based applications. This section presents the unified cybersecurity analytics model built for educational organizations.

Step III: Build a Unified Cybersecurity Analytics Model

Enterprise architecture offers a comprehensive view of the educational system, which eases the burden of costly errors brought on by the haphazard and unplanned use of various information and communication technologies. Enterprise architecture enables seamless user operations, unifies access to all content, and promotes connections between people, technology, and content. Determining business, information, applications, and technology concepts is necessary for enterprise design and development. Integrating educational data with learning resource information can monitor learning outcomes in near real-time, fully linking to other data through various services. It creates an SLE with a range of activities. It makes dependable connectivity to use an education cloud to retrieve and deliver data. It creates consolidated identity and electronic payment systems for internet services. It enables easy data sharing, application reuse, and service repurposing between academic institutions.

The development of unified data analytics model will include the following activities:

1. Educational Data Management System (EDMS) caters to all the necessary modules to meet the data requirements for teaching & learning, data delivery, and management.
2. The LMS covers the components of teaching and professional development.
3. Data integration and the transformed data are loaded into an Educational Data Warehouse.
4. It can create data view dashboards for stakeholders interested in education data.
5. It can be built with open standards to align smart education architecture.

Requirements

Security architecture for educational institutions facilitates integrating various protections into a more robust overall protection. It is the foundation for all educational institutions' cybersecurity requirements. The SLE is intelligent, aware, and autonomous. The security architecture for SLE can be designed with many emerging technologies. The core competencies of the cybersecurity system include systems, data, and applications.

1. Application security covers blockchain and financial technology (or FinTech), risk and decision-making, reliability, data privacy, and spam detection. SEIs must integrate and deploy automation, Big Data (Jeffrey & Young, 2017), and AI to handle the continuously rising warnings and crises.
2. Data security encompasses social network security, vulnerability forecasting, cyber-ML, digital forensics, and insider attack detection.
3. System security offers network, cloud, IoT, virus, and autonomous protection.

Security Concerns

According to various cyber security frameworks (such as NIST, ISO 27000, and CIS 20), the SLE has many issues in a distributed context, including accessibility, data integrity, validity, confidentiality, and security. Hence, the security architecture must include the features of privacy of data, communication security, access control, identification, non-repudiation, integrity, availability, and confidentiality. The security architecture's performance must include the characteristics of usability, safety, dependability, scalability, accuracy, and performance.

Security Data Sources

The numerous data sources from where data is collected for the security architecture of SLE are application, endpoint, network, and user data.

- Apps Data collects diverse data to analyze calls, data exchange, and commands for installing the representatives on the cyber security apps.
- Endpoint Data for analysis includes internal endpoints such as files, processes, RAM, registry, connections, and many more.
- Network Data can be gathered from the network to analyze packets, net flows, DNS, and IPS data with the help of the network equipment.
- User Data can be collected for analyzing user access and activities from Active Directory, Proxy, remote login or virtual private networks (VPN), and the corresponding apps.

Goals

The unified cybersecurity data analytics model aims to provide a coordinated collection of applications to manage the production and dissemination of advanced analytics. The fact that the existing unified platform maintains the data makes it trustworthy and transparent. It is typically hybrid or cloud-based, scalable to handle huge volumes of data, and cloud-based. It includes a variety of analytics and tooling, including open-source and for-profit solutions, and a large number of profiles. E-Learning analytical techniques (Palanivel & Chiralekha, 2018) were introduced to create a unified analysis of the vast amounts of data produced by learning actors.

Stakeholders and Terminology

Various stakeholders, technologies, and terms used in the proposed architecture are listed below:

- Authorized users are teachers, students, parents, educators, governing bodies, etc.
- Cybersecurity attacks in SLE are denial of service, probe, malware, zero-day, phishing, sinkhole, and user root attacks
- Data access privileges are authorization, authentication, and access control (AAA).
- Data models and visualization tools are MicroStrategy, OBIEE, Tableau, etc.
- Data suppliers are digital locker, individual identity, SMS, email, payment, Hyperledger, security, data center, analytics, research network, and social networks.
- Data visualization are charts, pivot tables, and drill-downs available.
- Databases are Oracle, SQL Server, MySQL, etc.
- Educational institutions are schools, colleges, universities, training centers, etc.
- Educational software is portal, LMS, gateway, data lake/warehouse, content storage, blockchain contracts, notification, publish/subscribe, monitoring, digital identity, etc.
- Emerging technologies include AI/ML/DL, Blockchain, IoT, 5G, and data mining.
- ETL tools are Informatica, SSIS, etc.
- Networking components are routers, switches, servers, etc.
- Numerous market risks include Trojan horses, harmful spyware, computer worms, botnets, spam, phishing, SQL Injection attacks, Cross-Site Scripting (XSS), buffer overflows, etc.
- Real-world scenarios are traffic lights, autopilots, industrial robots, and control systems,
- Research networks are Research Gate, Academia, Google Scholars, etc.
- Smart devices are smartphones and IoT devices.
- Social networks are Twitter, Facebook, Instagram, YouTube, etc.
- Technologies used in the learning infrastructure are smart educational solutions, cloud storage, virtualization, educational networks, research networks, mobile networks, etc.
- Various attack types are malware, spam, insider threats, network intrusions, false data injection, and malicious domain names used by botnets.

The Unified Cybersecurity Data Analytical Model

The unified cybersecurity model seeks to guide a coordinated set of tools for managing data, analytics, and deployment. The suggested unified cybersecurity model has pipeline services, data storage, virtual data, analytics, and consumption capabilities, and it can consume various information from various sources. as shown in Figure 5. The unified cybersecurity model is well-governed and can be deployed in the cloud, on-premises, or hybrid. This virtual data may contain the Data Warehouse (Leo Willyanto Santoso & Yulia 2017) and the Data Lake (Dawn Clement, 2021) that are integrated via a data fabric.

Figure 5. A Unified Cybersecurity Data Analytical Model

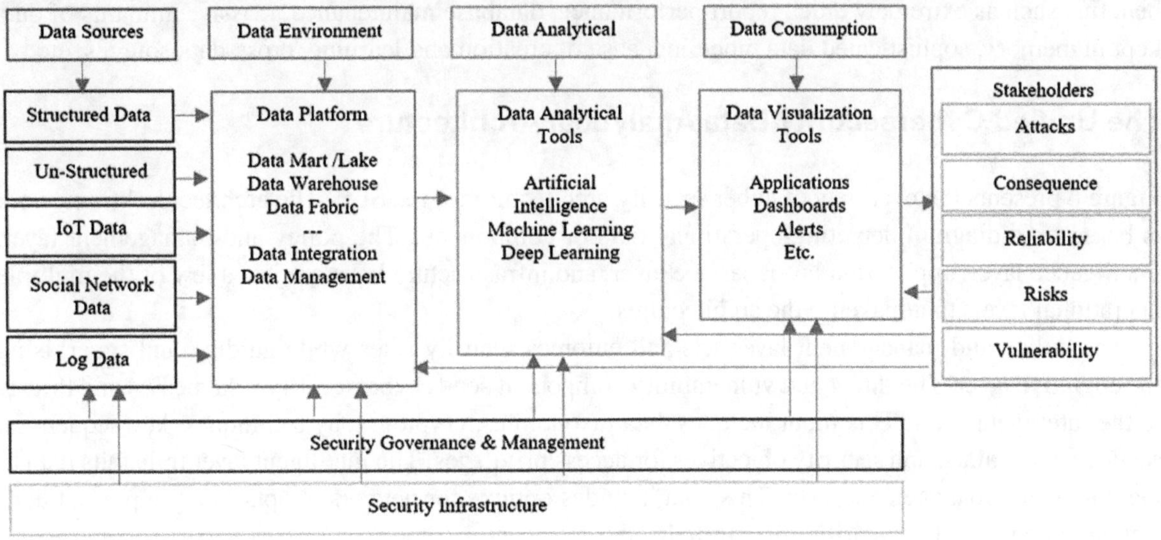

Most of the conventional BI environments have tools for ETL tools to load into a database, data model, and visualize the data tool. The proposed model delivers advanced calculations and a Datahub for external BI tools to connect with the data platform for massive data integration. The major components are data extraction, database, modeling, and visualization.

1. Data Extraction can use Direct Data Mapping technology (David Menninger, 2021) to extract data from the data sources as a full or incremental load. It can pull data from almost all conventional databases and cloud Apps stored on on-premises or cloud storage.
2. The data has then loaded into memory. Once the data (or database) is loaded into the in-memory database engine, the joins defined in the schema are precomputed at the end of the load. This pre-computation leads to the extreme performance of the reports.
3. The data modeling appears in physical and business forms. In the physical schema, users can build aliases to base tables, materialize views and create joins between various tables. Business schemas can present a flat, user-friendly interpretation of the physical schema to the user building the reports.
4. The data visualization has insights and dashboards that can be made on top of physical or business schemas. The users can make insights using various visualizations. The data visualization provides an interface with BI tools that can connect to the above schemas.

Advanced analytics for enterprise cybersecurity is a perspective, diagnostic, predictive, detective, and descriptive. The perspective describes the actions required for either an analysis or a solution. The diagnostic evaluation identifies the underlying causes of incidents and threats. The predictive support the rising risk and potential dangers facing upcoming users and resources. The detective detects lateral movement, complex malware, skipped hazards, and hidden or unrecognized threats. The description compiles the effectiveness and status of the metrics and developments.

Compared to traditional business analytics (BI) tools, a unified cybersecurity model has numerous benefits, such as extremely quick report performance, database maintenance, massive amounts of data kept in memory, sophisticated data modeling, ease of creation and learning, cross-data sources, etc.

The Unified Cybersecurity Data Analytical Architecture

Figure 6 presents the overview of cyber security architecture for the SLE. The architectural framework is based on a diagram depicting operational tiers or components. The policy and management layer, intelligence layer, application layer, service layer, and infrastructure layer are just a few of the multiple operational levels that make up the architectures.

The policy and management layer sets and enforces security rules while guiding and supervising the cognitive layer. The threat and vulnerability component sends cybersecurity weaknesses and threats to the intelligent layer. This input includes data taxonomies, cryptography techniques, key sequences, security constraints, and security objectives for access privileges. The intelligent layer transmits data to the policy and management layer. This data includes options for network adaptation, the present configuration, and any irregularities discovered.

Figure 6. A Unified Cybersecurity Data Analytical Architecture for SLE

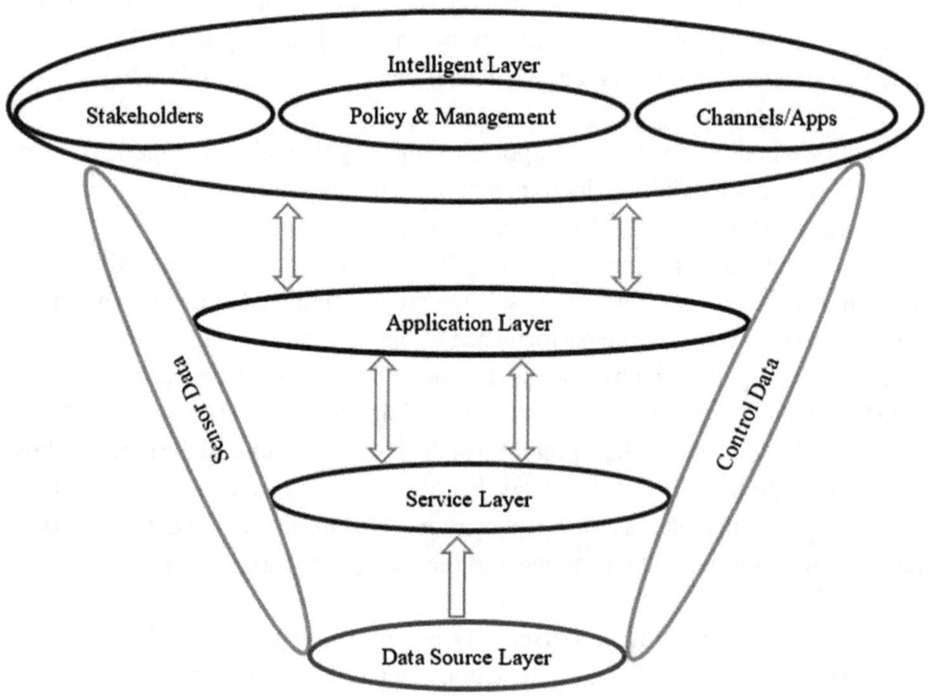

The intelligence layer implements cybersecurity adjustments in a network node and offers a cognitive method for decision-making. It uses the techniques of observation, assessment, decision-making, and action. The architecture, services, and business logic are all related to it. It monitors and updates cybersecurity features following the guidelines.

The application layer is concentrated on the security applications that end users access. Primary applications, cloud services, email, phone messaging, and collaboration software are just a few end-user apps. Data Centres, clouds, and local servers may all be required by an application. The service layer is primarily concerned with security activities, including portability, connectivity to service providers, network access to data services, and other features like location, messaging, remote connections, etc.

The infrastructure layer enables the service layer, giving the application layer permission. There are multiple security holes at each layer. Therefore, it is recommended to be adaptable in handling the serious dangers of cybersecurity. It includes several networked elements, wireless and cable networks between these devices, and security measures for network infrastructure. In the scenario of smart learning networks, the infrastructure layer comprises mobile tactical network elements that provide networking and informational capabilities to the end users. Developing networks, services, and application-building components are the most important basis.

Functional protection methods in each layer protect the information and data. The architecture's design allows for the flexible addition, removal, or modification of security features. All data types may be stored on this unified platform, which supports advanced analytics in a multi-cloud context. It implies making sure the data is accurate and compliant. The position ultimately governs the moral application of data to analytics. Decentralization has the drawback of complicating the regulatory capacity of the system, increasing the vulnerability of system issues.

The SLE goals are met via various progressive security measures, a distributed system, powerful network management, and incident reporting. Creating this architecture for unified data analytics can increase the effectiveness of educational data production, analysis, and usage for management and decision-making.

Unified Data Analytics Model Using ML Method

AI-based cybersecurity management systems (Balbix, 2022) can solve many cybersecurity challenges. AI can be applied in various areas of cybersecurity, such as password protection and authentication, phishing detection and prevention control, vulnerability management, network security, and behavioral analytics. ML is the most promising AI technology, typically used to automate analytical model building. Task automation, threat detection and classification, phishing, Webshell, and network risk score are all areas where ML can be used.

For advanced security analytics, ML algorithms can recognize and respond to threats on security apps. Big data sets of security events can be analyzed to find patterns in harmful activity and help accomplish this. When similar events are found, ML makes it so that the trained ML model can seamlessly handle them. Gartner's PPDR model (Yusuf Güven et al., 2022) allowed all security operations can be broken down into prediction, prevention, detection, reaction, and monitoring. ML can monitor user behavior, anti-malware, firewall application, network traffic analysis and intrusion detection, and anti-fraud. Network traffic analytics can detect attacks and abnormalities by thoroughly examining all the traffic at each tier. Figure 7 presents the algorithm-based ML classification method applied in the above architecture.

Figure 7. A Unified Data Analytical Model using ML

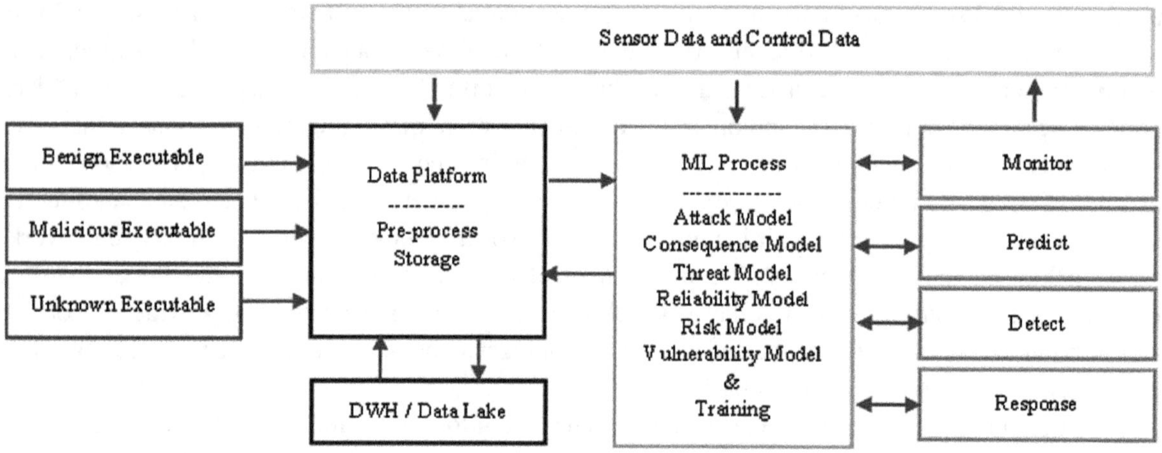

Data sets can be used to classify malware behavior using ML classification techniques. ML may be used in various cybersecurity sectors to improve security processes and make it simpler for security experts to swiftly detect, prioritize, handle, and fix new attacks.

Step IV: Evaluation of the Proposed Model

Evaluation of the proposed model is done based on the properties of reliability, validity, and objectivity. Table 2 shows the results of the assessment of the model.

Table 2. The results of the Evaluation of the Proposed Model

S/N	Properties/Aspects	Reliability	Validity	Objectivity
1	Responsibility (Administrative)	High	High	High
2	Responsibility (Stakeholders)	High	High	High
3	Application or Apps	High	Medium	Medium
4	Social Aspects	High	Medium	Medium
5	Cybersecurity Practices	High	High	Medium

VI. DISCUSSION

Recent years have seen an increase in cybersecurity risks and attacks due to the expanding use of smart devices and digitization. Every day, malicious acts against intelligent systems occur, including ransomware, malware assaults, zero-day attacks, cryptography, DoS, data breaches, phishing scams, and social engineering ruses. Cybercrime has the potential to disrupt activities, cause harm to individuals and enterprises, and have severe financial repercussions.

Modern technology can make everyday operations predictable and lessen security personnel's weariness. Implementing the data analysis, detecting, identifying, and minimizing potential device hazards is simple by building a cyber-security model for SLE. The cyber-security model can continually enhance analysts' presence in the alert system by concentrating on important notifications and minimizing the chance of missing important events.

Intelligent techniques can continuously improve cyber security efforts, protect the environment from vulnerabilities and attacks, and speed up the response time to incidents. They can be thought of as providing automation, a current arsenal, deeper investigations, thorough investigations in less time, alarm prioritization, improved vulnerability management, and high Data Center uptimes in cybersecurity. Fraudulent conduct can be found using ML and DL algorithms. With AI, educational institutions can process large datasets more efficiently, create a specific model for each use case, and apply a specialized data mining technique to examine zero-day vulnerabilities.

FUTURE ENHANCEMENTS

Technology has a significant impact on the digital transformation of the educational sector. It enables stakeholders to work together for sustainable development in an integrated and coordinated manner. Data communication, network connectivity, adaptability, and scalability of sophisticated systems are some research objectives in HEIs.

1. Smart security can function with stakeholders' individualized data.
2. Introducing blockchain technology to HEIs improves security.
3. Recommender systems can offer stakeholders guidance and suggestions.
4. Advanced data visualization can enhance the exploitation of both students and educators.

In addition to the difficulties above, SLEs face numerous problems concerning governance, data analysis, administration, and human-centricity. For HEIs to make important data-driven decisions, research on a data platform and distributed data authority models is required. Since SLE is where most cyberattacks occur, cyber security is now an essential component of the learning environment. Educational institutions should take precautions to protect themselves online. For secure networking and environments, new design techniques must be developed.

CONCLUSION

Cyber threats are expanding and changing quickly. Various malicious activities, such as phishing, spear-phishing, drive-by, password, and denial of service, bring these security problems. Having a live internet connection, cybersecurity mainly protects against risks to the system's hardware, software, and data. The business environment must deploy cybersecurity to prevent unauthorized access to its databases and processes.

This chapter offers a comprehensive analysis of cyberattacks from the perspective of a cutting-edge spectrum of applications. Various scenarios have been used to analyze the most recent research in each area of intelligent learning in hybrid and multi-cloud architectures. This cybersecurity architecture's relevant characteristics and security may be advantageous to an adaptive education model. The functional aspects of the architecture were designed based on a thorough analysis of the SLEs. The many layers encompass many options for identifying and explaining assaults, from network analysis and logic to security involvement and analytics, considering their strong interdependencies.

Author Contributions: Palanivel Kuppusamy and Suresh Joseph K have equally contributed to this work in all aspects with more implementation-related efforts. All authors have read and agreed to the published version of the manuscript.

Funding: This research received no external funding.

Conflicts of Interest: The authors declare no conflict of interest.

REFERENCES

Abel, R. (2017). *Shaping the Educational Technology Innovation Ecosystem*. https://er.educause.edu/articles/2017/7/shaping-the-educational-technology-innovation-ecosystem

Afridhi & Palanivel. (2022). Digital Forensics Triage Classification Model using Hybrid Learning Approaches. *International Journal of Innovative Research in Computer Science & Technology, 9*(3), 29-39. doi:10.55524/ijircst.2022.10.3.7

Aguilar Quintero, N. A., Velásquez Pérez, T., & Castro Silva, H. F. (2019). Information security model. Case study higher education institution. *Journal of Physics: Conf. Series, 1257*. 10.1088/1742-6596/1257/1/012014

Alcon, J. (2016). *13% Of The Higher Education Sector has been Infected with Ransomware, Vendor Risk Management*. https://www.bitsight.com/blog/higher-education-infected-with-ransomware

Alsulami, A. A., & Zein-Sabatto, S. (2020). Detection and Defense from False Data Injection Attacks in Aviation Cyber-Physical Systems Using Artificial Immune Systems. *IEEE, Int. Conf. on Computational Science and Computational Intelligence*, 69-75. 10.1109/CSCI51800.2020.00019

Arina, A., & Anatolie, A. (2021). Cyber Security Threat Analysis in Higher Education Institutions as a Result of Distance Learning. *International Journal of Scientific & Technology Research, 10*(3), 128–133.

Asif Khan & Hussain. (2010). Cyber Security Quantification Model. SIN'10, Taganrog, Rostov-on-Don, Russian Federation.

Augusto-Gonzalez, J., Collen, A., & Evangelatos, S. (2019). *From the Internet of Threats to the Internet of Things: A Cyber Security Architecture for Smart Homes*. IEEE Xplore.

Babu. (2018). A Review on Cybersecurity Threats and Statistical Models. *Mater. Sci. Eng., 396*. 10.1088/1757-899X/396/1/012029

Balbix. (2022). *Using Artificial Intelligence in Cybersecurity*. https://www.balbix.com/insights/artificial-intelligence-in-cybersecurity/

Bandara, I., Ioras, F., & Maher, K. (2014). Cyber Security Concerns in E-Learning Education. *Proceedings of ICERI2014 Conference*, 728-734.

Barabde, K. P., & Gaud, V. Y. (2019). A Survey of Data Mining Techniques for Cyber Security. *Journal of Emerging Technologies and Innovative Research*, *6*(5), 360–364.

Behura, D. (2021). *Cybersecurity: Proactive Leadership Strategy for Future-Focused Educational Institutions*. Education Business Unit, TCS. https://www.bluevoyant.com/resources/cybersecurity-in-higher-education/

Berman & Buczak. (2019). *A Survey of Deep Learning Methods for Cyber Security Information*. . doi:10.3390/info10040122

Bonderud, D. (2021). *What is Multicloud, and What are its benefits for Higher Ed?* https://edtechmagazine.com/higher/article/2021/11/what-multicloud-and-what-are-its-benefits-higher-ed-perfcon

Burgos Salazar, J., & Campos, P. G. (2009). Model for information security in IT. *CEUR Workshop Proceedings*, *488*, 234–253.

Chassidim, H., Perentis, C., Toch, E., & Lepri, B. (2020). Between Privacy and Security: The Factors that Drive Intentions to use Cyber-Security Applications. *Behaviour & Information Technology*. Advance online publication. doi:10.1080/0144929X.2020.1781259

Choi, Y. H., Liu, P., Shang, Z., Wang, H., Wang, Z., Zhang, L., Zhou, J., & Zou, Q. (2020). Using deep learning to solve computer security challenges: A survey. *Cybersecurity*, *3*(1), 15. doi:10.118642400-020-00055-5

Ciufudean C, (2014). *Cyber Security Model of Artificial Social System Man-machine*. doi:10.4018/978-1-4666-6324-4.ch031

Clement, D. (2021). *Data Lakes and Modern Analytics for Education*. https://www.bluegranite.com/blog/data-lakes-and-modern-analytics-for-education

Cobb, C., Sudar, S., Reiter, N., Anderson, R., Roesner, F., & Kohno, T. (2018). Computer security for data collection technologies. *Development Engineering*, *3*, 1–11. doi:10.1016/j.deveng.2017.12.002 PMID:30555887

Darling-Hammond, L., Flook, L., Cook-Harvey, C., Barron, B., & Osher, D. (2020). Implications for the educational practice of the science of learning and development. *Applied Developmental Science*, *24*(2), 97–140. doi:10.1080/10888691.2018.1537791

Ellis, L. (2019). Artificial Intelligence for Precision Education in Radiology – experiences in radiology teaching from a UK foundation doctor. *The British Journal of Radiology*, *92*(1104), 20190779. doi:10.1259/bjr.20190779 PMID:31646896

Fargana, N., & Abdullayeva, J. (2020). Deep Learning in Cybersecurity: Challenges and Approaches. *International Journal of Cyber Warfare & Terrorism*, *10*(2), 82–104. doi:10.4018/IJCWT.2020040105

García-Tudela, P., Prendes, P., & Solano-Fernández, I. M. (2021). Smart Learning Environments: A Basic Research Towards the Definition of a Practical Model. *Smart Learning Environments*, *8*(1), 9. Advance online publication. doi:10.118640561-021-00155-w

Government of Rwanda. (2020). *An Architecture for the Integrated Education Management Information System, Towards the Integration of the EMIS in Rwanda*. Report.

Hernández Sampieri, R., & Mendoza Torres, C. P. (2018). *The Quantitative, Qualitative and Mixed Routes Research Methodology*. McGraw-Hill Interam.

Huawei. (2018). *Smart Education Scenarios*. Huawei Technologies Co., Ltd.

Islabudeen, M., & Kavitha Devi, M. K. (2020). *A Smart Approach for Intrusion Detection and Prevention System in Mobile Ad Hoc Networks against Security Attacks, Wireless Personal Communications*. Springer. doi:10.100711277-019-07022-5

José, B., & Montealegre, R. (2016). *Measurement of Cybersecurity Maturity in Colombian MSMEs*. https://www.mckinsey.com/capabilities/risk-and-resilience/our-insights/organizational-cyber-maturity-a-survey-of-industries

Juliza, J., & Jemmy, M. R. (2018). Cyber-Physical System (CPS): State of the Art. *Int. Conf. on Computing, Electronics and Electrical Engineering (ICE Cube).*

Kärkkäinen, A. (2013). *A Cyber Security Architecture for Military Networks Using a Cognitive Network Approach* [Ph.D. Thesis]. NDU Course Library.

Kim, B. H., & Oh, S. Y. (2014). A Study on the SMART Education System Based on Cloud and N-screen. *Journal of the Korea Academia-Industrial Cooperation Society*, *15*(1), 137–143. doi:10.5762/KAIS.2014.15.1.137

Kreculj, Kovacevic, Krulj, & Dihovicni. (2021). The IoT in Education and Teaching. *XXVII Skup Trendovi Razvoja: "On-Line Nastava Na Univerzitetima"*, 6433, 407-410.

Kurt, S. (2015). *Educational Technology: An Overview, Teaching & Learning*. https://educationaltechnology.net/educational-technology-an-overview/

Labs, C. (2021). *Artificial Intelligence in Cybersecurity: AI Cyberattacks, Securing Your Ecosystem with AI, and More*. https://www.xcubelabs.com/blog/artificial-intelligence-in-cybersecurity-ai-cyberattacks-securing-your-ecosystem-with-ai-and-more/

Laković, L., Ognjanović, I., Šendelj, R., & Injac, O. (2021). Semantically enhanced cyber security model for industry 4.0: methodological framework. *25th Int. Conf. on Information Technology (IT)*, 1-4. 10.1109/IT51528.2021.9390120

Latchoumi, Reddy, & Balamurugan. (2020). Applied Machine Learning Predictive Analytics to SQL Injection Attack Detection and Prevention. *European Journal of Molecular & Clinical Medicine*, *7*(2), 3543–3553.

Li, G., Sharma, P., Pan, L., Rajasegarar, S., Karmakar, C., & Patterson, N. (2021). Deep Learning Algorithms for Cyber Security Applications: A Survey. *Journal of Computer Security*, *29*(5), 447–471. doi:10.3233/JCS-200095

Limba, Plėta, Agafonov, & Damkus. (2017). Cyber Security Management Model for Critical Infrastructure. *International Journal Entrepreneurship and Sustainability Issues, 4*(4), 559-577. DOI: doi:10.9770/jesi.2017.4.4

Maranga, M. J., & Nelson, M. (2019). Emerging Issues in Cyber Security for Institutions of Higher Education. *Int. J of Computer Science and Network, 8*(4), 371–379.

Murad, R., Hussin, S., Yaacob, M. H., & Ahmad, A. (2019). Mobile Service Delivery Mechanism in Smart Education: Conceptual Framework. *International Journal of Academic Research in Business & Social Sciences, 9*(2), 1242–1253. doi:10.6007/IJARBSS/v9-i2/5948

Palanivel K (2020). Emerging Technologies to Smart Education. *International Journal of Computer Trends and Technology, 68*(2), 5-16. doi:10.14445/22312803/IJCTT-V68I2P102

Palanivel, K., & Chiralekha, T. (2018). Big Data Reference Architecture for E-Learning Analytical Systems. *International Journal on Recent and Innovation Trends in Computing and Communication, 6*(1), 55–67. doi:10.17762/ijritcc.v6i1.1381

Potluri, Mangla, & Satpathy. (2020). Detection and Prevention Mechanisms for DDoS Attack in Cloud Computing Environment. *11th ICCCNT, IEEE Explore, 49239.*

Rosmansyah, Y., Putro, B. L., Putri, A., Utomo, N. B., & Suhardi. (2022, January 4). Simple Model of Smart Learning Environment. *Interactive Learning Environments*, 1–22. Advance online publication. doi:10.1080/10494820.2021.2020295

Sabillón, R. (2019). Audits in Cybersecurity: A Model of General Application for Companies and Nations. *RISTI - Rev. Ibérica Sist. e Tecnol. Information (Basel)*, (32), 33–48. doi:10.17013/risti.32.33-48

Santhosh Raj, P., & Silambarasan, G. (2017). Role of Data Mining in Cyber Security. *International Journal of Engineering Science and Computing, 4*(4), 13932–13935.

Santoso, L. W., & Yulia. (2017). Data Warehouse with Big Data Technology for Higher Education. *Procedia Computer Science, 124*, 93–99. doi:10.1016/j.procs.2017.12.134

Sarker, I. H. (2021). Deep Cybersecurity: A Comprehensive Overview from Neural Network and Deep Learning Perspective, SN. *Computer Science, 2*(3), 154. doi:10.100742979-021-00535-6

Soegoto, E. S., & Rinaldy, M. F. (2020). Smart Campus with A Learning Management System. *IOP Conf. Ser.: Mater. Sci. Eng., 879.*

Sonawat, R. (2021). *EdTech in Higher Education: Digital Equity & Cybersecurity are Concern Areas.* https://www.expresscomputer.in/news/edtech-in-higher-education-digital-equity-cybersecurity-are-concern-areas/74792/

Stefanini. (2021). *The New Role of Artificial Intelligence in Cybersecurity: How Can It Protect Your Business?* https://stefanini.com/en/trends/news/role-of-artificial-intelligence-in-cybersecurity-to-protect-busi

Topal. (2022). *Cybersecurity in Higher Education: Problems and Solutions*. https://www.toptal.com/insights/innovation/cybersecurity-in-higher-education

Trim, P. R. J., & Lee, Y. I. (2021). The Global Cyber Security Model: Counteracting Cyber Attacks through a Resilient Partnership Arrangement. *Big Data Cogn. Comput.*, *5*(3), 32. doi:10.3390/bdcc5030032

Trubina, I. I., Shutikova, M. I., Braines, A. A., Dzamykhov, A. K., & Dzamykhova, M. T. (2019). Monitoring The Assessment of Student Educational Performance: Information Aspects. In Education Environment for the Information Age, Vol 69. European Proceedings of Social and Behavioural Sciences (pp. 932-938). Future Academy. doi:10.15405/epsbs.2019.09.02.104

UNESCO. (2017). *Education for Sustainable Development Goals Learning Objectives*. https://unesdoc.unesco.org/ark:/48223/pf0000247444

Varona Taborda, M. A., Montano Collazos, F. A., Escobar Marulanda, C. A., & Márceles Villalba, K. (2021). Dynamic Cybersecurity Model based on ISO standards for Higher Education Institutions in Colombia. *Revista Ingeniería Solidaria*, *17*(3), 1–21. Advance online publication. doi:10.16925/2357-6014.2021.03.05

Veerendra, U. U., Ravitheja, B., & Veeresh, K. (2017). Data Mining for Security Applications, International *Journal of Core Engineering & Management,* 38-44.

Venugopal, Shenoy, Kumar, Pushpa, Venkatesh, Sunil, & Roopa. (2020). A Systematic Study and Comprehensive Comparison of Online Teaching and Learning (OTL) Apps for Measuring the Quality of User Experience. *International Journal of Scientific Research*, *9*(7), 864–890.

Wilbanks, L. R. (2016). *Cyber Security Requirements for Institutions of Higher Education*. https://fsaconferences.ed.gov/conferences/library/2016/NASFAA/2016NASFAACybersecurityRequirementsforIHEs.pdf

Xingjie, Y., & Huaqun, G. (2019). A Survey on IIoT Securit. *IEEE VTS Asia Pacific Wireless Communications Symposium (APWCS)*, Singapore.

Yeleswarapu, P. (2021). *Cybersecurity and EdTech: Securing the Cyberspace for Online Education*. https://www.blusapphire.com/blog/cybersecurity-in-edtech

Young. (2017). *'Precision Education' Hopes to Apply Big Data to Lift Diverse Student Groups*. Digital Learning in Higher Ed. https://www.edsurge.com/news/topics/digital-learning-in-higher-ed

Yusuf Güven, Y., Gülgün, S., Manav, C., Bakır, B., & Zeynep Gürkaş Aydın, G. (2022). Multiple Classifications of Cyberattacks using Machine Learning. *Electrica.*, *22*(2), 313–320. doi:10.54614/electrica.2022.22031

Chapter 7
Integrating Ed Tech and Cybersecurity Into the Curriculum

Deepa V.
https://orcid.org/0000-0001-8028-5429
SRM Institute of Science and Technology, India

Sivakumar B.
SRM Institute of Science and Technology, India

Swathi Mirthika G. L.
SRM Institute of Science and Technology, India

Abinaya K.
SRM Institute of Science and Technology, India

ABSTRACT

The chapter aims to discuss how people interested in incorporating different aspects of cyber security into the curriculum in higher education, corporate learning, and non-traditional learning environments can do so. Due to the COVID-19 outbreak, more businesses are switching to online platforms, which has resulted in a dramatic spike in the need for cybersecurity controls. The objective is to share how the immense impact of educational technology (ED Tech) in the age of COVID-19 lockdown is digitally focused on educational content and the basic need to be flexible and adaptable for students. Overall, this chapter proposes that the need for cyber security is becoming a more crucial facet of life. So, the report by intelligence system can examine threats and the platforms/applications for processing data can be examined. Cyber ED Tech protects against a variety of attacks, including cloud security breaches, denial of service (DoS), malware, zoombombing, password policy violations, and so on.

DOI: 10.4018/978-1-6684-6092-4.ch007

INTRODUCTION

The COVID-19 coronavirus pandemic has brought forth an exceptional situation all over the nation. The COVID-19 (coronavirus disease) pandemic shattered education systems in most countries, concerning the limited educational options for many learners of all ages. This paved the way for more than 1.7 billion learners, including those in developing and low-income countries, to receive a high-quality education in safe environment (United Nations, 2020). In order to stop the spread of virus and lessen its effects, this emergency in the sphere of education has resulted in widespread shutdown of face-to-face operations for educational institutions in more than 190 nations. By mid-May 2020, more than 1.2 billion students at all levels of education worldwide will have ceased attending face-to-face sessions, according to statistics from the United Nations Educational, Scientific, and Cultural Organization (UNESCO).

To the hindrance of lower-income nations and regions as well as rural areas where migrant populations tend to be concentrated, UNESCO has identified significant gaps in educational outcomes that are related to the unequal distribution of teachers in general and of the best-qualified teachers (Messina, D. and García, 2020). On January 30, 2020, the World Health Organization (WHO) General Director designated the COVID-19 outbreak a Public Health Emergency of International Concern (PHEIC), and nations started implementing a various policy measure to stop the virus' spread. As soon as the COVID-19 epidemic was classified as a worldwide pandemic on March 11, 2020 (WHO), containment procedures were quickly adopted. In addition to the disruption of face-to-face teaching and the varying success of alternatives to traditional education, the pandemic's other direct and indirect effects made it harder for families to assist children and teens in their academic endeavors. The shocks and stress suffered by individuals who had close family members afflicted by the virus, as well as the learning restrictions brought on by kids having to study at home, reduced their ability to learn. Furthermore, instructors are forced to instruct from their homes because the demands of coursework must be balanced out, sharing little and providing access to communication and digital gadgets for the lucky few.

Although different online learning tools and programmers cannot guarantee that students will learn correctly, the useful tools for instructors to ensure that their students continue to learn after COVID-19 by allowing them to connect and communicate online. Even though COVID-19 has presented many issues and hurdles in the lives of students, teachers, and parents, there are several ways in which technology has improved children's academic performance. Additionally, it has sparked in the kids a drive, enthusiasm, and an interest in knowledge. Higher-semester students, or those who have just completed six semesters, are not only self-motivated to study but also make use of such platforms by participating in webinars, online meetings, and conversations to learn more about their intrinsic abilities and character traits.

In the world of cybersecurity, ED Tech tools are nothing "new." Although ED Tech have always been utilized to train ambitious professionals, the pandemic's usage of them has increased the visibility of ED Tech in cyber classrooms. Institutions may adopt the US NIST (National Institute of Standards and Technology) Cybersecurity Framework as a collection of recommendations and other tools in their efforts to strengthen cybersecurity. Integrating ED Tech into the curriculum, cybersecurity also refers to reducing risks associated with data accessibility—ensuring users can use the data when needed and data security—protecting data from unauthorized modifications. Cyber concerned regulations and standard pointers have focused on gateways or firewalls and enabled device connections to virtualize cyber sessions using EdTech. Because of the widespread demand for cyber ranges in the classroom, cyber teachers can now able to design engaging, interactive learning experiences for their students, not limited to K-12.

Therefore, the chapter aims to discuss and examine potential issues caused by the fast adoption of commercial digital learning solutions. These solutions business models, which rely on user data for profit-making, may not always be motivated by best pedagogical practices. Additionally, criticism about how ED tech is redefining and condensing ideas of learning has been growing even before COVID-19. The article also questions the thesis that technology can and should address the problem with education. Such technological development, often seen as neutral, is strongly tied to educationalization, or the process of forcing ever-more-complex social issues upon education.

Thus, the objective is to share how the pandemic had repercussions on schools and education systems, in addition to the individual and collective effects it had on students, teachers, and school personnel. This aims to prioritize cybersecurity for end-users and challenges through attainment processes and needs to impose regulations with standards for making individual learning upgradeable. By examining cybersecurity in the education sector as a substantial national policy concern rather than a specific danger, the institutions need to take it on independently. The focus is on the danger of cyberattacks increasing throughout the higher education industry and in the program curriculum.

With the aforementioned background information, the proposed chapter will develop a technique to incorporate subject of cybersecurity in the curriculum and the current stage of cybersecurity awareness in ED Tech. The chapter will detail the institutional capacity to handle the regular and continued contact of educational activities even during pandemic situations like COVID-19.

BACKGROUND

The background section discusses the existing related works on the importance of cybersecurity education and the most likely threats offered in higher education institutions.

Education Advancement

The COVID-19 has quickly become an incitement for numerous businesses to look at cutting-edge solutions, from OTT platforms to virtual classrooms. A new, more efficient way to educate pupils has undoubtedly been established by the shift to learning apps for kids and online learning (Couldry and Yu 2018). The majority of online education systems place a strong emphasis on future-ready abilities like critical thinking and flexibility. The effectiveness of online learning systems is significantly influenced by these critical elements. In lieu of conventional face-to-face classroom instruction, we forecast that new learning techniques like live broadcasts and virtual reality experiences will take over. The learning might then turn into a lifestyle ingrained in everyday activities.

Figure 1. Strategies of education advancement
Source: 29 Countries of Latin America and Caribbean Economic Commission for Latin America and the Caribbean (ECLAC), on the basis of Information System on Educational Trends in Latin America (SITEAL), "Sistematización de respuestas de los sistemas educativos de América Latina a la crisis de la COVID-19", 2020 [online] https://www.siteal.iiep.unesco.org/respuestas_educativas_covid_19.

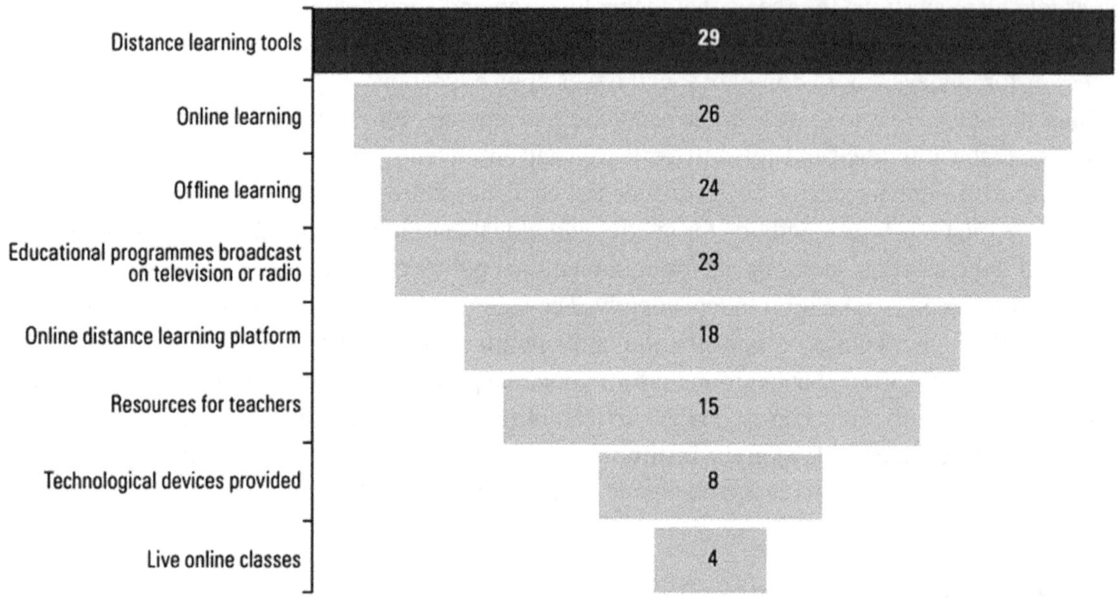

The advancement and datafy in education led to the expansion of data mining for data gathering and enhancing education. The logic of unlimited data flow becomes the beginning point for enhancing education, and this conclusion justifies increased types of data gathering (which translates into a bigger market for suppliers). Here, the logical conclusion is that additional data would be desirable for the education system (v3-volume, velocity, variety). The anticipated following stages in evolution are various wearable technologies and Internet of Things (IoT) solutions, up till all components of the educational process are converted into continuous data flows (Couldry and Yu 2018). While these flows bring in money for ed-tech businesses, their value to students and instructors is debatable. The neoliberal premise, however, that people and educational institutions have an ethical duty to datafy submit in the name of improved education, is what has brought about these changes (Birch et al., 2020).

Learning Through Platforms/Applications

The techniques used a variety of support mechanisms, including giving teachers access to resources, creating peer networks inside and between schools, and providing timely leadership direction. To promote teacher professional development, a number of resources were employed, mostly depending on online learning platforms, systems that allowed instructors to connect with other teachers, and virtual classrooms (Reimers and Schleicher 2020). The integration of digital tools into preservice teacher education courses and classroom activities could help future instructors accept the fundamentals of digital education. Through various research initiatives and long-term strategic efforts, the use of digital tools and settings in teacher education has been structured (Eklund 2018). In the COVID-19 pandemic situation, many of the online education sites and applications are handing out free access to their paid courses.

Drive to Online Learning

Some online learning methods have come under fire for disregarding established pedagogical principles, best practices, and prior research. On social media, well-known experts have questioned what motivates some people, groups, and businesses to provide advice with such zeal, wondering whether their motivation is determined by commercial factors (Siemens 2020). Concerns regarding privacy, monitoring, the influence on students' lives, and human dignity have also been raised by the hasty adoption of learning platforms and online learning (Harwell 2020). Others have drawn attention to the possible drawbacks if hasty solutions for educational technologies are used without considering their ramifications (Selwyn 2020a). As a result of emerging technology, it faces more significant challenges from hackers, who quickly developing sophisticated methods to commit cybercrime (St. Amour 2020). As more and more security holes in schools and colleges are made public, it would not be wrong to say that cyberattacks are becoming more common in the education sector.

Figure 2. Drive to online learning

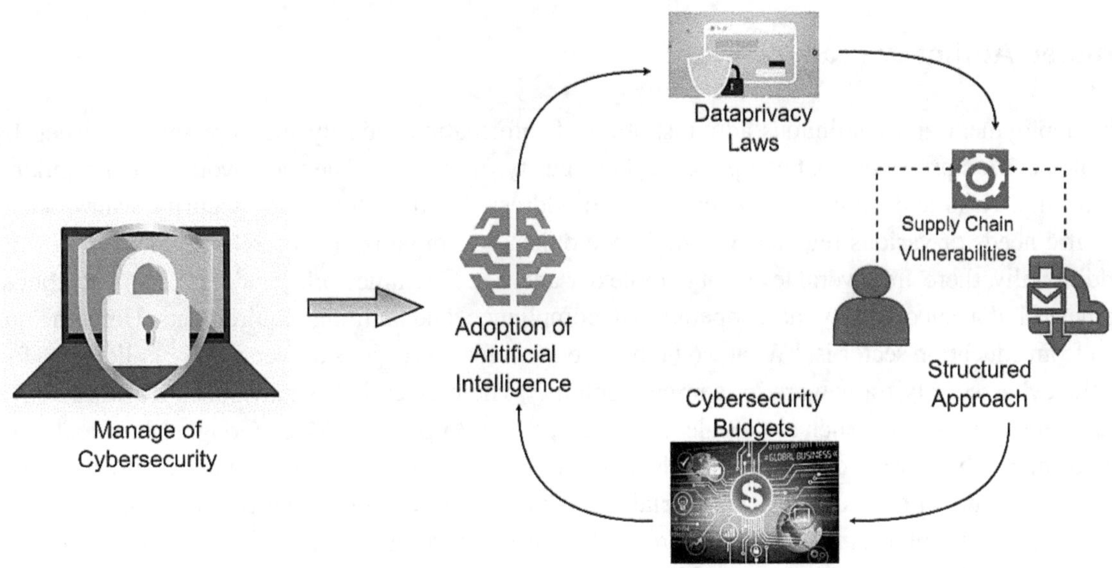

Need of Cybersecurity as Curriculum

Cybersecurity is the practice of applying protection and safeguards to data, systems, networks, and technology. It is marketed as a comprehensive strategy to enhance data privacy, and has safeguards in place to prevent unauthorized access to data and hide individuals from different types of data monitoring. Cybersecurity also has to do with reducing risks related to data availability (ensuring users can access data when needed) and data integrity (protecting data from unauthorized modifications), so it's important to pay attention to the security of the systems and networks where data is stored. When EdTech programs and regulations are adopted, cybersecurity should be taken into account for a variety of reasons. The risk of cyber mishaps and assaults should eventually decrease as a result of cybersecurity factors. These may result in privacy violations for students and instructors, disruptions of EdTech programs, and other harms, including financial losses for schools or families. All of these factors may also serve to undermine public confidence in the use of technology in education more generally.

Cybercriminals can easily access children's networks at school and home because they are all connected to the same network. These institutions, students, and their residences are vulnerable to both internal and external threats. Such assaults have a disastrous effect on faculty, staff, parents, and administrators as well as students. Leaders in the education industry should adopt a proactive stance by giving priority to crucial reforms in how they safeguard the personal information of their staff and students. Schools can prevent possible attacks by prioritizing important areas to reduce the harm that can be caused by an unavoidable cyber threat by having a proactive game plan. From the sixth grade onward, educational institutions should include cybersecurity curricula as a crucial component of digital education. Cyberattacks in the education sector are neither more common nor more severe than in other sectors, despite the industry experiencing significant issues like a lack of financing, resources, and staffing. In reality, they appear to be becoming more common year after year as more and more breaches, not limited to K–12 and higher education, are widely disclosed. In particular, public K–12 schools offer the soft targets that hackers are looking for in educational institutions.

Trusted Authority Frameworks

The deployment and continuous administration of information security measures are governed by a set of specified processes that comprise a cybersecurity framework. The frameworks act as a guide for controlling risks and minimizing exposures. To address certain information security issues, such as specific needs or various regulatory compliance objectives, organizations might develop frameworks. Additionally, there are several levels of complexity and size for frameworks, and it is crucial to choose a framework that successfully meets operational, compliance, and auditing requirements. Here, the question from education sector is, "What would be a concern for prestigious universities or colleges to focus on the cybersecurity framework in their curriculum?" The pandemic has galvanized learning delivery and interaction via tools such as Google Classroom, WhatsApp, Zoom Meet, Google Meet, and others. The primary objective of cybersecurity education in schools is to inform young internet users about the possible dangers of browsing different social media platforms. Therefore, educational institutions must assess their particular dangers and comprehend what information is exposed to unauthorized access. Furthermore, the frameworks are used by information security experts to specify and rank the tasks needed to manage security and accommodate the precise requirements outlined in the standard or rule.

FEATURES OF CURRICULUM CYBERSECURITY

Enabled Device Connection

The unique opportunities of the Internet of Things (IoT) in education are creating useful IoT apps, networking possibilities, and wirelessly connected gadgets. An IoT is any network of gadgets that are linked to the internet and are used for communication, data collection, or process control. IoT is used in many different sectors and offers almost infinite choices for linked devices. IoT in education simply refers to the use of smart building IoT technologies in learning spaces, including school buildings, buses, classrooms, etc. So, education professionals and school administrators are starting to see the advantages of using IoT technology on a greater scale in educational settings as smart classroom solutions with a vast difference in attention too. Cybersecurity education shouldn't be restricted to the classroom, whether it's online or not. Teachers and students are more likely to be the targets of hacking efforts as they spend more time online since most home networks do not provide the same enhanced firewalls or security as those provided by institutions, and it is crucial to follow safe internet practices. Additionally, some sensing technology can make changes or alert messages in electronic displays when the event of an intruder occurs. Fig. 3 depicts the challenges of IoT in education, and the explanation shows the necessity of device connection.

Figure 3. Challenges of IoT in Education

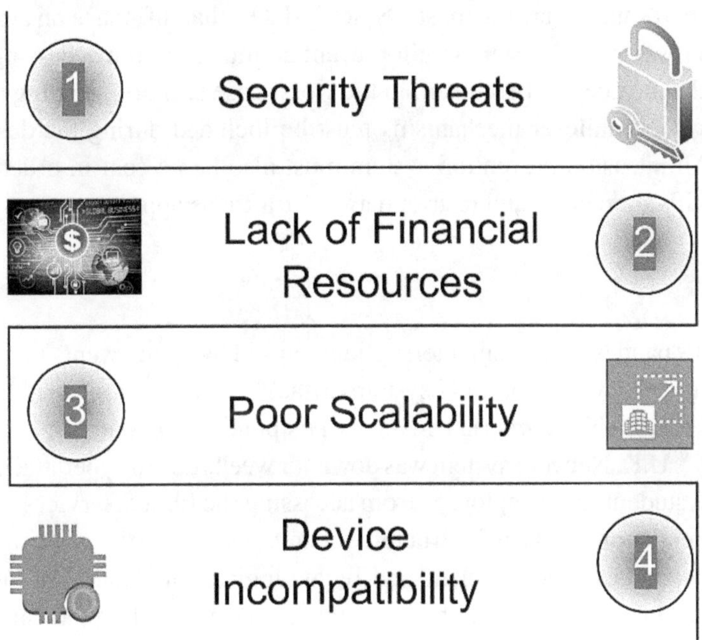

Availability

The accessibility of free programs like G suite / Google Workspace and Office 365 A1 for 5,700 schools; workshops, training sessions, and seminars on the use of eLearning; the usage of ICT tools; the prioritization of curricula; and affective learning; and infrastructure plans for renovation, replacement, furnishing, and the ability to adapt school spaces in preparation for the start of classes. Many schools have also used the subject of coexistence in education and socio-emotional support as a point of reflection and advice. The Ministry produced materials for teachers to deal with the workload or overload, and provided guidance for families and their socio-emotional well-being (Mineduc 2020). The Preferential School Subsidy Law 5 was also loosened by the authorities in April 2020, allowing schools to use the funds for technological resources, hygienic upkeep, cleaning and disinfecting of infrastructure, funds for modifying infrastructure, and other COVID-19 (Superintendencia de la Educación 2020)-related activities. In addition, from May to November, the Agency of Educational Quality switched its strategy of support and evaluation to an online modality, in which 846 schools from across the country participated in "mentorships," "remote visits," (with a simpler instrument than face-to-face), and "Agency Connects," (a virtual space where schools with noteworthy practices can share their positive experiences), among which the mentorships were the best attended. The same organization also organized a "Citizen Consultation" in August 2020 to address the question: "What is educational quality in the context of the pandemic?" (With a view to reconsidering online assistance). More than 37,226 people participated in this consultation, with 71% of them being parents or guardians. The primary findings were that the socio-emotional settings of students were critical to learning; that it was necessary to continue with online learning and develop it with additional tools and resources; and that student engagement and interaction were crucial.

The systems, apps, and data are accessible to users whenever required and make usage easier. The Denial-of-service attacks (DoS), in which the attacker prevents users from accessing data, systems, devices, or other network resources, are the most frequent attacks that influence on availability. An internal system network denial-of-service system might prevent an intruder from accessing the data it needs to function, rendering the intruder inoperable or, in the worst-case scenario, leading the system in danger. Redundancy pathways and failover mechanisms must be included during the design stage to prevent availability issues. An intrusion prevention system must also be present in order to monitor network traffic patterns, identify anomalies, and restrict network traffic as appropriate.

Confidentiality

During the COVID-19 pandemic, system interruptions caused by cyber events may be highly prevalent. The K-12 education sector may have robust IT systems to tackle the technological issues of online learning. In 2020, (BBC News 2020a) Northumbria University postponed examinations, and (BBC News 2020b) Newcastle University's U.K. Network system was down for weeks due to cyberattacks. Similar assaults in April 2021 prevented students and employees from accessing the library services, the learning management system, and the entire on-site IT infrastructure for days, leading to the postponement of courses and assessments at the National College of Ireland and Technological University Dublin (Cisomag 2021). In the same month, a ransomware assault on the University of Portsmouth in the United Kingdom caused an 11-day campus closure and postponed the start of the semester (Fatkin 2021). Similar attacks forced the University of Hertfordshire to suspend online sessions and postpone exams by taking down their whole IT infrastructure and blocking access to cloud-based services (University of Hertfordshire 2021).

The protection of confidentiality guarantees that unauthorized users cannot access the transmitted data. The software, processes, other technologies, and/or people might all be users. A system should be designed with sufficient control mechanisms to ensure confidentiality and rules governing whether authorized users are allowed and not allowed to do with the data. The degree of secrecy rises with the sensitivity of the data. As a result, all critical data should constantly be under control and observation. Data must be safeguarded both within and outside of the system when it is stored (data), transferred (data in the process), and processed (processing under control) in order to guarantee confidentiality in systems (data usage). Data that is currently in use may be protected in memory. While cryptography is good for maintaining the secrecy of data both on the server system and in process, it should be utilized with care in time-sensitive systems because of the computational cost and delay it imposes.

Authenticity

Higher education is not simply another cybersecurity-vulnerable industry; rather, there are a number of elements that make it a distinctive target. First off, due to the volume and variety of data they hold, the range of online behaviors they engage in, and their overall processing capability, educational institutions have an extremely complicated digital footprint (Singar and Akhilesh 2020). The most digitally transformed educational institutions have ongoing processes for creating and consuming data from registrars, faculty documentation, access cards, etc. Furthermore, big data analytics and educational data mining are being employed to enhance instructional materials and aid educators in understanding the unique requirements of students and their performance via the use of EdTech. The educational sector's concerns about students' privacy have long been raised by such data gathering activities (Peterson 2016). Another major issue here is authenticity, since it is difficult to safeguard such a vast volume of different data and it makes more vulnerable to online attacks.

The authenticity is the capacity to verify that no unauthorized alterations have been made to a system or its data. The security guards against illegal changes to hardware, operating systems, and applications, in addition to data, are measured. The hashing refers to a cryptographic technique to convert a data element or a file into a brief string of numbers called a message digest (MD) or hash. If the algorithm performs correctly, the MD is specific to the data being hashed, so any modification to the data will result in an entirely new digest. Therefore, the changes to data may be detected right away by comparing the digests generated by a Secure Hash Algorithm (SHA). Additionally, methods must be in place to identify authenticated violations and return any impacted systems or data to their original states.

Integrity

The COVID-19 made the education sector digital and less manual in its handling of payments, which led to the invisibility of data. The control of personal data makes the education sector susceptible to cyberattacks, not only K-12. The current rise in financial gain and data theft has made cyber security a problem. Since universities and colleges handle huge amounts of cash online, become attractive targets for hackers or intruders who are primarily motivated by the digitization of transaction flows.

Here, integrity is the protection of data from random or intentional changes and the certainty of complete data, which is more critical. The Risk-based validation is the difficult element of cybersecurity for transaction systems and even recognize data theft. Even more challenging is that it goes unnoticed for months, and often the victim is unaware of the loss until a third party finds out about it (Synopsys 2020). The Cyclic Redundancy Check is recognized to provide authenticity protection in automotive systems against unintentional or benign mistakes, but it is unsuitable for guarding against deliberate data tampering. Therefore, cryptographic checksums should be included in the sensitive data to ensure it is non-duplicable. The primary criterion to be addressed in the curriculum is to feed the significant ED technologies related Apps that are trending or available in the market for operational activities.

Non-Repudiation

Although authenticity and non-repudiation are closely related, they have distinct roles at security levels. The authenticity validates the message sender and source, while non-repudiation verifies the message's validity and legitimacy. It seems to be difficult to prevent the theft of data and ensure the accuracy level. Some popular tools, like digital signatures (data is a unique identifier of an individual person) and biometrics (hard to deny or falsify the data). As described, the ability to provide or database the information education system with a secure authentication process such as entering a PIN, scanning a fingerprint, or other biometric authentication methods is to be done. For instance, biometrics provide greater flexibility for the student information system. In most education systems, biometrics of human characteristics such as fingerprints or facial recognition is used for addressing attendance issues on time and identifying the students. With ED tech, it is proven and still changing the methods of identification in the education system to mark student truancy and report it. (Selwyn 2020a; b)

Online Application for Continued Personalization

The interactions between education and technology can be seen in the abundance of learning resources with open access or collaborative teaching and learning via ED Tech resources. In the world of COVID-19, we faced various real-world and hard-to-digital learning solutions for personalized learning resources. Due to the use of ED technology, exploration and innovative ideas have the outlook of online education on various platforms. Depending on the circumstances, the effect of converting the school to a virtual mode varies in severity. Given the difficulties of assessing standards from a distance, the school in the lockdown is unable to mitigate origin-based inequities. This happens despite the fact that the virtual school offers a relatively standard fundamental methodology, among whose features are the planning of online courses on apps and the deployment of learning materials with the most frequent use of teacher-prepared guides and videos. The K-12 education, public schools, and rural education sectors are increasingly using a variety of media to provide course material and are utilizing social media, video conferencing software, and online learning platforms to deliver their lectures. The instructors may provide course notes and multimedia materials to students using online learning tools like Google Classroom. The students may submit homework using the online learning environments, and instructors can monitor the progress. Online lectures and discussion forums may be organized with the use of videoconferencing solutions like Google Meet, Zoom, and Microsoft Teams. Additionally, several institutions are providing course materials through their websites and proprietary learning management systems (Ray & Srivastava 2020). The instructors are now using virtual labs or online simulations of experiments to assist and teach the curriculum courses for students. To ensure the education, new struggle and tackling of the online education made the ways for delivery of learning. Most importantly, the students seem to suffer with the online content and dedicate more time to digitalization learning environment. The transition to remote teaching and learning occurred very easily and distance teaching, co-teaching, and digital pedagogy techniques were established so that the instructors' and students' digital skills grew. In the Ministry of Education and National Agency of Education publications, the viewpoint was highlighted and stated that the instructors were unable to support the engagement and well-being of all learners, particularly pupils with special needs, and that this reduced the equity of teaching and the circumstances for learning throughout the distance learning time (FNAE 2020). Teachers and students both had various experiences with distance learning; for some, it was more stressful than in-person learning, while others thought it enhanced their well-being. Due to the absence of assistance, the situation for special care students has been the most difficult. With the aid of special needs instructors, these pupils were able to go on with their academics at school. Additionally, COVID-19 students who went through an educational transition phase performed worse on assessments and tests.

According to instructors, they generally use SMS-7%, Meta or Instagram-14%, printed work guides-23%, YouTube-26%, phone calls-30%, school textbooks-33%, Google Classroom or Zoom-34%, Meta WhatsApp-55%, email-63%, and other text-books-15% to communicate with their students (Elige Educar 2020). This shows the variety of approaches and forces taken by the instructors. Beyond educational interactions with students, 42% of instructors have gotten in touch with their students of every grade via social networks to see how they are faring throughout the outbreak of COVID-19, which results in a new way of communication. Due to the possibilities of the approaches and new modes of communication, activities that can hold students' attention are now possible. For instance, some instructors claim that they have persuaded bored students to participate in classroom activities by using rhymes, WhatsApp audio tales, tongue twisters, guessing games and exercises that promote relaxation and mindfulness (CIAE, Eduinclusiva Eduglobal 2020).

Recently, the lost learning opportunities and how they differed between student groups and at the level of each individual student information is still insufficient. The speak out by the group, system, and individual student levels is necessary to address the losses in online education learning. For these purposes, usually, the educators will gain from assessment data that is linked to students' continuous learning activities and that gives fine-grained information about how students proceed through the curriculum, particularly to address specific student needs. The Formative evaluation or Formative feedback has this as its intended function, and it necessitates that the assessments be closely related to teaching in terms of what they evaluate as well as in terms of when and how they utilize the information from the assessments. Teachers and students may have easier access to these tests if more digital platforms are used for learning and evaluation. These might take the shape of well-crafted evaluation assignments that are integrated into educational activities. Similarly, public schools and free subsidized private schools have relied on less effective methods of assistance including sending home manuals and tangible materials and communicating with parents by phone or email. The school administration must go on in order to sustainably secure the right to education for students and others. The instructors will be expected to supervise students' progress in their studies at home if they are unable to attend the class for whatever reason, including temporary closures.

CYBERTHREATS TOWARDS ED TECH

Cybersecurity Knowledge for Instructors

As reported by the Cybersecurity K-12 Research Center, among 348 publicly reported events involving 335 educational organizations across 43 states, were caused by the exploitation and misuse of technology and IT network systems. The schools exercise more caution in acquiring the right cyber security technologies and implementing current procedures with security policies in order to accommodate virtual learning. While there are numerous advantages to online learning for both students and instructors, it is more crucial than ever to bolster cybersecurity defenses for counter the new evolving threats. This section is intended to provide teachers, parents, and students the knowledge need to recognize common online risks as well as advice on cybersecurity best practices to help the securely ease into the academic environment. Due to the rush implementation of e-learning, there has been an uptick in cyberattacks and criminals are using the possibilities to scam schools, private information, or use ransomware to demand payment.

Phishing

The most popular method of cyber-attack employed by hackers to access educational institutions networks is phishing. It is a bogus email or website that seeks to gather sensitive data from users who fall for its trap, including debit/credit card numbers, passwords, and other personal information. In phishing emails, consumers are often asked to update their personal or financial information by following a link, downloading an attachment or opening a file that will infect their system with malware. These emails frequently take the form of legitimate notices from well-known companies. Phishing schemes sometimes take the shape of emails or instant messages and are intended to convince the recipient. To believe the source is legitimate in order to get access for their credentials, whether it may be for sensitive student information or private research.

Distributed Denial-of-Service (DDoS)

Cybercriminals try to overload a network server with service requests during denial of service (DoS) assaults, preventing users from accessing the server. Despite the fact that DoS assaults the server or makes the resources unavailable, distributed denial of service (DDos) attacks use multiple devices to flood the target. These include a "botnet," which is a network of infected computers capable of doing many tasks at once. The DDoS assaults are especially troublesome since it may linger for a few days to a few weeks, disrupting business operations and, in the case of educational resources, preventing students and staff from accessing vital resources.

IoT-based Vulnerabilities

When attempting to incorporate IoT devices into the educational environment, the development of a well-defined action plan is essential. The roles, permissions, and efforts for who will be in charge of maintaining IoT devices, rules for data protection, and other things should all be included in the security plan. The identified flaws are often caused by the fact that security is frequently overlooked during product development and is only taken into account as an extra layer rather than as a design requirement and utilize the security strategy of network segmentation. To create distinct network domains for various IoT device types by segmenting the network into several subnetworks or segments, limiting their ability to communicate with one another. By lessening network congestion, such a method may assist improve overall security while simultaneously enhancing speed. It's essential to provide administrators, instructors, teaching staff and students with IoT security awareness training. To provide security against hacking attempts, authentication and authorization should be guaranteed at all times while interacting with the IoT solution.

Data Breach

The use of encryption to secure the data is one of the best methods to lower the risk of a data breach. The Educational institutions utilize encryption to make sure that only authorized individuals with the encryption key may access the data. The safeguard of the keys and the use of encryption on any sensitive data ensures complete security.

Password Policy

The suggestions pertain to the accounts of the instructors and support employees. Everyone accessing the school system should use strong, and unique passwords for all user account. The guidance for developing the are accounts are:

- enforcing complex and secure passwords.
- each accounts have secure passwords with a minimum of 7-14 alphabets and special characters.
- make sure don't let users re-use their old passwords.
- every 120-90 days, force accounts to change their passwords.
- using two-factor authentication for the accounts of the administrative and instructional personnel.

The password policy should advise all faculty, staff, and students to use unique passwords for each account the instructors have, including those at home and at school. The need to work with the board of trustees to do a risk assessment and create a policy on password if the school doesn't already have one.

Cybersecurity Awareness for Students

As Ed Tech reports, students are impacted by malicious online behavior in a number of ways, usually the form of ransomware and fraud. The number of possible known vulnerabilities has dramatically increased as more students attend courses using their own laptops and home Wi-Fi networks. For instance, the potential of digital applications to considerably speed and enhance the entire procedures associated with collecting payments in schools is tremendous. The well-known small-scale developments like "cashless" cards represent the trend toward digitally enabled payment capabilities that are based on open standards and do not bind a school to a specific card manufacturer or hardware solution.

Malware

Most people are aware that malware is a kind of cyberattack that could harm a target. In fact, individuals run the danger of having their devices infected with malware when they download files from the internet. The victim may even be able to install and use the application, but they also unknowingly installed malicious software that allows hackers to access the PC. So, it can make a virtually data theft process more difficult to spot.

Cyber Predators

People are able to conceal their identity or even act otherwise. For kids and teenagers using the internet, predators can occasionally pose a serious risk. Online predators may attempt to seduce young people into interactions or even in-person meetups. Sometimes predators will urge that children and email images of themselves or obscene content. As a result, it's crucial to infuse in children the importance of being vigilant when using the internet.

Online Gaming

By overcoming a challenging opponent, confronting an online bully, or sending virtual currency can establish rapport and acquire trust. This might result in offensive remarks, webcam conversations, or even in-person encounters. It's critical that parents constantly watch their children's gaming and that students are made aware of the dangers of the internet.

Malicious Advertisement

By purchasing ad space from advertising networks and then uploading infected photos with harmful code, cybercriminals may start advertising campaigns. They intend for these advertisements to appear on trustworthy websites in the hopes of individuals will either click on them under the impression that they are trustworthy advertising or let them load and harm your computer in this manner before the malicious ads are found and taken down. Adware and malicious are the fact that both assaults depend on internet advertising to wreak harm.

ROLE OF KNOWLEDGE AND CONTENT STRATEGY-CYBERSECURITY

In general, the management of an institution's information security will focus on the policies and procedures that instructors are expected to follow in order to maintain the privacy and security, authenticity, and accessibility of data and other important assets. The role of Knowledge management consists of information and insight where the process of enabling and strengthening capabilities to undertake operations of embedded in technology, systems, and processes in networks. The conventional method for managing information security comprises completing a threat analysis to determine risks to the privacy, integrity, and accessibility of data systems, which is then followed by risk assessment that entails the use of safeguards to minimize those risks. With this, the primary objectives of information security within education sector not limited to K-12 are:

- to minimize the risk of institutions and organizations terminating operations;
- to preserve data confidentiality;
- to ensure the integrity and reliability of data resources;
- to confirm the continuous availability of data resources and online operations; and
- to ensure compliance with national security laws and privacy policies.

Therefore, the management of information security entails the implementation and ongoing maintenance of information security policies and processes in order to reduce the number of possibilities for risks such as data theft.

PROCUREMENT APPROACH TO GOVERNMENT MEDIATION INTO ED TECH

Although individual responsibility is crucial for effective cybersecurity practices, risks shouldn't be shifted to educational institutions because they are end users of technology themselves and lack the resources, know-how, and capacity to defend against cyberthreats. This is crucial for low- and middle-income nations, because structural problems are at the basis of widespread cyber vulnerability. It makes the case for a sectoral strategy to securing education in which governments play three key roles: a supplier, a facilitator, and a promoter for cybersecurity, drawing on research that evaluates the responsibility of government in cybersecurity policies (Bartlett 2018).

An insufficient awareness of the cybersecurity threats facing the sector and the most susceptible targets has resulted from the absence of event reporting to a centralized source for information collection in education. To address the distinct security settings of universities, governments might work with educational institutions to support the construction of sector-specific Information Sharing and Analysis Centres (ISACs). ISACs are non-profit organizations that are widespread in various industries worldwide and serve as essential information sources on cyberthreats. Additionally, ISACs are responsible for monitoring, early threat alerts, penetration tests, identifying vulnerabilities, and promoting best practices. There aren't many instances of information sharing in higher education now. The Research and Education Networks Information Sharing and Analysis Center (RENISAC) in the United States, for instance, provides services to over 650 institutions (REN-ISAC n.d.). In May 2021, five research sector security groups from the U.K., U.S., Canada, and Australia formed a new collaboration for cybersecurity threat information sharing in response to the surge of ransomware attacks against higher education. This effort is the most current to enter the global arena (McKenzie 2021).

The Governments may take a number of actions to encourage the best cybersecurity practices in classrooms. In many countries, sector-specific guidance is available for the finance, healthcare, energy, and other sectors. One of these is the provision of sector-specific guidance on the minimum cybersecurity measures and standards that educational institutions must adopt as identified by regulators. By defining cybersecurity for the educational sector and identifying best practices for security and resilience, it should provide a shared language. A more general regulatory framework on data protection and privacy laws, like the General Data Protection Regulation (GDPR) in Europe, can also be linked to provisions on cybersecurity standards for education. This has improved cybersecurity policies in the education sector, as some reports have shown (RSM 2020). The Governments may also provide free toolkits to educational providers that include questionnaires and checklists to assist in assessing their cybersecurity to pinpoint any gaps.

There are various instances when governments may urge high-educational institutions to make use of the cybersecurity knowledge of their faculty members and to support cybersecurity education. The government's involvement in initiative activities shouldn't be limited to designating universities as centers of excellence; rather, they should also provide financing and form alliances to assist institutions achieve long-term compliance with the accreditation standards. The global EdTech system is expanding quickly. The government should be in charge of regulating it. Therefore, as part of the various frameworks that apply to other private sector hardware and software suppliers, EdTech should be required to abide by specified national cybersecurity policy guidelines. The EdTech providers may be required to sign security contracts in order to get permission to join the market and be included in this database. The agreements between educational institutions and EdTech providers are one way to do this and the Governments may encourage by publishing sample security agreements that may be used as a guide for purchasing EdTech. The inclusion of security measures in such agreements may also assist in the creation of cybersecurity-specific terminology for use in education and the identification of minimal best practices in software development necessary to provide security by design across the entire product life cycle. The Ministries of Education could set up a national organization whose primary deals would be to certify the safety of EdTech products and list them in a database to help schools and teachers decide what to buy or how to use a certain EdTech product.

RESEARCH FUTURE DIRECTIONS

The education programme designed for instructors and mentors may also include cybersecurity modules in their curricula. The instructors will also provide pupils with appropriate assistance if they have actually taught in the educational programme. More critically, cybersecurity themes should be included in the teaching methodologies. People of the future will be able to comprehend how to defend themselves against cyber-attacks. Additionally, to guarantee that most educational institutions are incentivized to include the programme in their curriculum, the government should reimburse costs associated with adopting a cybersecurity programme in schools. Additionally, by being more aware of cybersecurity issues, children may learn how to defend themselves online. Young internet users may learn how to be safe and secure online, which is more vital. Teachers lack the cybersecurity expertise needed to educate their pupils despite the lack of access and demographics to technology. Future generations will be able to comprehend how to safeguard their data and information against unlawful access in this manner. However, research has shown that locals have trouble embracing cybersecurity awareness training because they think nature would keep them safe.

CONCLUSION

The results of the study make it clear that educational institutions need to provide cybersecurity instruction. This is due to the fact that by raising cybersecurity knowledge via the curriculum, it may aid in defending individuals from a variety of online dangers. More significantly, cybersecurity has led internet users to become aware of their risks while utilizing various social media sites like Instagram, Meta, YouTube, WhatsApp, and Twitter. Additionally, by merely comprehending the detrimental effects that certain cyberattacks, like cyberbullying, have on other online users, people may learn how to avoid them. Additionally, having a basic understanding of cybersecurity may help internet users grasp the laws that apply to different types of cybercrime. The deployment of cybersecurity education, however, confronts a number of difficulties, from a lack of official backing to a lack of funding. More significantly, instructors' lack of knowledge and experience is problematic, particularly when they are supposed to teach cybersecurity to their students. Consequently, the best ways to safeguard adolescent internet users from cyberbullying and other online crimes must be developed by relevant parties, including the authorities, parents, instructors, and others. Furthermore, via campaigns that are engaging and engaging for kids, the media, including broadcasting and television, should assist in spreading awareness about the need for cybersecurity. This article makes the case that cyberthreats to the education sector should be seen as a national policy issue and tackled as an IT policy problem where risks are transferred to the designated institutions. However, the infection process and the potential results of a successful attack are frequently unknown.

REFERENCES

Bartlett, B. (2018). Government as Facilitator: How Japan is Building its Cybersecurity Market. *Journal of Cyber Policy*, *3*(3), 327–343. doi:10.1080/23738871.2018.1550522

BBC News. (2020a). *Northumbria University Hit by Cyber Attack*. https://www.bbc.co.uk/news/ukengland-tyne-53989404

BBC News. (2020b). *Newcastle University Cyber Attack to Take Weeks to Fix*. https://www.bbc.co.uk/news/uk-england-tyne-54047179

Birch, K., Chiappetta, M., & Artyushina, A. (2020). The problem of innovation in technoscientific capitalism: Data rentiership and the policy implications of turning personal digital data into a private asset. *Policy Studies*, *41*(5), 1–20. doi:10.1080/01442872.2020.1748264

CIAE. Eduinclusiva, Eduglobal. (2020). *COVID-19. Nuevos contextos, nuevas demandas y experiencia docente en Chile*. Retrieved from http://eduinclusiva.cl/wp-content/upl oads/2020/10/CIAE-COVID-VFinal-1.pdf

Cisomag. (2021). Top Irish Colleges Face the Ire of Ransomware Attacks. *Cyber Security Magazine*. https://cisomag.eccouncil.org/ransomware-attack-on-two-irish-colleges/

Couldry, N., & Yu, J. (2018). Deconstructing datafication's brave new world. *New Media & Society*, *20*(12), 4473–4491. doi:10.1177/1461444818775968

Educar, E. (2020). Situación de docentes y educadores en contexto de pandemia. *Reporte de Resultados*. Retrieved from https://eligeeducar.cl/content/uploads/2020/07/ Resultados_EncuestaEEcovid_SitioWeb_mi.pdf

Eklund, G. (2018). Master's thesis as part of research-based teacher education: A Finnish case. *Journal of Teacher Education and Educators, 8*(1), 5–20. doi:10.23865/up.v13.1973

Fatkin, N. (2021). *University of Portsmouth Beefs up its Security After 'Cyber Incident' as Campus Reopens*. The News. https://www.portsmouth.co.uk/education/university-of-portsmouth-beefsup-it-security-after-cyber-incident-as-campus-reopens-3207773

FNAE. (2020). *Guidelines for primary education*. Opetushallitus. https://www.oph.fi/fi/koulutusja-tutkinnot/opetustoimi-ja-koronavirus

Harwell, D. (2020). Mass school closures in the wake of the coronavirus are driving a new wave. *Washington Post*. https://www.washingtonpost.com/technology/2020/04/01/online-proctoring-college-exams-coronavirus/

McKenzie, L. (2021). Global Higher Ed Collaboration to Share Cyberthreat Intelligence. *Inside Higher Ed*. https://www.insidehighered.com/quicktakes/2021/05/26/global-higher-ed-collaboration-share-cyberthreat-intelligence

Messina, D., & García, L. (2020). Estudio diagnóstico sobre docentes en América Latina y el Caribe. Documento de Trabajo, Santiago, United Nations Educational, Scientific and Cultural Organization (UNESCO).

Mineduc. (2020). *Apoyos del Mineduc durante la pandemia COVID-19.* Ministerio de Educación de Chile. Retrieved from https://www.mineduc.cl/apoyos-del-mineduc-durante-la-pan demia-del-covid-19/

Peterson, D. (2016). Edtech and Student Privacy: California Law as a Model. *Berkeley Technology Law Journal, 31*(2), 961–996.

Ray, S., & Srivastava, S. (2020). Virtualization of science education: A lesson from the COVID-19 pandemic. *Journal of Proteins and Proteomics, 11*(2), 77–80. doi:10.100742485-020-00038-7 PMID:33132627

Reimers, F., & Schleicher, A. (2020). *Schooling Disrupted. In Schooling Rethought. How the COVID19 pandemic is changing education.* OECD.

REN-ISAC. (2021). Retrieved from https://www.ren-isac.net/about/index.html

RSM. (2020). *Impact of the GDPR on Cyber Security Outcomes.* https://assets.publishing.service.gov.uk/government/uploads/system/uploads/attachment_data/file/906691/Impact_of_GDPR_on _ cyber_security_outcomes.pdf

Selwyn, N. (2020a). *After COVID-19: The longer-term impacts of the coronavirus crisis on education.* Monash University. https://educationfutures.monash.edu/all%2D%2D-present/after-covid-19

Selwyn, N., Hillman, T., Eynon, R., Ferreira, G., Knox, J., Macgilchrist, F., & Sancho-Gil, J. M. (2020b). What's next for Ed-Tech? Critical hopes and concerns for the 2020s. *Learning, Media and Technology, 45*(1), 1–6. doi:10.1080/17439884.2020.1694945

Siemens, G. [@gsiemens]. (2020). *Research pundits. A Google scholar search of prominent voices quickly reveals those who have earned the right to provide guidance* [tweet]. Retrieved from https://twitter.com/gsiemens/status/1246920826282110976

Singar & Akhilesh. (2020). Role of Cyber-Security in Higher Education. In Smart Technologies: Scope and Applications (pp. 249–264). Singapore: Springer.

St. Amour, M. (2020). Privacy and the online pivot. *Inside Higher Ed.* https://www.insidehighered.com/news/2020/03/25/pivot-online-raises-concerns-ferpa-surveillance

Superintendencia de la Educación. (2020). *Superintendencia de educación flexibiliza uso de la SEP para implementar estrategias de seguridad sanitaria por COVID-19.* Retrieved from https://www.supereduc.cl/prensa/superintendencia-de-educacion-flexibiliza-uso-de-la-seppara-implementar-estrategias-de-seguridad-sanitaria-por-covid-19/

Synopsys Cybersecurity Research Center. (2020). *Peril in a Pandemic: Mobile Security*. https://www.synopsys.com/software-integrity/resources/analyst-reports/mobile-application- security-covid.html

United Nations. (2020). *COVID-19 could lead to millions of unintended pregnancies, new UN-backed data reveals.* https://news.un.org/en/story/2020/04/1062742

University of Hertfordshire. (2021). *Important Information – Mobile Application Cyber Attack.* https://www.herts.ac.uk/ study/service-update

ADDITIONAL READING

Burton, J., & Lain, C. (2020). Desecuritising Cybersecurity: Towards a Societal Approach. *Journal of Cyber Policy*, *5*(3), 449–470. doi:10.1080/23738871.2020.1856903

Rid, T. (2013). More Attacks, Less Violence. *The Journal of Strategic Studies*, *36*(1), 139–142. doi:10.1080/01402390.2012.742012

Stone, J. (2013). Cyber War Will Take Place! *The Journal of Strategic Studies*, *36*(1), 101–108. doi:10.1080/01402390.2012.730485

Williamson, B., Potter, J., & Eynon, R. (2019). New research problems and agendas in learning, media and technology: The editors' wishlist. *Learning, Media and Technology*, *44*(2), 87–91. doi:10.1080/17439884.2019.1614953

Chapter 8
Integration of STEAM Education Supports the Future of Cybersecurity

Dana L. Smerda-Mason
New Jersey City Univeristy, USA

ABSTRACT

Our society exists in a 21st century digital world, reliant on technology to function. Daily lives are reliant on the technological functions of the modern world, and often leave us vulnerable to evolving cyber attacks globally. Staying ahead of cyber criminals is a difficult task, but one of the most important defenses we have in maintaining online safety. It is essential to develop students to not only be aware of how to keep themselves safe in a digital world, but also to be creative innovators to help thwart criminal attempts online. Through the implementation of STEAM education, students can be exposed to developing new collaborative and creative skills that can help inspire future computer scientists and policymakers tasked with battling the frontier of cybersecurity.

INTRODUCTION

Our society exists in a 21st century digital world, reliant on technology to function. Our lives fit in the palm of a hand, and with a few clicks an abundance of private information that ranges from financial information, medical records, to trade secrets can easily be accessed. In today's modern world, research and education are more accessible to people from anywhere they live than ever before thanks to modern technology solutions. Although this easy access is essential for business practices and functioning in the modern world, it can leave us vulnerable to cybercriminals working to develop new ways to benefit from accessing our private information. These threats are not unique to any one part of the world, but are universal in nature and target every individual regardless of origin or lifestyle.

Cybercrimes are defined as "criminal offenses committed via the Internet or otherwise aided by various forms of technology, such as the use of online social networks to bully others or sending sexually explicit digital photos with a smartphone" (Thompson Reuters, 2022). Other examples have developed

DOI: 10.4018/978-1-6684-6092-4.ch008

over time to include email and Internet fraud, theft of data financial or otherwise, cyberextortion, cyberespionage (FBI, 2022), or cryptojacking. The first conviction of an act of cybercrime occurred in 1982, when Ian Murphy was found guilty of hacking the American Telephone Company (Mfitzgerald, 2004). Although cybercrimes have been affecting global society on a variety of levels this is still a relatively new field of criminal activity, which evolves with the nuances in modern daily life that can provide new opportunities for cyberattacks.

As our world continues to adapt to changes and challenges that arise, new opportunities for cyberattacks present. In 2020, the health crisis of the Covid-19 pandemic forced businesses to consider an operational shift. The workplaces of these companies quickly pivoted from the public office environment with security structures in place, to home-based workspaces and learning environments. This type of change provided a new accessibility among cyber criminals, and business experienced 50% more cyberattacks on a weekly basis in the final quarter of 2021 (Brooks, 2022).

The private sector was not alone in this cybersecurity siege. Healthcare experienced an increase in weekly cyberattacks by 71%, and the military and government sector experienced a 47% increase at this time. The education and research sector increased as well, suffering with 75% more interference from cybercriminals, and was the most targeted sector worldwide in 2021 (Brooks, 2022). Cybercrime patterns adapted to the changes experienced by the physical world, and new innovations threatened global safety and security.

The nature of data breaches is moving beyond our regular world of expectation, and evolving to new areas. Instead of focusing on financial transactions, or the personal or business use of technology, cybercriminals are now focusing on one act that can influence the lives of many, even those who are not using technology. These types of attacks can easily shut down the day-to-day operations of major cities, disrupt the supply chain. and delay trade and commerce. In other circumstances, cybercriminals are using their skills to find vulnerabilities within the energy grid, all of which affect the safety of citizens in counties across the world. These types of attacks are creatively implemented so they can easily go undetected from parties unsuspecting issues of these natures.

For example, the SolarWinds data breach was an unusual occurrence that began with malicious code being embedded to the Orion system servicing over 33,000 customers. SolarWinds sent out an email to their customers with information about routine software updates, which unexpectedly included the hacked code (Jilbilian & Canales, 2021). This established a backdoor to the IT systems of various customers, which affected 18,000 individuals, many of which belonged to Fortune 500 companies and United States government agencies, leaving them exposed to spyware. Although these types of threats can now be prevented by many larger companies, smaller and medium sized organizations struggle to compete against cybercriminals attacking their systems, causing concern for customers and businesses alike.

Another example focuses on affecting people regionally, as opposed to directly disrupting the technological infrastructure to multiple individuals. Ransomeware was confirmed by the FBI as having been used to suspend operations of the Colonial Pipeline in May of 2021 (Panettieri, 2021). This particular attack affected 5,500 miles of pipeline that provides fuel to over 14 states in the United States, and leaving people without the necessary fuel supply for daily functions. This type of attack targeted and disrupted the infrastructure and supply chain, which is predicted to be a more commonly threatened area by cyber criminals in the near future (Brooks, 2022).

Occurrences such as these indicate a shift in how cybercrimes have affected individuals thus far. People are more aware now than ever that their passwords need to be protected, online financial transactions should be especially guarded, and are becoming more accustomed with what to identify regarding phishing and clickbait communications designed to lure them into unsafe situations. Individual companies are structured to keep customer's sensitive information secure, while thwarting attempts by hackers to impede technological interruptions. Society's knowledge of cyber security is reminiscent of the needs of the 20th century, and it is imperative we find new ways to prepare people and IT professionals to anticipate the developing changes in the field of cyber security. 21st century problems will not be successfully solved if experts are looking to the past for answers. To successfully do this, we need to start educating people differently so that they will not only be aware of how to keep themselves safe as individuals, but can also be empowered to contribute to the growing field of cybersecurity to make a positive impact on society.

Underrepresentation and Self-Efficacy

Cybercriminals are finding a variety of ways to penetrate security. In order to keep up with the developing nature of cyberthreats it is important to develop the next generation of thinkers to not only know how to keep themselves safe, but also have a full understanding of how cyber criminals are thinking. One way of developing this type of future support is through enhancing our educational approach in the classroom to incorporate learning activities that will encourage students' creativity and help them develop important 21st century skills earlier in their educational experience. Incorporating an approach such as STEAM education will help engage a variety of students, and ultimately produce lifelong learners who will better understand the future needs of cybersecurity to keep up with the evolving nature of these types of threats.

STEAM education is a convergence education approach that blends together the domains of science, technology, engineering, arts and design, and math. These domains are integrated to more efficiently solve issues that appear in society, as well as in the modern world of scientific innovation (Herr et al., 2019). The arts and design were incorporated as a 21st century necessity to add to encourage creativity and innovation in developing solutions that were more applicable to the world as a whole.

Currently the United States is facing an issue where there is a shortage of individuals in the technical fields that produce computer science engineers. According to a 2013 study conducted by A Partnership for a New American Economy, only 4.4% of graduating students from high schools in the United States were moving into technical fields in higher education (Land, 2013). Of the countries included in this study, the United States had the lowest rate, with countries such as China at 33.9% enrollment, and Singapore with 31.2% enrollment both leading the world in this area. The findings of this study helped indicate that American students felt intimidated by the technical fields and chose to engage in the liberal arts for their future course of study. In time, this low self-efficacy within this area of learning will affect our nation's ability to innovate, and can impact and limit our ability to react to cybercrimes most effectively.

When evaluated along with the growing need for cybersecurity professionals, this becomes a problematic statistic. Currently, the job outlook in the cybersecurity field for the 2020-2030 decade is predicting a much faster than average growth rate of 33% (US Bureau of Labor Statistics, 2022). In just 2021 alone, the New York Times estimated the creation of 3.5 million new jobs globally in cyber security. This includes C-level positions in the field as well as cyber project managers, information security analysts, systems and cybersecurity engineers, penetration testers, malware analysts, and cybersecurity consultants (Drexel, 2021). The minimum educational requirements for this field start with a bachelor's degree, and professionals can continue to grow and develop by obtaining certifications and staying abreast of advances associated with evolving aspects of the field.

In addition to general student interest, it is imperative that there is diversity among those that work within this particular field. The National Science Foundation has included a term called the Missing Millions in their 2030 vision for education. This refers to the need for representation from minorities, females, and other underrepresented groups of the general population to join careers related to the technical fields (Blatecky, et. al., 2021), as they are not developing a professional interest in science through the conventional learning models. This mission focuses on providing a path to STEM education, and solving supply issues in lower income communities, to ensure that students are properly exposed to these fields earlier in life.

The intention with this particular vision is that younger students will develop a healthy interest through STEM education studies, and overcome their uncertainties that prevent them from pursuing technical fields later in their academic journey. Cybercrime is an area that affects every individual in the world regardless of race, gender, religion, social economic status, or national origin. In order to properly protect those potentially affected from cyber threats there needs to be sufficient representation to understand the nuances and variety of opportunities in which cyber criminals threaten the lifestyles of each individual. Students' personal belief in their own academic abilities plays a significant role in future professional paths, and it is important to help foster an engaging relationship with studying science, technology, engineering, math, and the arts to help encourage students to pursue these types of careers,

Self-efficacy theory was a concept established by Albert Bandura in 1977, which stated that one's own beliefs about their personal capabilities directly affected their ability to be successful (Barni, et. al., 2019). This is determined through four categories, the first of which is known as mastery experience, where if an individual has been able to succeed in a particular area, they automatically decide that they are good in this practice. The same applies though if they fail, which reinforces the personal belief that this is not an activity they in which they have potential. This strongly affects the future abilities of an individual in an area and can cause them to continue to struggle instead of master the skill at hand (Lopez-Garrido, 2020).

Students' own actions supply the data relied on to make their future decisions. Therefore, it is important to positively engage students at an early age in STEAM education. By doing so at an early age, students can engage with less opinion of their own capabilities and can naturally develop their interests in the technical fields. This task becomes easier as we incorporate the arts by way of the STEAM method of learning (Hunter-Doniger, 2019). When the arts are incorporated to a convergence education approach earlier on, students who normally are less interested in the technical subjects begin to engage and find confidence to try new things.

Vicarious experience is the second domain where people measure their own personal abilities against the abilities of others in their environment (Valiante, n.d.). If someone who an individual determines to possess generally the capabilities or less is able to accomplish something, they themselves will believe that they also can accomplish this challenge as well. The decision is sometimes made in a negative way for them if they witness another individual that they believe has more advanced capabilities than themselves struggle with a particular skill. They often have the element of challenge reinforced, that contributes to labeling that achievement accordingly. It is not uncommon that they develop the personal belief that they would be unable to develop that skill based on the observation of another individual's experience.

This is one reasons why it is important that students see female and minority representation in the field of technology. When students see people like themselves, specifically women and minorities, in these types of fields they can more easily identify with these career paths (Salter, 2019), and provide greater diversity within the technical fields. This will help build self-efficacy in students because they feel that they belong and are supported, resulting in new perspectives to solutions in various areas of cybercrime. This type of thought-product provides a winning result for all parties involved, not just females and minorities entering this particular field (Salter, 2019).

Social persuasion is another domain where individuals develop their beliefs based on the messages, either positively or negatively, received from their environment (Cherry, 2020). Having a support network, versus an environment with negative reinforcement on an individual will affect future success. Students that come from households with strong beliefs about gender roles, or lack of funding to encourage students to explore a new interest will play a substantial role in an individual's developing sense of personal capabilities. Conversely, having educators, family, friends, community members, or professionals from the field of future interest offer suggestions, resources, advice, and encouragement can inspire an individual to take on and conquer a challenge that arises.

For example, a student who is the first to pursue higher education in their family may have more doubt about their potential, as opposed to a student that comes from a family of graduates who have always expected them to embark on the same path. When challenges arise, there is less support at home to rely on for help, and it is easy to allow these limitations determine their achievements. Someone with a strong family history of college-graduates can easily reach out to a relative for direction, or encouragement when these same feelings arise, and receive the help they need to overcome obstacles to keep moving forward. Social persuasion occurs in varying ways for different individuals, and can be a factor in students' pursuing the technical fields later in life.

The final domain relates to beliefs developed based on an individual's psychological state. If someone is coping with a physical or mental ailment, this will also affect their beliefs about their own personal capabilities at that time (Akhtar, 2008). Being aware of one's own health concerns, can limit an individual's understanding of their potential. It can be as simple as recovering from a physical injury and knowing they cannot complete a task until they are healed as a result, or it can be something related to their mental state that prevents them from having a clear understanding of their capabilities. This domain reminds us that our physical and mental states also play a part in determining beliefs about our personal success in a particular area.

Each of these areas affect how a student learns in their scholastic environment. The personal data is received from their young experiences immediately, and begins to develop permanent understanding of what they feel is true about their own capabilities. Students who are educated earlier on with technical skills have the benefit of developing a positive relationship with this area of study, and are able to contribute to our national ability to innovate on a professional level, ultimately affecting our global standing (Land, 2013) with cyber security.

It is often that negative personal beliefs can be determined early in life, limiting the student's potential or willingness to explore new areas of learning. If students grow up to feel that others always know more about technology than they do, they risk remaining a victim in the future, resisting the willingness to make change. To help students overcome this it is important that they have a chance to experience a creative approach to learning earlier in their school experience. This will help provide a platform to develop their creativity through important 21st century skills so that they will be more open to having different learning experiences especially in the technical fields as they continue their personal development.

Changes in Technology Effect Brain Function in Education

A constant and reliable aspect observed throughout history is change. Since the first cybercrime occurred, we are seeing this same evolution in this field as well. Evolution is evidenced in nature, and we are able to see these types of trends in our general processes and expansion of technology. To help anticipate changes in this area, it is important to understand how changes in technology are affecting society to try to anticipate more secure solutions in cybersecurity. Brain function research shows us that technology is influencing our neuroplasticity. Cortical plasticity of sensory representation is enhanced by activities where fingers are frequently engaged in operation, such as with activities like playing an instrument, or using technology (Korte, 2020).

Not everyone in society plays an instrument, but a majority of people use digital media and technology on a regular basis. At the beginning of 2022, the world population was at 7.9 billion people, and 5.2 billion of the population were regularly using the Internet for personal and business purposes (Miniwats Marketing Group, 2022). This was a 1335% growth in digital use since 2000, and speaks to a change in the somatosensory cortex as a result of the intense reliance on technology, affecting the cortical processes of brain usage in modern society (Korte, 2020).

In examining our society's evolution of technology, it began with physical solutions to issues, followed by more sophisticated ones to make life easier. Life in the 21st century is rapidly moving to symbiotic future solutions that would continue to transform our world, and suppress the simple physical origins of the solutions initially developed (Osiurak, Navarro, & Reynaud, 2018). Between changes in brain physiology, routines, and technology, new cybersecurity needs are in demand. To continue supporting progress in modern life, education also has had to undergo a variety of evolutionary changes as well to prepare students to succeed in a 21st century world. Education becomes the point of convergence between the needs to prepare the future innovators, while acknowledging that the neurophysiology of students living at this time in history also requires a new approach to learning.

Changes in education began to shift with the inception of convergence education in the later part of the 20th century. To meet the needs of these changes, the educational world embraced a method of convergence education. This model incorporated elements of many subjects in a single lesson while presenting learning experiences. This was done specifically to increase student experience in the areas of innovation and problem-solving, by bringing in helpful elements available from a variety of domains to create solutions (Herr, et. Al., 2019).

This model was inspired by the exciting advances occurring in the middle part of the 20th century, and was developed as an educational response to prepare for technological innovation. The 1960's space race experience began to ignite wonder in people everywhere as they looked to the skies and wondered about possibilities that lie ahead. The personal computer was an advent that began to introduce the daily use of technology into common households, and the workplace. As a nation, many individuals were inspired to contribute through their personal studies developing in the technical fields.

STEM Becomes STEAM: A Brief Overview

At this time in the 20th century, society was beginning to benefit from a faster pace of technological development, and theorists sought to adapt education to meet these modern needs. They began by incorporating science, technology, engineering, and math initially, which became a popular learning domain known today at STEM (Dalton, 2019). The technical skills and thinking taught by STEM education programs aimed to prepare students to fill employment positions in highly paid technical fields (Reitenbach, 2015). Gradually, students developed new skills to meet the growing needs for innovative minds to establish the United States as a global leader in world innovation.

Students were more prepared for the modern workforce as a result of this form of convergence education, and became strong contributors to modern innovation. Critical thinking, problem-solving, innovation, collaboration, became elements naturally associated with the technical fields as a result of the convergence education approach, which attracted individuals naturally adept in these particular domains to pursue study in STEM courses (Liao, 2016). Higher education began to adopt this model as a result of the comprehensive approach to learning that was natural in STEM education, and also to meet the needs of the developing workforce. The initial success of this learning model seemed to be a solution to the needs that emerged from the innovative technical fields.

The end of the 20th century drew nearer, and the needs of the modern workforce continued to change and adapt as ideas that were once considered sophisticated were now transforming to a symbiotic level of innovation (Osiurak, Navarro, & Reynaud, 2018). Contributors that had a STEM background all seemed to be educated in the same processes, which began to slow innovative contributions. These individuals shared a convergent thinking approach to problem-solving, where they were working to produce a single correct solution. Additionally, there were challenges in communicating many of the brilliantly developed ideas to the general public with utilitarian success, which affected early adoption of processes and types of technology (Reitenbach, 2015).

While initially relying on the STEM learning model, it was believed that this convergent thinking approach had once been thought to be the gateway to future innovative success. Over time there were signs that there were some needs left unaddressed, and progress was slowing. STEM was beginning to show its limitations. Robust problem solving was lacking, and communication and creativity, especially among collaborative partners, was becoming an increasing issue in the field. Reevaluation of these arising challenges prompted *Massachusetts Institute of Technology* (MIT) to develop a new approach that started with the text *Learning to Communicate in Science and Engineering*. This book was a requirement for incoming students and attempted to provide new strategies for clearer communication to peers in their field, as well as with contributors existing in other aspects of the innovation process, through a variety of situations utilizing case study examples (Reitenbach, 2015).

While important changes were being made in the STEM model, there were new needs demanded by the innovative fields. In the early part of the 1990's it became apparent that the element of design was lacking and changes needed to be made to incorporate creativity so that American innovation could continue to remain as the technological though-leaders of the world. It was at this time that a new seat at the STEM table was formed, which invited professionals from the field of the arts and design to add a new element to the collaborative team through inclusion and representation. The advent of the STEAM model of learning was dawning.

21ST CENTURY SOLUTIONS WITH STEAM EDUCATION METHODS

To prepare for the shift into the 21st century, the STEM model was expanded. The new model in convergence education became known as STEAM, which included the element of the arts and design to the evolving STEM approach. This evolution in innovation infused both the learning and development approaches with skilled professionals from the arts, which distributed new importance to the element of design. This brought new concepts to the convergent thinking world.

By having arts professionals involved in the development of new innovation, it was easier to develop new products and procedures. Arts professionals by trade rely on divergent thinking for their development process, which was previously underutilized in the 20th century STEM approach (Land, 2013). Arts professionals would collaborate by sharing a variety of ideas that would be developed as potential options with the group of thinkers, until the best possibility emerged as a solution. In this process, collaborators were not trying to find the one correct answer to solve the challenge at hand, but instead would explore and vet a variety of options and then logically decide on which was most efficient.

Incorporating the arts into innovation is not a new or foreign concept. In fact, many famous individuals known for their innovative contributions in the world also had experience in the arts. Leonardo da Vinci was a well-known painter as well as an inventor, while it may be lesser known that Albert Einstein played violin, and Steve Jobbs was a guitarist in addition to their contributions from the technical fields (Roebelen, 2011). Incorporating the arts into education and arts-professionals into the collaborative process promotes a unique element of creativity.

Arts professionals are considered to be risk-takers, which supports healthy discourse and collaboration when developing new processes and products (Robelen, 2011). They are fearless with sharing ideas because it is understood that all ideas will not be the correct answer, but every thought shared productively could spark a new thought in the mind of another collaborator, which brings the group closer to a polished solution. These skills were the perfect complement to the technical expertise of the STEM innovators and helped develop more advanced ideas, as well as contributed to more effective and attractive design popularity when brought to market (Harris & deBruin, 2018).

Diversity in thinking and expertise were essential elements infused into the world of innovation to help grow to a new level of success. This diversity included the expert contributions from arts professionals as well as individuals with a technical background, but does not end there. Diversity in gender, race, as well as interest and experience are imperative for the future of American innovation. This approach brings together the best in understanding the various life experiences of our diverse population, and helps offer nuanced and niched elements to vary a solution and make it more impactful for our society as a whole.

When engaging students to enter the technical fields, encouragement alone will not provide the diversity necessary for a growing economy. A natural attraction to this field of study must occur within a wide variety of people, which happens authentically when the arts are incorporated (Hunter-Doniger, 2018). Individuals who would normally pass on this area of study have a renewed interest because their skills and expertise are welcomed to the collaboration table.

In observing these types of evolution in the field of innovation, we understand that the greatest changes that we experience in our world are born out of intention towards developing a practical solution as a necessity. This path then can evolve from a physical need, to a more sophisticated solution, and eventually into a symbiotic one (Osiurak, Navarro, & Reynaud, 2018). In observing understanding the success that the STEAM approach has brought to the world of innovation, the needs of the workforce would be changing rapidly. It became important for the field of education to shift as well, to produce professionals that would have modern skills to contribute to this field, especially the growing needs of the evolving cybersecurity field.

PREVENTION OF CYBERCRIME THROUGH 21ST CENTURY LEARNING

The ability to address future cybercrime requires an understanding of criminal theories blended with 21st century understandings and learning approaches. This will help develop students in a way that they are poised as adults not only to fight existing attacks, but also prevent cyberthreats. The four Cs are an element of 21st century learning that helped bring STEM to a new level of efficacy as STEAM education. In addition to problem-solving, quality innovation and education now rely on collaboration, communication, critical thinking, and creativity (Silva, 2009).

The element of creativity is enhanced through the application of the arts and design in the 21st century classroom, which contributes to a rich experience of communication and collaboration within the group of student innovators. Cybercriminals are already using many of these same tactics to creatively develop and carry out their next attack, and having an understanding of the modern innovative process will help students become cybersecurity professionals who are capable of anticipating threats. When properly addressed in 21st century learning, these become curricular elements that can help future cybersecurity professionals stay ahead of criminal activity and attempt to maintain safe digital operations of institutions in education, the private sector, as well as household personal users.

Whether these skills are used for the good of the community, or negatively for personal gain through crime, processes are always improving and evolving. Just as scientists and innovators learn from their failed designs to create a stronger future solution, so do cyber criminals. It is important that educators develop new ways to approach their curricula by infusing it with 21st century learning opportunities earlier in the elementary school experience to positively impact student achievement in the areas of STEAM education and cybersecurity.

One way to introduce these elements is to infuse the understanding of real-world issues related to the cybersecurity world into problem-based and project-based learning experiences. Project-based learning is a method of continuous learning where students identify issues that are relatable to them in the real world, and conduct research to better understand and develop a solution (Wolpert-Gawron, 2015). Usually, the solution is presented in a multimedia approach which incorporates elements of 21st century tools at their disposal. Their completed project not only demonstrates their understanding of a concept, but also their understanding of how it affects others as well as employs their creativity to develop a solution and convey their findings to a wider audience in some capacity.

Crime Pattern Theory is a great place to start in helping students understand the challenges faced in cybersecurity. This theoretical framework was developed by Paul and Patricia Brantingham and incorporates a variety of elements of social routine with detailed specifics of a geographical area to identify patterns of criminal activity to anticipate and prevent future occurrences (Brantingham & Brantingham, 2021). Details such as demographics, activities in the area, neighborhoods, paths between neighborhoods as well as fringe sections of a location, all coupled with the social economic tapestry associated with the area can provide a multitude of information related to the criminal activity and potential occurrences in a specified location. Another benefit to this approach is that baseline data of frequency, location, and natures of offenses can be identified and established as a baseline understanding in a particular area. This data can be used for future analysis if frequency fluctuates, or if new forms of activity emerge and affect the normal expectations.

Students can learn a lot about their community's relationship to cyber security practices, while engaging in a project centered around this topic. Crime Pattern Theory naturally provides a structure to help students understanding how crimes are identified in different areas, and can be related to the field of cyber security. Students can actively survey community and family members to understand about the actions they take to keep their digital use safe.

There are many benefits to exposing students learning about cybersecurity to project-based activities. Students are able to explore with some autonomy and questioning in this type of structure, while experiencing a more transparent and responsive means of learning and strengthening classroom culture with peers (Fester & Starkey, 2022). The role of the educator shifts as well, from leading the class in discussions to facilitating while students-driven learning experiences authentically occur. Additionally, they are producing work that is akin to projects required of them in the workforce, helping them gain experience beyond the classroom that builds their confidence and positively reinforces self-efficacy.

The sociology that is related to cybercrime and its effects on society can also be a strong topic to build project-based learning experiences from. Rational Choice Theory is a criminology framework that states how behavior is driven by a balance of costs and rewards. People make choices about their actions based on how much benefit they receive from that choice, and if it outweighs the costs involved (Nickerson, 2021). When the action they chose becomes less beneficial, their choices change, and they begin to find other means of benefitting.

This aligns with Maslow's Hierarchy of Needs, which states that there are a hierarchy of basic psychological and physiological needs that humans have which motivate actions that are taken in different situations in life (Cherry, 2022). This can be applied to the understanding of criminal psychology and viewed through the lens of Rational Choice Theory. Having an understanding of the motivating factors of cybercriminals can help identify potential vulnerabilities in networking and provide a basis for designing solutions.

An aspect of cybersecurity is not only identifying network vulnerabilities and assessing damage from cyber criminals, but it also requires a knowledgeable base of legal minds, and policy makers. When cybercrimes occur, it is imperative that action be taken and consequences administered to the offenders. We were reminded of this in 2021 when the social media company Meta, most commonly known for Facebook and Instagram, had been facing scrutiny in congressional hearings. Meta's practices regarding how it collects algorithmic data and makes personal suggestions, as well antitrust concerns had been called in to question, and are under review by the Federal Trade Commission (FTC) (Duffy, 2022).

During these hearings it was apparent how important is was to have a basis of knowledge in technology. Policymakers and federal officials involved in these hearings must have a full understand of the nuances of the social media platform operations behind the scenes so that the most appropriate solutions for safety can be agreed upon, and fair consequences can also be assigned when appropriate. A project-based activity centered around the policy that guides and regulates technology should also be integrated into the classroom experience. This helps students to understand the relationship between ethics and cybersecurity, and discuss the guidelines and legal policy that establishes precedent in society's response to regulatory obligations.

Computer programming is a skill that all students will benefit from having in the future workforce, including policymakers leading society in the 21st century. Many individuals born in the 20th century were not raised with the emphasis on these skills, and are in the process of learning through computer science certifications and courses. Being able to instill this important skill in the youth of the 21st century will help prepare them for a variety of well-compensated positions in the technology industry post-graduation. Educators themselves may be less comfortable with teaching computer science as a result, but can benefit from the educational options that exist to support their students towards mastering these important skills.

Beginning computer science platforms such as Code Combat, Code Academy, Kodable, Code FWD, and Google's CS First platforms all support students with fun activities to learn basic computer science principles to be competitive in the future, many of which are offered free of charge to anyone with Internet access. Self-efficacy can be low in students and educators that find challenge in these developing skills, and so finding ways to differentiate learning experiences help reengage students of all abilities. For this Code.org provides a varied platform with a gamified learning approach for beginners of all ages. Gamification is an approach that engages their sense of fun, while having them navigate through entertaining modules that help develop problem-solving skills as they become more familiar with computer science.

Beginning courses are available for students of all ages, pre-readers included, to meet the age-appropriate individual needs of newcomers regardless of when they begin their computer science journey. There are varying courses that focus on CS Fundamentals for beginners, and CS Discoveries for helping students with web design elements such as HTML, Java, and CSS. High school students and older can benefit from the more advanced CS Principles, and Code.org also provides cybersecurity and encryption lessons to teach the basics to prepare students with the future needs for cyber security.

Not all students are immediately attracted to learning computer science, and free-will becomes a stronger factor in student success with each year that passes in a student's development. To help add the elements of art and design, engineers at Amazon's Project STEM have developed curriculum to help students design scenes and solve digital problems through the use of computer science, while drawing on their creative backgrounds. These approaches work on developing creativity with computer science skills early on before students have the chance to make a limiting decision on their own personal capabilities in the area of cybersecurity.

Schools also host Hack-a-thon events, and white-hat-hacking challenges to empower students with real-time problem-solving experiences in friendly team competitions. This helps students realize they can impact the world around them at a younger age, and become aware of the beginning nuances of the cybersecurity field instead of waiting until adulthood. Programs for youth of all ages are available through the National Security Agency (NSA), where students learn white hat hacking skills through 43 different camp programs (Blakemore, 2015). These summer camps are currently being hosted by 29 different universities throughout the United States and provide the education needed to help develop future NSA contributors.

These experiences layer positive data related to students' understanding of their technological capabilities, ultimately fortifying their self-efficacy and helping them develop confidence to explore this field post-graduation, as opposed to be intimidated by it. With these skills, students have a front seat at developing cutting edge cybersecurity skills and learning about established criminology theories. Understanding concepts such as Routine Activities Perspectives can help students better understand the importance of learning skills to take an active role to combat cybercrime. This framework observes criminal offenses from the point of view of the offender. It proposes that crimes are committed when two main factors converge with a willing and motivated criminal offender: An accessible target becomes present, and a lack of police presence or other capable guardians such as friends, security, or a variety of bystanders (NSW Department of Attorney General and Justice, 2011). This is generally associated with the Problem Analysis Triangle as a means of depicting the convergence of these elements, as well as how these elements are always present in all varieties of criminal activity.

It is easy to associate this theory with crime that is physically occurring because it is something individuals can bear witness to, and possibly avoid or prevent. It is not uncommon that visual environmental indicators present themselves in a situation, which can alert people to proceed cautiously in a particular environment. Sensing danger can help individuals keep themselves safe, or provide a presence of support if they see a vulnerable party in their proximity. There may be a motivated criminal, but the target can avoid the area, or bystanders could present themselves as capable guardians to deter criminal activity.

When dealing with cybercrime, these indicators are neither visual nor tangible, and thus more difficult to identify. Online targets are constantly accessible, and the role of capable guardians only exists in preventable software measure. Motivated offenders can operate unseen as they target and work to penetrate vulnerable areas of online systems. Under the cover of the digital world, it becomes easy for motivated cybercriminals to continue to test safety measures for faults without being seen.

Due to this unique nature, one of the best defenses to fighting cybercrime is to anticipate digital vulnerabilities and flaws in security plans, and prevent criminal activity from occurring. These nuances in cybercrime can be introduced to students while they are learning about cyber safety and digital citizenship. This is an attribute of the modern world that society will always be living with, and criminals operating in this arena are developing creative approaches to prey on their victims. It is increasingly more important to motivate students to develop skills that will help them be confident contributors to this field in their future.

Tiered Response to Cybersecurity as a Result of Educational Implementation

Future Recommendations

Through the process of developing our educational approaches to prepare and inform society with the nuanced skills to combat cybercrimes, we stand to produce individuals with a tiered relationship to the efforts of fighting cyberattacks. Having strong computer science professionals programming and supporting through their efforts in white hat hacking, and battling cyber criminals through creative technological solutions will help society safely adapt with the changing world. Not everyone is interested in the computer programming side of this field, but with this type of a background individuals who are less interested in working in the technology side of cybersecurity will be skilled with the proper understandings needed to make intelligent policy that meets the needs of society related to technology. Others can participate in litigation or other aspects that support the growing needs of the cybersecurity field to properly design consequences to appropriately fit crimes and bring justice to affected parties.

For this reason, everyone should be trained to understand cybercrimes as well as the use of safe technology and digital citizenship earlier in their academic experience. At the very least a stronger more-aware society of users is produced, and they will have a better understanding of how to use technology in the day-to-day functions with better security, while also having a clear path to solutions should they become successfully targeted by a cyberattack. An informed future generation of users is an excellent first defense against the attempts of cybercriminals. All individuals using technology in the 21st century should be aware of what precautions to take, which starts with simple maintenance of personal devices.

For example, it is important to stay current with software updates so that when companies identify and provide solutions to vulnerabilities in their products, users are ensured that they are relying on the strongest, and most up-to-date versions. Establishing multi-factor authentication for accounts can provide a 99% protection from hackers (CISA, n.d.). Not only does it provide an additional layer of protection from gaining unwanted access to personal accounts, it also and helps alert users when unauthorized personnel are attempting to access these accounts so they can immediately take action and protect their private information.

Additionally, the password chosen for each account can make a difference in online security as well. Many are adopting the use of a password manager to help not only create unique passwords, but help users not duplicate the use across online accounts they intend to keep safe (Cunningham, 2019). To support these areas of prevention, users must be able to identify clickbait, and phishing messages. These types of scams lure users to open messages or click on links on the Internet that bring them to unsecure locations. Phishing attacks account for 90% of data breaches in corporations according to research from IBM conducted in202. Since the Covid-19 pandemic these types of cyberthreats have risen two percentage points and are also affected by supply chain uncertainty (Rosenthal, 2022). It is becoming more important than ever that all technology users are aware of basic preventative practices, and changing tactics from hackers to help maintain safe and healthy function of their personal technological needs.

CONCLUSION

Cybercrime is a universal area of life that societies across the world will constantly be affected by, and we need to learn how to develop ways to keep ourselves safe through creative and innovative approaches. This beings with changing our approach to education so that we can attract more people to pursue technical fields of study and choose to be a part of the cybersecurity solution that we desperately need. Developing people at a younger age with modern skills necessary in the 21st century will not only support the modern world with skilled computer scientists, but also help produce diverse teams of people capable of informing policy to regulate and measure the effectiveness of cybersecurity laws. It is imperative that we have an informed society of individuals with enough understanding of the vulnerabilities and aggressive digital capabilities of criminals to properly develop and educate others on guidelines for daily security measures, or develop effective accountability for those who engage in cybercrime activities.

REFERENCES

Akhtar, M. (2008, November 8). *What is self efficacy? Bandura's 4 sources of efficacy beliefs*. Positive Psychology. Retrieved from http://positivepsychology.org.uk/self-efficacy-definition-bandura-meaning/

Barni, D., Daioni, F., & Benefene, P. (2019, July). *Teacher's self-efficacy: The role of personal values and motivations for teaching*. Frontiers in Psychology. Retrieved from https://www.frontiersin.org/articles/10.3389/fpsyg.2019.01645/full#:~:text=Teachers'%20self%2Defficacy%2C%20namely,being %20in%20the%20working%20environment

Blakemore, E. (2015, July 15). The NSA has a summer camp for cyberspies. *Smithsonian Magazine*. Retrieved from https://www.smithsonianmag.com/smart-news/nsa-has-summer-camp-cyberspies-180955999/

Blatecky, A., Clarke, D., Cutcher-Gurshenfeld, J., Dent, D., Hipp, R., Hunsinger, A., Kuslikis, A., & Michael, L. (2021, October 3*). The missing millions: Democratizing computation and data to bridge digital divides and increase access to science for underrepresented communities.* National Science Foundation OAC. Retrieved from https://www.rti.org/publication/missing-millions/fulltext.pdf

Bossler, A. M., & Berenblum, T. (2019, November 18). Introduction: New directions in cybercrime research. *Journal of Crime and Justice, 24*(5). doi:10.1080/0735648X.2019.1692426

Brantingham, P., & Brantingham, P. (2021, January 22). Crime pattern theory. *Criminology and criminal justice: Oxford research encyclopedias.* Retrieved from https://oxfordre.com/criminology/view/10.1093/acrefore/9780190264079.001.0001/acrefore-9780190264079-e-8

Brooks, C. (2022, January 21). Cybersecurity in 2022: A fresh look at some very alarming stats. *Forbes.* https://www.forbes.com/sites/chuckbrooks/2022/01/21/cybersecurity-in-2022--a-fresh-look-at-some-very-alarming-stats/?sh=6f9527556b61

Cherry, K. (2020, July 22). *Self efficacy and why believing in yourself matters.* Verywellmind. Retrieved from https://www.verywellmind.com/what-is-self-efficacy-2795954

Cherry, K. (2022, February 14). *Maslow's hierarchy of needs.* Verywellmind. Retrieved from https://www.verywellmind.com/what-is-maslows-hierarchy-of-needs-4136760

Coble, S. (2022, April 1*). House passes better cybercrime metrics act.* Info Security Group. https://www.infosecurity-magazine.com/news/house-passes-better-cybercrime/

Cunningham, A. (2019, August 5). Why you need a password manager: Yes, you. *The New York Times.* https://www.nytimes.com/wirecutter/blog/why-you-need-a-password-manager-yes-you/

Dalton, W. (2019). *What is STEM? Pearson accelerated pathways.* Retrieved from https://pearsonaccelerated.com/blog/stem

Demand continues to rise for cybersecurity professionals. (2021, July 21). The college of computing and informatics. Drexel university. https://drexel.edu/cci/stories/cyber-security-job-outlook/#:~:text=The%20current%20cybersecurity%20job%20outlook,for%20those%20pursuing%20cybersecurity%20positions

Duffy, C. (2022, January 17). *Here's how US lawmakers could finally reign in Facebook.* CNN Business. Retrieved from https://www.cnn.com/2022/01/17/tech/meta-facebook-regulation/index.html

Fester, J., & Starkey, E. (2022, March 11). *Three reasons why PBL is an effective solution for teachers.* Edutopia. Retrieved from https://www.edutopia.org/article/3-reasons-why-pbl-effective-option-teachers

Four things you can do to keep yourself cybersafe. (n.d.). Cybersecurity and Infrastructure Security Agency (CISA). https://www.cisa.gov/4-things-you-can-do-keep-yourself-cyber-safe

Harris, A., & de Bruin, L. R. (2018). Secondary school creativity, teacher practice and STEAM education: An international study. *Journal of Educational Change*, *19*(2), 153–179. https://doi.org/10.1007/s10833-017-9311-2

Herr, D. J. C., Akbar, B., Brummet, J., Flores, S., Gordon, A., Gray, B., & Murday, J. (2019, August). Convergence education- an international perspective. *Journal of Nanoparticle Research*, *2019*(21), 229. https://doi.org/10.1007/s11051-019-4638-7

Hunter-Doniger, T. (2018). Art infusion: Ideal conditions for STEAM. *Art Education*, *2*(71), 22–27.

Jilbilian, I., & Canales, K. (2021, April 15). The US is readying sanctions against Russia over the SolarWinds cyberattack. *Business Insider*. https://www.businessinsider.com/solarwinds-hack-explained-government-agencies-cyber-security-2020-12

Korte, M. (2020, June 22). The impact of the digital revolution on human brain and behavior: Where do we stand? *Dialogues in Clinical Neuroscience*, *22*(2). https://www.ncbi.nlm.nih.gov/pmc/articles/PMC7366944/

Land, M. H. (2013). Full STEAM ahead: The benefits of integrating the arts into STEM. *Procedia Computer Science, 20*. doi:10.1016/j.procs.2013.09.317

Liao, C. (2016). From interdisciplinary to transdisciplinary: An arts-integrated approach to STEAM education. *Art Education*. Retrieved from https://draweb.njcu.edu:2068

Lopez-Garrido, G. (2020, August 9). *Self-efficacy theory*. Simply Psychology. Retrieved from https://www.simplypsychology.org/self-efficacy.html

Mfitzgerald. (2004, January 8). *Nine famous hacks*. ExtremeTech. https://www.extremetech.com/extreme/55530-nine-famous-hacks

Miniwats Marketing Group. (2022). *World Internet usage and population statistics 2022 year-Q1 estimates. Internet world stats: Usage and population*. Retrieved from https://www.internetworldstats.com/stats.htm

Nickerson, C. (2021, December 15). *Rational choice theory*. Simply Psychology. Retrieved from https://www.simplypsychology.org/rational-choice-theory.html

Osiurak, F., Navarro, J., & Reynaud, E. (2018, March 7). How our cognition shapes and is shaped by technology: A common framework for understanding human tool-use interactions in the past, present, and future. *Frontiers in Psychology*. Advance online publication. doi:10.3389/fpsyg.2018.00293

Panettieri, J. (2021, June 7). *Colonial Pipeline cyberattack: Timeline and ransomeware recovery details*. MSSP Alert. https://www.msspalert.com/cybersecurity-breaches-and-attacks/ransomware/colonial-pipeline-investigation/

Reitenbach, G. (2015). From STEM to STEAM education. *Power*, *159*(6), 6–6.

Robelen, E. (2011, December 7). STEAM Experts make case for adding the arts to STEM. *Education Week, 1*(6).

Rosenthal, M. (2022, January 12. Must-know phishing statistics: Updated 2022. *Tessian*. https://www.tessian.com/blog/phishing-statistics-2020/

Routine activity theory: Crime prevention. (2011). New South Wales department of attorney general and justice. Retrieved from https://www.crimeprevention.nsw.gov.au/Documents/routine_activity_factsheet_nov2014.pdf

Salter, N. (2019, February 27). *The importance of minority leader representation*. Ohio State University Fisher College of Business. https://fisher.osu.edu/blogs/leadreadtoday/blog/the-importance-of-minority-leader-representation

Silva, E. (2009). Measuring skills for 21st century learning. *Phi Delta Kappan, 90*(9), 630-634. doi:10.1177/003172170909000905

Thompson Reuters. (2022). *Cybercrimes*. Findlaw. https://www.findlaw.com/criminal/criminal-charges/cyber-crimes.html

UKEssays. (2018). *Applying Criminological Theories to Cyber Crime*. Retrieved from https://www.ukessays.com/essays/criminology/explaining-cybercrime-using.php?vref=1

U.S. Bureau of Labor Statistics. (2022, April 18). *Occupational outlook handbook*. U.S. Bureau of Labor Statistics. https://www.bls.gov/ooh/computer-and-information-technology/information-security-analysts.htm

Valiante, G. (n.d.). *Self-efficacy: The exercise of control: An outline composed by Gio Valiante*. Emory University. Retrieved from https://www.uky.edu/~eushe2/Pajares/effbook3.html

What we investigate: The cyber threat. (2022). Federal Bureau of Investigation. https://www.fbi.gov/investigate/cyber

Wolpert-Gawron, H. (2015, August 13). *What the heck is project based learning?* Edutopia. https://www.edutopia.org/blog/what-heck-project-based-learning-heather-wolpert-gawron

Chapter 9
The Importance of the Use of Technology in the Education of Refugee Populations in Sub-Saharan Africa in the Digital Age:
Case of Central African Refugees at Gado Badzere Refugee Camp and Possible Solutions to Education

Sedar F. Pougaza
New Jersey City University, USA & Stockton University, USA

ABSTRACT

Despite having multiple strategies to provide better education to refugee populations around the world, the use of technology to teach refugees in conflict zones in the Sub-Saharan African countries especially in the Central African Republic (CAR) remains a key challenge for many organizations and nations. The purpose of this chapter is to show how the use of technology combined with effective leadership in the education of Central African refugees at Gado Badzere refugee camp can improve learning and teaching in the digital age. The Central African Republic, considered as a war-torn nation, continues to struggle with its education. Examples of technologies acting as indispensable tools to effectively teach 21st century competencies to Central African refugees living in the low-resource community of Gado-Badzere refugee camp and possible solutions to education in the CAR are given in this chapter. The data used is from international organizations and non-governmental organizations.

DOI: 10.4018/978-1-6684-6092-4.ch009

INTRODUCTION

This chapter focuses on the use of technology in the education of refugee populations in Sub-Saharan Africa in digital age - particularly in the Central African Republic. While refugees are regrouped in specific areas, one of their basic needs which is education needs attention. This chapter helps international organizations, local governments, non-governmental organizations, educators, teachers, parents, educational technology leaders, and stakeholders to understand how technology, combined with leadership, improves learning for refugee populations and to some extent, students in developing countries. It provides sufficient background information regarding its topic because it is based on the realities of refugee populations of the Central African Republic and access to education at Gado Refugee Camp and the whole country these days. Studies by Shah et al. (2015) showed that a boost must be given to refugee education. Furthermore, Culbertson et al. (2019, p.3) concluded in their research that technology can be used in the education of refugee populations. Here, trends in situation of the Central African refugees from age 0 to 60 from 2012 to the present time are illustrated. The data used is specifically from the United Nations Educational, Scientific and Cultural Organization (UNESCO), United Nations High Commissioner for Refugees (UNHCR), the World Bank DataBank and Action Against Hunger (AAH) and Save the Children (SC). Multiple trips in the Central African Republic, conversations with the citizens, teachers, students, parents, professionals in education and stakeholders in this country, and working closely with scholars such as professor Laura Zieger and Professor Christopher Shumberg contributed to this case study. Also, conversations with refugees like Paula who is a mother of two children and used to live at Gado-Badzere refugee camp in Cameroon and decided to live near Douala, the capital city of Cameroon, so her children could have access to education confirmed that the limited and inefficient education provided at camp could be improved with the use of technology for instance digital technology.

According to Pougaza, education is one of the positive externalities of the French colonization that was imposed on the country. He also pointed out that the legal system is based on French law, as the educational system is based on the French educational system. Furthermore, he suggested that this institution has to be adapted to the realities of the Central African Republic. In the beginning, the objective was to train the elite to take over the responsibilities after the colonial administration disappeared. Few people were trained or educated leading up to independence. Following Pougaza, statistics from the United Nations Educational, Scientific and Cultural Organization (UNESCO) showed that the trend is that 37.4% of literacy (age 15 and over can read and write), secondary school enrollment was 17% (2020), and education expenditures were 1.8% of gross domestic product. The adult (15+ and both sexes) literacy rates were 71% (2006 Regional average). The youth literacy rates for 15-24 years of age for both sexes were 48.2% in 1988, 71.8% (2006 Regional average), for male 62.6% (1988), 76.8% (2006 Regional average), and for female 67.1% (2006 Regional average). There are more schools in the center of the country because of the concentration of population and political strategies. These schools mostly, private education is reserved for the rich and middle class. Currently, the challenges to education in the Central African Republic are lack of infrastructure, depreciation of infrastructure, limited use of technology at higher education, non-existence of the use of technology at K-12, lack of enhancement of the professional development of teachers, and lack of new strategies and approaches for Central African Republic's education system.

Realities of Refugee Populations of the Central African Republic and Access to Education at Gado Refugee Camp and the Whole Country

In its 2020 report titled "Stop the War on Children: Gender Matters" where it uses research from the Peace Research Institute Oslo (PRIO) and its own analysis of the United Nations' data on grave violations in 2018, the organization Save the Children Federation identified the Central African Republic as one of the ten (10) worst conflict-affected countries to be a child. It also points out that children who live in conflict zones are at the highest risk of experiencing loss of education, lacking basic resources, psychological stress, hunger and violence. Yet, the ongoing conflicts coupled with the political unrest in the Central African Republic continue to increase poverty and have a disastrous effect on its populations singularly nearly 500, 000 refugees in neighboring countries awaiting uncertain return because they have lost houses, farms, small businesses, cattle, hospitals and schools due to war or armed conflicts. This an endless nightmare.

The Central African Republic (CAR) is in Central Africa, and it has a surface area of 623,000 square kilometers with a population of 4.9 million. It has 37.4% of literacy (age 15 and over can read and write), 17% of school enrollment secondary in 2020, and education expenditures of 1.8% as part of its Gross Domestic Product (GDP). Its Human Development Index is 188 (out of 188 countries ranked). There is only one national university in CAR. The national university is called Universite de Bangui and was created in 1969. Strikes and unrest on the campus of University de Bangui are very common. The university which is supposed to be the place of peace and knowledge is very often subjected to a place of violence. Students protest because of the government does not improve their condition of study and does not pay their scholarships. Professors and administrators can decide to stop teaching and working for a long period to force the government to listen to their complains and solve their problems. The Lack of infrastructure and limited use of technology in higher education are present in the country. Students do not have fast or powerful Wi-Fi networks accessible. The use of technology is inexistent at K-12. In some areas of the country, students seat on ground in a classroom of big capacity with only one teacher (case of Ecole Damala Direction Filles, for instance). Some schools in the capital (example of Ecole de N'Dres and lycée d'État des Rapides) in the capital city experiencing decay (depreciation) and lack of good teachers.

The CAR has been among the ten most under-reported humanitarian crises for five years in a row. According to United Nations High Commissioner for Refugees (UNHCR), there are more than 500, 000 refugees from the Central African Republic at Gado Badzere refugee camp in Cameroon located in the west of the Central African Republic. Children are among these refugees who escaped from the Central African Republic civil war. Children fleet with their parents the countrysides of the northwest of the country around Bouar where the rebels attack very often. The charts below constructed with data from UNCHR show the trends of the Central African refugees in Cameroon from 2012 to the present time in 2021 and the reality that the Central African Republic has more refugees in Cameroon than Nigeria and Chad.

Figure 1. Central African refugees in Cameroon from 2012 to 2019

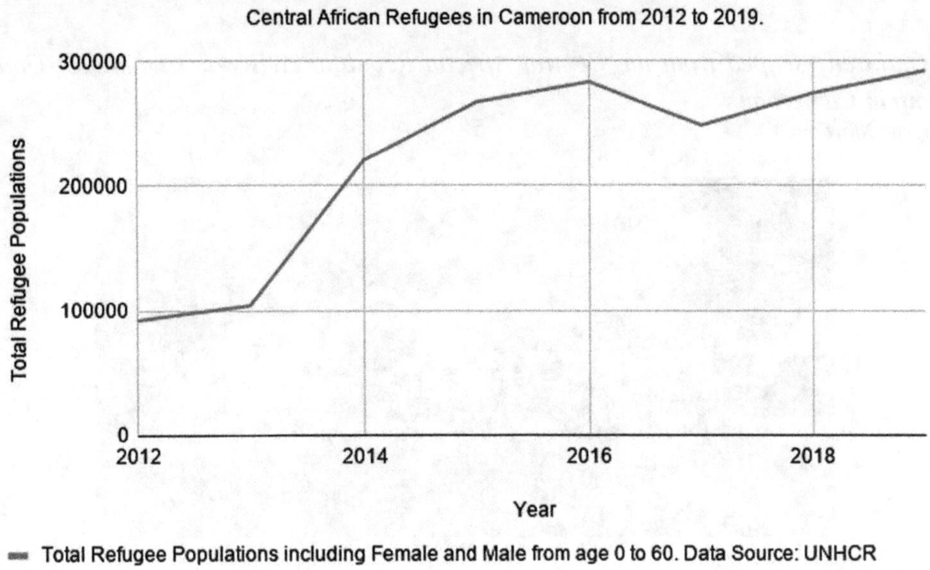

Figure 2. Refugees in Cameroon as of 2/28/2021.
Data source: UNHCR, the UN Refugee Agency

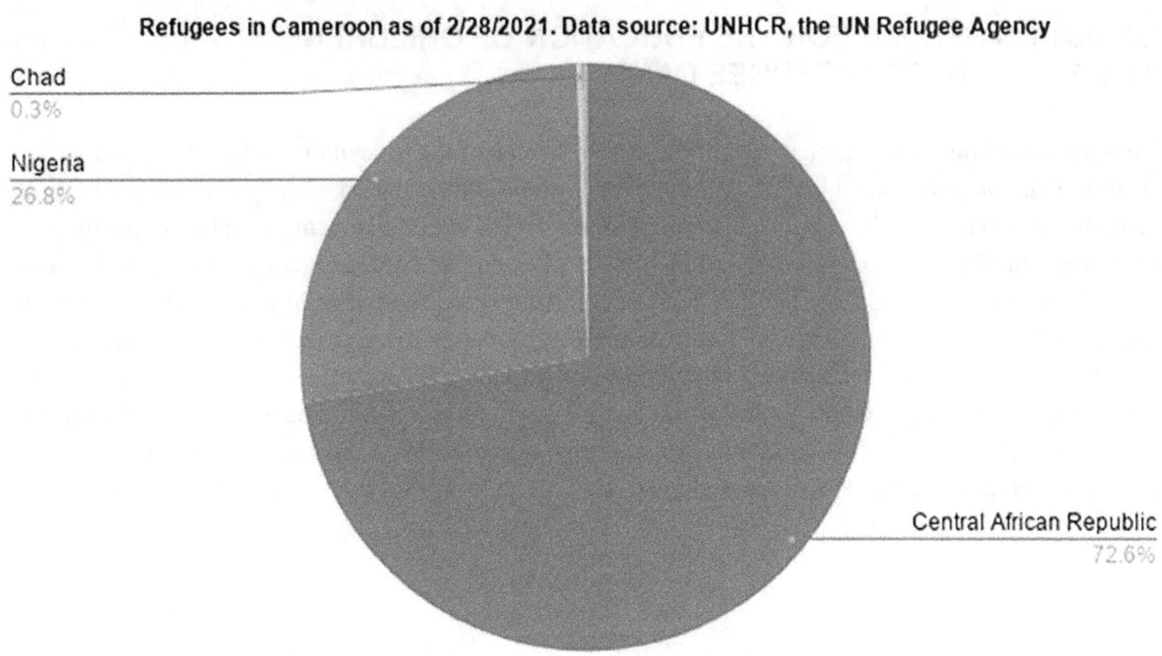

United Nations aid agencies are struggling to meet the needs of Central African refugees in Gado refugee camp. A tent as shown in the picture below, was built at Gado Badzere camp in Cameroon to provide basic education to children escaped from the Central African Republic civil war.

Figure 3. Children escaped from the Central African Republic civil war studying at Gado Badzere refugee camp in Cameroon.
(Photo by Eugene Nforngwa).

Since the population of the Gado Badzere refugee camp has exploded from just 1,000 refugees in January to 25,000 today, there is a need to create a conducive environment for the children in Gado Badzere refugee camp to learn and instructors to continue provide education.

LOGISTICS NEEDED FOR THE EDUCATION OF CHILDREN AT GADO BADZERE REFUGEE CAMP

Non-governmental organizational organizations have been helping to revitalize refugee education (Shah et. al. 2015). The government in the Central African Republic should work closely with the international community to have prefabricated container classrooms with social distancing installed close the army checkpoint in Gado Badzere refugee camp particularly and the conflict zone in the Central African Republic in general to educate k-12 students by offering them fundamental skills and competencies necessary for them to cope with the rapid changes in globalization and technological advancements of the twenty-first century. Changing the methods of providing education to Central African refugees at Gado Badzere refugee camp regarding the change in paradigms will be beneficial in improving the quality and relevance of education for those refugee populations. With the coronavirus situation and its impacts on education, digital resources aligned to a curriculum should be used to continue learning at Gado Badzere refugee camp.

RELEVANCE OF TECHNOLOGY FOR LEARNING AND TEACHING AT GADO BADZERE REFUGEE CAMP AND POSSIBLE SOLUTIONS TO EDUCATION IN THE CENTRAL AFRICAN REPUBLIC

Research shows that there are multiple ways in which technology can be used in the refugee context for example providing internet connectivity and access, supporting communication with family and friends, providing education and employment opportunities, facilitating distribution of housing and other resources, and providing a record of information about a displaced person's identity (Culbertson et. al. 2019). In the case of Gado Badzere refugee camp, the school supplies for the use of technology in the education of the Central African refugees are tablets, laptop computers, smartphones, solar charger and computer applications in French and English languages to be installed on tablets, smartphones and laptop computers. With connectivity to internet, Central African refugees can also use these technologies to communicate with family and friends while getting education. According to Culbertson et. al., refugees place a high value on internet and mobile connectivity for the reasons of keeping in touch with family and friends, maintaining documentation regarding their identity and experiences, and access information and support. The use of technology for education purposes is the most important in the case of Central African refugees at Gado Badzere refugee camp.

The digital learning tools that can be used to provide learning to Central African refugees at Gado Badzere refugee camp are as follows: African Storybook (ASb), which focuses on literacy with reading materials that are free for download, translation in multiple languages and use. ASb contains storybooks that are engaging, colorful and more relevant to the student's lives and experiences. With this ASb, teachers with some minimum training can help students at Gado Badzere refugee camp who cannot effectively work independently to use Kolibri offline learning system and do reading practice with digital books in kolibri on daily basis. Another tool to make high quality education technology available in low-resource community of Gado Badzere refugee camp with limited or no access to the internet is Aflatoun. Its content can be uploaded on a Raspeberry Pi device and any device that receives a Wifi signal. It has various digital products for children, young people, teachers and organizations to overcome the challenges of modern teaching, improve learning and create engaging materials. Aflatoun is also a digital financial education for children and youth with its online-offline tablet, online zoom and teams laptop, offline PC, free basics online-offline smart phone and online-offline games. The online-offline games allow for the use of gamification that incorporates simulation with a game to effectively teach Central African refugees resilience, team work, creativity and core competencies that refugee populations will need to succeed in the current century. Duolingo is another technological tool that can be used in the education of Central African refugees at Gado Badzere camp to teach languages such as English, academic French and basic Spanish. It is a free application-based language instruction that can be installed on tablets and cellphones. Virtual reality technology can be used to improve teaching in the Central African Republic because education is another area where virtual reality (VR) has been adopted for teaching and learning situations. Virtual Reality (VR) is the use of computer modelling and simulations which help a person in interacting with artificial 3D environment that shows reality with help of some interactive devices worn in form of googles, headsets, gloves or body suits which can send and receive information (Gandhi et al. 2018). VR is able to present complex data in an accessible way to students in the Central African Republic (CAR) which is both easy to learn and have fun. The advantage of the VR is that it enables large groups of students to interact with each other as well as within a three dimensional environment. VR environment is implemented for teaching aid such as in virtual classroom, virtual library and virtual lab. Also these students can interact with the objects in that environment to discover more about them because they feel "immersed" (plunged, absorbed or engaged) in the virtual world as if they are in the virtual world itself as all they can watch is their rendered movements (movements sent in) in virtual environment.

In one year, the knowledge of students in learning these digital learning tools will greatly improve because Rind et. Al. in their empirical study to evaluate the impact of Introduction of Smart Technology and Learning (INSTAL) project on students' academic performance in terms of students' science scores have found that students' science scores improved by 10% in one year and 23% in two years with the use of Information and Communication Technologies (ICT) -based facilities under INSTAL (Rind et. Al. 2022, December 6).

With the rapid changes in globalization and technological advancements of the twenty-first century, what are the possible solutions for improving education in the Central African Republic?

The CAR needs to develop a long-term school infrastructure construction plan. For example, every year on the state budget, 10 classrooms are built in such a way as to reduce the pupil-to-room ratio to an acceptable level. In addition, it has to lower student-teacher ratios (lower number of students for every teacher in a school). Furthermore, it has to invest in the improvement of teacher quality and enhancement of the professional development of teachers by following these steps: First, testing the level of K-12 teachers and civil servants from 2022 to separate those who the quality deemed acceptable from others. Second, reaching out to those who do not have a qualification by subjecting them to selective training of varying duration (four years for elementary teachers, three years for high school and college teachers) in order to fish out those that the current system has made unproductive. Finally, laying off those who did not hold to the end of this training by paying them all the benefits. This solution applies also to educational advisers, leaders and supervisors after year 2022.

In the short term, implement a mandatory training for the new civil servants on pedagogy so they can work for two years in K-12 before entering job in their fields. The country should embrace the "training as needed" approach. This could be done through the fact that the department of education and the labor department should work closely so as to train each year only teachers who will be immediately integrated. The training could end in June and in July the teacher completes all the administrative formalities and then in September he/she returns to his/her teaching position. If there is no need in a field of study (subject of French for instance) with considerable number of teachers already trained, it is necessary to suspend the training of teachers in this field of study for a few years. There is also the need to increase the level and quality of training at Ecole Normale Superieure (ENS), Ecole Nationale d'Instituteurs (ENI) and Centre Pedagogiques Regionaux (CPR). The teachers are in majority low qualified. Their selection must be made throughout a training process without any complacency of favoritism. The department of education should exclude the one who does not have the minimum acceptable level and make the one who does not the average grade repeat the training. Another important aspect is to strengthen the monitoring and evaluation mechanism by taking action to ban apparent teacher evaluations by an evaluator where the teacher to be evaluated offers rotisserie chicken and drink (such as wine or beer) to the evaluator or pedagogical advisor to be awarded a higher grade and good evaluation. This practice must be punished with the rigor, if necessary, create a secret service or watchdog for education. Teachers with poor performance should be fired and the good ones should receive good pay and even raise. A competition should be created to stimulate cost and quality consciousness so private and public schools must be able to take pride in their high-quality work. The Central African Republic should make the teaching profession attractive. To do this, several approaches could be considered. Here are some of them: First, either the State increases the salaries (wages) of K-12 and Higher Education teachers. Either the State decides that elementary teachers enter the public service directly with a fairly high index scale and not as a trainee. Next, redefine the career plan of teachers by leaving exit doors that is to say, under certain conditions, lay off the teachers after a few years of practice (to be defined) by reserving a quota for them during judicial tests to train them to be civil administrators, etc. Additionally, encourage gender equality in hiring process by making teaching more attractive to bright women. Furthermore, the country should facilitate collective bargaining so teachers can bargain collectively and have good pensions.

CONCLUSION

Education is the future of the Central African Republic and its economy. This chapter shows the importance of a solid foundation of technology use in the education of Central African refugees at Gado refugee camp. All the technologies mentioned above will improve learning and teaching at Gado Badzere refugee camp and by extension education in the Central African Republic. Combined with an effective leadership, these selected technologies will help in closing or avoiding the gaps in education that are hard to catch up in the Central African Republic affected by armed conflicts, civil war and political unrest despite its numerous natural and mineral resources and its young population. The computer applications could be used to provide Central African refugees at Gado Badzere camp with the four broad twenty-first century competencies such as digital literacy (Basic, scientific, economic, and technological literacies. Visual and information literacies. Multicultural literacy and global awareness), inventive thinking (Adaptability, managing complexity, and self-direction. Curiosity, creativity, and risk taking. Higher order thinking and sound reasoning), effective communication (Teaming, collaboration, and interpersonal skills. Personal, social, and civic responsibility. Interactive communication), and high productivity (Prioritizing, planning, and managing for results. Effective use of real-world tools. Ability to produce relevant, high-quality products) by taking into account the realities of the Central African refugees, the global pandemic and considering the help of international community, non-profit organizations and local government working side by side in this digital age. This case study is also a part of the agenda for future research consisting on exploring the implementation of emerging technologies (Virtual Reality technology, for instance) to enhance learning and teaching and also improve performance at the workplace at this era where virtual learning is more required. Government in the Central African Republic should subsidize the supply of education by making direct payment to public schools and indirect payment to private schools in the form a targeted tax cut.

REFERENCES

Action Against Hunger. (2021). *Central African Republic. Human Development Index.* Central African Republic I Hunger Relief in Africa I Action Against Hunger.

Aflatoun International. (2021, January 7). *Digital Learning.* Digital Learning.

Bourgois, X. (2021, January 19). *Thousands of Central Africans seek refuge in Cameroon.* UNHCR The UN Refugee Agency. https://www.unhcr.org/en-us/news/latest/2021/1/6006a3fc4/thousands-central-africans-seek-refuge-cameroon.html

Culbertson, S., Dimarogonas, J., Costello, K., & Lanna, S. (2019). *Crossing the Digital Divide: Applying Technology to the Global Refugee Crisis*. RAND Corporation Provides Objective Research Services and Public Policy Analysis I RAND. https://www.rand.org/content/dam/rand/pubs/research_reports/RR4300/RR4322/RAND_RR4322.pdf

Duolingo. (n.d.). *Learn a language for free. Forever.* https://www.duolingo.com/

France 24. (2021, January 27). Haut-Commissariat pour les Refugies, Camp de Gado. *Violences en Cengtrafrique: alerte a la frontiere camerounaise.* https://youtu.be/fSa2GDXJ_jU

Gandhi, R. D., & Patel, D. S. (2018). Virtual reality - Opportunities and Challenges. *International Journal for Research in Applied Science and Engineering Technology, 5*(1), 482-489. www.irjet.net

Kindzeka, M. (2017, October) *Many More Refugees Flee CAR Violence to Cameroon.* https://www.voanews.com/africa/many-more-refugees-flee-car-violence-cameroon

Pougaza, S. (2008). *Essay on Transformational Growth in the Central African Republic from its independence to the present time.* Published by Academia.

Reimers, F., & Chung. (2016). *Teaching and learning for the twenty-first century: Educational goals, policies, and curricula from six nations.* Harvard University Press.

Rind, A. A., Asad, M. M., Marri, S. A., Sherwani, F., & Rehman, F. U. (2022, December 6). How Integration of information and communication technologies impact academic achievement? An empirical study on Sindh education foundation. *Journal of Applied Research in Higher Education, 14*(4), 1761–1772. doi:10.1108/JARHE-05-2021-0177

Save the Children. (2021). *2020 report, Stop the War on Children: Gender Matters.* https://www.savethechildren.org/us/charity-stories/10-worst-conflict-affected-countries-to-be-a-child

Shah, R., & Lopes Cardozo, M. (2015). Chapter 11: The politics of education in emergencies and conflicts. In T. McCowan & E. Unterhalter (Eds.), *Education and international development: An introduction* (pp. 181-200). Bloomsbury. https://www.africanstorybook.org/

The World Bank Group. (2018). *Country Profile. Central African Republic.* worldbank.org

The World Bank Group. (2021, March 19). *DataBank World Development Indicators (WDI). Central African Republic.* https://databank.worldbank.org/reports.aspx?source=2&country=CAF#

UN Refugee Agency. (2020, April 6). How to ensure everyone can continue learning amid the coronavirus situation. In *Connected education: resources, considerations & guidance.* UNHCR. https://www.unhcr.org/en-us/5e787bea

UNCHR. (2021a, January 19). *Central Africans Fleeing post-election insecurity cross into Cameroon. Since December, nearly 5,000 Central Africans have crossed into Cameroon.* https://www.youtube.com/watch?v=KNQBNCFjVtI

UNCHR. (2021b, January 30). *Central African Republic situation*. Author.

UNHCR. (n.d.). *The UN Refugee Agency (2001-2021). Refugee Data Finder*. https://www.unhcr.org/refugstatistics/download/?url=LwOoL9

Chapter 10
Computational Thinking, 21st Century Skills, and Robotics

Carol Munn
https://orcid.org/0000-0003-2320-4252
New Jersey City University, USA

ABSTRACT

This chapter explores a unique framework that conveys engagement and innovation with diverse learning experiences focusing on the implementation of computational thinking and 21st century skills as essential elements in a robotics education program. Engineering design applications with robots create an atmosphere in which students apply abstract mathematics and science concepts. The robot and its technology immersed in the field of education create excitement in the minds of children by giving them powerful hands-on tools stretching across the science, technology, engineering, and mathematics (STEM) fields. The combination of robotics education and computational thinking skills unlocks creative and innovative sparks through fun and engaging hands-on activities. Robots provide a fascinating powerful learning opportunity that reinforces 21st-century skills in tech-savvy language familiar to today's students.

INTRODUCTION

Computational thinking is an essential skill for the 21st century learner, but is seemingly underdeveloped within the standards of the education system. "Computational thinking (CT) is a transversal and complex competence that goes beyond the use of computers and writing code. It is considered an ideal medium for the development of 21st-century skills" (Acevedo-Borrega et al., 2022, p. 1). Critical thinking, collaboration, communication, and creativity linked with problem-solving creates an extensive toolkit for engagement for all in the classroom. Computational thinking skills are molded in many different and diverse forms and can be applied to all areas of computer literacy. The computer literacy environment unfolds the understanding and application attributed to computational thinking. Nicoletti and Suemasu (2021) stated,

DOI: 10.4018/978-1-6684-6092-4.ch010

The cultural assimilation of the computer presence will give rise to computer literacy. This phrase is often taken as meaning knowing how to program or knowing about the varied uses made of computers. But true computer literacy is not just knowing how to make use of computers and computational ideas. It is knowing when it is appropriate to do so. (p.1)

Using analytic and algorithmic concepts and strategies, computational thinking is related to computer literacy with strengths in formulating, analyzing, and solving problems. The aim is to establish a channel for students to enhance their ability to formulate questions, articulate answers, and solve problems. According to Witherspoon et al. (2017), computational thinking brings to the classroom exciting and innovative activities, including robotics, through hands-on application platforms not only in the science and mathematics curriculum, but also in language arts, visual arts, social studies, foreign language and more. Within the past few years, the momentum of computational thinking integration within the K-12 education system is slowly extending and infiltrating across the STEM fields, in which the computational thinking skillset gap is quite evident at the intermediate school level (Computer Science Teachers Association [CSTA], 2017; Grover & Pea, 2013).

The educational field places the essence of the computer combined with abstract innovation to drive understanding and engagement in the power of thinking. Hence, big ideas emerge and explode through innovative disruptive paradigms to turnkey the status quo in future-drive classrooms. According to Papert (1993), "You can't think seriously about thinking without thinking about thinking about something" (p. 10). In society, a natural human method of understanding is thinking something through, from start to finish. Kordaki and Kakavas (2017) explained that a specific way of thinking reverts to the relationship between abstraction and the orderly process of algorithmic problem-solving, which contribute either directly or indirectly to the learner mastering skills involved with computational thinking. It is all about making computing cool and abstractions coming alive.

COMPUTATIONAL THINKING

Jeanette Wing, a forerunner in the field of computer science, promoted computational thinking in 2006 as a fundamental and operational stepping stone in human analytical skill and thought process as it relates to computer science and all professional fields. Fields such as engineering, medicine, manufacturing, education, finance, health science, and cybersecurity, utilize some form of computational thinking every day. With that ideology, Wing (2006) described computational thinking in terms of (a) abstraction, (b) decomposition, (c) system analysis, and (d) modularity to include more abstract ideology specifications. Within her research studies, Wing (2006) realized that focusing just on the mathematical aspects of solving problems was not sufficient, whereas within the computational thinking structure there was an intersection between logical thinking and systems thinking, allowing for the mixing of many other thought processes such as "compositional reasoning, pattern matching procedural thinking, and recursive thinking" (p. 1). Computational thinking was instrumental in formulating the framework evident by reconstructing, rethinking, and addressing the mental process of inquiry into solving all types of real-world problems (Lee et al., 2014).

Beside the contours of solving real-world problems, students' engagement, interactivity, and passion are part of the active learners' mindset, which absorbs new and innovative methods of digital literacy education. According to Wing (2017), "Computational thinking is the new literacy of the 21st century"

(p. 3) and computational thinking is defined as "the thought processes involved in formulating a problem and expressing its solution(s) in such a way that a computer-human or machine-can effectively carry out" (p. 8). With the direction of computational thinking expanding into other educational fields, Wing (2017) redefined and adjusted her description to include the "deeper thought process as a mental activity in formulating a problem to admit a computational solution" (p. 8) and can be carried out by a human or machine.

Computational thinking ideology revolves around complexities, patterns, and the telling of a story. It is human nature to tell stories and, in computational thinking world, the student stories provide further evidence thorough patterns and real-world connections (Patton, 2015). The individual stories saturate the overarching utilization and relationship between computational thinking and robots in hands-on classroom activities, providing the way for 21st century learner skillset to grow in education system. Recent studies indicate that computational thinking is no longer a single skill taught in the computer science field (V. Barr & Stephenson, 2011; Nicoletti & Suemasu, 2021; Shute et al., 2017; Wing, 2006). Many academic fields now incorporate computational thinking skills, noting their value in promoting critical thinking skills, whether in technology, science, mathematics, language arts, history, art, or other curricular fields. Computational thinking is a set of skills that materializes in cross-curricular academic areas. For example, in Spanish class, a computational thinking lesson would have students identify word patterns and structures in Spanish. Next, the students would compare the results to the English version and further explain the similarities and differences to a classmate. In computer science, a computational thinking lesson manages an unplugged or nontechnology hands-on coding activity that can easily translate to a robot carrying out a task.

Computational Thinking Model

Computational thinking is segmented into four steps involving a process to establish a solution to a problem. Computational thinking is a logical and sequential method starting with a problem and then breaking it down into smaller, manageable components. Each step is connected or linked in some way within the four pillars of computational thinking: decomposition, pattern recognition, abstraction, and algorithm design. Thus, formulating a structure for teamwork activities in alliance with computational thinking to break down the problem into four steps creates a problem formulation that involves logical reasoning and visual notation to promote effective learning.

Each step is specifically defined to work together as a process to complete and solve problems. The decomposition steps entail the breaking down of a problem into smaller and more manageable pieces for the students to understand and work on. Pattern recognition is the method or way the student observes the patterns, similarities, and trends in the given information or data. Abstraction is an important step in identifying the basic ideas which create the patterns. Algorithm design is the sequential, step-by-step process and instructions which lead to the solution for the problem.

Like Resnick and Robinson (2017), Grover and Pea (2013), Ortiz et al. (2015) asserted that computational thinking is the 21st century literacy and can be implemented and sustained at all ages and disciplines in education. The core set of skills includes algorithm design, sequential process, collaboration, creativity, critical thinking, and innovation all built-in with hands-on activities. The authentic learning process lends itself and contributes to the students' hands-on experiences in the classroom and then to problem-solving in the real world.

According to Piaget, "Discovery learning—the idea that children learn best through doing and actively exploring—was seen as central to the transformation of the primary school curriculum" (McLeod, 2018, p. 10). Papert (2000) stipulated, "The sense of power comes here from being able to solve well-known or self-generated problems, puzzles, and paradoxes from personal knowledge using very general techniques that are all part of what I call 'technological fluency'" (p. 8). Papert's (2000) big idea framework connects the freedom to creatively think and apply learned knowledge within the classroom and boils over to the real-world. Computational thinking embodies the learning and methodology delivered through hands-on discovery learning and can be differentiated at the same time, paving the way for all students to be able to participate and apply learned skills and knowledge in all aspects of life.

21st Century Learner

Computational thinking poses a strong ideology based on problem-solving equally conveying an essential position with a target to establish a channel for 21st century learners through their ability to formulate questions, articulate answers, and solve problems in cross-curricular classroom activities. Computational thinking becomes a key component in the skillset necessary for the 21st century learner. As a backbone of sequential processes, computational thinking evolves into everyday real-world solutions to problems. Papert (1993) stated that computers process data in well-defined sequential steps. Just like computers handle data instruction, students engaged in problem-solving are using skills that are key elements within the computational thinking framework; the processing and analyzing of data in a series of steps.

The key processes necessary for 21st century learners are (a) systems thinking, (b) programming mindset, (c) active learning, (d) mathematics, (e) science, (f) judgment and decision-making, (g) good communication, (h) technology design, (i) complex problem solving, and (j) persistence (Kim et al., 2019); along with engagement, fun, and excitement. Computational thinking skills develop through creative play stand out as a methodology that helps inspire students to find meaning in doing and learning, experimentation, minds on thinking, hypothesis testing, and social interaction.

Computational thinking poses new quests and opportunities to interest today's learners in the classroom by implementing different technologies. "Solving problems, designing systems, and understanding human behavior by drawing on the concepts fundamental to computer science" (Wing, 2006, p. 33). With the increasing attention on the early stages of education, there is an exciting opportunity in today's school-level curriculum for the joining of the 21st century learner and computational thinking through a hands-on activity such as robotics. As this opportunity takes shape in education, computational thinking and robotics can help shape and support the education of children by developing their skills around logic, creativity, and problem-solving.

Computational Thinking: The 5th "C" of 21st Century Skills

In a recent article, "The 5th 'C' of 21st Century Skills? Try Computational Thinking (Not Coding)," Shuchi Grover (2018) addressed computational thinking as the "5th C" as part of the emerging skillsets that young students should be exposed to during their education. Grover reflected a need for "another core skill" (para. 4) in the classroom teaching toolkit for teachers in preparing students for the 21st century global world. According to Grover, "Computational thinking is not about how to use technology; rather, it lifts the hood on how digital solutions are designed using computational tools" (para. 21). With the hands-on activity, children can experience computational thinking and engineering processes which conduct an object to perform a certain way to accomplish a task.

In the study "Computational Thinking and Tinkering: Exploration of an Early Childhood Robotics Curriculum," Bers et al. (2014) provided evidence that children at an early age can understand and follow through on several different parts of "robotics, programming, and computational thinking" (p. 145). In this study, Bers et al. initiated the ideology of computational thinking and children's hands-on activities in the classroom. Throughout the program, students kept detailed daily journals which captured their experiences in real time and allowed them to go back and revise, reflect, and identify strength and weaknesses. Analysis of the student journals demonstrated progress in the development of these students' computational thinking and a correlation between successful collaborative work and a deeper understanding and proficiency in the application of key components of computational thinking (Bers et al., 2014). Wing (2017) described the ideology of computational thinking as "reformulating a seemingly difficult problem into one we know how to solve, perhaps by reduction, embedding, transformation, or simulation . . . using abstraction and decomposition when attacking a large complex task or designing a large complex system" (p. 33).

Computational Thinking in the Classroom

Today's teachers are challenged with covering the curriculum while meeting the unique demands of developing critical thinkers. Educators need to acquire knowledge and an understanding and classroom tools and lessons on how to foster and energize their classroom while utilizing computational thinking and engineering design. These processes can be fostered through hands-on applications with a robot. Wing (2008) stated, "I envision that computational thinking will be instrumental to discovery and innovation in all fields of endeavor" (p. 5).

In its true form, computational thinking is packed with diverse and engaging multiple open opportunities embracing all areas in the educational community. The classroom voice or creative chatter takes over and removes barriers with the remixing of knowledge pieces and skills essential for success within the chosen engaging platform. Opening the communication methods between teacher and student, as well as between student and student, can ultimately capture the spirit of one's own voice and build the collaboration and communication skills pertinent to the community and workplace. This process also touches on the leadership skills and confidence needed to solve problems and have meaning in life; all of which come full circle within computational thinking and the 21st century skill set.

According to Francis and Davis (2018), robots are powerful instruments to advocate for mathematics and problem-solving in today's classroom. Leading the way for this emersion are multiple student-understanding skills such as critical thinking, problem-solving, computational thinking, and creativity. Students are engaged no matter the results of their solution—correct or incorrect—driving their curiosity and insight into the mathematical applications and coherent spin-offs. This experience reiterates that computational thinking involves multifaceted areas such as arithmetic, coding, and logic representations.

According to Korkmaz (2016), programming with LEGO Mindstorms EV3 is an example of a "complex and abstract process" (p. 1) that leads to the education and application of a coding program involving the robot energizing the human creative and algorithmic design to solve problems through mindful thought processes. Korkmaz also revealed that students understand and grasp the ideas behind logical and sequential mathematical thinking skills, including solving real-world problems. The value helps to uncover the tools of creativity and critical thinking in the field of managing information. In addition, Korkmaz found the LEGO Mindstorms EV3 design activities maintained a positive involvement and influence in directing students to problem-solve. Computational thinking activities provide a lasting educational experience based on nontraditional teaching activities, and the EV3 programming is conducive to problem-solving skills (Korkmaz, 2016).

The level of involvement in computational thinking starts with the abstraction process which Wing (2017) claimed is the key component to carrying out and implementing the involved computational thinking skillset and is relevant to all students. Computational thinking is an essential core element within computer science education (Henderson et al., 2007), thus providing learners with hands-on opportunities to exhibit creativity, demonstrate sequential processes, and collaborate with peers. The three key dimensions of computational thinking are (a) computational concepts, (b) computational practices, and (c) computational perspectives (Brennan & Resnick, 2012, p. 1). The four pillars of computational thinking include (a) decomposition, or the breaking down of a complex problem into smaller, more manageable parts; (b) pattern recognition, or looking for similarities; (c) abstraction, or focusing on the important information only; and (d) algorithms, or developing a step-by-step solution to the problem (Wing, 2006, pp. 33–34).

Computational thinking power in the classroom comes in different forms such as "abstraction, recursion, and iteration, to process and analyze of data, and to create real and virtual artifacts" (V. Barr & Stephenson, 2011, p. 4). The artifacts can provide insight into the thinking process, the comfort level of trial and error, learning by doing, and figuring things out which are key concepts for students to digest and produce a workable solution to a problem. For example, students involved in an activity are more likely to use key computational thinking concepts; and the evidence appears as students talking to other students and using computational thinking-related vocabulary such as sequences, inputs, outputs, line detection, degrees, angles, move forward, looping, saved value, friction, and motion. Another interesting and important computational thinking skill is an observation by peers in the classroom that the students understand there is more than one way to come up with a solution, and flexibility ties in with the entire process. These concepts reestablish the constructionism theory and opportunities for students to move forward in their learning.

Computational Thinking and Robotics

According to Wing's (2017) revised definition of computational thinking, "Computational thinking is the thought processes involved in formulating a problem and expressing its solution(s) in such a way that a computer—human or machine—can effectively carry out" (p. 8). Computational thinking activities provide a lasting educational experience based on nontraditional teaching activities, and the EV3 programming is conducive to problem-solving skills (Korkmaz, 2016). Korkmaz (2016) suggested that programming with LEGO Mindstorms EV3 is an example of a "complex and abstract process" (p. 1), leading to the education and application of a coding program involving the robot energizing the human creative and algorithmic design to solve problems through mindful thought processes. The study revealed that students understand and grasp the ideas behind logical and sequential mathematical thinking skills including solving real-world problems (Korkmaz, 2016). The value helps to uncover the tools of creativity and critical thinking in the field of managing information. In addition, the LEGO Mindstorms EV3 design activities maintained a positive involvement and influence in directing students to problem-solve (Korkmaz, 2016).

Computational thinking and robotics create a special partnership that exposes unity with strong practical hands-on approaches to learning in the classroom. Recently, this partnership has been gaining ground as an energizing approach to the natural human instinct of computation providing a theoretical framework and foundation encompassing meaningful and essential practices for mastery by the students (Weintrop et al., 2016).

Robots and their diverse applications can be the driving, engaging resource in creating a new force for infusing computational thinking skills within a classroom. Introducing robotics education provides a viable opportunity to pursue within a curriculum. As a learning tool, robots primarily engage students in activities that use visual block-based coding to perform simple or complex tasks (Barker et al., 2012). Robotics education can provide a focus on the measurement of transferrable computational thinking skills in intermediate and middle school robotics (Koh et al., 2013; Lin, 2015). With elements of innovation, creativity, and collaboration, robotics education acts as a viable and exciting means of engaging digitally literate students.

Papert (1993) referred to education, computers, and computer culture as providing "new opportunities for imagination and creativity" (p. 37) and formulating a climate for computational thinking activities involving computers and robots. Both peripherals have the potential to interlock all these fields with engaging hands-on activities which provide and foster computational thinking in keeping with stimuli of innovation (Alimisis, 2013). Expressed in terms of an all-in-one technological learning tool, computational thinking and robotics programs enhance the hands-on applications which engage and drive the student's thinking process with engaging and enlightening activities which crisscross the entire curriculum (Eguchi, 2014, p. 34).

An earlier attempt to define computational thinking was constructed by Seymour Papert (1980). According to the Logo Foundation (n.d.), Papert, identified as the "father of LOGO" (para. 4) programming (computerized educational programming system), described computational thinking in terms of a fundamental human experience powerful enough to tie everyday real-life experiences with conceptual, computational procedures. As the root of computational thinking, LOGO developer Daniel G. Bobrow detailed computational thinking as an operational and fundamental guide to help students in the process of critically thinking within the mathematics forum and solving problems (L'Amoreaux, 2019; Logo Foundation, n.d.; Papert, 1980). The LOGO programming reinforced the shifting of computer applications with a "new conceptual framework for thinking" (Papert, 1980, p. 184). Later, Papert (1996) expanded on the concept by re-empowering critical thinking and systematic strategies as an accelerant for solving problems.

Computational thinking and robotics programming utilize a specialized visual language that relies on easily recognized images which initiate a response by sparking an interest that advances into powerful inspiration, problem-solving, and collaboration. Martin (2016) reported, "Computational thinking has its core interest in thinking in multiple levels of abstraction and conceptualization . . . it is being seen at the center of learning in math, science, and engineering" (p. 24). In keeping with the curriculum areas, Hutchison et al. (2016) stated that the area of language arts literacy and programming is an "evolving form of literature" (p. 493) in attaining a core set of computational thinking skills, leading to the augmentation of communication outlets between different and diverse learning skills within an environment conducive to the education field.

Robots promote a playful learning environment in which students can be free to create, re-construct, imagine, and obtain various levels of abstraction and decomposition in the classroom (Barker et al., 2012). "Using robotics introduces students to emerging and innovative technological creations, as well as encouraging their participation in the act of making, which, in turn, nurtures them to become active creators rather than consumers of technological products in the future" (Eguchi, 2014, p. 30).

ROBOTICS IN THE CLASSROOM

A robot is an automatic device (machine) that performs a difficult task, by way of an intricate strand of commands through a computer program. Robotics education provides a learning environment or playground to promote socioemotional skills of engagement, collaboration, communication, and teamwork (Bers, 2008). The educational robotics programs are referred to as "all-in-one technological learning tools" (Eguchi, 2014, p. 34) that intermix the hands-on applications that drive the focus back to the student with engaging and enlightening activities which crisscross the entire curriculum. Repurposing robots as a teaching tool for computational thinking creates vibrant and engaging "learning hubs" and "centers of change" (Teich, 2019, para. 1).

According to Resnick and Robinson (2017), LEGO Mindstorms robotics "remixing is aligned with our core values of openness and creativity" (p. 103). Resnick (2018) illustrated scenarios in which students are involved in hands-on activities from building, coding, and executing the designed program on a robotic unit to fit the classroom activity. The association between building the LEGO EV3 robot and programming constitutes an alliance rich in creativity and computational thinking illuminating a powerful voice in the world of education. The robotics education platform represents a real, concrete, physical, and tangible option that allows students to comprehend the learning processes such as abstraction, construction, and evaluation (Resnick & Robinson, 2017). In another study, Chaudhary et al. (2016) provided data based on the infusion of robotics and programming, characteristics consistent with the technology-based groundwork consisting of lessons and activities which foster teamwork as well as problem-solving, creativity, collaboration, and project management.

Robots and their technology, such as coding, provide a fluid vehicle and an excellent opportunity for the tech-savvy 21st century learner to attain a solution for a real-world simulated engineering problem. Each robot maintains and expresses specific mannerisms and within each unit, there is a rationale derived as an asset in classroom applications (Ntemngwa & Oliver, 2018). Each with a unique characteristic to inspire curiosity and imagination while increasing the methodology of the 21st century learner. There is an exciting gateway created through computational thinking. Robotics can help shape and support the education of children by developing skills around logic, creativity, and problem-solving. Robotics, along with its programming applications, create an "iterative exploration" of computational thinking's four key elements (Grover & Pea, 2013, p. 40). Successful integration involving computational skills and robotics (coding applications) in the classroom, joining with authentic connections make key strides in the educational initiatives within computer literacy (Ottenbreit-Leftwich & Yadav, 2021).

21st Century Learner

Computational thinking entails a strong ideology based on problem-solving, equally conveying an essential position in cross-curricular classroom activities. As such, computational thinking becomes a key component in the skillset necessary for the 21st century learner. As a backbone of sequential processes, computational thinking evolves into everyday real-world solutions to problems. Papert (1993) stated that computers process data in well-defined sequential steps. Just like computers handle data instruction, students engaged in problem-solving are using skills that are key elements within the computational thinking framework; the processing and analyzing of data in a series of steps. Likely, the emphasis being placed on computing abilities within emerging and global education environments, computational thinking competency is considered a fundamental skillset to establish a channel for 21st century learners to enhance their ability to formulate questions, articulate answers, and solve problems.

The key processes necessary for 21st century learners are (a) systems thinking, (b) programming mindset, (c) active learning, (d) mathematics, (e) science, (f) judgment and decision-making, (g) good communication, (h) technology design, (i) complex problem solving, and (j) persistence (Kim et al., 2019). Along with these skills, engagement, fun, and excitement are essential elements involved in any classroom project in conjunction with the participants' understanding and experiences when using robotics. The thought of computational thinking connecting with robots as creative play in the classroom stands out as a methodology that helps students experience joy, meaning in doing and learning, experimentation, minds-on thinking, hypothesis testing, and social interaction.

The robotics curriculum focuses on the 21st century learner by providing hands-on learning, tinkering, and learning-by-doing, including problem-solving, sequential applications, and fundamental engineering concepts as innovative and engaging experiences (Scaradozzi et al., 2015). These experiences build the skills that are necessary for the students and create "playful learning" (Bers, 2008, p. 1) experiences for engaging students in a younger age group. Included in this exploration is a "gateway for helping children learn about mathematical concepts" (Bers, 2008, p. 3) and revitalizes classroom instruction to include all learners. Schools are utilizing robotics as a concrete physical tool in hands-on activities within the context of the specific academic domain. Computational thinking and robotics can aid in identifying and exploring deeper cognitive thinking techniques within the minds of younger students.

Computational thinking poses new quests and opportunities to draw interest in today's learners in the classroom by implementing different technologies, encompassing "solving problems, designing systems, and understanding human behavior by drawing on the concepts fundamental to computer science" (Wing, 2006, p. 33). With the increasing attention on the early stages of education, there is an exciting opportunity in today's school-level curriculum for the joining of the learner to robots and computational thinking. Alden and Tramonti (2020) stated, "Educational robotics and STEM do constitute a suitable framework for the development of these specific skills" (p. 1). As this opportunity takes shape in education, computational thinking and robotics can help shape and support the education of children by developing their skills around logic, creativity, and problem-solving.

The education curriculum has taken a positive turn by driving attention to the addition of robotics education and computational thinking skills with new and invigorating hands-on, creative classroom activities and lessons. Curriculum initiatives need to move forward and not stay with past stagnate technology applications in the classroom. In recent years, robotics education has been gaining speed and momentum, becoming an essential part of a school's curriculum (Francis & Davis, 2018). Subsequently, the educational framework has taken on a new configuration for students to engage as "better thinkers" by combining robots and computational thinking skills such as a sequential and abstract perception of a proposed real-world problem within the classroom (Resnick & Robinson, 2017, p. 48). A cohesive bonding of computational thinking and robotics education can effectively redirect the school curriculum to embrace these 21st century applications for the 21st century learner and the future global workforce.

Constructionism and 21st Century Skills

As the 21st century classroom emerges, Papert's (1993) theory of constructionism takes on a new light with the union of computational thinking and robotics. The connections are created to invoke thinking and learning as erecting knowledge construction in a way that allows the free flow of creative ideas following through the educational context of developing and learning. There are four pillars to constructionism: (a) learning by doing; (b) objection recognition, or supporting the development of ways of thinking and learning about abstract phenomena; (c) powerful ideas, and (d) self-reflection (Bers, 2012, p. 4). These four pillars can be expanded into the cross-cutting theoretical framework, which connects computational thinking and robotics education through diverse hands-on classroom activities.

Children think differently than adults do; their minds are open with no constraints or predetermined assumptions, putting cognitive skills, creativeness, and behaviors in motion to lead to discoveries and "big ideas" (Papert, 2000). Along with the hands-on and learning-by-making (constructionism), Papert (1993) referenced and refined the creativity of children's natural curiosity as an adventure that opens the mental activities leading the way to computational thinking. Interactivity, engagement, and passion navigate the students of today to the mindfulness of active learners in the new century of digital education. Children's innate inquisitiveness for exploring and playing is bursting with borderless ideas immersed in thinking and tinkering. "Seymour focused on how, as a child, he fell in love with gears, and that love for a material changed his self-perception and allowed him to become more interested in learning about math, science, and engineering" (Ryan, 2017, para. 3).

The "builder" in a child evolved from "Piagetian Learning" which described children as "doing without being taught," through the natural process of curiosity and exploration without boundaries or limitations (Papert, 1993, p. 7). In the transition from concepts and ideas to products and solutions, providing children with materials to physically build or code present a unique and valuable opportunity to take the lead and search out various resources, including tangible manipulatives to engage in the logical and sequential thinking of computational thinking. With constructivism as a background to constructionism, "constructionism states that children learn better when making their projects, constructing their ideas, and designing their solutions to problems . . . providing tools for children to playfully design their own objects to think with" (Bers, 2012, p. 14; Bers, 2008; Kafai & Resnick 1996).

Additionally, constructionism, as it progresses in a classroom, inspires children to become inventors, designers, and programmers and promotes and encourages peer learning by engaging and exploring engineering, science, and other fields of study. All are leading toward computational thinking concepts and skills associated with the construction paradigm of ideas and thoughts to craft human knowledge into the design and evaluation of problems and solutions which are part of everyone's brain (Bers, 2012, p. 14). Creating various opportunities for children to develop their ideas and projects, substantiating the validity of constructionism; computers are power tools combined with other peripherals, such as robots, to provide robust and playful opportunities to foster the designing and constructing ideas.

Accordingly, Papert (1993) stated that once children are involved in this activity, there is an upsurge in engagement and exploration, which lends itself to complex and multifaceted outcomes reflecting their thought processes and solutions. This process authenticates the finding from Bers (2012), in which children become "creators of interactive content, as opposed to consumers of information" (p. 15). Children are absorbed in the action of learning by doing, playing, investigating, and uncovering their thought processes with various applications and platforms regarded as computational thinking and problem-solving (Papert, 1993). According to both D. Barr et al. (2011) and Wing (2006), students who were exposed in the early stages of education to computational thinking skills possess advanced processing skills over those of students who have not been exposed earlier on to those skills. The student is the central player in constructionism, applying hands-on activities which revolve around the self-directed learning cycle to support meaningful methods of reshaping and restructuring through the mindful thought process. The process encourages the mind to dig further into the thinking process, analyze it, and make decisions based on the gathered information. Critical exploration and encouragement of self-expression create insights into "how children are seeing the problem" which prompts meaningful exchanges of ideas and thoughts to help in solving issues (Barker et al., 2012, p. 12).

In the classroom, digital tools, including robots, have found their place among the basic classroom tools and instruments. Bers (2008) referred to the tools as an intellectual way of thinking and connecting the "powerful ideas" described by Papert (1993) as a continuum of mixing new and old ideas creating new possibilities to disperse knowledge. Adding to the excitement and inquisitiveness of today's digital learners, the education phenomenon of computational thinking and robots enlivens the regular daily classroom events. Transformation to this digital technology connects knowledge-based activities to various skills such as "critical thinking, problem-solving, creativity, strategizing, and originality" (Bates, 2016, p. 18). From concept to hands-on knowledge-based activities, computational thinking skills restructure learning and applications throughout the students' lifetime to include, "how to find, evaluate, analyze, apply and disseminate information, within a particular context" (Bates, 2016, p. 19). Continuing with the constructionist philosophy, hands-on application learning and robots address social skills such as collaboration, communication, frustration, and anxiety to provide an authentic real-world learning experience in a safe-zone environment.

FUTURE DIRECTIONS

The opportunity, spontaneity, and unpredictability in absorbing critical 21st century skills are evident within the limitless computational thinking framework available in today's classroom to enable the power of imagination and curiosity of children to investigate and create the unknown. This framework advances the restructuring of today's education system to integrate computational thinking into the classroom and provide students with the opportunity to interact with a familiar and disruptive tool, the robot. Creating controlled chaos invoking the energy of disruption as it may seem, students are fascinated and completely mesmerized by the opportunity to learn and understand containing spur-of-the-moment, unpredictable, and random actions provided by robotics. Exposing students to computational thinking skillset in relation to computer science education at a younger age is a major viable solution that can entice the interest and the imagination of our young future scientists. Curriculum adjustments should include more tinkering, figuring out how things work, and exploring the real-world activities for all. In doing so, these computational thinking-enriched, hands-on activities attract today's 21st century learner in taking part in becoming young computer scientist, roboticists, programmers, engineers, web designers, and coders.

Concurrently, computational thinking and robotics can be fine-tuned to include vastly low- to high-grade, hands-on applications and create innovative waves within the pre-K–12 education field. Computational thinking activities create forward momentum in the classroom and provide outlets for the emerging and innovative ideology which students today will need to understand and apply in the real world. The culmination of thinking and sequential writing is the basis for innovative approaches in the classroom. No matter what role a robot takes on in the classroom technology curriculum as a tool, peer, or tutor, make no mistake the interactive teaching methodology can provide the opportunity to move forward in all areas of the education system.

Lastly, computational thinking through the lens of a child lends itself to a playground of creativity, imagination, and the wonder of play. With the addition of the playful instrument of the robot, the future-driven classroom is alive with engaging, exciting, and limitless learning opportunities for all students. The curiosity and sense of innovation motivate the digital learner and feed upon the natural sense of exploring new and exciting ideas and challenges. A student's passion and interest spark an innovative and creative thinking process with purpose, exploration, determination, tinkering, and imagination driving students closer to the solution. Seen through the naked eye of the child, no boundaries exist with limitless opportunities to move like synchronized gears in motion, making connections, developing critical thinking skills, and igniting curiosity to go beyond and venture into the inquisitive thought patterns that promote 21st century skills.

REFERENCES

Acevedo-Borrega, J., Valverde-Berrocoso, J., & Garrido-Arroyo, M. del C. (2022). Computational thinking and educational technology: A scoping review of the literature. *Education Sciences*, *12*(1), 39. doi:10.3390/educsci12010039

Alden, D., & Tramonti, M. (2020). Computational design thinking and physical computing: Preliminary observations of a pilot study. *Robotics*, *9*(3), 71. doi:10.3390/robotics9030071

Alimisis, D. (2013). Educational robotics: Open questions and new challenges. *Themes in Science & Technology Education, 6*(1), 63–71. https://files.eric.ed.gov/fulltext/EJ1130924.pdf

Barker, B. S., Nugent, G., Grandgenett, N., & Adamchuk, V. I. (2012). *Robots in K-12 education: A new technology for learning*. IGI Global. doi:10.4018/978-1-4666-0182-6

Barr, D., Harrison, J., & Conery, L. (2011). Computational thinking: A digital age skill for everyone. *Learning and Leading with Technology*, *38*(6), 20–23. https://files.eric.ed.gov/fulltext/EJ918910.pdf

Barr, V., & Stephenson, C. (2011). Bringing computational thinking to K-12: What is involved and what is the role of the computer science education community? *ACM Inroads*, *2*(1), 48–54. doi:10.1145/1929887.1929905

Bates, T. (2016). *Teaching in a digital age: Guidelines for designing teaching and learning* (1st ed.). SFU Document Solutions.

Bers, M. U. (2008). *Blocks to robots: Learning with technology in the early childhood classroom*. Teachers College Press.

Bers, M. U. (2010). The TangibleK robotics program: Applied computational thinking for young children. *Early Childhood Research & Practice*, *12*(2). https://files.eric.ed.gov/fulltext/EJ910910.pdf

Bers, M. U. (2012). *Designing digital experiences for positive youth development: From playpen to playground*. Oxford University Press. doi:10.1093/acprof:oso/9780199757022.001.0001

Bers, M. U. (2018). *Coding as a playground: Programming and computational thinking in the early childhood classroom*. Routledge.

Bers, M. U., Flannery, L., Kazakoff, E. R., & Sullivan, A. (2014). Computational thinking and tinkering: Exploration of an early childhood robotics curriculum. *Computers & Education*, *72*, 145–157. doi:10.1016/j.compedu.2013.10.020

Brennan, K., & Resnick, M. (2012). *New frameworks for studying and assessing the development of computational thinking* [Paper presentation]. The Annual Meeting of the American Educational Research Association. https://web.media.mit.edu/~kbrennan/files/Brennan_Resnick_AERA2012_CT.pdf

Chaudhary, V., Agrawal, V., & Sureka, A. (2016). *An experimental study on the learning outcome of teaching elementary level children using Lego Mindstorms EV3 robotics education kit*. https://arxiv.org/pdf/1610.09610.pdf

Computer Science Teachers Association. (2017). *CSTA K-12 computer science standards, revised 2017*. https://www.csteachers.org/page/about-csta-s-k-12-nbsp-standards

Eguchi, A. (2014, July). Robotics as a learning tool for educational transformation. In *Proceedings of the 4th International Workshop Teaching Robotics, Teaching With Robotics, 5th International Conference Robotics in Education* (pp. 27–34). https://www.terecop.eu/TRTWR-RIE2014/files/00_WFr1/00_WFr1_04.pdf

Francis, K., & Davis, B. (2018). Coding robots as a source of instantiations for arithmetic. digital experiences in mathematics education. *Digital Experiences in Mathematics Education*, *4*(2-3), 71–86. doi:10.100740751-018-0042-7

Grover, S. (2018, February 25). *The 5th "C" of 21st century skills? Try computational thinking (not coding)*. https://www.edsurge.com/news/2018-02-25-the-5th-c-of-21st-century-skills-try-computational-thinking-not-coding?

Grover, S., & Pea, R. (2013). Computational thinking in K–12: A review of the state of the field. *Educational Researcher*, *42*(1), 38–43. doi:10.3102/0013189X12463051

Henderson, P. B., Cortina, T. J., Wing, J. M., & Hazzan, O. (2007, March). Computational thinking. *ACM SIGCSE Bulletin*, *39*(1), 195–196. doi:10.1145/1227310.1227378

Hutchison, A., Nadolny, L., & Estapa, A. (2016). Using coding apps to support literacy instruction and develop coding literacy. *The Reading Teacher*, *69*(5), 493–503. doi:10.1002/trtr.1440

Jawawi, D., Jamal, N., Abdul Halim, S., Sa'adon, N., Mamat, R., Isa, M., Mohamad, R., & Abdull Hamed, H. (2022). Nurturing secondary school student computational thinking through educational robotics. *International Journal of Emerging Technologies in Learning*, *17*(3), 117–128. https://www.learntechlib.org/p/220514/. doi:10.3991/ijet.v17i03.27311

Kafai, Y. B., & Resnick, M. (1996). *Constructionism in practice: Designing, thinking, and learning in a digital world*. Erlbaum.

Kim, S., Raza, M., & Seidman, E. (2019). Improving 21st-century teaching skills: The key to effective 21st-century learners. *Research in Comparative and International Education, 14*(1), 99–117. doi:10.1177/1745499919829214

Koh, K. H., Repenning, A., Nickerson, H., Endo, Y., & Motter, P. (2013, March). Will it stick? Exploring the sustainability of computational thinking education through game design. In *SIGCES '13: Proceeding of the 44th ACM technical symposium on computer science education* (pp. 597–602). 10.1145/2445196.2445372

Kordaki, M., & Kakavas, P. (2017, July). *Digital storytelling as an effective framework for the development of computational thinking skills* [Paper presentation]. *The International Conference on Education and New Learning Technologies*, Barcelona, Spain. 10.21125/edulearn.2017.2435

Korkmaz, Ö. (2016). The effect of Scratch- and LEGO Mindstorms EV3-based programming activities on academic achievement, problem-solving skills, and logical mathematical thinking skills of students. *Malaysian Online Journal of Educational Sciences, 4*(3), 73–88. https://files.eric.ed.gov/fulltext/EJ1106444.pdf

L'Amoreaux, C. (2019, February 1). *Who is Seymour Papert (and why does it matter)?* https://www.claudialamoreaux.com/who-is-seymour-papert-and-why-does-it-matter/

Lee, I., Martin, F., & Apone, K. (2014). Integrating computational thinking across the K–8 curriculum. *ACM Inroads, 5*(4), 64–71. doi:10.1145/2684721.2684736

Lin, V. (2015). *Computational thinking and technology toys* [Unpublished undergraduate thesis]. Wellesley College. https://repository.wellesley.edu/thesiscollection/307

Logo Foundation. (n.d.). *Logo resources: Archive*. https://el.media.mit.edu/logo-foundation/ resources/archive.html

Martin, S. (2016). *A descriptive and explorative case study of a scratch programming experience involving the creation of a lunar simulation/model with grade six learners* [Unpublished master's thesis]. University of Calgary. doi:10.11575/PRISM/24707

McLeod, S. A. (2018, June 6). *Jean Piaget's theory of cognitive development.* https://www.simplypsychology.org/piaget.html

Nicoletti, M. D. C., & Suemasu, E. (2021). Thoughts on computational thinking. *Academia Letters. Article, 1045*. Advance online publication. doi:10.20935/AL1045.5

Ntemngwa, C., & Oliver, J. S. (2018). The implementation of integrated science technology, engineering, and mathematics (STEM) instruction using robotics in the middle school science classroom. *International Journal of Education in Mathematics, Science and Technology, 6*(1), 12–40. http://dergipark.ulakbim.gov.tr/ijemst/article/view/5000195373/5000183562 doi:10.18404/ijemst.380617

Ortiz, A. M., Bos, B., & Smith, S. (2015). The power of educational robotics as an integrated STEM learning experience in teacher preparation programs. *Journal of College Science Teaching*, *44*(5), 42–47. doi:10.2505/4/jcst15_044_05_42

Ottenbreit-Leftwich, A., & Yadav, A. (2021). *Computational thinking in preK-5: Empirical evidence for integration and future directions*. ACM and the Robin Hood Learning + Technology Fund. https://www.acm.org/binaries/content/assets/education/ct_prek-5_web.pdf

Papert, S. (1980). *Mindstorms: Children, computers, and powerful ideas* (1st ed.). Basic Books.

Papert, S. (1993). *Mindstorms: Children, computers, and powerful ideas* (2nd ed.). Basic Books.

Papert, S. (1996). An exploration in the space of mathematics educations. *International Journal of Computers for Mathematical Learning*, *1*(1), 95–123. doi:10.1007/BF00191473

Papert, S. (2000). What's the big idea? Toward a pedagogy of idea power. *IBM Systems Journal*, *29*(3 & 4), 720–729. doi:10.1147j.393.0720

Patton, M. Q. (2015). Qualitative research & evaluation methods: Integrating theory and practice. *Sage (Atlanta, Ga.).*

Piaget, J. (1954). *The construction of reality in the child.* Basic Books. doi:10.1037/11168-000

Resnick, M. (2018, September 16). *Computational fluency*. https://medium.com/@mres/computational-fluency-776143c8d725

Resnick, M., & Robinson, K. (2017). *Lifelong kindergarten: Cultivating creativity through projects, passion, peers, and play*. The MIT Press. doi:10.7551/mitpress/11017.001.0001

Ryan. (2017, February). Tinkering about thinking about Seymour. *Exploratorium*. https://www.exploratorium.edu/tinkering/blog/24?page=56

Scaradozzi, D., Sorbi, L., Pedale, A., Valzano, M., & Vergine, C. (2015). Teaching robotics at the primary school: An innovative approach. *Procedia: Social and Behavioral Sciences*, *174*, 3838–3846. doi:10.1016/j.sbspro.2015.01.1122

Shute, V., Sun, C., & Asbell-Clarke, J. (2017). Demystifying computational thinking. *Educational Research Review*, *22*, 1–18. doi:10.1016/j.edurev.2017.09.003

Teich, A. G. (2019). *Repurposing school libraries as vibrant hubs and centers of change*. https://www.techlearning.com/resources/repurposing-school-libraries-as-vibrant-hubs-and-centers-of-change

Weintrop, D., Beheshti, E., Horn, M., Orton, K., Jona, K., Trouille, L., & Wilensky, U. (2016). Defining computational thinking for mathematics and science classrooms. *Journal of Science Education and Technology*, *25*(1), 127–147. doi:10.100710956-015-9581-5

Wing, J. M. (2006). Computational thinking. *Communications of the ACM*, *49*(3), 33–35. doi:10.1145/1118178.1118215

Wing, J. M. (2008). Computational thinking and thinking about computing. *Philosophical Transactions of the Royal Society A: Mathematical, physical, and engineering sciences, 366*(1881), 3717–3725. doi:10.1098/rsta.2008.0118

Wing, J. M. (2017). Computational thinking's influence on research and education for all. *Italian Journal of Educational Technology*, *25*(2), 7–14. doi:10.17471/2499-4324/922

Witherspoon, E. B., Hugashi, R., Schunn, C., Baehr, E., & Shoop, R. (2017). Developing computational thinking through a virtual robotics programming curriculum. *ACM Transactions on Computing Education*, *18*(1), 1–20. doi:10.1145/3104982

Chapter 11
Using Hybrid Gamification to Build Community and Self-Efficacy Among Diverse University STEM Students

Karen J. Cotter
New Jersey City University, USA

ABSTRACT

Technology is all around us and has become ubiquitous in everyday life. Today's Generation Z college students are the first coeds who have never lived without technology. It is incorporated throughout their day and in a plethora of ways in college campuses. Many professional STEM jobs go unfilled annually, especially by diverse individuals. Many underserved, first-generation, African American, Latinx, and female students arrive on campus with disadvantages that create barriers to success. Increasing the number of STEM graduates to fill these jobs requires innovative ways to support and retain these underserved students. STEM Bridge programs across the country use various strategies to engage, retain, and graduate STEM majors. This chapter presents research on the unique use of hybrid gamification as an educational technology strategy, in a Bridge STEM program, to foster a sense of community and self-efficacy to support STEM majors as they persist to a STEM degree.

INTRODUCTION

Today's Generation Z university population has never lived without technology. "They are also digital natives who have little or no memory of the world as it existed before smartphones" (Parker & Igielnik, 2020). In the not-too-distant past, stereotypical images of 18-year-old boys in dorm rooms surrounded by gaming consoles come to mind when people think of individuals who spend a lot of time using technology or gaming. While younger men (18–29) make up an extremely large share of the people who do engage with video games (gamers) (Brown, 2017; Pew Research, 2019), today's gamer is not that stereotype. Today's gamer includes the seasoned lawyer buying coffee, the harried parent buying groceries, and

DOI: 10.4018/978-1-6684-6092-4.ch011

the university student. While many college-age students, mostly male, may identify as gamers, there are more than 5 billion people worldwide who call, text, tweet, browse, shop, or play games on their mobile devices (Kumar, 2017). People who have access to technology often have a range of platforms from which to choose, including gaming consoles, computers, tablets, watches, and the device most people carry with them everywhere: the mobile phone.

Currently, half of the time spent gaming on the internet occurs on mobile devices, an increase from 27% in 2013 (Gough, 2019). The use of gamification, the integration of game-like elements woven into routine tasks (Deterding, 2011), permeates even the most common areas of our lives (Erenli, 2013) and can motivate users/gamers to engage with these apps. Companies offer promotions and rewards for ordinary, daily activities. When consumers earn points toward a free coffee with the Starbucks app or when they receive grocery store coupons from their local store app, they are more likely to continue supporting these brands and are often motivated to continue engaging with that app to level up and earn more rewards. Additionally, easy access to technology on one's mobile devices, and the plethora of apps for games, entertainment, and communication, or learning can make a gamer of anyone with access to technology.

Using a mobile device for daily activities is not the only way gamification has impacted people's lives. Gaming is used to connect, engage, and interact with acquaintances, friends, and family, as well as strangers. Immediate access to multiplayer games such as *League of Legends, Fortnite,* or *Minecraft* encourages interactions that promote engagement with these groups. These connections also allow for strangers from diverse communities throughout the world to make connections. Face-to-face (F2F) gatherings once limited by proximity and size of a location can now be accessed via technology. Since COVID we have seen these venues (Zoom, Google Meet, etc.) open these once limited get-togethers to potentially hundreds of people all over the globe. These types of gatherings were once beyond the reach of most people. The opportunities to connect outside a physical neighborhood, workspace, community, or has become limitless.

Subsequently, the use of mobile devices is an obvious tool to engage this population of Gen Z students. The potential to build a sense of community and self-efficacy using their phones may support their persistence to a STEM degree. Additionally, the use of both F2F and hands-on STEM activities may allow for students to manifest creativity and collaboration while working with their peers. It has been shown that teamwork motivates students to complete the task at hand and allows them to be involved in a creative and meaningful scientific process (Estrada et al., 2016). Interaction within a peer group also fosters and builds a sense of belonging and that promotes a sense of community and self-efficacy (Bandura, 1986; Kuchynka et al., 2019; McMillan & Chavez, 1986). The use of a hybrid gamification model seeks to foster this sense of community and self-efficacy.

Participation in activities that use gamification has shown to increase persistence among college STEM students (Graham et al., 2013). Research specifically focused on the importance of community suggests that the social nature of gamified activities may support a students' sense of community and belonging which may contribute to increased self-efficacy (Alvarez & Oliveria-Smith, 2013; Gilliam et al., 2017; Thiry, 2017; Whittaker & Montgomery, 2012). Part of Bandura's (1994) social cognitive theory states that the resolve to persevere comes from social modeling, or seeing peers succeed. As students engage in community-based activities their self-efficacy, the confidence in one's own abilities, may also contribute to a persistence toward attaining a STEM degree (Gilliam et al., 2017; J. J. Lee & Hammer, 2011; Marczewski, 2013; McGonigal, 2011a).

The use of gamified orientation has been shown to increase retention and persistence among the STEM Success Academy students since its inception in May 2017 (Brown, 2017; Vanyi, 2018). How then might the use of this hybrid gamification model impact sense of community and self-efficacy for diverse, underserved over a 10-week period? The author implemented a hybrid gamification strategy over a 10-week period using the *Social Scavenger* game app and five F2F STEM activities throughout the STEM bridge program. The gamified orientation model was extended throughout the program to support an increased sense of community and self-efficacy ultimately impacting improved retention.

THEORETICAL APPROACHES SUPPORTING GAMIFICATION TO DEVELOP SENSE OF COMMUNITY AND SELF-EFFICACY

Self-Efficacy: Core Construct of the Social Cognitive Theory

Purposefully blending students' independent learning experiences with team collaboration using gamification may help to foster a sense of community among the diverse, underserved STEM students (Soldner et al., 2012). As feelings of belonging grow within the community, self-efficacy can be affected. Perceived self-efficacy, or "people's belief about their capabilities to produce designated levels of performance that exercise influence over events that affect their lives" is part of Bandura's (1994, p. 2) social cognitive theory.

A person's belief that challenges are not insurmountable but are instead opportunities to learn is a tenet of self-efficacy. A strong sense of self-efficacy is important when faced with challenging situations. This is particularly applicable to STEM students. A STEM major will take many demanding courses in pursuit of their degree. The ability to work through obstacles with the confidence that challenges can be overcome and knowing how to face challenge are tenets of self-efficacy.

Similarly, Dweck's (2006) mindset theory describe a person having a growth mindset or a fixed mindset. Someone with a fixed mindset believes that this is a mindset you are born with. If a task is too hard someone with a fixed mindset mentality believes that there is a lack of a skill and will give up easily. The belief is that they are good at something or not, and that potential is predetermined and unalterable. Someone with a growth mindset believes challenges foster growth. This person likes to try new thing, understands that feedback is constructive, and that there is room for progress and hard work will foster development (Dweck, 2006). Understanding self-efficacy in this context helps students to realize that self-efficacy can be developed.

Bandura's (1986) social cognitive theory illustrates a three-prong ecological approach that include, personal factors (persistence), environmental influences (sense of community) and behavior (self-efficacy) (Figure 1). This model when looked at along side Dweck's (2006) Mindset Theory may help to illustrate the dynamic and flexible nature how interactions between peers may contribute to a student's sense of self-efficacy and persistence as it related to the environment they are engaged with.

Figure 1. Social Cognitive Theory (Self-Efficacy) – Mindset Relationship
Note. From Social Cognitive Theory, by A. Bandura, 1986

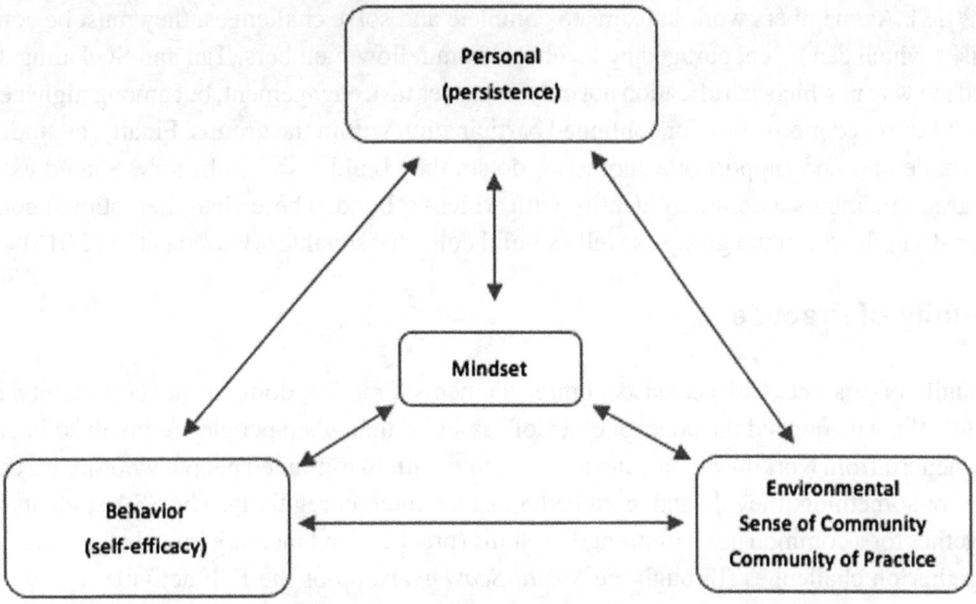

With these two theories in mind, the potential impact of gamification on student's sense of community (environmental influences) and self-efficacy (behavior) may relate to a student's alteration in persistence (personal). By introducing gamification into the environment (community), both personal factors (persistence) and behavior (self-efficacy) may be impacted.

Sense of Community

A sense of belonging is a basic human need. Once basic human physiological needs (food, water, air) and safety needs are met, the sense of belonging or love must be addressed to enable humans to be receptive to other, higher needs such as self-esteem (Maslow, 1981). Vygotsky (1980) noted the integral relationship of social interaction in the development of cognitive growth as part of a constructivist worldview. The importance of membership in a community plays a significant role in the creation of a sense of belonging. This process of membership and participation in a community helps develop students' perceptions of self-efficacy.

McMillan & Chavis (1986, p. 9) define sense of community as "the feeling that members have of belonging, the feeling that the members matter to one another and to the group, and a shared faith that their needs will be met through their commitment to be together." There are four components that contribute to a sense of community: (a) membership, (b) influence, (c) integration, and (d) fulfilment of needs through shared emotional connection. Membership reflects investment in the group with a right to belong because the requirements of membership have been met. The SSA students must meet the requirements of the program (apply and be accepted) to become a part of this group.

When feelings of emotional safety and belonging are generated, individuals may feel empowered to participate more actively and to influence fellow group members. The shared experiences foster understanding of others' needs, values, and opinions. Members tend to take risks to lead, support, and work to complete challenges with their teams. Social support from peers creates a strong sense of community (Baker, 2013). As members work in teams to complete and solve challenges, they must be comfortable taking risks which can be encouraged by feedback from fellow members. Tan and Sockalingam (2015) presented the way in which gamification not only improves task engagement, but among higher education students, it improved motivation for continued participation within the groups. Finally, as students work through challenges and support one another to do so, they build a shared history. Shared experiences provide group members a common identity with which to bond. These shared emotional connections can foster strength within the group as well as build collectivist values (Estrada et al., 2016)

Community of Practice

A community of practice (CoP) consists of three elements: practice, domain, and community. Lave and Wenger (1991), who created the concept of a CoP, asserted that when people are involved in communities, they benefit from working among and participating with like-minded people who share a concern or a passion for something; they do and learn better as they interact regularly. The SSA students willingly come together for a common goal: to strengthen skills (practice) and increase knowledge. When students work together on challenges (through the *Social Scavenger* app or the F2F activities) they work as a community of practice (Andrade & de Carvalho, 2015; Lave & Wenger, 1991). The shared domain of interest is the attainment of a STEM degree. Each member comes to the STEM community with different levels of expertise and understanding. As challenges are faced, each community member contributes their specific expertise, so they learn from each other. As the group successfully completes challenges, the sense of belonging grows stronger and supports deeper interactions among group members. SSA students work together on their mobile devices and F2F to problem solve, coordinate, and get information to practice skills based on STEM content. Additionally, social presence, motivation, and collaboration combine to create a healthy community of practice (Andrade & de Carvalho, 2015).

Theory of Gamified Learning

Most of the research about gamification focuses on the effect it has (or does not have) on learning in the classroom. The theory of gamified learning provides a two-fold process for student learning opportunities (Landers, 2015). While this theory does not specifically address gamification as it relates to a sense of community and self-efficacy it does relate the two processes of this theory that support these additional components.

Landers (2015) stated that "gamification can target a behavior or attitude that we already know affects learning and that makes existing instruction more effective" (para. 7). This theory offers a framework to scaffold both the building of a student's sense of community as well as to increase intrinsic motivation and self-efficacy through gamification (Banfield & Wilkerson, 2014; Hazan et al., 2018). The awareness of the student's sense of community and self-efficacy is identified before the addition of the gamification. The outcome is then measured to determine the extent to which gamification strengthened or causally affected behavior or attitudes as they related to students' sense of community and self-efficacy (Landers & Landers, 2015).

The use of the *Social Scavenger* mobile app over a 10-week period set forth to encourage team members to engage with one another and help to engage in three distinct areas: 1) to foster a sense of community among individual team members and the SSA group at large 2) to engage with campus resources 3) participate in STEM and STEM-related activities. Engaging with the *Social Scavenger* app challenges were not only an individual activity but also intended to encourage interactions among team members and across teams. Gamification for this program was not meant to impact specific learning outcomes but add elements designed to engage students in the overall program and as such, encourage teammates to persist ultimately foster increased student engagement (Arnold, 2014; Dennis et al., 2005; Hamari et al., 2014).

Gamification is not meant to replace high-quality instruction, but the addition of gamified elements, a kind of experiential learning (Kolb, 1984) that may increase student engagement in an otherwise routine learning experience (Banfield & Wilkerson, 2014; Landers, 2015). The challenges on the *Social Scavenger* app motivates students to participate through elements of gameplay: rules, goals, voluntary participation, and feedback (Arnold, 2014; McGonigal, 2011a) as do the F2F STEM challenges. Students engaged in all these elements participated individually and with peers as they participated in tasks throughout the SSA. As students become more engaged, they encourage team members to participate. Through ongoing gamification, whether through the *Social Scavenger* app activities or the F2F team STEM challenges, the building of a community is cultivated (Dewey, 1928; de Santana et al., 2016).

Landers (2015) presented several psychological theories that connect gamification and its principles to learner engagement as it builds a sense of community and self-efficacy among peers. The theory of gamified learning targets changes in behavior and/or attitude that make learning more effective to the conditioning, or the creation, of a positive association to the beneficial activity. Expectancy theory ties gamification to the impact on human motivation. Increasing intrinsic motivation through gamification can improve student self-efficacy (Banfield & Wilkerson, 2014). Play theory supports the concept that games are powerful contributors to human happiness and motivation. Goal-setting theory which incorporates specific, measurable, attainable, relevant, and timely (SMART) goals. All these theories integrate facets of what is engaging and enjoyable about gaming: goals, rules, voluntary participation, and feedback (McGonigal, 2011a; Vygotsky, 1980).

Whether the SSA students are interacting with their team through the *Social Scavenger* app or challenging other teams during the F2F team STEM challenges, students experience opportunities to develop a sense of community with their teams and the larger cohort of STEM students. The frequent mobile collaboration, as well as the regular F2F meetings, cultivate a sense of community. Continuous and consistent opportunities to collaborate with a community of peers impacts self-efficacy through support and encouragement and allows students an opportunity to observe and practice persistence. The belief that they can complete the challenges and encourage their teammates to do the same will serve to build self-efficacy, persistence, and a sense of community among the STEM students.

PATHWAYS AND BARRIERS TO PERSISTENCE AMONG DIVERSE, UNDERSERVED STEM STUDENTS

STEM Bridge Programs and Gateway Support Programs

The need to support diverse, underserved students as they embark on challenging STEM majors continues to be an important focus for of higher education. Especially if they strive to contribute to a more diverse STEM workforce. There are a range of bridge programs that endeavor to support these students in several different ways. Similar in many ways, each seeks to support diverse, underrepresented STEM students in one of three ways: (a) transition from high school to college, (b) transfer student assimilation or (c) transition from college freshman to sophomore year. Bridge programs can also vary in other ways 1) the diversity of students accepted 2) length of programs and the kinds of programs offered. Most of the programs vary in timeframe and can run from five days to 10 weeks. 3) Some take place only during the summer and others are offered throughout the year. Positive attitudinal changes are evident in short programs as well as longer programs. The bridge programs help to improve students' sense of belonging and encourage relationship-building among peers who share the similar goal of persistence to a STEM degree (Ashley et al., 2107).

Many of these programs are geared toward supporting a range of diverse students which include diverse, underserved racial-ethnic minorities, females, both highly academically prepared and/or academically underprepared students, as well as several unspecified students. A summary of 30 different STEM bridge programs over a period of 25 years was compiled to understand the different offerings among these programs (Ashley et al., 2017). Programs include research opportunities, mentorships, peer support, academic assistance, career counseling, and occasions to develop close-knit cohorts. Among the many differing programs 14 specific goals are structured into three general categories 1) academic success, 2) psychosocial support and 3) department-level content goals. Many of these STEM programs include summer bridge programs that offer academic courses, reinforcement of basic study skills, social and cultural events, as well as opportunities for summer research. The focus on pre-freshman programs, personalized academic support, and tutoring help to prepare students for the rigor of STEM curricula (Estrada et al., 2016). These programs, students have experienced positive social and peer interactions which impacted self-efficacy. Strong feelings of self-efficacy have been shown to be a predictor of "academic and STEM-specific achievement" (Flynn, 2016; Holmquist et al., 2013; Kuchynka et al., 2019).

While these programs have distinctive timeframes and methods, this author has not found a program that spans the length of time (10-weeks) or uses the methodology (hybrid gamification) to create or build a sense of community or belonging. The program discussed in this chapter is unique and, as of this publication, is the only university known to date that continued the gamified orientation using a hybrid gamification throughout the 10-week program.

Gamification: Motivation, Engagement and Persistence

Gamification research focuses on the impact of gamified elements as they influence intrinsic motivation and self-efficacy in higher education (Banfield & Wilkerson, 2014; Graham et al., 2013; Tan & Sockalingam, 2015). Gamification is an active learning strategy. Active learning is not a new concept and can be traced to early educational pedagogical theorists such as Dewey, Piaget, and Vygotsky. Gamification involves students in self-directed learning which allows them to construct meaning from their experiences. Constructivism, or learning through active engagement, is student-centered and self-directed because students seek knowledge to support what they want or need to learn. A few psychological theories support the idea that gamification supports engaged learning and affects motivation (Hamari et al., 2014; Landers, 2015).

"Using game-based mechanics, aesthetics and game thinking can engage people, motivate action, promote learning, and solve problems" (Kapp, 2012, p. 10) and aligns with techniques that are intended to leverage people's desire to engage in social networks (Arnold, 2014). Additionally, the use of game metaphors in a different setting increases motivation, commitment, and can influence user behavior

(Kiryakova et al., 2014). Research shows that gamification positively affects a student's membership or belonging in a group and impacts intrinsic motivation (Chavis et al., 2008; Hamari et al., 2014; Pink, 2009).

Different from didactic instruction, active learning often occurs through play (Banfield & Wilkerson, 2014). Gamification, the "idea of using elements of game design in non-game contexts, products, and services to motivate desired behaviors" (Deterding, 2012, para. 2) and is an active learning, constructivist pedagogy which engages and motivates learners. Gamification may influence student engagement and intrinsic motivation and may strengthen problem-solving skills and help students acquire broader knowledge (Šćepanović et al., 2015). Gamification employs four techniques: (a) appropriate challenges that utilize specific strategies and tasks for problem-solving skills, (b) intrigue, (c) opportunity to lead players to excitement or relief in the game "journey," and (d) promotion of competition and teamwork among peers (Ibanez et al., 2014). There is increased engagement among students when a challenge or task is tied to realistic problems (Martens et al., 2004), has clear objectives, and is developed with an understanding of the targeted learners (Gutierrez, 2015). The use of gamification in online and F2F applications has been shown to increase motivation using social engagement components. This, in turn, has the potential for developing growth mindset to take on difficult assignments (Rabah et al., 2018).

While research shows that teams score more points when competing than do individuals, the ability to make connections through play fostered connections that supported a sense of belonging. Students feel more related to fellow students within teams, thereby improving group play (Bovermann & Bastiaens, 2018).

Pink (2009) examined the impact of autonomy, mastery, and purpose on motivation. These characteristics are comparable with the game characteristics that McGonigal (2011a) describes as goals, rules, feedback, and voluntary participation, which help to establish the connection between gamification and its use in nongame situations such as in this program. As with any well-designed game, gamified material needs to be representative of design that focuses on "meaningful choices in the pursuance of interestingly hard goals" (Deterding, 2012, para.5). These align with the game elements that create engagement, mastery, and a feeling of accomplishment that the player must overcome a challenge (McGonigal, 2011a). Gamification pedagogy, an active learning approach, provides an example of immersive, experiential learning used to increase student engagement without deflation of educational credibility (Banfield & Wilkerson, 2014) and indicates it may help foster a sense of community and impact self-efficacy.

Barriers to Persistence Among Diverse, Underserved STEM Students

"The problem of STEM attrition appears to be more vexing for specific student populations. Degree attainment for females and underrepresented STEM students is lower for them than for all undergraduates as a whole" (Soldner et al., 2012, p. 312). Underrepresented students who are less likely to persist to a STEM degree are identified as African American/Black, first-generation, Hispanic/Latinx, Native American/American Indian and/or women (Crisp et al., 2009; Estrada et al., 2016; Freeman et al., 2017; Graham et al., 2013).

To improve representation and increase diversity for all demographic groups, several supportive programs should be implemented and monitored. Access to STEM gateway or bridge programs, enrichment of STEM educational programs, increase experiential learning, and a variety of individual and group activities should not only be offered, but should be directly aimed at support for students in preparation for STEM professions. This encouragement will help to retain and graduate these students (National Academy of Sciences, Engineering, and Medicine, 2018).

Little research has been conducted to better understand the factors that influence Hispanic students to persist in a STEM major. A few reasons have been put forth, including a lack of engaging pedagogy, the discouraging nature of introductory classes, or lack of preparation of the students for engagement in challenging classes. Other research indicates that STEM degree persistence can be related to a student's first semester GPA and whether they are enrolled in mathematics and science "gatekeeper courses." Authors posit that attending an HSI may be an important point of access for students in STEM fields and may provide a more equitable outcome for Hispanic students (Kezar & Holcombe, 2017; Thiry, 2017).

Most research supports the creation of community-based learning opportunities and participation in community learning for minority students in general. The "development of learning communities to promote community engagement in the comprehensive academic and social integration of URM students, specifically for first-generation, low-income students" is critical to minority student success (Kezar & Holcombe, 2017; Kuchynka et al., 2019; Whittaker & Montgomery, 2012, p. A50). On-campus social support from faculty and peer groups benefits African American and Latinx students as well (Baker, 2013). The benefit is that collectivist values may be more apparent and easier to access for underrepresented minorities when implicit bias does not need to be overcome (Baker, 2013; Crisp et al., 2009; Estrada et al., 2016; Kaufman et al., 2008).

Understanding that underrepresented minorities (URM) may be less likely to form study groups, gamification may serve as membership in a community. This approach may offer a way for students to communicate with peers and receive support when faced with challenging situations (Baker, 2013; Graham et al., 2013; Thiry, 2017). Peer support and academic performance have been positively correlated with membership in a strong ethnic and social network and are more helpful than multiple, varied supports (Kezar & Holcombe, 2017).

Finally, the literature identifies several topics for further research on the impact of gamification on persistence of STEM students to a degree. Few recent studies show consistent or definitive effects on learning, motivation, and engagement when using gamification in summer STEM bridge, gateway, or preparation programs. Research is lacking on gamification (either through a mobile app, F2F activities, or a combination of both) as it relates to building a sense of community and self-efficacy for diverse, underserved students as they persist to a STEM degree.

IMPLEMENTATION, OUTCOMES AND RECOMMENDATIONS

The focus of this study was to understand the impact of gamification—the integration of game design elements into a nongame application, task, or situation to make it more engaging and to encourage participation (McGonigal, 2011a; Treiblmaier et al., 2018)—among diverse, underserved STEM students' sense of community and self-efficacy as it relates to persistence toward a STEM major. The STEM Success Academy (SSA) program ran over a 10-week period. Rising sophomores enrolled in the selective SSA summer program took STEM classes that included General Chemistry I, Calculus I, Physics I and/or STEM Careers in the Fall of 2019 (STEM Success Academy, 2019).

Context

The STEM Success Academy (SSA) began in 2017 as part of a 5-year HSI STEM grant awarded to the university by the U. S. Department of Education to retain undergraduate STEM students and increase graduation rates. It was implemented in an accredited, public, HSI, 4-year institution. The university has an enrollment of 6,508 students (U.S. News and World Report, 2018) and comprises a population consisting of 38.2% Hispanic, 22.3% White, 22.2% Black or African American; and 18.3% Asian, nonresident alien, ethnicity unknown, and other. This New Jersey university is one of the most diverse cities in the United States and minutes away from New York City (College Factual, 2019).

The first year of the SSA program a began with a gamified orientation and was used to launch this program each subsequent year. The gamified orientation included the use of the *Social Scavenger* app in which small teams of four to five students competed against one another. The culminating activity for the day was a competitive STEM team activity. In the third year (2019), the gamified orientation activities were completed as they had been in previous but were then continued throughout the 10-week SSA program. The hybrid gamification approach included the continued use of the *Social Scavenger* mobile app and added five, biweekly face-to-face (F2F) collaborative, team, STEM challenges.

Participants

The participants were composed of students (aged 18 and above) who applied and were accepted by the SSA program for the summer of 2019. This program was part of a 5-year HSI STEM grant awarded in 2016 by the U.S. Department of Education to retain undergraduate STEM students and increase graduation rates. This grant, in its third year at the time of this study, was designed for students who plan to major in a STEM discipline. Students were selected for the 10-week program through an application process on the university website. The SSA accepted 30 students in the program for the summer of 2019. Two students did not complete the admission requirements and did not attend the Summer SSA; therefore, the sample was ($n = 28$).

A nonprobability, convenience sample of SSA students who were accepted into the program ($n = 28$) comprised the sample. These students took Pre-Calculus, Prep for General Chemistry or Prep for Physics; and the Career Directions in STEM classes during the 10-week program.

Hybrid Gamified Strategies

The *Social Scavenger* app challenges were designed specifically for the ten-week program with emphasis on three distinct areas 1) to foster a sense of community among individual team members and the SSA group at large 2) to engage with campus resources 3) participate in STEM and STEM-related activities. Having the ability to communicate with one another through mobile devices enabled team members to both connect individually and begin to build team relationships. Some of the challenges included 1) creating a *WhatsApp* chat group with their team members 2) securing a study buddy from a shared course 3) sharing a favorite place to study 4) collecting supplies for the F2F team STEM challenges and 5) attending Supplemental Instruction on a regular basis. Points were earned for both individual completion as well as for full team involvement. The ability to communicate via student mobile devices allowed team members to stay in touch 24/7. The use of the mobile app tended to reinforce information from the orientation and served to foster support for the team community. Some of the *Social Scavenger* app challenges are described in Table 1.

Table 1. STEM Success Academy Social Scavenger App Challenges and Descriptions for Orientation and Continuance of Similar Challenge During 10-week SSA Program

Challenge Name	Social Scavenger App Challenge Description for Orientation	Social Scavenger App Challenge Description Revised for 10-Week SSA Program
Shore Up Your Team! (Community Building)	Come up with a team logo (it could be all of you in a pic) and use it as your team icon. Make sure to include your team color! Be creative ☺ Download the school app for notifications – opt-in.	~Your part of the team matters! Sign into Social Scavenger as an INDIVIDUAL using your team color first, and your first name second (ex: Yellow Karen). That way you can compete for your team twice! The more of your team members that complete each challenge, the more points your team earns (on top of the team challenges). You got this!! BONUS - First team signed up gets an additional 100 points!! ~ Add another "study buddy" in Navigate app. Screenshot the study buddy and upload!
Get it Guarini (Campus Resources)	Find one of our awesome volunteers (hint: look for the black STEM Academy t-shirts) at the library to get a QR code. Hit the complete button to scan the QR code. Add a caption as to how you can "ask a Librarian" if you need a resource.	Visit the Library website. Go to--> Library resources-->databases by subject--> science and technology--> computing--> library information and technology abstract (LISTA). Login and search "stem careers" in the search bar. Pick one abstract you think is interesting (abstracts are about a paragraph long, so read it!) Screenshot your article (include the title)
"Vogue" (Academic Support)	Ever dreamed of being on the cover of a magazine! Here's your chance! Find the SI classrooms where Supplemental Instruction will be located during the summer (did you think it was Sports Illustrated?) and what days and times it will be available. Create a "cover shot" with your team and the magazine cover in the background. EXTRA points if the school's mascot can be seen!	Attend at least one session of SI (11:00 am – 11:50 am). Upload a pic of you and your SI Instructor EACH time you attend. **Bonus** – for more team members who attend
Safety First (STEM)	Get a teammate dressed up as safely as possible using a minimum of 3 pieces of protective gear, but the safer and more ridiculous they look the better. Find what you need in the science labs on the 3rd floor, Science Building (Room 330)	~In preparation for the Rube Goldberg final challenge: It's not too late to TEXT your list!! Use this "how-to" to prepare for Thursday's challenge (https://www.wikihow.com/Build-a-Homemade-Rube-Goldberg-Machine). TEXT a list of materials you will bring!

The second gamification strategy involved a series of F2F STEM challenges. The entire cohort of STEM Success Academy students assembled every two weeks to compete against the other teams in solving a STEM-focused challenge. While they didn't know the specifics of these challenges before, there were often *Social Scavenger* weekly challenges that encouraged preparation for these F2F challenges. For example, students would earn points for gathering recycled materials or brainstorming with their team members. This encouraged student communication between the F2F challenges as well as building anticipation for what the next STEM challenge would be. Some of the F2F challenges included EdTech strategies such as *Kahoot!*, *Breakout EDU*, or building a "tower" using a limited amount of common everyday materials that would withstand the force of "wind." The last challenge was to build a Rube Goldberg device from recycled materials.

Over the course of ten weeks, teams worked to earn points individually as well as with their team from both the *Social Scavenger* challenges and the F2F challenges. A running point total was reported out at each biweekly meeting. The culmination of the program brought the STEM cohort together for a final challenge, to build a Rube Goldberg device to get a ball in a cup using only recycled materials.

Points from this final activity were added to the 10-week running total. The team with the highest point total after the last challenge were awarded with an Apple product for each team member.

Outcomes

The correlation to the impact of gamification on diverse, underserved STEM students' sense of community and self-efficacy as it relates to their persistence toward a STEM degree was the focus of the study. Data were collected from pre- and postsurvey data from the SCI-2 and GSE Scale, individual interviews, a focus group, program coordinator surveys, and archival data. These data helped to reveal how the addition of gamification to the program affected the participants' sense of community, self-efficacy, and sense of persistence during the 10-week program.

Overall, five distinct themes emerged 1) a majority of participants (88%) indicated that involvement in the gamified activities created a strong sense of community 2) all students interviewed indicated they would continue to pursue a STEM major (as of Spring 2020) 3) participation in the *Social Scavenger* challenges supported a sense of belonging and contributed to the sense of community felt by undergraduates 4) participants indicated the F2F challenges were more impactful and engaging and allowed them to work confidently and collaboratively to problem-solve with conviction. This confidence and motivation demonstrated a growth mindset consistent with self-efficacy and, finally, 5) most students (88%) stated that being involved in the gamified activities motivated them to persist to complete the challenges and they would not have worked as hard or been as involved if not for the gamified activities. Finally, and unexpectedly, a few students exhibited leadership characteristics as they consistently encouraged participation and motivated team members throughout the duration of the program.

Recommendations

The judicious use of Educational Technology by incorporating gamified elements into a summer bridge program can add motivation and engagement to higher education activities. The implementation of such elements in a 10-week bridge program shows promise for impacting diverse, underserved STEM students' sense of community and self-efficacy. The use of sustained gamification motivated students to engage with their own team members and the SSA community. This resulted in a more cohesive cohort. The engagement of the gamified activities within the community seems to have impacted an increase student persistence toward a STEM degree. This author posits that the results may warrant the continued implementation of this type of intervention in other programs that seek to build community and self-efficacy as a method to retain and graduate STEM undergraduates. If gamified interventions continue to produce positive results (i.e., continued retention and persistence of diverse, underserved STEM students to a STEM degree) consideration of additional ways to implement these methodologies should be considered. Professors that teach in such programs might contribute to the F2F challenges as it relates to their field or suggest online challenges that directly relate to course curricula. Reaching out for student input on future challenges ideas may also help to encourage student engagement. The innovative use of gamification in these types of support programs might be a way to engage the GenZ STEM students in a way that excites them to persist in these challenging majors.

There are few, if any, studies on the use of sustained gamification strategies in any STEM bridge programs, as of the writing of this chapter. While there have been successful uses of gamified strategies in specific university courses, a review of literature illuminates a gap showing that there has been no sustained use of gamified strategies for STEM bridge programs. This chapter offers a way in which gamified interventions have impacted the program and resulted in positive outcomes for diverse, underserved students and their ability to persist to a STEM degree.

CONCLUSION

Increasing the number of diverse, underserved students who graduate prepared to work in a professional STEM career is a goal for numerous colleges and universities. Approximately one third of diverse, underserved students enter college with an interest in earning a STEM degree yet only about 16% of these students go on to graduate with a degree in that field (Estrada et al., 2016; NSC Research Center, 2015). Supporting diverse, underserved STEM students to persist toward a STEM degree is imperative if we are to graduate students who are prepared to enter the STEM workforce. The number of openings in STEM fields need to be filled with a demographic that is reflective of our diverse country. The addition of confident, well-prepared STEM graduates into the STEM workplace will allow for appropriate representation in STEM fields.

Higher education institutions offer bridge programs that may include innovative ways to support and retain these diverse, underserved students until graduation. The 10-week SSA program designed and implemented gamified strategies for use throughout the program with the focus on fostering community building to improve self-efficacy and encourage persistence to pursue a STEM degree. While technology is ubiquitous among the GenZ population the judicious use of Educational Technology can be most impactful when it is used purposefully.

The addition of hybrid gamification strategies in this SSA bridge program showed an impact on both sense of community and perceived self-efficacy among the participants. The perception of increased sense of community and self-efficacy reported by the participants when using gamified activities supported students' commitment to pursue a STEM degree. Ultimately, this type of gamified intervention has the potential to increase the number of STEM graduates who are prepared to join the professional STEM career workforce.

ACKNOWLEDGMENT

Research funding was provided by the U.S. Department of Education Project No. P031C16055 NJ) and supported by New Jersey City University.

REFERENCES

Alvarez, I. M., & Olivera-Smith, M. (2013). Learning in social networks: Rationale and ideas for its implementation in higher education. *Education Sciences*, *3*(3), 314–325. doi:10.3390/educsci3030314

Andrade, A., & de Carvalho, C. V. (2015). To enliven virtual communities of practice through gamification. *EAI Endorsed Transactions on Serious Games*, *1*(4), e6. doi:10.4108g.1.4.e6

Arnold, B. J. (2014). Gamification in education. *Proceedings of the American Society of Business and Behavioral Sciences*, *21*(1), 32–39. http://asbbs.org/files/ASBBS2014/PDF/A/ArnoldB(P32-39).pdf

Ashley, M., Cooper, K. M., Cala, J. M., & Brownell, S. E. (2017). Building better bridges into STEM: A synthesis of 25 years of literature on STEM summer bridge programs. *CBE Life Sciences Education*, *16*(4), es3. doi:10.1187/cbe.17-05-0085 PMID:29146667

Aynsley, S. A., Nathawat, K., & Crawford, R. M. (2018). Evaluating student perceptions of using a gamebased approach to aid learning: Braincept. *Higher Education Pedagogies*, *3*(1), 70–81. doi:10.1080/23752696.2018.1435296

Baker, C. N. (2013). Social support and success in higher education: The influence of on-campus support on African American and Latino college students. *The Urban Review*, *45*(5), 632–650. doi:10.100711256-013-0234-9

Bandura, A. (1986). *Social foundation of thought and action*. Prentice Hall.

Bandura, A. (1994). Self-efficacy. In V. S. Ramachaudran (Ed.), *Encyclopedia of human behavior* (Vol. 4, pp. 71–81). Academic Press.

Banfield, J., & Wilkerson, B. (2014). Increasing student intrinsic motivation and self-efficacy through gamification pedagogy. *Contemporary Issues in Education Research*, *7*(4), 291–298. doi:10.19030/cier.v7i4.8843

Bovermann, K., & Bastiaens, T. (2018, June 25). Using gamification to foster intrinsic motivation and collaborative learning: A comparative testing. In Proceedings of EdMedia + Innovate Learning (pp. 1128–1137). Association for the Advancement of Computing in Education (AACE).

Brown, A. (2017, September 11). *Younger men play video games, but so do a diverse group of other Americans*. Pew Research Center. https://www.pewresearch.org/fact-tank/2017/09/11/younger-men-play-video-games-but-so-do-a-diverse-group-of-other-americans/

Buckley, P., & Doyle, E. (2014). Gamification and student motivation. *Interactive Learning Environments*, *24*(6), 1162–1175. doi:10.1080/10494820.2014.964263

Cain, J., & Piascik, P. (2015). Are serious games a good strategy for pharmacy education? *American Journal of Pharmaceutical Education*, *79*(4), 47. doi:10.5688/ajpe79447 PMID:26089556

Chavis, S. M., Lee, K. S., & Acosta, J. D. (2008). *The Sense of Community Index (SCI) Revised: The reliability and validity of the SCI-2* [Paper presentation]. The 2nd International Community Psychology Conference, Lisbon, Portugal. http://dl.icdst.org/pdfs/files/f458f0f15016819295377e5a979b1893.pdf

Crisp, G., Nora, A., & Taggart, A. (2009). Student characteristics, pre-college, college, and environmental factors as predictors of majoring in and earning a STEM degree: An analysis of students attending a Hispanic serving institution. *American Educational Research Journal*, *46*(4), 924–942. doi:10.3102/0002831209349460 de Santana, S. J., Souza, H. A., Florentin, V. A., Paiva, R., Bittencourt, I. I., & Isotani, S. (2016, April). A quantitative analysis of the most relevant gamification elements in an online learning environment. *Proceedings of the 25th International.* 10.1145/2872518.2891074

Dennis, J. M., Phinney, J. S., & Chuateco, L. I. (2005). The role of motivation, parental support, and peer support in the academic success of ethnic minority first-generation college students. *Journal of College Student Development, 46*(3), 223–236. doi:10.1353/csd.2005.0023

Deterding, S. (2012). Gamification: Designing for motivation. *Interaction, 19*(4), 14–17. doi:10.1145/2212877.2212883

Deterding, S., Dixon, D., Khaled, R., & Nacke, L. (2011, September). From game design elements to gamefulness: Defining gamification. In *Proceedings of the 15th International Academic MindTrek conference: Envisioning future media environments* (pp. 9–15). ACM. 10.1145/2181037.2181040

Dewey, J. (1928). Body and mind. *Bulletin of the New York Academy of Medicine, 4*(1), 3–19. https://www.ncbi.nlm.nih.gov/pmc/articles/PMC2393849/pdf/ bullnyacadmed00900-0005.pdf PMID:19311595

Dichev, C., & Dicheva, D. (2017). Gamifying education: What is known, what is believed and what remains uncertain: A critical review. *International Journal of Educational Technology in Higher Education, 14*(1), 9. doi:10.118641239-017-0042-5

Dweck, C. S. (2006). *Mindset: The new psychology of success.* Random House Digital, Inc.

Erenli, K. (2013). The impact of gamification-recommending education scenarios. *International Journal of Emerging Technologies in Learning, 8*(S1), 15–21e. doi:10.3991/ijet.v8iS1.2320

Estrada, M., Burnett, M., Campbell, A. G., Campbell, P. B., Denetclaw, W. F., Gutiérrez, C. G., Hurtado, S., John, G. H., Matsui, J., McGee, R., Okpodu, C. M., Robinson, T. J., Summers, M. F., Werner-Wasburne, M., & Zavala, M. (2016). Improving underrepresented minority student persistence in STEM. *CBE Life Sciences Education, 12*(3), es5. doi:10.1187/cbe.16-01-0038 PMID:27543633

Flynn, D. T. (2016). STEM field persistence: The impact of engagement on postsecondary STEM persistence for underrepresented minority students. *Journal of Educational Issues, 2*(1), 185–214. doi:10.5296/jei.v2i1.9245

Fosse, T. H., Buch, R., Säfvenbom, R., & Martinussen, M. (2016). *The impact of personality and self-efficacy on academic and military performance: The mediating role of self-efficacy.* Academic Press.

Freeman, A., Becker, S. A., & Cummins, M. (2017). *NMC/CoSN horizon report: 2017 K.* The New Media Consortium.

Funk, C., & Parker, K. (2018, January 9). *Diversity in the STEM workforce varies widely across jobs.* https://www.pewsocialtrends.org/2018/01/09/diversity-in-the-stem-workforce-varies-widely-across-jobs/

Gilliam, M., Jagoda, P., Fabiyi, C., Lyman, P., Wilson, C., Hill, B., & Bouris, A. (2017). Alternate reality games as an informal learning tool for generating STEM engagement among underrepresented youth: A qualitative evaluation of the source. *Journal of Science Education and Technology*, *26*(3), 295–308. doi:10.100710956-016-9679-4

Gough, C. (2019, October 15). *Topic: Mobile gaming*. https://www.statista.com/topics/1906/mobile-gaming/

Graham, M. J., Frederick, J., Byars-Winston, A., Hunter, A. B., & Handelsman, J. (2013). Increasing persistence of college students in STEM. *Science*, *341*(6153), 1455–1456. doi:10.1126cience.1240487 PMID:24072909

Hamari, J., Koivisto, J., & Sarsa, H. (2014, January). *Does gamification work? A literature review of empirical studies on gamification* [Paper presentation]. The 47th Hawaii International Conference on System Sciences (HICSS). 10.1109/HICSS.2014.377

Hazan, B., Zhang, W., Olcum, E., Bergdoll, R., Grandoit, E., Mandelbaum, F., Wilson-Doenges, G., & Rabin, L. A. (2018). Gamification of an undergraduate psychology statistics lab: Benefits to perceived competence. *Statistics Education Research Journal*, *17*(2), 255–265. doi:10.52041erj.v17i2.169

Holmquist, C., Gable, R. K., & Billups, F. D. (2013). The relationship between self-efficacy and persistence in adult remedial education. *NERA Conference Proceedings 2013*. https://opencommons.uconn.edu/nera_2013/17

Ibanez, M. B., Di-Serio, A., & Delgado-Kloos, C. (2014). Gamification for engaging computer science students in learning activities: A case study. *IEEE Transactions on Learning Technologies*, *7*(3), 291–301. doi:10.1109/TLT.2014.2329293

Inocencio, F. (2018, December 13-16). *Using gamification in education: A systematic literature review* [Paper presentation]. *Thirty Ninth International Conference on Information Systems*, San Francisco, CA, United States.

Kapp, K. M. (2012). *The gamification of learning and instruction*. Wiley.

Kezar, A., & Holcombe, E. (2017). *Creating a unified community of support: Increasing success for underrepresented students in STEM*. A final report on the CSU STEM Collaboratives Project. Pullias Center for Higher Education. https://pullias.usc.edu/download/creating-a-unified-community-of-support-increasing-success-for-underrepresented-students-in-stem/

Kiryakova, G., Angelova, N., & Yordanova, L. (2014). Gamification in education. *Proceedings of 9th International Balkan Education and Science Conference*.

Kolb, D. A. (1984). *Experiential learning: Experience as the source of learning and development*. FT Press.

Kuchynka, S., Findley-Van Nostrand, D., & Pollenz, R. S. (2019). Evaluating psychosocial mechanisms underlying STEM persistence in undergraduates: Scalability and longitudinal analysis of three cohorts from a six-day pre-college engagement STEM academy program. *CBE Life Sciences Education, 18*(3), ar41. doi:10.1187/cbe.19-01-0028 PMID:31441721

Kumar, V. (2017, March 26). *Big data facts*. https://analyticsweek.com/content/big-data-facts/

Landers, R. N. (2015). Developing a theory of gamified learning: Linking serious games and gamification of learning. *Simulation & Gaming, 45*(6), 752–768. doi:10.1177/1046878114563660

Landers, R. N., Bauer, K. N., Callan, R. C., & Armstrong, M. B. (2015). Psychological theory and the gamification of learning. In T. Reiners & L. Wood (Eds.), *Gamification in education and business* (pp. 165–186). Springer. doi:10.1007/978-3-319-10208-5_9

Landers, R. N., & Landers, A. K. (2015). An empirical test of the theory of gamified learning: The effect of leaderboards on time-on-task and academic performance. *Simulation & Gaming, 45*(6), 769–785. doi:10.1177/1046878114563662

Langendahl, P. A., Cook, M., & Mark-Herbert, C. (2016). *Gamification in higher education: Toward a pedagogy to engage and motivate*. Department of Economics, Swedish University of Agricultural Sciences.

Lave, J., & Wenger, E. (1991). *Situated learning: Legitimate peripheral participation*. Cambridge University Press. doi:10.1017/CBO9780511815355

Lee, J. J., & Hammer, J. (2011). Gamification in education: What, how, why bother? *Academic Exchange Quarterly, 15*(2), 146. https://mybrainware.com/wp-content/uploads/2017/11/Gamification_in_Education_What_How_Why.pdf

Lee, Y. H., Dunbar, N., Kornelson, K., Wilson, S. N., Ralston, R., Savic, M., Stewart, S., Lennox, E., Thompson, W., & Elizondo, J. (2016). Digital game-based learning for undergraduate calculus education: Immersion, calculation, and conceptual understanding. *International Journal of Gaming and Computer-Mediated Simulations, 8*(1), 13–27. doi:10.4018/IJGCMS.2016010102

Machajewski, S. T. (2017). *Application of gamification in a college STEM introductory course: A case study* [Doctoral dissertation]. Northcentral University. doi:10.13140/RG.2.2.27751.34728

Marczewski, A. (2013). *Gamification: A simple introduction*. Andrzej Marczewski.

Maslow, A. H. (1981). *Motivation and personality*. Harper and Row.

McGonigal, J. (2011a). *Reality is broken: Why games make us better and how they can change the world*. Penguin Press.

McGonigal, J. (2011b, January 22). Be a gamer, save the world. *The Wall Street Journal*. https://myweb.uiowa.edu/dlgould/lifeclas/docs/Be%20a%20Gamer,%20Save%20the%20World%20(1.22.11)docx.pdf

McMillan, D. W., & Chavis, D. M. (1986). Sense of community: A definition and theory. *Journal of Community Psychology, 14*(1), 6–23. doi:10.1002/1520-6629(198601)14:1<6::AID-JCOP2290140103>3.0.CO;2-I

National Academies of Sciences, Engineering, and Medicine. (2018). *Indicators for monitoring undergraduate STEM education*. National Academies Press.

National Student Clearinghouse Research Center. (2015, April 22). *Persistence & retention–2015*. https://nscresearchcenter.org/snapshotreport-persistenceretention18/

Ortiz Rojas, M. E., Chiluiza, K., & Valcke, M. (2016). *Gamification in higher education and stem: A systematic review of literature* [Paper presentation]. *8th International Conference on Education and New Learning Technologies: EDULEARN 16*, Barcelona, Spain. 10.21125/edulearn.2016.0422

Parker, K., & Igielnik, R. (2022, April 1). *On the cusp of adulthood and facing an uncertain future: What we know about gen Z so far*. Pew Research Center's Social & Demographic Trends Project. Retrieved July 19, 2022, from https://www.pewresearch.org/social-trends/2020/05/14/on-the-cusp-of-adulthood-and-facing-an-uncertain-future-what-we-know-about-gen-z-so-far-2/

Pew Research. (2019, June 12). *Demographics of mobile device ownership and adoption in the United States*. https://www.pewresearch.org/internet/fact-sheet/mobile/

Pink, D. H. (2009). *Drive: The surprising truth about what motivates us*. Penguin.

Rabah, J., Cassidy, R., & Beauchemin, R. (2018, November). *Gamification in education: Real benefits or edutainment* [Paper presentation]. 17th European Conference on e-Learning, Athens, Greece. 10.13140/RG.2.2.28673.56162

Šćepanović, S., Žarić, N. A. Đ. A., & Matijević, T. (2015, September 24–25). *Gamification in higher education learning: State of the art, challenges, and opportunities* [Paper presentation]. In the Sixth International Conference on e-Learning (eLearning-2015), Belgrade, Serbia.

Soldner, M., Rowan-Kenyon, H., Inkelas, K. K., Garvey, J., & Robbins, C. (2012). Supporting students' intentions to persist in STEM disciplines: The role of living-learning programs among other social-cognitive factors. *The Journal of Higher Education*, *83*(3), 311–336. doi:10.1353/jhe.2012.0017

Tan, J., & Sockalingam, N. (2015). *Gamification to engage students in higher education* [Working paper]. https://ink.library.smu.edu.sg/lkcsb_research/4740

Thiry, H. (2017). Undergraduate degree: Increasing Latino retention and completion. *Underrepresented Minorities in STEM Fields*, 66. https://par.nsf.gov/servlets/purl/10049620#page=68

Toyama, K. (2015, October 29). The looming gamification of higher ed. *The Chronicle of Higher Education*. https://www.chronicle.com/article/the-looming-gamification-of-higher-ed/

Treiblmaier, H., Putz, L. M., & Lowry, P. B. (2018). Setting a definition, context, and theory-based research agenda for the gamification of non-gaming applications. *Association for Information Systems Transactions on Human-Computer Interaction*, *10*(3), 129–163. doi:10.17705/1thci.00107

Vanyi, J. (2018). *The impact of a gamified orientation on predominantly underrepresented minority, undergraduate student success and retention in a STEM academy program* (Publication No. 10937459) [Doctoral dissertation, New Jersey City University]. ProQuest Dissertations and Theses.

Vygotsky, L. S. (1980). *Mind in society: The development of higher psychological processes*. Harvard University Press. doi:10.2307/j.ctvjf9vz4

Whittaker, J. A., & Montgomery, B. L. (2012). Cultivating diversity and competency in STEM: Challenges and remedies for removing virtual barriers to constructing diverse higher education communities of success. *Journal of Undergraduate Neuroscience Education*, *11*(1), A44. https://www.ncbi.nlm.nih.gov/pmc/ articles/PMC3592737/ PMID:23493445

KEY TERMS AND DEFINITIONS

Active Learning: Any learning or course related activity in which students in a class session are engaged and not just watching, listening, and taking notes.

Bridge Programs: Any program that is designed to help students transition students from high school into higher education learning environments.

Community of practice (CoP): Introduced by Lave and Wenger (1991), a CoP comprises members with varied interests, differing contributions, and varied viewpoints who "share understandings concerning what they are doing and what that means in their lives and for their communities" (p. 98).

Diverse, Underserved Populations (DUS): Students with one or more of the following characteristics: first generation, low income, female, and/or a racial-ethnic minority (e.g., African American, or Black, Asian, Hispanic or Latinx, Native American, Non-resident alien). These students have been historically underrepresented in higher education institutions.

First-Generation: A student whose parent or parents did not earn a four-year college degree.

Generation Z: A group of people (students) who were born between1997 and 2012.

Persistence: As it relates to a program or university, persistence is the percentage of students who return to college, at any institution, for their second year (National Student Clearinghouse Research Center, 2015).

Retention: The practice in higher education, to keep students enrolled in the community college, college, or university they are attending.

Social Scavenger: A mobile app that allows "building and running mobile-based scavenger hunts as an engagement platform to facilitate mobile fun" (Social Scavenger, 2019). This app was used for the NJCU orientation and was then built to be used throughout the entire 10-week SSA program.

STEM Success Academy (SSA): A 10-week summer program designed to prepare rising sophomores and transfer students for enrollment in General Chemistry I, Calculus I, and Physics I in Fall 2019 (Grew, 2016).

Chapter 12
The Effects of a Technology-Enriched Classroom on Student Learning:
The Smart Classroom Model

Fırat Sarsar
https://orcid.org/0000-0002-3611-8137
Faculty of Education, Ege University, Turkey

Özge Andiç Çakır
Faculty of Education, Ege University, Turkey

Gülben Çalış
Faculty of Education, Ege University, Turkey

Beril Ceylan
https://orcid.org/0000-0002-2440-0434
Faculty of Education, Ege University, Turkey

Alev Ateş-Çobanoğlu
https://orcid.org/0000-0002-8319-9822
Faculty of Education, Ege University, Turkey

Orhan Dağdeviren
Faculty of Education, Ege University, Turkey

Mehmet Emin Kaval
School of Dentistry, Ege University, Turkey

ABSTRACT

Smart classrooms are created by using smart environments equipped with various software and hardware devices and applications. The smart classroom is the integration of advanced teaching technologies into

DOI: 10.4018/978-1-6684-6092-4.ch012

the classroom environment beyond the traditional classroom environment in order to contribute to the development of the student's learning ability and participation in the lesson. In general, the concept of the smart classroom will be discussed in this chapter from two aspects: (1) physical and (2) instructional. These two aspects are important in terms of showing how learning processes are affected in terms of educational technologies. This chapter also includes the outputs and experiences of the ongoing technology-enriched smart classroom project supported by a scientific research fund of Ege University.

INTRODUCTION

Education in the 21st century presents new learning approaches and technological opportunities. Learners and educators try integrating technology into the learning environments to acquire new learning skills. New learning methods and approaches have also changed the structure of learning environments, which can be flexible physical environments and online platforms with technology. Using technological systems fills the gap between learners' skills and their learning process. Technological systems are essential to a new era in global education (Phoong, Phoong, Moghavvemi & Sulaiman, 2019). The Organization for Economic Co-operation and Development (OECD) explains that digital smart technologies, learning analytics, and learning objectives will transform education into automated digital tasks and more equal and strategic education (OECD, 2019).

As a discipline, educational technology (EdTech) has many definitions for developing and integrating new technologies and changing points of view. In a recent definition, EdTech is defined as "the study and ethical application of theory, research, and best practices to advance knowledge as well as mediate and improve learning and performance through the strategic design, management and implementation of learning and instructional processes and resources" (AECT, 2022). In their analysis of educational technology research trends, Dağhan & Gündüz (2022) implied that the EdTech definitions have also covered ethical practices since the 2000s, primarily because of easy access to information via the internet. Frankenfield (2022) noted that EdTech involves implementing new learning technologies to improve learning outcomes and enhance individualized education that assists learners and teachers in learning-teaching. Such technology use and integration of learning interaction in the classroom can transform the classrooms into a smart learning environment. The Industrial Revolution emphasizes that human-machine interactions and education performed rapid, robust, and qualified connections for individuals. Fourth Industrial Revolution and Information 4.0 have examined the pedagogical approaches and the impacts of intelligent learning environments. Smart learning environments have filled the gaps between holistic informational context and high-level thinking processes (Lorenzo, Gallon, Palau & Mogas, 2021). A smart classroom is a future technology engagement between multidisciplinary eras and the context. For this reason, it is essential to understand learning environments and their relation to education systems.

At the beginning of the 2000s, smart classrooms were defined as technological support in traditional face-to-face classrooms that combined active learning and educational technologies (Niemeyer, 2003). The technologies are computers, data projectors, smart boards, and other learning tools. The term "smart class" was first used to differentiate it from the concept of a "computer lab class" (Li, Kong, & Chen, 2015). It is seen that the smart classroom is defined as a classroom equipped with an interactive whiteboard to support real-time interaction between teachers and students and to perform learning activities (Zhao, 2008; cited in Li, Kong, & Chen, 2015).

However, today, smart classrooms integrate digital learning activities, context-aware technologies, data analysis techniques, and interactive structures. The smart classroom is technology-enriched (Li, Kong, & Chen, 2015). Shen, Wu & Lee (2014) define smart classrooms include LED character displays, mobile devices, multi-touch displays, computers, smartphones, servers, and other systems to manage attendance and real-time feedback. Smart classrooms combine cameras, sensors, Internet of Things (IoT) systems, real-time services, software, and asynchronous and synchronous communication tools (Han & Xu, 2021). As a newer definition, a smart classroom is a physical classroom created by integrating advanced educational technologies (Lu, Yang & Shi, 2021). Cebrián, Palau & Mogas (2020) stated that a smart classroom is a culture of enriching learning experiences between adaptive and intelligent systems and education. All these definitions explain that smart classrooms are multidisciplinary environments with education and engineering structures and parameters.

Integrating educational technology through smart classes is possible to have positive pedagogical impacts. The present chapter focuses on the contributions of smart classes at the higher education level. It helps to fill the gap in the smart class literature regarding affective aspects while discussing the effect of indoor environmental conditions on learning. Finally, the preliminary results of the Ege University Smart Classroom project were reflected to analyze the findings in a multidisciplinary manner.

SMART CLASSROOM CHARACTERISTICS

Higher education institutions use technology to shape education as personalized and smart structures. According to students' opinions, instructed materials, the internet, digital devices, and smart technologies reflect modern learning and communication environments (Alfoudari, Dururgbo & Aldhmour, 2021). This means that a smart classroom is shaped in terms of learners' needs, including digital devices, learning strategies, activities, and classroom integration.

The smart classroom facilitates technology for active, social, and learner-centered learning. Theoretically, as Kwet and Prinsloo (2020) mentioned, smart classrooms include cameras, sensors, smart devices, and IoT systems to collect data about student participation, facial expressions, bodily postures, and engagement. In addition, smart classroom technologies contribute dynamic and flexible opportunities for monitoring teaching and learning administration. A popular form of analytics defined by D'Mello (2017) is "affect analysis" which assesses emotions and moods expressed in smart classrooms. Smart classroom research includes technological implementations and educational adaptations. Learning environments tend to be individual, collaborative, adaptive, intelligent, social, multidisciplinary, ubiquitous, flexible, and interactive (Alfoudari, Dururgbo & Aldhmour, 2021). In addition, technology-supported learning environments provide empirical data for usefulness, ease of use, and functional design (Li, Yang & MacLeod, 2019).

A smart classroom has positive effects on learners. Technology gives flexibility for student-centered learning. Learners can control deep cognitive engagement, motivation, and other contributors (Lu, Xie, Lui, 2022). Learners create new learnings with the aid of educators leading to impressive and attractive instructional design. Learners' academic performance, knowledge sharing, planning skills, reflective thinking, and technology abilities increase during the smart classroom teaching and learning process (Phoong, Phoong, Moghavvemi & Sulaiman, 2019). The other situation is about formative evaluation. Attendance, performance, interactive feedback, attitudes, and constructive records are used in these systems as alternative assessments (Shen, Wu & Lee, 2014). The educator needs to be informed about the automation of real-time feedback (Tissenbaum and Slotta, 2019) highlighted movements (that give information about student improvement), and future learning supports to lead the classroom with the ability of time management.

Learning limitations and necessities are changing with technological improvements. The research that combines theory and practice is leading in this area. Smart classrooms are high-tech learning environments that support responsive instructional learning situations with student-centered activities led by educators. Many studies in the instructional technology era focus on the effects and contributions of smart classrooms. Many researchers across the world implemented and investigated smart classroom technology at various levels and disciplines, e.g., at Indian secondary schools, Baby and Chellamani (2018) found out that among most 150 secondary school students had positive responses for having erased whiteboard, digital projector, smart board, and laptop in their class. Besides technological devices, the students in that survey also provided positive feedback for the techno-pedagogical aspect of smart classes. Such as the use of audio-visual tools by teachers, real-world learning through demonstration, brainstorming, storyboard telling, teamwork at computers, and puzzles and games. Baby & Chellamani (2018) also collected reflections from teachers and principals about the effectiveness of smart classes on learners and reported that most teachers agree that students developed self-confidence and skill in using technology tools for learning, exploring, writing, reading, and self-expression. It was mentioned that smart class motivates them to attend classes and interact with others healthily and richly regularly. Hence, the principals and parents had positive views on the contributions of smart class for developing 21st-century skills among their children.

Another study by Li, Yang, and Macleod (2019) on smart classes focuses on the preferences of preservice teachers for smart classes and connectedness. The participants were 462 preservice teachers with at least one-semester experience in the smart class. Li et al. (2019) found that connectedness is a critical factor positively and significantly associated with all smart classroom features included in the study. These features were "inquiry learning, student negotiation, reflective thinking, functional design, multiple sources, usefulness, and ease of use". Moreover, it was reported that the freshman preservice teachers with high technology self-efficacy levels mostly preferred constructivist smart classroom learning environments.

Li, Kong and Chen (2015) stated the basic features of enriched/smart classes:

1. They are classrooms enriched with technology, blending physical and virtual learning environments, sensitive to context, and automatically adjusting environmental parameters such as light and indoor air temperature.
2. It offers course content, interaction support, and constructivist learning tools to support learners' active, learner-centered, individual or group learning, collaborative, mobile, or virtual learning in different ways.
3. Collects, records, and analyzes the learners' data to make the most appropriate educational and scientific decisions.
4. It is an open learning environment that aims to bring learners to a different learning context. In this way, it increases learners' motivation to learn, develops their creativity, and provides them with a practical hands-on learning experience.

Smart classrooms include individual and group activities. These activities include constructive and interactive content supporting active, inquiry, collaborative, cognitive, and adaptive learning processes.

Smart classrooms motivate learners and permit them to manage their learning processes (Bouslama & Kalota, 2013; Li et al., 2015). Also, these classrooms allow learners to be more social. They generate the information into knowledge with fruitful discussions.

SMART CLASSROOM INDOOR ENVIRONMENTAL CONDITIONS

The indoor environmental conditions of buildings usually include factors such as (1) thermal environment, (2) sound and noise level, (3) light and illumination level, and (4) air quality. The effects of these indoor environmental conditions on users can vary according to demographic characteristics and the actions of users in different areas of the indoor area (Kocaman, 2021). In addition, the purpose of the use of buildings can change the effect of indoor conditions on users. For this reason, it should be ensured that the indoor environmental conditions in buildings that serve various purposes in daily life (e.g., schools, hospitals, offices) are suitable for the basic needs of different users in those buildings. Especially the indoor environmental conditions in educational buildings significantly affect students' learning process and efficiency (Burunkaya & Duraklar, 2022; Saini & Goel, 2019; Suleman & Hussain, 2014). Since this is a crucial subject for education, many researchers have studied this topic. With subjective and objective measurements, Lee et al. (2012) examined the relationship between indoor environmental quality and learning performance in university air-conditioned classrooms. They evaluate indoor air temperature, relative humidity, airflow velocity, mean radiant temperature, CO_2 concentration, sound pressure level, illumination level, user activity, clothing insulation level, learning performance (calculation, reading, comprehension, and writing), and perceived indoor environmental quality in four classrooms and four large amphitheaters. They concluded that all indoor environmental quality complaints had a similar effect on learning performance, and there was a good correlation between learning performance and the number of complaints. Bakó-Biró, Clements-Croome, Kochhar, Awbi, & Williams (2012) investigated the effects of ventilation on students' performance in eight primary schools in England. Carbon dioxide concentrations and other parameters were monitored for three weeks in two selected classes in each school. Students and teachers in the classrooms studied were often exposed to unacceptably poor air quality conditions (CO_2 concentration at 1500 ppm levels). Study findings showed that low classroom ventilation rates significantly reduced students' attention and alertness and negatively affected memory and concentration. According to the results, it has been revealed that the physical environment affects teaching and learning. Keis, Helbig, Streb, & Hille (2014) examined the effect of lighting on students' performance. In this context, they selected 58 high school students from four classes in two schools. In both schools, one classroom was equipped with blue-enriched white lighting, and the adjacent classroom was chosen as a controlled environment under standard lighting conditions. They evaluated the effect of classroom lighting on performance using psychological tests. The results revealed that compared to standard lighting conditions, blue-enriched white light has beneficial effects on students' performance and concentration. Haverinen-Shaughnessy & Shaughnessy (2015) estimated the effects of classroom ventilation speed and indoor air temperature on academic achievement using a multi-level approach in 140 classrooms in 70 elementary schools in the United States. They analyzed data on students' socioeconomic variables and standardized test scores. The results showed that providing adequate ventilation and thermal comfort in the classrooms can significantly improve students' academic achievement. Sarbu & Pacurar (2015) examined how indoor environmental conditions affect students' academic performance during the cooling season in a field study. Thermal comfort and air quality were evaluated in two university classrooms, and they developed a student performance prediction model based on attention tests. They performed three simple correlations to estimate indoor air temperature, relative humidity, and CO_2 concentration and tests. The model results showed that indoor environmental conditions could significantly affect students' performance. However, maximum performance in the cooling season was achieved at an indoor air temperature of 27°C. Sala & Rantala (2016) aimed to determine the effect of the acoustic environment in school classrooms in Finland. The activity noise levels of the classrooms, background noise levels, and acoustic parameter measurements were made, and the relationships between them were examined. Background noise levels and acoustic parameters were measured in empty classrooms, and activity noise levels were measured during classroom instruction. Study results showed that only a few classes met the acoustic criteria of the Finnish national standard. In addition, most classrooms had higher background noise and activity noise levels for listening and communication. According to the results, it has been revealed that the acoustic environment in these school classrooms is harmful to students' vocal communication and learning. Jiang, Wang, Liu, Xu, & Liu (2018) investigated the relationship between indoor air temperature and learning performance by controlling thermal comfort parameters (indoor air temperature, relative humidity, and airflow velocity) under different conditions. In the field study, six groups were formed to participate in all experiments under six different indoor air temperature conditions by keeping the CO_2 concentration, acoustics, and lighting at the same level. During the experiments, students rated their perceptions of thermal sensation, comfort, and satisfaction. Tests consisting of ten items were applied to the students to evaluate their performance. The study's results proved that thermal discomfort caused by high or low indoor air temperatures negatively affected students' learning performance. The highest performance was at a temperature of about 14°C. Bajc, Banjac, Todorović, & Stevanović (2019) presented an experimental analysis of the relationship between thermal comfort and student productivity in a university classroom in Belgrade during the heating season. In this study, they measured four scenarios with different indoor comfort conditions. Together with the measurements, they surveyed students' feedback about thermal comfort and indoor environmental conditions. They calculated the predicted mean vote and percentage of dissatisfaction with respect to ISO 7730 and ASHRAE 55 thermal acceptability as measured with a metric system. They also evaluated student productivity using new tests designed following the purposes of the research. Research findings reveal that high indoor air temperatures and carbon dioxide concentration negatively affect student productivity. Almaqra et al. (2019) aimed to examine the effects of caffeine consumption and indoor air temperature on the performance of university students through a performance experiment. Eighteen undergraduate university students participated in the study. They examined students' performance at three different indoor air temperatures (16, 23, and 30°C) in a heated room, keeping the relative humidity level constant at 32.8%. The results revealed that indoor air temperature has a significant effect on performance. In addition, it was determined that the performance was maximum at 23°C, and decreased at higher and lower temperatures. In summary, the results of the studies mentioned above show that it is important to meet the educational buildings' indoor conditions according to the students' needs.

Smart classrooms created for this purpose contribute significantly to setting optimum indoor environmental conditions with the ability to automatically adjust light, indoor air temperature, and air cleanliness and collect data to optimize pedagogical decisions. To ensure that a classroom is smart, it should be ensured that the equipment that will monitor and reliably control the indoor environmental parameters should be placed in the classroom (Yan et al., 2017). Runathong et al. (2017) developed a classroom environment monitoring system that monitors and controls the classroom environment's lighting and indoor air temperature in real time, including a design that beneficially uses the applications of the concepts of the internet of things (IoT) and cloud computing. It can make the necessary adjustments by using the data regarding the appropriate light and indoor air temperature set-point defined to ensure the student's comfort. The results show that the concept and prototype of the system are working correctly.

Moreover, another exemplary design scheme for the classroom monitoring system was proposed by Liu et al. (2020). Thanks to this system, which is suitable for school administrators to see the actual situation of the classroom environment, school administrators can perform real-time collection and monitoring of classroom environment parameters such as indoor air temperature, relative humidity, smoke concentration, and light intensity. The test of the application was carried out by remotely controlling the curtain, light, fan, and other equipment to ensure the comfort of the classroom. The results show that the system can detect and control the environmental parameters in the classroom in real time and provide the comfort of the classroom environment. However, these studies have yet to investigate the effect of these and similar systems on the level of classroom learning. Burunkaya and Duraklar (2022) conducted at a high school in Ankara and compared the academic achievement of students studying in a smart classroom environment with those studying in a traditional classroom environment. The research included 24 students in the smart classroom (experimental group) and 24 in the traditional classroom (control group). In the smart classroom they created, the researchers followed the data of light intensity, indoor air temperature, relative humidity, air cleanliness, sound intensity and distribution, and dust and particle amount on mobile with the software they developed. In addition, 5-point Likert scale satisfaction questionnaires were applied to the students in this classroom about the measured indoor environmental conditions. According to the results of these questionnaires, the needs of the students in terms of indoor environmental conditions were determined, and the indoor environmental conditions were adjusted accordingly. Experimental and control groups attended 30-hour lessons given by the same teachers in five different branches every week for five weeks and then took the same exam. While the average exam results of the students studying in the smart classroom environment was 85, the average of the students studying in the classical classroom environment was 74. These results revealed that the students educated in the smart classroom environment were more successful than those educated in the classical classroom environment. In other words, when indoor conditions are controlled, it has been observed that students' success and efficiency in learning increase.

The importance of classroom environment parameters, especially air quality, has increased after the COVID-19 pandemic. In 2021, a Ministry-wide transformation was initiated in Quebec, Canada, to measure and monitor schools' air quality with sensors and keep it at the values specified in the standards. Priority has been given to placing the sensors in naturally ventilated classes that do not have a mechanical ventilation system and where windows and doors must be opened to allow air exchange (https://www.quebec.ca/en/education/preschool-elementary-and-secondary-schools/air-quality-schools).

When commercially offered classroom management systems are examined, it is seen that these systems start with student attendance control, material sharing, library tasks and monitoring of homework, and continue with systems that provide smart board management, teacher-student, student-student interaction in the classroom. It is also seen that there are systems that allow students to interact with their smart devices in the classroom (https://www.lightspeedsystems.com/solutions/lightspeed-classroom-management/). There are also systems where VR/AR technology is integrated into classrooms (https://www.classvr.com/case-studies/). In addition, today, the use of economic systems such as Google Cardboard is increasing in classrooms.

TECHNOLOGY-ENRICHED SMART CLASSROOM PROJECT

A scientific research fund of Ege University supports a technology-enriched smart classroom project. The smart classroom project aims to integrate technology effectively into educational processes. This project also brings together academics from different disciplines, creating a different perspective for smart classrooms. Bringing together the fields of education, engineering, and health in a research process under the headings of classroom environment and technology is extremely important in evaluating the results in a multidisciplinary manner.

The project targets to examine various variables that affect learning in technology-enriched learning environments at the higher education level. In this context, it is aimed to investigate the effects of the indoor environmental conditions of the classroom as an enriched learning environment and the instructional design process on the learning of university students.

In this context, within the scope of this project, the following parameters were experimentally analysed:

- the thermal comfort of the classrooms,
- the amount of CO_2 in the environment,
- noise level,
- level of illumination,
- classroom design,
- technologies to interact with,
- learning processes,
- student-learning material interaction,
- learning materials,

It is aimed to perceive the effects of variables such as the effects of such variables in the classroom environment as attention and learning performance changes. The class created within the project's scope aims to follow these processes and understand the impact of environmental conditions on learning. In addition, this project will reveal the level of meeting the optimum expectations of the applications and classroom designs to be made at the higher education level. One of the essential variables affecting learning processes is how the learning environment is designed. In the current smart classroom project, the smart classroom is built on a specific design. (See Figure1). The aim of this first design, in which there is no outside intervention, and the inside intervention is done manually, is to determine the optimum features of the classroom environment. The smart classroom is planned to provide an interactive environment both inside and outside the classroom, thanks to the use of the internet. In light of the factors affecting the classroom learning environment, the effective communication of the technologies used with each other creates a classroom model with a high level of efficiency and effectiveness.

Figure 1. Literature in structural classroom policies

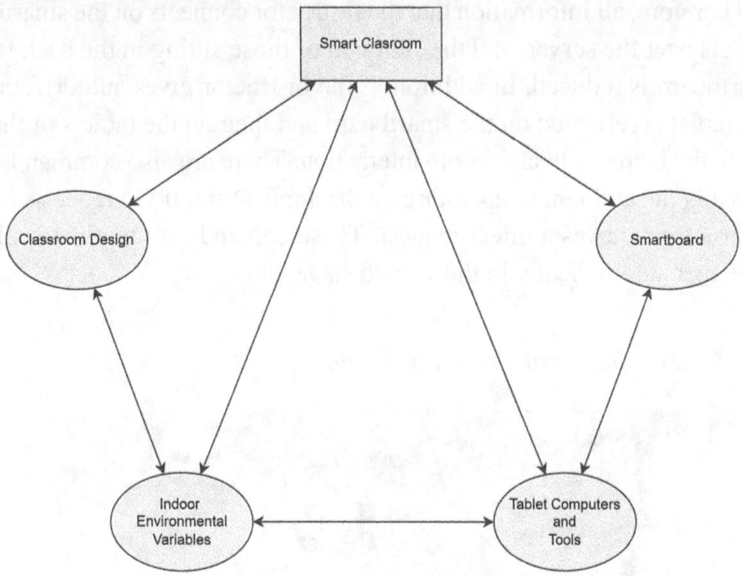

As seen in Figure 1, literature has been used in structuring classroom technologies, and tools that will provide data about environmental conditions have been added to the classroom environment. The tablets used during the lesson were directly integrated into the smartboard. The Smart Classroom Application was designed for the students' feedback, such as indoor air temperature, light, and humidity levels in the classroom. For example, when the students' requests to increase the indoor air temperature in the classroom reached 70%, a warning message was sent to the instructor, and information was given about the necessary interventions. All data in the classroom environment was recorded and stored instantly. The smart class has two main elements in this context. In-class environment data (indoor air temperature, relative humidity, illuminance, sound, CO_2) and data on which the instructional application is provided (e.g., participation of the students, distribution of the presentations, and interaction through the presentations, reflecting the students' views). In-class environment data are kept on instant movements in the classroom, as seen in Figure 2 below. The same data was kept both at the front and the back of the classroom and it was ensured that the entire classroom environment was reflected. In addition, the back and front data were correlated and deviations were prevented. In addition, visualization of the data was made and an interface was developed to enable users to read it.

Figure 2. In-class environment data

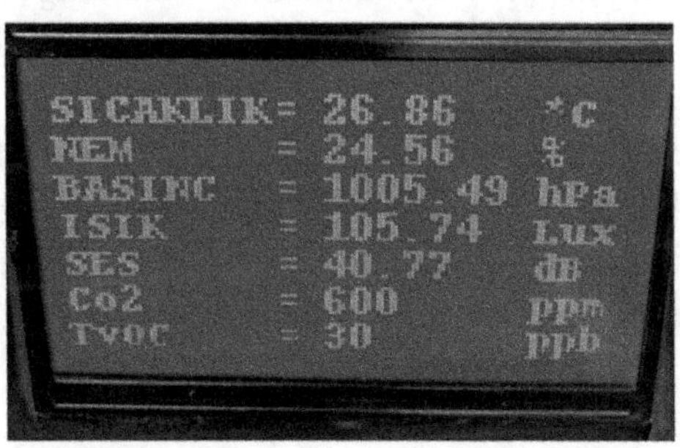

As seen in Figure 3, the data provided by the instructional application was planned to support students' in-class learning. Therefore, all information that the instructor connects on the smartboard is distributed to all students' tablets over the server, and the situation of those sitting in the back row missing what is visible on the smartboard is reduced. In addition, if the instructor gives authorization, the behavior of any student on the tablet is reflected on the smartboard and then on the tablets of the other classmates, which contributed to the increase in classroom interaction. There are also commands such as turning on the light and increasing the ambient temperature on the application. If the requests for these commands reach 70%, the instructor receives a direct request. These demands are met manually in the first stage and are aimed to be met automatically in the second stage.

Figure 3. Data provided by the instructional application

In this case, there are also some limitations. For example, while the project was carried out during the epidemic period, necessary precautions were taken to maintain distance in the classroom environment, while the emotional changes of the students were not clearly captured on the cameras due to the necessity of wearing masks. Laughter and boredom were tried to be perceived not from facial expressions, but from general physical movements. However, the epidemic situation has also made it possible to test a hybrid learning environment. In order to ensure that students maintain social distancing, some of the students attended the lesson remotely, and some of them were face-to-face. It has been observed that the students who attend the lesson remotely follow an interactive process at least as much as the students in the classroom. However, since they are primarily in their own learning environment, they were excluded from the classroom environment data. An additional application has been developed in order to monitor the data generated in all of these processes.

The smart classroom application is developed to aid in data visualization for students and instructors in an IoT-based class setting. The application utilizes data collected by other components of the smart classroom to better represent the classroom environment to its occupants. By connecting to a remote data source, the application fetches data collected from sensors strategically placed inside and outside the smart classroom. This includes indoor air temperature, relative humidity, atmospheric pressure, noise level, CO_2, and light intensity.

Figure 4. Data in classroom

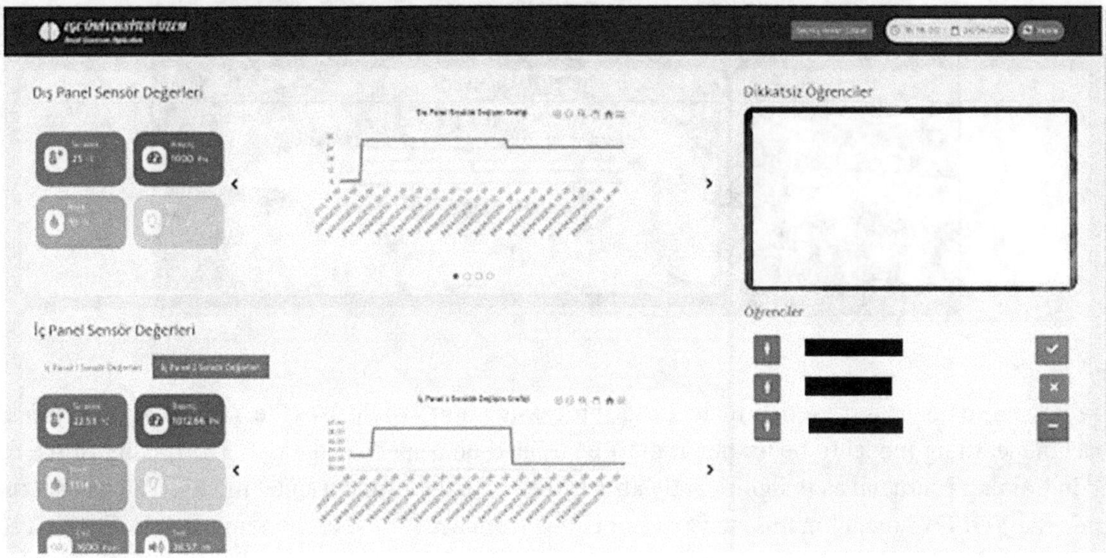

The application allows a user to look at the data history by searching for data values within a specific period allowing the observation of the classroom environmental changes over time, which may be necessary for student performance studies concerning their learning environment. Other than the representation of collected data, the smart classroom application utilizes artificial intelligence and machine learning to detect inattentive students in the classroom. During a lecture or a class session, a camera actively capturing the images of students in the classroom relays this data to a yolov5 trained machine-learning model. This model, in turn, determines inattentive students by their body language, which includes hand movements, sitting posture, and general facial direction. The application records these labeled images of inattentive students throughout the lesson. These records can later be used to correlate the inattentiveness rate of students in the classroom with the average class performance in a given subject or course.

Figure 5. Average classroom

A classroom image is passed on to the image processing unit, which uses the YOLOv5 algorithm. For a machine learning model to be usable, it must be trained on a specific dataset. The quality of the data used in training is crucial as it significantly affects the accuracy of the trained model. The dataset used to train the YOLOv5 model in this study was obtained from a recorded classroom session. The first step in preparing the training data was to extract an image sample from the video. This was done via a tool on a Linux-based computer called ffmpeg. A total of 1,284 images were obtained from a 107-minute class recording. After the data set to be used in the training of the object detection model was assembled, the images were labeled manually. Image tagging means identifying and tagging specific details in an image. In this case, students who were distracted by each visual were identified and labeled, and the visuals were labeled. Inattentive students were identified by their body posture. For example, a student was labeled careless if he was leaning over his phone or away from the instructor, playing with an object, or sitting in a hunched position. As all students in the class wore face masks, it was difficult to focus their attention on facial expressions, so body language was used. Through a data labeling platform called cvat.org, each image was manually labeled for careless students. The data is downloaded and uploaded to another platform called roboflow.com after being tagged with annotations showing inattentive students. It is a computer vision developer framework for data collection, processing, and model training. In this platform, the data is divided into three; training (87%), valid (9%), and test (4%) data. It is then processed with some enhancements to give a more robust model. These enhancements include adjusting images' brightness, exposure, flip, and noise.

The model is trained on Google's Colab, a cloud-based notebook that allows users to write and execute the python code used for the YOLOv5 model discussed in this study. Colab makes it easy to execute python code without downloading dependencies that often conflict and cause problems on the host. After the image input size, batch size, bus, model configuration, and weight path are defined, the YOLOv5 model is trained on an epoch value of 500. A python code is executed for object detection using the weights of the trained model. The careless student is identified in the image and is labeled with "careless student" above them.

The preliminary results of the project conducted at Ege University in the higher education level revealed that both students and instructors are satisfied with the smart classroom activities. In general, smart classroom technologies are becoming the most important outputs of educational technologies. According to the preliminary analysis results, when the students (n = 25) were asked to evaluate the course process in the smart classroom on a scale of 1 to 5, the average score was 4.48. The results revealed that 55.17 percent of students gave 5 points, 37.93 percent awarded 4 points, and 6.90 percent awarded 3 points. When students were asked to rate the teaching process of the course on a 5-point scale, an average of 4.55 points was attained. Sixty-five percent of the students scored five points, 27.59 percent scored four points, 3.45 percent scored three points, and 3.45 percent scored two points. In addition, they reported that interacting with others in the smart classroom settings and observing the entire process in real-time was a novel experience. According to the thoughts of the instructors, teaching in this smart classroom setting supplemented with technology is (i) a different experience, (ii) excitement, (iii) anxiety, and (iv) happiness. Teachers in smart classrooms remarked that it was fascinating to instruct in such a setting. They expressed anxiety about employing such technology to manage the course, but their experience was favorable. When asked to evaluate the instructional materials utilized in the technology-enhanced smart classroom environment during the pilot implementation, the students' scores averaged 4.62 out of 5 points. Students have favorable impressions of the instructional materials utilized in the course.

During the current project, both environmental conditions and educational methods were analysed and continue to be monitored. By observing the students' behaviour, the obtained results in consideration of the students' response to a change in environmental conditions are matched. The most significant finding from these first results is that environmental variables (indoor air temperature, relative humidity, illuminance, sound, CO_2) influence the learning processes. In the smart classroom settings, it was ensured that the environmental variables changed when the students reached an average level of demand based on their particular preferences. For instance, when 70% of the students indicated that they thought the environment to be warm, this heat exchange was conducted in accordance with student preferences.

CONCLUSION

When we look at the last 20 years of world history, we observe that while technology enters our lives very quickly, it also emerges at the same speed. Some technologies give way to other new ones, while others disappear. However, this does not change the fact that technology is an indispensable part of our lives. The transformation of technology from a luxury tool to a tool for compulsory use necessitates us to examine, manage, and use technology processes in more detail and more clearly. Smart classrooms are learning environments enriched with technology. This enrichment process can become more effective with meaningful data on the use of technology. In other words, it is necessary to use the technologies by being aware of their advantages and disadvantages. Keeping this balance depends on collecting data with different variables in ample processes and analyzing this data. The data analysis findings are critical for comprehending the processes of smart classrooms. In this chapter, the preliminary results of a research project are included to raise awareness of smart and/or technology-supported classrooms. These preliminary results showed that technology-supported smart classrooms and the lessons taught using these technologies were found to be positive for students. Even though students can use these technologies no matter their feelings, teachers might have some barriers. While these barriers were initially frightening, they soon became comfortable and excited. These preliminary results show that instructors in smart classroom environments have more anxiety than students. For this reason, improving the technology knowledge of the instructors in/for smart classroom environments may be necessary. It is also important to prepare the instructors for the process, update the curriculum according to the smart classroom environment, and have an effective technology integration process.

Another critical dimension is the development of systems with artificial intelligence applications that might give automatic responses. Thus, data-driven automated processes are not able to dependent on humans, such as automatically climate of classrooms based on student data. However, it has been observed that the creation of smart classrooms is still not economical in terms of cost. It would be expensive to make an organization fully intelligent. Institutions need to believe in the effectiveness of such learning environments and adopt this as their policy. For this reason, it is important to increase the number of smart classroom-based projects, to follow the learning processes, and to share their outputs.

In general, it has been observed that the learners have a positive attitude due to the appropriate and meaningful use of technology. In addition, it has been observed that students use existing technologies more effectively as they get used to the process and environment. Instead of placing many technological products that are ineffective in learning processes in classroom environments, it would be more appropriate to place technologies that support learning processes. It is a fact that technology design into the classroom will not make sense unless it is integrated educationally in an effective way. It should be remembered that the classroom environment is not only about technology, but also depends on the learners' many emotional, internal, physical, and psychological variables. Therefore, all variables related to external factors must be controlled to a minimum during the time the learners spend in the classroom. It should also be considered that response of the individuals can be affected by many different variables, such as age, gender, past experiences, and attitudes toward the course. Another critical situation is that such studies require multidisciplinary collaboration not only in the field of education but also in more than one field, contributing to the formation of different perspectives towards the same situation and finding different solutions to the problems. It is expected that future studies will open new paths to understanding effective smart classroom settings by including different teaching/learning strategies, new technologies, different variables, and fields of study.

ACKNOWLEDGMENT

The effects of a technology-enriched classroom on students' learning: The Smart Classroom Model project (ID: SOA-2020-21447) was funded by Ege University Scientific Research Project Coordination.

REFERENCES

AECT (Association for Educational Communications and Technology). (2022). *The Definition and Terminology Committee*. Retrieved on November, 9, 2022 from https://aect.org/news_manager.php?page=17578#:~:text='Educational%20technology%20is%20the%20study,'

Alfoudari, A. M., Durugbo, C. M., & Aldhmour, F. M. (2021). Understanding socio-technological challenges of smart classrooms using a systematic review. *Computers & Education, 173*, 104282. doi:10.1016/j.compedu.2021.104282

Almaqra, A., Almuqri, M., Alshathri, A., Aloraini, A., Alrehaili, Y., & Bin-Mubarak, A., et all (2019). Effect of caffeine consumption and air temperature on student performance. In *ACM International Conference Proceeding Series*, (pp. 250–254). Association for Computing Machinery. 10.1145/3306500.3309991

Baby, N., & Chellamani, K. (2018). Implementation of smart classrooms among secondary schools in Puducherry Union territory. *Journal of Science Education and Technology*, *14*(1), 39–51.

Bajc, T., Banjac, M., Todorović, M., & Stevanović, Ž. (2019). Experimental and statistical survey on local thermal comfort impact on working productivity loss in university classrooms. *Thermal Science*, *23*(1), 379–392. doi:10.2298/TSCI170920160B

Bakó-Biró, Z., Clements-Croome, D. J., Kochhar, N., Awbi, H. B., & Williams, M. J. (2012). Ventilation rates in schools and pupils' performance. *Building and Environment*, *48*(1), 215–223. doi:10.1016/j.buildenv.2011.08.018

Bouslama, F., & Kalota, F. (2013). Creating smart classrooms to benefit from innovative technologies and learning space design. In *Proceedings of International Conference on Current Trends in Information Technology (CTIT)* (pp. 102-106). IEEE. 10.1109/CTIT.2013.6749486

Burunkaya, M., & Duraklar, K. (2022). Design and Implementation of an IoT-Based Smart Classroom Incubator. *Applied Sciences (Switzerland)*, *12*(4), 2233. Advance online publication. doi:10.3390/app12042233

Cebrián, G., Palau, R., & Mogas, J. (2020). The smart classroom as a means to the development of ESD methodologies. *Sustainability*, *12*(7), 3010. doi:10.3390u12073010

Class, V. R. (2022). *Case Studies*. Retrieved July 20, 2022, from https://www.classvr.com/case-studies/

D'Mello, S. K. (2017). Emotional Learning Analytics. In The Handbook of Learning Analytics. Edited (pp. 115–127). SOLAR, Society for Learning Analytics and Research. doi:10.18608/hla17.010

Dağhan, G., & Gündüz, A. Y. (2022). Research trends in educational technology journals between 2000 and 2018: A web scraping study. *Education and Information Technologies*, *27*(4), 5179–5214. doi:10.100710639-021-10762-2

Frankenfield, J. (2022). *EdTech*. Retrieved on November, 9, 2022 from https://www.investopedia.com/terms/e/edtech.asp

Han, Z., & Xu, A. (2021). Ecological evolution path of smart education platform based on deep learning and image detection. *Microprocessors and Microsystems*, *80*, 103343. doi:10.1016/j.micpro.2020.103343

Haverinen-Shaughnessy, U., & Shaughnessy, R. J. (2015). Effects of classroom ventilation rate and temperature on students' test scores. *PLoS One*, *10*(8), 1–14. doi:10.1371/journal.pone.0136165 PMID:26317643

Jiang, J., Wang, D., Liu, Y., Xu, Y., & Liu, J. (2018). A study on pupils' learning performance and thermal comfort of primary schools in China. *Building and Environment, 134*(November), 102-113. doi:10.1016/j.buildenv.2018.02.036

Keis, O., Helbig, H., Streb, J., & Hille, K. (2014). Influence of blue-enriched classroom lighting on students' cognitive performance. *Trends in Neuroscience and Education*, *3*(3-4), 86–92. doi:10.1016/j.tine.2014.09.001

Kocaman, E. (2021). *Ofis Binalarında Kullanıcıların Demografik Karakteristiklerinin İç Ortam Isıl Konfor Memnuniyetine Etkilerinin Analiz Edilmesi* [Unpublished master's thesis]. University of Ege, Izmir, Türkiye.

Kwet, M., & Prinsloo, P. (2020). The 'smart'classroom: A new frontier in the age of the smart university. *Teaching in Higher Education*, *25*(4), 510–526. doi:10.1080/13562517.2020.1734922

Lee, M. C., Mui, K. W., Wong, L. T., Chan, W. Y., Lee, E. W. M., & Cheung, C. T. (2012). Student learning performance and indoor environmental quality (IEQ) in air-conditioned university teaching rooms. *Building and Environment*, *49*(1), 238–244. doi:10.1016/j.buildenv.2011.10.001

Li, B., Kong, S. C., & Chen, G. (2015). Development and validation of the smart classroom inventory. *Smart Learning Environments*, *2*(1), 3. Advance online publication. doi:10.118640561-015-0012-0

Li, B. P., Kong, S. C., & Chen, G. (2015). A Study on the Development of the Smart Classroom Scale. In G. Chen, V. Kumar, V. Kinshuk, R. Huang, & S. Kong (Eds.), *Emerging Issues in Smart Learning*. Lecture Notes in Educational Technology. Springer. doi:10.1007/978-3-662-44188-6_6

Li, Y., Yang, H. H., & MacLeod, J. (2019). Preferences toward the constructivist smart classroom learning environment: Examining preservice teachers' connectedness. *Interactive Learning Environments*, *27*(3), 349–362. doi:10.1080/10494820.2018.1474232

Lightspeed Systems. (2022). *Create Engaging Learning Environments Anywhere*. Retrieved July 20, 2022, from https://www.lightspeedsystems.com/solutions/lightspeed-classroom-management

Liu, Z., Geng, L., & Xu, Y. (2020, January). Design of Monitoring System for Classroom Environment Parameter Based on Wireless Communication. In *2020 International Conference on Intelligent Transportation, Big Data & Smart City (ICITBS)* (pp. 502-505). IEEE. 10.1109/ICITBS49701.2020.00109

Lorenzo, N., Gallon, R., Palau, R., & Mogas, J. (2021). New Objectives for Smart Classrooms from Industry 4.0. *Technology. Knowledge and Learning*, *26*(4), 719–731. doi:10.100710758-021-09527-0

Lu, G., Xie, K., & Liu, Q. (2022). What influences student situational engagement in smart classrooms: Perception of the learning environment and students' motivation. *British Journal of Educational Technology*, *53*(6), 1–23. doi:10.1111/bjet.13204

Lu, K., Yang, H. H., Shi, Y., & Wang, X. (2021). *Examining the key influencing factors on college students' higher-order thinking skills in the smart classroom*. Academic Press.

Niemeyer, D. (2003). *Hard facts on smart classroom design: Ideas, guidelines, and layouts*. Scarecrow Press.

OECD. (2019). *Going Digital: Shaping Policies, Improving Lives*. OECD Publishing. doi:10.1787/9789264312012-

Phoong, S. Y., Phoong, S. W., Moghavvemi, S., & Sulaiman, A. (2019). Effect of smart classroom on student achievement at higher education. *Journal of Educational Technology Systems*, *48*(2), 291–304. doi:10.1177/0047239519870721

Québec. (2022). *Air quality in schools*. Retrieved July 20, 2022, from https://www.quebec.ca/en/education/preschool-elementary-and-secondary-schools/air-quality-schools

Runathong, W., Wongthai, W., & Panithansuwan, S. (2017). A System for Classroom Environment Monitoring Using the Internet of Things and Cloud Computing. In K. Kim & N. Joukov (Eds.), *Information Science and Applications (ICISA 2017)* (Vol. 424). Lecture Notes in Electrical Engineering, Springer. doi:10.1007/978-981-10-4154-9_84

Saini, M. K., & Goel, N. (2019). How smart are smart classrooms? A review of smart classroom technologies. *ACM Computing Surveys*, *52*(6), 1–28. Advance online publication. doi:10.1145/3365757

Sala, E., & Rantala, L. (2016). Acoustics and activity noise in school classrooms in Finland. *Applied Acoustics*, *114*, 252–259. doi:10.1016/j.apacoust.2016.08.009

Sarbu, I., & Pacurar, C. (2015). Experimental and numerical research to assess indoor environment quality and schoolwork performance in university classrooms. *Building and Environment*, *93*(P2), 141–154. doi:10.1016/j.buildenv.2015.06.022

Shen, C. W., Wu, Y. C. J., & Lee, T. C. (2014). Developing a NFC-equipped smart classroom: Effects on attitudes toward computer science. *Computers in Human Behavior*, *30*, 731–738. doi:10.1016/j.chb.2013.09.002

Suleman, Q., & Hussain, I. (2014). Effects of classroom physical environment on the academic achievement scores of secondary school students in kohat division, Pakistan. *International Journal of Learning & Development*, *4*(1), 71–82. doi:10.5296/ijld.v4i1.5174

Tissenbaum, M., & Slotta, J. D. (2019). Developing a smart classroom infrastructure to support real-time student collaboration and inquiry: A 4-year design study. *Instructional Science*, *47*(4), 423–462. doi:10.100711251-019-09486-1

Yan, L., Yiqun, Z., & Tengfei, L. (2017). Design of environmental monitoring system for intelligent classroom. *Electron Technology*, *46*(05), 38–41.

Chapter 13
Using Smart Phones as Educational Technology to Promote Effective Learning

Amir Manzoor
https://orcid.org/0000-0002-3094-768X
Karachi School of Business and Leadership, Karachi, Pakistan

ABSTRACT

Today, smartphones have become a very popular learning tool. More specifically, educators have been using smartphones to enhance their teaching and students' learning. Using smartphones, educators can ensure flexible course delivery and provide learners access to online learning resources. In this study, the author examines how smartphones can be used as an effective learning tool for distance education. This study utilized a survey of university students in Karachi, Pakistan to find the effects of using smartphones in their learning activities and what factors inhibit their use of smartphones in their learning.

1. INTRODUCTION

Educational Technology is the field of study that investigates the process of analyzing, designing, developing, implementing, and evaluating the instructional environment, learning materials, learners, and the learning process in order to improve teaching and learning (Mishra et al., 2009). In education, educational technology plays a very significant role by assisting academicians integrate new technologies and tools into their classroom. Academicians can use educational technology to make their classes more focused towards needs of learners. Educational technology provides unique opportunities for academicians to engage their students in unique, innovative, and equitable ways and to expand their network and connect with other teachers and educators (School of Education, 2022).

Technology, especially information and related technology, has affected every aspect of our lives. Today, the impact of information technology (IT) is very evident in academics. Smartphones have rapidly become an integral element of our daily routine (Fawareh & Jusoh, 2017). The global rise in the use of smartphones has transformed the world of academics in both developed and developing worlds (Tagoe,

DOI: 10.4018/978-1-6684-6092-4.ch013

2014; Aljaber, 2021). Learners are no longer solely dependent on paper-based learning resources. The learning now takes place synchronously and asynchronously across geographical boundaries (Aljohani & Chandran, 2019; Amaliyah et al., 2021; Younes et al., 2021).

In their inception, smartphones were mainly used as an alternative to digital camera. Over the time, smartphones have even replaced digital watches. It is rare to find someone who owns a smartphone as well as a digital camera and digital watch. A smartphone can be considered a mini computer itself (Fawareh & Jusoh (2017; Komalavalli et al., 2020;). Besides basic call features, smartphones provide many amazing, advanced features such as web surfing, email, photo/vide/document sharing, biometric, access to social media sites to mention just a few (Zaki, 2019). Arguably, smartphone is the single most important driver of exploding use of social media sites including Facebook (Masiu & Chukwuere, 2018). From learners' point of view, a smartphone is a smart device that they can use to gain instant access to knowledge and achieve their learning objectives (Astuti et al., 2020; Ta'amneh, 2021; Tortorella et al., 2021; Yulkifli et al., 2022). For example, students can use smartphones to take notes, connect with learning management system (LMS), watch and record videos of lectures, record audios of explanation, access online libraries, connect with the teachers, listen to news and podcasts, read e-books, attempt online tests and assessments, collaborate with their peers, manage their time effectively etc.

According to Sarfoah (2017), the increased proliferation of smartphones has resulted in an associated increase in the number of social media users and the developing world has surpassed developed world in terms of number of mobile phone users. According to newzoo.com (2022), Pakistan was placed among the top 20 countries with respect to number of smartphone users. Pakistan has been ranked among developing nations that are quickly adopting mobile and IT.

Today, smartphones are playing a very important role for educators to enhance their teaching and students' learning. Using smartphones, students can quickly access the learning materials and information online without a computer. They can also access various academic databases and learning management systems (LMS) (Masiu & Chukwuere, 2018; Alfawareh & Jusoh, 2014; Lutfi & Hidayah, 2021). The introduction of smartphones in learning environment is one of the latest and most significant trends in higher education. With smartphones, learning has become more flexible, cost-effective, and easy while overcoming various limitations of traditional on-campus classes (Valk, Rashid, & Elder, 2010; Semarayasa et al., 2018). To further enhance their learning, students can use their smartphones to download recorded online lectures and e-books and to record abstract ideas discussed in the class. After deliberation, these abstract ideas can then be converted into concrete ideas (Norries et al., 2011; Jatmiko et al., 2021). Academicians can use the smartphone to produce learning material at their convenience and disseminate to students. As such, smartphone is one the most important tools of educational technology that benefits both learners and teachers in innovative ways.

Realizing the importance and usefulness of smartphones, academicians around the globe have adopted smartphones into their teaching practices (Ismail et. al., 2013; Pullen et al., 2015). However, the literature is still uncertain about the degree to which smartphones contribute towards the academic performance of students (Ng et al., 2020;Madumere et al., 2020; Malik & Asnur, 2019). In many cases, the students are not ready for smartphone technology and therefore use of smartphone for learning is not feasible. In these cases, students use their smartphones mostly for entertainment purposes and to access social media rather than for learning purposes (Masadeh, 2021; Mihail-Văduva, 2020; Salehudin et al, 2020). Therefore, this study aims to examine what drives students use of smartphones for learning activities. The study uses Technology Adoption Model to investigate the factors or drivers of smartphone use for learning purposes. The literature on the subject is available in the context of developed world. However, there is still lack of studies on the same subject in the context of developing world especially when it comes to application of TAM in Pakistani context. Universities around the globe are incorporating online learning in their curriculum to enhance students' learning experience and institutional competitiveness (Mazzarol & Soutar, 2012; Hariadi et al., 2021). Pakistani universities are no exception and therefore it is very important to examine what drives Pakistani students use of smartphones in their learning activities and what is the impact of smartphone on their learning.

2. LITERATURE REVIEW

2.1 Role of Smartphones in Mobile Learning Environment

Mobile learning is a learning mode that integrates mobile and wireless computing to provide learning and teaching opportunities round the clock and across geographical boundaries (Sarfoah, 2017). In mobile learning, the role of smartphone is very important. Smartphones are equipped with advanced features such as touch screen, a wide variety of downloadable applications, and advanced computing ability (Alfawareh & Jusoh, 2014; Guntur & Setyaningrum, 2021; Rahmadi, 2020; Thomas, 2021). Smartphones support both offline and online learning. In offline learning, users can use smartphones to store learning materials. Due to increased storage capacity available with modern smartphones, students can store large amounts of learning materials. Students can access online learning management systems, register their courses, take quizzes, and submit their assignments online (Imwa & Cabral, 2022).

2.2 Smartphones' Impact on Student Learning

The use of smartphone by students involves both positive and negative effects depending on the way smartphone is used (Bukhori et al., 2019; Darko-Adjei, 2019). For example, smartphones can be a source of great distraction for students (Ejimonye & Eneogu, 2019). Students excessively using their smartphones may excessively use their phones to keep checking various notification in different applications. Doing so, they divert their focus from their studies. Dealing with this negative effective of smartphones is a big challenge for academician looking to embrace mobile learning (Ifeanyi & Chukwuere, 2018; Dwikoranto et al., 2020; Shakoor et al., 2021; OMAR, 2020).

As such, the smartphones can be considered a double edge sword where many applications of smartphones may produce negative effects on students due to addictive nature of smartphones (Kibona & Mgaya, 2015). These negative effects were confirmed by another study conducted on young female Korean university students. This study found that students using smartphones made students at high risk of addiction and these students perceived themselves less regulated (Lee et al.,2015). These findings were again confirmed by Ifeanyi and Chukwuere (2018). They found smartphones consumed most of the students' time and their academic performance was decreased. The excessive use of smartphones can also lead to various medical problems including brain damage (Lin et al., 2014). Use of smartphones can also produce positive impacts on students' learning activities (Sarfoah, 2017; Mohammad, 2019)

While use of smartphones in learning are numerous, there are still many factors that inhibit students' adoption of smartphones to enhance their learning. For example, one study found that students did not prefer using smartphone in their learning activities because the screen size of smartphones was smaller as compared to the screen size of a normal computer or laptop. This small screen size served as a distraction while using smartphones during class (Gikas & Grant, 2013; Fauziah & Sulisworo. 2021; Suryanti et al.,2021). As such, students may also find that smartphones make learning uncomfortable. Stable / reliable internet connectivity is another major prerequisite for successful adoption of smartphones for learning activities. Not all smartphones can support all types of learning materials e.g., high-definition recording of live lectures need powerful graphics. Many a times, the smartphones can get frozen thereby causing inconvenience for the users. Intruding calls may disturb the students while in class. Such calls can significantly distract learning by driving away students' focus (Sarfoah, 2017).

2.3 Technology Acceptance Model (TAM) and Smartphones in Learning

Mobile learning is very important to enhance distance learning (Suryanti et al.,2021). Due to their sophisticated needs, students are hesitant to carry full-fledge laptops and heavy books. They prefer to store all their learning materials in their smartphones (Tuncay, 2016). Usage of smartphones can help students enhance their learning as well as having more social interactions, learn in collaboration with other, and socialize (Soegoto, 2019; Sulistyorini & Widodo, 2022). In future, smartphones are expected to become the most significant tool used in the distance education (Ketheeswaran & Mukunthan, 2016). The universities in both developed and developing world are adopting mobile learning at a rapid pace. These universities have started to complement their conventional teaching and learning practices with mobile learning (WIPAWASOMBAT, 2021). To study the students' acceptance and use of smartphones in distance education, this study employs Technology Acceptance Model (TAM) (Davis et al.,1989; Davis. 1986) which is a widely used behavioral intention model that focuses on factors that affect users' use of technology. There exist various variations of TAM. However, all focusses on the factors that affect users' acceptance of technology-based systems (Ketheeswaran & Mukunthan, 2016). According to TAM, two factors determine technology acceptance by its potential users: (1) perceived usefulness, and (2) perceived ease of use (Davis, 1989). The actual system use is the endpoint where people use the technology. Behavioral intention is a factor that leads people to use the technology.

2.3.1 Perceived Ease of Use

Perceived ease of use of technology is an important predictor of technology use. Students can be inclined to use smartphones if they perceive it easy to use for learning activities (Sarfoah, 2017). This is important given that students do sometimes find it very difficult accessing learning material on their smartphones (Ifeanyi & Chukwuere, 2018; Clark, 2021). To promote mobile learning, it is important that students should be comfortable in using a smartphone for learning. It is important to note that in some cases students may already be familiar with smartphones and can use smartphones in mobile learning efficiently and effectively (Iqbal & Bhatti, 2015).

2.3.2 Perceived Usefulness

One important aspect of usefulness of smartphones is the ability to enable users to study anywhere and at any time, making learning more attractive (Iqbal & Bhatti, 2015). Smartphones help students in communication with their peers and teachers. Students also use smartphones to discuss the concepts with peers, download study materials, access recorded lectures/slides, and help in homework (Ifeanyi & Chukwuere, 2018; Toperesu,2020).

2.3.3 Perceived Usefulness

Students can use smartphones to register courses, consult class/examination schedule, check their grades, conduct group discussion, keep aware of school announcements, pay school/university fee etc, various other activities. In this way, smartphones are perceived very useful by the students in the learning activities (Alzougool & Almansour, 2017). In some cases, students have even adopted smartphones as a necessity for learning. These students used smartphones to share learning material among peers, record lectures, and share the same material using social media sites (Mohtar et al., 2013; Tunca, 2016). Smartphones can also significantly enhance student-teacher interaction to learn while on the move (Mallampalli et al., 2019; Ahmadi et al., 2022).

The use of smartphone can significantly enhance student's learning. Students can use smartphones to conduct research, obtain relevant information for their assignments/projects, and much more (Akaglo & Nimako-Kodu, 2019; Akkara, 2020). The use of smartphones can make course delivery in distance education very effective. Students can use smartphones to save their learning materials and e-books and interact with their teachers digitally without any geographical boundaries (Tuncay, 2016; Gromik & Litz, 2021). On the flip side, excessive use of smartphones can cause unwanted consequences such as negative impacts on physical, psychological, and social well-being of learners (Chen et al., 2021; SAl Miaraj & Bhat, 2021; REMUS et al., 2018; Kashif et al.,2020; Hayat, 2021). There exist a wide variety of smartphone models and platforms. Each year, several new models of smartphones are introduced. Each smartphone has its operating system. Both smartphone and its operating system uniquely present information on screen of smartphone. However, it appears this unique way of information presentation doesn't affect the students' perception and beliefs about the usability of the smartphones. Literature suggests that learning is more effective if the smartphones are equipped with QWERTY keyboard feature and a larger screen that makes it easy and efficient to access and navigate the course content (Huang, 2009; Dwikoranto et al.,2021).

3. CONCEPTUAL FRAMEWORK AND RESEARCH HYPOTHESES

Figure 1 shows the conceptual framework used in this study.

Figure 1. Conceptual framework

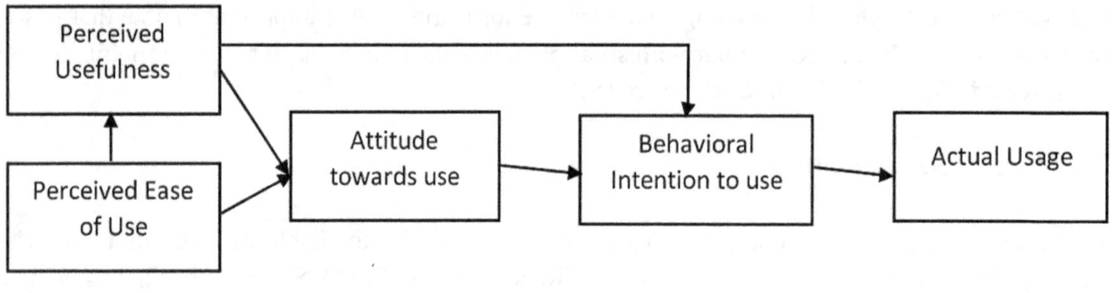

Following are the research hypotheses of this study.

H1: Perceived ease of use of smartphones has a significant impact on perceived usefulness of smartphones.
H2: Perceived ease of use of smartphones has a significant impact on attitude towards using smartphones.
H3: Perceived usefulness of smartphones has a significant impact on attitude towards using smartphones.
H4: Perceived usefulness of smartphones has a significant influence on behavioral intention to use smartphones.
H5: Attitude Towards Using smartphones has a significant impact on behavioral intention to use smartphones.
H6: behavioral intention to use smartphones has a significant impact on actual usage of smartphones.

4. METHODOLOGY

4.1 Research Instrument

The data for this study was collected using a questionnaire. The measures used in the questionnaire were adapted from available literature. Specifically, the scale used to measure perceived usefulness, perceived ease of use, attitude towards usage, behavioral intention towards usage, and actual usage were adopted from Adams, Nelson, and Todd (1992), Chin and Todd (1995), Corwin (1998), Davis et al., (1989), Szajna (1996), Venkatesh and Davis (2000), and Wallace (1998). A five-point Likert scale (where 1 = strongly disagree to 5= strongly agree) was used to measure all items. There were two parts of the questionnaire. The first part contained questions to collect demographic data. The second part contained items used to measure the variables included in the research framework.

4.2 Sampling Design

This questionnaire was administered on a sample of university students in Karachi. These students were selected using snowball sampling technique. All students were participating in distance education programs of different higher education institutions in Pakistan. The participants of the study had basic internet and computer skills. However, they had no prior mobile learning experience. The sample was balanced where 49% of participants were female and 51% were male.

5. DATA ANALYSIS AND RESULTS

We used confirmatory factor analysis (CFA) to establish construct reliability and validity. SmartPSLS statistical software was used for all statistical analyses. Multiple regression analysis and path analysis were used to examine the hypothesized relationships.

5.1 Instrument Validation

The model was tested to ascertain reliability of the research instrument. The procured specified by Cronbach (1951) was used to measure the internal consistency of the research instrument. As shown in Table 1, the values of Cronbach's alpha for all measures used in the research instrument were above .70 (Nunnally & Bernstein, 1994). Therefore, the research instrument was considered reliable.

Table 1. Reliability statistics

Measure	Cronbach's Alpha
Actual Use	0.713
Attitude Towards Use	0.927
Behavioral Intention	0.789
Perceived Ease of Use	0.869
Perceived Usefulness	0.903

5.2 Hypothesis Testing

H1 proposed that perceived ease of use of smartphones has a significant impact on perceived usefulness of smartphones. Looking at Table 2 and 3, we see that value of R^2 for Perceived Usefulness is 0.208 with $p< 0.05$. The path coefficient was 0.457 with p-value = 0.000. Therefore, H1 was supported. H2 and H3 proposed that perceived usefulness and ease of use have a significant impact on attitude toward using, respectively. Looking at Table 2 and 3, we see that perceived usefulness and ease of use explained 19.2% of the variance in attitude towards using ($R^2 = .192$, p=0.001). Both predictors significantly predicted attitude toward using ($\beta_{\text{perceived ease of use}} = .288$, p<.05) and ($\beta_{\text{perceived usefulness}} = .223$, p<.001). Hence, H2 and H3 are supported. Hypotheses 4 and 5 proposed that perceived usefulness and attitude toward using have a significant impact on behavioral intention to use. Looking at Table 2 and 3, we see that perceived usefulness and attitude toward using explained 22.2% of the variance in behavioral intention to use ($R^2 = .222$, p<.001). Both predictors significantly predicted behavioral intention to use ($\beta_{\text{perceived usefulness}} =$ 0.380, p<.05) and ($\beta_{\text{attitude toward using}} = 0.176.$, p <.05). Hence, H4 and H5 are supported. H6 proposed that behavioral intention to use has a significant impact on actual use. The results show that behavioral intention to use explained 3.6% % of the variance in actual use ($R^2 = .036$, p<.01). The predictor significantly predicted actual use ($\beta_{\text{behavioral intention to use}} = .190$, p<.001). Hence, H6 was supported.

Table 2. R^2 Values

	Original Sample (O)	Sample Mean (M)	Standard Deviation (STDEV)	T Statistics (|O/STDEV|)	P Values
Actual Use	0.036	0.046	0.019	1.886	0.060
Attitude Towards Use	0.192	0.209	0.059	3.262	0.001
Behavioral Intention	0.222	0.238	0.056	4.005	0.000
Perceived Usefulness	0.208	0.217	0.044	4.755	0.000

Table 3. Path coefficients

	Original Sample (O)	Sample Mean (M)	Standard Deviation (STDEV)	T Statistics (|O/STDEV|)	P Values
Attitude Towards Use -> Behavioral Intention	0.176	0.184	0.055	3.190	0.002
Behavioral Intention -> Actual Use	0.190	0.209	0.047	4.009	0.000
Perceived Ease of Use -> Attitude Towards Use	0.288	0.301	0.070	4.108	0.000
Perceived Ease of Use -> Perceived Usefulness	0.457	0.463	0.048	9.582	0.000
Perceived Usefulness -> Attitude Towards Use	0.223	0.221	0.068	3.269	0.001
Perceived Usefulness -> Behavioral Intention	0.380	0.383	0.062	6.121	0.000

6. DISCUSSION

The results show that students' intention to use smartphones significantly influences their actual use of smartphones. At the same time, students' perceived usefulness and attitude towards the smartphones significantly influences their behavioral intention to use smartphones. Students' perceived usefulness and perceived ease of use of the smartphones influence their attitude towards the use of the smartphones. Students' perceived usefulness of smartphones has greater influence than the student's perceived ease of use of smartphones. The results confirm TAM's suitability to predict actual use of technology with its relation to users' intention to use the technology. The students' perceived usefulness of smartphones has a direct impact on students' attitude and behavioral intention to use smartphones. We can say that perceived usefulness is the most significant driver of students' acceptance of smartphones in their learning activities. It also suggests that exposure to smartphones can be an important factor for students to develop their initial beliefs about smartphones. Students' behavioral intention to use smartphones is a significant predictor of their actual use of smartphones. As such, it can be said that students' adoption and use of smartphones is directly influenced by their beliefs and attitudes towards smartphones.

7. CONCLUSION

The findings of this study validate the application of TAM to explain and predict the acceptance of technology (smartphones) by the users (students). Students' perception and attitude are very significant influencers of actual use of smartphone by students. Perceived ease of use and perceived usefulness of smartphones are important predictors of students' perceptions of the smart phones. While designing mobile learning systems and its objects, academicians and practitioners must therefore consider both ease of use and usefulness to encourage use of these systems and objects by students.

8. PRACTICAL/MANAGERIAL IMPLICATION

There are two major implications of this study. First, the academicians and practitioners can use the conceptual model of this study to predict the factors that could enhance mobile learning in their respective context. The results of this study can serve as guidelines for designing learning objects in a mobile learning environment. The academicians and practitioners can also use the conceptual model as a tool to gauge students' acceptance of technology-based systems including mobile learning systems. Doing so, they could minimize the risks that students would reject the system. Early detection of risks would enable system designers to come up with measures that could ensure students' acceptance of the system. Since students' perceived ease of use of smartphones is a significant and direct predictor of their actual use of smartphones, it is important that students are introduced to smartphones and briefed about their use and benefits related to mobile learning. That would ease the task of getting their acceptance of mobile learning systems.

9. AREAS OF FUTURE RESEARCH

This study was a cross-sectional study. Future studies could be longitudinal where they could replicate the conceptual model of this study. Future studies could also use the extended TAM to gain more insights into how students' beliefs and attitudes towards smartphones could change overtime while they experience the use of smartphones.

REFERENCES

Adams, D. A., Nelson, R. R., & Todd, P. A. (1992). Perceives Usefulness, Ease of Use, and Usage of Information Technology: A Replication. *Management Information Systems Quarterly*, *16*(2), 227–247. doi:10.2307/249577

Ahmadi, F., Hapsari, I. P., & Artharina, F. P. (2022). Developing Android-based English Multimedia in Improving the Skill of Literary Criticism. *Journal of Nonformal Education*, *8*(1).

Akaglo, E., & Nimako-Kodua, J. (2019). *The effects of the use of mobile phones on second cycle students in Ghana.* Retrieved from https://www. myjoyonline. com/opinion/2019/February-15th/stu dy-the-effects-of-the-useof-mobile-phones-on-second-cycle-st
udents-in-ghana. php

Akkara, S. (2020, September). Enhancing Second Language Listening Skills Through Smartphones: A Case Study. In *Internet of Things, Infrastructures and Mobile Applications: Proceedings of the 13th IMCL Conference* (*Vol. 1192*, p. 347). Springer Nature.

Alfawareh, H. M., & Jusoh, S. (2014). Smartphones usage among university students: Najran University case. *International Journal of Academic Research Part B*, *6*(2), 321–326. doi:10.7813/2075-4124.2014/6-2/B.48

Aljaber, A. A. M. (2021). *The reality of using smartphone applications for learning in higher education of Saudi Arabia*. University of Glasgow.

Aljohani, N., & Chandran, D. (2019). *The role of individuals and social awareness in adopting mobile health applications in Saudi Arabia: A review and preliminary findings*. Academic Press.

Alzougool, B., & Almansour, J. (2017). *The use of smartphone for learning activities by University students in Kuwait*. 4th Teaching & Education Conference, Venice. Retrieved from https://www.researchgate.net/publication/320001995_the_use_of_smartphone_for_learning_activities_by_university_students_in_kuwaIT

Amaliyah, A., Agusmiati, S., Zakiyah, B., Ummah, W. K., Hasanah, U., & Abdullah, D. (2021). Accelerated e-Learning Implementation through Youtube Videos Using Smartphones. *Journal of Physics: Conference Series*, *1899*(1), 012155. doi:10.1088/1742-6596/1899/1/012155

Astuti, F. N., Suranto, S., & Masykuri, M. (2020). The appropriateness of developing the media: Experts' validation and students' response of learning media based on augmented reality technology for natural science lesson. *Journal of Physics: Conference Series*, *1567*(4), 042023. doi:10.1088/1742-6596/1567/4/042023

Bukhori, B., Said, H., Wijaya, T., & Nor, F. M. (2019). *The effect of smartphone addiction, achievement motivation, and textbook reading intensity on students' academic achievement*. Academic Press.

Chen, Y. Y., Medi, B., Safiy, A., Shamsudin, S. S. A. I. B., De Ng, K., & Malek, K. B. A. (2021). Smartphone Usage and Psychological Well-being among Malaysian University Students. *Global Business and Management Research*, *13*(2).

Chin, W. W., & Todd, P. A. (1995). On the Use, Usefulness, and Ease of Use of Structural Equation Modeling in MIS Research: A Note of Caution. *Management Information Systems Quarterly*, *19*(2), 237–246. doi:10.2307/249690

Clark, S. E. (2021). *Nursing Faculty Experiences With Mobile Technology Use in the Classroom* [Doctoral dissertation]. Walden University.

Corwin, T. A. (1998). *Prediction of and Differences in Computer Use: Universal Adoption of Notebook Computers at Three Undergraduate Institutions* [Unpublished Doctoral Dissertation]. Iowa State University.

Cronbach, L. J. (1951). Coefficient Alpha and the Internal Structure of Tests. *Psychometrika*, *16*(3), 297–334. doi:10.1007/BF02310555

Darko-Adjei, N. (2019). *The use and effect of smartphones in students' learning activities: Evidence from the University of Ghana*. Legon.

Davis, F. D. (1986). *Technology Acceptance Model for Empirically Testing New End-user Information Systems: Theory and Results* [Unpublished Doctoral Dissertation]. Massachusetts Institute of Technology.

Davis, F. D. (1989). Perceived Usefulness, Perceived Ease of Use, and User Acceptance of Information Technology. *Management Information Systems Quarterly*, *13*(3), 318–340. doi:10.2307/249008

Davis, F. D., Bagozzi, R. P., & Warshaw, P. R. (1989). User Acceptance of Computer Technology: A Comparison of Two Theoretical Models. *Management Science*, *35*(8), 982–1003. doi:10.1287/mnsc.35.8.982

Dwikoranto, D., Setiani, R., Prahani, B. K., & Mubarok, H. (2020). Mobile learning to improve student collaborative skills: An alternative to online learning in the era of Covid-19 pandemic. *Jurnal Penelitian Dan Pengkajian Ilmu Pendidikan. E-Saintika*, *4*(3), 259–271.

Dwikoranto, D., Setiani, R., & Tresnaningsih, S. (2021, December). Effectiveness of Mobile Learning to Increase Collaborative Ability and Science Process Skills of Students. In *International Joint Conference on Science and Engineering 2021 (IJCSE 2021)* (pp. 441-446). Atlantis Press.

Ejimonye, J. C., & Eneogu, N. D. (2019). Educational Use And Misuse Of Smartphones Among Economics Students In Tertiary Institutions In Enugu State, Nigeria. *ADECT 2019 Proceedings*.

Fauziah, R. N., & Sulisworo, D. (2021). The Development of Applications using Augmented Reality Technology as the Teaching Media of Special Mirror Lights. *Jurnal Pendidikan Fisika*, *9*(2), 117–124.

Fawareh, H. M. A., & Jusoh, S. (2017). The Use and Effects of Smartphones in Higher Education. *IJIM*, (11), 6.

Gikas, J., & Grant, M. M. (2013). Mobile computing devices in higher education: Student perspectives on learning with cellphones, smartphones & social media. *The Internet and Higher Education*, *19*, 18–26. doi:10.1016/j.iheduc.2013.06.002

Gromik, N., & Litz, D. (2021). Study Benefits of Smartphones: Perceptions of Female Emirati Pre-Service Teacher Undergraduates. *Education Sciences*, *11*(12), 817. doi:10.3390/educsci11120817

Guntur, M. I. S., & Setyaningrum, W. (2021). The Effectiveness of Augmented Reality in Learning Vector to Improve Students' Spatial and Problem-Solving Skills. *International Journal of Interactive Mobile Technologies*, *15*(5), 159. doi:10.3991/ijim.v15i05.19037

Hariadi, B., Sunarto, M. J., Sagirani, T., Amelia, T., Lemantara, J., Prahani, B. K., & Jatmiko, B. (2021). Higher Order Thinking Skills for Improved Learning Outcomes Among Indonesian Students: A Blended Web Mobile Learning (BWML) Model. *International Journal of Interactive Mobile Technologies*, *15*(7), 4. doi:10.3991/ijim.v15i07.17909

Hayat, F., Ahmad, D. S., & Ullah, M. K. (2021). Impact of Mobile Phone Use on Students' Moral and Learning Behaviour at Higher Secondary School Level. *International Research Journal of Education and Innovation*, *2*(2), 356–368. doi:10.53575/irjei.36-v2.2(21)356-368

Huang, K.-Y. (2009). Challenges in Human-Computer Interaction Design for Mobile Devices. *Proceedings of the World Congress on Engineering and Computer Science*.

Ifeanyi, I. P., & Chukwuere, J. E. (2018). The impact of using smartphones on the academic performance of undergraduate students. *Knowledge Management & E-Learning*, *10*(3), 290–308.

Imwa, M., & Cabral, P. B. (2022). The Potential of Using Smartphones in Teaching and Learning in Secondary School Education: A Literature Review Study-Time to Embrace the Mobile Devices in Classrooms. *Impact of Digital Transformation in Teacher Training Models*, 211-228.

Iqbal, S., & Ahmed Bhatti, Z. (2015). An investigation of university student readiness towards m-learning using technology acceptance model. *International Review of Research in Open and Distributed Learning*, *16*(4), 83–103. doi:10.19173/irrodl.v16i4.2351

Ismail, I., Bokhare, S. F., Azizan, S. N., & Azman, N. (2013). Teaching via mobile phone: A case study on Malaysian teachers' technology acceptance and readiness. *Journal of Educators Online*, *2*(1). Advance online publication. doi:10.9743/JEO.2013.1.3

Jatmiko, B., Hariyono, E., Lestari, N. A., & Prahani, B. K. (2021). MobLen Model for Enhancing Scientific Creativity of Physics Students: An Alternative in the Covid-19 Pandemic. *Journal of Physics: Conference Series*, *1805*(1), 012006. doi:10.1088/1742-6596/1805/1/012006

Kashif, M., Rehman, A. U., Javed, M. K., & Javaid, D. (2020). *Smartphone: A Big Threat for Student's Education. Irish Interdisciplinary Journal of Science & Research.*

Ketheeswaran, L. K., & Mukunthan, T. (2016). Smart Phones for Learning Purposes by Students Who Follows 'Diploma in Commonwealth Youth Development Programmes' in the Colombo And Batticaloa Centres of the Open University of Sri. *IOSR Journal of Humanities and Social Science, 21*(5). Retrieved from http://www.jmest.org/wp-content/uploads/JMESTN42350643.pdf

Kibona, L., & Mgaya, G. (2015). Smartphones' Effects on Academic Performance of Higher Learning Students: A Case of Ruaha Catholic University – Iringa, Tanzania. *Journal of Multidisciplinary Engineering Science and Technology*, *2*(4). http://www.jmest.org/wp- content/uploads/JMESTN42350643.pdf

Komalavalli, K., Hemalatha, R., & Dhanalakshmi, S. (2020). A Survey of Artificial Intelligence in Smart Phones and Its Applications among the Students of Higher Education in and around Chennai City. *Shanlax International Journal of Education*, *8*(3), 89–95. doi:10.34293/education.v8i3.2379

Lee, J., Cho, B., Kim, Y., & Noh, J. (2015). *Smartphone addiction in university students and its implication for learning. Emerging Issues in Smart Learning*. Springer-Verlag. doi:10.1007/978-3-662-44188-6_40

Lutfi, A., & Hidayah, R. (2021). *Gamification for Science Learning Media Challenges of Teacher and Expectations of Students*. Academic Press.

Madumere, C. P., Ekwelem, V. O., & Anike, C. J. (2020). Social media and smart phone usage among students in Nigeria: The implications to their academic activities. *Library Philosophy & Practice*.

Malik, A. R., & Asnur, M. N. A. (2019). Using Social Media As A Learning Media Of Foreign Language Students In Higher Education. *Bahtera: Jurnal Pendidikan Bahasa Dan Sastra*, *18*(2), 166–175.

Mallampalli, M. S., Anumula, V., & Akkara, S. (2019, October). Enhancing Second Language Listening Skills Through Smartphones: A Case Study. In *Interactive Mobile Communication, Technologies and Learning* (pp. 347–356). Springer.

Masadeh, T. S. Y. (2021). Smartphone Use In Learning As Perceived By University Undergraduates: Benefits And Barriers. *International Journal of Research-GRANTHAALAYAH*, *9*(3), 56–65. doi:10.29121/granthaalayah.v9.i3.2021.3764

Masiu, M. T., & Chukwuere, J. E. (2018). The Effect of Smartphones on Students' Academic Life: A Perceptive from a South African University. *International Conference on Business and Management Dynamics ICBM-2018.*

Mazzarol, T., & Soutar, G. N. (2012). Revisiting the global market for higher education. *Asia Pacific Journal of Marketing and Logistics*, *24*(5), 717–737. doi:10.1108/13555851211278079

Mihail-Văduva, D. (2020). The impact of a multimedia mobile application. *Proceedings of the IE 2020 International Conference*. 10.24818/ie2020.01.06

Mishra, P., Koehler, M. J., & Kereluik, K. (2009). Looking back to the future of educational technology. *TechTrends*, *53*(5), 49.

Mohammad, W. S. (2019). Work-related risk factors for Carpal Tunnel Syndrome among Majmaah University female touchscreen users. *Pakistan Journal of Medical Sciences*, *35*(5), 1221. doi:10.12669/pjms.35.5.683 PMID:31488982

Mohtar, N. M. M., Hassan, M. A., Hassan, M. S., & Osman, M. N. (2013). IOSR Journal Of Humanities and Social Science (IOSR-JHSS). *The Importance of Smartphone's Usage Among Malaysian Undergraduates*, *14*(3), 12–118.

newzoo.com. (2022). *Top Countries/Markets by Smartphone Penetration & Users*. Newzoo. https://newzoo.com/insights/rankings/top-countries-by-smartphone-penetration-and-users

Ng, S. F., Azlan, M. A. K., Kamal, A. N. A., & Manion, A. (2020). A quasi-experiment on using guided mobile learning interventions in ESL classrooms: Time use and academic performance. *Education and Information Technologies*, *25*(6), 4699–4719.

Norries, C., Hossain, A., & Soloway, E. (2011). Using smartphones as essential tools for learning: A call to place schools on the right side of the 21st century. *Educational Technology*, *51*(3), 18–25.

Nunnally, J. C., & Bernstein, I. H. (1994). *Psychometric Theory*. McGraw-Hill.

Omar, P. U. (2020). Smartphone usage among students at politeknik ungku omar. Jurnal Kejuruteraan, Teknologi dan Sains Sosial, 3(1).

Pullen, D. J-F., Swabey, K., Abadooz, M., & Sing, T. (2015). Malaysian university students' use of mobile phones for study. *Australian Educational Computing, 30*(1). Retrieved from http://journal.acce.edu.au/index.php/AEC/article/view/55

Rahmadi, F. (2020). *WhatsApp Group for Teaching and Learning in Indonesian Higher Education: What's Up?* Academic Press.

Remus, V., Cosmin, P., & Mihai, K. (2018). Study on technology as support for the activity of physical education and sport teachers in the primary and secondary education system of Cluj-Napoca. *Studia Universitatis Babes-Bolyai, Educatio Artis Gymnasticae, 63*(4).

SAl Miaraj, A. A., & Bhat, I. B. (2021). Prevalence of Text Neck Syndrome and Its Association with Mobile Phone Usage Among University Academic Staff. *Int J Phys Med Rehabil, 9*, 10.

Salehudin, M., Hamid, A., Zakaria, Z., Rorimpandey, W., & Yunus, M. (2020). *Instagram user experience in learning graphic design*. Academic Press.

Sarfoah, E. (2017). *Smartphone use for learning: A study on University of Ghana students* [Unpublished MPhil Thesis]. Department of Communication Studies, University of Ghana.

School of Education. L. U. of M. (2022, December 13). *What is Educational Technology—School of Education—Loyola Maryland*. https://www.loyola.edu/school-education/blog/2021/what-is-educational-technology

Semarayasa, I. K., Soegiyanto, K. S., Rahayu, S., & Hidayah, T. (2018, September). Impact of smartphones on the achievement of sepak takraw learners. In *International Conference on Science and Education and Technology 2018 (ISET 2018)* (pp. 237-240). Atlantis Press.

Shakoor, F., Fakhar, A., & Abbas, J. (2021). Impact of smartphones usage on the learning behaviour and academic performance of students: Empirical evidence from Pakistan. *Int. J. Acad. Res. Bus. Soc. Sci*, *11*, 862–881.

Soegoto, H. (2019). Smartphone usage among college students. *Journal of Research in Engineering and Technology*, *14*(3), 1248–1259.

Sulistyorini, E., & Widodo, P. (2022). The Utilization of the Deutsche Welle Learning Application in Teaching German Vocabulary. *International Journal of Linguistics, Literature and Translation*, *5*(1), 110–116.

Suryanti, S., Widodo, W., & Yermiandhoko, Y. (2021). *Gadget-Based Interactive Multimedia on Socio-Scientific Issues to Improve Elementary Students' Science Literacy*. Academic Press.

Szajna, B. (1996). Empirical Evaluation of the Revised Technology Acceptance Model. *Management Science*, *42*(1), 85–92.

Ta'amneh, M. A. A. A. (2021). The Use of Smartphones in Learning English Language Skills: A Study of University Students' Perspectives. *International Journal of Applied Linguistics and English Literature*, *10*(1), 1–8.

Tagoe, M., & Abakah, E. (2014). Determining distance education students' readiness for mobile learning at University of Ghana using the Theory of Planned Behavior. *International Journal of Education and Development Using Information and Communication Technology*, *10*(1), 91.

Thomas, A. D. (2021). *The Use of Smartphones by K-12 School Administrators: A Gratification Study* [Doctoral dissertation]. Tennessee State University.

Toperesu, B. (2020). *The impact of smartphone use on student learning experience in higher education in South Africa* [Master's thesis]. Faculty of Commerce.

Tortorella, G. L., Narayanamurthy, G., & Cauchick-Miguel, P. A. (2021). Operations Management teaching practices and information technologies adoption in emerging economies during COVID-19 outbreak. *Technological Forecasting and Social Change*, *171*, 120996.

Tuncay, N. (2016). Smartphones as tools for distance education. *Journal Of Educational And Instructional Studies in the World.*, *6*(2), 2146–7463.

Valk, J., Rashid, A., & Elder, L. (2010). Using mobile phones to improve educational outcomes: An analysis of evidence from Asia. *The International Review of Research in Open and Distributed Learning*, *11*(1), 117–140. https://www.irrodl.org/index.php/irrodl/article/view/794/1507

Venkatesh, V., & Davis, F. D. (2000). A Theoretical Extension of the Technology Acceptance Model: Four Longitudinal Field Studies. *Management Science*, *46*(2), 186–204.

Wallace, P. R. (1998). *Diffusion of Internet Adoption: A Study of the Relationship between Innovativeness, the Attitude of Teachers toward Using the Internet, and Internet Use* [Unpublished Doctoral Dissertation]. University of Tennessee, Knoxville, TN, United States.

Wipawasombat, M. O. (2021). *Characteristics of smartphone to support online study during COVID-19 situation* [Doctoral dissertation]. Thammasat University.

Younes, S. S., Alharbi, A. H., & Aboeldahab, M. M. (2021). Measuring the impact of an AI-enabled mobile application for university students. *Mobile Information Systems*.

Yulkifli, Y., Yohandri, Y., & Azis, H. (2022). Development of physics e-module based on integrated project-based learning model with Ethno-STEM approach on smartphones for senior high school students. *Momentum: Physics Education Journal*, 93–103.

Zaki, M. (2019). *The relationship between segmentation and question location within mobile video platforms for enhancing the ability of recall*. Academic Press.

Chapter 14
Digital Literacy for Students With Intellectual Disabilities

Patricia Holzman
A. Harry Moore School, New Jersey City University, USA

Wendy Thompson
A. Harry Moore School, New Jersey City University, USA

ABSTRACT

Safe use of media sources is a part of curriculums for all students, including those with intellectual disabilities. Educators are promoting cyber-wellness through social emotional learning (SEL) incorporated with digital and media literacy skills. When students are prepared to face risky online interactions, they are more equipped to safely navigate dangers encountered online. Students with intellectual disabilities may interact safely in virtual settings either for social activities, learning, or employment when prepared with appropriate functional skills and provided accessible methods and tools. Educators utilizing proven instructional strategies can support students with intellectual disabilities as they access the internet. Students' awareness of potential online dangers along with the development of digital literacy skills can motivate them to be positive online risk takers.

INTRODUCTION

The utilization of the internet and social media has become an integral part of most of our existences with many of us spending hours and hours scrolling through social media platforms. Many of us who consider ourselves "internet savvy" have fallen prey to schemes and viruses that interfere with our lives and the lives of people with whom we are virtually connected. So, we must use a preparative lens when we consider cyber safety of students with intellectual disabilities. Rosa's Law (2017) updated the term used to identify individuals with cognitive delays with onset at birth from "mental retardation" to "intellectual disabilities." The Individuals with Disabilities Education Act (IDEA, 2017) defines an intellectual disability as, "significantly subaverage general intellectual functioning, existing concurrently with deficits in adaptive behavior and manifested during the developmental period, that adversely affects a child's

DOI: 10.4018/978-1-6684-6092-4.ch014

educational performance." The goal is to have realistic guidelines which increase their safety but do not deny them the opportunity to access information and the social media available to them.

Statistics from the 2020–21 calendar year show 7.2 million or 15 percent of all public-school students aged 3 through 21 received some form of special education services under the Individuals with Disabilities Education Act (NCES, 2021). Of those students receiving special education services 6 percent were diagnosed with intellectual disabilities (U.S. Dept. of Education, 2022). A child diagnosed with an intellectual disability may have sitting and walking delays. They may also have problem-solving issues, difficulty with logical thinking, and trouble understanding the cause and effect regarding their actions. There is also the chance they will have difficulty interpreting social cues which would allow them to decipher between safe and unsafe situations (American Academy of Pediatrics, 2015). Understanding how these intellectual disability signs impact the learning process is imperative for productive teaching.

Legal Support

Keeping all school-age students safe needs to be a shared responsibility. Through legislation, government plays a big role regarding safe internet access in both the school and home environments. The short history of the Internet has seen few attempts to legally regulate use by adults. Holmes (2022) identified legislative attempts to regulate content available for children on the internet. With cyber security concerns on the rise throughout the K-12 learning environment, there are legal protections in place for students that govern the types and amounts of information that websites are allowed to gather based on the individual's age. The Federal Trade Commission's Children's Online Privacy Protection Act of 1998 15 U.S.C. 6501-6506 Children's Privacy (16 CFR Part 312) established the regulation of information retrieval and access for school age students. The Children's Internet Protection Act (CIPA) which was enacted by the United States Congress set parameters that schools are required to follow to guarantee internet safety in order to acquire E-rate discounts. As a result, school districts are obligated to have programs in place to ward against risks such as hacking and unauthorized access to students' information (CIPA, 2000). New legislation such as the Kids Online Safety Act (KOSA, 2022) has been presented to Congress. If KOSA is passed, it will give parents more control of their minor child's internet access.

The mission to keep children safe on the internet is a global concern. As broadband availability expands around the world so will the risk of exposure to possible malicious situations. Collaborations are on the rise globally to prevent and combat the dangers vulnerable children face while participating in online platforms. The Disrupting Harm Study for South Africa, surveyed parents and children to gain insight into online risks. Data derived from this ECPAT, Unicef, and International Police (2020) report regarding children's experiences and parents' concerns can be used to construct future internet safety legislation. In May of 2022 the European Commission adopted legislation entitled Better Internet for Kids (BIK+) (2022). This legislation defines children's online rights and strategies to provide further online safety protections for all children residing in countries of the European Union.

BACKGROUND

In March 2020, families around the world saw an unprecedented shift in the delivery of educational services to remote learning for many students. The initial onset of the Covid-19 pandemic forced students with intellectual difficulties and their educators into virtual arenas for learning and therapeutic services

(Kim and Fienup 2022). Kim and Fienup (2022) determined two major issues facing schools and parents attempting to make the successful shift to online learning. The first issue was the ability and resources necessary to access online learning, which varied depending on multiple factors (economic, location, and support). The second issue was related to the non-participation of those with the required equipment and ability to access online learning but did not participate due to lack of needed support (either human, material, or skill based). In response, schools developed emergency plans for online learning that required addressing these major accessibility issues. Yet, the discrepancy in educational and therapeutic services acquired during the pandemic led states to institute measures that required districts to offer students with all disabilities an opportunity to recover for lost time upon returning to in-person learning.

Remote learning also demonstrated the need for students with intellectual disabilities to be prepared to participate in online learning. This inclusion in the virtual classroom came with the added pressure to quickly help students gain and apply digital learning skills, many of which might not have seemed as important before in a face-to-face environment. During the height of the pandemic, students with intellectual disabilities were spending more instructional and social time online as quarantine limitations restricted their ability to participate in regular social outlets. Consequently, educators and caregivers supporting students with intellectual disabilities were then placed in the position of gatekeepers and facilitators for students' online use.

Borgstrom, Daneback, and Molin (2019) reviewed the current research on young people with intellectual disabilities and social media and found three recurring concerns, risks, vulnerabilities, and supports. The increase in virtual learning and technology use has had positive results but leads to a variety of potential hazards. Issues such as the sharing of personal information, exploitation, and privacy concerns are risks for all students. Students with intellectual delays can lack the skills necessary to distinguish between fact and opinion and, in extreme cases, between friendship and coercion. Therefore, digital literacy is an important skill for all students, especially those with intellectual disabilities. Reviewing current findings and practical applications for students with intellectual disabilities will support their positive use of technology in the classroom and beyond.

The Internet has opened doorways for students with intellectual disabilities to participate in social, recreational, and vocational activities that were previously limited by their physical location. School personnel and others responsible for student safety are facing concerns surrounding students with intellectual disabilities' ability to safely use the digital realm.. Digital literacy skills training has been promoted as a means of preparing students with intellectual disabilities to interact safely in the digital medium. Literacy skills are no longer limited to the ability to read and understand printed text but must also account for the ability to understand and relay information presented via digital formats. The determination of the level and type of support needed by a student with intellectual disabilities to participate safely in online activities is the initial step educators must take in preparing to address digital literacy skills training.

Utilizing cognitive strategies to directly and successfully teach students with intellectual disabilities the skills needed to safely participate in digital activities requires a multilevel approach of instruction. Current best practices for students with intellectual disabilities call for instruction that is broken into small parts (tasks), verbal and visual delivery of information, repeated assessment for understanding, along with multiple opportunities for practice, and reassessment and retraining for mastery. These strategies should also, to the degree possible, be employed for the delivery of instruction on digital literacy for students with intellectual disabilities.

Instructional material must be designed to address the varied learning styles of students. Materials may include but are not limited to digital storytelling, social stories, realistic practice activities, visually modeled task analysis, and trial and error opportunities. With the growth of virtual and augmented reality, their use has been recommended as a tool that may offer realistic application for the safe training of students with intellectual disabilities in a controlled environment (Zitter 2020). Today's student with intellectual disabilities, as a member of Generation-G (Gen-G), has had opportunities unlike those prior. These students are part of an era where technology has always been available for learning, social opportunities, and work interactions.

Initiatives such as W3C Web Accessibility Initiative (WAI) support educators working to integrate technology into the classroom through the application of Universal Design for Learning guidelines and assistive technology (CAST, 2018). Educators are also designing and implementing opportunities to incorporate the use of these technologies into the everyday life of students. Current research (Alfredsson Agren, Kjellberg, and Hemmingsson 2018) suggests that when provided with strategies supported with pictures and the reduction of the number of Internet- enabled devices used, students with Intellectual disabilities were able to interact through the internet effectively.

While technology is ever changing and adapting, we have found over the past 25 years that preparing students through experiential learning with problem solving skills has been most effective in supporting students' ability to generalize information. Understanding that our students often face deficits in areas of adaptive functioning with regards to conceptual understanding, as well as social and or practical skills, their use of the internet can be a scary place for teachers regarding their students. A surprising number of parents of individuals with intellectual disabilities in contrast perceive students' participation in online activities, according to Alfredsson Agren et al. 2020, via the internet and social media, as a benefit providing opportunities for social outlets that,with support and monitoring, outweigh the risk.

In accordance, Buijs et al. (2016) found in their study that it was important to discuss with individuals with intellectual disabilities the possible dangers that they may face in online situations. These discussions need to be clear, concise, and most importantly ongoing. While the risks change daily, the ability to mobilize resources to combat them takes time and planning. Classroom teachers seeking to support students' "cyber-wellness," defined as a sense of "positive wellbeing in online spaces, including awareness of how to behave appropriately and protect oneself" (Lewin et al., 2021, p.1) must, along with discussion, devise strategies that address risky factors while not shying away from the difficult topics of bullying, sexual exploitation, cyber-crimes including financial manipulation.

As in all things in education, accountability matters. How do we address these concerns with an effective approach? That is the question facing educators. What strategies can be utilized to promote cyber-wellness for our students with intellectual disabilities? How do we adapt current strategies to meet the experience levels of ourselves and our students? Who will assess our students for proficiency? What measures can students be given to determine competency? The truthful answer to most of these questions is there is not one measure, means, or answer to this complicated issue. The answers in most cases will be found through trial and error.

DIGITAL LITERACY

According to U.S. Digital Literacy (2016), classrooms today function in Web 2.0 and Social 3.0 domains that require students to be participatory learners in an ever-expanding social arena. The digital and media skills that are essential for any learner of the 21st Century are imperative for students with intellectual disabilities. Yet, the ability to differentiate these skills to a comprehensive level of understanding for varied functional ranges of students with disabilities is not an easy task.

Researchers are calling on educators to not just focus their attention on cyber wellness, but wellness (Lewin et al. 2021). The suggestion is made that rather than our primary focus being on prevention, we should be preparing students to be compassionate, self-aware, empathetic, and self- reliant. Aligning these skills with training in digital literacy that is geared towards the user's comprehension ability will grant them the skills to manage their virtual experiences.

The focus of digital literacy media skills for students with intellectual disabilities should be shifting to include functional digital literacy skills according to Cichak et al. (2015). Establishing and using personal email accounts, learning to manage social bookmarks, and utilizing cloud services for storage of documents are skills that students with intellectual disabilities need but also open the doors to online risks.

Instructional Strategies

Colclasure, Thoron, and LaRose (2019) suggest to effectively teach students with intellectual disabilities modifying the following instructional strategies is imperative. Chunking of concepts is a process that allows more complex material to be taken in and processed before adding additional information. Modeling can be done by teachers and/or peers as it provides early exposure to the concept thus preparing the students with intellectual disabilities for future interactions. They also point out that direct application and repetition of the material being taught is important, meaning it may offer students with intellectual disabilities a more direct connection to the information which might prove more meaningful. The types of strategies found to be effective in the classroom can also be transferred to learning online when composed of the correct instructional materials.

Instructional Material

There are a variety of free resources online readily available to help promote cyber safety for children and young adults. Cyber Safety: Protect our People and our Science, (U.S. Department of Health and Human Services, 2020) an activity book designed to promote online safety for kids, offers an online pledge that kids, parents, and educators can take to prompt discussion on digital literacy skills. The Cyber Peace Foundation (2019) developed a guide for adolescents that defines digital literacy and describes the 8 components of digital literacy. The State of New Jersey's Office of Consumer Affairs offers a free PDF that can be downloaded for Middle School students. Educators should try adapting one of these examples to offer leveled instruction for students with intellectual disabilities. While the information and resources are there, how to make them instructionally ready for all students must be addressed.

Students with intellectual disabilities who respond best to more concrete material may require low-tech or high-tech assistive technology options. Each student's form of communication must also be counted in the preparation of materials when planning for instruction on digital literacy. Those students with speech and language impairments may benefit from the use of speech to text applications to assist in online communication. Meeting students with intellectual disabilities at their level of communication is imperative for their understanding and transfer of knowledge to real world applications.

The gap in use of the internet by individuals with disabilities and those without is not as wide as it once was. Much of the research fails to account for individuals with intellectual disabilities in their numbers according to Werner and Shpigelman (2019). The authors identified information communication technology, in particular social media, as a basic ingredient of interactions between individuals. Yet, Caton and Chapman (2016) suggested that there are indicators of youth with intellectual disabilities embracing social media to a larger extent than adults with intellectual disabilities.

The standard practice of inclusion of students with intellectual disabilities requires the differentiation of learning material. UDL accommodations are helpful in opening the online world for students with intellectual disabilities but may not be enough. The student with an intellectual disability may also need additional context clues as well as visual and auditory support to bring meaning to current products. Students who also use assistive technology may necessitate even more specialization in content delivery to ensure their interactions are beneficial. Teaching users how to engage assistive technology features that are built into many newer devices or online services can offer a quick means for students who struggle with written text to access the content with text to speech application. Symbol support for words is another means of enabling students with intellectual disabilities to gain a clearer understanding. A feature that originally began as an assistive technology option but has since become a widely popular component of most software, speech to text, can support students with intellectual disabilities in communication in virtual environments as well.

Student and Educator Communication Dynamics

The importance of shared communication cannot be overstated for students with intellectual disabilities. It is imperative to keep in mind that the hours that students spend in school daily can be more time than they spend with family. Therefore, the push should be to engage in and encourage meaningful communication between teachers and students and among groups of students. Through examining research McLaughlin (2008) noted,

The emotional availability and sensitivity of adults in a child's life has a powerful impact on the ability of the child to contain, regulate, feel, ignore and reflect upon feelings. The child learns early on from the reactions of adults how his/ her feelings will be managed and responded to, and these are internalized. (p. 361)

Developing communication patterns with your students is a key to being able to successfully present information that can become student knowledge. Productive communication needs to be a shared experience in which information, questions, and concerns are respectfully exchanged to create an environment of open dialogue. Creating a classroom atmosphere which becomes a safe space for students that encourages communication should always be the goal. This is in the hands,the words, or actions of the educator. Being conscientious of word choices and tone is important to the communication process. Students need to see the educator or instructor as an active, empathic, and unbiased listener in all communication exchanges. This ease of communication develops the skills needed for interpersonal communication and group communication, which will hopefully transfer to future situations for students.

Communicating safety concerns regarding current risky online situations and even the potential risk of other online situations needs to be introduced clearly and with respect to each student's communication style and mode. According to the American Psychological Association (APA) (2001), it is a priority that educators make an emotional connection with students to create a supportive communicative exchange. Being aware that each student is an individual and requires different attention at various times is also important. Presenting lessons in different modes needs to be in the forefront of all lessons but especially those lessons which address the safety of students with intellectual disabilities.

SCENARIOS AS A LEARNING TOOL

Scenarios as instructional tools can present realistic images, which can allow students with intellectual disabilities the opportunity to recognize the signs of potential risks and allow problem solving in a safe setting. The fear of students with intellectual disabilities being victimized while interacting with social media or other platforms cannot push us to encourage less interaction. The benefits of students' desire to participate in the same activities as their peers without intellectual disabilities need to be considered. Therefore, while comprehensive and concise plans in place can lessen fear, we must remember it cannot eliminate the potential risks. We can inform our students of the potential risks by having the opportunity to explore these dangers in a variety of manners. Instructional support can help provide the transfer of skills for when a student is no longer in the classroom setting.

The following are scenarios as examples of risks facing students with intellectual disabilities in online situations and tried solutions to support student safety and cyber-wellbeing. These scenarios should be presented to ignite open conversations in which students freely share ideas and experiences during problem-solving sessions. Educators prompting these discussions should provide open-ended questions but can also add their experiences when students are having difficulty sharing. A target goal for the following scenarios is to instill an awareness of possible online risks and not to scare students with intellectual disabilities to the point of not engaging online at all. It is also important for students to know that it is always okay to reach out to someone they trust for guidance.

Scenario 1: The Risk of Online Multi-User Games

Bailey, a 14-year-old boy with mild intellectual disabilities, loves to play Fortnight. He started playing the free version when an online "friend" he met in the game directly messaged him while playing. This new friend asked Bailey for his credit card information to purchase skins so that they could keep playing together. Bailey did not readily have access to his parent's credit card. Yet, he did not immediately want to say no to his new online friend. He might consider asking for use of the credit card by saying he wanted to move further into the game.

What Should Bailey Do?

It is difficult, if not impossible, to find a young person who does not participate in some form of online gaming. Though many families set time parameters on gaming hours, a general conversation with their child may be enough to relay the importance of not sharing personal information with other online gamers. Safe interactions which involve just game play within a gaming situation can help students with intellectual disabilities build social interaction skills.

The issue is not gaming but being in a situation which allows strangers to interact using a pseudonym. In the world of massively multiplayer online (MMO) games, the open platform allows for random groups of gamers to be formed. Chatting within the game is part of the experience as the game players are trying to work together to accomplish a task. This chat experience can lead to adding stranger profiles to your friend lists which can lead to more online game interactions. Prolonged and multiple online interactions can be interpreted as budding friendships, especially for those who have difficulty with in-person social interactions. This sense of friendship gives a potential victimizer the opportunity to present questions which can divulge important and personal information from the innocent gaming participant.

Acknowledging that you cannot prepare for every conceivable scenario that may occur, it is important to engage the individual with intellectual disabilities in discussions that address topics surrounding friendship and boundaries. Role play is an excellent way to help demonstrate the dos and don'ts when it comes to sharing personal information with others in virtual environments. Acting out questions and responses that incorporate when to ask a trusted person in their home or school environment if it is okay to share information with another online gamer is a good strategy. Again, the objective is not to prevent the individual with intellectual disabilities from participating. It should focus on helping the individual learn strategies to protect themselves in virtual environments.

Scenario 2: Expense/Gambling Associated With Online Gaming

Gail, an 18-year-old girl with mild intellectual disabilities, enjoys playing online games. In some of the online games Gail plays, she has the opportunity to purchase additional tokens to extend her play time. Gail is currently playing a game where she has met her daily limit of free play and to continue, she will have to pay. This is the third time this week that Gail has purchased additional time in the game and is over the budget she set for play. Gail does not have her own source of income. Yet, she feels that she must keep playing. If she continues on this path, she will have to find a way to acquire more money.

What Should Gail Do?

Online gaming can offer an additional concern for students with intellectual disabilities in the expenses associated with play. While initial play can be free for online games, upon entry, players are often required to purchase subscriptions within the game. This, along with the added cost of in-game purchases of equipment, special characters, and "prize boxes", may lead individuals seeking a deeper level of play and the opportunity to connect with others into serious financial territory.

Setting hard limits on spending and supervising purchases over the agreed upon limits should be a part of the online agreement contract between the student with intellectual disabilities and their care person. Establishing the boundaries can help keep a student with intellectual disabilities from being coerced into overspending. Discussing and reviewing games beforehand can also act as an additional means of establishing spending limits. Introducing monetary responsibility through online gaming participation is an opportunity that may lead to the generalization of healthy financial practices in off-line activities.

Creating storyboards addressing the pull of spending money to get greater access to different aspects of online gaming can provide students with a nonthreatening means of discussion and problem-solving opportunities in the classroom setting. Another way of having students gain an understanding of unhealthy or dangerous online interactions is by having students select different scenario situations from a box and act out the scenario. This can provide another opportunity for discussion and assist students in finding the power within to seek help when and if a situation arises. The goal is always to provide multiple means of exploration of these topics for full understanding.

Scenario 3: Cyberbullying

Jaquan, a 15-year-old boy with mild intellectual disabilities and a slight speech impairment, enjoys using his Xbox™ to play video games. He heard a group of kids at school talking about a new multiplayer game. Jaquan remembered the name of the game and signed into play. After signing in and joining the group, Jaquan saw in the chat that a player told the other players not to choose him for a team because he was "slow." Still wanting to play online games and be part of the group, Jaquan signed into play multiple times and each time he read negative comments about himself.

What Should Jaquan Do?

This may be the most difficult situation to address. All students want to feel connected, and social media is a means of connecting to friends when not in the classroom environment. Intellectual disabilities are often not considered visual disabilities like an orthopedic disability would. That does not mean it excludes students with intellectual disabilities from feeling different from their peers without disabilities. The emotional devastation caused by cyberbullying is painful to all and can be a private pain when a student does not feel safe confiding in a peer or adult. So how do we approach this risk when we may not be aware it is currently happening? We need to define all aspects of cyberbullying clearly and carefully. Stopbullying.gov (2022) defines cyberbullying as the following.

Cyberbullying is bullying that takes place over digital devices like cell phones, computers, and tablets. Cyberbullying can occur through SMS, text, and apps, or online in social media, forums, or gaming where people can view, participate in, or share content. Cyberbullying includes sending, posting, or sharing negative, harmful, false, or mean content about someone else. It can include sharing personal or confidential information about someone else causing embarrassment or humiliation. Some cyberbullying crosses the line into unlawful or criminal behavior.

Social stories developed to introduce positive and negative speech can be a powerful way to help students with intellectual disabilities to begin to foster a sense and understanding of self-protectiveness. When a student with intellectual disabilities is self-aware of language that is hurtful or harmful, they are given the opportunity to seek resources to remove the negative person or themselves from the situation. The use of online scenarios that are adaptable to facilitate the inclusion of students with intellectual disabilities may demonstrate ways of addressing disruptive behavior.

Scenario 4- Social Media Intimidation/Cyberbullying

Sam, a 16-year-old girl with moderate intellectual disabilities, has a friend who has begun interacting with people in an online forum. The forum encourages violence against women and her friend has been sharing images he received from others in the group on his social media. Sam is now also receiving the images on her social media feeds, and they upset her.

What Should Sam Do?

A risk for anyone who actively engages in exchanges on any social media platform is online bullying or intimidation whereby an individual or group actively engages in acts that are intentionally designed to cause emotional harm or embarrassment to others. A characteristic of individuals with intellectual disabilities that increases this vulnerability is their limitations in social skills. Shree and Shukla (2016) delineate the following as aspects of social skills, "interpersonal skills, social responsibility, self-esteem, gullibility, naïveté (i.e., wariness), social problem solving, and the ability to follow rules/obey laws and to avoid being victimized." (p.11)

Youth with intellectual disabilities are seen as vulnerable to intimidation in the virtual world. Self-concept is acknowledged as largely a reflection of others towards the individual (Popovici and Buica-Belcia 2013). The student with intellectual disabilities who experiences cyberbullying while they are seeking to expand their social landscape in the virtual world can undergo damage to their self-esteem. The increase in online social interactions for students with intellectual disabilities with the easy access of mobile devices makes it harder for care providers to monitor interactions. Thus, this expands the need for open discussion and communication between the students with intellectual disabilities and care persons. A strategy that encourages positive risk behaviors in online situations should be part of the training for safe online interactions. Online trolling of social media sites can offer real examples that help students pinpoint negative language and inappropriate interactions.

Scenario 5: Sexual Exploitation

Ang, a 14-year-old boy with moderate intellectual disabilities, struggles with making friends. He has started posting pictures to a social media app. Ang thinks it is cool and safe because his older cousin does it all the time. His parents are aware that he joined this social media app. Ang's parents looked at his friends' list which consisted of his cousins, other family members, and a few classmates. So, they felt this was a safe and age-appropriate use of social media for their son. Ang received a random friend request from a profile name he does not know. He accepted and received a direct message from his new friend. The conversation started without any red flags or uncomfortable indications. Eventually Ang is asked for personal information and inappropriate photos.

What Should Ang Do?

Sexual exploitation is generally an uncomfortable online topic to discuss. The possible outcomes are so devastating that we try to remove it from ever being in the realm of possibility for anyone we know or love. Students with intellectual disabilities are often perceived as vulnerable to exploitation and unable to navigate unhealthy social interactions. A 2018 report by Joseph Shapiro for National Public Radio (NPR) identified people with intellectual disabilities as being at an elevated rate for acts of sexual assault in comparison to their non-disabled peers.

People with intellectual disabilities are sexually assaulted at a rate seven times higher than those without disabilities. That number comes from data run for NPR by the Justice Department from unpublished federal crime data... Predators target people with intellectual disabilities because they know they are easily manipulated and will have difficulty testifying later. These crimes go mostly unrecognized, unprosecuted, and unpunished. And the abuser is free to abuse again. (Shapiro, 2018)

Social media apps have rules that lead to inappropriate material being removed when discovered. This unfortunately does not impede those who have the intent to victimize from pursuing private contact with innocent individuals. The use of social media to groom and exploit youth with intellectual disabilities is a risk that needs to be addressed. Prevention of exploitation requires recognition of its dangers. Preventive practices that isolate the individual with intellectual disabilities from access or participation in online activities also limit their ability to gain the skills necessary to discriminate between safe and dangerous situations. As the use of virtual and online environments continues to expand into most facets of our daily life, individuals with intellectual disabilities are going to organically become a part of the mass use, thus, increasing their exposure to risky situations.

Careful consideration of the needs of individuals with intellectual disabilities should be the first step in addressing safe online participation. As students with intellectual disabilities reach their teenage years and beyond, it is important to recognize them as maturing individuals and not children. We want them to have experiences that align with their age. Preparing the individual with intellectual disabilities for risk of exploitation and sexual harassment should be discussed using the language system that supports the individual's ability to comprehend and relate understanding. Role-playing and control situations are also valuable strategies to utilize in helping the individual with intellectual disabilities gain protective tactics to support safe online interactions.

Scenario 6: Effective Online Communication

Amanda, a 20-year-old girl with an intellectual disability and a communication disorder, must meet with a new therapist. Amanda's previous therapist changed jobs and is no longer in her health care network plan. Amanda uses an augmentative and alternative communication device (AAC) and has a personal support assistant. Amanda's health plan is transitioning to virtual visits, but Amanda has never participated in a virtual session. This situation is causing Amanda great anxiety which might interfere with a successful therapeutic process. She would like to be able to share privately with her new therapist without her support person.

What Should Amanda Do?

The individual with intellectual disabilities who uses the internet for social interaction, entertainment, and/or communication requires a way to express and demonstrate comprehension. These students often are faced with difficulty related to their deficits in reading, writing, and spelling when offline. Transferring these difficulties online and the ability to find information, sites, or preferred entertainment can lead to frustration and an unwillingness to participate. Those individuals with moderate to severe cognitive impairments who struggle with communication and comprehension may require the assistance and support of alternative communication systems. Adapting such a communication system to assist in online communication can be daunting. Though accessibility designs are more prevalent than in the past, they are often not enough for the more involved user.

Utilizing picture/object-based symbols to allow for user response along with speech to text/to speech features can be used as strategies to support engagement. Symbol based systems may also be a means to support reading and writing online. Developing a personalized online communication system which offers the user the most optimal opportunity to interact with others can facilitate online communication providing support for the more involved user. The designation of a single device that contains the individual's personal accommodations which students can be taught to access will simplify the process for the user and the care person offering support.

Scenario 7: Lack of Opportunity

Yosef, a 9-year-old boy with moderate intellectual disabilities likes anime and wants to watch his favorite show online. In school he uses a system with symbols to communicate with his friends about the show and the new season that has just started. Even though the series is age appropriate for Yosef at home his parents think he should only watch it on TV. They have blocked Yosef from searching for the online stream. Yousef is becoming frustrated and upset.

What Should Yosef Do?

A major risk for students with intellectual disabilities regarding online use is lack of access. This includes the risk of being blocked from accessing online resources by care persons for fear of possible perceived risk. Educators and care persons seeking to protect individuals who they deem vulnerable from possible danger may actively limit their opportunities to access online environments, thus preventing them from gaining the skills they would need to be self-reliant in online settings. Chadwick (2019) advocates for the right of individuals with intellectual disabilities to be assessed on a personal level for risk factors connected to online access. His findings suggest "taking a risk-averse approach may not be in the best interests of people with ID and may serve to further increase digital exclusion preventing development of online competence and resilience." (p.7) A preferable approach would be to review the individual case to determine the supports necessary to promote positive risk factors that contribute to individuals with intellectual disabilities inclusion in virtual environments.

Scenario 8: Parent Involvement

Albert is a ten-year-old boy with a mild intellectual disability. He has been playing an online community game. His parents are aware of the time Albert spends playing games on his computer, but they have not investigated the games he is playing. His parents had basic safety conversations with Albert about strangers in the world but did not consider the need to have that discussion regarding strangers online. Albert's mother approaches Albert about needing to get ready to go out while he is playing an online game on his laptop. Albert nods and then tells his mother that he needs a minute to say good-bye to his friend. His mother has been unaware Albert has been playing any type of games that involve chatting with strangers. Her reaction is one of shock and fear. His mother demands that Albert stop playing that game and all multiplayer games. Albert tries to explain that he is making friends, but this upsets his mother even more.

What Should Albert Do? What Should Albert's Parents Do?

As with all challenges that occur in the school setting, collaboration between home and school helps ensure the successful transfer of skills to real-world experiences. Though schools can use best practices to inform students of all the potential dangers lurking on the web with the goal of building strong digital citizenship skills, technology use happens outside of the classroom as well. A student left alone with their laptops, tablets, and phones is not uncommon and that is the same for students with intellectual disabilities. Both educators and parents would like to think that the young technology user will only use websites that have been verified as safe. The idea of them wandering onto unknown sites where interactions might be confusing is very often not considered as a possibility.

Parents might have their own feelings about technology due to past experiences, both safe and unsafe. Parents who have had unsafe experiences might have set parameters for technology use that are too stringent. Though this option might be what a parent feels is the safest option, it does not teach a child with intellectual disabilities what to avoid. When rules are even lessened a bit later, the now young person can be unprepared for any challenges. Conversations between parent and child can allow parents to share their concerns. It will also give the child the opportunity to teach their parents aspects of multiplayer games. With full understanding from all parties, realistic rules can be set which allow the child with intellectual disabilities the ability to continue playing multiplayer games. Communication between school and home regarding all aspects of educational goals is important to the success of students with intellectual disabilities

The possibilities garnered by access to the internet are constantly changing and students with intellectual disabilities should be active participants in the experience. The internet allows the user to obtain information, provides social interaction, and opportunities for education and employment. Research and practical observation have shown that the inherent risk involved in being active in social media and online activities is a shared danger for all users. While the debate of its risk versus reward value for individuals with intellectual disabilities continues to be argued, there is no argument on their right to choose to be included.

The risks which include exposure of personal information, exploitation, and privacy concerns must be addressed. The research into the cyber-wellness of individuals with intellectual disabilities is growing but remains focused heavily on those categorized as having a mild to moderate disability. Most data collected is from the perspectives of educators and care persons, not the individuals with intellectual difficulties themselves. The difficulties involved in gaining access to these participants and communicating effectively with them have been difficult for researchers to overcome. Yet, there remains a need to understand the complex relationship between students with significant intellectual disabilities and their use of the internet. Distinguishing between risks and benefits for these users adds an additional level of concern for educators and care persons.

The protective instincts of those supporting students with intellectual disabilities can be detrimental to their rights to access and must be weighed against their potential to gain from positive-risk situations. Preparing students for online participation can be one means of reducing the prospect of danger. Digital media literacy has been advanced as an instructional method that equips students with the skills to combat online perils. This avails them of the knowledge necessary to be good cyber-citizens and makes them aware of risky online situations through early awareness, access, and participation. Students with intellectual disabilities can benefit from digital learning when these skills are provided using instructional strategies that acknowledge their diverse needs.

Instructional techniques that have been proven effective with individuals with intellectual disabilities, chunking, modeling, direct instruction and repetition can be utilized to prepare students for online participation. Educational personnel are establishing opportunities for learning that are accessible with the development of UDL aligned activities in class and online. Advocating for maintaining individualization in the determination of resources and support systems for individuals with intellectual disabilities will help to establish guidelines for success.

Preparation for students with intellectual disabilities to fully embrace the online experience encompasses the distinction of their limitations and ways to facilitate their communication and understanding. Instructional strategies that incorporate symbol representation, text to speech, and speech to text will go a long way in supporting cognitive differentiation. Recognition of a student with intellectual disabilities' need for routine and repetition should also include the use of technology. The suggestion of dedicating a device, which can be customized to the user, has been found to be beneficial for training and access in helping to reduce the cognitive load for students with intellectual disabilities.

Outside of abstaining from all things online, there is no way to ensure that students with intellectual disabilities are not at risk in online environments. Yet, there are a variety of resources available to help prepare students for the risk they will potentially face. Adapting these resources for students with intellectual disabilities can be done effectively. Start with the current system in place for offline learning and communication and integrate it into a functional structure for online support that encompasses the needs of the user. Individuals with intellectual disabilities may continue to require personal physical support to interact in virtual environments.

CONCLUSION

Students with intellectual disabilities have the right to be included in the same activities as their peers without disabilities. Educators, parents, and caregivers have no control of the risks that lurk online. We can do our best to prepare students for these challenging situations by utilizing realistic case scenarios, open discussion, and individualized support. Cyber-security should not be a hindering factor to student participation online for enjoyment, socialization, and or learning. Educators should focus on determining the most effective means of preparing students to be successful through adapting positive risk strategies and digital literacy skills training.

REFERENCES

Alfredsson Ågren, K., Kjellberg, A., & Hemmingsson, H. (2018). Access to and use of the internet among adolescents and young adults with intellectual disabilities in everyday settings. *Journal of Intellectual & Developmental Disability*, *45*(1), 89–98. doi:10.3109/13668250.2018.1518898

Alfredsson Ågren, K., Kjellberg, A., & Hemmingsson, H. (2020). Internet opportunities and risks for adolescents with intellectual disabilities: A comparative study of parents' perceptions. *Scandinavian Journal of Occupational Therapy*, *27*(8), 601–613. doi:10.1080/11038128.2020.1770330 PMID:32538241

American Academy of Pediatrics. (2015). *Children with intellectual disabilities*. https://www.healthychildren.org/English/health-issues/conditions/developmental-disabilities/Pages/Intellectual-Disability.aspx

American Psychological Association (APA). (2001). *Developing adolescents: A reference for professionals*. American Psychological Association.

Borgström, Å., Daneback, K., & Molin, M. (2019). Young people with intellectual disabilities and social media: A literature review and thematic analysis. *Scandinavian Journal of Disability Research*, *21*(1), 129–140. doi:10.16993jdr.549

Buijs, P. C., Boot, E., Shugar, A., Fung, W. L., & Bassett, A. S. (2016). Internet safety issues for adolescents and adults with intellectual disabilities. *Journal of Applied Research in Intellectual Disabilities*, *30*(2), 416–418. doi:10.1111/jar.12250 PMID:26914835

CAST. (2018). *Universal Design for Learning Guidelines version 2.2*. Retrieved from http://udlguidelines.cast.org

Caton, S., & Chapman, M. (2016). The use of social media and people with intellectual disability: A systematic review and thematic analysis. *Journal of Intellectual & Developmental Disability*, *41*(2), 125–139. doi:10.3109/13668250.2016.1153052

Chadwick, D. D. (2019). Online risk for people with intellectual disabilities. *Tizard Learning Disability Review*, *24*(4), 180–187. doi:10.1108/TLDR-03-2019-0008

Federal Communications Commission. (2020, April 28). *Children's Internet Protection Act*. Retrieved August 1, 2022, from https://www.fcc.gov/consumers/guides/childrens-internet-protection-act

Cihak, D. F., Wright, R., Smith, C. C., McMahon, D., & Kraiss, K. (2015). Incorporating functional digital literacy skills as part of the curriculum for high school students with intellectual disability. *Education and Training in Autism and Developmental Disabilities*, *50*(2), 155–171. https://www.jstor.org/stable/24827532

Colclasure, B. C., Thoron, B. C., & LaRose, S. E. (2019, November 5). *Teaching Students with Disabilities: Intellectual Disabilities*. AEC599/WC261. Retrieved August 4, 2022, from https://edis.ifas.ufl.edu/publication/WC261

Cyber Peace Foundation. (2019). *Cyber Safety Booklet for Children for Adolescents*. New Delhi, India; Cyber Peace Foundation. Retrieved August 5, 2022, from https://www.cbse.gov.in/cbsenew/documents/Cyber%20Safety.pdf

ECPAT, INTERPOL, & UNICEF. (2022). *Disrupting Harm in South Africa: Evidence on Online Child Sexual Exploitation and Abuse*. Global Partnership to End Violence against Children. Retrieved November 27, from https://www.unicef.org/

European Commission. (2022). *A European Strategy for a Better Internet for Kids*. Retrieved Nov. 25, 2022, from https://digital-strategy.ec.europa.eu/ en/policies/strategy-better-internet-kids

Federal Trade Commission. (1998). *Children's Online Privacy Protection Act of 1998 15 U.S.C. 6501-6506 Children's Privacy (16 CFR Part 312)*. ftc.gov/legal- ibrary/browse/statutes/childrens-online-privacy-protection-act

Holmes, E. N. (2022). *Children and the Internet: Legal Considerations in Restricting Access to Content*. Congressional Research Service. Retrieved July 17, 2022, from https://crsreports.congress.gov/product/pdf/R/R47049

Individuals with Disabilities Education Act (IDEA). Section 300.8 (c)(6) (2017). Retrieved July 10, 2022, from http://sites.edu/gov.idea/regs/b/a/300.8/c/6

Kids Online Safety Act. S.3663 - 117th Congress. (2022). Retrieved July 10, 2022, from https://www.congress.gov/bill/117th-congress/senate-bill/3663/text

Kim, J. Y., & Fienup, D. M. (2022). Increasing access to online learning for students with disabilities during the COVID-19 pandemic. *The Journal of Special Education*, *55*(4), 213–221. https://doi.org/10.1177/0022466921998067

Lewin, C., Niederhauser, D., Johnson, Q., Saito, T., Sakamoto, A., & Sherman, R. (2021). Safe and responsible internet use in a connected world: Promoting cyber-wellness. *Canadian Journal of Learning and Technology*, *47*(4). https://doi.org/10.21432/cjlt28069

McLaughlin, C. (2008). Emotional well-being and its relationship to schools and classrooms: A critical reflection. *British Journal of Guidance & Counselling*, *36*(4), 353–366. https://draweb.njcu.edu:2085/10.1080/03069880802364486

National Center of Educational Statistics. (2021). *Students with Disabilities*. Retrieved July 15, 2022, from https://nces.ed.gov/programs/coe/indicator/cgg

New Jersey Division of Consumer Affairs. (2022). *Cyber Safety for Middle Schoolers: Activity and Quiz Book*. New Jersey Division of Consumer Affairs.

Popovici, D.-V., & Buică-Belciu, C. (2013). Self-concept pattern in adolescent students with intellectual disability. *Procedia: Social and Behavioral Sciences*, *78*, 516–520. https://doi.org/10.1016/j.sbspro.2013.04.342

Rosa's Law. 74 FR 55947, Oct. 29, 2009, as amended at 82 FR 31913, July 11, 2017. https://www.govregs.com/regulations/expand/title34_chapterVI_part668_subpart_section668.231

Shapiro, J. (2018, January 8). *The sexual assault epidemic no one talks about*. NPR. Retrieved August 18, 2022, from https://www.npr.org/2018/01/08/570224090/the-sexual-assault-epidemic-no-one-talks-about

Shree, A., & Shukla, P. C. (2016). Intellectual disability: Definition, classification, causes and characteristics. *Learning Community-An International Journal of Educational and Social Development, 7*(1), 9. doi:10.5958/2231-458x.2016.00002.6

StopBullying.gov. (2022). *What is cyberbullying*. Retrieved July 16, 2022, from https://www.stopbullying.gov/cyberbullying/what-is-it

United States Department of Education. (2022). *IDEA section 618 data products*. Retrieved July 10, 2022, from https://data.ed.gov/dataset/idea-section-618-data-products

United States Department of Health & Human Services. (2020, April 23). *Safety for Kids Activity Book - National Institutes of Health*. NIH Provides Cyber Safety Resources for Children and Families. Retrieved August 3, 2022, from https://www.cit.nih.gov/sites/default/files/NIH-Cyber-Safety-for-Kids-Activity-Book.pdf

United States Digital Literacy. (2016). *Web 2.0 to Social 3.0*. US Digital Literacy. Retrieved August 13, 2022, from http://digitalliteracy.us/web-2-0-to-social-3-0/

Web Accessibility Initiative (WAI). (2022). *Home*. Initiative (WAI). Retrieved August 10, 2022, from https://www.w3.org/WAI/

Werner, S., & Shpigelman, C.-N. (2019). Information and communication technologies: Where are persons with intellectual disabilities? *Israel Journal of Health Policy Research*, *8*(1). https://doi.org/10.1186/s13584-018-0282-4

Zitter, L. (2020, August 7). How VR and AR can be used to support students with special needs. *TechLearning-Magazine*. Retrieved July 17, 2022, from https://www.techlearning.com/how-to/how-vr-and-ar-can-be-used-to-support-students-with-special-needs

KEY TERMS AND DEFINITIONS

Communication: The concept of exchanging thoughts and ideas orally, by sign language, through written words, facial expressions, hand gestures, or the use of an augmentative and alternative communication device.

Instructional Strategies: Planned techniques used by educators to encourage student involvement and foster learning.

Internet Use: Use of the world wide web to gain information, be entertained, or communicate.

Online Risk: The potential of interacting with any dangerous situations such as cyber bullying and sexual harassment while interacting with others on the internet.

Positive Risk: The use of potentially dangerous interactions online for practical training.

Scenario: A story or possible events which can be used as examples for investigation and learning.

Social Media: Internet applications and websites which are used for entertainment and communication.

Universal Design for Learning: The plan to ensure the educational process provides multiple means of learning opportunities to meet the needs of all users.

Web 2.0 and Social 3.0: The term describing the asynchronous use of the internet for communication and the growing use of collaboration applications for synchronous communication.

Chapter 15
Making Learning Environments More Inclusive for All Students With Educational Technology

Kathryn Nieves Licwinko
https://orcid.org/0000-0003-4430-9934
Wayne Township Public Schools, USA

ABSTRACT

The placement of students with disabilities in the inclusion setting alongside their peers has increased in recent years due to a variety of federal mandates. Technology has become an important component of this learning experience since digital tools and resources can provide students with support while accessing the grade-level curriculum. This chapter addresses the various ways that technology can be utilized in the inclusion classroom, including assistive technology, mainstream educational technologies, and accessible digital resources. The existing research tends to focus on how specific tools can be integrated, but this chapter synthesizes this information to show educators how technology can be leveraged to support all learners in the classroom. The intent of this chapter is to share research-supported strategies for making classrooms more inclusive using available technologies.

INTRODUCTION

There are approximately 240 million students around the world who are classified with a disability (UNICEF, 2021). The UNICEF (2021) report found that across countries, even students with similar classifications can have very different life experiences and can have different levels of societal participation. Providing access to assistive technologies, related services, and social norms are all essential to creating an inclusive societal mindset (UNICEF, 2021). Despite the global consensus on the importance of education, including the United Nations' fourth Sustainable Development Goal (SDG), focusing on providing equitable, inclusive, and quality education for all students (United Nations, n.d.), only 68% of countries in 2020 had defined "inclusive education" within their national education policies (UNICEF, 2021).

DOI: 10.4018/978-1-6684-6092-4.ch015

In the United States, 7.3 million students qualify for special services (United States Department of Education, 2021). Within this population of students, 65 percent spend 80 percent or more of their school day in the general education classroom, learning alongside their peers (United States Department of Education, 2021). The number of students who spend most of their day in this setting has been rising in recent years, demonstrating a shift toward inclusion. The history of educating learners with disabilities within the United States was not always inclusive. Previously, this population of students was segregated from their peers in the same school building, or in earlier circumstances, they may not have received public education at all (Osgood, 2005). Activism and movements led to a spotlight on this issue, bringing more awareness to the fact that students with disabilities deserved access to an equal education.

In the United States, No Child Left Behind (NCLB) was adopted in 2001, which addressed the fact that all students, including those with disabilities, needed to have access to the general education curriculum and teachers who were highly qualified in specific subject matter (Friend et al., 2010). In 2004, the reauthorization of the Individuals with Disabilities Education Act (IDEA) placed a focus on the least restrictive environment, which meant that students with disabilities should be placed in the general education setting to learn amongst their peers "to the maximum extent possible" (IDEA §300.114(a)). More recent history has shown the Every Student Succeed Act (ESSA), which was adopted in 2015. This mandate continued to address that students with disabilities need access to the general education setting to be better prepared for life after their secondary education.

Despite the United States mandates, the word "inclusion" does not appear in federal documentation and mandates (Grynova & Kalichenko, 2018). Internationally, the first time that term was used within the field of special education was in the Salamanca Statement in 1994 (Francisco et al., 2020). During that event, 92 countries signed the statement and subsequent framework, dedicating themselves to creating schools that "include everybody, celebrate differences, support learning and respond to individual needs" (UNESCO, 1994, p. III). There has been some debate over the exact criteria to constitute an inclusive school. Some common characteristics of inclusive education include: (a) students with disabilities attending their home school, as opposed to being segregated in a specialized school, (b) a positive environment where all students feel welcomed, (c) placement for all students in the general education classroom, (d) the modification or adaptation of curriculum and instruction based on individual student needs, (e) social inclusion support, and (f) training and resources about inclusion (Chambers, 2020).

In the United States, more schools are turning toward inclusion to lessen the achievement gap between students with disabilities and their peers and provide access to the curriculum for all learners. These models look different between states and even districts. In some districts, students with disabilities have a harder time getting the opportunity to access an inclusive education (Kozleski, 2020), which can eliminate the opportunity for active involvement. In other districts, involvement in general education can include lesson participation, active engagement in activities, and progress within appropriate academic learning objectives (Quick et al., 2017). Other criteria for successful inclusion of individuals with disabilities include access to learning, provision of accommodations, and appropriate social engagement with peers (Bakken, 2019).

Technology became prevalent as classrooms became more inclusive of students with learning differences. Access to digital tools and resources can allow students to meaningfully participate in their classes while providing them with the support they need (Okolo & Diedrich, 2014). According to Thomas et al. (2019), three main technology categories fall under special education technology: (a) assistive technology (AT), (b) accessible instructional materials, and (c) educational technologies. Each category has a different function within the inclusion classroom, but it still provides the accommodations a student might need. Furthermore, these special education technologies can support not only a student with an Individualized Education Program (IEP) but also any student present in the classroom.

THE EVOLUTION OF ASSISTIVE TECHNOLOGY

Assistive technology is commonly associated with special education. Assistive technology, or AT, is outlined in the Individuals with Disabilities Education Act (IDEA). The term is defined as any item or service "used to increase, maintain, or improve the functional capabilities of children with disabilities" (Individuals with Disabilities in Education Act, 2004). Assistive technology is a part of the IEP process and is often discussed at annual review meetings to determine if specific tools will help the student find success. Typically, this conversation occurs between the IEP team members, including the student, parents or family members, teachers, case managers, or therapists. School perspectives on assistive technology often vary. Some school districts may fully understand the necessity and value of assistive technology. In contrast, others may need more time to see how impactful and inclusive these tools are for students (Schaff, 2018).

The selection of assistive technology can help a student to communicate and learn in a general education classroom (Chambers, 2020). However, technology is not limited by screens and highly complex devices. Assistive technology has three classifications: high-tech, mid-tech, and low-tech. A high-tech device would be a piece of specialized equipment, such as an eye-gaze system or switches (Chambers, 2020). These tools are often recommended for students with specific functional needs and may require technology for day-to-day activities (Conderman, 2015). A mid-tech tool would be something that is not as complex but still requires a battery to operate, such as a calculator or an audiobook system (Bouck & Satsangi, 2020). Low-tech tools may not be digital but still meet the IDEA definition of assistive technology by improving the function of a child with a disability. These tools may include pencil grips, a visual schedule, or a graphic organizer (Chambers, 2020). Unlike high-tech or mid-tech tools, low-tech assistive technology does not require training and is fairly low cost for schools (Chambers, 2019).

Assistive technology often provides opportunities for students with disabilities to meaningfully engage in the general education classroom. Some students, especially individuals with physical disabilities, face difficulty accessing the general education classroom with their peers (Behrmann, 1994). However, these students can now experience meaningful participation in the general education classroom through the continuous development of technology tools. A study by Siu and Lam (2012) found that when a Braille keyboard was provided to a student with a visual impairment, they were less likely to be segregated and join inclusion classrooms. Assigning assistive technology to a student can potentially impact their feeling of belonging in the inclusion classroom (Chambers, 2020). Suppose students interact with an augmentative and alternative communication (AAC) device. In that case, it increases the opportunity for the student to be included in the classroom with their peers by allowing for communication between both parties (Aftab et al., 2021). According to Owour et al. (2018), this increase in social inclusion is not about simply assimilating into the "existing societal parameters" but rather giving students with disabilities their self-determination through assistive technology (p. 2).

Assistive Technology Selection

There are proposed frameworks that educators should consider when making assistive technology decisions for students. The Student, Environment, Tasks, and Tools (SETT) Framework is one tool the IEP team can use. Developed by Zabala (1995), each part of the SETT framework must be discussed. This framework maps out the types of conversations the IEP team should have when deciding on assistive technology, including (a) the student's strengths, needs, and future goals, (b) the organization and instructional style of the class, and (c) the types of lessons and activities conducted in the class (Zabala, 1995). These conversation topics can help the team decide whether technology is appropriate and necessary for the student. This framework was eventually transitioned to ReSETTing, which required that the IEP team frequently revisit conversations about assistive technology to make adjustments based on student needs (Zabala et al., 2005). The Matching Person and Technology (MTP) model is similar in perspective and requires that both personal and environmental considerations must be reviewed when making assistive technology decisions (Scherer et al., 2007).

The rate at which students with disabilities are assigned assistive technology varies and highly depends upon their classification (Bouck & Long, 2021). Currently, students with high-incidence disabilities are less likely to be assigned an assistive technology tool, including students with specific learning disabilities or Attention-Deficit Hyperactivity Disorder (Bouck et al., 2012). These students, however, are also more likely to be placed in an inclusion, general education classroom (United States Department of Education, 2021). By contrast, students with low-incidence disabilities are more likely to be assigned more specific assistive technology (Bouck et al., 2012). These disabilities, including deaf-blindness, intellectual disabilities, and multiple disabilities, were integrated into the general education classroom less frequently (United States Department of Education, 2021). Consequently, a student's chances of having more specialized devices in the inclusion setting were smaller.

The Shift to Mainstream Tools

Assistive technology has evolved. Previously, IEP teams were more likely to assign highly specialized equipment to support student needs (Nepo, 2017). However, these tools often made students stand out from their peers (Alnahdi, 2014). As a result, more complicated assistive technologies were abandoned by students (Peterson-Karlan, 2015). Overall, students tend to lean toward devices they have used before (Satsangi & Miller, 2017). For example, a student with a specific learning disability may have previously been assigned an electronic speller or dictionary to help with their writing. However, if a student has never used that type of hand-held device before, they are more likely to reject it in favor of the spell check and dictionary built into a traditional laptop or tablet. Similar, the social acceptance of a digital tool was a consideration for students when using assistive technology. If a student is assigned a device that is similar in appearance and function to that of their general education classmates, the students were able to assimilate easier into the inclusion classroom (Bouck et al., 2012).

A recurring theme in assistive technology research is that students with disabilities are leaning toward mainstream technologies. Since many accommodations or adaptations previously assigned through specialized equipment are now built into mainstream devices, they provide an easier way to meet student needs (Nepo, 2017). Laptops, tablets, and cell phones all have various accessibility features, which often mirror the functionality of specialized assistive technology devices. For example, a study by Dale and Grut (2015) found that students with Attention Deficit Hyperactivity Disorder (ADHD) used mainstream software to support their day-to-day planning, scheduling, and time management. Another study by Nordström et al. (2018) found that students with specific learning disabilities were given more learning opportunities by accessing text-to-speech and speech-to-text technologies. In both of these studies, the students could utilize more mainstream technologies to find support and success instead of being assigned a more specialized, separate device.

1:1 Devices and Their Impact on Assistive Technology

One initiative that has greatly impacted the evolution of assistive technology and its role in the classroom is the 1:1 device initiative. Within this program, every student is provided with a computing device, such as a laptop or tablet, to use for schoolwork throughout the duration of the school day (Cho & Littenberg-Tobias, 2016). The purpose of this initiative is to encourage collaboration while continuing to build the other 21st century skills: critical thinking, creativity, and communication (Kee & Samsudin, 2014). Prior to the COVID-19 pandemic, a survey by the EdWeek Research Center found that 66 percent of high schools, 65 percent of middle schools, and 42 percent of elementary schools had implemented this type of initiative (Klein, 2021). By contrast, after a year of the pandemic, 90 percent of middle and high schools and 82 percent of elementary schools had adopted 1:1 devices for each student (Klein, 2021). As 1:1 device initiatives become more commonplace in districts around the country, more students are turning toward these devices as supportive technology. Within these programs, every student receives the same device, regardless of whether or not they are classified with a disability.

A student is more likely to use their 1:1 device because it is considered socially acceptable by the student population (Satsangi et al., 2019). Using the same device as their classmates allow the student to easily join the lesson, especially in the inclusion setting (Bouck et al., 2012). Additionally, many technology companies are looking to make devices more accessible for all users. In a study of using mobile devices as assistive technology, Ismaili and Ibrahimi (2017) found that separate assistive technologies are becoming more obsolete as modern devices, like smartphones, are designed with all users in mind. This idea of universal accessibility provides anyone who is using a device with the ability to use some of the accessibility features, including voice typing, text-to-speech, and word prediction software. In a classroom setting, these considerations mean that all students would be able to take advantage of supports embedded within a district-provided device.

Chrome, Apple, and Windows devices each have accessibility features that can be used to provide accommodations and modifications for students, including text-to-speech, speech-to-text, screen magnifiers, and screen color contrasts (Nieves, 2021). Students can utilize these tools for reading, writing, visual, and mobility support. Browsers such as Google Chrome, Edge, Safari, and Firefox also provide accessibility tools for students (Ok & Rao, 2019). In both of these situations, specific tools do not have to be manually added to the device of a student with a disability. Instead, every child with a device has the ability to try out and use these features during instruction. Even web conference platforms have accessibility features embedded into their interface. When schools were virtual and hosting synchronous sessions through web conference tools, accessibility was factored into many commonly used platforms. For example, Zoom had a spotlight feature and backchannel to benefit students (Dolamore, 2021), as well as transcripts.

As an example, take a group of students in a high school inclusion English classroom. They are assigned to read an online article to help make a connection between current events and their current whole class novel. A few students have specific learning disabilities centered on reading. After the directions, these students plug their headphones into their Chromebooks and begin to use the built-in text-to-speech function to listen to one paragraph of the article at a time. They use their digital highlighter to bold the key information and support their comprehension. Meanwhile, another student nearby does not have an IEP. She is still able to plug in her headphones and listen to the article because she feels it will help her focus on the content. Other students decide just to dive into the article and read silently. In this example, students have the agency to choose the technology tool for themselves and are not restricted to accessibility features based on whether or not they have an IEP.

In another inclusion classroom, a group of middle schoolers is independently practicing after a math lesson. Several students with reading challenges decide to listen to the word problems read aloud and complete their work on paper. Other students need access to manipulatives to help understand the concepts and log onto a virtual manipulative website to help visualize the problem. A few students receive the accommodation of access to a calculator during independent practice and decide to use a virtual version on their computer for easy access. In this inclusion class, students are given a choice to decide which supports work for them. They can activate these features on their own without needing an entirely separate device, giving them more independence and discretion as they work.

As more schools are shifting toward the assigning of 1:1 devices, this development has the potential to influence the role of assistive technology in the classroom. There will still be a need for highly specialized equipment, especially in circumstances where an individual may need technology tools to complete daily functional activities. However, many features are being integrated into these everyday technology devices. Students will have the ability to openly use their supportive tools in a general education classroom, and their peers can utilize the same resources as they work. There is no classification required to utilize these supports, making these resources available to use for all students in a classroom (Nepo, 2017).

Frameworks for Choosing Mainstream Technologies

While access to mainstream technologies, such as laptops, accessibility features, mobile devices, and apps, has benefits with social inclusion, there are problems with this access. Whereas most assistive technology requires an evaluation of the child's individual needs before assigning a device, teachers can assign readily available apps without an evaluation (Evmenova, 2020). As teachers learn about new apps, extensions, or technology tools, they can jump right into assigning them to a student without stopping to fully understand a student's individual needs (Evmenova, 2020). Similarly, there is often an issue with free versions of apps, where a fully paid version has different features and functions, so teachers need to be aware of these multiple versions (Peterson-Karlan, 2015). In the same way that teachers need to use a formal framework to make data-driven decisions on which assistive technology to assign to a student, a framework needs to be applied to adopt mainstream technology as assistive technology.

The SETT framework for assistive technology can also be used in this circumstance, as the criteria are still applicable to 1:1 devices or daily use tools. Even if a teacher is considering using an accessibility feature on a laptop or tablet, they can still evaluate the student's strengths and performance, the learning environment, the learning tasks, and the tools to find success from SETT (Zabala, 1995). Technology assignments, especially when adding extensions or apps, still require these considerations before providing the tool to the student. Before downloading a new tool to all student devices, a teacher needs to consider whether this technology will actively benefit each individual student. A tool that is comfortable for one student may not necessarily work for another, even if they have the same classification. As a result, the teacher needs to still do formal evaluations, even in the face of the constant new app and extension options on mainstream devices.

Another option for considering which mainstream technology to assign is the TECH framework, which can be used to select, integrate, and evaluate the effectiveness of a technology tool (Evmenova & King-Sears, 2013; King-Sears & Evmenova, 2007). The TECH framework focuses on both assistive and instructional technologies, making it a strong resource for reviewing mainstream apps and resources, as well as more specialized equipment (Evmenova & King-Sears, 2013; King-Sears & Evmenova, 2007). TECH requires teachers to (a) target both the needs of the student and the intended learning objectives, (b) examine the available technology tools and resources that can be selected, (c) create ways to bring the technology into classroom activities and lessons, and (d) handle the integration process through the frequent monitoring of the technology's impact on how the student is learning (Evmenova, 2020). Whereas SETT is normally dedicated to assistive technology, TECH allows for mainstream technologies to be considered when supporting a student with a disability in the inclusion setting.

THE IMPACT OF TECHNOLOGY ON INSTRUCTION

A combination of instructional and assistive technologies are integrated into inclusion classrooms (King-Sears & Evmenova, 2007). Educational technology, along with accessible digital materials, is considered to be the other two classifications of special education technology paired with assistive technology (Thomas et al., 2019). While assistive technology has a formal definition through IDEA, educational technology has a "broader" definition (Israel et al., 2021). Educational technology is defined as "the study and ethical practice of facilitating learning and improving performance by creating, using, and managing appropriate technological processes and resources" (Januszewski & Molenda, 2008, p. 1). In connecting this definition to special education technology, educational technology would be any tool available to all students for the purpose of improving student learning outcomes and performance. However, unlike assistive technology, which has an associated legal mandate, educational technology is not subjected to legislation focused on students with disabilities (Thomas et al., 2019).

Accessible materials are similarly outside the legal mandates for students with disabilities (Thomas et al., 2019). Accessible materials are defined by the National Center on Accessible Materials (n.d.) as any print or digital resource that was created specifically to be used for learners with diverse needs, where accessibility is maintained regardless of the format of the resource. Both accessible resources, along with instructional technologies, can be used to increase learning opportunities for all students in the classroom, including both students with disabilities and their peers. However, to effectively implement these tools to support learners, schools need to participate in evidence-based instructional practices to support the needs of all learners, including Universal Design for Learning (UDL) and data-informed instruction (Quick et al., 2017).

Universal Design for Learning and Technology

Universal Design for Learning (UDL) is a framework that adopts the general education curriculum but provides flexibility and multiple pathways for meeting the learning objectives (Chita-Tegmark et al., 2012). Building off of concepts in neuroscience, learning sciences, and cognitive psychology (CAST, 2011), UDL allows the content to become more accessible for all learners in the classroom. This framework requires teachers to consider potential barriers to understanding the content, embed appropriate support to achieve learning objectives, and provide modifications or adaptations to ensure the success of all learners (Nicholl et al., 2013). There are three guiding principles of the UDL framework: multiple means of engagement, representation, and action and expression. Multiple means of engagement refers to helping students become motivated to take part in the learning process (CAST, 2018). Multiple means of representation requires learning materials to be presented in a variety of ways, so students have various pathways toward comprehending the information (CAST, 2018). Within multiple means of action and expression, students have the choice to showcase what they have learned and demonstrate their understanding (CAST, 2018).

The UDL framework can be effectively paired with technology. The characteristics of UDL can blend harmoniously with technology by matching a student's individual learning needs and allowing them to find success in the classroom (More & Travers, 2012). Since UDL positively impacts both students with disabilities and their peers (McGuire-Schwartz & Arndt, 2007), the use of technology within this framework also has the capacity to be beneficial for all students in the classroom.

Multiple Means of Engagement

Within multiple means of engagement, the "why" of learning becomes the focus (CAST, 2018). During the planning phase, a teacher should consider how to incorporate options for recruiting interest, sustaining effort and persistence, and self-regulate (CAST, 2018). When planning, Jung (2021) recommends designing engagement strategies by thinking about the students in a class who are often the least engaged during lessons. Aiming for these students will help to engage more students in the class (Jung, 2021). Some options for increasing engagement within the UDL framework can include: offering choices for seating preferences or student groups, utilizing problem or project-based learning, integrating formative assessment techniques, and integrating resources that connect to students' cultures and interests (Hovey et al., 2021).

Collaboration is often considered a way to increase engagement for students. Collaborative experiences allow for ways to practice learning goals while continuing to build a strong classroom community. Digital tools can be utilized to support this engagement technique. For example, teachers could use Google Jamboard to share reflections on a topic in class. Before learning about a new event in history, students could use this space to share information they already know about the topic. Since Jamboard allows for multimodal posting options, such as hyperlinks, text, audio files, video files, sticky notes, and images, students can collaborate to share and learn alongside their peers (Rao et al., 2021). Students can also use video recording platforms, such as Flip, to collaborate asynchronously. They can record themselves in a variety of formats to share and discuss the outcomes from the lesson while replying to their classmates, thus building their level of engagement with the material.

Project- or problem-based learning (PBL) is another way to blend technology and the UDL guideline of multiple means of engagement. The learning within PBL involves the student creating their own project based on a specific problem or question that is meaningful to them (Walsh & Dalton, 2021). In a study by Walsh and Dalton (2021), students accessed multiple means of engagement through a project-based learning experience where students designed tactile picture books or literary elements for individuals who were visually impaired or blind. The students were engaged in the work because they could select an area of interest (Walsh & Dalton, 2021). This experience also led to persistence as students worked through their projects to share with an authentic audience (Walsh & Dalton, 2021).

Multiple Means of Representation

Under multiple means of representation, students will be provided with various methods of obtaining the information within a lesson. In this guideline, students should be given options for perception, language and symbols, and comprehension (CAST, 2018). These categories allow for students to provide alternatives for information, receive support in learning new terms and vocabulary, and build background knowledge to help their overall understanding of a new topic. Determining how to differentiate content in a variety of ways to make it more accessible for students might seem initially challenging, but given all the features, apps, and extensions that can be built into a student's device, finding alternate representations can become easier for teachers to achieve (Jung, 2021).

One example of multiple means of representation would be providing a smartpen for students to use in the classroom. A study by Boyle and Joyce (2019) focused on this type of support. A group of students in an inclusion language arts class was split into two groups, where both groups contained both students with and without disabilities. One group was taught to use the smartpen for recording notes during lectures. The students in this group received higher scores and achieved higher than the other group (Boyle & Joyce, 2019). This study exemplifies the benefit of having access to digital support by all learners within an inclusion classroom. Not only did the individuals with an IEP receive high achievement with the aid of the smartpen, but their peers also outperformed their classmates with this support.

Virtual math manipulatives also fall under multiple means of representation. Virtual manipulatives are "technology-enabled visual representations of a dynamic mathematical object" that allow the user to manipulate and demonstrate their mathematical understanding (Moyer-Packenham & Bolyard, 2016, p. 3). Examples of these digital manipulatives can include fraction pieces, geoboards, money pieces, or visual number lines. These resources have been documented as beneficial for students with disabilities, specifically in developing a conceptual understanding of mathematical topics and skills (Shin et al., 2017). However, there is an issue with accessing the tangible version of these resources after elementary school. Virtual manipulatives provide the opportunity to receive support, but in a way that is more engaging and developmentally appropriate for secondary school (Bouck et al., 2019). Digitizing these resources also offers the opportunity to extend the visual, concrete practice to students in the general education classroom who do not have an IEP or a disability classification but would still benefit from the extra support during the learning process.

In the previous discussion of the evolution of assistive technology, accessibility features were addressed. These features are built into every device, and all users have access to these tools and resources. In addition to these preset features, users can customize their device's browser to include extra extensions or apps to provide supplemental support during instruction. An example might include a picture dictionary, where students can double-click on a word while independently reading and see a visual to represent the definition of that word. Since these apps and extensions are available for all students to download, a teacher can extend the opportunity to utilize these resources to all learners in the classroom (Ok & Rao, 2019).

Multiple Means of Action and Expression

Since multiple means of action and expression focuses on the "how" of learning, this guideline emphasizes the need for students to have options when demonstrating their learning (CAST, 2018). Students need options for physical action, expression and communication, and executive functions (CAST, 2018).

Instead of using one singular measure to determine a student's level of understanding of a topic, this guideline requires that consideration be given to the strengths of each student when determining how they can best demonstrate their knowledge.

One of the ways to exemplify this UDL guideline using technology is to give students a choice in how they want to compose a response. In a history class, instead of having all students write a response to a document-based question, students could have the autonomy to choose the way they want to respond. For example, some students might feel that writing is their strength and will decide to explore that option. Other students might feel more comfortable verbalizing their thoughts aloud and will choose to record their answers. Even still, some students may prefer to create a presentation or a video to showcase their responses. Each of these options will still meet the targeted learning objective but allows students the opportunity to make the decision on the method of execution for themselves.

Multiple means of action and expression move beyond just choosing how to demonstrate understanding; it also requires students to set goals and monitor their progress, building the necessary executive functioning skills (CAST, 2018). Rao et al. (2021) suggest using a checklist on Google Keep to allow students to keep track of the work they have completed. In a study focused on using UDL within elementary computer science, the teachers used checklists as both a way for students to self-monitor throughout the project while also giving a space for the teacher to provide feedback (Israel et al., 2020). From a technology perspective, teachers could use a collaborative document between themselves and the student for the checklist. The student can update their progress accordingly, and the teacher can leave comments. By adding technology to this option, the teacher has the opportunity to embed helpful links, videos to self-created screencasts, or audio feedback to make the comments more meaningful to their students.

Technology and Accessible Materials

If a teacher is considering the UDL framework to ensure inclusivity and accessibility for their students, they need to address the accessibility of the resources they provide. There is a responsibility for educators to ensure that resources are appropriately modified, so they are equitable for all learners (Swenson & Ryder, 2016; Rice & Ortiz, 2021). Given that accessible learning materials are one of the categories of special education technology (Thomas et al., 2019), it is important for teachers to be proactive in modifying and adapting the resources they are sharing (Rice & Ortiz, 2021).

Since many digital resources automatically have features to make digital resources more accessible, the teacher just needs to support students in implementing each feature. For example, a student reading a text on the computer could activate the text-to-speech feature on their device to listen to the information at their own speed. A screen reader could be enabled to read any images presented on the page, so the student does not miss any key details. Other tools for accessible resources include closed captioning when presenting videos and access to audiobooks (Hashey & Stahl, 2014). Audiobooks provide a way for students to read whole class novels alongside their peers, while closed captioning can make video content more accessible. Video transcripts can also be integrated into resources to add another element to media-based content.

SOLUTIONS FOR INCLUSIVE TECHNOLOGY EDUCATION

As technology continues to update and evolve, the opportunity presents itself for solutions to be found within inclusive education. Some of the current problems with technology are a disconnect between technology and instructional objectives or curriculum, lack of training and expertise in technology used by both the student and the teacher, and the fast-paced nature of technology, which lends itself to being quickly outdated (Thomas et al., 2019). Additionally, obstacles such as a lack of access to accessible technology, lack of technical support for devices and technologies, and lack of support from administration can also impact technology integration in the inclusion setting (Israel et al., 2021).

In general, special education teachers tend to have positive feelings toward assistive technology, especially within the inclusion setting (Mohamed, 2018; Satsangi et al., 2019). However, these positive feelings do not undermine the need for technology-related training. Teachers need to have some level of familiarity with accessibility and technology to decrease barriers facing students with disabilities (Shaheen & Lazar, 2017). While researchers have frequently recommended integrating more assistive technology training in teacher preparation programs (Parette et al., 2005), an alternate solution is needed to support teachers currently in the field. For in-service teachers, ongoing learning is a good way to provide training. Hayes (2013) addressed a school district in California that provided a digital library of technology resources related to special education that teachers could explore independently. Other options to overcome the training barrier include learning from building colleagues or from the students themselves (Hayes, 2013). Ideally, a school district would provide the training on the devices, but in circumstances where this may not be feasible, these solutions could be alternatives.

Aside from a lack of teacher training, there is often a lack of student training that corresponds to technology usage (Thomas et al., 2019). The absence of these training opportunities is especially problematic, considering the fact that students are supposed to use the tools autonomously to support their learning. Simply passing along a new device and having students teach the technology to themselves is ineffective (Boyle & Kennedy, 2019). Instead, teachers need to provide opportunities for modeling how to use the technology (Boyle & Kennedy, 2019). Teachers should actively use supportive technology in their lessons to properly show students how to use the tools. For example, a language arts teacher working on a writing mini-lesson may use dictation instead of typing to show how to compose a text. This modeling allows the students to see how to properly use the technology while helping to normalize accessibility tool usage in the inclusion classroom. Furthermore, students need opportunities to practice using technology tools (Boyle & Kennedy, 2019). Teachers should provide adequate time to explore and learn a new technology before they are expected to use the tool within the context of a lesson or activity.

There is an existing barrier to accessibility features in the classroom, specifically for schools that have a mixture of different devices in an inclusion setting. Uniform terminology is often nonexistent across platforms and devices (Shyyan et al., 2016). The name of the text-to-speech service on an iPad or iPhone differs from the naming convention on a Chromebook or an Android device. In these circumstances, teachers need to be cognizant of the various names. At the beginning of the year, teachers can provide an overview of the accessibility features on the different devices the students are using but use generic names when referring to them in the classroom. For example, a teacher might encourage their entire class to use speech-to-text. Rather than telling students to go to a specific accessibility feature by name, this generic statement includes all the different voice typing technologies that students may use in the class.

FUTURE TRENDS IN INCLUSIVE TECHNOLOGY

As new technologies continue to emerge and become more commonplace in education, their roles will expand within inclusive classrooms. When more emerging technologies are used in the classroom for instructional purposes, a discussion will occur about how these tools could help to make learning more inclusive. The research has started to shift toward a discussion of how augmented and virtual reality is beneficial in education. Aside from being a way to engage students in the content, this technology also has the potential to be effective in supporting student needs. For example, augmented reality can allow students to visualize and determine relationships between concepts that are not tangible or concrete, including scientific concepts such as molecules (Walker et al., 2017). The research already suggests that augmented and virtual reality are supportive for individuals with disabilities and help increase inclusivity (McMahon & Walker, 2014). However, future research trends will likely shift toward how this type of technology supports all learners in the inclusion classroom.

In assistive technology, as more mainstream technologies are being designed with all users in mind (Ismaili & Ibrahimi, 2017), there may be a decreased need for separate devices and equipment. There is a rise in mainstream products becoming more inclusive, adding new apps and features that consider the varying needs of all users while making these tools accessible to everyone. While this shift has already started within assistive technology discussions, the trend will likely continue with each new device update. Students can customize their support and get the resources they need on the smaller, portable devices used by their peers in their classes. These resources will be openly available for anyone who needs them, leading to a learning environment where all learners feel accepted and included. Furthermore, as these updates occur, the stigma will continue to decrease regarding accessibility features and assistive technology.

REFERENCES

Aftab, M. J., Bano, H., Qureshi, M. S., Nadeem, H. A., & Qamar, A. M. (2021). Role of assistive technology in promotion of inclusive education for children with disabilities: Special educator's perspective. *Multicultural Education, 8*(1), 325–334.

Alnahdi, G. (2014). Assistive technology in special education and the universal design for learning. *The Turkish Online Journal of Educational Technology, 13*(2), 18–23.

Bakken, J. P. (2019). Special education for young learners with disabilities: An introduction. In F. E. Obiakor & J. P. Bakken (Eds.), *Special education for young learners with disabilities* (pp. 1–14). Emerald.

Behrmann, M. (1994). Assistive technology for students with mild disabilities. *Intervention in School and Clinic, 30*(2), 70–81.

Bouck, E., & Satsangi, R. (2020). Maths assistive technology to support inclusion. In D. Chambers (Ed.), *Assistive Technology to Support Inclusive Education* (pp. 51–68). Emerald Publishing.

Bouck, E. C., Flanagan, S., Miller, B., & Bassette, L. (2012). Rethinking everyday technology as assistive technology to meet students' IEP goals. *Journal of Special Education Technology, 27*(4), 47–57.

Bouck, E. C., & Long, H. (2021). Assistive technology for students with disabilities: An updated snapshot. *Journal of Special Education Technology, 36*(4), 249–257. https://doi.org/10.1177/0162643420914624

Bouck, E. C., Matthews, L. A., & Peltier, C. (2019). Virtual manipulatives: A tool to support access and achievement with middle school students with disabilities. *Journal of Special Education Technology, 35*(1), 51–59.

Boyle, J. R., & Joyce, R. L. (2019). Smartpen technology for note taking in inclusive English/language arts classes. *Reading & Writing Quarterly, 35*(6), 525–538.

Boyle, J. R., & Kennedy, M. J. (2019). Innovations in classroom technology for students with disabilities. *Intervention in School and Clinic, 55*(2), 67–70.

CAST. (2011). *Universal design for learning guidelines version 2.0.* CAST.

CAST. (2018). *Universal design for learning guidelines version 2.2.* http://udlguidelines.cast.org

Chambers, D. (2019). *Assistive technology to enhance inclusive education.* Oxford Research Encyclopedia of Education. doi:10.1093/acrefore/9780190264093.013.155

Chambers, D. (2020). Assistive technology supporting inclusive education: Existing and emerging trends. In D. Chambers (Ed.), *Assistive technology to support inclusive education* (pp. 1–18). Emerald Publishing.

Chita-Tegmark, M., Gravel, J., Serpa, M., Domings, Y., & Rose, D. (2012). Using the universal design for learning framework to support culturally diverse learners. *Journal of Education, 192*, 17–22.

Cho, V., & Littenberg-Tobias, J. (2016). Digital devices and teaching the whole student: Developing and validating an instrument to measure educators' attitudes and beliefs. *Educational Technology Research and Development, 64*(4), 643–659.

Conderman, G. (2015). Assistive technologies: A lifeline for learning. *Kappa Delta Pi, 51*(4), 173–178.

Dale, O., & Grut, L. (2015). Mainstream ICT can support children and adolescents with ADHD and/or autism in their everyday activities. *Studies in Health Technology and Informatics, 217*, 679–684.

Dolamore, S. (2021). Accessibility features in Zoom to improve quality in the MPA classroom. *Journal of Public Affairs Education, 27*(3), 376–379. https://doi.org/10.1080/15236803.2021.1929020

Evmenova, A. (2020). Implementation of assistive technology in inclusive classrooms. In D. Chambers (Ed.), *Assistive technology to support inclusive education* (pp. 177–194). Emerald Publishing.

Evmenova, A. S., & King-Sears, M. E. (2013). Technology and literacy for students with disabilities. In J. Whittingham, S. Huggman, W. Rickman, & C. Wiedmaier (Eds.), Technological tools for the literacy classroom (pp. 83-104). IGI Global.

Francisco, M. P. B., Hartman, M., & Wang, Y. (2020). Inclusion and special education. *Education in Science, 10*(9). https://doi.org/10.3390/educsci10090238

Friend, M., Cook, L., Hurley-Chamberlain, D., & Shamberger, C. (2010). Co-teaching: An illustration of the complexity of collaboration in special education. *Journal of Educational & Psychological Consultation, 20*(1), 9–27.

Grynova, M., & Kalinichenko, I. (2018). Trends in inclusive education in the USA and Canada. *Comparative Professional Pedagogy*, *8*(2), 28–34.

Hashey, A. I., & Stahl, S. (2014). Making online learning accessible for students with disabilities. *Teaching Exceptional Children*, *46*(5), 70–78.

Hayes, H. B. (2013, April 2). *How to help teachers integrate assistive technology into the classroom*. EdTech Magazine. https://edtechmagazine.com/k12/article/2013/04/how-help-teachers-integrate-assistive-technology-classroom

Hovey, K. A., Lohmann, M. J., & Gauvreau, A. N. (2021). Enhancing learning for all students: Using a UDL framework to create expert learners. In A. M. Quinzio-Zafran & E. A. Wilkins (Eds.), *The New Teacher's Guide to Overcoming Common Challenges: Curated Advice from Award-winning Teachers*. Routledge.

Individuals with Disabilities Education Act, 20 U.S.C. § 1400 (2004).

Ismaili, J., & Ibrahimi, E. H. O. (2017). Mobile learning as alternative to assistive technology devices for special needs students. *Education and Information Technologies*, *22*(3), 883–899.

Israel, M., Jeong, G., Ray, M., & Lash, T. (2020). Teaching elementary computer science through universal design for learning. In *Proceedings of the 51st ACM Technical Symposium on Computer Science Education* (pp. 1220-1226). ACM.

Israel, M., Marino, M. T., Yan, W., & Samuels, J. H. (2021). Using technology to support effective inclusive elementary schools. In *Handbook of Effective Inclusive Elementary Schools* (pp. 483–506). Routledge.

Jung, L. A. (2021). Lesson planning with universal design for learning: Intentionally using UDL principles upfront means making fewer adaptations later— and reaching more students. *Educational Leadership*, *78*(9), 38–43.

Kee, C. L., & Samsudin, Z. (2014). Mobile devices: Toys or learning tools for the 21st century teenagers? *The Turkish Online Journal of Educational Technology*, *13*(3), 107–122.

King-Sears, M. E., & Evmenova, A. S. (2007). Premises, principles, and processes for integrating technology into instruction. *Teaching Exceptional Children*, *40*(1), 6–14.

Klein, A. (2021, April 20). *During COVID-19, schools have made a mad dash to 1-to-1 computing. What happens next?* EdWeek. https://www.edweek.org/technology/during-covid-19-schools-have-made-a-mad-dash-to-1-to-1-computing-what-happens-next/2021/04

Kozleski, E. B. (2020). *NEPC review: Special education and distance learning: Supporting students through the pandemic (ExcelinEd, June 2020)*. National Education Policy Center. https://nepc.colorado.edu/thinktank/special-education-pandemic

McGuire-Schwartz, M., & Arndt, J. (2007). Transforming universal design for learning in early childhood teacher education from college classroom to early childhood classroom. *Journal of Early Childhood Teacher Education*, *28*(2), 127–139.

McMahon, D., & Walker, Z. (2014). Universal design for learning features and tools on iPads and iPhones. *Journal of Special Education Technology, 29*(2), 39–49.

Mohamed, A. H. (2018). Attitudes of special education teachers towards using technology in inclusive classrooms: A mixed-methods study. *Journal of Research in Special Educational Needs, 18*(4), 278–288. https://doi.org/10.1111/1471-3802.12411

More, C. M., & Travers, J. M. (2012). What's app with that? *Young Exceptional Children, 16*(2), 15–32.

Moyer-Packenham, P. S., & Bolyard, J. J. (2016). Revisiting the definition of a virtual manipulative. In P. S. Moyer-Packenham (Ed.), *International Perspectives on Teaching and Learning Mathematics with Virtual Manipulatives* (pp. 3–23). Springer.

National Center on Accessible Educational Materials. (n.d.). *AEM basics*. http://aem.cast.org/about/aem-basics.html#.W3G3bS2ZNok

Nepo, K. (2017). The use of technology to improve education. *Child and Youth Care Forum, 46*(2), 207–221.

Nicholl, B., Flutter, J., Hosking, I., & Clarkson, P. (2013). Transforming practice in design and technology: Evidence from a classroom-based research study of students' responses to an intervention on inclusive design. *Curriculum Journal, 24*(1), 86–102. https://doi.org/10.1080/09585176.2012.744696

Nieves, K. (2021). Building inclusive learning environments with 1:1 devices. *Journal of Special Education Technology, 36*(1), 54–59.

Nordström, T., Nilsson, S., Gustafson, S., & Svensson, I. (2018). Assistive technology applications for students with reading difficulties: Special education teachers' experiences and perceptions. *Disability and Rehabilitation, 14*(8), 798–808. https://doi.org/10.1080/17483107.2018.1499142

Ok, M. W., & Rao, K. (2019). Digital tools for the inclusive classroom: Google Chrome as assistive and instructional technology. *Journal of Special Education Technology, 34*(3), 204–211. https://doi.org/10.1177%2F0162643419841546

Okolo, C. M., & Diedrich, J. (2014). Twenty-five years later: How is technology used in the education of students with disabilities? Results from a statewide study. *Journal of Special Education Technology, 29*(1), 1–20.

Osgood, R. L. (2005). *The history of inclusion in the United States*. Gallaudet University Press.

Owuor, J., Larkan, F., Kayabu, B., Fitzgerald, G., Sheaf, G., Dinsmore, J., ... MacLachlan, M. (2018). Does assistive technology contribute to social inclusion for people with intellectual disability? A systematic review protocol. *BMJ Open, 8*(2), e017533.

Parette, H. P., Peterson-Karlan, G. R., & Wojcik, B. W. (2005). The state of assistive technology services nationally and implications for future development. *Assistive Technology Outcomes and Benefits, 2*(1), 13–24.

Peterson-Karlan, G. R. (2015). Assistive Technology Instruction within a Continuously Evolving Technology Environment. *Quarterly Review of Distance Education, 16*(2).

Quick, C., Ryndak, D., & Taub, D. (2017). Research and evidence-based practices to promote membership and learning in general education for students with extensive support needs. *Inclusion*, *5*(2), 94–109.

Rao, K., Torres, C., & Smith, S. J. (2021). Digital tools and UDL-based instructional strategies to support students with disabilities online. *Journal of Special Education Technology*, *36*(2), 105–112.

Rice, M., & Ortiz, K. (2021). Evaluating digital instructional materials for K-12 online and blended learning. *TechTrends*, *65*(6), 977–992. https://doi.org/10.1007/s11528-021-00671-z

Satsangi, R., Miller, B., & Savage, M. N. (2019). Helping teachers make informed decisions when selecting assistive technology for secondary students with disabilities. *Preventing School Failure*, *63*(2), 97–104.

Schaaf, M. J. (2018). Editorial: Technology adoption, acceptance, satisfaction, and benefit: Integrating various assistive technology outcomes. *Special Education Technology*, *33*(3), 171–181. doi:10.1177/0162643417753561

Scherer, M. J., Jutai, J., Fuhrer, M., Demers, L., & Deruyter, F. (2007). A framework for modeling the selection of assistive technology devices (ATDs). *Disability and Rehabilitation. Assistive Technology*, *2*(1), 1–8. doi:10.1080/17483100600845414

Shaheen, N. L., & Lazar, J. (2017). K-12 technology accessibility: The message from state governments. *Journal of Special Education Technology*, *33*(2), 83–97.

Shin, M., Bryant, D. P., Bryant, B. R., McKenna, J. W., Hou, F., & Ok, M. W. (2017). Virtual manipulatives: Tools for teaching mathematics to students with learning disabilities. *Intervention in School and Clinic*, *52*, 148–153.

Shyyan, V. V., Thurlow, M. L., Larson, E. D., Christensen, L. L., & Lazarus, S. S. (2016). *White paper on common accessibility language for states and assessment vendors*. University of Minnesota, Data Informed Accessibility–Making Optimal Needs-Based Decisions (DIAMOND). https://nceo.umn.edu/docs/OnlinePubs/DIAMONDWhitePaper.pdf

Siu, K., & Lam, M. (2012). Public computer assisted learning facilitates for children with visual impairment: Universal design for inclusive learning. *Early Childhood Education Journal*, *40*, 295–303.

Swenson, S., & Ryder, R. E. (2016). *Dear colleague: Virtual schools*. Department of Education, Office of Special Education and Rehabilitative Services. https://www2.ed.gov/policy/speced/guid/idea/memosdcltrs/dcl–virtual-schools–08-05-2016.pdf

Thomas, C. N., Peeples, K. N., Kennedy, M. J., & Decker, M. (2019). Riding the special education technology wave: Policy, obstacles, recommendations, actionable ideas, and resources. *Intervention in School and Clinic*, *54*(5), 295–303.

UNESCO. (1994). *Final report: World conference on special needs education: Access and quality*. UNESCO.

UNICEF. (2021). *Seen, counted, included: Using data to shed light on the well-being of children with disabilities*. UNICEF.

United Nations. (n.d.). *The 17 Goals.* United Nations Department of Economic and Social Affairs: Sustainable Development. https://sdgs.un.org/goals

United States Department of Education, National Center for Education Statistics. (2019). *Digest of education statistics, 2018 (NCES 2020-009).* nces.ed.gov/fastfacts/display.asp?id=59

Walker, Z., McMahon, D., & Rosenblatt, K. (2017). Beyond Pokémon: Augmented reality is a universal design for learning tool. *SAGE Open*, (October-December), 1–8.

Walsh, B., & Dalton, B. (2021). Build a better book: Enriched literacy-project-based learning for multilingual students. *Journal of Adolescent & Adult Literacy*, *65*(4), 361–365.

Zabala, J. (1995). *The SETT framework: Critical areas to consider when making informed assistive technology decisions* (ERIC Document Reproduction Service No. ED381962). Region IV Education Service Center. https://eric.ed.gov/?id=ED381962

Zabala, J., Bowser, G., & Korsten, J. (2005). SETT and ReSETT: Concepts for AT implementation. *Closing the Gap*, *23*(5), 1–4.

Chapter 16
Virtual Exchange Experiences Energized by an Educational Technology Paradigm Shift

Patricia Szobonya
https://orcid.org/0000-0003-4655-313X
Rockland Community College, USA

Catherine M. Roche
Rockland Community College, USA

ABSTRACT

Asynchronous and synchronous modes of online communication utilizing a variety of technology applications provide students with opportunities to engage in both student-to-student and team discourse. Through experiential and project-based learning, students develop skills in digital literacy, virtual teamwork, empathy, and cross-cultural communication—all requisite 21st century skills for employment. The authors will showcase their virtual exchange collaborations utilizing the latest educational tech tools. Challenges, considerations, and opportunities inherent in developing and delivering virtual exchange projects plus student reflections will be shared. Teaching strategies that embrace a diversity, inclusion, equity, and social justice learning environment will be discussed.

INTRODUCTION

Although the rise of globalization is often attributed to advances in communication, transportation, and commerce, technology is the driving force responsible for connecting people, goods and services, information, and ideas across international borders. The sporadic lockdowns and quarantines demanded during the pandemic precipitated an increased societal reliance on and utilization of technology for people's mere existence. This dependence and sometimes vulnerability was a reminder that we are indeed all connected and encounter similar challenges.

DOI: 10.4018/978-1-6684-6092-4.ch016

In spite of hardships endured during the pandemic, challenges of various types were ubiquitous even before. The detrimental effects of climate change on current natural world, anxiety about employment and personal finance affecting families' welfare, and relentless geopolitical strife and political friction are a few of the universal concerns that affect daily life, today.

Therefore, to tackle these critical issues, multilateral partnerships and intercultural alliances that unite individuals through their collective efforts are imperative. Endeavors of this magnitude, however, will require an awareness and understanding of the values, behavior, and attitudes of other cultures. Possessing intercultural knowledge can serve as a prerequisite for working harmoniously toward solving or at least alleviating the issues facing civilization today and tomorrow.

Educators can do their part by preparing students to succeed in their globalized, continually changing, and uncertain world. Global issues should be introduced juxtaposed with opportunities for binational team and student-to-student discourse and collaboration.

A traditional approach for internationalizing the curriculum has been the availability of short and long-term study abroad programs. According to the Open Doors report on international educational exchange, the number of undergraduate students participating in such programs was increasing annually (Institute of International Education, Inc., n.d.). Despite this positive trend, however, the percentage of community college and marginalized students participating remained low (Palmer, 2021). Financial constraints combined with a lack of time, work conflicts, and family responsibilities; these are the principal factors contributing to disappointing numbers.

Due to travel restrictions and intermittent global outbreaks of COVID-19 that compelled cancellation of programs from 2020 to 2022, study abroad percentages plummeted dramatically. However disappointing this may have been, the pandemic has prompted newfound interest in virtual exchange. According to O'Dowd (2021), virtual exchange is an inaccurate term, as it suggests that the exchange is not real and perhaps secondary to study abroad. On the contrary, virtual exchange is an expedient learning paradigm. By leveraging technology, barriers are eliminated granting all students the opportunity for an intercultural experience. Historically underrepresented populations who have been excluded from study abroad programs due to the factors previously mentioned are now included with an equitable chance to develop their intercultural awareness and competency.

VIRTUAL EXCHANGE

The introduction of synchronous and asynchronous communication tools has played an integral role in the evolution of virtual exchange. New and improved video-conferencing platforms and apps, the availability of smart mobile phones and texting, and the growth of social media have altered the landscape of telecommunications. A host of technology tools, many of which are free, are available with additional tools continually being introduced.

Under the direction of faculty facilitators, two classes from different countries and perhaps different disciplines work together using a variety of asynchronous and/or synchronous digital tools to engage in intercultural communication and collaboration. Similar to activities in the traditional classroom, no two collaborations are identical, as each is uniquely designed and delivered by trained faculty partners from institutions around the world.

The Stevens Initiative

The Stevens Initiative was inspired by the work of J. Christopher Stevens, U.S. Ambassador to Libya (Stevens Initiative, 2022). His Peace Corp teaching assignment in Morocco framed his devotion to the people and youth of the Middle East North Africa (MENA) region.

Unfortunately, in 2012, Ambassador Stevens was killed in the terrorist attack on the U.S. Embassy compound in Benghazi, Libya. Established in 2015, this eponymous initiative serves as a tribute to him and as his legacy to continue the goal of connecting students in the MENA region with students in the U.S. by providing opportunities for person-to-person dialogue. The Stevens Initiative awards grants for virtual exchange programs through the support of multilateral partnerships including the Stevens family, the U.S. Department of State, the U.S. government, the Bezos Family Foundation, Google, and the governments of Morocco and the United Arab Emirates. The initiative is administered by The Aspen Institute (http://www.aspeninstitute.org), a global nonprofit Washington DC-based educational and policy studies organization.

Advantages to Students

Virtual exchanges provide advantages to all stakeholders, namely students, faculty, institutions, and perhaps ultimately the local community and/or the world. The obvious intercultural communication skills that students develop are just one kind of numerous skills to be acquired. Through interactions on binational teams, students examine their own culture from different perspectives. This self-examination leads to an understanding of how others perceive them and their culture and the basis for that perception. Collaborations enable students to appreciate and navigate differences diplomatically. Students develop relationships with students across the globe with some budding friendships continuing beyond the collaboration.

While working in a team-oriented and project-based learning environment, students develop skills in digital communication, empathy, negotiation, critical thinking, decision making, problem solving, and entrepreneurial thinking. These skills correspond with the eight career ready workplace competencies identified by the National Association of Colleges and Employers (2022): Career and self-development, communication, critical thinking, equity and inclusion, leadership, professionalism, teamwork, and technology.

The above skills are commonly referred to as soft skills or 21st Century skills, as they are transferable, versatile, and thus desired in prospective job applicants in varied industries around the globe. During the pandemic, remote work arrangements prevailed in business sectors out of necessity and were enabled by the availability of technology. The flexibility and convenience resulting from remote work has reinforced a frequently sought-after employee wish for work/life harmony. When working remotely, geographic borders are irrelevant, enabling work to encompass a 24/7 global environment. Since remote arrangements provide advantages to both employees and employers, some interim changes may become permanent. The ability to self-manage and lead while participating with domestic or global parties in virtual team meetings is an additional 21st Century skill. Virtual exchange activities prepare students for employment in an ever-changing workplace empowered by technology (Dondi et al., 2021).

United Nations Sustainable Development Goals

Earlier virtual exchanges concentrated primarily on learning outcomes directly correlated to developing intercultural awareness. Today, however, many virtual exchanges continue this focus, but approach it by addressing one or more of the 17 United Nations Sustainable Development Goals (UN SDGs). The goals are befitting the entire world, as they present vital issues seeking urgent solutions affecting us all. Integrating the SDGs into a virtual exchange project brings awareness of and action toward creating a sustainable environment for present and future generations (United Nations, 2022).

Many of the 17 goals are interconnected, so that achieving one will positively impact one or more others. Besides commitments from governments around the world and local, national, and international partnerships, human advocacy is necessary to reach SDG targets by 2030. Innovative and creative ideas effectuated through student research, brainstorming, communication, collaboration, and activism in virtual exchange projects can support these efforts.

Generation Z

Community colleges are a microcosm of society, as they encompass a diverse population in terms of age, gender, gender identity, sexual orientation, race, ethnic background, socioeconomic status, and college readiness. Born between 1996 and 2012, members of Generation Z (Gen Z) are the traditional-aged students pursuing higher education. Throughout their formative years, this cohort has been exposed to political, economic, social, and, more recently, health crises through Facebook, Twitter, TikTok, Instagram, and Snapchat news feeds. Domestic and global turmoil has shaped the attitudes of these digital natives, propelling them into action. Whether it be social justice issues, climate change, ubiquitous mass and school shootings, abortion and voting rights or a host of other issues, Gen Z uses technology as their catalyst for activism toward change (Parker & Igielnik, 2020).

Although the younger members of this generational cohort are not yet eligible to exert their political power at the ballot box, they demonstrate soft power in the digital world. In the U.S., recent and proposed changes to long-standing legislation have not been well received by many members of Gen Z. Their displeasure has been voiced through influencers and online activism (Kingsberry, 2022).

Their commitment to equality, diversity, human rights, and sustainability combined with a penchant for a digital lifestyle indicates that Gen Z wishes to be involved in experiential learning projects that can make a difference. Educators can satisfy their interests by launching high-impact learning experiences as defined by the American Association of Colleges and Universities (2022). For example, some of the high-impact practices espoused by this organization that correspond to virtual exchange and 21st Century skills are collaborative work and projects, common intellectual experiences, diversity/global learning, internships, service learning, and undergraduate research.

Advantages to Faculty

Students are not the only stakeholders who benefit from involvement in virtual exchange. Faculty, too, can augment their cultural knowledge base concomitant with utilization of technological tools and contemporary learning paradigms. The movement toward diversity, equity, and inclusion has been reaffirmed by the persistent digital divide and the social justice awakening and protests of 2020. Therefore, culturally responsive teaching has garnered interest, as it is a student-centered approach that embraces inclusivity and appreciates cultural awareness. It draws upon every student's unique cultural background and identity and eschews attempts to homogenize students into uniformity. Students' race, culture, and ethnicity are regarded as assets to be nurtured and valued, not as liabilities to be corrected or even expunged. Adopting such a paradigm satisfies diversity, equity, and inclusion efforts as well as virtual exchange activities at the same time (Wlodkowski & Ginsberg, 1995).

Involvement in virtual exchange can reinvigorate and motivate faculty, serving as a remedy for burnout. Besides the intrinsic value of serving students' needs and the addition of pedagogical skills to one's teaching repertoire, the extrinsic value of professional advancement can be acknowledged. Participation in professional development workshops and the implementation of teaching strategies such as culturally responsive teaching can provide efficacious evidence to a faculty dossier prepared for reappointment, tenure, promotion or awards. In addition, collaborating with a faculty member at a global institution enlarges a faculty member's network of colleagues. Opportunities for scholarship through exchange of pedagogy, collaboration on research projects and grants, and preparation of proposals for workshop and conference presentations can be pursued.

Advantages to Institutions

Higher education administration is ultimately charged with crafting institutional strategic plans. These plans structure the direction a campus will follow as it moves toward accomplishing its mission, vision, goals, and objectives. An institutional commitment that provides students with a global perspective and 21st Century skills can increase student enrollment and retention, while simultaneously delivering an inclusive image and message to the community.

SUNY COIL

A well-known virtual exchange platform is State University of New York (SUNY) Collaborative Online International Learning (COIL). In 2006, Jon Rubin, a Film/New Media Professor at SUNY Purchase, conceived this faculty-driven grassroots project. Prof. Rubin served as Director of COIL from its inception until 2017. He is a pioneer in virtual exchange and continues to advocate through COIL Consulting and COIL Connect, organizations he founded and which support the development of COIL initiatives at institutions of higher learning.

Through distribution four times a year, a COIL Partnership Bulletin lists faculty who are interested in finding a partner with whom to collaborate. The bulletin provides a brief overview of a proposed project, and faculty who are interested are encouraged to contact the faculty member to discuss the possibility of working together. If a match is made, the next step is to contact the campus COIL Coordinator, so that the required training may commence.

COIL is inherently an inclusive paradigm, as it is the channel through which students and faculty from different cultures are brought together in a learning environment (SUNY COIL, n.d.). COIL expands the horizons of students by opening up the world to them, as some may not have traveled outside the country or even beyond their own locality. Students have person-to-person conversations enabling the development of empathy and elimination of any prevailing stereotypes generally promulgated by the media.

COIL Network and Rockland Community College

Rockland Community College (RCC) is one of 64 campuses in the SUNY system of higher education. In 2014, RCC became a member of the SUNY COIL Network. Since then, the COIL Network has grown exponentially through the addition of SUNY campuses, global partner institutions, and, more recently, non-SUNY campuses across the U.S.

RCC has offered collaborations in a variety of departments, such as Art, Business, English, Hospitality, Legal Studies, Multicultural Studies, Political Science, Science, and Speech. To the credit of the dedicated COIL faculty who have expended time and effort to serve students and their institution, many of these collaborations have been sustainable throughout the years. The COIL partners regularly discuss improvements and reflect upon the technology used, ensuring that it is the optimal choice for their projects.

Besides offering professional development training, partnering opportunities, resources, and support, the SUNY COIL Center (n.d.) has worked with third-party organizations and governmental bodies to identify grant opportunities for faculty. Between 2015 and 2017, SUNY COIL was the recipient of two major grant initiatives that focused on COIL exchanges in different parts of the world. The Stevens Initiative focused on the MENA region, while the U.S.-Mexico Multi-State Project focused on Mexico.

COIL projects are scaffolded to build student confidence and motivation. Projects commence with an icebreaker activity that serves as both a welcome and an introduction. Short video or audio segments are uploaded in which students share information about themselves and their culture (e.g., language, dress, food, pop culture, greetings, and rituals). These visible aspects of culture are positioned at the tip of Hall's cultural iceberg model, as they are the external and observable aspects of culture that are above the water (Lazarus, 2017). As tasks in the project advance, however, conversations relating to cultural aspects that are internal, not as easy to observe, and below the water reveal deeper aspects of culture such as attitudes and values (Lazarus, 2017).

In the next section, the authors will share details about virtual exchange projects that they developed and delivered from 2015 to 2022 with higher education institutions in China, Colombia, Iraq, Jordan, Mexico, Morocco, and the Netherlands. All collaborations were conducted in English.

Virtual Exchange Collaborations

China

China's Social Credit Score

This East-West collaboration of business students was conducted via Skype for a six-week duration. Weekly activities were assigned, providing opportunities for students to connect virtually and discuss relevant international business and cultural topics. Several classes included guest speakers who presented on issues involving cultural protocol, artificial intelligence, family dynamics, and alternative lifestyles. The students met in binational teams to contrast and compare behavior in both countries.

One study focused on the data used in the social credit score in China to the U.S. credit score. Ethical issues were raised concerning privacy and the personal and economic impact the scores had on individuals. Students determined that both scores had positive and/or negative repercussions enabling or limiting purchasing power. In addition, the social score in China has further implications where restrictions based on certain social behavior were enforced. For example, a low social score could prohibit an individual from making dinner reservations or limit travel. As China and the U.S. have a 12-hour time difference, alternate arrangements were necessary for students to meet synchronously. The students in China resided in a dorm and were able to return to the classroom in the late evening while U.S. students met in their scheduled class at 8 a.m. Students engaged in live synchronous discussions while learning to adjust to cultural and language obstacles, even with English as the lingua franca. Outside of the classroom, the students communicated via WhatsApp.

Colombia

Peacebuilding

Virtual exchange provides the perfect opportunity to develop and apply 21st Century skills such as critical thinking, problem-solving, and collaboration that foster international peacebuilding. This six-week asynchronous collaboration began with student introductory videos posted in Flipgrid to initiate classroom community. The icebreakers presented an opportunity for students to express themselves through information such as their field of study, family life, hobbies, and favorite things. The peacebuilding project was facilitated through Padlet, where binational teams collectively selected an international issue that was relevant in both countries. Teams were required to develop an achievable strategy to raise awareness about the selected issue. For example, creating a poster, organizing a protest, conducting an educational presentation or scheduling a fundraiser. It was understood that "building world peace" literally would be unattainable in six weeks, yet creating an action plan with measurable goals in raising awareness was feasible.

The students communicated on WhatsApp and through text messaging to determine what changes they would like to see in their communities. Topics ranged from gun violence, poverty, hunger, equal education, bullying, and domestic violence. The collaboration process took place via Google Docs and Slides. The teams showcased their results in a final PowerPoint or video presentation uploaded to Padlet. This collaboration provided individuals across diverse social, economic, and cultural backgrounds a chance to devise a plan collectively while forming a shared identity within the group. This collaboration highlighted the UN SDGs # 1, 2, 4, 5, and 16.

The Influence of Culture and the Macroenvironment on Global Marketing Strategy

The module learning outcomes of this eight-week collaboration included the development of intercultural communication skills and cultural intelligence through virtual teamwork activities, the application of a situational analysis (PESTLE) to determine potential for product or service introduction in Colombia and the U.S., and creation of a business model canvas to illustrate the business model of a product or service.

Binational teams were populated with 40 Colombian and 24 U.S. students. Some of the Colombian students were taking International Business in the classroom, while others were connecting remotely from home using Microsoft Teams. The U.S. students were enrolled in a remote synchronous section of Principles of Marketing delivered via Blackboard. Pre-collaboration tasks were introduced in both classrooms via Kahoot and Padlet, and students were permitted to choose the technology best suited for sharing their ideas outside of class. Among the tools selected were WhatsApp, Discord, and Google Drive. Synchronous binational meetings in Zoom were scheduled during class time for presentations of PESTLE research and subsequently the business model canvas. The one-hour time difference between the two countries was considered in planning synchronous meetings to be held during class time. The time the classes were scheduled to meet was synchronized as the Colombian class met at 8 a.m. while the U.S. class met at 9 a.m. on the same weekday (Chartered Institute of Personnel and Development, 2021).

Mexico

Electronic Waste in the U.S.

This six-week collaboration involved students from the U.S. who were studying law and students from Mexico who were studying electronic engineering. While both courses had distinct learning objectives, converging goals into an impact cultural themed project fostered values in business and global citizenship. The students in the U.S. garnered cultural connections through an interview, whereas the students in Mexico obtained understanding of Americans' shopping preferences through a consumer survey. As the electrical engineering students developed e-gadgets and toys, in consonance with the course learning outcomes, the "distribution and sale" in the U.S. component was added. This element engendered the skill of the U.S. students to research and convey the requirements of U.S. patent law.

The student teams showcased their collaborative efforts in Facebook subgroups. Photos of the e-gadgets and toys or designs of such were posted on the main wall of the Facebook closed private group. A binational comparative analysis on electronic waste and recycling habits completed the project. U. S. students identified a product they recently purchased and described its life cycle, including how it was or would be disposed of. The students enjoyed the supplemental topics of study that ordinarily would not have been introduced in their course. This collaboration highlighted UN SDGs # 3, 6, 7, 11, 13, 14, and 15.

Morocco

Activism and Youth: Motivation

The respective countries involved in this collaboration were widely known for political and social movement demonstrations often involving youth participation. This six-week asynchronous project examined the motivation of younger generations in their experience within such movements. The students prepared video introductions to break the ice and posted them on the main wall of a Facebook closed private group. Within subgroups, binational teams determined why young people were motivated to participate in such activism including movements centering radical ideologies. The students were transparent in sharing that both countries lacked opportunities to support and positively influence youth. Responses further suggested that young people often felt isolated and powerless to effectively create change and that they were very concerned about the future. The groups provided multi-perspective solutions that included educational, social or physical activities to occupy youths' time. The students bonded in the collaborative process, often using the instant messaging feature in Facebook throughout the day and beyond the virtual exchange component. UN SDGs #10 and 16 were highlighted in this project.

Comparison Between the Black Lives Matter and the Arab Spring

The Black Lives Matter Movement originating in the U.S. and the Arab Spring protests occurring throughout the Middle East over a decade ago were explored, considering their success and achievements. In this asynchronous collaboration, the participants introduced themselves to the class utilizing Flipgrid.

The students created brief videos sharing their field of study, preferences, and hobbies. Students also were asked to post a cultural image on the Padlet wall, advancing cultural exploration.

For the six-week duration, binational teams communicated via email and texts to determine the skills and strategies that foster peaceful protests. The teams compared both movements through detecting and analyzing the elements of success and failure. Padlet was used to provide instructions, present the documentaries showcasing the movements, and to create space for collaboration and reflection. Many students in the U.S. had never heard of the Arab Spring protests. A common reflection from students was that while the movements did not accomplish every demand, they certainly raised awareness of important issues. This collaboration highlighted UN SDGs # 5, 10, and 16.

Examining Culture: Waiting in Line

Through a cultural lens, this asynchronous collaboration involved a study of human behavior while performing an ordinary daily task revealed through images. Binational teams introduced themselves with a visual introduction through a photo or a video in a Facebook closed private group. Students who were uncomfortable with posting a self-image were encouraged to post a favorite cultural photo or video of a favorite place, artwork, architecture or traditional dish. Once acquainted, the teams collected images or videos of people in their country waiting in a line and posted them on the main wall of the Facebook page.

For the team project, images and videos posted by members were examined with detailed attention to the surrounding environment and cultural clues depicted. As pictures often tell a story not spoken, the students identified and discussed talking points that were revealed in the background. The specific behavior displayed in the act of waiting in a line was compared, as well as visuals captured displaying customs, religion, art, architecture, and facial expressions. These discussions cultivated fruitful conversation and appreciation of one another's culture. While the activity appears to be rudimentary, a complex intercultural discussion prevailed in explaining visual presuppositions. Students were asked to share their interpretations of the viewed behavior and draw conclusions based on comparing cultural and societal norms.

Examination of the Influence of Culture on Communication Styles: Focus on Employment Communication Through e-Portfolios

Students enrolled in Principles of Management were paired with Moroccan fourth year civil engineering students enrolled in an English language module. Despite the disparity in course content, student career goals, faculty backgrounds, and student demographics, faculty partners were able to establish common course learning outcomes.

After the requisite icebreaker activity in which students used their cellphone cameras to record an introductory video, the second task was completed via a Facebook closed private group. Students were asked to respond to various scenarios. For example, in one scenario, students were told that they were on their way to a coveted job interview. On the way to the interview they met a close friend who was very upset about a personal matter and wanted to talk right away. The situation created a dilemma: If the student stopped to console the friend, the student would undoubtedly miss the bus and be late for the job interview. Responses from the U.S. students indicated that they would go to the job interview as planned and speak to the friend afterwards. Although they were concerned about their friend, personal plans to arrive on time took priority. On the other hand, the Moroccan students offered to stay with the friend or even asked a family member to comfort the friend in their absence. These contrasting reactions were consistent with one of Hofstede's (n.d.) dimensions of culture: Individualism vs. collectivism. The U.S. is an individualistic culture whereas Morocco is a collective culture in which the welfare of the group supersedes the needs of the individual.

The last task in the project was creation of an e-Portfolio in which student reflections and other work was posted. The U.S. students used Digication, the campus supported e-Portfolio platform, while the Moroccan students chose one of the free e-Portfolio sites. A Google Form was used for assessment.

Cultural Influences on Consumer Behavior

Students in a marketing honors course worked with civil engineering students from Morocco in binational teams in Facebook closed private groups. They examined cultural values, interests, and behavior to determine influences on consumer buying behavior. The project began with an icebreaker followed by discussion responses to various scenarios such as What Would You Do? What If? and Completion Statements. Responses delved deeper into Hall's cultural iceberg as students learned more about each other's culture through disclosure of individuals' values, beliefs, behavior, and attitudes on various topics.

The final task focused on responses to a list of questions about buying behavior: Who influences your purchases? Where do you shop? Do you work? Are you influenced by social media? From their responses, the teams concluded that they had much in common regarding buying behavior. Findings revealed that in both countries families and social media exerted a strong influence on buying behavior. Although many global brands were available in Morocco, one observation was that Moroccan students were not as brand insistent as their U.S. team mates.

Contemporary Parallels of The Great Gatsby

This collaboration involved students from Morocco who were studying English literature and students from the U.S. who were enrolled in Multicultural Studies. Faculty partners creatively blended distinct course learning objectives implementing a collective literary and sociological analysis of *The Great Gatsby* characters in the context of the era, class, and geography (West & Fitzgerald, 2013). Initially the students created an icebreaker video in the Facebook closed private groups describing the student's field of study, favorite food, and hobbies. During the six-week project, the binational teams conducted character analysis by examining flaws and conflict based on gender, class, and societal expectations. The groups communicated through messaging or within their subgroups via Facebook. The final deliverable was a reaction paper critiquing social stratification within the context of *The Great Gatsby* including a cross-cultural analysis (West & Fitzgerald, 2013). This collaboration highlighted UN SDGs # 5 and 10.

Going Global From Within Local: Cultural Styles and Strategies Examined Through COIL Interactions

Students completed practical project-based tasks related to employment communication. Through binational team interactions in a Facebook closed private group, similarities and differences regarding employment practices in both countries were identified. English was used in a professional context equipping students to demonstrate language proficiency in the workplace. Team research concluded that resumés prepared in both countries included the same elements, but the Moroccan format was somewhat different. The frequently asked interview questions were the same, but some personal questions were asked in Morocco—questions that are illegal in the U.S. Similar to resumés, cover letters were formatted differently and were more detailed.

Transnational Education: Connecting Students Through a COIL Project

This collaboration was very similar to the previous one in terms of technology, outcomes, student population, and deliverables. However, the Moroccan engineering students and the U.S. business students required 10 weeks in order to accommodate holidays and spring break. The U.S. students recorded team video introductions at various locations around campus, rather than individual videos. This change in recording was decided because many students said they would feel more comfortable recording as a team and uploading to the Facebook closed private group. However, some students expressed that they would have preferred recording individually.

Developing Soft Skills Through an Intercultural COIL Lens

This five-week module was conducted in Slack with students from Business Communications and students from English for Professional Communication in Morocco. Although students from both classes were preparing for different careers, interpersonal skills transcend specific fields and are considered the hallmark of a professional. Since this was a shorter module than usual, the tasks were primarily discussion-based after the customary icebreaker. In binational teams students discussed the difference between hard and soft skills and provided examples of both. A link to a job posting students were currently or will be qualified for upon program completion was uploaded for discussion. After comparison, students concluded that many of the soft skills required were identical in both countries.

Exploring Soft Skills and Professionalism

The theme of this collaboration was similar to the previous one, except for three variables: Technology, duration, and the Moroccan class. The six-week module joined a Business Communications class with students enrolled in English teacher preparation in Morocco. Students uploaded a video introduction as the icebreaker and then shared job postings segueing into a discussion identifying hard and soft skills. To encourage additional student interaction, a global sharing panel was created in Padlet. This panel included questions pertaining to best practices for job interview preparation. Students discussed the topic of professionalism and were asked to complete the statement: "A good manager is one who …." Another Padlet panel was created for sharing cultural information, images, and artifacts.

The final assignment in Business Communications directed students to assume the role of marketing manager. Students were asked to compose a short persuasive memo report to their boss requesting that seven employees be enrolled in an intercultural training session focusing on Moroccan business practices and protocol. The training was costly, but necessary, since these employees would be working on a substantial marketing project with new clients in Morocco. The memo report served as a culminating activity, as they not only conducted further research on Morocco, but also added their own reflections resulting from their interactions with the Moroccan students.

Communicating Interculturally Through Technology

This Padlet collaboration involved Business Communications and an oral communications course in Morocco. A spring break in the U.S. and holidays in Morocco extended the collaboration to 10 weeks.

The principal learning outcome was the development of intercultural communication skills and cultural intelligence through virtual teamwork activities. After the usual video introductions, students were introduced to Geert Hofstede's (n.d.) six dimensions of culture plus their country's rankings on the dimensions. In binational teams, students discussed the dimensions and their agreement or disagreement with the rankings assigned to their countries. Specific examples of their culture that supported the rankings were requested.

Lastly, students discussed their culture by examining Hall's concept of high- and low-context cultures and how time and space are exhibited in cultural interactions (Lazarus, 2017). A Padlet panel was created for sharing of cultural artifacts such as videos, images or simply information representing everyday life.

Netherlands

Global Brand Marketing Strategies in the United States and the Netherlands

During a nine-week period, students enrolled in a hybrid Principles of Marketing class joined with business students at a university in Amsterdam. Both groups were preparing for employment as future members of a global virtual team or seeking employment abroad. The goal was to develop positive interpersonal relationships leading to professional success. In four binational teams populated by eight or nine students, team members researched global brands that conducted business in both countries. From their research, each team selected a different global brand and examined the brand's marketing strategy and performance in both countries.

The culminating project was a written report accompanied by a recorded team presentation showcasing recommendations on how the brand might improve its performance. Team communication was enabled by Google Docs and Skype. In addition, teams chose WhatsApp for video chats and communication.

Global Solutions Sustainability Challenge

In addition to COIL, the International Research & Exchanges Board (IREX) (n.d.a) is a nonprofit global education organization offering virtual exchanges in over 100 countries. The programs focus on empowering youth by equipping them with workplace skills enabling them to function and prosper as global citizens.

One of the programs that IREX facilitates is the Global Solutions Sustainability Challenge. This program connects students in Iraq, Jordan, and the U.S. to develop 21st Century workplace skills. Funding is provided by several foundations, governments, and grants from the Stevens Initiative (IREX, n.d.b).

Through a prescribed eight-week curriculum, binational teams communicate and collaborate asynchronously through Slack and synchronously through Zoom. Binational teams apply the business design process to identify a shared problem and a sustainable solution that addresses one of the UN SDGs. In recognition of the soft skills attained, students are awarded digital badges that can be shared on social media sites and displayed on resumés.

The project deliverables include submission of a business model canvas report and production of a short video. The top six teams are invited to pitch their idea to a panel of judges. Seed money is awarded to the top three teams to commence work on the proposed solution.

The following collaborations will describe three challenges involving students enrolled in a Principles of Marketing honors course and their MENA partners. Unlike the U.S. students, the MENA students were not enrolled in a specific class at their institution, but had voluntarily applied for acceptance to participate in the Challenge.

Iraq

Metamorphasystem

Students worked with their partners from a university in Iraq. The timing of this collaboration was Spring 2020, a semester which presented unprecedented challenges of its own as COVID-19 was spreading across the globe. The collaboration began in the classrooms; however, campus closings and quarantines necessitated rapid migration online. The Internet connections were somewhat sporadic and unreliable, in Iraq, forcing some students to abandon their classes. Nevertheless, remaining students and faculty partners expressed interest in continuing despite the involvement of fewer Iraqi students.

After icebreakers and brainstorming via synchronous and asynchronous discussions and teamwork in Slack, Zoom, and Google Docs, students identified a problem and offered a possible solution. Students developed a CAD drawing of a prototype called the metamorphasystem. This device enabled the conservation of water through recycling, as water conservation was the central problem the binational team chose to address.

The binational team conducted research about sustainability within the framework of the triple bottom line: people, planet, and profit. Through Zoom meetings, U.S. students observed the cultural dimension of Hofstede's (n.d.) individualism vs. collectivism as evidenced through the collective behavior of Iraqi students. Students shared details of everyday life in their countries, which often contradicted the media version and any preconceived notions they might have had. As a result of their involvement in the project, some of the students discovered a newfound interest in recycling, engineering, Arabic, and water conservation. This collaboration highlighted UN SDGs #3, 6, and 15.

I Don't Think My Brother Likes Me: Autism Awareness Alliance

The U.S. team on campus was part of a binational team working with students from a private university in the Kurdistan region of Iraq. After much discussion at Zoom meetings and in class, the "A Team" chose to address UN SDG #3 – Good Health and Well-Being, with a focus on autism. Students wanted to ensure that children with autism could lead healthy, happy, and productive lives. The solution proffered was the creation of a prototype—an illustrated, informative children's book called *I Don't Think My Brother Likes Me*. The intended audience was both children and parents or caregivers. The book explained autism in terms that a child could understand, and resources were provided at the end of the book to assist families around the world in identifying early signs of autism and where and how to seek proper diagnosis and treatment. A guest speaker who works with autistic children provided an informative lesson on the signs, prevalence, and different effects of autism on individuals and their families.

Besides the knowledge gleaned from the guest speaker, students conducted research to learn more about the autism spectrum. Research was shared on a Slack channel for the binational team, and Google Docs was used in the U.S. classroom for team sharing, brainstorming, and decision making. A team logo was created using Canva. Besides the required deliverables for the Challenge, students created a Web site using SquareSpace. In recognition of their efforts, judges awarded the binational team the designations of Honorable Mention and Unique Concept. This collaboration highlighted UN SDGs #3, 4, and 10.

Jordan

Meyah Irrigation System Technology

This binational team consisted of U.S. students working with students from a university in Amman. Through their joint efforts, the binational team discussed and proposed a smart-technology-based agricultural solution to help farmers around the globe optimize their utilization of water for irrigation. Discussion regarding the name of the prototype ensued with the name MIST (Meyah Irrigation System Technology), being chosen. MIST dispensed the exact amount of water for irrigation through coded algorithms.

Binational subgroups were established to work on various aspects of the project with information sharing conducted through corresponding Slack channels and in meetings. Google Docs and Blackboard discussion boards were used in the U.S. for decision making and polls. Binational teams met regularly via Zoom during U.S. class time as Jordanians accommodated the eight-hour time difference. Via Zoom, a SUNY faculty member with extensive experience working with irrigation systems in several countries provided information on systems and feedback on the prototype and solution.

A total of 27 teams from institutions in Iraq, Jordan, and the U.S. competed in this cohort of the Challenge. The binational team's creativity, innovation, and knowledge was recognized by the judges, as the team was awarded second place in the competition. This collaboration highlighted UN SDGs # 3, 6, and 15.

Student Reflections

"I should not feel embarrassed if my English is not perfect; people in other parts of the world are not going to judge me, as they understand I'm not native. Now I can feel brave, when speaking in other languages different than Spanish."

"I love the fact that I was able to practice my English. I definitely have to keep working on my English skills to avoid language barriers."

"Although I thought Dutch was the only language that the Dutch students spoke, I was shocked to find out that they did in fact speak English. My notion has changed for obvious reasons, and it made me think that American students should learn another language other than English as well."

"I always thought that Colombia was very poor and I might have judged it the wrong way due to stories I would hear on the news or from my friend. But, I saw that all of the country isn't like that, and that I actually shared a lot in common with them."

"The part I enjoyed the most was the PESTEL analysis, not only for what I found about the U.S., but especially for many interesting factors my teammates from the U.S. found about Colombia. They were not only focused on the typical things, but they looked for really interesting issues that I didn't even know about my country."

"With all the turmoil going on in this country, I felt as if America was looked down upon by a lot of other countries and considered a laughing stock of a country. I did not know if the Moroccan students

would take us seriously or not; I was not sure what preconceived ideas they had about us. Yes, my attitude changed. After speaking one-on-one with the Moroccan instructor, I was able to understand how tolerant Moroccans are of others of adversity and difference. They do not impose their beliefs, ideas or morals onto others. They value respect very heavily."

"The videos made me realize how similar we all really are even though they come from a totally different culture. I was also impressed by how well the Moroccans speak English. This assignment got me very excited to start the semester and I was hopeful that the project would go well and for further interactions between our two groups."

"Due to the differences in cultures, both the United States and Morocco have differences, when it comes to job interviews and the questions they are asked during the interviews. We discussed this on Facebook, through the COIL group, as well as in our classroom through discussions and different assignments. It was very interesting in two ways: The way job interviews are performed in a different country and the complex, and sometimes 'weird' questions that are asked."

"This project really tested my skills and applied what I was learning in a more real-world situation. I think you should continue doing this project for future classes, as I think it's what every marketing student needs to know exactly what they are in for."

"It was clever to do COIL for marketing class, as it helped solidify and underline the notion that all consumers have the same basic needs, and even wants. But, more importantly, it emphasizes the fact that people from all over the world have much more in common with each other than they think, and that underneath it all we are all still brothers and sisters."

"This project confirmed my belief that two nations can come together and create exceptional things without prejudice. I learned from this project that I can actually be a marketer if I want to. This project made me understand the power of marketing in business and encouraged me to continue on my long-term goal."

"I definitely learned that I need to improve my communication and organization skills in the future before officially entering the marketing field. I'm very used to working with and depending on myself. It is hard for me to trust other people's quality of work, but it's necessary for me to conquer that since I will always be working and collaborating with other people in my career."

"Overall, I am quite impressed with our Moroccan friends; even though they come from very different cultural backgrounds, we aren't that different. I hope just like we were able to see our common interest and not focus on what divides us and get along, I hope we as the next generation can see that politically and grow together instead of having conflict."

"I believe that it is an amazing experience for me to interact with students across the world and explore commonality and differences between cultures." "It was important to me that nations can help each other and work together. It's something that I wish politicians would be able to do more often. Seeing my fellow classmates and the students from Iraq working together as a team was something that I learned a lot from."

"One thing I learned about the United States is how our problems are relative to other parts of the world. I thought that problems were exclusive to each country. However, the problems in every country are similar or the same. The United States and Iraq both worry about water, oil and political instability. However, the scales of the problems are different. Relative to Iraq, the problems in the United States are not that bad. In Iraq, water scarcity is widespread across the country. Oil is the most important metric as most of their economy relies on oil."

"Seeing the daily hardships Iraqis face which do not stop them from striving for a good education and for improving their prospects, put the issues we face in perspective. It is easy to take all the infrastructure and services we have for granted and forget about challenges other students who are just like us have on top of everything else."

"I view Iraq differently from before simply because I didn't know much about Iraq before the Global Solutions Challenge. I can empathize with them and therefore can see them more as peers, rather than as people from across the world in a country I only hear about in the news."

"Through working on this project, I definitely gained some confidence. I had usually been the student who waited for direction to be given to me, or thought my ideas were not good enough. However, this autism project changed that for me. I had been a director and had to assign myself along with others different roles. I also felt very comfortable working with my classmates as it was a positive environment and felt eager to share my ideas. I realized my ideas were helpful and my input was just as important as anyone else."

"One of the tasks that I did not know that I would be able to complete was the children's story about autism. I spent the entire weekend thinking about what to write and eventually an impromptu writing style helped me come up with a story. The lesson I would say I learned is that when faced with a challenging assignment; the best thing to do is start it and it will begin to work itself out. The same thing applied when working on the Business Model Canvas."

"The most interesting and useful learning moment for me was being able to build something of our own, for the betterment of society from the ground up. All of the components in this project were very important and every team had a specific goal to help make the prototype and the business concept the best it can be. Overall, it shows the importance of teamwork and, in order to become successful, you need a good team. In addition, anything is possible, and it doesn't matter where you are in the world to make a difference."

"I had a great experience working with Jordanian students and being able to create a whole prototype based on an idea. This project has made me consider learning more about international business and how businesses grow from different parts of the world. I would love to visit Jordan, one day, and many countries around the world to learn about their cultures. I would love to explore other areas of sustainability and how to implement sustainability into businesses. In terms of skills, I would like to explore Slack and the business model more!"

"I learned that I could manage a team. Initially, when I was asked to be a team leader, I wanted to answer no. Some part of me just said do it. I was surprised to learn that I enjoy being a leader and being involved in more leadership roles in the future."

"I struggle with getting my voice heard and tend to work passively. Write a report—I'll do it myself. Make flyers—I'll do it myself. However, this wasn't an option for this project. Although it was difficult, I tried to take the initiative and communicated with my team members. Planning and meeting deadlines are something that I learned to be critical throughout the project. In the future, I'd apply the planning process, and I hope to continue to become an effective communicator."

"I learned and, in fact, I'm still learning the skills I experienced throughout this project. I will continue to learn how to share my ideas without fearing what will happen. In addition, when I was doing the Web site, I didn't know how to start it, but I still did it anyway. I'm taking this experience to not be afraid of starting something completely new and unfamiliar to me and explore it."

"I want to further my education in the environmental issues we currently have. As a long-term goal of mine, I also want to contribute to something that will help earth out in a positive way, whether it's forming an organization or having an eco-friendly and cruelty free business. Even though I've had this long-term goal for a while, this project has motivated me to continue pursuing it."

TECHNOLOGY AND VIRTUAL EXCHANGE

The latest technological advances have enhanced educational pedagogy and mobility in virtual exchange. In the aftermath of COVID-19 quarantines, there has been an increase in digital opportunities highlighting the demand for efficient technology and online functionality, as well as the expansion of virtual exchange relationships. Increasing global student online populations have galvanized educators to design virtual cross-cultural collaborations utilizing affordable and accessible contemporary digital modalities.

With the proliferation of collaborative digital resources in education and increased connectivity, virtual exchange can be easily incorporated into course curriculum. The success of virtual exchange partnerships relies heavily on the technological resources accessible between partnering institutions. Sufficient resources such as bandwidth, Internet speed, and accessibility have an impact on student participation and communication. Institutional support also plays a pivotal role, as administration is ultimately responsible for the selection and financing of innovative tech resources to accommodate international collaboration.

COVID-19 exposed many inequities in the field of technology prevalent on campuses around the world. Equity gaps revealed that many students were without use of electronic devices and access to the Internet. This prompted many institutions to create hotspots and electronic device loaner programs, which remain available today. Many students continue to rely on their mobile devices to conduct schoolwork and communicate. Successful contemporary collaborations utilize an equitable framework which encompasses educational mobility as well as digital accessibility. Each virtual exchange implies many other considerations and distinct alternatives, from language, class size, learner profiles, task sequences, calendar, time zone, support, and technologies. Thus, designing successful collaborations is both a process and a product.

Institutions experienced a rapid transformation, from teaching and learning face-to-face to teaching and learning via electronic platforms, much sooner than anticipated. This prompted many inexperienced faculty members to navigate digital and online pedagogy. Online teaching has become indispensable and is integrated across disciplines, requiring high quality professional training for educators to excel in this craft. While challenging for some, these contemporary digital modalities and platforms have also brought advantages for students. Equitable opportunities for student populations have been created through flexible options of online or blended platforms (Powell Sears, 2022). Students are empowered and take ownership in a format that suits them best, enhancing their learning and participation.

Developing a virtual exchange collaboration is rewarding for all participants. Embarking on a unique relationship with an educator from another country broadens personal development and enumerates an appreciation for another's values, beliefs, and practices, expanding global relationships. After finding a reliable partner to subscribe to this adventure, various components and considerations are necessary.

Initially, educators select the courses they will teach, which ultimately defines the intended learning objectives. These learning objectives lay the foundation for the planned collaborative activities and how educators will implement them through an international partnership enabled by technology.

Virtual Exchange and Modes of Course Delivery

Synchronous

Course design, whether synchronous, asynchronous, HyFlex, hybrid or a traditional face-to-face course, necessitates other considerations between educators when planning to incorporate a virtual exchange component.

In synchronous courses, students have the luxury of joining classes from anywhere around the world and meet on a regular basis. Communications between faculty and students are conducted instantaneously through real-time virtual interactions made possible through technology. Mobile devices, voice or video conferencing tools such as Skype, Facetime, Microsoft Teams, Google Voice, and the infamous Zoom are popular choices for creating synchronous learning environments. In this learning environment, students have access to the instructor while experiencing an interdependent environment. Students can interact with peers, offer encouragement, and receive instant feedback. To maximize student interaction in a synchronous environment, educators can utilize the camera function, screen share, breakout rooms, poll, and chat features.

Virtual exchange within a synchronous course can be easily implemented utilizing the digital tools mentioned above. Synchronous sessions can be scheduled if the timing permits for both institutions.

Asynchronous

Asynchronous learning environments provide opportunities for students to become independent learners. Faculty design and develop online courses are housed and accessed within the institution's learning management system (LMS). The LMS is utilized to facilitate the course, house the learning materials, and monitor student activity. While meeting times to conduct classes are not set, faculty can communicate with students through the course messaging features, discussion boards, email or by adding third party apps that foster additional student interaction and engagement. The structure of the course is outlined in the syllabus, and students self-navigate at their own pace and submit work electronically on established due dates. Students should be self-motivated and resourceful, as they will work independently.

Popular choices for LMS software are Blackboard, Canvas, Moodle, Edmodo, D2L, and Schoology (Fenton, 2018). Each LMS operates in a relatively similar fashion. Typically, the administration has the task of determining which LMS is most suitable for the institution, based on functionality, integration, and innovation, while balancing the financial aspect.

In asynchronous courses, virtual exchange can be embedded within the course structure, depending on the partnering instructors' goals and timing. As asynchronous learners work independently, a space for collaboration with binational partners must be available for students to communicate and interact. Partners decide which third party digital mediums will be most suitable to facilitate the collaboration. Some popular tools are VoiceThread, Flipgrid, Facebook or Padlet. Email, texts or chats can also generate student-to-student and faculty-to-student communications. The benefit of learning in an asynchronous environment is that students are offered the convenience to complete their coursework on their own schedule. Additional benefits include saving time and money in lieu of commute and travel expenses. In this format, a virtual exchange collaboration would likely be accomplished asynchronously as well.

Hybrid

The hybrid course model blends traditional face-to-face (or synchronous) classes with a portion of online (asynchronous) learning. Virtual exchange can be easily incorporated into either the synchronous or asynchronous portion of the hybrid model, contingent upon the usual considerations. In the hybrid model, students benefit by having physical access to the instructor, while enjoying the flexibility of working independently between face-to-face sessions. Also, the commute time and travel expenses are diminished.

HyFlex

The latest design in online teaching and learning, also expeditiously prompted by COVID-19, is the HyFlex model. The HyFlex model integrates synchronous remote instruction while conducting face-to-face classroom instruction that is live streamed, simultaneously. HyFlex requires an investment for the necessary equipment to deliver a streamlined uninterrupted class. An integrated HD two-way camera system with Zoom capabilities is used to capture movement of the instructor and students within the class via pan and tilt features. A microphone is used to detect and relay the sound. The faculty member is responsible for operating all the live streaming functionality and recording features, while facilitating the class with sound pedagogy (Beatty, 2022). Often, faculty have little experience and minimal training to operate the equipment, encountering disruptions and loss of student attention. Faculty may rely too heavily on their IT department, thus remaining inexperienced to resolve issues on their own (Beatty, 2022).

When students enroll in a HyFlex course, students take control over their preferred learning style and choose the format that suits them best. Having the responsibility of choice enhances student learning and motivation (Kohnke & Moorhouse, 2021). With HyFlex, students either select the remote synchronous learning option or the traditional face-to-face learning. The option may not be interchangeable. HyFlex, however, easily accommodates all students to learn remotely should future quarantines become a reality. As COVID-19 and other strains are still widely circulating, having a viable option of remote learning continues to be well received (Kohnke & Moorhouse, 2021).

Challenges in Electronic Platforms

Educators are challenged with delivering engaging courses, regardless of the chosen format. Contemporary learning environments offer varied remote options that create flexibility in adapting instruction to individual student's needs. Educators strive to develop skills that impact and promote student achievement equitably. Equitable education not only includes advancing diversity, equity, and inclusion in the classroom, but also ensures digital accessibility and universal design for learning (UDL) in electronic formats.

The UDL principles include multiple means of engagement (why), representation (what), and expression (how) (CAST, 2018). These principles can be implemented by presenting information in a variety of means, providing students with various ways to communicate, and encouraging students to demonstrate their competency in a format that best suits their preference. UDL explores different ways by which educators can meet students' needs proactively, while digital accessibility ensures students have equal access to electronic modalities and connections (Greene, 2022).

As synchronous courses have become increasingly available and utilize videoconferencing, the phenomenon of "Zoom fatigue" has become apparent (Ramachandran, 2021). Zoom fatigue can occur after staring at an electronic device for too long. While many individuals experience this mental exhaustion, sitting in front of the computer for long periods of time may also result in physical exhaustion (Ramachandran, 2021). In synchronous learning environments, many educators have experienced lecturing to students who keep their cameras turned off resulting in lecturing to "black boxes". Trained educators learn to implement electronic features such as polling, word clouds, breakout rooms, and chats to foster student engagement. Educators need to be proactive in using these features to encourage participation and enhance the interactive digital space.

Virtual Exchange Technology Tools

Emerging trends are indicators of innovation as a result of technological advancement. With educational technology, emerging trends further academic mobility and enable an increase in viable sustainable virtual exchange interactions. Binational collaborations are incorporated into course curriculum through digital platforms garnering international community-based dialogue. Innovative platforms provide colorful, stimulating, and user-friendly environments that enable students to communicate by posting text, videos, pictures, and Web links. Video features enable the instructor and fellow classmates to visually recognize one another, attaching names to faces. Interactions become more personalized, and the community dynamic is stronger.

While numerous technology choices are available to incorporate in a virtual exchange collaboration, the choice is contingent on what is accessible to both faculty and students. Many apps and software are available and favored for communication, such as social media platforms, WhatsApp, Flipgrid, and Zoom. Other tools are best suited for collaborative work such as Padlet, Trello, Slack, Google Workspace, and Facebook. These options will be explained in further detail below, along with the necessary technology and considerations for virtual exchange.

Social Media Platforms

In modern society, social media has fundamentally changed the way people communicate and interact. From becoming one of the most popular activities performed, users regularly visit venues such as Facebook, Twitter, YouTube, and other social platforms. A recent study by Experian Simmons found that 98% of people aged 18-24 years use social media frequently, if not daily (Gama, 2021). The ubiquity of social media and accessibility on mobile devices empower their constant use. The more connections created, the wider the social community extends. Social media platforms are interactive technologies that enable communication beyond geographical borders. Users exchange ideas, opinions, and their personal content such as videos and images. Social media are also used as a source of information; current events, news, political discourse, advertisements, and advocacy are often exchanged. Virtual platforms also provide community space for shopping, entertainment, support, and education.

Educators have successfully integrated learning into these virtual platforms aiding meaningful exchange and discourse between students. This digital space provides a mutual location for binational groups to explore one another's culture and collaborate on varied issues. Students develop understanding and empathy for one another, forming alliances through teamwork. The interaction exposes students to a multitude of viewpoints providing the opportunity to learn and respect differences. The authors have utilized social media platforms to facilitate their virtual exchange components, in particular Facebook, in earlier collaborations.

Facebook, a free social media networking site, accessible via mobile devices, is a popular choice for virtual exchange. Facebook enables the creation of a private customized group to house the virtual exchange project, with subgroups for individual team space. The main wall of the group provides space for students to showcase personalized icebreaker video introductions, images, and videos as well as the final deliverable project or presentation. Other social media platforms have been used in virtual exchange, such as Twitter, YouTube, and Instagram.

Prior to deciding which social media platform would be most suitable, the goals of the virtual exchange should be established by the faculty partners. The platform should effectively aid in student-to-student communication and the collaborative experience.

Disadvantages of Using Social Media

While social media have many positive attributes, some risks hinder their use in general and may have an impact on students' behavior when accessing virtual collaborative space.

Persistent data sharing within social media networks can increase personal security, identity theft, and data breaches, whereas too much private information is available in open networks. Seeking a social media platform, akin to Facebook, for virtual exchange can accommodate privacy (Drahošová & Balco, 2017).

Finally, censorship of social media can inhibit international communications and ties, thus impacting virtual exchange. Some countries ban or limit social media platforms altogether, while others terminate services at will. Partnering institutions determine mutually accessible social media platforms that will foster international collaborations, while remaining flexible in anticipation of change.

Video Conferencing Tools

Virtual exchange can be incorporated in various digital platforms. However, to interact with binational partners in real time, video conferencing tools are necessary. Video conferencing permits prompt interaction and an opportunity for immediate feedback, coupled with live video that may enhance cultural sensitivity and empathy. Student reflections often indicate that connecting with international counterparts through synchronous technology enhances connections and relatability. Some popular options for video conferencing are Zoom, Blackboard Collaborate, Skype, WebEx, Google Meet, Microsoft Teams, FaceTime, and WhatsApp.

Zoom, widely introduced during the pandemic, positively impacted education and virtual exchange. Zoom provides a host of features geared toward fostering engagement and interaction. Tools such as screen sharing, white board, chat box, breakout rooms, polling, and emoji features serve as interactive mechanisms to maintain students' attention. Zoom empowers users to create their own virtual background, thus enabling some aspect of privacy and creativity. Zoom also has a recording feature, where presentations or lessons can be recorded and uploaded for later screening. This feature promotes equity in learning for those students who require additional review. While many options exist for video conferencing, Zoom is popular because of the simplicity of functionality and the features provided (Novak & Watts, 2022).

Collaborative Apps

Padlet

Padlet is another popular platform used to house and implement virtual exchange. Padlet digitizes bulletin boards with selected wall styles and options for educational interaction. Padlet permits instant updates to rich media boards with posts, videos, and images. Members are invited to join a particular Padlet via a link or QR code, and can add content to the board. The QR code is similar to a barcode that can be scanned by using a camera app on a mobile device, thus making the link accessible. Padlet can be set to be private or public, making this a viable and interactive option for virtual exchange (Staake, 2021).

Trello

Like Padlet, Trello is a team software application utilizing virtual boards as team workspace. The free plan offers users up to ten boards, while Padlet offers three free boards. Trello manages virtual workspace and members' activity in creating, organizing, and monitoring team tasks. The platform enables communication with group members, file uploading, checklists, due dates, and designating tasks. Trello is a visual tool known for project management, while Padlet is more social media oriented (Van Gieson, 2018).

Flipgrid

Flipgrid is an interactive electronic tool popular for its video enhancing capabilities enabling students to post videos, images, text or documents within set "grids." The platform can be easily embedded into an LMS or social media platform via a Web link. Students can easily join the grid via the link or a QR code. The Flipgrid platform is user-friendly. Instructors can use the platform to create lectures, instructional videos or introductions for a more personalized experience. Students have the option of responding to the videos with a voice reply or text, along with the ability to upload rich media. Flipgrid offers an equitable aspect to those students who need time to reflect on their response. A student can retake a video until they are satisfied. Users can send emojis to enhance their messages creating a casual and social vibe. For virtual exchange collaborations, Flipgrid is an excellent way to provide interactive space for transnational students to visualize each other and promote a deeper connection. Visualizing group members and listening to voices fosters student engagement and builds the classroom community (Edwards, 2022).

Other Collaborative Apps

Other options for collaboration are Slack, VoiceThread, and Google Workspace. Slack is a popular messaging app featuring instant communication and team collaboration. Slack offers the ability to share files, archive and manage team projects, utilize chat rooms or direct messaging for communication between groups. The benefits are that it is easily integrated into other software applications and aids management of team collaborations.

VoiceThread is an app designed to share voices within a classroom community, perfect for international virtual collaborations. This app offers the option to upload content such as a lecture and respond to it with a video recording available to a group (Stachowiak, 2019). The group members can collaborate by responding individually with a video recording or text, engaging in asynchronous conversation. Listening to voices is said to create a stronger community than text dialogue (Educause, 2009). The app offers the ability to create five voice threads for free with a valid email address.

Google Workspace provides easy sharing ability through Docs, Sheets, Slides, and Forms. Students can create group projects while simultaneously working on the same file. Files can be shared with group members via email, and members may communicate using Google Chat.

Considerations in Planning a Virtual Exchange

Language

Language is a primary consideration, as it is the universal conduit student partners use to communicate. In bilingual-bicultural collaborations, English, the lingua franca, is used. Although English may not be the native language of most COIL partners, collaborations are usually conducted in English because many students are bi- or multilingual and are required to study the language. U.S. students are often surprised that their student partners speak English and speak it well. Students are pleased to have the opportunity to converse in English with their partners, as practicing improves their speaking confidence and ability.

Timing

Virtual exchanges across different time zones present challenges to both faculty and students, when planning synchronous meetings. Countries that follow Daylight Savings Time (DST) can present additional issues when scheduling. About 40% of countries observe DST by adjusting the standard time an hour ahead in the spring and by turning the clock back an hour in the fall (Buckle & Bikos, n.d.). Faculty must be aware that this change may occur during their collaboration.

Since the academic calendars of institutions differ from country to country, faculty must discuss their respective calendars when planning the dates of their collaboration. Religious and national holidays, seasonal academic breaks such as winter, summer, and spring break, and weekend designations can also vary and must be considered.

Sustainable Partnerships

Integrating virtual exchange across countries and disciplines requires partner compatibility. Sustainable partnerships serve to strengthen the context, scope, and longevity of successful binational student collaborations. Much time and effort are allocated into the development of a virtual exchange, so that it should be sustainable, not a one-time implementation, but an ongoing relationship that improves with time and experience. Selecting a partner that will continue to develop and improve the success of such collaborations is beneficial for a long-term commitment.

Upon meeting a potential partner, initial conversations should address the considerations the authors discussed in the previous section. This conversation will determine if a partnership is feasible. As partners are responsible for the development, design, implementation, and reflection of the virtual collaboration, a strong commitment is required. Communication is paramount, because it enables partners to negotiate confidently, share ideas, and understand each other's viewpoints. Sustainable partners typically embody honesty, empathy, synergy, and accessibility (Cunningham & Tedesco, 2002). Partners must be flexible, as changes can occur abruptly; for example, academic schedules have been affected by the pandemic, climate conditions, and political events. Sustainable partners often complement each other's craft, encourage student engagement, and embrace international collaboration.

Discipline

Interdisciplinary projects can elevate intellectual capabilities and enrich student learning. When partners offer additional resources in addition to their individual expertise, intellectual attention and sensitivities are elevated. When supplementary topics ancillary to their primary discipline are introduced, students broaden their education and enhance their learning experience (Háhn & Radke, 2020).

Soft Power

Virtual exchange aims to strengthen global allies and communities. It can serve as the vehicle to advance a country's soft power through a network of international relationship building. Soft power is achieved by attraction, a subtle persuasion, which can be forged through international relations via virtual exchange (Nye, 2017). Power dynamics, however, are not always equal and may cause friction in virtual collaborations. When one country is perceived as a superpower and the other a third world country, the imbalance may be reflected in student perspectives. This can impact trust, discourse, and meaningful engagement. While the goal of the collaboration is to foster an equitable experience for all constituents, power struggles should be confronted and resolved through meaningful dialogue. Dispelling stereotypes through discussion strengthens and promotes sustainable international relationships.

Partners should take the time to understand each other's culture, society, and politics. Regardless of a country's perceived status, domination or superiority in collaborations can create hegemony and subjugation of peers, negatively affecting outcomes. Successful virtual exchange can enrich this subtle power of persuasion through discourse, understanding and appreciation of culture, and trust between partnering countries, instructors, and students.

Extended Reality

Extended reality (XR) is an umbrella term under which virtual reality (VR), augmented reality (AR), and mixed reality (MR) fall. These three-dimensional environments will increasingly play a role in educational technology ((Rosenberg, 2022).

XR has already been integrated in the gaming industry, tourism, architecture, real estate, healthcare, and other businesses (Huspi, 2021). In the metaverse, educational environments will become VR, transforming a two-dimensional (2D) classroom into a three-dimensional (3D) immersive space where users can interact within a computer-generated virtual classroom (Meta, n.d.). The metaverse will provide digital space where students will interact and feel as if they are together. Currently, "metaversities" are exploring the use of virtual classrooms (Asiedu, 2022).

Meta, the parent company of Facebook, is funding the metaversity project, consisting of ten universities that will offer a VR classroom experience (Koenig, 2022).

Students utilize a headset to access the "metacampus," joining other students and the professor in the virtual classroom. Students digitally become part of the lesson; for example, in an anatomy class, a student has the ability to explore the human body by walking through it (NewsnReleases, 2022). Studies have shown that 40% of VR learners are more confident in applying what they have been taught and 150% more engaged. In addition, VR was found to be 400% faster than classroom-based learning (NewsnReleases, 2022).

Utilizing this emerging technology will benefit student learners by fostering equity in education through personalized interactive learning spaces. Simulated scenarios enable students to apply learned 21st Century skills, such as high impact projects designed to support learning by doing. For example, students can virtually tour partnering countries in 3D, broadening their international intellect. All participants of virtual exchange will be able to gather in one immersive space enriching the collaborative experience.

Adopting Accessibility Best Practices

With the increase of digital classrooms, digital accessibility ensures that all students and users can access Web content and engage within digital platforms equitably. Foremost, students need the Internet and an electronic device to access it. Notwithstanding the digital divide, digital accessibility has also become apparent following the COVID-19 pandemic. Digital accessibility includes the means to assist users with physical disabilities and those technologically challenged; the elderly, those that have slow bandwidth connection or outdated hardware and/or mobile devices (Ableser & Moore, 2018).

Digital accessibility employed in concert with UDL can serve to decrease the digital divide (Farry, 2021). UDL focuses on an equitable experience for all students with access to digital content (Ableser & Moore, 2018). UDL provides flexibility, for example by uploading both a liquid syllabus for visual learners and a PDF printable syllabus for those students who want to hold their learning contract. Including closed captions when displaying a video ensures that varied learners can understand the content and ALT tags for images. Employing practices such as these will promote an equitable learning experience in both the classroom and in virtual exchanges.

RECOMMENDATIONS

For all the advantages previously mentioned, virtual exchange is a win-win choice for everyone. Reinforcement of global competencies can be accomplished through critical thinking and problem-solving international collaborations that address global issues. Twenty-first Century skills are gained and benefit students in their roles as responsible global citizens.

Students participating in virtual exchange collaborations should be recognized for their educational and intercultural achievements. Digital badging, electronic symbols evidencing completion, would showcase their successful participation in virtual collaborations and serve as an additional credential to prospective employers.

While virtual exchange is widely known, its exposure should be increased and institutionally supported across campuses. Administration can encourage virtual exchange opportunities and promote its benefits to faculty, staff, and students. Training opportunities need to be available and accomplishments of virtual exchange celebrated. Resources for faculty to attend in-person and virtual global conferences would foster international partnerships for future collaborations. Grant opportunities can be researched and shared across campus.

In terms of training, as digital technologies are increasingly integrated into education, the need for diversity, equity, and inclusion in a digital sense requires additional professional development for faculty. This involves their being able to create accessible content to all learners digitally while integrating the elements of UDL.

Gen Z, the generation with increased concern for global peace and activism, should have more virtual exchange opportunities available to foster international goals as outlined by the UN 17 SDGs. Gen Z has played a fundamental role in activism because of their unique lived experiences in the digital era. They recognize the need for allyship, transcending geographical borders as they will inhabit this world for decades to come.

Embracing the future integration of XR into virtual exchange will advance cultural awareness and acceptance of diversity, exponentially increase student engagement, and reinforce necessary 21st Century skills. The future evolution of immersive virtual exchange within the metaverse will be out of this world, literally.

CONCLUSION

Educators and students alike should continue to embrace virtual exchange as an opportunity to expand social, educational, and international networks. The interconnected nature of current digital world continues to unite people from various cultures, ethnicities, and personalities, with distinct social customs and norms. The proliferation of technology has made globalization possible, making communication and learning accessible to more people.

Through virtual exchange, students develop the 21st Century skills necessary to communicate and strengthen cross-cultural international relationships within emerging digital societies. Students realize firsthand that global concerns unite people, as outlined in the 17 UN SDGs. Through a combined international effort, resolutions to global problems can be addressed and developed. The 21st Century skills realized in virtual exchange prepare students to address and resolve intercultural challenges through meaningful discourse and negotiation. In essence, equipping a generation to work collectively and converge international partners to resolve global challenges in the future.

Virtual exchange across curriculum provides more students with the opportunity to explore diverse cultures, not just the small percentage that can study abroad. Increasing global citizenry experiences for underserved populations provides a level playing field in which all students can thrive personally, academically, and professionally. Gen Z, also known as the global generation, is not only very cognizant of world events and global injustices, but is taking an active role locally and internationally through social media. The generation to follow, Generation Alpha, will be even more entrenched in technology and will inherit these complex issues, bearing the need for more virtual exchange opportunities.

The sudden jolt in March 2020 that thrust educators and students into online learning has changed the educational technology landscape greatly. Faculty who in the past regarded online learning as inferior, see the many advantages to a well-planned and delivered online course. Students who typically preferred the classroom environment now recognize that the trade-off from in-person classes is the flexibility and convenience of learning online. As the anxiety first experienced in 2020 has decreased and comfort levels are on the rise, virtual exchange is now a paradigm to be seriously considered and adopted.

Educational technology will continue to alter the landscape of teaching and learning. Learning innovations through XR will advance equitable opportunities for students. Future immersive 3D experiences that join international students in a combined virtual space will strengthen bonds and contextualize the experience. Virtual exchange will become a valuable instrument in forging international collaborations, soft power, and lasting relationships.

REFERENCES

Ableser, J., & Moore, C. (2018, September 10). *Universal design for learning and digital accessibility: Compatible partners or a conflicted marriage?* https://er.educause.edu/articles/2018/9/universal-design-for-learning-and-digital-accessibility-compatible-partners-or-a-conflicted-marriage#:~:text=While%20UDL%20aims%20at%20a,%2C%20and%2For%20cognitive%20impairments

American Association of Colleges and Universities. (2022). *High-impact practices.* https://www.aacu.org/trending-topics/high-impact

Asiedu, K. G. (2022, July 20). *Meta's next big bet: The "metaversity."* https://www.protocol.com/enterprise/metaverse-in-education-morehouse-meta

Buckle, A., & Bikos, K. (n.d.). *How does daylight savings work?* https://www.timeanddate.com/time/dst/transition.html

CAST. (2018). *Universal Design for Learning Guidelines version 2.2.: Provide multiple means of representation.* https://udlguidelines.cast.org/representation

Chartered Institute of Personnel and Development. (2021, December 6). *PESTLE analysis.* https://www.cipd.co.uk/knowledge/strategy/organisational-development/pestle-analysis-factsheet#gref

Cunningham, L. C., & Tedesco, L. A. (2002). Mission possible: Developing effective educational partnerships. *Journal of Higher Education Outreach & Engagement*, *7*(1&2), 79. https://www.boisestate.edu/servicelearning/files/2012/01/Mission-Possible-Developing-EffectiveEducation-Partnerships.pdf

Dondi, M., Klier, J., Panier, F., & Schubert, J. (2021, June 25). *Defining the skills citizens will need in the future world of work.* https://www.mckinsey.com/industries/public-and-social-sector/our-insights/defining-the-skills-citizens-will-need-in-the-future-world-of-work

Drahošová, M., & Balco, P. (2017). The analysis of advantages and disadvantages of use of social media in European Union. *Procedia Computer Science*, *109*, 1005–1009. doi:10.1016/j.procs.2017.05.446

Educause. (2009). *Seven things you should know about... VoiceThread.* https://voicethread.com/resources/site/docs/ELI_VoiceThread.pdf

Edwards, L. (2022, May 23). *What is Flipgrid and how does it work for teachers and students? Tips and tricks.* https://www.techlearning.com/how-to/what-is-flipgrid-and-how-does-it-work-for-teachers-and-students

Farry, M. (2021, July 6). *An old problem in the new normal: The digital divide.* https://www.newamerica.org/the-thread/an-old-problem-in-the-new-normal-the-digital-divide/

Fenton, W. (2018, January 12). *The best (LMS) learning management systems.* https://www.pcmag.com/picks/the-best-lms-learning-management-systems

Gama, L. (2021, January 4). *Study finds 98 per cent of young Americans use social media monthly.* https://dagamawebstudio.com/study-finds-98-per-cent-of-young-americans-use-social-media-monthly/

Greene, C. (2022, June 3). *Digital accessibility's intersection with universal design for learning.* https://ctl.jhsph.edu/blog/posts/accessibility-intersection-with-UDL/

Háhn, J., & Radke, K. (2020). Combining expertise from linguistics and tourism: a tale of two cities. In F. Helm & A. Beaven (Eds.), *Designing and implementing virtual exchange – a collection of case studies* (pp. 11–22). doi:10.14705/rpnet.2020.45.1111

Hofstede, G. (n.d.). *National culture.* https://hi.hofstede-insights.com/national-culture

Huspi. (2021, October 19). *Great business benefits of XR for tourism businesses.* https://huspi.com/blog-open/great-business-benefits-of-xr-for-tourism-industry/

Institute of International Education, Inc. (n.d.). *U.S. Study Abroad.* https://opendoorsdata.org/annual-release/u-s-study-abroad/

International Research & Exchanges Board. (n.d.a). *About Us*. https://www.irex.org/about-us

International Research & Exchanges Board. (n.d.b). *Global solutions sustainability challenge*. https://www.irex.org/project/global-solutions

Kingsberry, J. (2022, June 28). *Gen Z is influencing the abortion debate - from TikTok*. The Washington Post. https://www.washingtonpost.com/nation/interactive/2022/gen-z-tiktok-abortion-debate/

Koenig, R. (2022, June 1). *With money from Facebook, 10 colleges turn their campuses into "metaversities."* https://www.edsurge.com/news/2022-06-01-with-money-from-facebook-10-colleges-turn-their-campuses-into-metaversities

Kohnke, L., & Moorhouse, B. L. (2021). Adopting HyFlex in higher education in response to COVID-19: Students' perspectives. *Open Learning: The Journal of Open, Distance and e-Learning, 36*(3), 231-244. doi:10.1080/02680513.2021.1906641

Lazarus, S. (2017, May). *The Cultural Iceberg and Communication*. www.emiworld.org/emi-tech/cultural-iceberg-communication

Meta. (n.d.). *Our story: Enter the future of learning*. https://about.facebook.com/immersive-learning/our-story/

National Association of Colleges and Employers. (2021, March). *Career Readiness: Competencies for a Career-Ready Workforce*. readiness-competencies-revised-apr-2021.pdf

NewsnReleases. (2022, April 7). *Engage XR partners with victory XR to launch 10 Meta funded metaversities*. https://newsnreleases.com/2022/04/07/engage-xr-partners-with-victory-xr-to-launch-10-meta-funded-metaversities/

Novak, J., & Watts, R. (2022, July 5). *Webex vs. Zoom: Which is best for your team?* Forbes. https://www.forbes.com/advisor/business/software/zoom-vs-webex/#:~:text=Both%20Webex%20and%20Zoom%20offer%20feature-rich%2C%20stable%20video%20conferencing,types%20of%20video%20conference%20users

Nye, J. (2017). Soft power: The origins and political progress of a concept. *Palgrave Communications, 3*(1), 17008. Advance online publication. doi:10.1057/palcomms.2017.8

O'Dowd, R. (2018). From telecollaboration to virtual exchange: State-of-the-art and the role of UNICollaboration in moving forward. *Journal of Virtual Exchange, 1*, 1–23. doi:10.14705/rpnet.2018.jve.1

Palmer, A. E. (2021, October 8). *Can community college students study abroad?* https://www.gooverseas.com/blog/can-community-college-students-study-abroad

Parker, K., & Igielnik, R. (2020, May 14). *On the cusp of adulthood and facing an uncertain future: What we know about Gen Z so far*. https://www.pewresearch.org/social-trends/2020/05/14/on-the-cusp-of-adulthood-and-facing-an-uncertain-future-what-we-know-about-gen-z-so-far-2/

Powell Sears, K. (2022, July 14). *Five ways online learning benefited some students.* https://www.insidehighered.com/views/2022/07/14/five-ways-online-learning-benefited-some-students-opinion

Ramachandran, V. (2021, February 23). *Stanford researchers identify four causes for "Zoom fatigue" and their simple fixes.* https://news.stanford.edu/2021/02/23/four-causes-zoom-fatigue-solutions/

Rosenberg, L. (2022, May 20). *VR vs. AR vs. Mr vs. XR: What's the difference?* Big Think. https://bigthink.com/the-future/vr-ar-mr-xr-metaverse/

Staake, J. (2021, January 22). *Padlet for teachers: The best tips, tricks, and ideas for your classroom.* https://www.weareteachers.com/padlet-for-teachers/

Stachowiak, B. (2019, January 15). *How to get students engaging with each other in online and blended classes.* https://teachinginhighered.com/2019/01/15/how-to-get-students-engaging-with-each-other-in-online-or-blended-classes/

Stevens Initiative. (2022, January 8). https://www.stevensinitiative.org/

SUNY COIL Center. (n.d.). *Welcome.* https://coil.suny.edu./

United Nations. (2022). *Do you know all 17 SDGs?* https://sdgs.un.org/goals

University of San Diego. (2022). *Virtual/hybrid/HYFLEX classroom technology setup.* https://www.sandiego.edu/its/support/classrooms/hybrid-classroom-technology.php

Van Gieson, L. (2018, January 31). *My top 5 (Free-ish) cool tools that integrate into Canvas.* https://wp.wpi.edu/atc-ttl/2018/01/31/my-top-5-free-ish-cool-tools-that-integrate-into-canvas/

West, C., & Fitzgerald, F. S. (2013). *The Great Gatsby.* Oxford University Press.

Wlodkowski, R. J., & Ginsberg, M. B. (1995, September 1). A framework for culturally responsive teaching. *Educational Leadership, 53*(1). https://www.ascd.org/el/articles/a-framework-for-culturally-responsive-teaching

ADDITIONAL READING

Coelen, R., & Gribble, C. (2020). *Internationalization and employability in Higher Education.* Routledge Taylor & Francis Group.

Commander, N. E., Schloer, W. F., & Cushing, S. T. (2022). Virtual Exchange: A promising high-impact practice for developing intercultural effectiveness across disciplines. *Journal of Virtual Exchange, 5*, 1–19. doi:10.21827/jve.5.37329

Educause. (2022, April 18). *2022 Educause Horizon Report: Teaching and learning edition*. 2022 EDUCAUSE Horizon Report | Teaching and Learning Edition. https://library.educause.edu/resources/2022/4/2022-educause-horizon-report-teaching-and-learning-edition

Helm, F., & Beaven, A. (2020). *Designing and implementing Virtual Exchange: A collection of case studies*. Research-publishing.net.

Jackson, J. (Ed.). (2020). *The Routledge Handbook of Language and Intercultural Communication.* Routledge. doi:10.4324/9781003036210

Satar Müge (Ed.). (2021). Virtual Exchange: Towards digital equity in Internationalisation. Research-publishing.net. doi:10.14705/rpnet.2021.53.9782490057955

KEY TERMS AND DEFINITIONS

Asynchronous: Online learning delivered with no predetermined meeting days or times. All instructional materials are housed in the learning management system.

COIL: Collaborative Online International Learning, a virtual exchange model pioneered by the State University of New York (SUNY) system of higher education.

Digital Literacy: The ability to navigate and use online resources and tools to create, evaluate, communicate, and share content in an ethically responsible and safe manner.

Global Solutions: Virtual exchange programs offered through IREX (International Research and Exchanges Board) and supported by the Stevens Initiative.

IREX: International Research and Exchanges Board, a global nonprofit organization that empowers youth through access to educational opportunities to develop skills for life and work as leaders and global citizens.

Metaverse: An immersive 3D extended reality (XR) world that includes augmented reality (AR), mixed reality (MR), and virtual reality (VR).

PESTLE: Political, Economic, Social, Technological, Legal, and Environmental, elements in the macroenvironment to be considered in strategic planning.

Soft Power: Power asserted by subtle persuasion and through relationship building as with virtual exchange.

Stevens Initiative: The legacy to former U.S. Ambassador to Libya, J. Christopher Stevens. Supports virtual exchange through grants and resources offering programs to youth in the MENA region to enhance job readiness and develop 21st Century skills.

Synchronous: Online learning delivered remotely on predetermined days and times via a video conferencing program.

United Nations Sustainable Development Goals (UN SDGs): Seventeen interconnected global goals established in 2015 that focus on sustainability, equity, and social justice for the well-being of present and future generations.

Chapter 17
Esports in Education:
An Overview

Veronica E. O'Neill
New Jersey City University, USA

ABSTRACT

This chapter provides an overview of a relative newcomer to education at all levels, esports. Esports has become very popular in recent years, and it is important for educators to understand the issues surrounding this activity, as well as the benefits to student participants with respect to the experience itself and to potential careers in the field. A brief history is provided and the issues surrounding esports in education are examined. Resources are provided relevant to starting an esports program at all levels: collegiate, secondary school, and middle school.

INTRODUCTION

When you think about college athletics, the first image that comes to mind is likely a football player, or a basketball star. Perhaps you think of a soccer goalie, or a baseball pitcher. The image of a swimmer or gymnast, working toward the next Olympic games, may be the first thing you see. Most of us do not conjure a vision of a gamer at a console. However, many colleges and universities have varsity level esports programs, and that number continues to grow. This growing movement has led to a call to officially recognize esports as a sport, and to bring it under the umbrella of NCAA sports (Kane & Spradley, 2017).

According to Kane and Spradley (2017):

Esports will be a general term that includes all the various esports leagues from around the world. Each league could be compared to a different sports league that plays the same sport such as the Ultimate Fighting Championship (UFC), Bellator and Invicta Fighting Championship. The various esports leagues have different rules, play different games, rank professionals differently and host tournaments and competitions. The consistent aspect throughout the leagues is that the competitors play video games and the athletes that win matches consistently could progress to a professional level. (Kane & Spradley, 2017)

DOI: 10.4018/978-1-6684-6092-4.ch017

There is no official or universal definition of esports, so the initial analysis begins with a dictionary. According to the Cambridge English Dictionary, a sport is "a game, competition, or activity needing physical effort and skill that is played or done according to rules, for enjoyment and/or as a job (Cambridge Dictionary, n.d.). Many have examined the amount of physical effort required to play esports, which varies with the game being played. Some of the games, such as those based on physical sports, require the player to be active. Others do not require as much physical movement, but may still require physical exertion. For example, some studies have shown that blood pressure and heart rate are elevated during game play (Kane & Spradley, 2017). The other criterion is the element of competition. While video gaming began as an individual activity, it has evolved into the possibility of multi-player gaming and team competition. Some games have recognized tournaments, with prize money available to the winners. These contests are often broadcast on television or streamed on the Internet (Kane & Spradley, 2017).

This chapter will be organized into six key sections:

1. Introduction
2. What is Esports?
3. Esports in Education
4. Issues in Esports
5. Best Practices
6. Future Research Directions

An explanation of the six key sections is included below.

The first section, "Introduction," focuses on introducing the purpose of this chapter.

The second section, "What is Esports?" focuses on defining esports. A brief historical review of some milestones in the esports movement is included.

The third section, "Esports in Education," provides a review of the establishment of esports teams at the post-secondary, secondary and middle school levels.

The fourth section focuses on several "Issues in Esports." These issues range from the place of women and minorities in eSports, to protecting the health and well-being of esports athletes.

In the fifth section, "Best Practices," the considerations when starting a new esports team are discussed.

In the sixth section, "Future Research Directions," recommended areas of future research will be presented. Concluding thoughts are shared on the need to further understand student and educator issues with esports.

What Is Esports?

Esports can be defined as "a computer-mediated form of competitive gaming within a multiplayer environment" (Delello et al., 2021). Neilsen (2019) offers another explanation, which may be more intuitive:

When people play video games competitively, they're playing esports, or electronic sports. Just like football players play football together, esports players play video games together. Baseball players fill stadiums, and so do esports players. It's a billion-dollar industry with more than 500 million people predicted to watch them in 2020. (Neilsen, 2019).

Although esports is relatively new compared to other sports, it has experienced massive growth. Revenue has increased dramatically, from $130 million in 2012, to $865 million in 2018. It is predicted to reach $1.79 billion by 2022 (Block & Haack, 2021). Viewership has also grown, for example, 99.6 million viewers watched the 2018 League of Legends World Championships. To contrast, Super Bowl LIII in 2019 drew 98.2 million viewers (Delello et al., 2021).

Esports is also gaining in prestige, as it is progressing toward becoming an Olympic sport. Esports was a demonstration sport at the 2018 Asian Games in Jakarta. At the 2022 Asian Games, now scheduled for September - October 2023, medals will be awarded in 8 different esports games, and 2 more games will be demonstration sports (Venkat, 2021; Olympic Council of Asia, 2022).

A Brief History of Esports

The late 70's and early 80's brought computer games to the mainstream. At that point, computer-based games such as *Space Invaders* and *Pac-Man* were found in arcades worldwide, and fans vied to see their names on the leaderboard. This type of game was brought into the home when Atari introduced *Pong*, a simple ping-pong game, for home consoles in 1975 (Delello et al., 2021).

As time went on, home consoles improved as new technology became available. For example, the Nintendo Entertainment System (NES) sold over 61 million units beginning in 1983. Momentum shifted to handheld units such as the Game Boy, introduced in 1989, and Nintendo DS beginning in 2005. However, game consoles still had significant sales, particularly Sony's PlayStation series, which began in 1994 and continues strong sales with its latest model, the PlayStation 5, introduced in 2020. PlayStation 2 consoles hold the record for most sales of a console, having sold over 157 million units (Mendoza, 2022).

South Korea is known for having the fastest Internet speeds on the planet. This came about because after the Asian financial crisis in 1997, the South Korean government made an economic decision to pivot from the chemical and industrial sectors and move toward becoming a leader in technology and knowledge-based industry. Due to low Internet fees, having Internet access in the home was widespread. Internet cafes, which are gathering places like coffee houses which feature computers for customer use and Internet access, were also established, providing gathering spots for gaming (Li, 2016).

"For South Koreans, gaming was a social activity, in contrast to the Westerners, who saw it as a solitary hobby, an inauthentic, artificial experience compared to more laudable physical sports" (Li, 2016, p. 36). The South Koreans also received sponsorship support directly from the game manufacturers. They developed a system of team houses, where players could practice ten or more hours a day, then retire to their bunks. Elite players had all their living needs met so they could concentrate on their game but had little involvement with life outside the gaming community (Li, 2016).

Esports became a global phenomenon, especially in Asia, Europe and North America. Esports was transformed from an unorganized activity in college dorms to a major business. Tournaments began to become common in the late 2000s, and many colleges began to organize teams (Kauweloa, 2021).

One reason for the exponential growth of esports is its appeal to spectators. Due to the development of widespread streaming services on the internet, it is no longer necessary to travel to an arena to watch an esports match. Teams at all levels stream their tournaments, providing commentary and multiple views of the action. While some spectators watch the events passively, a significant number of viewers interact with others, including the athletes and broadcasters, by using the live comment function on streaming platforms such as Twitch. The esports industry must support its athletes, passive spectators, and active spectators, to ensure that they to deliver a product that meets the needs of all parties (Stahlke et al., 2018).

There are not many qualitative studies examining why spectators choose to view esports events. Hamari and Sjöblom (2017) conducted such a study, and found that escapism, acquiring knowledge about the games being played, novelty, and esports athlete aggressiveness were positively found to predict the frequency of viewing esports events. While the games are played on a computer screen, images of the athletes are often included in the broadcast, in interviews and other segments. Athletes can demonstrate team spirit and aggressiveness toward their opponent, which can increase the interest of spectators in the match. Interestingly, the quality of the stream as far as graphics was not found to have a positive impact on frequency of viewing. This leads to a conclusion that sophisticated, cutting edge graphics are not necessary for esports games (Hamari & Sjöblom, 2017).

The isolation of COVID-19, and the shutdown of many sources of leisure activity made playing video games and watching esports tournaments an accessible and desirable pastime. Collegiate esports was relatively new at this time, and there were concerns that the movement would not survive the pandemic disruption. However, universities were quick to shift to online education, and esports was able to pivot to strictly online activities as well (Cote, et al., 2022).

Cote, et al. (2022) conducted a study of collegiate esports programs during the pandemic, to discover the impact of the disruption of normal life to esports programs. The first challenge they discovered was the cancellation of many esports events. This impacted the supporting personnel, such as coaches, broadcasters and social media creators, as well as the athletes themselves. After this initial reaction, programs began to adjust to a fully online model for esports. The lack of availability of space for practice and high-end technology was also a challenge. One reason that universities build esports arenas is that students don't have access to sophisticated technology at home. The athletes also had to adjust to a lack of communication with teammates during matches. A similar issue was noted by the broadcast staff, who were accustomed to having full access to players in person. A third challenge was the impact of COVID-19 on budgets, which threatened to shut down the young esports programs. The final challenge noted in the study was a shift in the social connections within the teams. All parties had to adjust to communication online and missed some of the bonding opportunities they had previously enjoyed. Despite all these challenges, most participants felt the future prospects for esports at the collegiate level were bright (Cote, et al., 2022).

ESPORTS IN EDUCATION

Space Invaders 1972

Stanford University hosted the first intercollegiate tournament in 1972, based on the game *Space Invaders*. Twenty-four players competed for a subscription to *Rolling Stone Magazine* (Delello et al., 2021).

The introduction of the Internet changed these competitions, as ownership of devices capable of playing competitive games became widespread. Additionally, players were now able to compete without travel, and matches could be livestreamed to viewers worldwide.

Before the current era of esports competitions began, teachers were often using technology to facilitate learning and engagement. Two examples of transitioning such technology into competitive events, while fostering teamwork, creativity, and STEM learning, are described below.

Minecraft (NYC Battle of the Boroughs)

Many educators are familiar with using the game *Minecraft* in the classroom. The game is very popular, and students often enjoy playing it. In 2016, Microsoft took *Minecraft* to another level, introducing *Minecraft: Education Edition*. This version is designed to allow students to explore STEM subjects and other subjects through the familiar gaming platform (Whitworth, 2022). *Minecraft: Education Edition* is well known as a game used in classrooms to allow students to build projects and learn STEM concepts. Many teachers have used *Minecraft* to have in-class challenges, introducing an element of competition among students (*Minecraft*, 2022).

Recently, *Minecraft* elevated this concept to a new level, sponsoring a city-wide competition in cooperation with the New York City Department of Education. In the first round, over 17,000 students and 250 educators participated in the Build a Better Tomorrow challenge, using New York City's One-NYC 2050 strategic plan to create a project that would improve the city's future (*Minecraft Education Edition*, 2021). For the final round, 20 teams of five middle and high school students from the five boroughs of New York City gathered for a building competition using *Minecraft Education Edition*. The teams were given a prompt and one hour to plan. Then they were given 30 minutes to create their entry within a 32x32 field. The students created projects that were judged on planning, collaboration, and esthetics, and demonstrated creativity, sustainability, and positive change for New York City. The students demonstrated leadership, teamwork, design and building skills (*Minecraft*, 2021). More than 450,000 spectators watched the live stream of the finals on Twitch, and 300,000 spectators watched the championship broadcast on ESPN (*Minecraft Education Edition*, 2021).

Microsoft (2022) provides free training to teachers who are interested in using *Minecraft: Education Edition* in an esports program. The training is delivered online and is self-paced. It covers the definition of esports, its benefits, using esports in schools, and career pathways. The training includes extensive support for establishing an esports program at your own school, with a focus on developing a safe environment, with student leadership and an inclusive environment. Specifics on creating and hosting a build challenge, similar to the one described above in New York City, are included to make the process easier for teachers. Last, but critically important, is a section on maintaining balance and moderation in your esports program to ensure student success (Microsoft, 2022).

Drones and the Drone Racing League

The Drone Racing League (DRL) is a professional competition series featuring some of the best drone pilots in the world racing identical drones through challenging courses in stadiums and arenas around the world. The pilots race identical drones, and wear goggles that stream video from the drone's camera. The pilots experience the race as if they are on the drone. These tournaments are televised around the world and are available to stream on demand. Prior to COVID-19, there were huge crowds of devoted fans who gathered to watch these contests in person. COVID-19 changed all that, and DRL pivoted to a virtual platform called the DRL Sim. (Drone Racing League, 2022).

DRL reports that during their 2021-22 season, their viewership reached 250 million households in 140 markets worldwide. This includes broadcasts on mainstream networks such as NBC Sports, as well as streaming over the Internet (French, 2022). DRL has grown dramatically due to increased television coverage, a new sponsor, Algorand, which has incorporated blockchain into the drone experience, a new game for mobile phones, and an actual racing drone that lets anyone stream their flying footage over the Internet (French, 2022).

Since the beginning of DRL, in addition to providing entertainment, the league focused on education. They originally focused on in-person experiences at the tournaments. However, as COVID-19 made this impossible, they moved this education initiative to the Internet. Students who are studying aeronautics and other STEM fields can access the DRL Sim at no cost. This is the same platform pilot candidates use to learn to control drones. In addition, lectures are provided by experts in the field, including drone pilots, to augment the hands-on flight experience. (Booton, 2020).

While the current focus on drone racing could be a passing obsession, there are many new career opportunities for skilled drone pilots. Competent drone pilots will soon have opportunities for employment in such mainstream corporations as Amazon. Amazon is currently testing its Prime Air delivery service, which will deliver items from Amazon warehouses to customers in just one hour using drone technology. These advanced drones will be able to operate safely without direct observation by the pilot because they incorporate a sense-and-avoid system to avoid people, pets, and other obstacles (Amazon, 2022).

Another emerging use of drones is as a passenger taxi. This futuristic idea is becoming a reality in Dubai, as well as other cities. The Dubai service offers aircraft which hold two passengers, are completely automated, and can be used to travel between any points in the city (Dubai Taxi, 2022). Dubai officials hope to convert 25% of all travel into self-driving flights by 2030 (Wray, 2020).

Drones are being embraced in the K-12 community as another tool to engage and educate students. Students can fly a drone and view the world from a different perspective. Drones can be incorporated into lessons about any subject, from mathematics to science to literature. Students are motivated and engaged in investigative learning, not just listening to a teacher, or reading a text. (Carnahan et al., 2016).

When implementing a drone program in a school, it is important to integrate the technology into the curriculum, to ensure that learning goals are achieved. Carnahan and Zieger have created a model called SOAR, (safety, operation, active learning, research), which can help teachers evaluate their plans and success in using drones to enhance student learning.

- Safety: must be a primary focus. Students must follow all safety instructions to protect themselves, their classmates and property
- Operation: the instructor must be comfortable in flying the drone, making minor repairs, and be able to coach students as they begin to learn to fly
- Active Learning: it is important that students are engaged in the activity and are active participants
- Research: this step is critical, as the instructor must continually evaluate if the use of the technology is delivering the desired results. Effective research in this space considers policy, professional development for teachers, and classroom implementation (Carnahan et al, 2016).

Carnahan et al. (2016) also provide an extensive guide on how to introduce the use of drones into the curriculum. Topics covered include how to learn to pilot a drone, licensing requirements, federal regulations about operating a drone, and teaching students to pilot a drone safely. Examples of activities using drones across the curriculum are also included to spark the imagination and help teachers establish a drone program (Carnahan et al., 2016).

Interest in creating formal drone racing leagues for high school students continues to grow. For example, in 2021 Trumbull County schools in Ohio began a drone program that included students building their own drones, earning FAA certification as drone pilots, and participating in formal tournaments against other high schools in the district. The schools partnered with an organization called Drones in School, and they hope to expand the program to other schools in the future (Coupland, 2021).

A similar program was launched in 2022 aimed at middle school students. The course "The Science of Drone Racing" was developed by DRL Academy and Draganfly. The interactive course will teach students how to fly, build and code drones (Williams, 2021).

Considering the interest in using drones commercially, colleges and universities are working to create programs that will prepare learners for these highly technical careers. For example, Warren County Community College in New Jersey offers several programs in Unmanned Systems, better known as Drone Technology. These programs range from Pilot Certification training, certificates in Drone Repair and Maintenance, and an Associate in Applied Science program in Unmanned Systems (Drone Technology). The intent of these programs is to provide hands-on training in state-of-the-art technology. This training prepares learners for many careers in unmanned aviation, in industries such as surveying, photography, search and rescue, and construction, to name just a few (Warren County Community College, 2022).

Establishment of Modern Esports at the Collegiate Level

The term esports refers to a plethora of different games that can be played competitively in various tournament formats. Each school determines which games it will compete in, and recruit players accordingly. Most players specialize in just one game, as the skill sets required for each game vary widely. The four main categories of esports games include:

- First-Person Shooter, including *Counter Strike: Global Offensive*
- Multi-player Online Battle Arena, such as *League of Legends*
- Player vs. Player, including sports games like the FIFA series
- Real-time Strategy, such as *Starcraft* (Hamari & Sjöholm, 2017)

Many colleges have developed a dedicated space for an esports arena. This may be restricted to the organized esports teams, or it may be open to others when there is no event or practice scheduled. In some cases, the space may also be used as a computer lab or classroom space. Venues for esports generally include spectator facilities for fans to attend in person, as well as broadcast facilities for streaming.

The University of Kentucky has made a significant commitment to esports. They designed and built a new facility to be the home base for the University's esports team. This facility was built with streaming in mind, and with deliberate attention to details such as lighting for tournaments and video production. One novel attribute is the University's pay-to-play model, which opens the facility to other campus denizens for a membership fee. The facility is also open to the greater community outside the university for a higher membership fee. The University established partnerships with outside parties to make this project a reality, including the University of Kentucky Federal Credit Union (UKFCU), who obtained the naming rights for the facility. University of Kentucky expects that the facility will contribute to recruitment of students and will lead to new revenue streams for the university. The University of Kentucky noted that student involvement in all phases of the project was a key part of the success of the UKFCU Esports Lounge (Stewart & Price, 2022).

In contrast, some facilities built for other purposes have been retrofitted to accommodate spectators at esports events. For example, the Staples Center in Los Angeles, now the Crypto.com Arena, hosted the 2013 and 2016 League of Legends World Championships, selling out all available seats (Jenny et al., 2018). This represents an opportunity to increase revenue through esports without the need to build an entire venue from the ground up. The arena benefits from increased revenue, and the spectators can enjoy the amenities of a world-class sports facility (Jenny et al., 2018). This trend may also represent an opportunity for colleges to retrofit existing sporting venues, such as their basketball arenas, to accommodate esports events rather than needing a purpose-built facility.

Scholarship Opportunities

Esports athletes are eligible for scholarships at many universities. Robert Morris University in Chicago offered the first scholarships in the United States to its varsity and varsity reserve squads. These scholarships totaled 70% and 35% of tuition, respectively (Miller, 2016).

According to NCSA College Recruiting, a service that assists athletes in the recruiting process for all college sports, scholarships most often range from $500 to $8,000 per year. However, some colleges offer full tuition scholarships to their recruited esports athletes. Harrisburg University made esports history in 2018, when it awarded full ride scholarships to all members of its 16-person roster (NCSA, 2022).

Scholarship recipients report that since some colleges do not accept esports as a true sport, they may not get the same perks offered to traditional athletes. For example, esports students often do not get the same priority registration privileges offered to athletes in traditional sports. This early registration allows the student-athlete to create a schedule that does not conflict with practice and game schedules. This can lead to a struggle to fit practice into a schedule and limit the student-athlete to practicing at night (Nelius, 2019).

Degree Opportunities

While many colleges and universities have embraced the idea of establishing esports teams, West Virginia University (WVU) has taken this idea to new heights. Starting in the Fall 2022 semester, WVU will offer an academic minor in esports. This program consists of 15 credits, with a core of 9 credits in esports history, ethics and regulatory issues. The remainder of the program will be electives chosen from courses such as business, marketing and promotion (West Virginia University, 2021).

WVU is also recruiting professional esports players to represent the university at the varsity level. The first such recruit, Noah Johnson, has a proven record at both the collegiate and professional level. Johnson reports that he spends 30 to 40 hours per week practicing esports, in addition to completing classwork for his Economics major (West Virginia University, 2021).

Other universities are also offering degrees in esports. For example, The Ohio State University is offering degree programs in game studies and esports. The program will include courses in esports management, game design, and the business of gaming, for example. The university has invested in a dedicated arena for esports, which will be used for tournaments, practice, and to teach skills such as broadcasting esports events (The Ohio State University, 2018). The arena includes 80 gaming computers, a virtual reality system, a competition venue for matches with other universities, and a broadcast booth (The Ohio State University, 2019).

Benedict College in South Carolina, an historically Black college, has established a bachelor's degree in Esports Administration. In addition to courses in esports and in sports management, the degree will feature gaming techniques, content development, and management skills for all aspects of the esports industry (Benedict College, 2021).

Careers in Esports

One focus of esports in education is preparing students for future careers. Although many assume that careers in this area revolve around playing games professionally or programming, opportunities for good jobs in the field are much broader (Ofgang, 2020).

- *Professional Athlete* - It is reasonable to think that many esports players at an elite level might dream of playing as a professional. This dream is supported by the availability of prize money even at the collegiate level, provided by game manufacturers and other sponsors. However, only a tiny percentage of collegiate players ascend to the professional ranks. With this in mind, many of the collegiate programs in esports also include other career opportunities.
- *Marketing* – Sports marketing is an important aspect of traditional sports and of esports. Top players endorse games and products and receive sponsorship money from game manufacturers and other sponsors. A recent study at University of South Florida showed that advertisements presented during sporting events had a positive effect on consumer wants and desires. It also looked at personal branding and found that it is not directly correlated with increase purchasing but may have an impact when the athlete has an established following (Winters, 2022). Students with an interest in marketing may want to explore this intersection of esports and marketing.
- *Broadcasting* - As with many other sports, the spectator experience, in person and online, is greatly enhanced by a quality broadcasting team, who can explain the action and add color and personality to the event.

"The commentator, or caster, is an essential component of the esports experience. Top broadcasters can become as well-known as star players, just as John Madden became one of the most famous names in football in the broadcast booth. A commentator can create a narrative from the game and give meaning to the action on screen. A combination of gameplay knowledge, familiarity with players, and energy is essential. As with traditional sports commentary, esports often employs a duo of play-by-play and analyst or color commentator" (Li, 2016, p. 48)

- *Venue Operations* – To effectively manage a sporting venue, many factors must be considered. Scheduling, maintenance, selecting concessionaires and game-day operations are just the beginning of the task of managing a venue. In today's world, environmental concerns are in the forefront. Sporting venues have unique operating characteristics, as they are often vacant, but when there is an event there is a tremendous need to make the vast spaces comfortable for participants and spectators alike. Sporting venues of all sorts consume a massive amount of energy and finding ways to optimize this consumption is critical (Elnour et al., 2022).
- *Game Development* – Video games are often updated in cycles, to address problems experienced by players, and to add additional experiences to keep player interest in the long term. Developers also work on new titles, to keep their sales stable. Career opportunities in game development may include graphic arts and design, writing, and programming (computerscience.org, 2022).
- *Venue Design* – As colleges and cities embrace esports, they often need to build a venue from scratch, retrofit existing space to a dedicated esports facility, or modify an existing arena to accom-

modate esports events. The successful completion of these projects requires a team which includes experts in design, building and technology (Jenny et al., 2018).

Competitive Structure

Colleges and universities wishing to establish a varsity esports program will often apply for membership in the National Association of Collegiate Esports (NACE). Their goal is to broaden acceptance of esports as a varsity program, and to establish standards for the sport. These would include aspects such as eligibility, path to graduation, competition and scholarships (NACE, 2022).

NACE had humble beginnings: in 2016, it had seven member institutions. As of 2019, the most recent data available, that number had grown to over 170 institutions. (Schnackner, 2021). Since the onset of COVID-19, many colleges and universities have found that esports was one of the only sports programs available through the pandemic (Schnacker, 2021).

Another major organization in college esports is the Collegiate StarLeague, which consists of about 700 college and university teams. The Collegiate StarLeague is now known as part of NACE StarLeague, as Playfly Sports acquired it in 2020 (Luongo, 2020). The teams who are full members of NACE play in the Varsity divisions of NACE StarLeague, while all other teams play in the Open divisions (Playfly ESports, 2022).

Other intercollegiate esports conferences have also been formed. For example, the Esports Clubs from all eight Ivy League colleges have formed the Ivy Esports Conference (IEC). The IEC was not formally recognized by the colleges, but the esports clubs seek to bring the same organization seen in traditional Ivy League sports to esports. The IEC conducts tournaments and oversees matches between its members in several esports titles (Carpenter, 2018).

Another example of a new esports conference comes from the Historically Black Colleges and Universities (HBCUs). The Black Collegiate Gaming Association (BGCA) was established in 2020. Their stated purpose is "to pivot men and women of color college students into the overall gaming industry, not only as consumers, but as contributors." (BGCA, 2020). They focus not only on the gaming itself, but on exposing participants to various aspects of the gaming industry and help them get internships and work experience in the corporate side of gaming. They hope to help students pay for their education through scholarships and have incentives to complete their degree. (SmithBarrow, 2020). To make this dream a reality, the BGCA has partnered with streaming service Twitch and an Atlanta non-profit, Cxmmunity (Diverse, 2020).

Each HBCU chooses its own focus in the esports industry. For example, Johnson C. Smith University incorporates esports into classes that focus on working in the field, instead of just playing. Tennessee State University works to incorporate esports into the traditional curriculum, improving teaching and learning in many different fields. Yet another approach is demonstrated at Kentucky State University, where the focus in on students creating games, which could lead to a lucrative career. (SmithBarrow, 2020).

The National Junior College Athletics Association Esports (NJCAAE) is the premier organization for two-year colleges participating in esports. Their focus is to improve retention and increase completion rates for participants. Currently they hold tournaments for their members in seven different games (NJCAAE, 2022).

NCAA

In 2019, the National Collegiate Athletic Association (NCAA) considered incorporating esports into its official collegiate programs. This inclusion would add legitimacy to esports and would encourage colleges and universities to offer scholarships to esports athletes. At the time, the NCAA declined to oversee esports, largely because NCAA athletes must be amateurs, thus they were not permitted to make endorsements or have sponsors. Successful esports athletes often have such deals with software companies and other corporations. In 2021, the NCAA policy changed, and its athletes are now permitted to license their name, image and likeness (NIL) to third parties (Moreno & Carter, 2021).

Another issue with current practices in esports is prize money. Sponsors and game manufacturers often offer prizes for winning tournaments. This can result in significant payments to team members. For example, Riot Games offers prize money for winning its League of Legends North American Collegiate Tournament. In 2014 and 2015, the University of British Columbia won the tournament, resulting in a $360,000 total prize for the student-led club team (Kauweloa & Winter, 2019).

This acceptance by the NCAA would let the esports programs take advantage of NCAA's experience in producing large tournaments. The focus of the NCAA on Title IX, which promotes equality for women in sports programs, would assist collegiate programs in recruiting women to their teams. The NCAA also has stringent rules for academic performance for athletes, which would ensure that esports athletes place an appropriate focus on completing a degree, not just playing esports. Last, the NCAA affiliation would lend legitimacy to esports programs (Moreno & Carter, 2021).

The NCAA, and its colleges and universities, would also benefit from this arrangement. The National Association for Collegiate ESports (NACE), has extensive experience with dealing with athletes' NIL arrangements. They could assist the NCAA in developing policies which fairly resolve any conflicts that arise from these player deals. Additionally, NACE has existing partnerships with sponsors who could be willing to support other sports as well. (Moreno & Carter, 2011).

Middle and High School

To ensure availability of quality athletes at the collegiate level, it is necessary to develop young athletes. Many school districts are embracing esports in middle school and high school. Rothwell and Shaffer (2019) note that many teachers incorporate the use of technology-based games into the curriculum, known as gamification. This technique can increase student engagement and motivation to learn. Introducing esports at this level can similarly allow students to embrace technology in an appropriate manner (Rothwell & Shaffer, 2019).

Esports at this level can improve students' skills in important areas such as teamwork, communication and problem-solving. These skillsets are highly valued by employers. Some research has found that using esports in the curriculum can improve student behavior, in areas such as attendance, and getting better grades (Rothwell & Shaffer, 2019).

Some experts have expressed concern that playing esports, especially violent games, may be risky for the health of young players. They argue that prolonged exposure to violence in the video game setting could carry over and increase the player's probability of being violent in the real world. Others express concern that the sedentary nature of playing on a computer might discourage physical activity and exercise in players (Rothwell & Shaffer, 2019).

A study of high school students found that non-gaming students and gaming students did not differ in well-being, self-efficacy, and loneliness. Gaming students did, however, display more symptoms of gaming addiction. The researchers suggest that more work needs to be done to differentiate between high gaming participation and actual gaming addiction. The study also suggested that participation in gaming allowed students to enhance mental well-being by bonding with other teammates through esports (Fiskaal et al., 2020).

In addition to skill building, participating in esports may open opportunities for college scholarships. Several colleges and universities offer financial support for esports athletes, similar to scholarships available to traditional athletes (Rothwell & Shaffer, 2019).

There are also career opportunities available to participants in esports. In addition to the possibility of playing eSports professionally, there are opportunities for careers in the technological and business sides of esports.

Recently, Barnegat High School in New Jersey became the first high school in the state to award a varsity letter for esports. Barnegat competes in the Garden State ESports League, and competes virtually with opponents in several games, including Overwatch, League of Legends, Rocket League and Super Smash Brothers Ultimate (Faughnan, 2021).

Varsity athletes must meet several guidelines determined by the state to be eligible for a varsity letter. For example, student athletes must maintain good grades and meet attendance requirements. One additional consideration is that many colleges and universities offer scholarships for varsity letter holders (Faughnan, 2021).

The Barnegat esports team consists of 25 athletes. They report that they have developed skills in strategy, teamwork, and eye-hand coordination. During COVID-19, the team played against other schools virtually. However, they look forward to participating in tournaments in other venues, such as the Rutgers ESports Stadium (Faughnan, 2021).

Esports teams are also becoming popular at the middle school level, providing a pathway to high school and collegiate teams. Educational video games such as *Where in the World is Carmen Sandiego* and *The Oregon Trail* have long been used in the classroom. Today, other competitive games such as *Fortnite* are used at this level. Chris Aviles, a middle school teacher in New Jersey, started the nation's first middle-school esports team, playing Rocket League. He notes that the game can be used to help students develop important qualities such as leadership, communication, and teamwork, just like traditional athletics (Aviles, 2019).

One important concern for younger players in esports is the need for balance. If a young person is to become proficient in esports, they must devote a significant amount of time to practice. This is a concern for many educators and parents. For example, an EdWeek Research Center study found the 88% of educators felt that student learning challenges increased with increased screen time. Over 80% of the educators felt student behavior worsened as screen time increased. The study noted that all screen time cannot be considered equally, and that the activity chosen has an impact. This demonstrates the importance of schools teaching healthy habits with respect to technology. One educator who was interviewed suggested that introducing esports to schools could help students make social connections in a purposeful implementation of technology (Sparks, 2022).

South Korea is the center of the esports universe, and many students dream of becoming professional esports players. To this end, they practice countless hours, and sometimes neglect their schoolwork. This can cause issues, as they need to excel at school to have a chance at admission to university. Parents are understandably concerned, since the chances of success at the professional level of esports are quite small. One American company has opened the Gen.G Elite ESports Academy, to address some of these concerns. The Academy provides school lessons in English that can lead to earning an American high school diploma. With that credential, some of its graduates have earned admission to American universities (Choe, 2021).

China is also taking action to ensure that school-age children are not spending too much time gaming at the expense of their studies. In 2021, China banned minors from playing video games during the school week and limiting them to playing only one hour on Fridays, weekends and holidays. Previously, a 2019 rule prohibited play between 10 pm and 8 am, and limiting play to 90 minutes on weekdays (Liao, 2021, August 30).

On the other hand, a poll of parents of children aged 11 to 18 found that playing esports games can help develop key skills such as teamwork, problem-solving and communication, as well as build confidence, leadership, and technological skills (Young, 2022) The study also found that parents would be in favor of their children finding careers in esports, in all aspects including marketing, technology, and broadcasting. However, the same study found 61% of the educational stakeholders polled did not believe there was sufficient evidence to show educational benefits from esports (Young, 2022).

Starting a Team

If an educator is interested in starting a high school esports club, there are several support mechanisms available. Marywood University in Scranton, Pennsylvania has created a four-session professional development opportunity for high school faculty members interested in starting an esports program. The certificate, "How to Start a High School ESports Program" is offered in four sessions, three virtual and one onsite at the Marywood University ESports Center.

There may also be a state-wide esports organization that can assist in starting an eSports team. For example, Garden State Esports (GSE) is a non-profit organization that was founded by New Jersey educators to create programs in which all students can grow socially, emotionally, and academically through participation in esports. GSE is free to all New Jersey educators and provides resources to help new programs become established successfully. They also schedule competitions among member schools, and they provide assistance for esports players to transition to college and university esports programs in New Jersey (Garden State Esports, 2022).

There are several books with valuable information for schools considering establishing an esports program. One of these, *The Esports Education Playbook: Empowering Every Learner Through Inclusive Gaming*, was written by educators at the high school level, and focuses on the mechanics of starting an esports team, and the benefits to students participating in the activity:

Social and emotional learning (SEL) is the process through which children and adults understand and manage emotions, set and achieve positive goals, feel and show empathy for others, establish and maintain positive relationships, and make responsible decisions. sports. Through esports, the SEL skills taught through traditional sports are available to a much wider audience. (Aviles et al, 2020, p. 59-61).

The book contains specific activities that can be incorporated into the esports curriculum to develop these important SEL skills.

ISSUES

Despite all the positive attributes of esports, and the benefits of playing, there are several major issues that must be addressed if esports is to truly realize its potential.

Diversity

AnyKey is an organization that advocates for diversity, inclusion and equity in gaming and streaming. According to their website "We are motivated by the dream of seeing the rainbow of humanity celebrated on the world's largest gaming stages" (AnyKey, 2022a). They provide training in making gaming more inclusive and welcoming. The organization strives to help create a gaming world that is diverse so that marginalized players, such as women, players of color, LGBTQ+ persons, older players and players with disabilities are all represented and welcome to play together (AnyKey, 2022a).

Organizers of gaming clubs can participate in online training such as "Inclusion 101", which gives specific action items and strategies to help achieve this diverse and welcoming atmosphere. They note that having policies is not enough, to truly become inclusive proactive measures are needed. They provide certification for trainers within gaming clubs, to train participants throughout the organization and ensure that every participant is aware of the need for diversity and inclusion (AnyKey, 2022b).

AnyKey also advocates the adoption of a Code of Conduct for all gaming organizations. Their model code, called the Keystone Code, focuses on four fundamental values; compassion, integrity, respect and courage. These values are important in the gaming realm as well as in everyday life (AnyKey, 2022c).

Gender Equality

Unlike most traditional sports, there is no inherent difference in performance between men and women due to physical attributes. However, this has not translated to equality and equal representation between the genders. (Rogstad, 2021).

According to the Pew Research Center, 43% of all U.S. adults play video games on a device such as a computer, television, game console or cellphone. This figure soars to 97% for teenage boys, and 83% of teenage girls. (Perrin, 2018). However, only 5% of professional esports players are women (Hilbert, 2019).

While many women play games, only a small percentage of them characterize themselves as gamers. The image of a gamer is often associated with a male-dominated community. It is interesting to note that this resistance to the term "gamer" does not equate to a lower participation in playing games. Women are also more likely to reject the term "tech nerd" and to characterize themselves as "tech savvy" (Kivijiarvi & Katila, 2022).

Female avatars are often oversexualized, with unrealistic body portrayals and overtly sexual behavior. Female gamers are often harassed in-game, which has a negative impact on the players. Some female players reported using a male avatar and in-game identity to avoid this issue. However, there are positive impacts for women who participate in gaming. For example, female gamers are three times more likely to attain a career in STEM fields, science, technology, engineering and mathematics, than their non-gaming counterparts (Kuss et al., 2022).

The performance of female gamers is equivalent to that of male players with equal practice. However, the dramatic imbalance between the genders cannot be ignored. One contributing factor could be the portrayal of female characters in many games, which can lead to objectification of female characters.

The anonymous character of the internet allows hostility and comments that would not be possible in the real world. This can be a disincentive for femaie game players (Ruvalcaba et al., 2018).

A recent study in Japan interviewed male and female players regarding the stereotypes present within esports. One woman reported that she was directly asked "Why are you playing games? You are a girl." (Madden et al., 2021). These types of attitudes may have a negative impact on women playing esports at all levels. There is also a stereotype that male players are more aggressive by nature than females, and therefore are more suited to esports play. This has not been supported by research, in fact, there is no difference between genders with respect to ability to learn and play esports (Madden et al., 2021).

A study was conducted regarding spectator comments on Twitch, directed at male and female gamers regarding play, the player and the gender of the player. In this analysis, 37% of the positive comments made about female players referred to their appearance, as opposed to 7.5% for male players. Female players also received 11 times the sexual harassment comments as their male counterparts. There is a need to conduct further research in this area, to determine how these findings impact participation in esports by women (Ruvalcaba et al., 2018).

There are still some issues that must be considered as esports becomes more widely accepted. Membership in collegiate esports teams is dominated by men, even though women are welcome to participate. For example, a recent study from North Carolina State University found that as varsity esports grows, women are increasingly marginalized. The researchers interviewed 21 esports leaders, both women and men. They found that as colleges invested more resources in building their varsity esports programs, women were pushed into club esports, and disenfranchised from the varsity programs (Taylor, 2020). Although coaches maintain that all are welcome to try out, many women do not have the experience and background to qualify for teams. If esports is to live up to its promise of being a level playing field that is gender neutral, focus must be on cultivating skill and developing players, and behavior such as harassment must not be tolerated (Taylor, 2020).

Darvin (2021) notes that female players often experience threats in the in-game chats, so many choose not to reveal their gender, or choose not to participate in esports. In addition to the inherent unfairness in this situation, these women may not benefit from scholarship opportunities for participation in varsity esports. The author notes that women are capable of competing in esports at the highest levels, so colleges must do more to ensure that women are offered the same opportunities as their male counterparts.

Proctor & Gamble, maker of Tampax and Always products, is trying to level the playing field by sponsoring a new tournament featuring *Valorant*, a first-person shooter game. The tournament will include mentoring for girls, giveaways and livestreams for viewers who cannot participate (Adams, 2022).

Another concern is the impact of Title IX on esports programs. This law requires that there be no sex-based discrimination in educational institutions. One manifestation of this requirement is the provision of equal opportunity to male and female athletes. It can be argued that there is no gender-based separation in esports, so the Title IX requirement is met. In practical terms, the prominence of men in esports could indicate that more must be done to encourage participation by women (Holden et al., 2022).

Racial Diversity

The current esports scene is dominated by white and Asian players. Fletcher (2020) examined the lack of black players and made several discoveries. First is a blatant prejudice, which manifested as Terrence Miller was subjected to blatant racist remarks and chat messages on the livestream during a major tournament in 2016. Second, these incidents are rare, quite possibly because there are so few black players at high levels. The bigger question is why this is the case, and what can be done to increase diversity. The author pointed to two barriers, structural and cultural. These include the high cost of gaming systems, a lack of public places to play esports, and that PC gaming is seen as the purview of white and Asian players (Fletcher, 2020). It is important to note that "rarely has diversity alone solved the problem of racism and inequality" (Fletcher, 2020, page 2676). More research is required to fully understand the forces at work in the esports realm.

Another organization working to bring esports to schools in urban and rural areas is the non-profit Varsity Esports Federation (VEF). VEF was started by Bubba Baeddert, who noticed that while over 1,500 schools had esports teams, these were concentrated in suburban areas. This effectively eliminates students in urban and rural areas from reaping the benefits of participation in esports. VEF seeks to level the playing field and enable these students who are economically challenged to reap the benefits of esports discussed above (Exley, 2021).

Asian members of American professional esports teams have also reported acts of harassment and violence directed at them in game and outside of esports. They noted that coming to America was the first time they had experienced such behaviors. They had not expected such racist treatment in America. If esports is to truly be representative of all races, this type of behavior cannot be permitted to persist (Liao, 2021).

Physical Activity

Many observers of the esports movement have expressed concern that playing esports can have a negative impact on health due to reduced physical activity. However, a 2022 study of professional esports players found that more than 90% of the athletes had high or moderate levels of physical activity. The study also found that about half of the athletes had a body mass index (BMI) in the normal range, refuting the idea that all esports players are overweight or obese (Giakoni-Ramirez et al., 2022)

Esports athletes at a Midwestern university were participants in a study that examined the relationship between exercise and reaction time. The subjects were evaluated with respect to their body composition, cardiorespiratory fitness, muscular endurance, muscular strength and flexibility. The participants also completed the Stroop Color Word Task to measure reaction time. This is a standard test in which subjects view a color word typed in color, and the subject presses a key to indicate the color of the word, not the word itself, as fast as possible. The study found there was a significant correlation between cardiorespiratory fitness and reaction time. No correlation was found with the other fitness dimensions tested. This suggests that esports athletes would benefit from regular aerobic exercise, which would positively impact overall health and reaction time (Dykstra et al., 2021).

A German study has shown that esports athletes have similar stresses to those experienced by traditional athletes during competition. Players at a high level must complete over 400 precise clicks per minute in many cases. Cortisol levels of players are analogous to those of race car drivers, and pulse rate can increase to 160 – 180 beats per minute, similar to marathon runners (Block & Haack, 2021)

Sports Injuries

A recent article in *Orthopedics Today* (Tingle, 2022) focused on injuries to esports athletes. Injuries may not be reported by esports athletes. Most of the injuries which are reported are overuse injuries in the hands and arms. This can result in pain in the wrist, elbow, and shoulder, which sometimes extends to the neck and lower back. There are sometimes nerve compression and tendinitis injuries, or problems such as carpal tunnel syndrome, can develop. Treatments can range from limiting time spent training, to changing the design of the mouse used as a game controller, to utilizing compression garments to support the injured area. Educating the athlete about ergonomics is key: orthopedic doctors say with proper treatment, these injuries can often be overcome. Without proper treatment, they may be career-ending and could cause permanent impairment. The doctors emphasize a team approach, with coaches and athletes working together with the medical team. Prevention of injuries is most important, including taking breaks, stretching, and warming up before play (Tingle, 2022).

A recent study examined the impact of a 6-minute walking break during a two-hour gaming session, versus a 6-minute passive resting break, versus continuous play. Twenty-one elite players completed several evaluations of executive function on day 1 as a baseline, then again in days 2, 3 and 4 after each trial. They also completed a survey capturing their impressions of the impact of the rest periods. The results showed that the active walking break resulted in faster solution times and faster planning times than the other two conditions. Actual game performance did not change under any of the conditions. However, 70% of the participants reported that the 6-minute walking break 'positively helped' their gaming performance compared to the passive break, by providing a mental break and allowing them to be physically active (DiFrancisco-Donoghue et al., 2021).

Dr. Elizabeth Matzkin also notes the importance of core training for esports athletes, for improved posture and body alignment during play. This type of exercise can also result in increased endurance and enhanced ability to focus during play (Tingle, 2022).

It is important to include other disciplines, including physical therapy, sports psychology, nutritionists, and ophthalmology. It is also critical that research in this area continue, to identify the most prevalent injuries and their causes, to make esports safer for young athletes. (Tingle, 2022).

It is clear that further research is required to enhance health and safety for esports athletes, especially young players. A focus on prevention and structured practice and tournament play, providing support and protection to athletes.

Violence

The esports world is not without controversy. By their very nature, many games have a violent element. This can range from hand-to-hand combat to first-person shooter elements. For example, PlayVS, an esports platform provider for amateur esports, recently added *Fortnight* to its list of available games. Some organizations, including the Kentucky Department of Education, have determined that it is not appropriate to have students shooting each other in esports. This is especially true considering the recent school shooting incidents in the United States. Thus, the Kentucky High School Athletic Association has banned its 47 schools from playing *Fortnight* in school-sponsored competition (Austin, 2020; PlayVS, 2022).

It should be noted that "a meta-analysis of video game violence provided no support for the hypothesis that violent video game playing is associated with higher aggression" (Ferguson, 2007). In a large longitudinal study of youth in Singapore, "current results suggest that it would require more hours of M-rated game play to produce clinically significant aggression than exist in a day. Therefore, data from this study do not suggest that aggressive video games contribute to real-world aggression" (Ferguson & Wang, 2019).

The Role of Sponsors

Unlike traditional sports, esports sponsors are primarily concerned with selling their product, the games themselves, to players and spectators. As such, they often recruit the most successful professional gamers to represent their brand. Additionally, they offer incentives and prize money for tournament winners at all levels. This focus on esports as a business can counter concerns about equality and diversity. Making esports a safe space for all players becomes secondary to the desire for business success. Hayday and Collison (2020) refer to this situation as a "fractured reality" between business and the potential for esports to create safe, inclusive gaming space.

Legal Issues

Several legal issues will have to be addressed if esports is to be widely accepted on college campuses. For example, there is a need to develop a policy to permit student-athletes who are legitimately using stimulants like Adderall or Ritalin for medical reasons to continue to participate in esports, while curtailing use for the intent of enhancing performance. It may be necessary to have all leagues adopt random testing to ensure the integrity of the sport (Holden, et al., 2020).

There is no current, single regulatory body for collegiate esports. As discussed earlier, NACE is an organization charged with the advancement of collegiate esports as a varsity program. Membership in NACE is voluntary, and in many cases, oversight is conducted by individual leagues and sponsors of tournaments. If the NCAA becomes involved in regulation of esports, many institutions which are not NCAA member institutions could be negatively impacted. They might not be able to compete for national titles and may be barred from competing with NCAA member institutions (Holden, et al., 2020).

ESPORTS BEST PRACTICES

Combining the experience of many esports pioneers, the list below contains some best practices for establishing a successful esports program at any level.

- Establish an atmosphere of diversity and inclusion. AnyKey is an advocacy group that focuses on making esports both diverse and inclusive. This concern includes the diversity with respect to gender, sexual orientation, race, disability and economic background. They have developed a Code of Conduct which they share freely with educators involved in esports. The Code of Conduct can be modified by the organization and accepted by all participants to guide interactions. They also provide specific suggestions that teams can use to recruit and retain players of all backgrounds, to truly embrace diversity (AnyKey, 2019).
- Encourage participation by students who do not see themselves as players but have different talents. Rudy Blanco, Director of Entrepreneurship and Gaming Programs for The DreamYard Project in New York City, states

Esports is so much more than just the game piece, there are opportunities for camera people, reporters, casters, and other game- related jobs. Let students come to that on their own and I think that that's the best place to start. Find a way to connect your passion with gaming to their passion, and then just follow it. (Bendici, 2021)

- Seek out the assistance of educators in your own district, as well as in your state, who will likely be happy to help you get started. The esports organizations described earlier, are also valuable sources of information and advice for new teams. Several books have also been published with step-by-step assistance in starting a new team at your school.

FUTURE RESEARCH DIRECTIONS AND DISCUSSION

To date, esports is still in a developmental stage in the education realm. Some research has been conducted, but the complications of the Covid-19 era may have impacted the results of those investigations. The time is right to continue these investigations in a world that has largely returned to normal circumstances. It is important that this research include issues of balance between esports and academics, protecting the health of student-athletes, and the diversity issues identified above. If esports is to thrive in schools, we must create and nurture programs that are safe spaces, and that teach life skills such as leadership and teamwork.

Darvin et al. (2020) conducted a study of hostile treatment of players within esports. They found that female players were more likely to experience hostility in gaming, while male players were more likely to participate in hostile actions in gaming. The team suggests that one reason for this hostile behavior is the anonymity offered by the streaming services, which permit spectators to hide their identity when posting comments during esports events. The team suggested that an artificial intelligence program like CATT, Chat Analysis Triage Tool, (Dormehl, 2018) used by law enforcement to track child predators, might remove this anonymity, and diminish the hostility.

"What does it take to get really good? You have to sacrifice everything else in your life," said Frank Lantz, director of the New York University Game Center (Li, 2016, p.5). While this may be true to perform at the highest levels in sports, it is critical that educators maintain balance, to ensure that students continue to make good academic progress while developing their esports skills, especially younger students.

According to a survey by the National Alliance for Youth Sports, about 70% of children stop playing sports by age 13 (Eng, 2021). The reason cited most often is that sports are just not fun anymore. This is understandable, because most teenaged players are vying for spots on high school teams and college scholarships. This causes a tremendous increase in pressure, which is amplified by pressure from coaches and parents (Eng, 2021).

According to the Centers for Disease Control and Prevention (CDC), only 57% of high school students play in organized sports, either at the high school or community level (Riser-Kositsky & Peele, 2021). Participation in organized sports is another area that was severely impacted by COVID-19, as schools closed and gatherings in the community were curtailed.

What is the impact of esports on the institution and on the individual athlete? Kurt Melcher, who started the first-ever varsity esports program at Robert Morris University in Chicago, shared his thoughts about the impact of esports on the student-athlete:

I see him walk around our campus wearing esports gear, either the warm-up hoodie or our uniform, and they walk around with a swagger because they are part of something bigger than just them. In the game now they're part of an esport department, they're part of an athletic department and they're part of a university and it matters (Melcher, 2015).

It is clear that esports today is dominated by males, but does it have to be that way? Skillz, a mobile esports and gaming company, holds diversity as a core value. Their staff includes women, and members of various minorities. It is obvious that these hires are not tokenism, rather, they are top talent who contribute to the success of the company (Florentine, 2015).

A recent study shed light on the challenges experienced by women in eSports. Elite level players and executives within the esports industry were interviewed about their experiences. These women had all "broken the glass monitor" and risen to prominence in the industry. Along the way, they experienced stigmas and disapproval from their families, and built communities with other players. The women noted a scarcity of female role models as they were building their careers. Many of the women also mentioned that they hid their gender from others to avoid toxic treatment. Others noted the existence of tokenism, that teams would only have one female member, and that there was a sense that the female player was not worthy of holding that spot. Some of the women reported physical threats leveled in-game based on their gender. They pointed out the need for mental toughness and grit to succeed in this environment. These negative aspects contribute significantly to the lack of female participation in organized esports. (Darvin et al., 2021).

In 2020, Keshia Walker vowed to change the male-dominated gaming industry by starting her own collegiate esports and gaming company. The Black Collegiate Gaming Association (BCGA) is trying to help Black college students prepare to work in the esports industry as creators and other careers. She notes that 73% of African Americans aged 13 or older identify themselves as gamers. However, only 3% of the workers in the gaming industry are Black, and only 1% are professional gamers. The company will offer curriculums to prepare students for positions in the field, as well as job counseling, networking and mentoring opportunities. BCGA also offers its member schools the chance to compete in tournaments against other members (Wright, 2020).

Differences between the genders extend to watching esports as well. Tang et al. (2021) notes that men and women watch sports, including esports, for different reasons. Women tend to view sports as a social event, which helps maintain relationships with their family and friends. Men, on the other hand, are most likely to watch sports to relax and escape from their day to day lives. One notable feature of esports is the ability of spectators to communicate with players in real time online. Spectators can also express support for their teams using animated emotes Tang, et al., 2021).

More study is needed to find the different preferences of males and females with respect to esports, so that more programming that is attractive to women can be offered to increase the market for esports viewing (Tang, et al., 2021).

Esports can offer a new dimension of freedom and enjoyment to students with disabilities. For example, Dan, a student with cerebral palsy, was outfitted with adaptive equipment that enabled him to play the soccer game *FIFA*. He controls the game using eye-gaze technology mapped to an Xbox controller and head switches to control the buttons in the game. Dan struggled to play at first, but quickly adjusted. Dan was able to compete in the inaugural FIFA competition designed specifically for disabled students at four colleges. The students who participated enjoyed the competition greatly, and developed skills such as teamwork, communication, decision making and resilience. The major obstacle is the price of equipment, as each student needs a solution tailored to their own disability. However, Microsoft has supported the initiative by providing equipment free to the four pilot schools. Hopefully, the tournament can be expanded in the future to all of the specialized colleges (Parker, 2021).

It is also interesting to note that the cybersecurity community has also adopted a competitive model to interest students in exploring the techniques of the cybersecurity industry. In 2010, over 600 high school teams participated in the CyberPatriot national competition. At such competitions, teams of five students compete online using CyberPatriot software to defend computer networks from real-life threats. This fun and exciting activity could help provide a steady stream of cybersecurity professionals to defend the world's computer networks (Business Insights: Essentials, 2010). The organizers of cybersecurity competitions are actively working toward making their competitions more appealing to spectators, modeling these visualizations on esports competitions (Peng, et al., 2020).

CONCLUSION

Is Esports a sport? If esports are to continue to grow and thrive at the collegiate level, a consensus must be reached as to whether esports is really a sport. This will determine where in an institution esports will reside and determine team makeup and availability of scholarships. Walton et al. (2020) have examined this issue from a legal perspective and note that currently, esports may reside within the athletic department, office of student affairs, or academic departments. Currently, college scholarships for esports are largely limited to male participants. If esports is formally deemed a sport, institutions could be found in violation of Title IX requirements that require equivalent treatment for male and female players with respect to scholarships and opportunities to play at the varsity level (Walton et al., 2020).

Taylor and Stout (2020) look to the two-tiered system of collegiate esports for some explanation of the inequality of gender in esports. While many believe this is due to an innate superiority of males with respect to playing the game, research has not demonstrated a significant difference in ability to succeed at esports. Varsity programs receive the bulk of support from colleges, ranging from scholarships and training facilities to support staff and physical trainers. These programs tend to be heavily weighted toward male players. In contrast, esports clubs are often student-run and organized loosely. Generally, clubs receive little or no financial support from their institutions. They are often more balanced with respect to gender and racial diversity (Taylor & Stout, 2020).

Although the goal of making esports a diverse, welcoming endeavor seems daunting, it is important that organizations at all levels embrace this ideal. One prime example of the effort is the esports organization at the University of California at Irvine (UCI). UCI is committed to making its esports community diverse and nurturing. They have established The UCI Esports Task Force for Diversity and Inclusion, with a charge to increase diversity and inclusion with respect to recruiting players and staff. The initiatives of this group include focusing on diverse applicant pools for staff positions. They also provide outreach programs such as tours and arena events to introduce local students in economically challenged areas and UCI students who may have never considered gaming to the university's esports programs. New players from within the university are invited to New Player Nights to experience the games and the esports arena. UCI Esports also runs a Girls and Gaming Summer Camp for young people in the community. The Task Force continues to seek ways to foster diversity and inclusion in UCI's esports community (Amazan-Hall, 2018).

A well-organized program of esports can enhance students' STEM learning. Students develop teamwork skills to solve problems and gain practical experience generating hypotheses and testing them. The successful team uses data and observation to develop new strategies to improve performance. Students develop technical skills as they work on creating livestreams and taped interviews. Students who may come from economically disadvantaged backgrounds can gain experience using technology that is unaffordable to their families. Finally, gaming is fun, and can expose underrepresented groups to STEM fields, including female students, students with disabilities and students of color (Raupp, 2020).

If esports is truly going to succeed in the long-term, much work must be done. However, the rewards that students may reap from being part of the team, and the exposure to new career possibilities, will far outweigh the difficulties that must be addressed.

REFERENCES

Adams, P. (2022, June 3). P&G's Always, Tampax sponsor esports tournament to break down gender barriers. *Marketing Dive*. https://draweb.njcu.edu/login?url=https://draweb.njcu.edu:2073/trade-journals/p-amp-gs-always-tampax-sponsor-eSports-tournament/docview/2675088378/se-2?accountid=12793

Amazan-Hall, K., Chen, J. J., Chiang, K., Cullen, A. L. L., Deppe, M., Dormitorio, E., Haynes, D., Kernan, J., Quanbeck, K., Romine, M., Ruberg, B., Song, J., Stepan-Norris, J., Steinkuehler, C., & Trammell, A. (2018). Diversity and inclusion in esports programs in higher education: Leading by example at UCI. *International Journal of Gaming and Computer-Mediated Simulations, 10*(2). https://www.researchgate.net/profile/Constance-Steinkuehler/publication/326759651_Diversity_and_Inclusion_in_Esports_Programs_in_Higher_Education_Leading_by_Example_at_UCI/links/5b7df52292851c1e12291b4e/Diversity-and-Inclusion-in-Esports-Programs-in-Higher-Education-Leading-by-Example-at-UCI.pdf

Amazon. (2022, June 13). *Amazon Prime Air prepares for drone deliveries*. https://www.aboutamazon.com/news/transportation/amazon-prime-air-prepares-for-drone-deliveries

AnyKey. (2019) *Diversity & inclusion in collegiate esports: Challenges, opportunities, and interventions*. https://anykey-resources.s3.amazonaws.com/publications/AnyKey+-+Diversity+%26+Inclusion+in+Collegiate+Esports+-+Challenges%2C+Opportunities%2C+and+Interventions+(Oct+2019).pdf

AnyKey.org. (2022a). *About*. https://anykey.org/en/about

AnyKey.org. (2022b). *Inclusion 101*. https://anykey.org/en/inclusion-101

AnyKey.org. (2022c). *Keystone Code*. https://anykey.org/en/keystone-code

Austin, E. (2020, Jan 30). Fortnite banned in high school esports: Kentucky official: 'No place for shooter games'. *Courier Journal*. https://draweb.njcu.edu/login?url=https://draweb.njcu.edu:2073/newspapers/fortnite-banned-high-school-eSports/docview/2348180941/se-2?accountid=12793

Aviles, C. (2019). Playing to win: Video games finally make a legitimate move into the classroom. *Tech & Learning, 40*(2), 20-21. https://draweb.njcu.edu/login?url=https://draweb.njcu.edu:2073/trade-journals/playing-win-video-games-finally-make-legitimate/docview/2282387302/se-2?accountid=12793

Aviles, C., Isaacs, S., Lion-Bailey, C., & Lubinsky, J. (2020). *The esports education playbook: Empowering every learner through inclusive gaming*. Dave Burgess Consulting, Incorporated.

Bendici, R. (2021). How to build an esports community. *Tech & Learning*. https://link.gale.com/apps/doc/A661267413/AONE?u=rocklandcc&sid=bookmark-AONE&xid=d80beb5b

Benedict College in South Carolina to offer a new major in Esports Administration. (2021). *Journal of Blacks in Higher Education (Online)*. https://draweb.njcu.edu/login?url=https://draweb.njcu.edu:2073/scholarly-journals/benedict-college-south-carolina-offer-new-major/docview/2556493790/se-2?accountid=12793

Black Collegiate Gaming Association. (2020). https://bcgausa.org/

Block, S., & Haack, F. (2021). Esports: A new industry. *SHS Web of Conferences, 92*. 10.1051hsconf/20219204002

Booton, J. (2020, March 20). DRL launches academy to give students remote access to STEM tools. *Sporttechie*. https://www.sporttechie.com/drl-drone-racing-league-launches-stem-academy-coronavirus-remote-learning

Carnahan, C., Zieger, L., & Crowley, K. (2016). *Drones in education: Let your student's imaginations soar*. International Society for Technology in Education.

Carpenter, N. (2018, April 23). *8 Ivy League esports clubs are set to form the Ivy Esports Conference*. https://doteSports.com/business/news/ivy-league-eSports-conference-22992

ComputerScience.org. (2022). *What is a video designer?* https://www.computerscience.org/careers/video-game-designer/

Cote, A. C., Can, O., Foxman, M., Harris, B. C., Jansen, J., Rahman, M. W. U., & Fickle, T. (2022). The COVID season: U.S. collegiate esports programs' material challenges and opportunities during the 2020-21 pandemic. *Games and Culture, 0*(0), 1–22. doi:10.1177/15554120221088116

Coupland, B. (2021, Nov. 22). Drones fly in to school curriculum. *The Vindicator*. https://www.vindy.com/news/local-news/2021/11/drones-fly-in-to-school-curriculum/

Darvin, L. (2021, Mar 12). At colleges nationwide, esports teams dominated by men. *The ConversationEducation*. https://draweb.njcu.edu/login?url=https://draweb.njcu.edu:2073/newspapers/at-colleges-nationwide-eSports-teams-dominated/docview/2500622467/se-2

Darvin, L., Holden, J., Wells, J., & Baker, T. (2021). Breaking the glass monitor: Examining the underrepresentation of women in esports environments. *Sport Management Review*, *24*(3), 475–499. Advance online publication. doi:10.1080/14413523.2021.1891746

Darvin, L., Vooris, R., & Mahoney, T. (2020). The playing experiences of esport participants: An analysis of treatment discrimination and hostility in esport environments. *Journal of Athlete Development and Experience*, *2*(1), 3. Advance online publication. doi:10.25035/jade.02.01.03

Delello, J. A., McWhorter, R. R., Roberts, P., Dockery, H. S., DeGiuseppe, T. & Corona, F. (2021). The rise of esports: Insights into the perceived benefits and risks for college students. *International Journal of eSports Research, 1*(1).

DictionaryC. (n.d.). https://dictionary.cambridge.org/us/dictionary/english/sport

DiFrancisco-Donoghue, J., Jenny, S. E., Douris, P. C., Ahmad, S., Yuen, K., Hassan, T., Gan, H., Abraham, K., & Sousa, A. (2021). Breaking up prolonged sitting with a 6 min walk improves executive function in women and men esports players: A randomised trial. *BMJ Open Sport & Exercise Medicine*, *7*(3), e001118. doi:10.1136/bmjsem-2021-001118

Diverse. (2020, August 4). Esports Enters HBCU Turf. *Diverse: Issues in Higher Education, 37*(14), 6. https://www.diverseeducation.com/sports/article/15107472/new-partnership-to-create-eSports-league-for-hbcus

Dormehl, L. (2018, April 25). To catch an on- line predator: New A.I. scours chatrooms looking for sex offenders. *Digital Trends.* Retrieved from https://www.digitaltrends. com/cool-tech/catt-algorithm-seeks-preda- tors-online/

Drone Racing League. (2022) https://thedroneracingleague.com/about-drl/

Dykstra, R., Koutakis, P., & Hanson, N. (2021). Relationship between physical fitness variables and reaction time in esports gamers. *International Journal of eSports Research*, *1*(1), 1–14. doi:10.4018/IJER.288540

Elnour, F. F., Himeur, Y., Petri, I., Rezgui, Y., Meskin, N., & Ahmad, A. M. (2022). Performance and energy optimization of building automation and management systems: Towards smart sustainable carbon-neutral sports facilities. *Renewable & Sustainable Energy Reviews, 162*, 112401. doi:10.1016/j.rser.2022.112401

Eng, J. (2021, October 8). 70% of kids in sports quit by their teens – here's how (and why) to keep them in the game. *Parents Together.* https://parents-together.org/70-percent-of-kids-in-sports-quit-by-their-teens-heres-how-and-why-to-keep-them-in-the-game
/

Exley, T. (2021, June 24). *Esports applications in multicultural issues.* https://www.varsityesportsfoundation.org/blog-list/2021/6/24/esports-applications-in-multicultural-issues

Faughnan, S. A. (2021, February 5) Competitive gaming: Now a varsity sport in Barnegat. *Tap Into Barnegat/Waretown*. https://www.tapinto.net/towns/barnegat-slash-waretown/sections/education/articles/competitive-gaming-now-a-varsity-sport-in-barnegat

Ferguson, C. J. (2007). The good, the bad and the ugly: A meta-analytic review of positive and negative effects of violent video games. *The Psychiatric Quarterly*, *78*(4), 309–316. doi:10.100711126-007-9056-9 PMID:17914672

Ferguson, C. J., & Wang, J. C. K. (2019). Aggressive video games are not a risk factor for future aggression in youth: A longitudinal study. *Journal of Youth and Adolescence*, *48*(8), 1439–1451. doi:10.100710964-019-01069-0 PMID:31273603

Fiskaali, A., Lieberoth, A., & Spindler, H. (2020). Exploring institutionalised esport in high school: A mixed methods study of well-being. *Academic Conferences International Limited*. https://draweb.njcu.edu:2072/10.34190/GBL.20.0

Fletcher, A. (2020, January). Esports and the color line: Labor, skill and the exclusion of black players. *Proceedings of the 53rd Hawaii International Conference on System Sciences*. 10.24251/HICSS.2020.325

Florentine, S. (2015). Women in tech: Why esports are a win for diversity. *Cio*. https://draweb.njcu.edu/login

French, S. (2022, February 19). *DRL viewership doubled in 2021-22 season, drone racing giant reports*. https://www.thedronegirl.com/2022/02/22/drl-viewership-doubled-2022/

Garden State Esports. (2022). https://gsesports.org/about/

Giakoni-Ramírez, F., Merellano-Navarro, E., & Duclos-Bastías, D. (2022). Professional esports players: Motivation and physical activity levels. *International Journal of Environmental Research and Public Health*, *19*(4), 2256. doi:10.3390/ijerph19042256 PMID:35206445

Hamari, J., & Sjöblom, M. (2017). What is esports and why do people watch it? *Internet Research*, *27*(2), 211–232. doi:10.1108/IntR-04-2016-0085

Hayday, & Collison, H. (2020). Exploring the contested notion of social inclusion and gender inclusivity within esport spaces. *Social Inclusion*, *8*(3), 197–208. doi:10.17645/si.v8i3.2755

Hilbert, J. (2019, April 9). *Gaming & gender: How inclusive are esports?* https://www.sportsintegrityinitiative.com/gaming-gender-how-inclusive-are-eSports/

Holden, J. T., Edelman, M., & Baker, T. A. (2020) A short treatise on esports and the law: How America regulates its next national pastime. *University of Illinois Law Review*. https://www.illinoislawreview.org/wp-content/uploads/2020/04/Holden.pdf

Business Insights: Essentials. (2010). 600 Teams Now Registered for Innovative Cybersecurity Competition. *Defense & Aerospace Business*.

Jenny, S. E., Keiper, M. C., Taylor, B. J., Williams, D. P., Gawrysiak, J., Manning, R. D., & Tutka, P. M. (2018). Esports venues: A new sport business opportunity. *Journal of Applied Sport Management, 10*(1), 34–49. Advance online publication. doi:10.18666/JASM-2018-V10-I1-8469

Kane, D., & Spradley, B.D. (2017, May 11). Recognizing esports as a sport. *The Sport Journal*. thesportjournal.org /article/recognizing-eSports-as-a-sport/

Kauweloa, N., & Winter, J. (2019). Taking college esports seriously. *Loading, 12*(20), 35–50. doi:10.7202/1065896ar

Kauweloa, N. S. (2021). The emergence of college esports in North America. In Y. J. Kal (Ed.), *Global esports: Transformation of Cultural Perceptions of Competitive Gaming*. Bloomsbury Academic. doi:10.5040/9781501368745.0022

Kivijärvi, M., & Katila, S. (2022). Becoming a gamer: Performative construction of gendered gamer identities. *Games and Culture, 17*(3), 461–481. doi:10.1177/15554120211042260

Kuss, D. J., Kristensen, A. M., Williams, A. J., & Lopez-Fernandez, O. (2022). To be or not to be a female gamer: A qualitative exploration of female gamer identity. *International Journal of Environmental Research and Public Health, 19*(3), 1169. Advance online publication. doi:10.3390/ijerph19031169 PMID:35162194

Li, R. (2016). *Good luck, have fun: The rise of esports*. Skyhorse Publishing.

Liao, S. (2021, April 7). Asian esports players, staffers speak out on "unspeakable" racism, harassment in America. *The Washington Post*. link.gale.com/apps/doc/A657697127/AONE?u=rocklandcc&sid=bookmark-AONE&xid=33fdae9a

Liao, S. (2021, August 30). China restricts young people to playing video games three hours a week. *Washington Post*. https://link.gale.com/apps/doc/A673700847/AONE?u=rocklandcc&sid=bookmark-AONE&xid=0aca8a9a

Luongo, C. (2020, September 17). *Colleagiate StarLeague, World Gaming Network acquired by Playfly Sports*. https://eSportsinsider.com/2020/09/collegiate-starleague-playfly-sports/

Madden, D., Liu, Y., Yu, H., Sonbudak, M. F., Troiano, G. M., & Harteveld, C. (2021). Why are you playing games? You are a girl! Exploring gender biases in esports. *CHI '21: Proceeding of the 2021 CHI Conference on Human Factors in Computing Systems*. 10.1145/3411764.3445248

Marywood University. (2021, Aug 7). *Professional continuing education esports certification. Targeted News Service*. https://draweb.njcu.edu/login?url=https://draweb.njcu.edu:2073/wire-feeds/marywood-university-professional-continuing/docview/2559052490/se-2?accountid=12793

Melcher, K. (2015). *Gamers: The rising stars of collegiate athletics*. TedXNapierville. https://www.youtube.com/watch?v=kcX11m1g3hs&t=818s

Mendoza, E. (2022, June 6). Ranked: The best-selling video game consoles of all time. *Visual Capitalist*. https://www.visualcapitalist.com/cp/ranked-the-best-selling-video-game-consoles-of-all-time/

Microsoft. (2022). *Microsoft ESports Teacher Academy (META)*. https://docs.microsoft.com/en-us/learn/paths/microsoft-eSpor ts-teacher-academy/

Miller, A. (2016, Jul 17). Esports just may pay for your college education. *Kitsap Sun*. https://draweb.njcu.edu/login?url=https://draweb.njcu.edu:20 73/newspapers/eSports-just-may-pay-your-college-education/do cview/1804581260/se-2?accountid=12793

Minecraft. (2021). *Finals: Battle of the Boroughs*. https://www.twitch.tv/videos/1057074324

Minecraft. (2022). https://education.minecraft.net/en-us/resources/stem-eSports -challenges

Minecraft Education Edition. (2021, December 2). *A city-wide eSports smack-down in New York: BOTB*. https://education.minecraft.net/en-us/blog/battle-of-the-bor oughs-eSports

Moreno, D. A., & Carter, A. B. (2021, October 8). *Will the NCAA's NIL ruling impact collegiate esports?* https://sportslitigationalert.com/will-the-ncaas-nil-ruling-impact-collegiate-eSports/#:~:text=As%20noted%20above%2C%20t he%20NCAA,violence%20of%20certain%20video%20games

NACE. (2022). *What is NACE?* https://naceSports.org/about/

NCSA. (2022). *Esports scholarships*. https://www.ncsasports.org/college-eSports-scholarships

Neilsen, L. (2019). *Esports, the down & dirty stats for educators – live from #ISTE19*. https://www.techlearning.com/news/eSports-the-down-and-dirty -stats-for-educators-live-from-iste19

Nelius, J. (2019). Excerpt: What it's like to go to college on an esports scholarship: Balancing practice and matches with academics, combating toxicity, and explaining esports to parents and professors. *TWICE: This Week in Consumer Electronics*, *34*(17), 16–17.

NJCAAE. (2022). *National Junior College Athletic Association Esports*. https://www.generationesports.com/njcaae

Ofgang, E. (2020). How to build an inclusive esports community: BX Start is focused on building an inclusive esports community from the ground up. *Tech & Learning*, 29. https://link.gale.com/apps/doc/A640002289/AONE?u=rocklandcc&sid=bookmark-AONE&xid=853ea267

Olympic Council of Asia. (2022). *Press Release*. https://oca-sia.org/news/3217-oca-press-release-oca-announces -new-dates-for-the-19th-asian-games-hangzhou.html

Parker, K. (2021). College identifies a game-changer for students with disabilities. *The Times EducationalSupplement.* https://draweb.njcu.edu/login?url=https://draweb.njcu.edu:2073/trade-journals/college-identifies-game-changer-students-with/docview/2553440846/se-2?accountid=12793

Peng, C., Stackpole, B., Richards, D., Schwartz, D., Weeden, C., Fogle, C., Walrond, V., Johnson, D., Marcovecchio, J., & Brown, C. (2020). Visualization for spectators in cybersecurity. *2020 IEEE Conference on Visualization for Cyber Security (VizSec).* 10.1109/VizSec51108.2020.00009

Perrin, A. (2018, September 17). *5 facts about Americans and video games.* https://www.pewresearch.org/fact-tank/2018/09/17/5-facts-about-americans-and-video-games/

Play, V. S. (2022). *High school eSports.* https://www.playvs.com/high-school

Playfly ESports. (2022). *NACE StarLeague.* https://playflyeSports.com/new-competitive-structure/

Raupp, A. B. (2020, April 16). *Esports and STEM education: A 2020 perspective.* Forbes. https://www.forbes.com/sites/forbestechcouncil/2020/04/16/esports-and-stem-education-a-2020-perspective/?sh=7c84fb9c4eae

Riser-Kositsky, M., & Peele, H. (2021, July 30). Statistics on school sports: How many students play sports? Which sports do they play? *Education Week.* https://www.edweek.org/leadership/statistics-on-school-sports-how-many-students-play-sports-which-sports-do-they-play/2021/07

Rogstad. (2021). Gender in eSports research: a literature review. *European Journal for Sport and Society,* 1–19. doi:10.1080/16138171.2021.1930941

Rothwell, G., & Shaffer, M. (2019). eSports in K-12 and Post-Secondary Schools. *Education Sciences, 9*(2), 105. doi:10.3390/educsci9020105

Ruvalcaba, O., Shulze, J., Kim, A., Berzenski, S. R., & Otten, M. P. (2018). Women's experiences in eSports: Gendered differences in Peer and Spectator Feedback during competitive video game play. *Journal of Sport and Social Issues, 42*(4), 295–311. doi:10.1177/0193723518773287

Sang-Hun. (2021, Jun 19). Inside the 'deadly serious' world of esports in South Korea. *New York Times.* https://draweb.njcu.edu/login?url=https://draweb.njcu.edu:2073/newspapers/inside-deadly-serious-world-eSports-south-korea/docview/2542803244/se-2?accountid=12793

Schnackner, B. (2021, November 3). *You think it's not a college sport? Buckle up as eSports is not a degree pursuit, too.* https://phys.org/news/2021-11-college-sport-buckle-eSports-degree.html

SmithBarrow, D. (2020, September 18). HBCUs entering the game: Black colleges join the esports bandwagon*: Washington Post.*

Sparks, S. D. (2022). Students Are Behaving Badly in Class. Excessive Screen Time Might Be to Blame. *Education Week, 41*(30). https://draweb.njcu.edu/login?url=https://draweb.njcu.edu:2073/trade-journals/students-are-behaving-badly-class-excessive/docview/2651398638/se-2?accountid=12793

Stahlke, S., Robb, J. & Mirza-Babaei, P. (2018) The fall of the fourth wall: Designing and evaluating interactive spectator experiences. *International Journal of Gaming and Computer-Mediated Simulations, 10*(1).

Stewart, M., & Price, H. (2022). Getting in the eGame: ESports Streaming Gives the University of Kentucky a New Way to Grow Revenue and Recruit Students. *Planning for Higher Education, 50*(2), 26–35. https://draweb.njcu.edu/login?url=https://draweb.njcu.edu:2073/scholarly-journals/getting-egame-eSports-streaming-gives-university/docview/2651853366/se-2?accountid=12793

Tang, T., Cooper, R., & Kucek, J. (2021). Gendered ESports: Predicting Why Men and Women Play and Watch ESports Games. *Journal of Broadcasting & Electronic Media, 65*(3), 336–356. doi:10.1080/08838151.2021.1958815

Taxi, D. (2022). *Drone taxi Dubai.* https://taxi-dubai.ae/drone-taxi-dubai/

Taylor, N. (2020, September 9). As collegiate eSports become more professional, women are being left out. *MedicalXpress.* https://medicalxpress.com/news/2020-09-collegiate-eSports-professional-women-left.html

Taylor, N., & Stout, B. (2020). Gender and the two-tiered system of collegiate esports. *Critical Studies in Media Communication, 37*(5), 451–465. doi:10.1080/15295036.2020.1813901

The Ohio State University. (2018, October 3). *The Ohio State University launches first-of-its-kind comprehensive esports program.* https://news.osu.edu/the-ohio-state-university-launches-first-of-its-kind-comprehensive-eSports-program/

The Ohio State University. (2019, September 11). *Ohio State eSports arena ready for play.* https://news.osu.edu/ohio-state-eSports-arena-open-and-ready-for-play/

Tingle, C. (2022). More research is needed on prevalence, incidence of injuries in eSports athletes. *Orthopedics Today, 42*(1), 10-12. https://draweb.njcu.edu/login?url=https://www.proquest.com/trade-journals/more-research-is-needed-on-prevalence-incidence/docview/2630948183/se-2?accountid=12793

Venkat, R. (2021, September 9). *Asian Games 2022: ESports to make debut; FIFA, PUBG, Dota 2 among eight medal events.* https://olympics.com/en/news/fifa-pubg-dota-2-eSports-medal-events-asian-games-2022

Walton, D. R., Lower-Hoppe, L. M., & Horger, M. (2020). Do eSports classify as intercollegiate sport? Legal analysis of Title IX. *Journal of Issues in Intercollegiate Athletics, 2020*(13), 94–118.

Warren County Community College. (2022). *Warren Unmanned Systems Technology programs*. https://www.warren.edu/drones/

West Virginia University. (2021, October 21). Game on: WVU prepping launch of eSports minor alongside development of new eSports team, top player already representing the gold and blue. *WVU Today*. https://wvutoday.wvu.edu/stories/2021/10/21/game-on-wvu-prepping-launch-of-eSports-minor-alongside-development-of-new-eSports-team-top-player-already-representing-the-gold-and-blue

Whitworth, S. (2022, April 22). *When was Minecraft: Education Edition launched? Exploring the history behind the game*. https://www.sportskeeda.com/minecraft/when-minecraft-education-edition-launched-exploring-history-behind-game

Williams, R. (2021, December 21). Drone Racing League & Draganfly go back to school. *Boardroom*. https://boardroom.tv/drone-racing-league-draganfly-stem-program/

Winters, M. (2022). *How sports marketing and athlete branding influence public consumption*. https://digitalcommons.usf.edu/cgi/viewcontent.cgi?filename=1&article=1669&context=usf_ourconference&type=additional

Wray, S. (2020, August 27). *Flying taxi trials in cities set to expand*. https://cities-today.com/cities-progress-flying-taxi-plans/

Wright, S. (2020, October 22). Black woman launches collegiate esports & gaming company: GameStop, Intel and Nacon Gaming agree to support. *Washington Informer*, *56*(1), 34.

Young, A. (2022, Feb 3). Online sports games like FIFA and F1 help children develop key skills. *Express*. https://draweb.njcu.edu/login?url=https://draweb.njcu.edu:2073/newspapers/online-sports-games-like-fifa-f1-help-children/docview/2625126097/se-2?accountid=12793

ADDITIONAL READING

Aviles, C., Isaacs, S., Lion-Bailey, C., & Lubinsky, J. (2020). *The esports education playbook: Empowering every learner through inclusive gaming*. Dave Burgess Consulting, Inc.

Collis, W. (2022). *The book of esports*. RosettaBooks.

Li, R. (2016). *Good luck, have fun: The rise of esports*. Skyhorse Publishing.

KEY TERMS AND DEFINITIONS

Avatar: The computerized character which represents an esports player in the game.
Console: The equipment used to play esports games, for example, a Playstation.

Esports: The playing of video games competitively at the professional, collegiate, or K-12 levels.

First Person Shooter (FPS): A game played through the eyes of the character controlled by the player.

Multiplayer Online Battle Arena (MOBA): A strategic video game in which two teams compete against each other on a battlefield. Each player controls a character.

NPC: A non-player character, which is controlled by the game itself, not by a competitor.

Twitch: A live-streaming platform that enables spectators to view a competition from remote locations.

Chapter 18
What's Next for Teacher Preparation Programs?

Joanna Antigone Antoniou
https://orcid.org/0000-0001-5287-3151
Passaic Public Schools, USA

ABSTRACT

This chapter provides context for teacher preparation programs to adjust their approach based on the lessons learned from emergency remote and hybrid instruction necessitated by the COVID-19 pandemic. This research makes reference to the TPACK framework and its impact on educator training and is framed on Bandura's theory of self-efficacy. A list of post-pandemic skills that teachers need is discussed, followed by suggestions for teacher preparation programs to address those skills. Any changes in teacher preparation programs must also be met with support for faculty of those programs. Finally, further research is suggested and discussed.

INTRODUCTION

The COVID-19 pandemic had an effect on all industries, and education was no exception. As the world of education has reopened post pandemic, schools and educators are still reflecting on the lessons learned from the emergency remote and hybrid instruction during the COVID-19 pandemic. Even as the landscape of education is shifting, novice teachers are in a unique position to need support acclimating to their new careers. The goal of this chapter is to delve into what teacher preparation programs can include to meet the ever-changing needs of novice teachers.

The technological, pedagogical, and content knowledge (TPACK) model has long been used to classify teachers' competencies in pedagogy, content, and technological knowledge. It provides a context, particularly for professional development and teacher preparation programs, to understand the various components of successful teaching and how they overlap. The COVID-19 pandemic had an incredible impact on education as well as on educators' approaches to teaching, and the lessons learned from mandated remote instruction continue to have an impact on teaching and learning. Now, post pandemic, when most students and teachers are back in face-to-face classrooms, the TPACK model can be viewed with a

DOI: 10.4018/978-1-6684-6092-4.ch018

new perspective in terms of how technology intersects with effective content and pedagogy knowledge. Further, this new perspective of effective teaching and learning with the proper use of technology has to be considered and applied in teacher preparation programs.

This chapter is organized into the following seven main sections, and described further below:

1. Understanding TPACK
2. Theoretical Framework
3. Teacher Preparation Programs
4. Skills Teachers Need Post Pandemic
5. Where Teacher Preparation Programs Go From Here
6. How to Support Faculty in These Shifts
7. Further Research

The first section, "Understanding TPACK," provides a brief background on the origins of the TPACK model as well as examples of how TPACK has been used extensively in education research. The chapter begins with this foundation, as it helps to frame the ideas of pedagogical, technological, and content knowledge, which are critical to all teachers and, therefore, foundational to the idea of how teacher preparation programs develop their courses and work. These competency areas are at the heart of every teacher preparation program, in which preservice teachers learn about pedagogical theory and applications, with respect to specific content and effective technology integration.

The second section encompasses the "Theoretical Framework" in which this research is grounded. Bandura's (1977) work on self-efficacy explains how an individual develops their sense of self-efficacy through various means. This theory is examined from the lens of teacher preparation. Framing the concept of teacher preparation programs on Bandura's theory of self-efficacy gives decision-makers a theoretical framework to understand how they can impact their students' confidence levels and abilities.

The third section, "Teacher Preparation Programs" delves into research concerning teacher preparation programs and how they have addressed TPACK skills into their curricula. Many teacher preparation programs in the United States are guided by the Council for the Accreditation of Educator Preparation (CAEP) standards for accreditation, that provide a standard for programs to develop clear goals for pedagogy and technology for their students. In this section, there will be discussion of how the COVID-19 pandemic has affected teacher preparation programs. This section also addresses the special considerations for novice teachers. Novice teachers' needs are important to consider and analyze particularly in relation to the teacher preparation programs. Decision-makers in teacher preparation programs can use the unique needs of novice teachers to make programmatic changes that may address some of their needs early on, even when they are placed in another school after graduating. Further, teacher preparation programs should strive to have completers who can reflect on the program in a positive manner and relate their knowledge development back to their experiences within the program.

The fourth section covers "Skills Teachers Need Post Pandemic." Teachers have always required certain skillsets, and using this lens, the discussion is focused on the particular TPACK skills that post pandemic teachers need. In reflecting on the emergency remote and hybrid instruction forced by the COVID-19 pandemic, some necessary skills for teachers stand out. In this section, these various skills are highlighted and discussed.

In the fifth section, "Where Teacher Preparation Programs Go From Here," there is a discussion of various ideas and techniques that programs should include for successful technology integration in a post pandemic world. These suggestions consider the special skills that post pandemic teachers need. This section is broken down further into multiple components, exploring the skills that have been exposed by various research studies for successful technology integration post pandemic. Each component is discussed and supported with literature and references that support the claim.

Since there are recommendations for improving teacher preparation programs, it is also critical to prepare for the changes that the higher education faculty will face. The sixth section, "How to Support Faculty in These Shifts," entails discussion of how higher education institutions can best support their faculty with the instructional changes needed to keep up with post pandemic education. Of course, as practicing teachers in schools need support and professional development, so do faculty and teacher educators. Since their modeling is a large component of a preservice teacher's first experiences with using technology, it becomes even more important for faculty of teacher preparation programs to be ready to use technology in transformative and innovative ways.

In the seventh section, "Further Research," ideas for further research and study are considered. At the time of publication, schools are still responding to the circumstances that the COVID-19 pandemic forced upon them. So, schools are still learning from the lessons of the pandemic and are continuing to reflect on their responses. As such, various areas of future research are suggested and discussed.

UNDERSTANDING TPACK

Origins of TPACK

TPACK is a framework developed by Matthew J. Koehler and Punya Mishra that describes three areas of knowledge that teachers develop for effective teaching (Koehler & Mishra, 2009). The premise of TPACK was extended from Lee Shulman's work on pedagogical content knowledge (Mishra & Koehler, 2006) and adds the component of technological knowledge and considers each component and the relationships between the three main knowledge components. While Mishra and Koehler (2006) did not purport that this theory was new, they emphasized that their views on addressing the overlaps of content knowledge, pedagogical knowledge, and technological knowledge are what makes their approach different. Figure 1 shows a visual representation of the TPACK framework. Koehler and Mishra (2009) described each component, but even before the pandemic, they admitted that that technological knowledge component is harder to define since technology changes quickly. Now, post pandemic, the landscape of educational technology and its use in the classroom has changed even more, making this area even more complex in its definition.

Figure 1. The TPACK Framework
Note. Reproduced by permission of the publisher, © 2012 by tpack.org

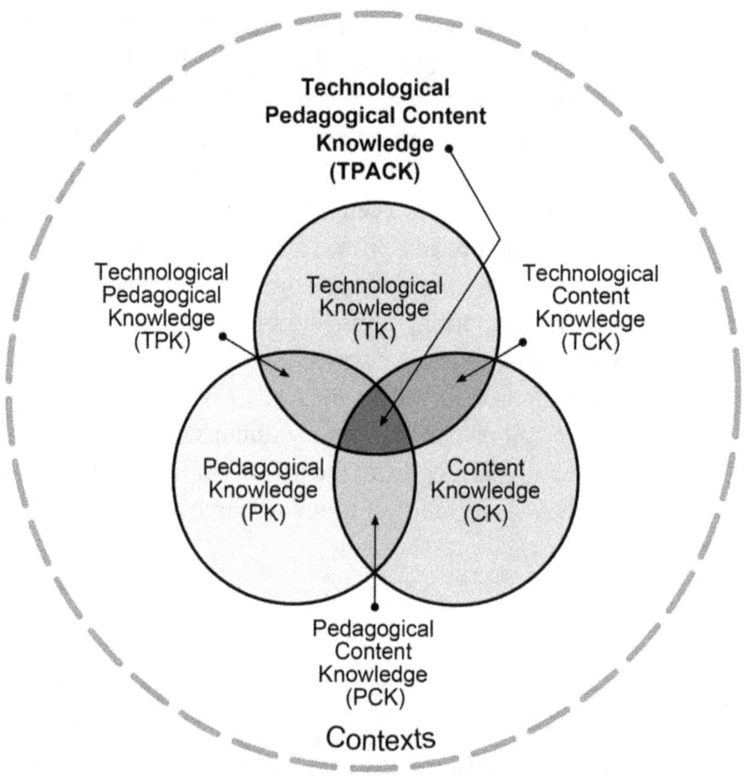

Overall, the TPACK framework models seven knowledge areas (see Figure 1). The three main knowledge areas are content knowledge (CK), pedagogical knowledge (PK), technological knowledge (TK). Additionally, the overlap of each of these knowledge areas are considered: technological pedagogical knowledge (TPK), technological content knowledge (TCK), pedagogical content knowledge (PCK), and finally, the overlap of all three knowledge areas is called TPACK. Each of the seven areas represents a portion of effective teaching that teachers should have and Koehler and Mishra (2009) asserted that the development of each of these areas makes for effective teaching. According to Koehler and Mishra (2009), the component of technology is extremely complex with regard to its intersection with pedagogy and content. A pencil or a blackboard could be considered technology, in that it is an instrument used in the classroom that affords certain benefits. Similarly, more modern technologies, such as computers, educational software, and the Internet, for example, also provide benefits in the classroom, and are more complex in their application. Teachers without experience may struggle to use the more complex technologies in their classrooms, particularly without any training.

TPACK in Education

As technology became more prevalent in classrooms, it became important to prepare teachers to use the technology. However, simply training teachers to use hardware and software in their classrooms was problematic on various levels (Mishra & Koehler, 2006). Theoretically, it has been established that a stand-alone professional development session or stand-alone college course on the use of technology will not make an impact on a teacher's technological pedagogical skills (Hu & Fyfe, 2010; Lewis, 2015). This stems from a belief that simply understanding how to use a technology equates to using it appropriately and meaningfully in pedagogy and content concerns. The TPACK framework suggests that it is not just the three areas of knowledge that are important for effective teaching, but also the overlaps of each of those three knowledge areas. TPK and TCK are actually separate from TK. Due to how fast technology can change, even before the COVID-19 pandemic, approaching technology training in this way for teachers may not have been as impactful on transforming pedagogy.

Still, the use of the TPACK framework has been used in research to assess teachers' self-efficacy in the various components, particularly with preservice teachers. In many studies using TPACK surveys and assessment tools, teachers often rated their TK components the lowest (Archambualt & Crippen, 2009; Byker, 2014; Hoffer & Grandgenett, 2012). Sometimes, teachers even separate the technological component from their other responsibilities in the classroom (e.g., pedagogy and content) and this may lead to the uncertainty about confidence and technology use in the classroom (Byker, 2014).

THEORETICAL FRAMEWORK

In his theory of self-efficacy, Bandura (1977) posited that an individual may develop self-efficacy from performance accomplishments, vicarious experiences, verbal persuasion, and physiological states. Three of these four concepts provide a theoretical foundation for this area of literature review and recommendations of teacher preparation programs and suggestions for novice teachers.

Within self-efficacy theory, the idea of performance accomplishments refers to the paradigm that an individual is likely to feel more confident in a task if they have previously accomplished another similar task (Bandura, 1977). This concept is foundational to student teaching during teacher preparation programs: Prior to becoming a full-fledged teacher, a preservice teacher is immersed in an authentic context classroom with a partner school. This can be in various forms, from random classroom visits to daily presence within a selected classroom. During their practicum, the preservice teacher is responsible for creating and facilitating lessons while the mentor teacher is still present. In an ideal situation, the mentor teacher would help plan the lessons and provide clear, consistent, and constructive feedback for the preservice teacher. In this way, the successful performance accomplishment would help that novice teacher feel more confident in their first years of teaching, since they have already accomplished the task of planning and conducting lessons.

Vicarious experiences are also central to Bandura's (1977) theory of self-efficacy. What an individual observes another doing may have an impact on their own confidence to accomplish the same or a similar task. The student teaching experience is central to this idea, as well. In the student-teaching classroom, a preservice teacher may initially observe the mentor teacher. In the observation, the preservice teacher can note what was effective, so that they can mimic the same when they in turn lead a lesson. In Antoniou's (2021) study of novice teachers, respondents reported that both watching mentor teachers and peer observations had a positive impact on their own self-efficacy to use technology in their lessons.

According to Bandura (1977), verbal persuasion, or coaching, is another element that has an effect on an individual's self-efficacy. In the student teaching model, a preservice teacher works with the classroom teacher, as well as faculty from higher education. In an ideal setting, the preservice teacher would get coaching from various individuals that would support them in their areas of struggle, encourage them in their areas of success, and ultimately, help them develop a sense of confidence. While not always possible, student teaching done in the same district where a novice teacher ultimately gets placed is helpful, because the novice teacher has already developed relationships with others in the school who can provide those coaching moments.

TEACHER PREPARATION PROGRAMS

During the pandemic, programs were forced to move completely online. Professors and teachers turned to conducting their lessons online using tools that they may have never used before. In some cases, curricula were transitioned from synchronous to asynchronous modalities, forcing the professor or teacher to adapt their pedagogical approach to teaching content.

How Do Teacher Preparation Programs Address TPACK Skills?

The International Society for Technology in Education (ISTE, 2022), publishes sets of standards for technology integration for teachers, students, coaches, and academic leaders. The ISTE teacher standards were created to support the integration of technology in classrooms and have gone through various iterations. Additionally, higher education programs align themselves with the Council for Accreditation of Educator Preparation (CAEP), which provides a set of standards for accreditation of their preparation programs. The CAEP framework for accreditation has stipulated that technology integration is critical in teacher preparation and should be embedded throughout the program (CAEP, 2019).

Even with both the ISTE standards and guiding CAEP standards, teacher preparation programs struggle with effective technology integration in their course of study. Many programs continue to offer stand-alone technology courses and fail to critically assess if students have achieved their technology standard goals (Lewis, 2015; Martin, 2015). As asserted by Mishra and Koehler (2006), teaching about technology on its own is not impactful for TPK or TCK. Preservice teachers have expressed a lack of confidence with using technology tools for effective pedagogy (Antoniou, 2021; Lei, 2009; Martin, 2015; Williams et al., 2009).

In addition to the technology courses offered by teacher preparation courses, there are ways that programs have explored the efficacy of technology integration. One way is to conduct preassessments and postassessments after receiving instruction on technology use. Another way is through conducting microteaching lesson studies, in which preservice teachers closely examine their use of technology in lessons, and reflect and address pedagogical concerns with the use of technology (Hoffer & Grandgenett, 2012). In this chapter, there is a discussion of ways that teacher preparation programs can continue to adapt to meet the needs of technology integration post pandemic.

The Impact of COVID-19 on Teacher Preparation Programs

During the COVID-19 pandemic, schools across the world were thrust into emergency remote teaching environments. Students and teachers stayed home to mitigate the spread of the virus, forcing schools to move the bulk of their education online, through both synchronous experiences and asynchronous activities. Teachers were faced with the challenges of moving their instruction and activities to digital means, whether or not they had experience doing so.

Teacher preparation programs include components in which preservice teachers participate in clinical practice. Student teaching is a critical component of the preservice teachers' training experiences (L. M. Anderson & Stillman, 2013). The time spent in the classroom with students allows the preservice teacher to employ the theoretical ideas and lessons they worked on during their preservice classes. During emergency remote instruction, preservice teachers missed out on critical face-to-face instructional time with students, components that are so integral to developing the preservice teachers' self-efficacy (Bandura, 1977). In particular, the experiences of preservice teachers truly varies based on their student teaching pairings (Assunção Flores & Gago, 2020). In institutions in Portugal, for example, practicum guidelines were revised to allow the cooperation between school-based mentors and preservice teachers to stay the same, but be conducted online (Assunção Flores & Gago, 2020). Further, the new guidelines stipulated changes if practical application could not be achieved in student teaching experiences and research components; instead, preservice teachers could plan based on theoretical frameworks of pedagogy and reflect on the "idealisation of practice" (Assunção Flores & Gago, 2020, p. 6).

These changes to practicum implementation have an impact on the first generations of novice teachers exiting teacher preparation programs since the pandemic first started. These novice teachers are entering the teaching workforce with less experience than they would have had if there were no emergency remote instruction (Choate et al., 2021). These novice teachers would need additional supports in their first years of teaching, particularly for teachers working under emergency certificates and the constraints on budgets meant to support new teachers (Choate et al., 2021).

Further, those same preservice teachers had to shift to virtual instruction. Teacher preparation programs are now considering how to add virtual instruction components to their programs, as the lessons learned from the COVID-19 experience in schools have had such an impact on teaching and learning. The lessons learned during the pandemic are already expanding the threshold of content learned during preservice programs. Suggestions for preservice modifications are discussed later in this chapter.

Special Considerations for Novice Teachers

Teacher preparation programs should consider what novice teachers need in order to best prepare them. Novice teachers often require many levels of support, but the levels of support may differ in each school. So, teacher preparation programs should aim to equip their completers with the skills necessary to adjust to their new career. The CAEP (2022) standards specify in a few areas why this is important. First, CAEP Standard 3 states, "The provider demonstrates the quality of candidates is a continuous and purposeful focus from recruitment through completion" (CAEP, 2022). Secondly, CAEP Standard 4 states, "The provider demonstrates the effectiveness of its completers' instruction on P-12 student learning and development, and completer and employer satisfaction with the relevance and effectiveness of preparation" (CAEP, 2022). Standard 4 continues with follow-up standards, which call for the satisfaction of both employers and completers (CAEP, 2022). For these reasons, it is important for teacher preparation programs to be thoughtful and reflective of the unique needs of novice teachers to develop their own programs with purpose.

Novice teachers usually require various levels of support in all areas of teaching. The level of support for novice teachers can be directly related to teacher retention and quality of teaching (Akiri & Dori, 2022; Ewing, 2021). Novice teachers work with a mentor teacher in their first years, but this can sometimes be a burden on the school system (Ewing, 2021). Mentors need training themselves on how to provide a comfortable support system for novice teachers (Spătărelu, 2020). Spătărelu (2020) investigated the integration of an external mentor to collaboratively coach and nurture, as opposed to internal mentors or colleagues, who are often too busy with their own work load to provide enough support to the novice teacher. One-on-one mentoring contributes to the greatest gains for a novice teacher, as opposed to group mentoring or mentoring networks (Akiri & Dori, 2022). Successful mentoring can lead to less teacher turnover and increase learning outcomes (Spătărelu, 2020).

Before and since the COVID-19 pandemic, novice teachers need support in all areas, including content, pedagogical methods, and technological guidance. Many school districts have brought in new technology to their schools since the pandemic. This has brought a new layer of additional considerations for novice teachers, who are already navigating the new environment of their school. Since the pandemic began, schools across the world may have introduced new technology, learning platforms, classroom hardware and other technological advancements to their classrooms in response to the need for remote and hybrid learning. All teachers, including novice teachers new to the school, would need proper support to use these resources. Novice teachers need additional professional development and support in the areas of integrating technology, assessment, and managing digital learning environments (De Vera et al., 2021).

An effective mentoring model can help provide a safe space for novice teachers to learn how to teach in their school placement using the school's technologies. A successful mentor can help the novice teacher increase their confidence in all areas of TPACK: technological, pedagogical, and content knowledge.

SKILLS TEACHERS NEED POST PANDEMIC

The landscape of teacher skills has changed post pandemic. Due to remote and hybrid instruction, new technologies were thrust into teachers' hands in an effort to keep teaching and learning going during emergency school closures during the pandemic. To comprehend the skills that teachers need, it is first imperative to have a better understanding of post pandemic classrooms and how educational technology is used in conjunction with content and pedagogical areas to deliver lessons. The following sections will highlight some of the critical skills that teachers need for success in post pandemic classrooms and schools.

Digital Skills That Include Virtual Learning Environments

During the pandemic, schools used virtual conferencing tools, learning management systems, digital platforms, and other technology tools to conduct digital learning. Post pandemic, schools continue to use these platforms, so teachers will still need initial and support training to understand how to best use these platforms for effective teaching and learning. Additionally, schools can use the increase in virtual learning options to increase their course offerings. If a school is using a platform which provides self-paced virtual courses, they can use that platform to provide courses that the school would not normally provide because they may not have had a certified teacher to teach it. Teacher preparation programs must keep up with the current demands of teaching and learning, and this includes a focus on virtual, hybrid, and blended learning environments (Darling-Hammond & Hyler, 2020).

For teachers, this means that they must be prepared to teach in any type of learning environment, whether it be face-to-face classrooms, hybrid instruction, fully virtual instruction, or asynchronous online courses. Each of these learning environments requires different skills and teacher competencies, particularly related to TPK and TCK. These skills are not only necessary in the case of another emergency remote learning situation, like the COVID-19 pandemic presented, but also since schools will employ more and more of these learning environments with the addition of more technology to their classrooms and curriculum. This skill makes a graduating preservice teacher a prime candidate to be a successful teacher.

Flexibility and Resilience

Emergency remote and hybrid instruction taught educators that they may need to quickly learn new skills in order to teach better. It is not so much the skills themselves that are necessary to learn; but rather, the ability to quickly learn new skills that teachers need to be successful. Flexibility is a primary skill that teachers need post pandemic. During the pandemic, when schools quickly introduced new platforms, teachers were required to adjust accordingly to change their lesson plans. Flexibility and responsiveness to students has always been a teacher skill, but with the fast-paced nature of post pandemic schools, this seems to be a skill that teachers need even more.

Teachers experienced anxiety during the pandemic, particularly with keeping up with the workload and demand of using new technologies quickly and effectively. With training, though, teachers showed a decrease in anxiety and fatigue with the technology use (Pozo-Rico et al., 2020). That decrease in anxiety around using technology can have an impact on the teachers' confidence levels and encourage them to use more technology effectively in their lessons.

Post pandemic teachers need to know that it is okay when a lesson gets derailed, or when technology stops working mid-activity. They need skills to assess a situation in the classroom and determine how to make it better. That act of resilience makes a difference in the classroom. Students and other adults respond to it, instead of resorting to the feelings of anxiety, as many did during the pandemic.

How to Create and Engage With a Professional Learning Network

During the height of the COVID-19 pandemic, teachers relied heavily on self-directed learning through their own professional learning networks (PLNs; Trust & Whalen, 2020). In a time when teachers were most overwhelmed and struggling to keep up with the daily challenges of emergency remote and hybrid teaching, teachers turned to others in the field for support, suggestions, and tutorials.

Finding and curating resources through a PLN is a skill that would greatly assist all teachers. This can be done through many social media platforms. Through PLN interactions, teachers can curate lesson and activity plans, share and elaborate on ideas, and reflect on their own practice with authentic feedback from others in the field. In a study of lessons learned from the pandemic, teachers self-reported that they used social media posts, internet searches, and asked for help on social media, among other strategies, as they prepared for remote teaching (Trust & Whalen, 2020). Networking with others through a learning network can be beneficial for teachers to find the resources they need. When developing a PLN, teachers can pinpoint the specific support that they need, as opposed to participating in a predetermined professional development opportunity that may not align with the teacher's current goals and struggles. The support that a preservice or novice teacher receives through an active and authentic PLN can be helpful in developing the confidence of the teacher (Kearney et al., 2019). In post pandemic education, participation in a PLC can positively affect teachers' confidence levels.

Ability to Access and Use Data

With the addition of digital platforms, many teachers now have access to more data about their students. The pandemic brought with it many digital platforms where students could participate in self-paced activities that could be self-graded. Online learning provided opportunities for teachers to have quick and easy access to student data files (Fuad et al., 2020).

Teachers need to develop the ability to find, understand, and access their student's data. Further, they need to be able to analyze student data and, where appropriate, merge with other data that would be helpful in understanding a student's progress. This is a true overlap of technological and pedagogical skills. Teachers should be able to use technology to assess their students and use the data to make informed decisions about students' progress. They should use student data to determine how to inform their next lesson.

WHERE TEACHER PREPARATION PROGRAMS GO FROM HERE

The COVID-19 pandemic was very impactful on all areas of education. During the pandemic, teachers used more educational technology tools because the classes were offered online. Teachers were forced to find new ways to connect and engage with their students, while still providing the same level of quality with covering their content. The lessons learned during the trying times of the COVID-19 pandemic could be applied not only to current teacher preparation programs, but also to the approach that these programs use to prepare new generations of teachers. Even after classrooms and schools safely reopened their physical doors, the pandemic continued to have an impact on teaching and learning. In moving forward from this experience, teacher preparation programs can develop a list of lessons learned to apply them to the revision of their programs and adoption of new or modified practices so that new cohorts of novice teachers can have sustained experiences with using technology in effective ways. The following sections highlight some of the insights that teacher preparations programs can reflect on while analyzing their own programs.

Modeling Technology Use in an Authentic Context

There are many variables within a classroom context, such as class size, technologies available, learning styles, and timing. For this reason, novice teachers should design technology-enhanced learning activities in a real-world context (Glazer et al., 2005; Nguyen & Bower, 2018). As compared to theoretical lesson design, authentic context provides the novice teacher with real-life challenges to increase their skill levels.

In an experimental study, the experimental group that was taught instructional technologies and how to use them to plan and teach lessons had more positive improvements in how to integrate technology than did the control group (Kartal & Dilek, 2021). The course that the experimental group took was focused on teaching methods and positively affected their TPK. Figg and Jaipal (2009) also asserted that TPK would be critical in teaching successfully with technology. Successful implementations of technology-enhanced lessons during a teachers' preservice experience would reduce the trial-and-error that might occur with a novice teacher (Figg & Jaipal, 2009).

The modeling of technology must come from an authentic context, and not from a stand-alone course on educational technology (Hu & Fyfe, 2010; Lewis, 2015). There is no one-size-fits-all approach to using technology effectively in education. Instead, teacher preparation programs should ensure preservice teachers have exposure to technology use in two areas. First, preservice teachers should see modeling of effective technology use by the faculty of the teacher preparation program. Secondly, they should be placed in a student teaching experience to observe authentic use of technology in the classroom, so that they can get first-hand exposure to strengths and challenges of using technology. These experiences would address competencies beyond the TK component of TPACK; they would address TPK and TCK.

During the height of the pandemic, the preservice teachers in preparation programs had abbreviated or nonexistent time in classrooms, since schools closed world-wide; but this time in a classroom is critical for a preservice teacher's self-efficacy (VanLone et al., 2021). Preservice teachers need the time to practice the knowledge they gain in their teacher preparation courses, with the support of a mentor teacher. This vicarious experience builds a preservice teachers' self-efficacy and knowledge to infuse technology in education.

Another way that teacher preparation programs can model the use of technology in an authentic context is by embedding the use of PLNs into the curriculum. Encouraging students to immerse themselves in real-time learning networks with others globally will start them on a path of understanding the need and benefits of collaborating and sharing with other educators. Faculty can do this by embedding the ideas of PLNs into their curriculum and ask students to join in on the conversation. They can have students reflect on the experience of using a PLN and how it has benefited their time in the classroom. Furthermore, faculty can model their own use of a PLN and explicitly show students how they use social media to enhance their own practice.

Observing a mentor or experienced teachers teach using technology, use technological pedagogical knowledge in an authentic context, and participate in a PLC are forms of "vicarious learning." According to Bandura (1977), vicarious learning can happen when an individual watches someone else complete a task. These experiences are critical in the development of a preservice teacher's knowledge and self-efficacy development.

Emphasis on Virtual Instruction

Teacher preparation programs should incorporate components related to the development, analysis, and assessment of virtual instruction models. Even when schools reopened after the initial school shutdowns, teacher preparation program leaders still showed an interest in and prioritization of virtual instruction components in their programs (Choate et al., 2021; VanLone et al., 2021). More exposure to technology during preservice results in a higher confidence which, in turn, increases abilities with technology (S. E. Anderson & Maninger, 2007).

This component may come with its own set of challenges. First, teacher preparation programs are attempting to implement new virtual or hybrid learning models within their existing budgetary constraints. Without additional resources, programs find it difficult to implement new mediums for conducting virtual instruction (Choate et al., 2021). Additionally, teacher preparation programs report that additional parental authorization is required when students are in a virtual setting and being recorded. These additional steps of producing signatures on forms with various languages is considered difficult to manage, particularly during the pandemic (Choate et al., 2021).

One way to embed the emphasis on specific virtual instruction skills is to embed micro-credentials into the teacher preparation program. Micro-credentials focus on a set of specific skills based on a teachers' performance and can range across many disciplines (Darling-Hammond & Hyler, 2020). Focusing professional development on micro-credentialing allows teachers to focus on the specific skills that they need and are more meaningful for their own practice and content (Hunt et al., 2020). Furthermore, decision-makers in teacher preparation programs should be thoughtful about future budgeting, to ensure that new technologies can be accommodated.

Embedded TPACK Skill Recognition

Including the TPACK framework within the teacher preparation program may have positive effects on students' understanding and application of these skills (Drajati et al., 2021; Kartimi et al., 2021; Miguel-Revilla et al., 2020). Though all teacher preparation programs already include components of pedagogy, content, and technological skills, the suggestion is to be deliberate in addressing TPACK understanding and knowledge.

Drajati et al. (2021) asserted that incorporating TPACK skills in lesson planning had a positive impact on teachers. Their recommendation was to suggest that teacher education programs incorporate TPACK into their program so that they have that experience as preservice teachers. In addition, Drajati et al. found that using TPACK in their lesson planning allowed these teachers to design critically to use technology in an effective manner. They implemented technology in different ways to address the issue of students not joining class due to poor Internet connections, by providing asynchronous technologically enhanced options to those students. Additionally, the teachers were more motivated to use technology they had not used before and analyze ways that it intersected with pedagogical skills.

In a study of preservice teachers over a 2-year period, Miguel-Revilla et al. (2020) used a questionnaire to assess the teachers' TPACK competencies before and after an applied intervention. The questionnaire, TPACK-21, was developed by Valtonen et al. (2017) and incorporates all the components of TPACK while including a 21st century perspective of the pedagogical component. Initially, teachers were not confident in integrating technology with their pedagogical skills, but after the intervention, they were able to articulate confidence.

In particular, Kartimi et al. (2021) found that enhancing preservice teachers' TPACK skills assisted with their online learning during COVID-19. In this study of chemistry teachers adapting to their virtual learning environments, the teachers recognized that their TPK was critical in keeping students engaged and motivated during remote instruction (Kartimi et al., 2021). The teachers were challenged with teaching critical thinking skills and keeping students on-task with practical skills in science. Additionally, they also had to determine how to assess students on the skills they acquired during this instruction, all without prior training in these modalities.

Coaching

Coaching during preservice school placements has been shown to make a positive impact on the teacher's abilities and competencies (Adulyasas & Temdee, 2021; Bozkurt, 2016; Cohen et al., 2020; Hofer & Grandgenett, 2012). One of the struggles of novice teachers is the need to learn strategies in their first years of teaching, but research has shown that those skills can be improved through a coaching model. Coaching, or verbal persuasion, is also one of the components of Bandura's (1977) theory of self-efficacy, and could be a critical factor in the way that people develop self-efficacy.

In a study that observed the impact of peer coaching on in-service and preservice teachers, Adulyasas and Temdee (2021) found that the coaching that centered around TPACK skills not only increased the teachers' TPACK competencies, but also had an impact on student performance. In this research, it was reported that before the peer coaching process, the teachers reported themselves to be at the lowest levels of TPACK understanding in that they could use the technology and recognize an alignment between the technology and the content. However, after the peer coaching model was employed, the same teachers could not only fully integrate technology effectively into their lessons, but could also evaluate the effectiveness in the classroom environment (Adulyasas & Temdee, 2021).

Coaching or mentoring during COVID-19 presented its own set of challenges. Teacher preparation programs should consider how they can allow for more flexibility in mentoring and coaching in the future. Coaching can occur virtually to ease time constraints and create innovative ways to accommodate coaching techniques (Assunção Flores & Gago, 2020). During the pandemic, preservice teachers needed very quick turnaround time from their mentors to provide feedback, simply based on the fast-paced nature of day-to-day instruction in remote school. Mentors found that virtualizing their mentoring process required long hours to provide quick feedback, but the online tools provided more flexibility (Assunção Flores & Gago, 2020).

Another way that teacher preparation programs can incorporate coaching is through peer coaching. Peer coaching can provide a safe place to provide and receive feedback from others in the same position in the hierarchy as the learner (Showers & Joyce, 1996). Through collaborative conversations with peers, teachers can develop their own knowledge and perspectives as well as increase reflective practices. The peer coaching model has shown some success in developing TPACK skills in preservice teachers (Jang & Chen, 2010).

Opportunities for Reflection

Teachers need opportunities to reflect on their practice in order to make a lasting impact (Glazer et al., 2005; Hu & Fyfe, 2010; Nguyen & Bower, 2018). Journaling is one way a teacher can reflect on their practice. After an initial trial of a technology or lesson, reflective journaling can provide the teacher an opportunity to modify their approach based on the demands of their classroom (Glazer et al., 2005).

Preservice teachers need time to reflect on the new teaching methodologies they use, especially with technology. The act of reflection can be extremely helpful in preparation programs, because the preservice teacher has mentor teachers and faculty with whom to share the reflection. Practitioners should ensure that they create those opportunities within the curriculum to allow for reflection. Those practitioners can provide expertise feedback on their reflection and help to build on the preservice teacher's learning experience.

Place Preservice Teachers in High-Demand Communities

As schools are faced with staffing shortages (Goldhaber et al., 2020), teacher preparation programs can place preservice teachers in communities of high-demand to help alleviate this burden (Darling-Hammond & Hyler, 2020; Goldhaber et al., 2020). According to Goldhaber et al. (2020), there may be a connection between proximity to a teacher preparation program and a school's staffing difficulties. One way to combat this is to place preservice teachers in schools where there is a high need for qualified staff. Where geographic distance is a concern, mentor teachers can use technology, like high quality audio and visual equipment, to virtually watch and mentor teachers (Goldhaber et al., 2020).

HOW TO SUPPORT FACULTY IN THESE SHIFTS

In the same way that teachers are required to adapt to the shifts in education with more technology, faculty at teacher preparation programs must also adjust to the new curricular approaches. This may require a deep dive into current curriculum and programmatic placings to determine what modifications are necessary. Decision-makers at teacher preparation programs should also be thoughtful about providing resources to their faculty, such as time, support, and well-rounded budgets, to accomplish their goals. As De Vera et al. (2021) stated,

Teacher education institutions must intensify in equipping teachers with knowledge on integrating technology in lesson preparations. The government must provide resources for the teachers that will help them prepare instructional materials such as ICT rooms, technicians for technical support, laptops, and internet connectivity. (p. 63)

Changes in curriculum will only be impactful if the faculty teaching these courses are well-versed and prepared. Faculty should be directly involved in planning for changes. There should be a clear expectation of including technology integration into course objectives, as opposed to the use of technology for productivity or presentation of material (Lewis, 2015).

Teacher educators should also visit schools to observe current situations. They should understand and be able to identify TPACK and the overlaps of each knowledge area in observations of teachers. The collaborations between teacher preparation programs and schools have never been more important. Understanding post pandemic schools is critical for teacher preparation, and the best way to accomplish this is to be in the classroom.

Connections with alumni can also make a big impact. During the pandemic, schools were using their alumni networks to work with preservice teachers, in the absence of in-person student teaching experiences (Darling-Hammond & Hyler, 2020). These alumni connections can also be helpful for faculty as they determine the current state of classrooms. As stated in the CAEP (2022) standards, teacher preparation programs should be reflective of their completers' effectiveness based on their preparation.

Faculty will also need support in professional development. Decision-makers should be thoughtful about giving faculty the time and resources to learn about new technologies. They should be given time to collaborate on lessons, and further, to reflect on their embedding of TPACK skills. Faculty should be encouraged to engage in PLNs on social media, for their own professional growth and to model proper use for the preservice teachers. Through abiding by given guidelines, such as the CAEP (2022) standards, faculty can establish their own competencies and can therefore assist their students with addressing technological and pedagogical skills (Lewis, 2015).

Certification requirements and mandatory exams for teacher certification may change in the wake of the pandemic (Hill, 2021). As states reconsider teacher certification processes, teacher preparation program faculty will be responsible for adjusting to correspond with any new guidelines. This requires that faculty remain flexible and resilient as well, because changes may occur quickly and without much notice.

FURTHER RESEARCH

Studies from the impacts of the COVID-19 pandemic will continue for years. As schools take the time to modify and reflect on new and modified practices, teacher preparation programs can continue to adapt to meet the new needs of teaching and learning. Future research is needed in this area to benefit novice teachers, teacher preparation programs, and schools.

The first area for suggested future research is in how teacher preparation programs can develop a structure to continuously adapt their curriculum and programming to align best with schools and the particular needs of preservice and novice teachers. This could include partnerships with receiving schools, clearly structured vertical articulation, and circle-back support from their graduated students. Further research is needed globally to determine how teacher preparation programs have evolved since the pandemic and how these enhancements have made an impact on novice teachers entering the workforce. For example, what new courses or course modifications were put in place that made an impact on preservice teachers' self-efficacy for using technology? Additionally, what methodologies were implemented in the teacher preparation program that exposed students to authentic applications of technology in classrooms?

A second area of further study that is needed is to assess the value of the changes brought since the pandemic. Longitudinal studies that follow preservice teachers through to their novice teacher days to assess how their preparation program has affected their self-efficacy in the areas of TPACK knowledge and their self-efficacy for technology use would be helpful in providing teacher preparation programs with data to modify their offerings. Studies that follow an individual from preservice to novice teacher may be helpful in understanding how teachers make that transition into their careers.

A third area of further research is to explore the value of mentor teachers' impact on a novice teachers' self-efficacy in the components of TPACK. Since mentor teachers are one of the largest sources of support for novice teachers, their impact should be studied in regard to the technological and pedagogical competencies of the novice teacher. What strategies can the mentor teacher employ to help a novice teacher with TPACK competencies? Do schools have the resources necessary to improve and modify mentoring so that it can address more TPACK components? Do schools continue to modify the mentor teachers' framework so that it addresses new needs of post pandemic novice teachers?

The fourth and final area of further research centers on the TPACK framework and how the pandemic may have affected its foundational presence in teacher preparation. Future research can focus on how necessary TPACK skills may differ between content areas or grade levels. For example, can a successful teacher have more PK skills than CK skills? Additionally, does having more TK balance a lower PK base? Mishra and Koehler (2006) discussed a balance of the three knowledge areas of TPACK. Post pandemic, are more novice teachers entering with more TK than PK or CK? How does this make an impact on the new generation of teachers and what effects does it have on students?

CONCLUSION

The COVID-19 pandemic affected education in many ways and, in turn, is changing the platform for teacher preparation. Teachers have reported that if they had been better prepared for teaching with technology and been more exposed to effective methods of teaching with technology, they would have had an easier transition to the emergency remote and hybrid teaching environments of the pandemic (Trust & Whalen, 2020). Teacher skillsets have been reprioritized post pandemic, and schools now need teachers who have strong pedagogical and technological skills. Teacher preparation programs need to ensure they are thoughtfully incorporating TPACK into their curriculum, for both preservice teachers and faculty.

Teacher preparation programs are well established in countries worldwide, but there is room for improvement, particularly for addressing current school needs. As Hoffer and Grandgenett (2012) explained,

> *Teacher preparation programs are typically educational "mosaics" with a variety of courses, student experiences, and instructional support mechanisms brought to bear on a student's targeted development into an effective teacher. Within such a program mosaic, it is obvious that TPACK should be examined in a variety of ways and at various points with a program to be truly useful for program refinement. (p. 102)*

In reflecting on the lessons learned from the pandemic, teacher preparation programs can use these experiences to modify their offerings and approaches to better prepare the next generation of teachers.

REFERENCES

Adulyasas, L., & Temdee, N. (2021). The effects of integrated technology-based approach and peer coaching in teaching geometry: A closer look at teachers' TPACK and students' understanding. *Turkish Journal of Computer and Mathematics Education*, *12*(3), 5695–5708. doi:10.17762/turcomat.v12i3.2244

Akiri, E., & Dori, Y. J. (2022). Professional growth of novice and experienced STEM teachers. *Journal of Science Education and Technology*, *31*(1), 129–142. doi:10.100710956-021-09936-x

Anderson, L. M., & Stillman, J. A. (2013). Student teaching's contribution to preservice teacher development: A review of research focused on the preparation of teachers for urban and high-needs contexts. *Review of Educational Research*, *83*(1), 3–69. doi:10.3102/0034654312468619

Anderson, S. E., & Maninger, R. M. (2007). Preservice teachers' abilities, beliefs, and intentions regarding technology integration. *Journal of Educational Computing Research*, *37*(2), 151–172. doi:10.2190/H1M8-562W-18J1-634P

Antoniou, J. (2021). *Perceptions of novice teachers' TPACK gained from teacher preparation programs: A mixed methods research study* (Publication No. 29065154) [Doctoral dissertation, New Jersey City University]. ProQuest Dissertations & Theses Global.

Archambault, L., & Crippen, K. (2009). Examining TPACK among K-12 online distance educators in the United States. *Contemporary Issues in Technology & Teacher Education*, *9*(1), 71–88. https://citejournal.org/volume-9/issue-1-09/general/examinin g-tpack-among-k-12-online-distance-educators-in-the-united-s tates/

Assunção Flores, M., & Gago, M. (2020). Teacher education in times of COVID-19 pandemic in Portugal: National, institutional and pedagogical responses. *Journal of Education for Teaching*, *46*(4), 507–516. Advance online publication. doi:10.1080/02607476.2020.1799709

Bandura, A. (1977). Self-efficacy: Toward a unifying theory of behavioral change. *Psychological Review*, *84*(2), 191–215. doi:10.1037/0033-295X.84.2.191 PMID:847061

Bozkurt, G. (2016). Mathematics teachers and ICT: Factors affecting pre-service use in school placements. *International Journal of Research in Education and Science*, *2*(2), 453–468. doi:10.21890/ijres.16161

Byker, E. (2014). Needing TPACK without knowing it: Integrating educational technology in social studies. *Social Studies Research & Practice*, *9*(3), 106–117. doi:10.1108/SSRP-03-2014-B0008

Choate, K., Goldhaber, D., & Theobald, R. (2021, April). The effects of COVID-19 on teacher preparation. *Phi Delta Kappan*, *102*(7), 52–57. doi:10.1177/00317217211007340

Cohen, J., Wong, V., Krishnamachari, A., & Berlin, R. (2020). Teacher coaching in a simulated environment. *Educational Evaluation and Policy Analysis*, *42*(2), 208–231. doi:10.3102/0162373720906217

Council for the Accreditation of Educator Preparation. (2019, February). *2013 CAEP standards*. https://caepnet.org/~/media/Files/caep/standards/caep-standards-one-pager-0219.pdf?la=en

Council for the Accreditation of Educator Preparation. (2022). *2022 initial level standards*. https://caepnet.org/~/media/Files/caep/standards/2022-initial-standards-1-pager-final.pdf?la=en

Darling-Hammond, L., & Hyler, M. E. (2020). Preparing educators for the time of COVID… and beyond. *European Journal of Teacher Education*, *43*(4), 457–465. doi:10.1080/02619768.2020.1816961

De Vera, J. L., Andrada, M. D., Bello, A. Q., & De Vera, M. J. D. (2021, June). Teachers' competencies in educational technology integration in instructional methodologies in the new normal. *Lukad: An Online Journal of Pedagogy*, *1*(1), 63–84. https://lukad.org/wp-content/uploads/2021/07/volume1_issue1_devera_et_al_June2021.pdf

Drajati, N. A., Rakerda, H., Sulistyawati, H., Nurkamto, J., & Ilmi, M. (2021). Investigating the adoption of TPACK-21CL by English pre-service teachers in a COVID-19 teaching practicum. *Indonesian Journal of Applied Linguistics*, *11*(1), 124–133. doi:10.17509/ijal.v11i1.34625

Ewing, L.-A. (2021). Mentoring novice teachers. *Mentoring & Tutoring*, *29*(1), 50–69. doi:10.1080/13611267.2021.1899585

Figg, C., & Jaipal, K. (2009). Unpacking TPACK: TPK characteristics supporting successful implementation. In I. Gibson, R. Weber, K. McFerrin, R. Carlsen, & D. Willis (Eds.), *Proceedings of SITE 2009–Society for Information Technology & Teacher Education International Conference* (pp. 4069–4073). Association for the Advancement of Computing in Education (AACE).

Fuad, M., Ariyani, F., Suyanto, E., & Shidiq, A. S. (2020). Exploring teachers' TPCK: Are Indonesian language teachers ready for online learning during the COVID-19 outbreak? *Universal Journal of Educational Research*, *8*(11B), 6091–6102. doi:10.13189/ujer.2020.082245

Glazer, E., Hannafin, M. J., & Song, L. (2005). Promoting technology integration through collaborative apprenticeship. *Educational Technology Research and Development*, *53*(4), 57–67. doi:10.1007/BF02504685

Goldhaber, D., Krieg, J., Naito, N., & Theobald, R. (2020). Making the most of student teaching: The importance of mentors and scope for change. *Education Finance and Policy*, *15*(3), 581–591. doi:10.1162/edfp_a_00305

Hill, J. (2021). Pre-service teacher experiences during COVID 19: Exploring the uncertainties between clinical practice and distance learning. *Journal of Practical Studies in Education*, *2*(2), 1–13. doi:10.46809/jpse.v2i2.18

Hoffer, M., & Grandgenett, N. (2012). TPACK development in teacher education: A longitudinal study of preservice teachers in a secondary M.A.Ed. program. *Journal of Research on Technology in Education*, *45*(1), 83–106. doi:10.1080/15391523.2012.10782598

Hu, C., & Fyfe, V. (2010). Impact of a new curriculum on pre-service teachers' technical, pedagogical and content knowledge (TPACK) [Paper Presentation]. In *Proceedings ASCILITE 2010* (pp. 184–189). https://www.ascilite.org/conferences/sydney10/procs/Chun_Hu-concise.pdf

Hunt, T., Carter, R., Zhang, L., & Yang, S. (2020). Micro-credentials: The potential of personalized professional development. *Development and Learning in Organizations*, *34*(2), 33–35. doi:10.1108/DLO-09-2019-0215

International Society for Technology in Education. (2022). *ISTE standards: Educators*. https://www.iste.org/standards/iste-standards-for-teachers

Jang, S. J., & Chen, K. C. (2010). From PCK to TPACK: Developing a transformative model for pre-service science teachers. *Journal of Science Education and Technology*, *19*(6), 553–564. doi:10.100710956-010-9222-y

Kartal, T., & Dilek, I. (2021). Preservice science teachers' TPACK development in a technology-enhanced science teaching method course. *Journal of Education in Science, Environment and Health*, *7*(4), 339–353. doi:10.21891/jeseh.994458

Kartimi, K., Gloria, R. Y., & Anugrah, I. R. (2021). Chemistry online distance learning during the COVID-10 outbreak: Do TPACK and teachers' attitude matter? *Indonesian Journal of Science Education*, *10*(2), 228–240. doi:10.15294/jpii.v10i2.28468

Kearney, M., Maher, D., & Pham, L. (2019). Investigating pre-service teachers' informally-developed online professional learning networks. *Australasian Journal of Educational Technology*, *36*(1), 21–36. doi:10.14742/ajet.4766

Koehler, M., & Mishra, P. (2009). What is technological pedagogical content knowledge? *Contemporary Issues in Technology & Teacher Education*, *9*(1), 60–70. https://citejournal.org/volume-9/issue-1-09/general/what-is-technological-pedagogicalcontent-knowledge/

Lei, J. (2009). Digital natives as preservice teachers: What technology preparation is needed? *Journal of Computing in Teacher Education*, *25*(3), 87–97. https://files.eric.ed.gov/fulltext/EJ835233.pdf

Lewis, C. L. (2015). Preservice teachers' ability to identify technology standards: Does curriculum matter? *Contemporary Issues in Technology & Teacher Education, 15*(2), 235–254. https://citejournal.org/volume-15/issue-2-15/current-practice/preservice-teachers-ability-to-identify-technology-standards-does-curriculum-matter/

Martin, B. (2015). Successful implementation of TPACK in teacher preparation programs. *International Journal on Integrating Technology in Education, 4*(1), 17–26. doi:10.5121/ijite.2015.4102

Miguel-Revilla, D., Martínez-Ferreira, J. M., & Sánchez-Agustí, M. (2020). Assessing the digital competence of educators in social studies: An analysis in initial teacher training in using the TPACK-21 model. *Australasian Journal of Educational Technology, 36*(2), 1–12. doi:10.14742/ajet.5281

Mishra, P., & Koehler, M. J. (2006). Technological pedagogical content knowledge: A framework for teacher knowledge. *Teachers College Record: The Voice of Scholarship in Education, 108*(6), 1017–1054. doi:10.1111/j.1467-9620.2006.00684.x

Nguyen, G. N. H., & Bower, M. (2018). Novice teacher technology-enhanced learning design practices: The case of the silent pedagogy. *British Journal of Educational Technology, 49*(6), 1027–1043. doi:10.1111/bjet.12681

Pozo-Rico, T., Gilar-Corbí, R., Izquierdo, A., & Castejón, J.-L. (2020). Teacher training can make a difference: Tools to overcome the impact of COVID-19 on primacy schools. An experimental study. *International Journal of Environmental Research and Public Health, 17*(22), 8633. doi:10.3390/ijerph17228633 PMID:33233750

Showers, B., & Joyce, B. (1996). The evolution of peer coaching. *Educational Leadership, 53*(6), 12–16. https://www.ascd.org/el/articles/the-evolution-of-peer-coaching

Spătărelu, E. M. (2020). Beginner teacher in the recent research: A review of literature. *Journal of Education Studies*, 2(2), 107–122.

Trust, T., & Whalen, J. (2020). Should teachers be trained in emergency remote teaching? Lessons learned from the COVID-19 pandemic. *Journal of Technology and Teacher Education, 28*(2), 189–199.

Valtonen, T., Sointu, E., Kukkonen, J., Kontkanen, S., Lambert, M. C., & Mäkitalo-Siegl, K. (2017). TPACK updated to measure pre-service teachers' twenty-first century skills. *Australasian Journal of Educational Technology, 33*(3), 15–31. doi:10.14742/ajet.3518

VanLone, J., Pansé-Barone, C., & Long, K. (2021). Teacher preparation and the COVID-19 disruption: Understanding the impact and implications for novice teachers. *International Journal of Educational Research Open, 3*, 100120. Advance online publication. doi:10.1016/j.ijedro.2021.100120 PMID:35059675

Williams, M. K., Foulger, T. S., & Wetzel, K. (2009). Preparing preservice teachers for 21st century classrooms: Transforming attitudes and behaviors about technology. *Journal of Technology and Teacher Education, 17*(3), 393–418.

KEY TERMS AND DEFINITIONS

CK: Content knowledge.

Education Post Pandemic: The concept of education and how it has been impacted by the COVID-19 pandemic.

Higher Education: Postsecondary education, usually at a 2- or 4-year institution.

Novice Teachers: Teachers who are new to the field and may have less than 5 years of experience.

PCK: Pedagogical content knowledge.

PK: Pedagogical knowledge.

Preservice Teachers: Individuals who are immersed a program to learn to become a teacher.

TCK: Technological content knowledge.

Teacher Preparation Programs: Programs at accredited institutions of higher education to prepare preservice teachers.

TK: Technological knowledge.

TPACK: Technological, pedagogical, content knowledge.

TPK: Technological pedagogical knowledge.

Chapter 19
Case Studies in Remote Living and Remote Learning

Cari Marks
New Jersey City University, USA

Christopher Shamburg
https://orcid.org/0000-0001-8413-0299
New Jersey City University, USA

ABSTRACT

Students and families who live in remote sections of the United States had unique challenges with remote learning during the COVID-19 pandemic. This multiple case study profiles four families in remote parts of Appalachia in the United States as they lived and learned during the shutdown. These stories highlight the struggles, innovations, and resilience of an often-neglected population in discussions of the digital divide. Each family portrait was developed through in-depth interviews with several generations and a review of related documents.

INTRODUCTION

When you think of the current trend of working remotely, you likely think of working from home. Most of us generally enjoy the opportunity to work from home as it allows us our chosen comforts and potentially the opportunity to sleep in a bit. However, what if your home were in a remote location, without strong, consistent Internet access? What if you also had children, and in addition to your work, you needed to help them with remote learning through the use of the Internet in that remote location?

The decisions, struggles, and rewards of families living at the end of the first quarter of the 21st century without access to broadband or strong, consistent Internet connectivity within their homes offers insights into our society's contemporary use of educational technology. As rural education becomes a growing concern globally, these cases and lessons are applicable across the world. In this chapter we profile four families in case studies who choose to live in more remote sections of Appalachia--in areas that do not offer affordable, reliable Internet access. Three of these families educate their children in public schools

DOI: 10.4018/978-1-6684-6092-4.ch019

and one homeschooled their children at the time. In this book on current trends, this chapter serves as a contrast: the background to the everyday uses of educational technology that most people in modern society intuitively accept as constants.

Families living in remote locations had always tried to maintain a balance between the use of technology and living in a home outside of ubiquitous technology access. When learning went remote for students in March 2020, these families living across the digital divide remained creative and intentional in their approaches to connecting their children with education and connecting themselves with necessary online tasks and work, even though the tasks became more difficult and less fulfilling. In 2013 physicist and futurist Michio Kaku predicted that soon networked technology will be "everywhere and nowhere, ubiquitous yet hidden, just like electricity and running water. The cloud will follow us silently and seamlessly, carrying out our wishes anytime, anywhere." This prediction would characterize the lives of many people in the developed world. However, we should temper Kaku's words with the prediction of a cable service technician working in a remote section of Appalachia who remarked to one of the interview participants, "When I saw the address, I was afraid it was here. The only way you'll get Internet access is if you can remove the top of that mountain."

The research in this chapter is based on extensive interviews, combined with contextual data from public records, about the families in Appalachia who have no, or severely limited, access to the Internet. Interviews with children and parents were synthesized with existing data such as census records and local laws, existing literature, national trends and school policies to create rich, detailed descriptions of their experiences dealing with Internet access during the COVID-19 shutdown. The COVID-19 shutdown is a catalyst and a trigger to examine a perennial issue in the United States–uneven Internet connectivity. While much existing research correlates connectivity with economic status, it must be noted that there are many living in the United States who have to negotiate a connected world, unconnected, without viable choices to live otherwise even though they work middle class jobs. This chapter will present descriptions of these families and their lives managing educational technology for the remote learning of their children as well as managing technology for their own jobs and lives as citizens.

Participants were selected based on where they lived and their level of Internet access, economic status was not a direct factor in their selection. Participants were initially recruited through the primary researcher's personal and professional network, as an educator in Appalachia for 19 years. During this first series of interviews, snowball sampling was used; the participating families were asked to help identify other families with limited Internet access in the area. The interviews were completed at the participants' homes and by phone. A total of six households were involved, and 24 interviews were conducted: 14 adults and 10 children ranging from elementary to high school age. The chapter will present four cases of the lives of these families, their technology needs, and their approaches to obtain and use technology.

There is a consensus that broadband Internet service is beneficial not only to education but also to economic development, healthcare, civic engagement, and agriculture (Whitacre, 2021). However, there is a debate concerning the pivotal factor of these benefits—availability or adoption of broadband technologies. Availability is the presence of the infrastructure and adoption is the opting-in of people to subscribe and use broadband services. Broadband availability has been shown to increase commercial firms' location decisions in rural areas (Kim & Orazem, 2017), migration to rural areas (Mahasuweerachai et al., 2010), home values (Deller & Whitacre, 2019), agricultural land values and profits (Kandilov et al., 2017), and farming productivity (Lopiccalo, 2020).

However, the focus on adoption is also important. Research has shown that adoption is pivotal for increases in income levels and job growth (Whitacre et al., 2014). Moreover, rural broadband adoption has been shown to increase civic engagement (Whitacre & Manlove, 2016). The National Telecommunications and Information Administration found a consistent 5–10 percentage gap between rural and urban residents for Internet use in places where broadband technologies were equitably available. The focus on availability and adoption can have profound consequences on policy decisions--whether state and federal programs should be focused on wires and satellites or subscriptions and training.

The issue of the digital divide in the rural United States was a problem before the pandemic. With sparse populations, difficult topographies, and lower levels of characteristics that correlate to adoption (e.g. education, income, younger populations), rural locations offer a difficult profit margin for Internet Service Providers (Whitacare, 2021). The lowered profit margin and difficulties in crossing over certain types of topography reduce the number of service providers who have bridged the digital divide with services comparable to those found in non-rural settings. Moreover, 58% of rural Americans believed that access to high-speed Internet was a problem in their area (Anderson, 2018). Pre-pandemic, the digital divide was salient in both urban and rural communities, with an estimated 30% of households with school age children without a connection or device for online learning (Chandra et al., 2020; Horrigan, 2020). Significantly, Horrigan's research points out that during the pandemic US schools were successful in getting devices to more students, yet not in increasing Internet access for educational use (2020).

During the beginning of the move to remote learning, only 28% of rural schools were able to provide HotSpots which provided access for their students, compared to 48% of urban schools, and rural schools were only able to provide devices to 48% of their students as opposed to 85% in urban districts (Gross & Opalka, 2020). Furthermore, Gross and Opalka found that rural districts were less likely to take attendance or monitor student engagement with courses and course materials during remote learning. Rural school districts in the United States did try innovative solutions: beyond providing hot spots, some districts created community maps for internet access, upgrading school wifi to reach parking lots, building workspaces in school parking lots, and moving wifi-enabled vehicles into rural areas (Nicola et al., 2020; Thompson, 2020). Others circumvented the need for Internet access by hand delivering printed packets and pre-loaded USB drives (Whitacre, 2021).

The definition of rural has grown in complexity and needs to accommodate diverse characteristics.. There is a growing movement to recognize rurality as a complex phenomenon (Ledger & Fuqua, 2021; Organization for Economic Cooperation and Development, 2019; Thier et al., 2021). The OECD (Organization for Economic Cooperation and Development has been moving to recognize that rurality involves diverse and complex socio-economic systems (OECD, 2006, 2019). Nevertheless, despite this diversity of 'rural' Mueller et al. (2021) found consistent effects of the COVID-19 pandemic on rural populations in the United States "with significant negative impacts on unemployment, overall life satisfaction, mental health, and economic outlook" (p. 1). Conversely, rurality, broadly speaking, can be a positive force in academic achievement. Rurality can be a boost to academic achievement for rural youth because of strong community capital and attachment that correlate to college completion (Byun et al. 2012; Petrin et al., 2014). One nuanced area of existing research on COVID in the rural United States is that rural adults were more likely to continue working (Brooks et al., 2021) but less likely to work remotely (Callaghan et al., 2021) than their urban and suburban counterparts.

The Reinback Family: "Getting Web"

William, Marie, and their two elementary school children, Michael and Autumn, live on more than 25 acres of land in a remote area which borders a national forest. Michael and Autumn enjoy exploring the woods and creeks to discover wildlife and evidence of wildlife, bike riding, and participating in imagination games they create based on their moments and moods. Their home is six miles from a main highway. On that highway, driving into the county, there is a sign announcing, "Entering Virginia's Technology Corridor"; however, the Reinback family does not have stable Internet access in their home. Before the shutdown, the family balanced the lack of stable Internet by spending mornings together "getting web" at a local coffee shop or the local public library. The time allowed the family to be a part of the local community, enjoy local fare, peruse book selections, support local businesses, while also providing the technology access necessary to pay their bills, download podcasts and apps, complete schoolwork, and participate in online forums. These were aspects of life that William and Marie felt were important for Michael and Autumn to understand. When schools shut down to operate remotely, the family's source of home Internet access–the coffee shop and the public library--shut down, too.

To assist all residents without Internet access, the county set up a mobile Internet HotSpot at the municipal recycling center, which the Reinback family had always called "the dump." The dump was located less than eight miles from the family's home, just off of the main highway. During the school shut down, when William took a day off from his job as an essential worker so that he may help with the children, William would drive Michael and Autumn—grades 1st and 3rd--to the dump with a variety of charging devices to ensure they would maintain enough battery life during their stay. The children would use the time at the dump to work on their school tasks or enjoy iPad time. Autumn liked to finish her school work and take her remaining time to watch YouTube videos; during the spring of the 2020 shutdown, Michael had no online school work, and used the majority of his time playing Internet-based apps and waving to people coming drop off their refuse--he had learned to be a friendly community member from the days of the public library and coffee shop trips. During his dump time, Michael particularly enjoyed playing an app that allowed him to type in comments and responses to his "friends" who were also playing the game, and he often created imaginary scenarios concerning where his "friends" were spending their web time--many times those imagined scenarios involved the minivans that were entering the dump site. Their father continued to attend and host zoom meetings, send emails, and receive/analyze data through Internet based platforms that were essential to his job that day while trying to take time to explain to Michael the way the Internet worked in other homes.

Marie was a high school teacher. She completed her master's degree and a certificate program during and post-shutdown. Marie would work in the school building as often as she was allowed to complete her work and her class work. When schools initially shut down in March 2020, Marie was provided with a MiFi device to allow her to gather whatever connection she could from her home. The MiFi device was helpful; however, Marie quickly learned that long videos, bulky websites with videos that would automatically play, and the use of multiple tabs at once were too much for the MiFi connection. For her students, Marie used Screencastify to create lessons to introduce concepts, apply literary terms, and appropriately summarize previous texts, but the MiFi did not provide a connection that was strong enough to allow her to save and share those screencasts with her students via Google Classroom; in fact, there were several times that Marie made screencasts which never succeeded in uploading, and thus the time she spent was wasted.

When Marie was unable to work within her school building, or was unable to post assignments from her home, she would drive to locations that also enabled strong Internet connection with Michael and Autumn. Marie would upload her screencasts from the grocery store parking lot that was ten miles from their home through the use of free wireless Internet supplied by a local Internet provider, or she worked from one of the school's parking lots which were even further. Marie's students completed assignments which included various technology based on students' own preferences--videos, Visme, Kami, Screencastify, SnapChat, online book creations, pdfs of photographs and artwork, Google platforms, etc.--and Marie would often make several trips to procure WiFi in order to view and score the students' work and provide feedback in a timely manner. There were several occasions that Marie would begin working in one location and then discover that the Internet connection was not strong enough to support her tasks, so she would then drive on to another location.

In the return to school in fall of 2020, on the days and weeks when local schools unexpectedly shut down and teachers were to instruct students from home, Marie would host Google Meets for her students--with her children in the back seat working on their own school work--from the grocery store parking lot. Marie tried once to host a meeting from her home, but she was unable to continue with an Internet connection long enough to say "hello"; that morning, to solve the problem, her husband made a last-minute decision to take the children to work with him, and she drove tearfully (and quickly) to the closest WiFi to connect with the last ten minutes of her first class. After learning that she would not be able to connect from home, Marie would also spend time completing online tasks with the children in the back seat as she was parked outside of the library, which had closed for patron's entry, but graciously (or accidently) left their Wi-Fi on. Several times, Marie connected with her students individually via Google Meet in order to discuss projects and papers that the students had completed; each of these meetings occurred in either her car, a picnic table outside of a location that provided free WiFi, or the school building.

For a few of her certificate course meetings, Marie needed to join the 7 p.m. meetings from her home when her husband was working out-of-town. In one meeting, Marie inquired if it could be possible to request that her peers to leave their cameras off, as she had discovered fewer "live feed" connections could enable her to remain in meetings from her home with an acceptable amount of lag, but she was told that she would just need to watch the class at a later time. Tearfully, Marie watched as her computer disconnected, and she began brainstorming where and how she would find the time to watch the hour-long session within the next few days.

In the fall of 2020, the school division provided a MiFi for Michael and Autumn to use, and each child was provided a Chromebook. To increase the reception of the MiFi device, William purchased and installed an Antenna Booster on the family's home. To represent attendance each day that schools were closed for cleaning, or closed based on CDC recommendations, the children were required to sign in via a Google form. The Google form was to be completed by each child and served to provide information for the children's teachers about whether the students needed assistance in their assignments. When the MiFi was unable to connect the children well enough to submit the Google form, Marie drove them to either a grocery store or a school parking lot to submit the form. Subsequently, Marie would receive information from her own school about her students' needs and would reach out to assist them as needed. The needs of Marie's students would take Marie and her children to parking lots to allow for Google Meets, emails, and phone calls; however, Michael and Autumn did not have the Internet access necessary to preview their day's tasks, though they often completed the form with the assumption that their assignments would be manageable. When the tasks did not prove to be understandable, or the tasks would not load, days became more stressful.

Autumn and Michael's school work expectations in the fall of 2020 were often to complete online programs--iStation, iXL, Reflex, or Frax--and other options that were provided on a digital choice board that was shared via Google Classroom in a Google slide deck. Unfortunately, Autumn and Michael struggled with accessing their work at the same time, and there was an even greater struggle when the access had multiple tiers of expectation: Michael needed to access google classroom to find his assignments and links, then watch videos or complete an online platform task, and then submit a final snapshot of his work; Autumn needed to open her Google Slides in order to choose the HotSpot link from a choice board, and then she needed to return to the Google Slides to enter the information she gained. The two children were unable to work simultaneously from home because of the immense amount of Internet connectivity to access data that was necessary for each of them; this meant that the completion of their assignments took a minimum of twice as long to complete.

The children's many Google Slides were filled with pictures, interactive sections, and HotSpots, and both Michael and Autumn were forced to wait an extended period of time before they were able to arrive at the necessary slide because the entire deck was simply too large to load. Each time Autumn would leave and return to the google slide deck to enter answers to questions after watching the associated video from which she was to be learning, the slide deck would reload. This reloading of the slide deck would often take several minutes, and occasionally the reloads just never happened. As 1st and 3rd graders, the children understood the tasks that they were being asked to complete, but as 1st and 3rd graders, they found it difficult to understand why they could not complete the tasks provided to them by their teachers. Neither of the children had found tasks to be a struggle when they worked within their classrooms prior to the shutdown, but suddenly they regularly felt incapable. Often the children's knowledge and focus on the topics provided as assignments were blurred by the simple fact that they could not record their understanding in a fluid, sequential method, as the assignments were designed.

Ultimately, each day of work turned into a test of patience rather than a time for learning. Autumn often worked for more than five hours to try to complete her tasks before she was in tears and told to stop trying by a parent. At that point, either William or Marie would drive the children out for Internet access again after dinner, and Autumn would try to finish her tasks while Michael began working on his tasks (if he had not started working before Autumn). The children's school tasks often took the family members back and forth in thirty-minute round-trip drives to town to gain Internet access several times a day. When the tasks could not be completed, Marie or Autumn would have to email teachers to explain the problem. After several unaided requests from Marie that Autumn be allowed to complete a different task than iXL due to the lag, and frustration, Marie reached out to the school's principal. The principal suggested that Marie look at Autumn's history in order to better track her daughter's actual work focus. Marie did check her daughter's history to discover that her daughter had once opened an extra YouTube tab to attempt to listen to music while she worked. The emails and phone conversations served to belittle any accomplishments that the Reinback family should have felt based on the immense amount of dedication they had shown the assignments in the course of the day, and instead served to increase the ever-present tension in their home.

In the summer of 2021 Marie was faced with unexpected health issues that were unrelated to COVID, and she learned that doctor's offices were recommending virtual visits to patients. She attempted to join her doctor's appointment from her home only to be told that she must also have cell phone access for a call. In tears, she explained to the nurse practitioner that she was not able to have access to both devices at the same time while she remained in her home. At first, the nurse practitioner stated that Marie would be unable to be seen that day given the parameters, but as Marie pleaded that the nurse practitioner look at her address on a map to understand the issue, there was a concession to her situation.

While Marie was working through her health issues, she was also faced with a cell phone concern: Marie's mother's cell phone plan was attached to Marie's. Unfortunately, her mother's 3G phone was no longer going to be accepted as a device the cell phone company supported. Marie's mother could not enter the store to work out the issue due to the shutdown, and Marie could not use her cell phone in her home to work through the issue. Marie was again left to drive away from her home to find cell phone service to address the issues which ultimately led to Marie shopping for a new device for her mother online. The struggle to exist in the COVID-shutdown society never ceased, and the battles against the constant problems were never won because there were no changes that Marie and William could make, other than to move from their home.

Concerning the children's education, Michael continued to miss his friends as the shutdown-impacts continued into his 2nd grade of school in the fall of 2021. Michael began to try to reach out to his peers through the creation of Google Documents--Michael had taken note of the fact that he and his friends could type back and forth to one another in the document and engage "in real time" conversations which he called "texting." Unfortunately, the Google Document did not update well from his home, and he often sat with his computer waiting for the document to update only to wait so long while the computer tried to load that the action timed out.

Equally often, Michael sent several emails to his friends and sat waiting for responses to come back--not understanding that not all of his friends were allowed to use email at home. Sometimes, he and his friends would make plans as they left school to try to "find one another" in the online Prodigy game that they had been told about as a math game at school because they could type messages to one another in the game, but Michael quickly discovered that it was difficult to navigate and find his friends in that platform. In the first fall 2021 parent/teacher conference, his teacher remarked that it seemed that Michael often "just wanted to lean over and talk to the person beside him" during reading time, and his teacher noted that Michael seemed incredibly focused on the use of his Chromebook. Marie was again left trying to explain that her son wanted to experience connections with his friends, and he did not feel satiated by the ones he was able to make from his home due to shutdown restrictions, lack of Internet access, and his age.

Marie tried to complete her online tasks before her children and husband were out of bed in the mornings, usually beginning around 4 am. She learned that she could have one website (as long as it did not have embedded videos), and three Google document or slides tabs open at one time, and she could generally toggle between them; sometimes, depending on the weather, the documents would freeze up as they attempted to continue to save her progress. It was not unusual for her progress to be paused at least 30 times in each half hour of work. This caused her immense amounts of frustration, and she was often on edge by the time she needed to begin to help Michael and Autumn. The feelings of frustration that are caused by Internet struggles are not feelings that most people understand, and when Marie would attempt to relay the struggles to her children's teachers or her co-workers, she was typically left with her stress and the feeling that she had been dismissed and disregarded.

The Dawson's Calculus

The Dawson family has three boys who attend the local schools. The family lives between two mountains, accessible by one road and without strong Internet connectivity. Prior to the shutdown, the family would complete updates and information downloads as they shopped for groceries at Kroger and Walmart which were tasks that the family needed to complete each week. Depending on the amount of homework, the crowd at the store, and the shopping list, they would spend one to two hours strolling periodically peeking into the backpack with the computer and phone to make sure the transfers were moving undisturbed. At other times, the family would complete their device updates and downloads as they ate dinner together at restaurants chosen for their available Wi-Fi service. On those days, the family was able to enjoy time together in a social setting while completing their necessary digital updates. The updating process was a part of their daily and weekly life, and the process was one that naturally fit into the tasks that their family was already completing. In fact, their lives and connections with one another were enhanced by the meals that the family enjoyed together in social settings as well as by the time that the family spent together purchasing the items that they needed for their week ahead.

When the COVID shutdown occurred, the family was no longer able to download as they shopped or ate dinner together in a public place as a social connection. The act of updating their devices a few times a week was no longer sufficient to their lives' requirements of digital work. The opportunity to naturally embed their devices into their lives as fulfilling mechanisms of enjoyment was no longer the use of the digital devices. The devices were now to use for work, and the expectation of what they were to do with the devices was no longer left to their own choices; the choices were being dictated by work and school tasks created by others who did not seem to understand or care about the access that the family lacked within their home.

After the shutdown occurred, Sylvia began the day by driving the kids to the school parking lot to download the assignments, and then she would drive them home to complete the work. Dave's job had moved to being online, so he was required to use their home's limited Internet data for his work each day. This meant that Dave's day was spent in their home--away from Sylvia and the boys for most of the day. Sylvia was left to struggle with the boys' educational technology needs by herself.

From the school parking lot each morning, the boys would download their work. Jake, the oldest son, was a student in AP Calculus. After the downloading process, once the family had returned home, Jake would often become frustrated with work because his assignment was to watch videos to learn how to complete the problems, but the videos he was tasked with watching were often more than ten minutes long. Jake had opened the necessary tabs to download the videos while he was in the parking lot each morning--attempting to complete several downloads at once in order to save as much time as possible-- but the videos would often not play through later because, unbeknownst to him, they had not fully buffered while the family waited at the school. As an AP Calculus student who had As in the course before the shutdown, Jake understood that getting behind in coursework was not optimal; however, after the shutdown, both Jake and his parents discussed and came to an agreement that As may no longer be feasible given the learning constraints imposed by their home's Internet access. Jake and his parents all understood that he always worked to complete his assignments to the best of his accessible abilities.

Jake's younger brother, Lance, was given the bi-weekly assignment (sometimes more frequently) of creating a video of himself completing a homework task. Once he had created the video, he was required to upload that video to an online platform or FlipGrid. The videos would rarely save when he made them with his Chromebook, but when the videos did save he had trouble getting them to upload. These struggles often meant that Lance was forced to make the videos again when he was driven back to the school parking lot. This meant that he had to "re-complete" his assignments. Sylvia explained that the boys' homework would often require three trips back and forth to the school in the course of each day; as the pandemic stretched on, this repeated trip became a cumbersome reminder of what their home's location was not able to support.

During the pandemic, teachers were available to assist students with their assignments; however, the typical way to reach teachers was through email or the Google form that was completed, so that often meant that students were unable to know that there was a problem because they were unable to look at the assigned tasks before submitting the Google form. Sylvia was as supportive of her children's education as she could possibly be, but she admitted that she often felt frustrated with their assignments which required trips back and forth to the parking lot for Internet downloads, uploads, and further assignment clarification. All of the boys expressed frustration in not being able to connect with their friends through social media and gaming platforms--frustrations that were both highlighted and exacerbated by the COVID shutdown. While their friends connected and continued to build worlds, experiences, and camaraderie, her boys were spending their time and bandwidth attempting to get their schoolwork completed.

Sylvia wanted the boys to connect with their peers, but between Dave's need for their data for his work and the school's need for their data for assignments, there was just no extra for the children's aspirations to socialize. The Dawson family's frustrations with accessing technology as expected by their school, work, and society was so exacerbated in the time of the pandemic shutdown that the family began to question their home's value in relation to their needs. Ultimately, the family made the decision to move; unfortunately, the move happened too late for the family to avoid the struggles experienced during the time of the shutdown.

The Toneti Family

The Toneti family lives nine miles from a major highway. David has a job as an essential worker whose schedule varies by week, and Mirabella is a teacher. David and Mirabella's two boys, Axel and Matteo, grew up spending time outdoors: fishing, exploring, and bike riding both around their home and when their family took their camper on vacations with their friends and other family members. The boys have always been involved in various sports and constantly engaging with peers. When the shutdown happened, the boys were in grades 8 and 9, and their social worlds changed. Many parents did not feel comfortable taking their children to other people's homes at the time of the shutdown, and the boys no longer met friends at the ballpark or on the field; instead, they were suddenly expected to meet up with their friends on social media or through the use of FaceTime. The Satellite Internet their family had been using as the only connectivity option that was available was suddenly insufficient for the family's needs.

Each month, Mirabella purchased 75 GB of satellite service to use at any time, and 50 GB of additional data to use during the 2-6 a.m. hours. Prior to the pandemic, this amount of data sufficed as both David and Mirabella were able to complete their necessary tasks from work, and Axel and Matteo had less need for the use of data. After the pandemic set in, and Mirabella and the boys were completing their work and school tasks from home (as well as adding increasing amounts of social Internet use), the amounts were no longer enough. Each month, the family would "run out" of data within the first week.

The pandemic had created a need for higher amounts of cell phone service as well as satellite data, and the family began to experience cell phone plan struggles. These problems meant that Mirabella was forced to spend several hours on several different days in parking lots attempting to converse with automated services, waiting for her cell phone providers to address her calls, or waiting for the provider to call her back about the issues. The cell phone providers insisted that Mirabella be able to make calls on the cell phones which were experiencing problems at the time of their calls, and Mirabella was unable to make calls from any of the family's cell phones from her home.

Alongside her role of problem-solver, Mirabella was a teacher who needed to use more than the limited amount of Satellite Internet to create and post assignments for her students, and often had to "add data" midday in order to complete her work; she also suddenly had the task of ordering her groceries for pick up which used larger amounts of data. Meanwhile, Matteo and Axel needed to use the family's Internet access to complete their school tasks, but Matteo just wanted to spend his hours using FaceTime, streaming videos, and connecting with friends through gaming systems. Matteo's personal enjoyment and needs in education had largely focused on peer driven activities, which were suddenly not a part of the online learning experiences being provided by educators. Education during the shutdown became increasingly more focused on the individual and individual tasks rather than individuals building group-created projects, and Matteo struggled to adjust and thrive in this environment.

Axel's grades began to decline at the time of the shut down. Axel was unable to load the practice website that he was supposed to use for his coursework once school shut down, and being an independent 9th grade student, he kept the problem to himself. His mother discovered that his grade was 50% and began questioning Axel about his work. Finally, Axel explained the issue: the website would never load from their home; the loading icon simply continued to spin. Mirabella reached out to his teacher about the issue asking if there could be a work-around for the problem. No alternatives were given because the website would load from the high school--even though the school was closed for students. Axel failed the course with a 50% He had completed all other assignments at 100% accuracy, but he could not complete the tasks related to the unloadable website. The failing of the course stopped Axel from continuing in the course of study, and the experience served to deter him from attempting to strive in his other courses: it was more guaranteed to not try and fail rather than waste hours working and still fail.

The following school year introduced 10th grade Axel to a new elective course to replace the failing grade through a new subject matter. This course also included software that Axel was unable to load from his home. As an option to potentially help solve the loading problem, Mirabella borrowed a MiFi device from the school division to assist the boys in their work completion. Unfortunately, the MiFi was unable to provide a connection that provided a viable resource--the MiFi connection simply did not have the connectivity from their home's location to support the use of a school Chromebook. The family tried installing an antenna that would serve to boost the MiFi's service in their home, but they simply could not use the MiFi for the tasks that the boys were being assigned to complete. After attempting to solve the problem, Mirabella reached out to the new course teacher. The teacher provided recommendations for ways that Mirabella could help Axel load the software, but the recommended ways never worked. Fortunately, the teacher did continue to inquire about Axel's progress with the software and recognized that a work-around was necessary. Axel's appreciation for the teacher's understanding was immense--the course became his favorite.

Throughout the shutdown, the boys felt compelled to socialize with their peers while their mother knew that she needed to complete her work. During the pandemic, there were times that Mirabella worked from the school parking lot to accomplish her work, after dropping Axel and Matteo off at their grandfather Poppy's house to use his faster Internet. Poppy lives further from a main road than Mirabella's family; however, his county created a membership cooperative in 1914 when landlines were established in his area. The membership cooperative was a way to collectively advocate for their telephony needs, and that membership has continued to support emerging technologies through offering high speed Internet to residents.

The boys experienced the Internet data limits and speed differences between their own home and their Poppy's. During separate interviews, both boys explained that they preferred staying with their Poppy because he did not limit their Internet access, and they were able to complete multiple online tasks at one time. From Poppy's house the boys were able to interact with their friends without having to stop because "mom said so" or because of the lag that so frequently plagued them at their home. The dissonance that was created between the boys and their parents during the time of the shutdown due to the expensive satellite issues that the family had within their home was noted often during the interviews with Mirabelle and David. From the boys' perspectives, their parents were the limiting factor to their socialization needs, but Mirabelle and David knew that the problem was ultimately outside of their control. Mirabelle said:

The boys have a fear of missing out on what their peers are taking part in, and I understand their inability to focus differently; they are children. They want and need social interactions, and we can't provide those interactions in face-to-face ways right now. None of us want to move--the boys won't even discuss that option--but David and I often talk about the 'what-ifs'. David and I always do the best we can for our boys, but the shutdown has really made us feel as if our best is never adequate.

Mirabelle and David made many trips to create opportunities for their children to access the Internet connections they needed for both educational and personal fulfillments.

McCalaster Family: Seven Generations in the Mountains

Getting "Web" affected broader social and civic aspects of the McCalaster Family's lives. For seven generations, the MacCalaster family has owned property located in the middle of a national forest; in fact, Jim remembers knowing nearby neighbors who were removed from property ownership in order to increase the number of acres claimed by the National Forest Service. Jim recalled that his neighbors were pressured to sell the family farm, but that the father of the household ensured a caveat existed that entitled the property owner to lifelong residence. This continuance of home was allowed until less than one week after the patriarch's untimely death, and then his wife was told she and their children must move. Jim remembers the mother and son being unexpectedly forced to find another home immediately. Jim knows that choosing to have a life in a remote area does not always follow the same comforts and consistencies as life lived in other places. Living in a remote area often requires acceptance and the willingness to pursue innovative and time-consuming workarounds.

At the time of the COVID shutdown, Beth's job suddenly required her to host Zoom meetings with her clients. She immediately learned that she could not host meetings from her home, so she began to search for new "office" locations in her car. At first, she drove with her MiFi to a parking lot that serves as a link for people on a trail system; unfortunately, the parking lot proved to be a bustling, noisy location filled with runners, cyclists, and horseback riders that made it difficult to concentrate on the meetings with her clients. Next, she began looking for Internet locations in town, and she found a few parking lots that remained quiet enough to host meetings, but Beth did not feel that she could connect with her clients from her driver's seat and behind a screen in the same way that she had connected with them prior to COVID in a face-to-face setting; in addition, the pervasive struggle for a strong Internet connection created an unwelcome, stressful hassle for Beth. Within three months of the shutdown and the start of online meetings, Beth stepped away from the job that she had held for nearly five years.

During the time of the shutdown, Jim and Beth assisted in caring for their two grandchildren, Ricky and Allie, ages 13 and 8. Beth took over the children's homeschool education as she had taken over her own son's nearly 20 years before. Beth looked for fellow homeschool groups, which she had found supportive during her own son's education, but she found that present-day homeschool support focused on the use of web platforms and programs rather than group activities. Beth knew that there was a lack of quality Internet connection from her own home and had experienced the lag and drag which kept progress from occurring when Jim tried to watch YouTube videos, so she pulled from resources that were tangible rather than digital. Her grandchildren spent time outside, creating artwork, gardening, reading, measuring, and cooking. When asked to complete a poem, however, the children's views on the Internet resurfaced: Ricky wrote poetry about how he missed the Internet because the Internet represented what he had used to access games and friends prior to moving to the remote home. Ricky understood that his friends and games were "still there," but he was just not in a place that allowed him to "be there, too."

Jim and Beth understood Ricky's frustration in the lack of viable Internet. Beth spoke of her longing for Internet access to keep Jim occupied with less risky tasks--if he could watch "how to" videos, then he would stay inside more often instead of climbing onto their roof to determine whether he could fix a problem or working so hard on manual tasks that he found around their property to complete. Jim is a person who is always working, and while Beth could generally find contentment in reading a book or working on her artwork, Jim could not. Beth strongly believed that an Internet connection that could support Jim's interests of task completion via video would enable him to slow down, but that connection was not one that their home was to provide.

Beth had her own personal wishes for technology, and she also had endured conversations about her technology availability on multiple occasions at her service provider's store--both her iPhone and her Apple watch quit working because they had not been updating. The store representative seemed unable to understand how it was possible that her devices had never experienced updates in the two years she had owned them, and Beth calmly tried to explain that it was quite likely that the devices attempted to update, but because the service was so unreliable, the devices eventually "gave up." The store representative's response of "well, at least you are lucky to live with such a beautiful view!" coupled with his recommendations that she improve her Internet connection provided Beth with a firm understanding of the representative's lack of understanding of her position. The representative did not grasp that she was already paying for the best connection she could receive or that she was paying for an amount of data that she could never access. He did not hear her issues of slower Internet speeds as the truths that they were: unacceptable, insufficient, and unusable. He did not understand that the updates that her devices kept attempting were using data without a final outcome of update completion--and thus wasting her data. Beth was left frustrated with the encounter of yet another person who did not understand and did not care to try. She was left with the option of buying new devices to start the cycle again.

Jim and Beth also had Internet concerns that represented their responsibilities as citizens. When the shutdown occurred, they were told that their banking needs needed to be taken care of online--even though they were unable to complete online tasks from their home. When they had to complete their taxes that year, the documents had to be downloaded and emailed. The task of submitting taxes is one that (including completing the form) would take a connected adult about 15 minutes. Jim was unable to obtain access to the form. He tried to use his cell phone to act as a HotSpot to the site, but the indicator "just kept spinning." He had to drive nearly fifteen miles to town, find and then connect to WiFi outside of a local business, download the tax document, come home and print the copy, sign the copy, take photos, and then drive back to the service area to upload the final copy. The struggle took days because of the need of gathering information, entering and reentering information, driving, and printing, and the reward of completing the task felt minimal because submitting taxes is simply a chore that all citizens complete. In recounting the story, Jim shook his head slowly, just as he had as he retold the story of the close neighbors who had been relocated by the National Forest.

ANALYSIS AND CONCLUSION

The value of the Internet and technology were never questioned by these adults or children. The need for Internet access and devices was understood by all of those interviewed, and the ownership of multiple devices was cited as important for both social and learning reasons. The children interviewed viewed the Internet as a school connection, social conduit, and popular cultural platform to which they lacked access. The adults interviewed focused on the practical aspects of Internet use: schoolwork for their children, taxes, paying bills, selling on eBay, managing accounts. The struggles that adults experienced were different from the struggles the children recognized: adults struggled to find and utilize the Internet to complete societal tasks and to help their children complete their own educational tasks. Adults felt a great deal of pressure to find connectivity time for their children at specific times of the day, and adults also had to contend with their own job responsibilities vying for connectivity time within the times their children were learning while supporting their children's learning.

Before the pandemic getting Internet access was special and convenient enough to be an enjoyable family tradition—all heading to the library or enjoying a leisurely morning coffee treat, for example. Now, as their necessity increased and the available places dwindled, creativity and patience became more important. There needed to be both an intentionality and a flexibility in their lives.

There was intermittent access for most of the families at their homes, though nothing close to broadband. For students who lacked accessible broadband from their home, downloading school videos took much longer, and sometimes videos could not even be downloaded without physically going elsewhere to access Internet services--and the children would not know if the videos would download from home until they tried and failed, meaning that they wasted data on downloads without even gaining access to the downloaded materials. Students who were working without broadband Internet, no matter their grade level, spent more time focusing on gathering the content materials they needed to begin working on their assignments rather than the assignments themselves. Once students without broadband access had completed the work, there was then another struggle to share the work with teachers in the way it had been assigned; many students were unable to upload the content that they had created in the ways it had been required for final submission. This meant another trip to Wi-Fi in order to turn in their work. Students were focusing less on the content and more on the processes required to find and share the content.

Students were assigned tasks that required multiple applications to be open and running at the same time. Those without broadband access in their homes found this expectation impossible. Bandwidth within the homes had become a limited commodity. When the service slowed due to increased data usage, the same tasks were still required to be completed. Families with several children had to repeatedly make the choice on who got to do their work during a particular class or day. Who chose whose work was most important to complete?

This research highlights a population that is mostly silent and invisible to the digital ecosystem of 21st Century life in the United States. Education and collaboration were not possible for every student at the same standard; job access and economic opportunities were not possible for every citizen at equal levels of access; civic and collaborative engagement between young people were disparate, and models for those engagements were not present in households. How large is the divide that has existed between those with broadband access and those without and what will the future impacts be for those who have existed across this divide? In 2020-2022, the time of the COVID-19 Pandemic and the year following, those without access to broadband Internet were isolated from jobs and education, necessary daily tasks, and peer connections unless they stepped outside of their homes to cross mountains to find what they needed.

There were two major themes that cut across the families. The first one was the need to get online with intent and innovation—organizing a family's day and week around travel to Internet HotSpots. Moreover, these were not designated spaces for children to complete work—they were parking lots, garbage dump sites, and grocery stores–hardly designed with the intention of a year's worth of schoolwork. All of the families studied had the means to move to a more connected location. A second theme that permeated our conversations was the internal debate, shared by individuals and discussed among family members, of moving to a location that provided better connectivity. Throughout most of the conversations, the overwhelming pull of home kept them put. However, there was always the allure of better resources for the children and easier participation in social activities–from renewing a driver's license to learning what streaming services offered.

The purpose of this research was to gather information through interviews to explain educational lives of children and their families during the pandemic in areas of Appalachia. The need for study arose to explore the experiences of families and students who lived in remote areas and did not have full access to the Internet. The families lived in remote areas and had access to minimal to non-existent Internet access attained by MiFi devices, HotSpots, and Satellite Internet. These families were adults and school-aged children. The adults were expected to complete tasks which utilized the Internet for both work and necessary life tasks; the children were expected to complete tasks which utilized the Internet for school. The children wished for Internet access to connect with their friends and family during the shutdown, and the adults attempted to fulfill these wishes as best they could given their living situation. These cases demonstrate the delicate and awkward dance within and among living conditions, lifestyle choices, technology, civic participation, family responsibilities, and 21st century American education.

REFERENCES

Anderson, M. (2018). *About a quarter of rural Americans say access to high-speed internet is a major problem.* Pew Research Center FactTank. https://www.pewresearch.org/fact- major-problem/

Brooks, M., Mueller, J., & Thiede, B. (2021). Rural-urban differences in the labor-force impacts of COVID-19 in the United States. *Socius: Sociological Research for a Dynamic World, 7*. Advance online publication. doi:10.1177/23780231211022094 PMID:36466734

Byun, S., Meece, J., & Irvin, M. (2012). Rural-nonrural disparities in postsecondary educational attainment revisited. *American Educational Research Journal, 49*(3), 412–437. doi:10.3102/0002831211416344 PMID:24285873

Callaghan, T., Lueck, J., Trujillo, K., & Ferdinand, A. (2021). Rural and urban differences in COVID-19 prevention behaviors. *The Journal of Rural Health, 37*(2), 287–295. doi:10.1111/jrh.12556 PMID:33619836

Chandra, S., Chang, A., Day, L., Fazlullah, A., Liu, J., McBride, L., & Weiss, D. (2020). *Closing the K–12 digital divide in the age of distance learning*. Common Sense and Boston Consulting Group. https://www.commonsensemedia.org/sites/default/files/uploads/pdfs/common_sense_media_report_final_6_29_12-42pm_web_updat
ed.pdf

Deller, S., & Whitacre, B. (2019). Broadband's relationship to rural housing values. *Papers in Regional Science, 98*(5), 2135–2156. doi:10.1111/pirs.12450

Gross, B., & Opalka, A. (2020). *Too many schools leave learning to chance during the pandemic.* Center on Reinventing Public Education. https://www.crpe.org/sites/default/files/final_national_sample_brief_2020.pdf

Horrigan, J. (2020). *Census Pulse data shows some growth in computer access for students, but not much for internet availability at home.* Benton Institute for Broadband & Society. https://www.benton.org/blog/digital-tools-learning

Kaku, M. (2013). A scientist predicts the future. *New York Times.* https://www.nytimes.com/2013/11/28/opinion/kaku-a-scientist-predicts-the-future.html

Kandilov, A., Kandilov, I., Liu, X., & Renkow, M. (2017). The impact of broadband on US agriculture: An evaluation of the USDA broadband loan program. *Applied Economic Perspectives and Policy, 39*(4), 635–661. doi:10.1093/aepp/ppx022

Kim, Y., & Orazem, P. (2017). Broadband internet and new firm location decisions in rural areas. *American Journal of Agricultural Economics, 99*(1), 285–302. doi:10.1093/ajae/aaw082

Ledger, S., & Fuqua, M. (2021). Disruption, diversity, and dynamic developments in rural education during COVID-19. *Australian and International Journal of Rural Education, 31*(1), 1–7. doi:10.47381/aijre.v31i1.297

LoPiccaloK. (2020). Impact of broadband penetration on US farm productivity. SSRN. doi:10.2139/ssrn.3749647

Mahasuweerachai, P., Whitacre, B., & Shideler, D. (2010). Does broadband access impact migration in America? Examining differences between rural and urban areas. *The Review of Regional Studies, 40*(1), 5–26. doi:10.52324/001c.8158

Mueller, J., McConnell, K., Burow, P., Pofahl, K., Merdjanoff, A., & Farrell, J. (2021). Impacts of the COVID-19 pandemic on rural America. *Proceedings of the National Academy of Sciences of the United States of America, 118*(1). Advance online publication. doi:10.1073/pnas.2019378118 PMID:33328335

Nicola, T., Gable, A., & Ash, J. (2020). *The Response of rural districts to the COVID-19 pandemic.* National Center for Rural Education Research Networks. https://cepr.harvard.edu/files/cepr/files/ncrern_report.pdf

Organization for Economic Cooperation and Development. (2006). *The new rural paradigm: Policies and governance.* https://www.oecd.org/cfe/regionaldevelopment/thenewruralparadigmpoliciesandgovernance.htm

Organization for Economic Cooperation and Development. (2019). *OECD Regional outlook 2019: Leveraging megatrends for cities and rural areas.* Organization for Economic Co-operation and Development. doi:10.1787/9789264312838-

Petrin, R. A., Schafft, K. A., & Meece, J. L. (2014). Educational sorting and residential aspirations among rural high school students: What are the contributions of schools and educators to rural brain drain? *American Educational Research Journal*, *51*(2), 294–326. doi:10.3102/0002831214527493

Thier, M., Longhurst, J., Grant, P., & Hocking, J. (2021). Research deserts: A systematic mapping review of US rural education definitions and geographies. *Journal of Research in Rural Education*, *37*(2). Advance online publication. doi:10.26209/jrre3702

Thompson, S. (2020). *Wi-Fi equipped school buses to prepare students for homeschooling*. School Bus Fleet. https://www.schoolbusfleet.com/10112966/wi-fi-equipped-school-buses-to-prepare-students-for-rhomeschooling

Whitacre, B., Gallardo, R., & Strover, S. (2014). Does rural broadband impact jobs and income? Evidence from spatial and first-differenced regressions. *The Annals of Regional Science*, *53*(3), 649–670. doi:10.100700168-014-0637-x

Whitacre, B., & Manlove, J. (2016). Broadband and civic engagement in rural areas: What matters? *Community Development (Columbus, Ohio)*, *47*(5), 700–717. doi:10.1080/15575330.2016.1212910

Whitacre, B. E. (2021). COVID-19 and rural broadband. *Choices*, *36*(3), 1–10. doi:10.2139srn.3898548

Chapter 20
Blended Learning in Higher Education

İbrahim Halil Özdemir
https://orcid.org/0000-0001-9291-7112
Graduate School of Educational Sciences, Ege University, Turkey

Fırat Sarsar
https://orcid.org/0000-0002-3611-8137
Faculty of Education, Ege University, Turkey

Steve W. Harmon
Faculty of Professional Education, Georgia Institute of Technology, USA

ABSTRACT

With the integration of technology into learning environments, traditional learning approaches have begun to leave their place to current learning approaches. One of the current learning approaches that has been popularly used recently is blended learning. Because of the various advantages it provides, blended learning is preferred by learners, teachers, and educational institutions. With the current COVID-19 pandemic, higher education institutions' interest in blended learning has increased. This growing interest raises the issue of how efficient blended learning should be. In this context, researchers investigated the requirements of effective blended learning for higher education institutions in this chapter. In the chapter, the researchers also discuss the contents of blended learning models that can be used in higher education, current research, blended learning adoption process in higher education, and tips for effective blended learning.

INTRODUCTION

Rapid developments and evolution in information and communication technologies (ICT) also affect learning processes. With the influence of such developments, the integration of technology into traditional learning environments has accelerated. This technology integration enables the use of some alternative approaches, methods, and research topics for learning environments. One of these alternative approaches

DOI: 10.4018/978-1-6684-6092-4.ch020

is blended learning. Various definitions have been made in the literature for blended learning. Graham (2006) introduced one of the first definitions of the blended learning approach and defined blended learning as the process of combining traditional teaching methods with computer-assisted teaching. In other words, blended learning is an important and frequently used approach in learning practices due to the advantages offered by both online learning and traditional learning methods (Castro, 2019). According to Broadbent (2017), the blended learning process offers the advantages of both face-to-face and online learning techniques if it is effectively and well planned. One of the most important criteria for an effective blended learning practice is the selection of the most suitable model for the target audience (Horn & Staker, 2017). There are several models of blended learning in use. "Station Rotation, Lab Rotation, Individual Rotation, Flipped Classroom, Flexible Model, A la Carte Model, and Enriched Virtual Model" (Blended Learning Models, No Date) are some of the most frequently used models for effective blended learning. Through these models, blended learning use in higher education can be expanded. Higher education curricula are generally suitable for the implementation of various learning approaches with different content and learner characteristics (Khin, 2021). Blended learning brings a number of advantages to higher education institutions. These advantages can be categorized under the following headings: temporal, spatial, interactional, and financial (Alammary, 2019).

Blended learning in higher education can be more effective with a systematic and wisely planned adoption strategy (Anthony et al., 2020). Implementation and adoption of blended learning has emerged as an important variable for education, accreditation, and innovative vision policies of higher education institutions (Porter & Graham, 2016; Porter, Graham, Bodily & Sandberg, 2016). In this regard, different models for a systematic and well-planned blended learning adoption are presented in the literature.

Based on this information, this section discusses blended learning, blended learning in higher education, blended learning models for higher education, and implementation of blended learning.

BACKGROUND

Blended Learning

Different approaches are continuously being developed in the creation and distribution of knowledge in the learning practices. New learning and instructional techniques and methods often accompany these approaches. In current reports and practices on these approaches, the blended learning approach attracts great attention. Various definitions of blended learning have been made in the literature. According to Allen and Seaman (2010), blended learning is defined as the blend of face-to-face (traditional) and online learning content in a certain systematic framework. Put simply, blended learning is a planned implementation of traditional learning and online learning practices based on theoretical foundations (Graham, 2013). Ateş-Çobanoğlu (2020) presents an up-to-date definition of blended learning as an instructional design approach that combines advantages of both traditional learning and online learning to reduce time spent in traditional face-to-face classroom environments, provides peer learning opportunities, and supports the learning process by making use of online learning communities.

According to Hrastinski (2019), blended learning is a learning approach in which online learning and traditional learning environments are combined with a holistic perspective. Picciano (2021) emphasizes that in the definition of blended learning, various learning environments are a blending process rather than a combination.

So and Bonk (2010) stated that some questions should be asked for a correct blending process. These questions are as follows:

1. Which parts of the learning process will take place online, and which parts will be traditional face-to-face?
2. When should online and traditional face-to-face learning environments be used in the learning process?
3. How should the online and traditional face-to-face learning environments be blended into the learning process?

Graham (2006) defined blended learning as the blending of face-to-face learning environments and learning environments provided by computers and visualized it as given in Figure 1.

Figure 1. Blended Learning Structure
(Graham, 2006)

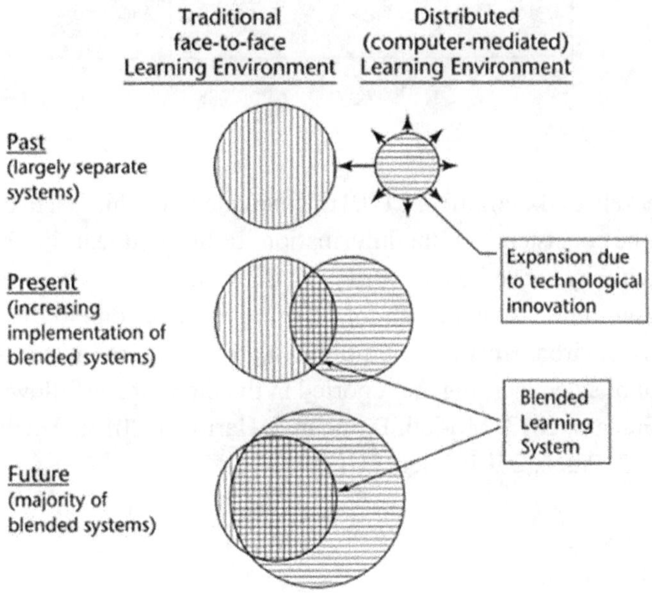

A similar situation of uncertainty in the definition of blended learning is also observed in the effectiveness of blended learning. Different views have been put forward regarding the effectiveness of blended learning (Dziuban, Graham, Moskal, Norberg, 2018). In this context, the MIX taxonomy developed by Margulieux, McCracken, and Catrambone (2016) aims to resolve inconsistencies about the effectiveness of blended learning. The foundations of the taxonomy are the dimensions of instructional experiences that make up the current pedagogical approach to blended learning. The structure of the taxonomy is indicated in Figure 2.

Figure 2. MIX Taxonomy

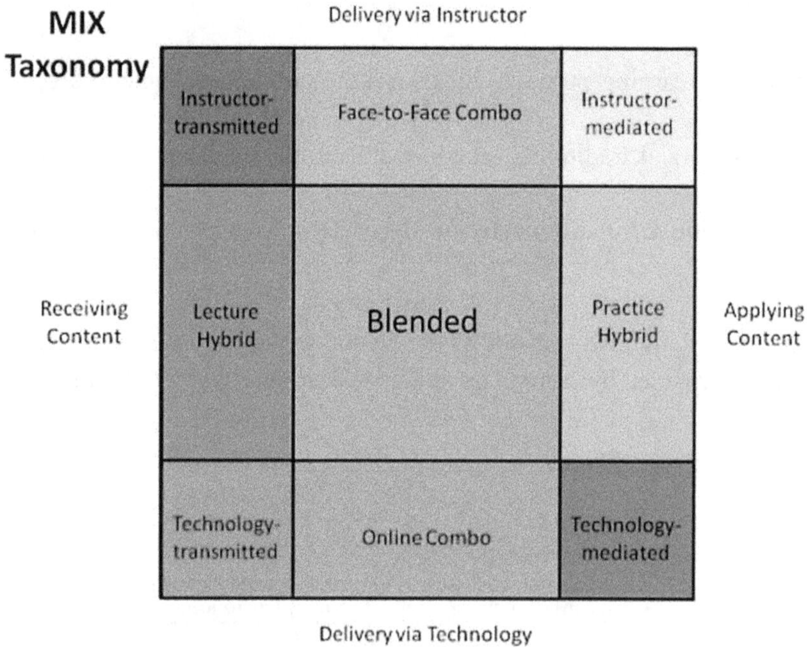

Margulieux, McCracken, and Catrambone (2016) concluded that this is a taxonomy that can be used in the classification of the consistency of the information for blended learning in the existing literature as a result of the research they carried out to verify the taxonomy.

Blended learning is an important approach for learning practices due to the various advantages offered by online learning environments and traditional learning environments (Castro, 2019). Several important advantages of blended learning are reported in the literature as follows (Anthony et al., 2019; Anthony et al., 2020; Graham, 2013; Moskal, Dziuban & Hartman, 2013; Özdemir, Ateş-Çobanoğlu & Sarsar, 2021; Tayebinik & Puteh, 2013; Yuen, 2010):

- Provides financial savings
- Provides temporal flexibility
- Provides spatial flexibility
- Presents alternatives in terms of teaching methods
- Promotes and increases in-class interaction (Learner-Learner, Learner-Teacher, Learner-Content)
- Increases resource and material diversity
- Ensures security for applied lessons
- Increases class engagement
- Offers cooperative learning opportunities

Among the primary aspects that contribute to the advantages of blended learning and its effectiveness, educational technology rank first. Bordoloi, Das, and Das (2021) stress the importance of incorporating educational technologies into contemporary learning processes.

Educational Technologies and Blended Learning

Throughout history, educational technology has been defined in a variety of ways, taking into account the characteristics of the time period and technological developments. The utilization of instruments in education forms the foundation of the initial definitions. The subsequent eras' definitions focused on the design and implementation of the learning process and the enhancement of the performance of the learners. Today, the Association for Educational Communications and Technology (AECT) definitions are recognised as references in the definitions of educational technology. In this context, the current definition of educational technologies by AECT (2017);

"Educational technology is the study and ethical application of theory, research, and best practices to advance knowledge as well as mediate and improve learning and performance through the strategic design, management and implementation of learning and instructional processes and resources."

With the establishment of a definition for educational technology, the present shift in learning techniques throws into question the efficiency and competence of traditional learning methods (Singh, Steele, & Singh, 2021). This circumstance elevates contemporary learning techniques to a prominent position and promotes the development of these approaches through the use of educational technologies. In light of this knowledge, blended learning, which is a contemporary learning strategy, stands out as an effective and efficient learning approach that takes advantage of educational technology's capabilities.

The advancements and improvements in educational technology allow the application of a variety of pedagogical strategies in the learning process. This circumstance is advantageous for the application of blended learning in educational processes (Castro, 2019). Due to its structure, blended learning might sustain its development in conjunction with educational technology in the current period, in which online access to knowledge is easier in accordance with the opportunities provided by educational technologies (Khalil, Abdel Meguid, & Elkhider, 2018). In addition, the strategic design of learning processes to enhance performance, based on the current concept of educational technology, provides an effective blended learning process. However, it is essential to emphasize the concept of educational technology in the design of blended learning processes in order to boost the permanency of the learning experiences (Rao, 2019).

Through providing the possibility to govern the learning process, educational technology facilitates the demonstration of blended learning's benefits. Moreover, recent technological advancements facilitate the implementation of blended learning (Khalil, Abdel Meguid, & Elkhider, 2018). In this context, it is unavoidable for an effective learning process to incorporate educational technology as a reference point in the blended learning method to be employed in learning activities.

Blended learning is being used in higher education to improve learning processes and learning performance by embracing educational technology and its benefits. Blended learning has a critical importance in the future policy planning of higher education institutions in consideration of the Covid-19 pandemic.

Advantages of Blended Learning in Higher Education

With the impact of developments and transformations in technology, higher education curricula and learning processes have also evolved and been revised (Dunn & Kennedy, 2019). This development and transformation has also affected some other variables of the higher education process (Castro, 2019). The pedagogical and methodological approaches in higher education programs are one of these variables. With the latest developments and transformations, blended learning has become a frequently used approach by higher education institutions (Alammary, Sheard, & Carbone, 2014; Castro, 2019; Okaz, 2014). Blended learning offers many advantages for higher education institutions since it systematically and wisely blends the pros of the traditional learning and online learning methods (Adams, Tan, Sumintono and Oh, 2020; Bailey, 2021; Castro, 2019; Fisher, Perényi, and Birdthistle, 2021; Heilporn, Lakhal, and Bélisle, 2021; Holmes and Prieto-Rodriguez, 2018; Jones and Sharma, 2019; Kacetl and Semradova, 2020; Müller and Mildenberger, 2021; Okaz, 2014; Suartama, Setyosari, and Ulfa, 2019). The blended learning approach can produce cost savings both for the higher education institution and for learners in terms of the great learner population in higher education (Castro, 2019). If blended learning is carried out effectively and in a planned way, it saves time in the classroom and improves time management (Müller & Mildenberger, 2021). In addition, blended learning increases access for learners and higher education instructors (Jones & Sharma, 2019). With increased access, school attendance of learners increases. Blended learning, by its nature, offers alternatives to teaching staff and higher education institutions in terms of teaching methods (Antwi-Boampong, 2020). Blended learning, which includes different communication channels (face-to-face and online communication channels), also strengthens the communication of learners among themselves and with instructors (Okaz, 2014). With strengthened communication, learner-learner, learner-instructor, and learner-content interactions can be improved (Bailey, 2021; Holmes & Prieto-Rodriguez, 2018; Kacetl & Semradova, 2020). With changes in the distribution of information, as well as the developments and transformations in technology, blended learning has diversified and facilitated the access of both learners and instructors to academic resources (Holmes & Prieto-Rodriguez, 2018). In addition, blended learning increases access opportunities to academic content through versatile access to resources. Blended learning is also preferred by higher education institutions for security purposes. A reliable and secure educational environment can be created through the affordances of blended learning in online education, especially in applied courses such as field studies (for example, courses in engineering education or medical education) (McCutcheon, O'Halloran, & Lohan, 2018). Another advantage of blended learning in higher education is increased engagement (Adams, Tan, Sumintono and Oh, 2020; Heilporn, Lakhal and Bélisle, 2021). Blended learning can increase learner engagement and, therefore, offers efficiencies in time-saving, management, interaction, and flexible access, as well as providing possibilities for alternative teaching methods (Fisher, Perényi, & Birdthistle, 2021). These advantages are summarized in Figure 3.

Figure 3. Advantages of Blended Learning

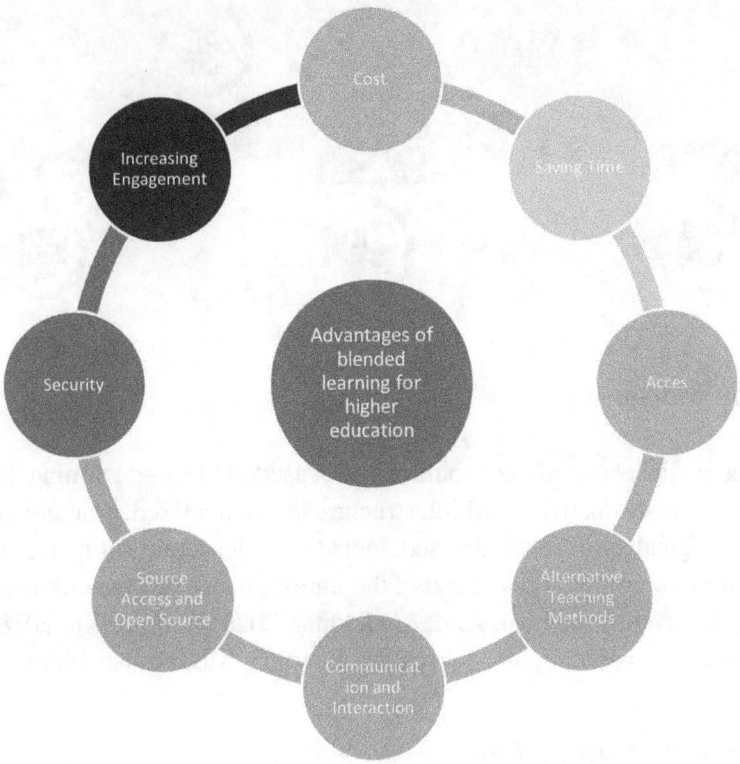

The many advantages of Blended Learning spark an increasing interest and adoption of it in higher education. To help guide faculty who are considering adopting a blended learning approach, we present different models and suggestions for a successful implementation process.

Blended Learning Models for Higher Education

Many different models for blended learning have been presented by researchers. These models focus on the physical characteristics of the learning process rather than the psychological characteristics and pedagogical conditions of the target group (Hrastinski, 2019). Effective implementation of the blended learning process in higher education is possible with an instructional design and the use of the most appropriate blended learning model suitable for the target audience (Graham, 2009). There are many different models for higher education depending on the target audience. Accordingly, frequently used blended learning models are shown in Figure 4.

Figure 4. Blended Learning Models

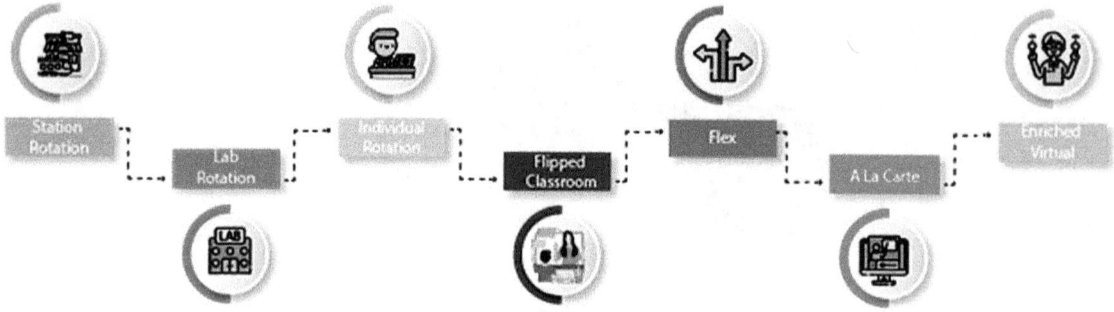

Station Rotation Model

The Station Rotation model is one of the popular models used in blended learning. Station Rotation is a model that provides a transformative transition structure through a fixed structure between the stations where different pedagogical approaches are used, including at least one online learning station, by putting the learners into 3 or 4 groups. The context of the stations may differ according to the applied group and content (Ayob, Abd Halim, Zulkifli, Zaid, & Mokhtar, 2020; Truitt & Ku, 2018). A scheme of the Station Rotation model is given in Figure 5 (Blended Learning Models, No Date).

Figure 5. Station Rotation Model Structure

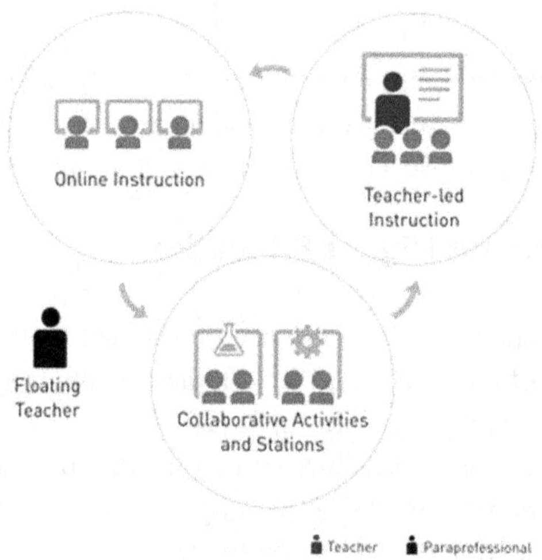

Lab Rotation Model

The Lab Rotation model is similar to the station rotation model in terms of implementation method and structure. In this model, an alternating transition takes place between the stations where different pedagogical approaches are used. Unlike the station rotation model, however, the Lab Rotation model includes online learning carried out in school computer laboratories. A visual drawing of the Lab Rotation model is given in Figure 6 (Blended Learning Models, No Date).

Figure 6. Lab Rotation Model Structure

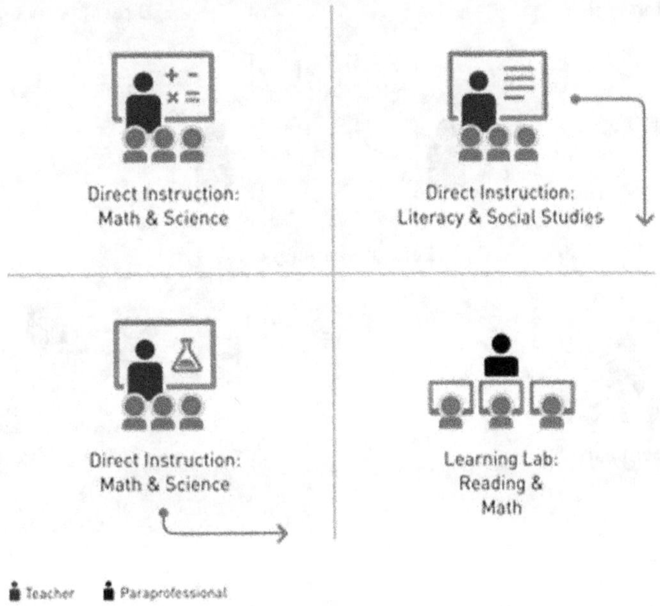

Individual Rotation Model

In the Individual Rotation model, students alternate between stations within a plan created by the teacher or educational software. Unlike the station rotation and lab rotation models, students do not have to experience all stations. Students only experience specially planned stations. A Schema of the Individual Rotation model is given in Figure 7 (Blended Learning Models, No Date).

Figure 7. Individual Rotation Model Structure

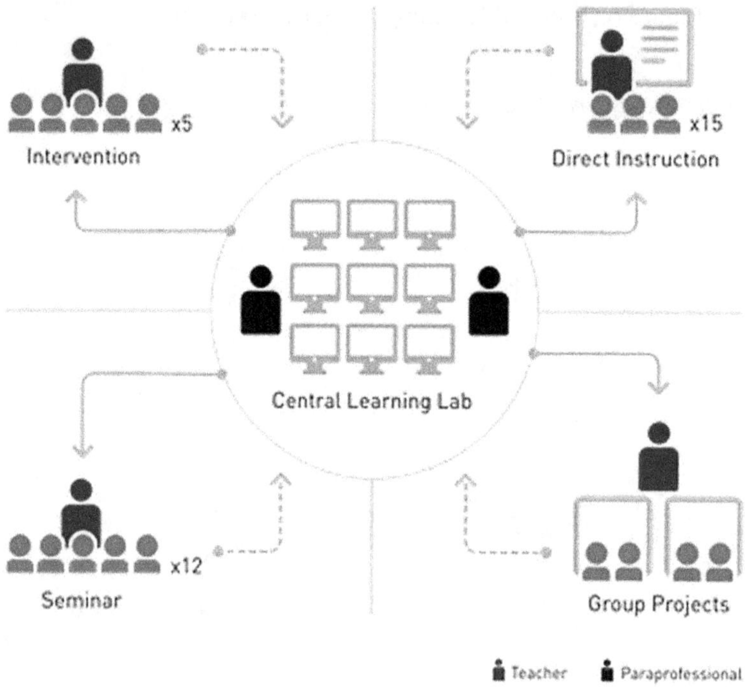

Flipped Classroom

Contrary to the usual teaching practices, the Flipped Classroom approach enables learners to carry out practical studies and projects in the school and classroom environment, while acquiring theoretical knowledge online from home. This allows efficient and economical use of time in the classroom (Blended Learning Models, No Date). In the Flipped Classroom model, the role of teachers is to be a guide Students have more responsibility for their learning and it is therefore a learner-centered model (Lai & Hwang, 2016). The Flipped Classroom model offers improved learner-learner, learner-teacher, and learner-content interactions by giving learners more time for interaction (Akçayır & Akçayır, 2018). It has a positive effect on student performance (Strelan, Osborn, & Palmer, 2020). Due to these advantages, the Flipped Classroom model is frequently used in many disciplines of higher education (Hao, 2016). A schema of the Flipped Classroom model is given in Figure 8 (Blended Learning Models, No Date).

Figure 8. Flipped Classroom Model Structure

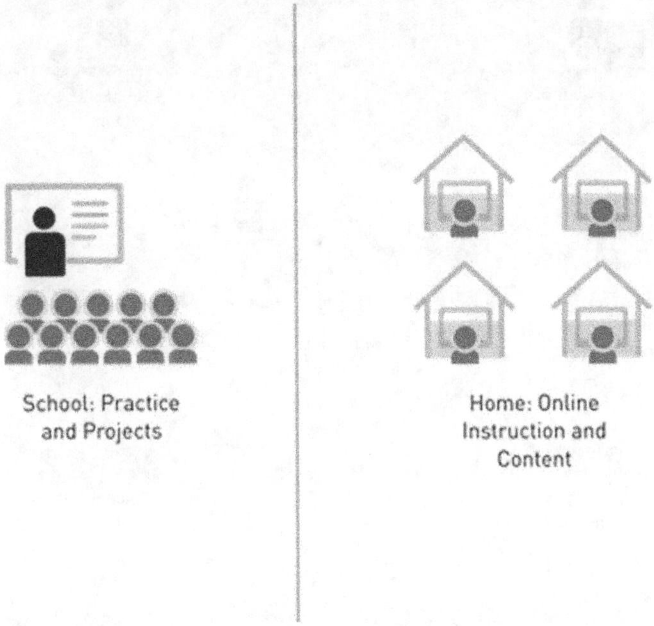

Flex Model

In the flexible model, the main focus of online learning, the learning process, and learning activities are developed in line with the needs of the learners. Learners can move flexibly between learning activities designed specifically for them (Blended Learning Models, No Date). In the flexible model, the process is learner-centered. Learners can receive teachers' guidance on issues they need support from while achieving their learning goals (Ayob, Abd Halim, Zulkifli, Zaid, & Mokhtar, 2020). A visual drawing of the flexible model is given in Figure 8 (Blended Learning Models, No Date).

Figure 9. Flex Model Structure

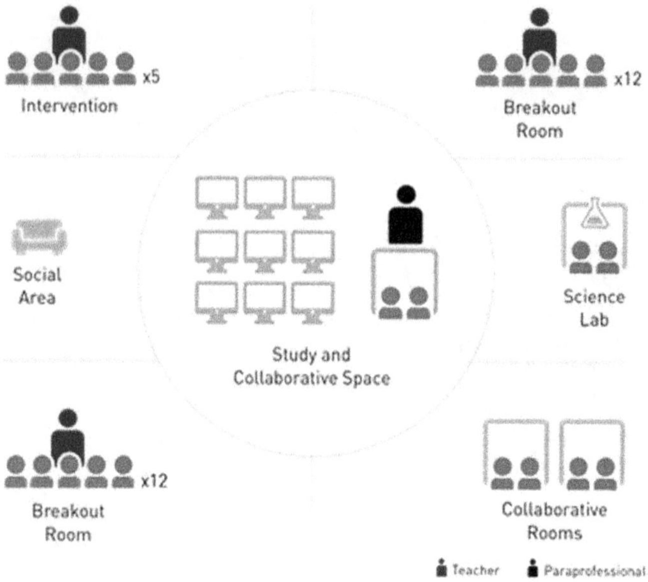

A La Carte Model

The A La Carte Model is a blended learning technique in which learners and instructors implement online learning because of a lack of traditional teaching resources (time, space, material, etc.). The A La Carte model, therefore, offers flexibility to learners and instructors (Blended Learning Models, No History; Wang, Zhang, & Lovell, 2021) but may suffer from a lack of intentional design. Much of the emergency shift to remote teaching caused by the COVID-19 pandemic falls under this model. A schema of the A La Carte model is given in Figure 10 (Blended Learning Models, No Date).

Figure 10. A La Carte Model Structure

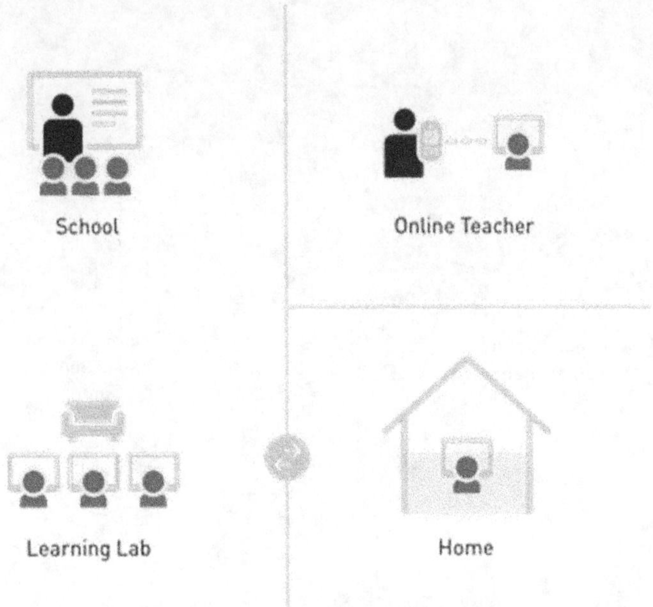

Enriched Virtual Model

The Enriched Virtual model is a blended learning method in which learners carry out most of the learning process online at home or anywhere outside of the school; face-to-face lessons, on the other hand, are carried out when deemed necessary. Unlike Flipped Classroom, the enriched virtual model does not require learners to attend school face-to-face every day. Instead, special sessions are held when learners need to meet with teachers. (Blended Learning Models, No History). A diagram of the Enriched Virtual model is given in Figure 11 (Blended Learning Models, No Date).

Figure 11. Enriched Virtual Model Structure

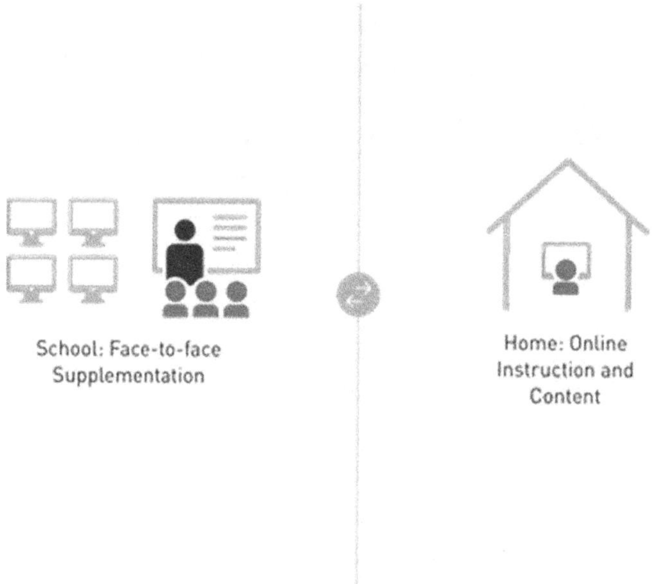

Practical Examples of Blended Learning Models to Be Used in Higher Education

With the increasing use of the blended learning approach in higher education, applied studies have been carried out by researchers to explore the effectiveness of blended learning models and their impact on the learning process.

Castedo et al. (2019) applied an experimental design to measure the effectiveness of the problem-based learning with flipped classroom model in higher education and the effect of the flipped model on absenteeism and exam participation. The study was conducted with 152 engineering students. While the first group (80 students) was exposed to a course taught in a flipped classroom, traditional learning methods were used in the second group (72 students). Their findings indicated that the flipped classroom model had a positive effect on the learning process. According to the other findings obtained from their study, the flipped classroom significantly increased attendance and exam participation.

Dandashly, Barbar, and Antoun (2019) aimed to determine the effect of blended learning strategies carried out using the Station Rotation model on the academic success of teacher candidates. They used an experimental design with quantitative research methods. The control group (25 pre-service teachers) was exposed to 2 lessons using traditional teaching methods (Lesson 1: Teaching Methods, Lesson 2: Fundamentals of Education), while the experimental group was exposed to 2 lessons using blended learning (Lesson 1: Teaching Methods, Lesson 2: Fundamentals of Education). Their findings revealed that blended learning had a significant positive effect on academic achievement in the teaching methods course. Their findings also showed that there was no significant difference between the groups in the course on the fundamentals of education. Researchers emphasize that the reason for not reaching a significant difference is due to the content of the course, or it may be due to the teachers' attitudes to apply innovative methods in the context of the course content.

Cai, Yang, Gong, Macleod, and Jin (2018) examined the development and implementation of a blended learning model in their study. The authors also aimed to measure the effectiveness of the Lab Rotation model in the learning process. A total of 277 pre-service teachers participated in their study. Their results pointed out that the Lab Rotation model had a significant effect on the learning process. Also, they found that various materials used in the Lab Rotation model had a significant positive impact on the student learning process.

Deepa, Reba, Santhanamari, and Susithra (2021) aimed to reveal the effectiveness of the environments used to provide virtual laboratory experience within the scope of the enriched virtual model. A total of 70 undergraduate students participated in their study and the findings showed that the enriched virtual model had a positive effect on the learning process. In addition, the researchers determined that student participation increased with the use of the enriched virtual model.

EFFECTIVE BLENDED LEARNING FOR HIGHER EDUCATION: ADOPTING BLENDED LEARNING

In the present century and also in the future, technology will inevitably have a global impact on the teaching/learning process. With the current and expected advancesof technology, change and transformation of instructional approaches are inevitable (Dunn & Kennedy, 2019). Blended learning emerged accordingly and has been used frequently in recent years; accordingly, its adoption in higher education has increased, and more examples are emerging regarding its use (Pelletier et al., 2021). With blended learning, problems faced by higher education institutions such as the rising costs, disruptions in accessing school, non-attendance, need for quality and effective teaching, and physical environment inadequacies can be addressed in novel ways (Castro, 2019). An effective blended learning implementation in higher education is possible if higher education institutions adopt systematic and well-planned approaches within the framework of a theoretical model. Institutional adoption of blended learning is important for the teaching and institutional policies of higher education institutions (Spring, Graham, & Hadlock, 2016). With the increasing prevalence of blended learning worldwide, creating an adoption plan for blended learning has become a necessity for higher education institutions (Anthony et al., 2020; Darling-Hammond, and Hyler, 2020; Martin-Garcia, Martinez-Abad, and Reyes-Gonzalez, 2019). For a successful adaptation of blended learning in higher education, learners, educators, and policymakers of higher education institutions should act collaboratively (Anthony et al., 2020). In this context, some models have been developed for the adoption of blended learning.

Models of Blended Learning Adoption

Some models have been developed for the effective adoption of blended learning in higher education institutions (Antwi-Boampong, 2020; Graham, Woodfield, & Harrison, 2013). Through these models, the adoption process implemented by higher education institutions can be analyzed and evaluated.

The blended learning adoption model developed by Graham, Woodfield, and Harrison (2013) consists of a three-stage structure as indicated in Figure 12.

Figure 12. Blended Learning Adoption Model introduced by Graham, Woodfield, and Harrison (2013)

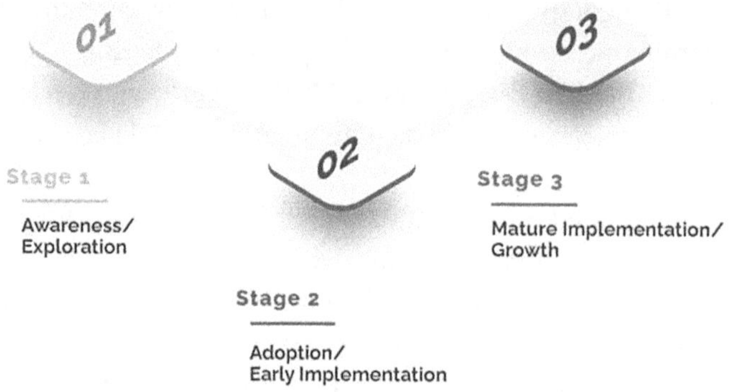

Stage 1 – Awareness and Discovery

The first stage of this model is Awareness and Discovery. In this stage, higher education institutions without a strategy and plan for adaptation of blended learning begin to work on creating a strategy. The academic leadership of higher education institutions should examine and explore blended learning in detail and determine its fit with the goals of the institution clearly (Graham, Woodfield, & Harrison, 2013; Porter, Graham, Spring, & Welch, 2014). The main goal at this stage is to provide institutional support for higher education faculty members to raise awareness for the implementation of blended learning (Porter, Graham, Spring, & Welch, 2014). According to Porter, Graham, Bodily, and Sandberg (2016), higher education institutions should develop an institutional definition for blended learning at this stage.

Stage 2 – Adoption – Early Implementation

The second stage is Adoption and Early Implementation. In the Adoption-Early Implementation stage, the blended learning adoption process and practice trials begin (Graham, Woodfield, & Harrison, 2013). Application trials are carried out with highly motivated academic staff within the institution. In addition, determination of the most suitable blended learning model for the institution's target audience is necessary at this stage (Graham, Woodfield, & Harrison, 2013; Porter, Graham, Spring, & Welch, 2014). Institutional administrators should implement a technological support system for learners and instructors during the Adoption-Early Implementation process. However, developing supporting courses and workshops for teaching staff is also important in preparing blended courses (Graham, Woodfield, & Harrison, 2013). Moreover, the higher education institution should officially develop a model blended course and present it to its stakeholders for early application and analysis (Porter, Graham, Bodily, & Sandberg, 2016).

Stage 3 - Mature Application - Growth

The third stage of this model is Mature Implementation and Growth. In this stage, effective blended learning strategies, a blended learning structure, and support for blended learning are developed through the administrative processes of higher education institutions. An effective and successful blended learning adoption can be achieved through these practices (Graham, Woodfield, & Harrison, 2013). At this stage, an official definition of blended learning should be made and accepted by the higher education institution. For a successful application of blended learning, project champions of academic units should be selected at this stage and a structure supporting these champions should be created (Graham, Woodfield, & Harrison, 2013). Also, a well-planned technological infrastructure should be created and implemented. Furthermore, instructors should be motivated and encouraged for the implementation of blended learning within the institution (Porter, Graham, Spring, & Welch, 2014).

Unlike the adoption model developed by Graham, Woodfield, and Harrison (2013), Antwi-Boampong (2020) has developed the "Faculty Blended Learning Adoption Model". This model emerged based on the teaching staff's experiences with blended learning (Antwi-Boampong, 2020). The model is shown in Figure 13.

Figure 13. Faculty Blended Learning Adoption Model
(Antwi-Boampong, 2020)

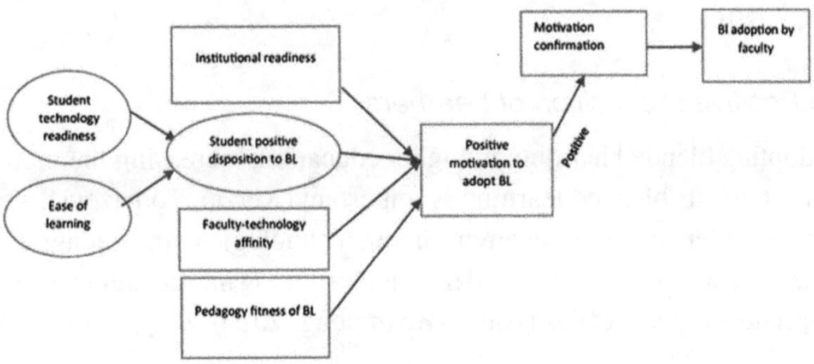

Antwi-Boampong (2020) emphasizes four key points in the model he developed. These points are the readiness of higher education institutions, the instructor-technology relationship, the pedagogical relevance of blended learning, and the positive disposition of learners.

i. Readiness of Higher Education Institutions for Blended Learning

For an effective blended learning adoption process, higher education institutions should perform a preparatory process that includes strategic, structural, and support elements (Graham, Woodfield, & Harrison, 2013). Higher education institutions should clearly state the strategies, objectives, and resources for the widespread adoption and implementation of blended learning throughout the institution. In addition, a suitable infrastructure for blended learning should be created by performing a proper resource management process. During the establishment of the infrastructure, a Learning Management System should be implemented by the institution (Antwi-Boampong, 2020). Definitions for blended learning should be made by the institution and a suitable blended learning model for the institution should be determined. Also, blended learning adoption leaders should be selected and assigned to the units (Antwi-Boampong, 2020; Graham, Woodfield, & Harrison, 2013; Porter, Graham, Spring, & Welch, 2014). Higher education institutions should motivate the teaching staff towards blended learning and organize training programs for them (Antwi-Boampong, 2020).

ii. Instructor-Technology Relationship

The blended learning approach cannot be considered without technology due to its unique structure and theoretical framework. Considering this fact, the role of technology skills is very critical in the effective adoption of blended learning (Castro, 2019). Accordingly, instructors as practitioners of blended learning are expected to have a positive relationship with technology (Al-Maroof, Al-Qaysi, Salloum, & Al-Emran, 2021). With this positive relationship, higher education institutions could develop technology-oriented educational content and instructors can choose the appropriate technology for the pedagogical methods and techniques they use in learning practices (Antwi-Boampong, 2020).

iii. Pedagogical Relevance of Blended Learning

Blended learning is suitable for using different teaching methods and techniques as it offers a blend of advantages of traditional and online teaching methods. Therefore, instructors should be familiar with the possibilities provided by this convenient structure and put them into practice in the learning process (Antwi-Boampong, 2020).

iv. Promoting the Positive Disposition of Learners

In the process of adopting blended learning in higher education, increasing the motivation of the learners and the instructor towards blended learning is important (Keržič, Tomaževič, Aristovnik, & Umek, 2019). Accordingly, in a blended learning environment technological and pedagogical affect should be encouraged by higher education institutions and instructors, taking into account the learner characteristics and creating appropriate learner profiles (Antwi-Boampong, 2020).

SUGGESTIONS FOR SUCCESSFUL IMPLEMENTATION OF BLENDED LEARNING

For a successful implementation of blended learning in higher education, some additional variables need to be taken into account (Bruggeman et al., 2021). Considering these variables, we offer some suggestions for higher education institutions and for instructors in adopting blended learning.

Suggestions for Higher Education Institutions

Higher education institutions have important responsibilities in the adoption of blended learning. Higher education institutions are expected to perform effective and successful management of the adoption process. Some suggestions for higher education institutions to effectively fulfill their responsibilities and manage the process are presented below (Anthony et al., 2019; Anthony et al., 2020; Antwi-Boampong, 2020; Bruggeman et al., 2021; Castro, 2019; Galvis, 2018; Graham, Woodfield, & Harrison, 2013; Porter, Graham, Bodily, & Sandberg, 2016; Porter, Graham, Spring, & Welch, 2014; Sandanayake, 2019; Stoffregen et al., 2016):

1. Identifying the strategies of the institutional and theoretical frameworks.
2. Developing an institutional definition for blended learning.

3. Planning and managing the resources needed to adopt blended learning.
    a. Human resources management
    b. Cost management
    c. Physical and virtual environment management
4. iv. Planning the technical infrastructure required for blended learning and putting the plan into action.
5. v. Increasing motivation among the institution's faculty and staff for blended learning practices.
6. vi. Planning and organizing training courses on technologies and pedagogical approaches that instructors should use in blended learning practices.
7. vii. Establishing a commission and assigning unit/departmental leaders for implementation of blended learning.
8. viii. Organizing informative seminars and training to increase students' readiness for blended learning.

SUGGESTIONS FOR INSTRUCTORS

In the process of adopting blended learning, instructors also have some responsibilities. The following steps are some suggestions for instructors to fulfill these responsibilities in the implementation process (Anthony et al., 2020; Antwi-Boampong, 2020; Bruggeman et al., 2021; Galvis, 2018; Graham, Woodfield, and Harrison, 2013; Martin-Lucas, Torrijos-Fincias, Serrate-Gonzalez, and del Dujo, 2021; Porter, Graham, Bodily, & Sandberg, 2016; Previtali & Scarozza, 2019; Sanchez-Gomez, Martin-Garcia & Mena, 2020):

1. Conducting an instructional design process required to implement the strategy and theoretical frameworks developed by the institution in courses.
2. Integrating various technologies or technological materials into lessons.
3. Increasing the variety of materials in lessons and considering multimedia principles.
4. Paying attention to the use of various pedagogical approaches in lessons.
5. Putting students at the center of the learning process.
6. Taking initiatives to increase the motivation of students. Using motivation models when required (ARCS, ARCS-V)(Ma ve Lee, 2021).
7. Providing rapid feedback to students during the learning process.
8. Observing learner needs
9. Insisting on success even in failures.
10. Planning time management realistically and wisely.
11. Avoiding hesitation to share problems and needs with the institution management or unit leader.
12. Evaluating performance in the process with a critical perspective.

FUTURE RESEARCH DIRECTIONS

Future research can carry out applied studies on the blended learning adoption process in higher education, taking into account the theoretical foundations in this section. In addition, there are deficiencies in the literature regarding the adoption of blended learning in higher education. At this point, meta-analysis studies to be carried out will contribute to the literature.

CONCLUSION

The popularity of blended learning, a promising learning and teaching approach of the future, is currently increasing. With this increasing popularity, effective implementation of blended learning emerges as an important need. Therefore, one of the most important variables in this process is constructing informative blended learning models. However, most of these models focus on the physical characteristics of the learning process rather than their psychological components and features. For this reason, learner characteristics and learner needs should also be considered during the implementation planning of the models.

Many higher education institutions have implemented blended learning in learning and teaching processes due to its various advantages and the emerging body of research on it. One of the most important considerations for higher education institutions is the diffusion and adoption of blended learning. Institutions should use blended learning adoption models for systematic and wisely-planned implementation of blended learning within the appropriate institutional and theoretical frameworks. In this regard, higher education institutions may use the "Blended Learning Adoption Model" developed by Graham, Woodfield, and Harrison (2013) and the "Faculty Blended Learning Adoption Model" of Antwi-Boampong (2020). Furthermore, institutions should consider the needs of their stakeholders, instructors, and learners in the process of adopting blended learning. At this point, the main responsibility of institutions is to ensure the management of processes considering strategy, structure, and support aspects. On the other hand, instructors also have some responsibilities such as integrating pedagogical approaches and the latest technologies into the learning process in accordance with the blended learning approach. In addition, instructors should put students at the center of the learning process by motivating learners in blended learning environments.

Effective and successful implementation of blended learning can be done through a systematic and planned roadmap developed in cooperation with all stakeholders. As technology becomes increasingly and more tightly integrated into society and our daily lives, it is important that our higher education institutions acknowledge this interweaving, and not just stay current with it, but lead in taking advantage of the learning affordances it provides. Blended learning has an important role yet to play for 21st-century learners.

REFERENCES

Adams, D., Tan, M. H. J., Sumintono, B., & Oh, S. P. (2020). Blended Learnıng Engagement In Hıgher Educatıon Instıtutıons: A Dıfferentıal Item Functıonıng Analysıs Of Students'backgrounds. *Malaysian Journal of Learning and Instruction*, *17*(1), 133–158. doi:10.32890/mjli2020.17.1.6

Akçayır, G., & Akçayır, M. (2018). The flipped classroom: A review of its advantages and challenges. *Computers & Education*, *126*, 334–345. doi:10.1016/j.compedu.2018.07.021

Al-Maroof, R., Al-Qaysi, N., Salloum, S. A., & Al-Emran, M. (2021). Blended learning acceptance: A systematic review of information systems models. *Technology, Knowledge and Learning,* 1-36.

Alammary, A. (2019). Blended learning models for introductory programming courses: A systematic review. *PLoS One*, *14*(9), e0221765. doi:10.1371/journal.pone.0221765 PMID:31487316

Alammary, A., Sheard, J., & Carbone, A. (2014). Blended learning in higher education: Three different design approaches. *Australasian Journal of Educational Technology*, *30*(4). Advance online publication. doi:10.14742/ajet.693

Allen, I. E., & Seaman, J. (2010). *Class Differences: Online Education in the United States*. Sloan Consortium. https://files.eric.ed.gov/fulltext/ED529952.pdf

Anthony, B., Kamaludin, A., Romli, A., Raffei, A. F. M., Nincarean, A. L., Eh Phon, D., Abdullah, A., Ming, G. L., Shukor, N. A., Nordin, M. S., & Baba, S. (2019). Exploring the role of blended learning for teaching and learning effectiveness in institutions of higher learning: An empirical investigation. *Education and Information Technologies*, *24*(6), 3433–3466. doi:10.100710639-019-09941-z

Anthony, B., Kamaludin, A., Romli, A., Raffei, A. F. M., Phon, D. N. A., Abdullah, A., & Ming, G. L. (2020). Blended learning adoption and implementation in higher education: A theoretical and systematic review. *Technology, Knowledge and Learning,* 1-48.

Antwi-Boampong, A. (2020). Towards a faculty blended learning adoption model for higher education. *Education and Information Technologies*, *25*(3), 1639–1662. doi:10.100710639-019-10019-z

Ateş-Çobanoğlu, A. (2020). From Ubiquitous to Ubiquitous Blended Learning Environments. In G. Durak & S. Çankaya (Eds.), *Managing and Designing Online Courses in Ubiquitous Learning Environments* (pp. 215–232). IGI Global. doi:10.4018/978-1-5225-9779-7.ch011

Ayob, N. S., Abd Halim, N. D., Zulkifli, N. N., Zaid, N. M., & Mokhtar, M. (2020). Overview of blended learning: The effect of station rotation model on students' achievement. *Journal of Critical Reviews*, *7*(6), 320–326.

Bailey, D. (2022). Interactivity during Covid-19: Mediation of learner interactions on social presence and expected learning outcome within videoconference EFL courses. *Journal of Computers in Education*, *9*(2), 291–313. doi:10.100740692-021-00204-w

Blended Learning Models. (n.d.). *Blended Learning Universe*. https://www.blendedlearning.org/models/

Bordoloi, R., Das, P., & Das, K. (2021). *Perception towards online/blended learning at the time of Covid-19 pandemic: an academic analytics in the Indian context*. Asian Association of Open Universities Journal.

Broadbent, J. (2017). Comparing online and blended learner's self-regulated learning strategies and academic performance. *The Internet and Higher Education*, *33*, 24–32. doi:10.1016/j.iheduc.2017.01.004

Bruggeman, B., Tondeur, J., Struyven, K., Pynoo, B., Garone, A., & Vanslambrouck, S. (2021). Experts speaking: Crucial teacher attributes for implementing blended learning in higher education. *The Internet and Higher Education*, *48*, 100772. doi:10.1016/j.iheduc.2020.100772

Cai, J., Yang, H. H., Gong, D., MacLeod, J., & Jin, Y. (2018, July). A case study to promote computational thinking: The lab rotation approach. In *International Conference on Blended Learning* (pp. 393-403). Springer. 10.1007/978-3-319-94505-7_32

Castedo, R., López, L. M., Chiquito, M., Navarro, J., Cabrera, J. D., & Ortega, M. F. (2019). Flipped classroom—Comparative case study in engineering higher education. *Computer Applications in Engineering Education*, *27*(1), 206–216. doi:10.1002/cae.22069

Castro, R. (2019). Blended learning in higher education: Trends and capabilities. *Education and Information Technologies*, *24*(4), 2523–2546. doi:10.100710639-019-09886-3

Dandashly, N. A., Barbar, A., & Antoun, M. (2019). The effects of using blogs and webquests in teaching education postgraduate courses. *Global Journal of Information Technology: Emerging Technologies*, *9*(1), 12–19. doi:10.18844/gjit.v9i1.4018

Deepa, M., Reba, P., Santhanamari, G., & Susithra, N. (2021). Enriched blended learning through virtual experience in microprocessors and microcontrollers course. *Journal of Engineering Education Transformations, 34*, 642-650.

Dunn, T. J., & Kennedy, M. (2019). Technology enhanced learning in higher education; motivations, engagement and academic achievement. *Computers & Education*, *137*, 104–113. doi:10.1016/j.compedu.2019.04.004

Dziuban, C., Graham, C. R., Moskal, P. D., Norberg, A., & Sicilia, N. (2018). Blended learning: The new normal and emerging technologies. *International Journal Of Educational Technology İn Higher Education*, *15*(1), 1–16. doi:10.118641239-017-0087-5

AECT Definition & the Terminology Committee. (2017). *Educational technology: A new definition*. Association for Educational Communications & Technologies. Retrieved from https://aect.org/aectnews.php

Fisher, R., Perényi, Á., & Birdthistle, N. (2021). The positive relationship between flipped and blended learning and student engagement, performance and satisfaction. *Active Learning in Higher Education*, *22*(2), 97–113. doi:10.1177/1469787418801702

Galvis, Á. H. (2018). Supporting decision-making processes on blended learning in higher education: Literature and good practices review. *International Journal of Educational Technology in Higher Education*, *15*(1), 1–38. doi:10.118641239-018-0106-1

Graham, C. R. (2006). Blended learning systems: Definition, current trends and future directions. In C. J. Bonk & C. R. Graham (Eds.), *The handbook of blended learning: Global perspectives, local designs* (pp. 3–21). Pfeiffer.

Graham, C. R. (2009). Blended learning models. In *Encyclopedia of Information Science and Technology* (2nd ed., pp. 375–382). IGI Global. doi:10.4018/978-1-60566-026-4.ch063

Graham, C. R. (2013). Emerging practice and research in blended learning. Handbook of Distance Education, 3, 333-350. doi:10.4324/9780203803738.ch21

Graham, C. R., Woodfield, W., & Harrison, J. B. (2013). A framework for institutional adoption and implementation of blended learning in higher education. *The Internet and Higher Education*, *18*(7), 4–14. doi:10.1016/j.iheduc.2012.09.003

Hao, Y. (2016). Exploring undergraduates' perspectives and flipped learning readiness in their flipped classrooms. *Computers in Human Behavior*, *59*, 82–92. doi:10.1016/j.chb.2016.01.032

Heilporn, G., Lakhal, S., & Bélisle, M. (2021). An examination of teachers' strategies to foster student engagement in blended learning in higher education. *International Journal of Educational Technology in Higher Education*, *18*(1), 1–25. doi:10.118641239-021-00260-3 PMID:34805484

Holmes, K., & Prieto-Rodriguez, E. (2018). Student and staff perceptions of a learning management system for blended learning in teacher education. *Australian Journal of Teacher Education (Online)*, *43*(3), 21–34. doi:10.14221/ajte.2018v43n3.2

Horn, M. B., & Staker, H. (2017). *Blended: Using disruptive innovation to improve schools*. John Wiley & Sons.

Hrastinski, S. (2019). What do we mean by blended learning? *TechTrends*, *63*(5), 564–569. doi:10.100711528-019-00375-5

Jones, K. A., & Sharma, R. S. (2019). An experiment in blended learning: Higher education without lectures? *International Journal of Digital Enterprise Technology*, *1*(3), 241–275. doi:10.1504/IJDET.2019.097846

Kacetl, J., & Semradova, I. (2020). Reflection on blended learning and e-learning–case study. *Procedia Computer Science*, *176*, 1322–1327. doi:10.1016/j.procs.2020.09.141

Keržič, D., Tomaževič, N., Aristovnik, A., & Umek, L. (2019). Exploring critical factors of the perceived usefulness of blended learning for higher education students. *PLoS One*, *14*(11), e0223767. doi:10.1371/journal.pone.0223767 PMID:31751345

Khalil, M. K., Abdel Meguid, E. M., & Elkhider, I. A. (2018). Teaching of anatomical sciences: A blended learning approach. *Clinical Anatomy (New York, N.Y.)*, *31*(3), 323–329. doi:10.1002/ca.23052 PMID:29352730

Lai, C. L., & Hwang, G. J. (2016). A self-regulated flipped classroom approach to improving students' learning performance in a mathematics course. *Computers & Education*, *100*, 126–140. doi:10.1016/j.compedu.2016.05.006

Ma, L., & Lee, C. S. (2021). Evaluating the effectiveness of blended learning using the ARCS model. *Journal of Computer Assisted Learning*, *37*(5), 1397–1408. doi:10.1111/jcal.12579

Margulieux, L. E., McCracken, W. M., & Catrambone, R. (2016). A taxonomy to define courses that mix face-to-face and online learning. *Educational Research Review*, *19*, 104–118. doi:10.1016/j.edurev.2016.07.001

Martín-García, A. V., Martínez-Abad, F., & Reyes-González, D. (2019). TAM and stages of adoption of blended learning in higher education by application of data mining techniques. *British Journal of Educational Technology*, *50*(5), 2484–2500. doi:10.1111/bjet.12831

Martín-Lucas, J., Torrijos-Fincias, P., Serrate-González, S., & del Dujo, Á. G. (2021). Teaching use intention and self-perception of bLearning in higher education1 Intención de uso y autopercepción docente del bLearning en educación superior. *Review of Education, 391*, 199–224.

McCutcheon, K., O'Halloran, P., & Lohan, M. (2018). Online learning versus blended learning of clinical supervisee skills with pre-registration nursing students: A randomised controlled trial. *International Journal of Nursing Studies, 82*, 30–39. doi:10.1016/j.ijnurstu.2018.02.005 PMID:29574394

Moskal, P., Dziuban, C., & Hartman, J. (2013). Blended learning: A dangerous idea? *The Internet and Higher Education, 18*, 15–23. doi:10.1016/j.iheduc.2012.12.001

Müller, C., & Mildenberger, T. (2021). Facilitating flexible learning by replacing classroom time with an online learning environment: A systematic review of blended learning in higher education. *Educational Research Review, 34*, 100394. doi:10.1016/j.edurev.2021.100394

Okaz, A. A. (2015). Integrating blended learning in higher education. *Procedia: Social and Behavioral Sciences, 186*, 600–603. doi:10.1016/j.sbspro.2015.04.086

Özdemir, İ. H., Ateş Çobanoğlu, A., & Sarsar, F. (2021). Blended Learning Adaptation in Higher Education. In Technology Readings in Education 2021 (pp. 639-649). Pegem Academy Publications.

Pelletier, K., Brown, M., Brooks, D. C., McCormack, M., Reeves, J., & Arbino, N. (2021). *EDUCAUSE Horizon Report, Teaching and Learning Edition*. EDUCAUSE. https://library.educause.edu/-/media/files/library/2021/4/2021hrteachinglearning.pdf?la=en&hash=C9DEC12398593F297CC63440 9DFF4B8C5A60B36E

Picciano, A. G. (2021). Theories and frameworks for online education: Seeking an integrated model. In *A Guide to Administering Distance Learning* (pp. 79–103). Brill.

Porter, W. W., & Graham, C. R. (2016). Institutional drivers and barriers to faculty adoption of blended learning in higher education. *British Journal of Educational Technology, 47*(4), 748–762. doi:10.1111/bjet.12269

Porter, W. W., Graham, C. R., Bodily, R. G., & Sandberg, D. S. (2016). A qualitative analysis of institutional drivers and barriers to blended learning adoption in higher education. *The internet and Higher education, 28*, 17–27. doi:10.1016/j.iheduc.2015.08.003

Porter, W. W., Graham, C. R., Spring, K. A., & Welch, K. R. (2014). Blended learning in higher education: Institutional adoption and implementation. *Computers & Education, 75*, 185–195. doi:10.1016/j.compedu.2014.02.011

Previtali, P., & Scarozza, D. (2019). Blended learning adoption: A case study of one of the oldest universities in Europe. *International Journal of Educational Management, 33*(5), 990–998. doi:10.1108/IJEM-07-2018-0197

Rao, V. (2019). Blended Learning: A New Hybrid Teaching Methodology. *Online Submission, 3*(13).

Sánchez-Gómez, M. C., Martín-García, A. V., & Mena, J. (2020). Blended learning in tertiary education: Teachers' beliefs according to the technology acceptance model. *International Journal of Learning Technology*, *15*(4), 341–359. doi:10.1504/IJLT.2020.113883

Sandanayake, T. C. (2019). Promoting open educational resources-based blended learning. *International Journal of Educational Technology in Higher Education*, *16*(1), 1–16. doi:10.118641239-019-0133-6

Singh, J., Steele, K., & Singh, L. (2021). Combining the best of online and face-to-face learning: Hybrid and blended learning approach for COVID-19, post vaccine, & post-pandemic world. *Journal of Educational Technology Systems*, *50*(2), 140–171. doi:10.1177/00472395211047865

So, H. J., & Bonk, C. J. (2010). Examining the roles of blended learning approaches in computer-supported collaborative learning (CSCL) environments: A Delphi study. *Journal of Educational Technology & Society*, *13*(3), 189–200.

Stoffregen, J. D., Pawlowski, J. M., Ras, E., Tobias, E., Šćepanović, S., Fitzpatrick, D., ... Friedrich, H. (2016). Barriers to open e-learning in public administrations: A comparative case study of the European countries Luxembourg, Germany, Montenegro and Ireland. *Technological Forecasting and Social Change*, *111*, 198–208. doi:10.1016/j.techfore.2016.06.030

Strelan, P., Osborn, A., & Palmer, E. (2020). The flipped classroom: A meta-analysis of effects on student performance across disciplines and education levels. *Educational Research Review*, *30*, 100314. doi:10.1016/j.edurev.2020.100314

Suartama, I. K., Setyosari, P., & Ulfa, S. (2019). Development of an instructional design model for mobile blended learning in higher education. *International Journal of Emerging Technologies in Learning*, *14*(16), 4. doi:10.3991/ijet.v14i16.10633

Tayebinik, M., & Putch, N. (2012). Blended and e-learning. *IMACST*, *3*(1), 103–110.

Truitt, A. A., & Ku, H. Y. (2018). A case study of third grade students' perceptions of the station rotation blended learning model in the United States. *Educational Media International*, *55*(2), 153–169. doi:10.1080/09523987.2018.1484042

Wang, T., Zhang, T., & Lovell, B. (2021). Faces a la carte: Text-to-face generation via attribute disentanglement. In *Proceedings of the IEEE/CVF Winter Conference on Applications of Computer Vision* (pp. 3380-3388). 10.1109/WACV48630.2021.00342

Yuen, A. H. K. (2010). Blended learning in Higher Education: An Exploration of Teaching Approaches. *Proceedings of the 18th International Conference on Computers in Education.*

Chapter 21
Workplace Learning Trends: Third-Party Resources as Part of an Organizational Learning Content and Knowledge Strategy

Remberto Jimenez
https://orcid.org/0000-0002-7829-5887
New Jersey City University, USA

Veronica E. O'Neill
New Jersey City University, USA

ABSTRACT

This chapter will review the concept of third-party resources for workplace learning and how organizations can use this as part of a greater learning content and knowledge strategy. This chapter will define what constitutes third-party libraries, such as LinkedIn Learning, Udemy, EmTrain, and Skillshare, and how these tools can support corporate goals. This includes looking at how third-party libraries are being used to bolster both employee retention efforts as well as general employee upskilling. Workplace learning is no longer the purview of HR or corporate leadership. The benefits and challenges of implementing such solutions are discussed. Future areas of research are also reviewed.

INTRODUCTION

Since the start of this decade, the world has changed dramatically both in terms of our personal lives and our work lives. The Covid-19 pandemic has, for better or worse, changed the ways that we interact with each other and in the ways that we utilize technology to support these interactions. The workplace was no exception; it too had to change and evolve. Strategies around employee retention and employee upskilling became an immediate necessity and had to be addressed as employees considered changing their careers as part of the "great resignation." Organizations must consider the ways in which workplace learning can support both corporate imperatives and the needs of their employees.

DOI: 10.4018/978-1-6684-6092-4.ch021

Workplace learning is not a new concept. Different names and constructs have been used over the years to describe the teams and people in the workplace learning function. Learning organizations may be called corporate universities, learning and development teams, employee experience, or human performance. Staff titles can vary as well. Roles such as instructional designers, manager of learning and development, managers of training, or even Chief Learning Officers can be found in the smallest to largest of organizations. Some roles, such as sales enablement coordinators, business operations specialists, and organizational effectiveness managers, may not have obvious titles that link to the learning function, but support the learning function for specific parts of a business.

Regardless of the name, the core of workplace learning remains the same. Workplace learning has always been tasked with supporting the core functions of an organization by training its workers. Lui-Abel (2011) notes that "organizations have always relied on their training departments to ensure workers possessed appropriate skill sets to do their job" (p. 407). Whether you are upskilling your employees with the latest compliance and regulatory requirements, or enhancing employee knowledge and skills to perform more complex tasks, workplace learning is a necessary element in both the development of a "pipeline of talent" and in employee retention efforts.

Workplace learning affects every industry, regardless of whether it is a corporate environment, an educational setting, or even a government agency. Even educational institutions have a workforce that needs to be supported with proper workplace learning. Workplace learning has a role to play in the success of any enterprise. One way to support these workforces is through the use of third-party resources.

Third-party resources are a type of educational technology that can be utilized by the workplace learning professionals to enhance training outcomes. Educational technology enables workplace professionals to consider what programs, tools, and resources can be used to support the learning function in relation to the goals and objectives within any given organizational structure. More importantly, through these tools and resources, workplace learning focuses on driving initiatives that relate back to corporate requirements and initiatives that can change at any time, based on local market conditions.

This chapter focuses on the use of third-party resources to support both corporate and employee related goals and imperatives. Before third party libraries can be explained, the intersection of what we mean by work and learning must be discussed. To help begin the conversation, a brief review of the history of workplace learning is explored in the next section.

A BRIEF HISTORY OF WORKPLACE LEARNING

Workplace learning has a history as long as work itself. Apprentices learned their trade at the feet of a master craftsman long before formal workplace training was established. As early as 1812, German and Prussian armies used wargames to allow soldiers to develop their skills before engaging in conflict with the enemy (Lewis, 2016). The late 1800's saw the rise of formal training schools and company-specific training programs for employees (Lewis, 2016). The use of role-playing scenarios, which are still common in live training settings, dates back to 1910, when Moreno described the technique (Lewis, 2016).

A turning point in workplace training began when Frederick Taylor described his theory of scientific management. In his own words, "The principal object of management should be to secure the maximum prosperity for the employer, coupled with the maximum prosperity for the employee" (Taylor, 1911). Taylor's focus to achieve this maximization was to discover the methods which allow workers to reduce unproductive time and produce results in the shortest possible time (Lewis, 2016). Taylor's influence is still seen in modern life, in fields ranging from education to manufacturing. Today's management techniques, including strategic planning, can trace their roots back to Taylor's work (Blake and Moseley, 2011).

During wartime, the need for effective workplace training became even more evident. Trained and efficient workers were needed to support the war effort in shipyards and factories. This need became more pronounced as many experienced workers enlisted in the armed forces to fight for their country, especially during World War I and World War II. (Lewis, 2016).

Individualized instruction became prevalent in the 1950's as workplace learning became focused on individual employees. Tasks were broken into discrete steps, and employees were evaluated during an activity following the learning. The use of virtual reality in training began during this period as well, although it would not be widespread for many years. (Lewis, 2016).

A new era began in the 1960's, as computerized instruction was born. This period also saw the establishment of the first of the corporate universities: General Electric's Crotonville (Rio, 2018) was started in the mid 1950's. McDonald's Hamburger University, founded by McDonald's to train its franchisees and managers was launched in 1961 (Rio, 2018). Diana Thomas, a representative of Hamburger University explains, "Hamburger U. is the center of excellence that ensures that the standards of quality, service, value and cleanliness are maintained here and around the world (Morais, Lopes & Jordão, 2011).

Computer-based training became prevalent in the 1980's and 1990's. Rather than gather in groups with an instructor, employees interact with an educational platform that provides information and uses evaluation activities to ensure comprehension. The technique of gamification began to develop momentum in the early 2000's (Lewis, 2016). Massive Open Online Courses (MOOCs), gained prominence in adult learning in 2008, and social networking sites later became an important vehicle to deliver training (Lewis, 2016).

Since the start of the 2020's, and COVID-19 pandemic, trends such as the Great Resignation and the Great Reshuffle are now being examined through various lenses of employee retention strategies. Learning and development opportunities to develop and upskill employees are one of the many elements being considered to support such efforts. As such, the role of workplace learning is even more important as the world looks to the future and deals with the realities that have unfolded since the start of the pandemic.

To support such efforts, investments are being made to bolster existing workplace learning programs, while other organizational entities are building out their nascent learning and development strategies. Workplace learning is no longer a supplementary function, but a critical one if organizations hope to compete for talent across each industry. Although workplace learning can take on many forms, the concept of third-party content as part of learning knowledge and content strategy must be considered to support the current and future needs of an organization.

DEFINING THE WORKPLACE

To define the workplace, we must first define the term work. Cairns and Malloch (2011) define work as "an enabled purposive effort by an individual to initiate or respond to an issue or problem in a range of situations for some perceived productive end…this emphasizes that the action is intentional engagement by an individual" (p. 6). Work itself is not just a location, but a learning process as well; since learning through work involves meaning making and experiences that add to each worker (Cairns, 2022, p.21).The first few decades of the 21st century have seen the broadening of how we define work and workplace. Working is no longer the purview of a specific physical location or time.

Workplaces can be in-person, remote, or hybrid environments as well. Iqbal et al., (2021) describe hybrid work environments as a system that enables employees to work from home or the office, and provide both the company and employee with a mutually beneficial arrangement, such as cost savings and limited commuting time. Similar to colleges and universities that also offer online classes, there are opportunities to work from home through other flexible arrangements.

Every organization has their mission, vision, and values on how they operate. Beyond these aspirational guidelines, they also have key roles and functions to support their overall organization mission. Each role must also have a predetermined list of tasks and functions that are to be performed. As such, each of these roles has specified knowledge, both unique to the company and specific for a given role or profession. The knowledge needed to perform a function can vary from role to role, from division to division, or even country to country. In other words, there is not one single body of knowledge, but perhaps multiple bodies of knowledge that can exist with the landscape that is an organization.

According to Wenger-Trayner and Wenger-Trayner (2015), the real body of knowledge of any profession is the "community of people who contribute to the continued vitality, application, and evolution of a practice" (p. 52-53). In organizational structures, you may have different divisions and levels of expertise that exist based on the roles and functions that are involved. Each of these roles constitutes different professions and areas of focus that form their own respective body of knowledge. As such, each of these professional occupations consist of "different communities of practice that are involved in the research, teaching, management, regulation, associations and other relevant dimensions" (p. 57).

Each of these communities come together to form a complex "landscape of practice" that evolves overtime. The knowledge needed to perform a function becomes part of the formal and informal workplace learning environments that can be both enterprise-wide or local to a given department or market. This in turn provides the information needed to create more formalized structures for learning. Specifically, the formal and informal elements of knowledge needed to perform a role informs the workplace learning strategy to be implemented within an organization.

Therefore, workplace learning sits at the intersection between work and the knowledge needed to perform the work required. Depending on the role and the work required, it may necessitate the formation of various learning programs to address the landscape of practices within an organization. Yet, understanding what learning can look like in such complex landscapes must be discussed to support the overall organizational needs and requirements of any workplace.

LEARNING WITHIN THE WORKPLACE

Cairns and Malloc (2011) define learning as "the outcome of an enabled active intentional interactional engagement in experiences and thinking" (p. 9). Hase and Blaschke (2012) describe learning as a "just in time phenomenon where opportunities to learn must be harnessed when the occasion presents itself, regardless of whether we are looking for them or not" (p.81). As such, learning can happen anytime, anywhere, and the opportunity for learning may present itself at any time.

Learning in the workplace is more than just providing employees with their annual compliance training and their new hire tasks. It is about empowering the worker to not just do their job, but to prepare them for the ongoing learning that will be required for future job opportunities, or changes to the business. O'Connor and Lynch (2011) note how an empowered, engaged individual is a productive individual; an alienated or stagnate individual simply does not care" (p. 421).

In short, we need to consider empowering workers to become life-long learners to support organizational goals and requirements. The life-long learner is not just limited to academia or to individualized personal efforts. Learning and doing so continuously is now part of the job and a requirement to support a potentially successful career. Employees must continue to learn on the job and pivot as organizational changes emerge.

Many employees were required to shift to a remote mode of doing work during the pandemic. For those same employees training that was once conducted in person is now being conducted through some form of video communication tool, such as Zoom or Google Meet, or through e-learning. During the pandemic, many of these workers did not have the convenience of walking to the next cubicle or office to ask their more tech-savvy coworker for help or guidance. They had to learn how to be self-sufficient in the new environment, and they had to learn quickly. This meant shifting one's mindset, learning new technologies, and in other cases, learning new processes and procedures to get the job done. Learners needed to engage their "learning muscles" in order to survive and thrive in the new normal.

Simultaneously, corporate leadership needed to look to learning professionals to support workplace learning as a necessary element in both the development of a pipeline of talent and in employee retention efforts. By empowering employees, organizations began to supply the tools they need to be successful and to consider potential opportunities for their career, regardless of whether those opportunities are internal or external to the organization.

In the workplace learning occurs on the job, in a meeting, or throughout various interactions with our colleagues and peers. Learning in the workplace can be both formal and informal. It can happen at any time and requires today's workers to be ready to take control of their growth and develop agency when educational opportunities arise. Since unique types of growth are required across different levels of organization, there is a varied set of competencies and knowledge that must be understood for a worker to perform effectively. This can vary significantly by role, division, function, or even country.

There is a bigger problem that needs to be considered. Specifically, is it possible to provide training and guidance across every single topic area related to a specific job or work function? The reality is that it may not be feasible depending on the limitations that exist within a given organization. These limitations can include cost, labor, and limitations related to the number of instructional designers and content creators on staff.

It may also be unrealistic to cover every single possible nuance in a complex organization. This may necessitate the use of subject matter experts within each department to play a role in upskilling or knowledge content creation. Normally, these subject matter experts have their own operational roles and functions and may not always be available to provide the expertise or knowledge needed to support such efforts by the learning team.

The learning and development function (L&D) is being tasked, now more than ever, to help upskill and retain employees. Thanks in part to the 2020 COVID-19 pandemic, and what many are titling as the great resignation, employees are no longer content with remaining in their previous roles or even within a given company. According to Pew Research Center (2022), among the top reasons for this include low pay, no opportunities for advancement, and feeling disrespected at work. From April to June of 2021 11 million workers left their jobs (U.S. Department of Labor, 2021).

Employees want to be empowered and compensated accordingly for their work. The days of staying at the same job for years is not a realistic model. Employees feel that they can go to another job and create a more beneficial situation for themselves. This is espsically the case of the employee who sees no path forward in terms of new opportunities or in term of higher wages. As such, it becomes important for an organization to find different ways to support employees and to provide them with the tools and resources to satisfy their needs, while also retaining them in the process.

Workplace learning cannot solve every single possible need and want of an individual employee, however, it can help in three critical areas. The first one refers to the area of employee upskilling: finding ways to ensure that your employees are getting the knowledge and the resources that they need to be able to perform their jobs. In some cases this also includes upskilling employees to perform expanded duties that have emerged with the realignment of resources, thanks in part to both the COVID-19 pandemic and the great resignation.

The second area of focus is to help expand employees' abilities and knowledge by providing them access to training on more advanced topics or areas that could help them to develop in their careers. This training may help them qualify for a new position or undertake a new set of responsibilities. This enrichment opportunity could include topics such as advanced Microsoft Excel skills, leadership competencies, and programming and script language knowledge. Many employees are eager to change careers or get promoted to satisfy their new realities. Providing upskilling with a focus on career growth and potential movement will go a long way towards motivating employees, quelling any issues of dissatisfaction or perceived lack of mobility in their current role.

Finally, learning and development can provide access to learning tools that cover current trends and happenings in an organization. This includes everything from harassment prevention tactics, diversity, equity and inclusion strategies, cyber security best practices, as well as empathy and workplace interactions. This will help ensure that the workplace function is being proactive and is addressing topics of the day that may be challenging to discuss in some circles.

However, not every organization has the ability, economically or physically, to produce all of this content internally. This can be for a variety of reasons including but not limited to, a lack of expertise in a given topic or subject area, lack of resources to actually build the content, or lack of reputable sources within the organization to ensure the accuracy of the content. In short, this motivates employers to look outside their own organizations in search of third-party content to supplement whatever gaps exist in the learning and knowledge strategy.

EDUCATIONAL TECHNOLOGY AND MULTIMEDIA LEARNING IN THE WORKPLACE

Third-party educational technology involves the disciplined application of knowledge for the purpose of improving learning, instruction and/or performance (Spector, 2015) and are not just for K-16 academic environments. Educational technologies, also known as instructional communication technologies (ICTs), have been used in various different settings for decades, such as corporate, government, and nonprofit organizations.

Examples of educational technologies that have been used in workplace learning include, Learning Management Systems (LMS), e-books, podcasts, videos, online scavenger hunts, as well as e-learning modules. Some organizations are exploring the use of virtual reality, augmented reality, and mixed reality technology for their employee onboarding programs. Others are beginning to explore potential future technologies including augmented, virtual,and mixed realities to be used for learning. As new technologies and media emerge, there will be more opportunities for organizations to consider these tools as potential options to support their learning efforts.

One of the more common types of educational technologies that are found in workplace environments are e-learning modules. Clark and Mayer (2014) describe e-learning as any type of instruction delivered through a device that is intended to support the learning function. Traditional e-learning is thought to be limited to the standard compliance videos that include multiple-choice quizzes as part of a knowledge check. Mayer and Clark's definition highlights how any form of electronic delivered instruction can be used to support learning.

This can include but is not limited to videos, PDF documents, podcasts or vodcast, websites, and any other type of electronic based medium. Some would consider multimedia as a subset of this division of tools. Mayer (2021) notes how learners can gain a better understanding of a topic when content is presented with both video and pictures, but not by words alone (p. 3). Considering the variety of tools that are available to instructors it would make sense that instructors can both reuse existing resources such as YouTube videos, or construct their own multimedia content (e.g., screencasts, infographics, or interactive quizzes). Yet instructors must always take a learner-centered approach when it comes to both selecting and creating multimedia tools and resources (Mayer, 2021; Lawson & Mayer, 2021; Mayer 2014).

Multimedia content is typically accessed from a learning management system (LMS). An LMS is a central hub of learning that serves as the access point to self-paced, hybrid, and live courses, while also tracking employee progress and completion rates (Jimenez and O'Neill, 2022). From a corporate or workplace learning perspective, there are various LMSs that can provide these services including, SumTotal, Cornerstone, Edapp, and Schoox.

Even prior to the COVID-19 pandemic organizations and workplaces were exploring different ways of presenting their content, such as in-person learning activities, synchronous or asynchronous online activities, and varieties of hybrid solutions. This is no different than what has been occurring in higher education or K-12 education levels. The focus in the workplace is in finding more and more ways to support employee value propositions. In academic institutions the goal is to make sure the learners are provided the opportunity to enhance their learning and overall knowledge while preparing for future careers.

In corporate environments learning and development is seen through the lens of employee benefits, employee upskilling, and talent retention. The modes for learning must still provide opportunities for employees to grow and to develop and construct new levels of knowledge. However, workplace learning is required to play a dual role as it must meet organizational requirements and endeavor to use effective instructional design and instructional communication technologies. Therefore, it becomes even more important for instructional designers and all employees involved in workplace learning to understand the instructional strategies needed to support their learners while also understanding the goals and objectives of every aspect of their organization.

LOOKING AT THIRD PARTY LEARNING CONTENT

For the purposes of this chapter, third-party learning content will be defined as any content that can be obtained, purchased or otherwise, from a third party. In essence, it is any content that was not created by an organization and is available through a subscription or available at no cost through a commons license, or other shareable license. Examples of third-party resources for workplace learning include: LinkedIn Learning, Udemy/Udemy for Business, Pluralsight, 360Learning, EmTrain, Skillshare, and Opensesame. Some of the platforms, like LinkedIn Learning, are topic agnostic and offer a wide breadth of content. Some third-party platforms are targeted to specific topics, such as Pluralsight, which offers information technology related skills. Opensesame offers human resources courses that can develop soft skills and other human resource-related topic areas.

Many of these third-party resources offer subscription services that are relatively easy to implement and use. For example, a standard subscription to the LinkedIn Learning library provides employees with access to thousands of courses. Employees can be assigned specific courses, but they may also choose topics that interest them. Some subscription services offer enterprise plans in which you can get significant benefits and discounted pricing based on the volume of licenses purchased. These enterprise subscription services provide transparency in terms of content reporting of your user base. This content can optionally be passed back to your company's LMS to track overall progress and course consumption.

Some learning platforms such as LinkedIn Learning or Cornerstone Knowledge, the knowledge platform associated with Cornerstone LMS, offer a variety of topics and content that range from podcasts, videos, white papers, to short TikTok-like videos. Many of these third-party systems are constantly upgrading their libraries with a variety of content using different modalities to support their audiences and to showcase the benefits of their solution. It becomes a competitive advantage for these organizations to showcase why their content library is better suited to the needs and wants of their clients.

Massive Online Open Courses (MOOCs) have also emerged as another alternative for third party resources. The earliest idea of MOOCs can be traced back to when the Massachusetts Institute of Technology's (MIT) OpenCourseWare (OCW) initiative was founded in 2002. During this time, MIT decided to take its classroom-based courses and make them available for free to teachers, college students, and all kinds of independent and lifelong learners (Haber, 2014). The first official MOOC can be traced back to the work of Siemens and Downes and their course: Connectivism and Connective Knowledge (Haber, 2014). Since that time, numerous MOOC consortiums were formed and provided educational content taught from its prestigious professors. Udemy, Udacity, edX, and Coursera are among the many providers that offer a variety of courses and subscription services that could support the learning needs of an organization.

The basic premise of a MOOC is that it is a free, online course that anyone with an Internet connection can sign-up for and take (Billsberry, 2013). There are MOOC providers that can supply a certificate of completion for a small fee. Learning in MOOCs differs from traditional classrooms or higher education online courses since they are typically open to an unlimited number of learners (Tang, 2021; Milligan and Littlejohn 2016; Tang et al. 2016). To succeed in such courses, learners require a high level of self-regulation (Kizilcec et al. 2017; Littlejohn et al. 2016). MOOCs differ from online offerings from suppliers such as the Khan Academy or material on video sharing websites (e.g., YouTube) in that they tend to offer a course covering a subject fully rather than the useful nuggets (Billsberry, 2013).

MOOCs offer an alternative for micro-credentialing that could be attractive to some employers. They also tend to offer an a la carte approach where organizations can invest in individual courses for their employees. MOOC providers, such as Udemy, offer specialized enterprise solutions such as Udemy for Business which can provide relevant content to support organizational needs. However, not all organizations may be in the economic position to pay for such services.

Some organizations may direct employees to use free services such as YouTube, TikTok, or Vimeo because they can provide a library of professional and specialized content. Not all employees may not be comfortable with these platforms, and not all content is created equal. Many of these are free resources and the qualifications of the creator of the content may be difficult to ascertain. There are some outstanding creators who are on YouTube, such as Leila Gharani, who offers extremely valuable and well-thought-out Microsoft Excel videos at no cost. In addition to her YouTube channel, she also offers a variety of courses, some for a fee, from her website (https://www.xelplus.com/) as well as on LInkedin Learning as well. These YouTube videos may be valuable assets for any learning knowledge strategy that include Excel skills.

Another free resource that can be equally helpful are podcasts. In its most basic form, "Podcasting is simply the creation and distribution of audio files in a series, and podcasts are consumed in a variety of ways, such as computers, mobile devices, and smart speakers, typically without a cost" (Shamburg, 2020). More and more people are looking at podcasts as an alternative to learning new things (Shamburg, 2020, Edison Research 2019). Companies should be considering this growing popular medium that supports learning as part of their recommended solution suite for their employees.

There are some podcasts that could be used to supplement key areas of knowledge and business such as the "$100 MBA Podcast," which offer a 10-minute set of episodes that focus on strategies of successful business owners and managers. "The Manager Tools'' podcast covers a variety of topics including communicating better with employees, deciding who to promote, and improving interview tactics. On the "Engaging Leader podcast," tips are offered on a variety of topics including communicating with Millennials and Generation Z employees, becoming more emotionally transparent, and creating better connections at work. A third example of a business relevant podcast is "The BBC Business Podcast.'' This podcast covers a range of topics from global news to trends in healthcare, technology, startups, and more.

In short, podcasts can offer an alternative to support employee learning that can cover a vast array of topics and subject areas. Podcasts can also be listened to at work or even outside of the workplace. They do not require any special equipment, which could also offer a viable alternative for companies that may not possess a large learning and development budget.

Free content should not be summarily dismissed from any learning content and knowledge management strategy. Free libraries of content have their place just like purchased libraries of content. Depending on the industry and level of topics needed, a hybrid solution or mix of purchased and free libraries can help push the boundaries on addressing the learning needs of any organization and help control costs.

BENEFITS AND CHALLENGES OF THIRD-PARTY RESOURCES

The first benefit of a third-party library is the plethora of content available. The subscription model for many of these libraries is one of their key selling point. Here, employees obtain access to a large range of content for a nominal fee. For example, in LinkedIn Learning one could actually search for the topic of change management and come up with hundreds of possible courses and materials that could support learning about this topic. Some of these are sub-modules within a greater curriculum, and in other cases they may be stand-alone videos that vary in terms of detail and in terms of scope. The benefit that these libraries can offer is a variety of content that may serve novice, intermediate, and advanced users. It can be a supporting set of tools for any employee group regardless of their skill set or comfort level with a given content area.

The second benefit is the just-in-time nature that these libraries can provide. Employees may have an immediate need to access key content to help them in resolving a problem, or some sort of pertinent issue related to a work task. For example, perhaps they need a reliable source on performing a return on investment (ROI) calculation that will be needed for an upcoming meeting. Alternatively, you could have a non-financial employee who needs a crash course of business financials. They could obtain this information in real time from a course subscription to a resource such as LinkedIn Learning. In short, third-party resources offer the just-in-time resources that can help employees to get what they need and move forward with their desired task.

The third benefit is third party resources can be scalable solutions for an organization. Many of these resources offer both enterprise and individually purchased licenses. Depending on the size of the organization and the budgetary constraints that may exist, libraries can be purchased to meet the needs of the budget. Sometimes buying an enterprise license for the entire company may be cost-prohibitive. There may be some cases where targeting key employees and only purchasing licenses based on a specific talent development need can also be part of the knowledge strategy. Other employees can continue to use the free resources available in YouTube and in the other free platforms.

Third-party libraries can also present challenges for the organization. The first challenge is the same as one of the benefits: there is a plethora of content that may make it difficult for an employee to find an appropriate course or topic. The challenging part of this is in finding the right content within a reasonable amount of time for some users. Employee populations usually have limited time for training. Workers need to get access to knowledge quickly and as efficiently as possible. Some organizations have pilot groups that review the content on the platform and develop a list of suggested recommended courses. This list can be used by leaders and other colleagues in the workforce. This will provide a level of credibility for the courses since someone has already reviewed and vetted the material for relevance and relative accuracy. In other organizations, the employees are left to their own devices to search and find courses that meet their needs.

The second challenge that employees might encounter with third-party resources is that not all of the courses lead to a certification or credential. Some employees may value this type of certification, and may opt to look at Massive Online Open Courses (MOOCs), or accredited certificate programs at universities and colleges to help support their credentialing needs. Not all third-party resources offer formal credentialing. Some offer badging and completion certificates for select courses.

The third challenge is that these libraries, especially those using the subscription model, may be too expensive for some organizations. There are many small organizations that may not have the funding to purchase libraries of content. This may raise questions of equity and fairness when it comes to purchasing library licenses for select employees.

A fourth challenge is that these resources may promote passive forms of learning. There are several strategies to incorporate active learning strategies in third-party resource usage. In many cases these third-party libraries may offer a multiple-choice quiz or knowledge check to help reinforce some of the concepts covered in a given course. However, this may not be the best way to apply what was learned. Instructional designers can add opportunities for reflection, and other active learning strategies to augment watching a third-party course or content.

For example, sample worksheets could be used by a leader and their direct reports to discuss what was learned and how it is applied. Some of these discussion worksheets may includes discussions to further understand that ways that the newly learned skills will be applied in an upcoming project. The worksheet can provide leaders with the means to evaluate the learners' experience with the content and its relevancy to their job function. This is supported by Lawson and Mayers's 2021 study on generative learning theory.

Lawson and Mayer (2021) describe generative learning theory as meaningful learning that occurs when learners engage in appropriate cognitive processing during learning (Fiorella & Mayer, 2015, 2016; Mayer, 2020; Wittrock, 1974, 1989). This includes active cognitive processes to support deeper learning. For example, prompting learners to generate an explanation leads to better learning, specifically from a multimedia lesson (Lawson & Mayer, 2021, p.1882). So-called passive multimedia lessons could be become more active and engaging when learners provide explanations of what they learned and how they can apply such learnings to their job. Therefore, critical deeper thinking can occur in these kinds of scenarios when learning is not passive. Ultimately the goal would be to create opportunities for critical thinking and demonstration of the new skill or knowledge. This can be done through on-the-job follow-up, coaching sessions, or even as part of an employee development plan.

In short, there are many benefits when it comes to the usage of third-party resources for learning and development. The challenge is in finding the content and finding ways to support the learning function through active learning strategies. Active learning strategies can be introduced in conjunction with these resources to offer an opportunity to support learners' self-efficacy, autonomy, and agency.

DEVELOPING A LEARNING CONTENT AND KNOWLEDGE STRATEGY

Before an organization can start looking externally at the plethora of content resources and providers that are out there, it must develop a learning knowledge and content strategy. Specifically, an analysis of an organizations' needs that both can and can't be met through the creation of internal content by internal resources. Once identified, the search begins on what external platforms or resources offer content that would meet their needs. In short, a learning knowledge and content strategy focuses on the learning collateral that an organization uses, which could be purchased, freely accessed, or internally created, to support the developmental needs of its employees. A learning knowledge and content strategy containing three key elements that can be used to support organizational goals and requirements.

The first is a base of internally created learning content. What content is the learning and development team creating and managing? This content, created by either internal organizational resources, or contractors, will have minimum cost implications to the organization. The focus on the content is specific to key processes that may be unique to a team or organization. For example, this may relate to training that supports key business processes such as a sales cycle, accounts payable system, or even an employee hiring request. These content pieces can be formal e-learnings, zoom recordings, or even one-page walkthroughs of key business processes.

The second part of the strategy is purchased learning content. The Learning and development team needs to determine what learning content must be purchased from external vendors in order to address regulatory, mandatory, and compliance-related requirements. This content may be purchased in conjunction with human resources, legal and compliance, and other entities within an organization. These are meant to be very specific, and in some cases required pieces of content. They should be prioritized with their own separate budget and looked at with the help of key subject matter experts across each of their respective domains. Examples of this kind of content include harassment prevention, cyber-security awareness and prevention, diversity, equity and inclusion, and regulatory-specific content.

The third part of this strategy refers to third-party learning resources. Third-party libraries consist of individual or enterprise-wide subscription services to support a variety of employee skill development topics. Some of these libraries could be free, such as YouTube. The topics covered in these libraries may be niche or broad depending on the provider.

These resources can service a large swath of your employee population, while also trying to keep some of the cost down. Once the content and strategy are understook the process of looking for appropriate vendors can begin. Networking with colleagues in other organizations who are in a similar function can be helpful in obtaining unbiased reactions to using these subscription services. Connecting to communities on LinkedIn, Facebook, or Twitter can offer a variety of potential vendors and subscription services that may meet the organizational needs. This is the case now more than ever since employee learning and development programs are considered a key component of any employee retention and upskilling program.

Not every organization has instructional designers who can build content. Even for the organizations that do have instructional designers, there are questions of the scalability of their development efforts to create content that can address the differing needs of employees. The one-size-fits-all approach is not realistic in terms of content development, and is both physically and economically not feasible or sustainable. However, supplementing courses through third-party resources such as Massive Online Open courses (MOOCs), and through third-party course libraries, such as LinkedIn Learning, Emtrain, and SkillShare, become potential alternatives that can support the needs of different organizations regardless of size or cash-flow. The immediate challenge is that there may be the perception and reality of what material from each of these content areas is viable for the learners of an organization. One recommendation is to start small and validate the content with experts in your organization. For example, if there are four negotiation courses that may meet the needs of your team that can be completed in LinkedIn Learning, then it may be prudent to get identified subject matter experts to take the courses and provide their feedback on which ones will best serve the needs of the organization. This will help create greater employee engagement as they realize that the material is credible and that the content is relevant and viable towards supporting organizational needs. Moreover, it will help to create a selected library of recommended content that can be communicated to the employee population. For employees, it will help teams maximize their time so they take the courses that are most relevant based on pre-selected lists of course recommendations.

Figure 1. Learning Knowledge and Content Strategy

Learning Knowledge and Content Strategy

Internally Created Content	Purchased Content	Third Party Resources
• Internally created content is created by either internal organizational resources, or contractors. • The focus on the content created is specific to key processes that may be unique to a team or organization.	• This can be one or more pieces of content that have been purchased to support a specific organizational need. • Usually, this type of content, or materials, support a key mandatory, regulatory, or compliance driven initiative (e.g., Harassment Prevention, Cybersecurity, Diversity, Equity, and Inclusion).	• Third party resources consist of individual or enterprise-wide subscription services to support a variety of employee skill development topics. • The topics covered in these libraries may be niche or broad depending on the content provider.

Content across the three pillars varies and can include multimedia materials (e.g., e-learning, videos, audio books, and podcasts) to static PDF and text-based documentation.

FUTURE RESEARCH AND CONCLUSION

Third-party content resources offer an alternative for all types of organizations. Learning and development no longer needs to be driven by what content is created by instructional designers or by subject matter experts within a given organization. Learning materials can now be purchased through libraries of content that will support the various and dynamic needs of organizations. Workplace learning is no longer just about conducting in-person training and creating custom learning modules. It is also about managing knowledge and managing the strategy on how you disseminate that knowledge across your learner base; in this case, your fellow employees. LinkedIn learning, Udemy, Skillshare, and Emshare offer a variety of options, but there are many others including other massive online open courses platforms that are available.

The proliferation of third-party content will continue as more and more content is generated. Currently, TikTok is looking at new ways of monetizing their content through TikTok Learning. Other organizations will probably follow a similar path as well. In short, there are a variety of opportunities for organizations to upskill and train their employees. This will support both employee value propositions and retention efforts, despite the challenges and in some cases, the economic realities.

There are various different models that may work for an organization. Depending on the size and budgetary constraints there may be opportunities for single license usage, or enterprise-level/organizational licensing. In cases where there are not as many options due to budgetary constraints, there are free resources that are still able to support the learning function such as YouTube. Again, the pros and cons of these different platforms need to be compared and vetted towards available funding, knowledge needs, and employee requirements.

Further studies will be needed to determine the efficacy and overall effectiveness of these resources and platforms. Many of these platforms will offer videos and content, but may not offer ways to actively use the content unless the employee applies it specifically to a work task. For example, LinkedIn Learning provides quizzes at the end of some of their modules.

Beyond that it is a question of looking at how instructional designers and or coaches can work with employees to understand and take what they have learned and apply in the context of their jobs. This will help employees take on a more active approach to their learning. Therefore, further studies and research is recommended when it comes to applying active learning strategies to third-party resource content.

This also includes a variety of content that can range from both beginner, intermediate, to more advanced topics. The effectiveness of such content needs to be evaluated and discussed by users and professionals. Finally, reinforcing the idea that learning is an active process and that just because one watches a video does not necessarily mean that learning and retention occurred. Applying generative learning theory so learners can explain what they learned can help to create more active engagement.

Following the creation of a learning content strategy, learning and development professionals can curate content and resources to address the ever-growing needs of their organizations. Learning & development is no longer just the department that manages a LMS, or creates instructor led and computer based e-learning. Content curation and knowledge management of these resources are natural outgrowths of the learning function within an organization. The content of others can be remixed and repurposed to support the needs of our learners both today and in the years to come.

REFERENCES

Billsberry, J. (2013). MOOCs: Fad or Revolution? *Journal of Management Education*, *37*(6), 739–746. doi:10.1177/1052562913509226

Blake, A. M., & Moseley, J. L. (2011) Frederick Winslow Taylor: One Hundred Years of Managerial Insight. *International Journal of Management*, *28*(4), Part 2. https://www.researchgate.net/profile/Anne-Blake/publication/286930119_Frederick_Winslow_Taylor_One_Hundred_Years_of_Mana gerial_Insight/links/5670846c08aececfd5532970/Frederick-Wins low-Taylor-One-Hundred-Years-of-Managerial-Insight.pdf

Cairns, L. G. (2022). Learning and work: theories and developments. In M. Malloch, L. Cairns, K. Evans, & B. O'Connor (Eds.), The SAGE Handbook of Learning and Work (pp. 80–98). Sage Publishing.

Cairns, L. G., & Malloch, M. S. (2011). Theories of Work, Place and Learning: New Direction. In The SAGE Handbook of Workplace Learning. SAGE Publications.

Chapman, P., Selvarajah, S., & Webster, J. (1999). Engagement in multimedia training systems. *Proceedings of the 32nd Hawaii International Conference on System Sciences.*

Chen, D.-W., & Catrambone, R. (2014). Effects of Multimedia Interactivity on Spatial Task Learning Outcomes. *Proceedings of the Human Factors and Ergonomics Society Annual Meeting*, *58*(1), 1356–1360. doi:10.1177/1541931214581283

Clark, R. C., & Mayer, R. E. (2016). *E-learning and the science of instruction: Proven guidelines for consumers*. John Wiley & Sons. doi:10.1002/9781119239086

Edison Research. (2019a). *The podcast consumer*. Available at: www.edisonresearch.com/wp-content/uploads/2019/04/Edison-Res earch-Podcast-Consumer-2019.pdf

Haber, J. (2014). MOOCs. The MIT Press.

Hase, S., & Blaschke, L. (2022). Heutagogy, Work and Lifelong Learning. In M. Malloch, L. Cairns, K. Evans, & B. O'Connor (Ed.), The SAGE Handbook of Learning and Work (pp. 80–98). Sage Publishing.

Hase, S., & Blaschke, L. M. (2021). Heutagogy and Work. In S. Hase & L. M. Blaschke (Eds.), *Unleashing the Power of Learner Agency*. EdTech Books. https://edtechbooks.org/up/work

Iqbal, K. M., Khalid, F., & Barykin, S. Y. (2021). Hybrid Workplace: The Future of Work. In B. Khan, M. Kuofie, & S. Suman (Eds.), *Handbook of Research on Future Opportunities for Technology Management Education* (pp. 28–48). IGI Global. doi:10.4018/978-1-7998-8327-2.ch003

Kizilcec, R. F., Pérez-Sanagustín, M., & Maldonado, J. J. (2017). Self-regulated learning strategies predict learner behavior and goal attainment in Massive Open Online Courses. *Computers & Education*, *104*, 18–33. doi:10.1016/j.compedu.2016.10.001

Lawson, A. P., & Mayer, R. E. (2021). Benefits of Writing an Explanation During Pauses in Multimedia Lessons. *Educational Psychology Review*, *33*(4), 1859–1885. doi:10.100710648-021-09594-w PMID:33776377

Lewis, D. (2016). *The History of Training and Development (Infographic)*. https://www.allencomm.com/blog/2016/04/history-training-development-infographic/

Lui-Abel, A. (2011). Identifying and classifying corporate universities in the United States. In M. Malloch, L. Cairns, & K. Evans (Eds.), The SAGE handbook of workplace learning (pp. 407-419). SAGE Publications Ltd. doi:10.4135/9781446200940.n30

Marsick, V., Fichter, R., & Watkins, K. (2022). From work-based learning to learning based-work: exploring the changing relationship between learning and work. In M. Malloch, L. Cairns, K. Evans, & B. O'Connor (Eds.), The SAGE Handbook of Learning and Work (pp. 80–98). Sage Publishing. doi:10.4135/9781529757217.n12

Matthews, P. (1999). Workplace learning: Developing an Holistic Model. *The Learning Organization, 6*(1), 18–29. https://citeseerx.ist.psu.edu/viewdoc/download?doi=10.1.1.990.9914&rep=rep1&type=pdf

Mayer, R. C. (2021). *Multimedia Learning* (3rd ed.). Cambridge University Press.

Mayer, R. E. (2014). The cognitive theory of multimedia learning. In R. E. Mayer (Ed.), *The Cambridge handbook of multimedia learning* (2nd ed., pp. 43–71). Cambridge University Press., doi:10.1017/CBO9781139547369.005

Milligan, C., & Littlejohn, A. (2016). How health professionals regulate their learning in massive open online courses. *The Internet and Higher Education, 31*, 113–121. doi:10.1016/j.iheduc.2016.07.005 PMID:27928198

Morais, T., Lopes, P., & Jordão, F. (2011). *Organizational culture and human resources' training and development: A study about the McDonald's Hamburger University*. https://repositorio-aberto.up.pt/bitstream/10216/71466/2/16005.pdf

O'Connor, B., & Lynch, D. (2011). Partnerships between and among education and the public and private sectors. In M. Malloch, L. Cairns, & K. Evans (Eds.), The SAGE handbook of workplace learning (pp. 407-419). SAGE Publications Ltd. doi:10.4135/9781446200940.n31

Pew Research Center. (2022). Majority of workers who quit a job in 2021 cite low pay, no opportunities for advancement, feeling disrespected. *Pew Research Center Newsletter*. https://www.pewresearch.org/fact-tank/2022/03/09/majority-of-workers-who-quit-a-job-in-2021-cite-low-pay-no-opportunities-for-advancement-feeling-disrespected/

Rio, A. (2018). *The future of the corporate university*. Chief Learning Officer. https://www.chieflearningofficer.com/2018/05/03/future-corporate-university/

Shamburg, C. (2020). Cases of successful independent educationally oriented podcasters. *E-Learning and Digital Media, 17*(6), 505–520. doi:10.1177/2042753020946281

Spector, J. M. (2015). *Foundations of educational technology: Integrative approaches and interdisciplinary perspectives*. Routledge. doi:10.4324/9781315764269

Tang, H. (2021). Person-centered analysis of self-regulated learner profiles in MOOCs: A cultural perspective. *Educational Technology Research and Development*, *69*(2), 1247–1269. doi:10.100711423-021-09939-w

Taylor, F. W. (1911). *The Principles of Scientific Management*. Harper and Brothers.

Wenger-Trayner, E., & Wenger-Trayner, B. (2015). Learning in a landscape of practice: a framework. In E. Wenger-Trayner, M. Fenton-O'Creevy, S. Hutchinson, C. Kubiak, & B. Wenger-Trayner (Eds.), *Learning in landscapes of practice* (pp. 51–78). Routledge.

KEY TERMS AND DEFINITIONS

Educational Technology: Any medium, digital or otherwise, that can be used to support the learning function in a variety of environments including academic, corporate, and government.

Great Resignation: (Also known as the great reshuffle) is the period of time starting from the 2020 Covid-19 pandemic where employees resigned from their job, in some cases without another job already secured.

Internally-Created Learning Content: This content, created by either internal organizational resources, or contractors, where the focus on the content is specific to key processes that may be unique to a team or organization.

Learning Knowledge and Content Strategy: A framework that focuses on the learning collateral that an organization uses, which could be purchased, freely accessed, or internally created, to support the developmental needs of its employees.

Learning Organization: A formal organized body created to develop key employee skills and knowledge to support organizational requirements and needs.

Purchased Learning Content: Content that is purchased by an organization to address a specific mandatory, required or regulatory need (i.e., cybersecurity and harassment prevention).

Third-Party Learning Resources: Any content that can be obtained, purchased or otherwise, from a third party to support learning in the workplace.

Workplace: Any location or place where work can be performed for an organization; this includes both physical and virtual locations.

Workplace Learning: At the intersection of work and the knowledge needed to perform a job-related function, lies the conglomeration of formal or informal learning program(s) tasked with supporting the training of its employee base.

Compilation of References

Abel, R. (2017). *Shaping the Educational Technology Innovation Ecosystem.* https://er.educause.edu/articles/2017/7/shaping-the-educational-technology-innovation-ecosystem

Ableser, J., & Moore, C. (2018, September 10). *Universal design for learning and digital accessibility: Compatible partners or a conflicted marriage?* https://er.educause.edu/articles/2018/9/universal-design-for-learning-and-digital-accessibility-compatible-partners-or-a-conflicted-marriage#:~:text=While%20UDL%20aims%20at%20a,%2C%20and%2For%20cognitive%20impairments

Acevedo-Borrega, J., Valverde-Berrocoso, J., & Garrido-Arroyo, M. del C. (2022). Computational thinking and educational technology: A scoping review of the literature. *Education Sciences, 12*(1), 39. doi:10.3390/educsci12010039

Action Against Hunger. (2021). *Central African Republic. Human Development Index.* Central African Republic | Hunger Relief in Africa | Action Against Hunger.

Adams, P. (2022, June 3). P&G's Always, Tampax sponsor esports tournament to break down gender barriers. *Marketing Dive.* https://draweb.njcu.edu/login?url=https://draweb.njcu.edu:2073/trade-journals/p-amp-gs-always-tampax-sponsor-eSports-tournament/docview/2675088378/se-2?accountid=12793

Adams, D. A., Nelson, R. R., & Todd, P. A. (1992). Perceives Usefulness, Ease of Use, and Usage of Information Technology: A Replication. *Management Information Systems Quarterly, 16*(2), 227–247. doi:10.2307/249577

Adams, D., Tan, M. H. J., Sumintono, B., & Oh, S. P. (2020). Blended Learnıng Engagement In Hıgher Educatıon Instıtutıons: A Dıfferentıal Item Functıonıng Analysıs Of Students'backgrounds. *Malaysian Journal of Learning and Instruction, 17*(1), 133–158. doi:10.32890/mjli2020.17.1.6

Adulyasas, L., & Temdee, N. (2021). The effects of integrated technology-based approach and peer coaching in teaching geometry: A closer look at teachers' TPACK and students' understanding. *Turkish Journal of Computer and Mathematics Education, 12*(3), 5695–5708. doi:10.17762/turcomat.v12i3.2244

AECT (Association for Educational Communications and Technology). (2022). *The Definition and Terminology Committee.* Retrieved on November, 9, 2022 from https://aect.org/news_manager.php?page=17578#:~:text='Educational%20technology%20is%20the%20study,'

AECT Definition & the Terminology Committee. (2017). *Educational technology: A new definition.* Association for Educational Communications & Technologies. Retrieved from https://aect.org/aectnews.php

Aflatoun International. (2021, January 7). *Digital Learning.* Digital Learning.

Afridhi & Palanivel. (2022). Digital Forensics Triage Classification Model using Hybrid Learning Approaches. *International Journal of Innovative Research in Computer Science & Technology, 9*(3), 29-39. doi:10.55524/ijircst.2022.10.3.7

Aftab, M. J., Bano, H., Qureshi, M. S., Nadeem, H. A., & Qamar, A. M. (2021). Role of assistive technology in promotion of inclusive education for children with disabilities: Special educator's perspective. *Multicultural Education, 8*(1), 325–334.

Aguilar Quintero, N. A., Velásquez Pérez, T., & Castro Silva, H. F. (2019). Information security model. Case study higher education institution. *Journal of Physics: Conf. Series, 1257*. 10.1088/1742-6596/1257/1/012014

Ahmadi, F., Hapsari, I. P., & Artharina, F. P. (2022). Developing Android-based English Multimedia in Improving the Skill of Literary Criticism. *Journal of Nonformal Education, 8*(1).

Ain, A., Bhuyan, M. H., Bhattacharyya, D. K., & Kalita, J. K. (2016). Rank Correlation for Low-Rate DDoS Attack Detection: An Empirical Evaluation. *International Journal of Network Security, 18*(3), 474–480.

Akaglo, E., & Nimako-Kodua, J. (2019). *The effects of the use of mobile phones on second cycle students in Ghana*. Retrieved from https://www. myjoyonline. com/opinion/2019/February-15th/stu dy-the-effects-of-the-useof-mobile-phones-on-second-cycle-st udents-in-ghana. php

Akçayır, G., & Akçayır, M. (2018). The flipped classroom: A review of its advantages and challenges. *Computers & Education, 126*, 334–345. doi:10.1016/j.compedu.2018.07.021

Akhtar, M. (2008, November 8). *What is self efficacy? Bandura's 4 sources of efficacy beliefs*. Positive Psychology. Retrieved from http://positivepsychology.org.uk/self-efficacy-definition-ba ndura-meaning/

Akiri, E., & Dori, Y. J. (2022). Professional growth of novice and experienced STEM teachers. *Journal of Science Education and Technology, 31*(1), 129–142. doi:10.100710956-021-09936-x

Akkara, S. (2020, September). Enhancing Second Language Listening Skills Through Smartphones: A Case Study. In *Internet of Things, Infrastructures and Mobile Applications: Proceedings of the 13th IMCL Conference* (*Vol. 1192*, p. 347). Springer Nature.

Alammary, A. (2019). Blended learning models for introductory programming courses: A systematic review. *PLoS One, 14*(9), e0221765. doi:10.1371/journal.pone.0221765 PMID:31487316

Alammary, A., Sheard, J., & Carbone, A. (2014). Blended learning in higher education: Three different design approaches. *Australasian Journal of Educational Technology, 30*(4). Advance online publication. doi:10.14742/ajet.693

Alcon, J. (2016). *13% Of The Higher Education Sector has been Infected with Ransomware, Vendor Risk Management*. https://www.bitsight.com/blog/higher-education-infected-with -ransomware

Aldawood, H., & Skinner, G. (2018, December). Educating and raising awareness on cyber security social engineering: A literature review. In *2018 IEEE International Conference on Teaching, Assessment, and Learning for Engineering (TALE)* (pp. 62-68). IEEE. 10.1109/TALE.2018.8615162

Alden, D., & Tramonti, M. (2020). Computational design thinking and physical computing: Preliminary observations of a pilot study. *Robotics, 9*(3), 71. doi:10.3390/robotics9030071

Alfawareh, H. M., & Jusoh, S. (2014). Smartphones usage among university students: Najran University case. *International Journal of Academic Research Part B, 6*(2), 321–326. doi:10.7813/2075-4124.2014/6-2/B.48

Alfoudari, A. M., Durugbo, C. M., & Aldhmour, F. M. (2021). Understanding socio-technological challenges of smart classrooms using a systematic review. *Computers & Education, 173*, 104282. doi:10.1016/j.compedu.2021.104282

Alfredsson Ågren, K., Kjellberg, A., & Hemmingsson, H. (2018). Access to and use of the internet among adolescents and young adults with intellectual disabilities in everyday settings. *Journal of Intellectual & Developmental Disability, 45*(1), 89–98. doi:10.3109/13668250.2018.1518898

Alfredsson Ågren, K., Kjellberg, A., & Hemmingsson, H. (2020). Internet opportunities and risks for adolescents with intellectual disabilities: A comparative study of parents' perceptions. *Scandinavian Journal of Occupational Therapy, 27*(8), 601–613. doi:10.1080/11038128.2020.1770330 PMID:32538241

Alimisis, D. (2013). Educational robotics: Open questions and new challenges. *Themes in Science & Technology Education, 6*(1), 63–71. https://files.eric.ed.gov/fulltext/EJ1130924.pdf

Aljaber, A. A. M. (2021). *The reality of using smartphone applications for learning in higher education of Saudi Arabia.* University of Glasgow.

Aljohani, N., & Chandran, D. (2019). *The role of individuals and social awareness in adopting mobile health applications in Saudi Arabia: A review and preliminary findings*. Academic Press.

Allen, I. E., & Seaman, J. (2010). *Class Differences: Online Education in the United States*. Sloan Consortium. https://files.eric.ed.gov/fulltext/ED529952.pdf

Almaqra, A., Almuqri, M., Alshathri, A., Aloraini, A., Alrehaili, Y., & Bin-Mubarak, A., et all (2019). Effect of caffeine consumption and air temperature on student performance. In *ACM International Conference Proceeding Series*, (pp. 250–254). Association for Computing Machinery. 10.1145/3306500.3309991

Al-Maroof, R., Al-Qaysi, N., Salloum, S. A., & Al-Emran, M. (2021). Blended learning acceptance: A systematic review of information systems models. *Technology, Knowledge and Learning,* 1-36.

Alnahdi, G. (2014). Assistive technology in special education and the universal design for learning. *The Turkish Online Journal of Educational Technology, 13*(2), 18–23.

Alotaibi, F., Furnell, S., Stengel, I., & Papadaki, M. (2016). A review of using gaming technology for cyber-security awareness. *International Journal of Information Security Resources., 6*(2), 660–666. doi:10.20533/ijisr.2042.4639.2016.0076

Alsulami, A. A., & Zein-Sabatto, S. (2020). Detection and Defense from False Data Injection Attacks in Aviation Cyber-Physical Systems Using Artificial Immune Systems. *IEEE, Int. Conf. on Computational Science and Computational Intelligence*, 69-75. 10.1109/CSCI51800.2020.00019

Alvarez, I. M., & Olivera-Smith, M. (2013). Learning in social networks: Rationale and ideas for its implementation in higher education. *Education Sciences, 3*(3), 314–325. doi:10.3390/educsci3030314

Alzougool, B., & Almansour, J. (2017). *The use of smartphone for learning activities by University students in Kuwait.* 4th Teaching & Education Conference, Venice. Retrieved from https://www.researchgate.net/publication/320001995_the_use_of_smartphone_for_learning_activities_by_university_students_in_kuwaIT

Amaliyah, A., Agusmiati, S., Zakiyah, B., Ummah, W. K., Hasanah, U., & Abdullah, D. (2021). Accelerated e-Learning Implementation through Youtube Videos Using Smartphones. *Journal of Physics: Conference Series, 1899*(1), 012155. doi:10.1088/1742-6596/1899/1/012155

Amazan-Hall, K., Chen, J. J., Chiang, K., Cullen, A. L. L., Deppe, M., Dormitorio, E., Haynes, D., Kernan, J., Quanbeck, K., Romine, M., Ruberg, B., Song, J., Stepan-Norris, J., Steinkuehler, C., & Trammell, A. (2018). Diversity and inclusion in esports programs in higher education: Leading by example at UCI. *International Journal of Gaming and Computer-Mediated Simulations, 10*(2). https://www.researchgate.net/profile/Constance-Steinkuehler/publication/326759651_Diversity_and_Inclusion_in_Esports_Programs_in_Higher_Education_Leading_by_Example_at_UCI/links/5b7df52292851c1e12291b4e/Diversity-and-Inclusion-in-Esports-Programs-in-Higher-Education-Leading-by-Example-at-UCI.pdf

Amazon. (2022, June 13). *Amazon Prime Air prepares for drone deliveries*. https://www.aboutamazon.com/news/transportation/amazon-prime-air-prepares-for-drone-deliveries

American Academy of Pediatrics. (2015). *Children with intellectual disabilities*. https://www.healthychildren.org/English/health-issues/conditions/developmental-disabilities/Pages/Intellectual-Disability.aspx

American Association of Colleges and Universities. (2022). *High-impact practices*. https://www.aacu.org/trending-topics/high-impact

American Psychological Association (APA). (2001). *Developing adolescents: A reference for professionals*. American Psychological Association.

Anderson, M. (2018). *About a quarter of rural Americans say access to high-speed internet is a major problem.* Pew Research Center FactTank. https://www.pewresearch.org/fact- major-problem/

Anderson, L. M., & Stillman, J. A. (2013). Student teaching's contribution to preservice teacher development: A review of research focused on the preparation of teachers for urban and high-needs contexts. *Review of Educational Research, 83*(1), 3–69. doi:10.3102/0034654312468619

Anderson, S. E., & Maninger, R. M. (2007). Preservice teachers' abilities, beliefs, and intentions regarding technology integration. *Journal of Educational Computing Research, 37*(2), 151–172. doi:10.2190/H1M8-562W-18J1-634P

Andrade, A., & de Carvalho, C. V. (2015). To enliven virtual communities of practice through gamification. *EAI Endorsed Transactions on Serious Games, 1*(4), e6. doi:10.4108g.1.4.e6

Anft, M. (2020). An Emerging Threat: Ransomware. *The Chronicle of Higher Education.* https://bit.ly/3z1j1sx

Annasingh, F., & Veli, T. (2016). An investigation into risks awareness and e-safety needs of children on the internet. *Interactive Technology and Smart Education, 13*(2), 147–165. doi:10.1108/ITSE-09-2015-0029

Anthony, B., Kamaludin, A., Romli, A., Raffei, A. F. M., Phon, D. N. A., Abdullah, A., & Ming, G. L. (2020). Blended learning adoption and implementation in higher education: A theoretical and systematic review. *Technology, Knowledge and Learning,* 1-48.

Anthony, B., Kamaludin, A., Romli, A., Raffei, A. F. M., Nincarean, A. L., Eh Phon, D., Abdullah, A., Ming, G. L., Shukor, N. A., Nordin, M. S., & Baba, S. (2019). Exploring the role of blended learning for teaching and learning effectiveness in institutions of higher learning: An empirical investigation. *Education and Information Technologies, 24*(6), 3433–3466. doi:10.100710639-019-09941-z

Antoniou, J. (2021). *Perceptions of novice teachers' TPACK gained from teacher preparation programs: A mixed methods research study* (Publication No. 29065154) [Doctoral dissertation, New Jersey City University]. ProQuest Dissertations & Theses Global.

Antwi-Boampong, A. (2020). Towards a faculty blended learning adoption model for higher education. *Education and Information Technologies*, *25*(3), 1639–1662. doi:10.100710639-019-10019-z

AnyKey. (2019) *Diversity & inclusion in collegiate esports: Challenges, opportunities, and interventions.* https://anykey-resources.s3.amazonaws.com/publications/AnyKey+-+Diversity+%26+Inclusion+in+Collegiate+Esports+-+Challenges%2C+Opportunities%2C+and+Interventions+(Oct+2019).pdf

AnyKey.org. (2022a). *About.* https://anykey.org/en/about

AnyKey.org. (2022b). *Inclusion 101.* https://anykey.org/en/inclusion-101

AnyKey.org. (2022c). *Keystone Code.* https://anykey.org/en/keystone-code

Archambault, L., & Crippen, K. (2009). Examining TPACK among K-12 online distance educators in the United States. *Contemporary Issues in Technology & Teacher Education*, *9*(1), 71–88. https://citejournal.org/volume-9/issue-1-09/general/examining-tpack-among-k-12-online-distance-educators-in-the-united-states/

Arctic Wolf-Educause. (2021) *Arctic EWS research paper: A strong case for the utility of cybersecurity monitoring in higher education.* Educause. https://library.educause.edu/-/media/files/library/2021/11/arcticsecurityeducause.pdf

Arina, A., & Anatolie, A. (2021). Cyber Security Threat Analysis in Higher Education Institutions as a Result of Distance Learning. *International Journal of Scientific & Technology Research*, *10*(3), 128–133.

Arnold, B. J. (2014). Gamification in education. *Proceedings of the American Society of Business and Behavioral Sciences*, *21*(1), 32–39. http://asbbs.org/files/ASBBS2014/PDF/A/ArnoldB(P32-39).pdf

Ashley, M., Cooper, K. M., Cala, J. M., & Brownell, S. E. (2017). Building better bridges into STEM: A synthesis of 25 years of literature on STEM summer bridge programs. *CBE Life Sciences Education*, *16*(4), es3. doi:10.1187/cbe.17-05-0085 PMID:29146667

Asiedu, K. G. (2022, July 20). *Meta's next big bet: The "metaversity."* https://www.protocol.com/enterprise/metaverse-in-education-morehouse-meta

Asif Khan & Hussain. (2010). Cyber Security Quantification Model. SIN' 10, Taganrog, Rostov-on-Don, Russian Federation.

Assunção Flores, M., & Gago, M. (2020). Teacher education in times of COVID-19 pandemic in Portugal: National, institutional and pedagogical responses. *Journal of Education for Teaching*, *46*(4), 507–516. Advance online publication. doi:10.1080/02607476.2020.1799709

Astuti, F. N., Suranto, S., & Masykuri, M. (2020). The appropriateness of developing the media: Experts' validation and students' response of learning media based on augmented reality technology for natural science lesson. *Journal of Physics: Conference Series*, *1567*(4), 042023. doi:10.1088/1742-6596/1567/4/042023

Ateş-Çobanoğlu, A. (2020). From Ubiquitous to Ubiquitous Blended Learning Environments. In G. Durak & S. Çankaya (Eds.), *Managing and Designing Online Courses in Ubiquitous Learning Environments* (pp. 215–232). IGI Global. doi:10.4018/978-1-5225-9779-7.ch011

Augusto-Gonzalez, J., Collen, A., & Evangelatos, S. (2019). *From the Internet of Threats to the Internet of Things: A Cyber Security Architecture for Smart Homes*. IEEE Xplore.

Austin, E. (2020, Jan 30). Fortnite banned in high school esports: Kentucky official: 'No place for shooter games'. *Courier Journal*. https://draweb.njcu.edu/login?url=https://draweb.njcu.edu:2073/newspapers/fortnite-banned-high-school-eSports/docview/2348180941/se-2?accountid=12793

Aviles, C. (2019). Playing to win: Video games finally make a legitimate move into the classroom. *Tech & Learning*, *40*(2), 20-21. https://draweb.njcu.edu/login?url=https://draweb.njcu.edu:2073/trade-journals/playing-win-video-games-finally-make-legitimate/docview/2282387302/se-2?accountid=12793

Aviles, C., Isaacs, S., Lion-Bailey, C., & Lubinsky, J. (2020). *The esports education playbook: Empowering every learner through inclusive gaming*. Dave Burgess Consulting, Incorporated.

Aynsley, S. A., Nathawat, K., & Crawford, R. M. (2018). Evaluating student perceptions of using a gamebased approach to aid learning: Braincept. *Higher Education Pedagogies*, *3*(1), 70–81. doi:10.1080/23752696.2018.1435296

Ayob, N. S., Abd Halim, N. D., Zulkifli, N. N., Zaid, N. M., & Mokhtar, M. (2020). Overview of blended learning: The effect of station rotation model on students' achievement. *Journal of Critical Reviews*, *7*(6), 320–326.

Babu. (2018). A Review on Cybersecurity Threats and Statistical Models. *Mater. Sci. Eng.*, *396*. 10.1088/1757-899X/396/1/012029

Baby, N., & Chellamani, K. (2018). Implementation of smart classrooms among secondary schools in Puducherry Union territory. *Journal of Science Education and Technology*, *14*(1), 39–51.

Bachelet, M. (2021). *Statement by the United Nations High Commissioner for Human Rights on Venezuela. 46th session of the Human Rights Council.* https://www.ohchr.org/EN/NewsEvents/Pages/DisplayNews.aspx?NewsID=26874&LangID=E

Bailey, D. (2022). Interactivity during Covid-19: Mediation of learner interactions on social presence and expected learning outcome within videoconference EFL courses. *Journal of Computers in Education*, *9*(2), 291–313. doi:10.100740692-021-00204-w

Bajc, T., Banjac, M., Todorović, M., & Stevanović, Ž. (2019). Experimental and statistical survey on local thermal comfort impact on working productivity loss in university classrooms. *Thermal Science*, *23*(1), 379–392. doi:10.2298/TSCI170920160B

Baker, C. N. (2013). Social support and success in higher education: The influence of on-campus support on African American and Latino college students. *The Urban Review*, *45*(5), 632–650. doi:10.100711256-013-0234-9

Bakken, J. P. (2019). Special education for young learners with disabilities: An introduction. In F. E. Obiakor & J. P. Bakken (Eds.), *Special education for young learners with disabilities* (pp. 1–14). Emerald.

Bakó-Biró, Z., Clements-Croome, D. J., Kochhar, N., Awbi, H. B., & Williams, M. J. (2012). Ventilation rates in schools and pupils' performance. *Building and Environment*, *48*(1), 215–223. doi:10.1016/j.buildenv.2011.08.018

Balbix. (2022). *Using Artificial Intelligence in Cybersecurity*. https://www.balbix.com/insights/artificial-intelligence-in-cybersecurity/

Bandara, I., Ioras, F., & Maher, K. (2014). Cyber Security Concerns in E-Learning Education. *Proceedings of ICERI2014 Conference*, 728-734.

Bandura, A. (1977). Self-efficacy: Toward a unifying theory of behavioral change. *Psychological Review*, *84*(2), 191–215. doi:10.1037/0033-295X.84.2.191 PMID:847061

Bandura, A. (1986). *Social foundation of thought and action*. Prentice Hall.

Bandura, A. (1994). Self-efficacy. In V. S. Ramachaudran (Ed.), *Encyclopedia of human behavior* (Vol. 4, pp. 71–81). Academic Press.

Banfield, J., & Wilkerson, B. (2014). Increasing student intrinsic motivation and self-efficacy through gamification pedagogy. *Contemporary Issues in Education Research*, *7*(4), 291–298. doi:10.19030/cier.v7i4.8843

Barabde, K. P., & Gaud, V. Y. (2019). A Survey of Data Mining Techniques for Cyber Security. *Journal of Emerging Technologies and Innovative Research*, *6*(5), 360–364.

Barker, B. S., Nugent, G., Grandgenett, N., & Adamchuk, V. I. (2012). *Robots in K-12 education: A new technology for learning*. IGI Global. doi:10.4018/978-1-4666-0182-6

Barki, L., Shidling, A., Meti, N., Narayan, D. G., & Mulla, M. M. (2016). Detection of distributed denial of service attacks in software defined networks. *IEEE International Conference on Advances in Computing, Communications and Informatics (ICACCI)*, 2576-2581.

Barni, D., Daioni, F., & Benefene, P. (2019, July). *Teacher's self-efficacy: The role of personal values and motivations for teaching*. Frontiers in Psychology. Retrieved from https://www.frontiersin.org/articles/10.3389/fpsyg.2019.01645/full#:~:text=Teachers'%20self%2Defficacy%2C%20namely,being %20in%20the%20working%20environment

Barr, D., Harrison, J., & Conery, L. (2011). Computational thinking: A digital age skill for everyone. *Learning and Leading with Technology*, *38*(6), 20–23. https://files.eric.ed.gov/fulltext/EJ918910.pdf

Barr, V., & Stephenson, C. (2011). Bringing computational thinking to K-12: What is involved and what is the role of the computer science education community? *ACM Inroads*, *2*(1), 48–54. doi:10.1145/1929887.1929905

Bartlett, B. (2018). Government as Facilitator: How Japan is Building its Cybersecurity Market. *Journal of Cyber Policy*, *3*(3), 327–343. doi:10.1080/23738871.2018.1550522

Bates, T. (2016). *Teaching in a digital age: Guidelines for designing teaching and learning* (1st ed.). SFU Document Solutions.

BBC News. (2020a). *Northumbria University Hit by Cyber Attack*. https://www.bbc.co.uk/news/ukengland-tyne-53989404

BBC News. (2020b). *Newcastle University Cyber Attack to Take Weeks to Fix*. https://www.bbc.co.uk/news/uk-england-tyne-54047179

Behrmann, M. (1994). Assistive technology for students with mild disabilities. *Intervention in School and Clinic*, *30*(2), 70–81.

Behura, D. (2021). *Cybersecurity: Proactive Leadership Strategy for Future-Focused Educational Institutions*. Education Business Unit, TCS. https://www.bluevoyant.com/resources/cybersecurity-in-higher-education/

Bendici, R. (2021). How to build an esports community. *Tech & Learning*. https://link.gale.com/apps/doc/A661267413/AONE?u=rocklandcc&sid=bookmark-AONE&xid=d80beb5b

Benedict College in South Carolina to offer a new major in Esports Administration. (2021). *Journal of Blacks in Higher Education (Online)*. https://draweb.njcu.edu/login?url=https://draweb.njcu.edu:2073/scholarly-journals/benedict-college-south-carolina-offer-new-major/docview/2556493790/se-2?accountid=12793

Berman & Buczak. (2019). *A Survey of Deep Learning Methods for Cyber Security Information.* . doi:10.3390/info10040122

Bers, M. U. (2008). *Blocks to robots: Learning with technology in the early childhood classroom.* Teachers College Press.

Bers, M. U. (2010). The TangibleK robotics program: Applied computational thinking for young children. *Early Childhood Research & Practice*, *12*(2). https://files.eric.ed.gov/fulltext/EJ910910.pdf

Bers, M. U. (2012). *Designing digital experiences for positive youth development: From playpen to playground.* Oxford University Press. doi:10.1093/acprof:oso/9780199757022.001.0001

Bers, M. U. (2018). *Coding as a playground: Programming and computational thinking in the early childhood classroom.* Routledge.

Bers, M. U., Flannery, L., Kazakoff, E. R., & Sullivan, A. (2014). Computational thinking and tinkering: Exploration of an early childhood robotics curriculum. *Computers & Education*, *72*, 145–157. doi:10.1016/j.compedu.2013.10.020

Betsch, C., Böhm, R., Korn, L., & Holtmann, C. (2017). On the benefits of explaining herd immunity in vaccine advocacy. *Nature Human Behaviour*, *1*(3), 1–6. doi:10.103841562-017-0056

Bhuyan, M. H., Bhattacharyya, D. K., & Kalita, J. K. (2015). An empirical evaluation of information metrics for low-rate and high-rate DDoS attack detection. *Pattern Recognition Letters*, *51*, 1–7.

Bild. (2017). *German media: Russians intended to use nuclear weapons in 2008*. Retrieved from: resonancedaily.com: http://www.resonancedaily.com/index.php?id_rub=2&id_artc=42590

Billsberry, J. (2013). MOOCs: Fad or Revolution? *Journal of Management Education*, *37*(6), 739–746. doi:10.1177/1052562913509226

Birch, K., Chiappetta, M., & Artyushina, A. (2020). The problem of innovation in technoscientific capitalism: Data rentiership and the policy implications of turning personal digital data into a private asset. *Policy Studies*, *41*(5), 1–20. doi:10.1080/01442872.2020.1748264

Black Collegiate Gaming Association. (2020). https://bcgausa.org/

Blake, A. M., & Moseley, J. L. (2011) Frederick Winslow Taylor: One Hundred Years of Managerial Insight. *International Journal of Management, 28*(4), Part 2. https://www.researchgate.net/profile/Anne-Blake/publication/286930119_Frederick_Winslow_Taylor_One_Hundred_Years_of_Managerial_Insight/links/5670846c08aececfd5532970/Frederick-Winslow-Taylor-One-Hundred-Years-of-Managerial-Insight.pdf

Blakemore, E. (2015, July 15). The NSA has a summer camp for cyberspies. *Smithsonian Magazine*. Retrieved from https://www.smithsonianmag.com/smart-news/nsa-has-summer-camp-cyberspies-180955999/

Blatecky, A., Clarke, D., Cutcher-Gurshenfeld, J., Dent, D., Hipp, R., Hunsinger, A., Kuslikis, A., & Michael, L. (2021, October 3*). The missing millions: Democratizing computation and data to bridge digital divides and increase access to science for underrepresented communities*. National Science Foundation OAC. Retrieved from https://www.rti.org/publication/missing-millions/fulltext.pdf

Blended Learning Models. (n.d.). *Blended Learning Universe*. https://www.blendedlearning.org/models/

Block, S., & Haack, F. (2021). Esports: A new industry. *SHS Web of Conferences, 92*. 10.1051hsconf/20219204002

Boettke, P., & Powell, B. (2021). The political economy of the COVID-19 pandemic. *Southern Economic Journal, 87*(4), 1090–1106. doi:10.1002oej.12488 PMID:33821055

Bonderud, D. (2021). *What is Multicloud, and What are its benefits for Higher Ed?* https://edtechmagazine.com/higher/article/2021/11/what-multicloud-and-what-are-its-benefits-higher-ed-perfcon

Booton, J. (2020, March 20). DRL launches academy to give students remote access to STEM tools. *Sporttechie*. https://www.sporttechie.com/drl-drone-racing-league-launches-stem-academy-coronavirus-remote-learning

Bordoloi, R., Das, P., & Das, K. (2021). *Perception towards online/blended learning at the time of Covid-19 pandemic: an academic analytics in the Indian context*. Asian Association of Open Universities Journal.

Borgström, Å., Daneback, K., & Molin, M. (2019). Young people with intellectual disabilities and social media: A literature review and thematic analysis. *Scandinavian Journal of Disability Research, 21*(1), 129–140. doi:10.16993jdr.549

Bossler, A. M., & Berenblum, T. (2019, November 18). Introduction: New directions in cybercrime research. *Journal of Crime and Justice, 24*(5). doi:10.1080/0735648X.2019.1692426

Bouck, E. C., Flanagan, S., Miller, B., & Bassette, L. (2012). Rethinking everyday technology as assistive technology to meet students' IEP goals. *Journal of Special Education Technology*, *27*(4), 47–57.

Bouck, E. C., & Long, H. (2021). Assistive technology for students with disabilities: An updated snapshot. *Journal of Special Education Technology*, *36*(4), 249–257. https://doi.org/10.1177/0162643420914624

Bouck, E. C., Matthews, L. A., & Peltier, C. (2019). Virtual manipulatives: A tool to support access and achievement with middle school students with disabilities. *Journal of Special Education Technology*, *35*(1), 51–59.

Bouck, E., & Satsangi, R. (2020). Maths assistive technology to support inclusion. In D. Chambers (Ed.), *Assistive Technology to Support Inclusive Education* (pp. 51–68). Emerald Publishing.

Bourgois, X. (2021, January 19). *Thousands of Central Africans seek refuge in Cameroon*. UNHCR The UN Refugee Agency. https://www.unhcr.org/en-us/news/latest/2021/1/6006a3fc4/thousands-central-africans-seek-refuge-cameroon.html

Bouslama, F., & Kalota, F. (2013). Creating smart classrooms to benefit from innovative technologies and learning space design. In *Proceedings of International Conference on Current Trends in Information Technology (CTIT)* (pp. 102-106). IEEE. 10.1109/CTIT.2013.6749486

Bovermann, K., & Bastiaens, T. (2018, June 25). Using gamification to foster intrinsic motivation and collaborative learning: A comparative testing. In Proceedings of EdMedia + Innovate Learning (pp. 1128–1137). Association for the Advancement of Computing in Education (AACE).

Boyle, J. R., & Joyce, R. L. (2019). Smartpen technology for note taking in inclusive English/language arts classes. *Reading & Writing Quarterly*, *35*(6), 525–538.

Boyle, J. R., & Kennedy, M. J. (2019). Innovations in classroom technology for students with disabilities. *Intervention in School and Clinic*, *55*(2), 67–70.

Bozkurt, G. (2016). Mathematics teachers and ICT: Factors affecting pre-service use in school placements. *International Journal of Research in Education and Science, 2*(2), 453–468. doi:10.21890/ijres.16161

Brantingham, P., & Brantingham, P. (2021, January 22). Crime pattern theory. *Criminology and criminal justice: Oxford research encyclopedias.* Retrieved from https://oxfordre.com/criminology/view/10.1093/acrefore/9780190264079.001.0001/acrefore-9780190264079-e-8

Brennan, K., & Resnick, M. (2012). *New frameworks for studying and assessing the development of computational thinking* [Paper presentation]. The Annual Meeting of the American Educational Research Association. https://web.media.mit.edu/~kbrennan/files/Brennan_Resnick_AERA2012_CT.pdf

Broadbent, J. (2017). Comparing online and blended learner's self-regulated learning strategies and academic performance. *The Internet and Higher Education, 33*, 24–32. doi:10.1016/j.iheduc.2017.01.004

Brooks, C. (2022, January 21). Cybersecurity in 2022: A fresh look at some very alarming stats. *Forbes*. https://www.forbes.com/sites/chuckbrooks/2022/01/21/cybersecurity-in-2022--a-fresh-look-at-some-very-alarming-stats/?sh=
6f9527556b61

Brooks, M., Mueller, J., & Thiede, B. (2021). Rural-urban differences in the labor-force impacts of COVID-19 in the United States. *Socius: Sociological Research for a Dynamic World, 7*. Advance online publication. doi:10.1177/23780231211022094 PMID:36466734

Brown, A. (2017, September 11). *Younger men play video games, but so do a diverse group of other Americans*. Pew Research Center. https://www.pewresearch.org/fact-tank/2017/09/11/younger-men-play-video-games-but-so-do-a-diverse-group-of-other-america
ns/

Brown, G., & Susskind, D. (2020). International cooperation during the COVID-19 pandemic. *Oxford Review of Economic Policy, 36*(Supplement_1), S64–S76. doi:10.1093/oxrep/graa025

Bruggeman, B., Tondeur, J., Struyven, K., Pynoo, B., Garone, A., & Vanslambrouck, S. (2021). Experts speaking: Crucial teacher attributes for implementing blended learning in higher education. *The Internet and Higher Education, 48*, 100772. doi:10.1016/j.iheduc.2020.100772

Brush, K. (n.d.). *Disaster recovery plan.* TechTarget. https://www.techtarget.com/searchdisasterrecovery/definition/disaster-recovery-plan

Buckle, A., & Bikos, K. (n.d.). *How does daylight savings work?* https://www.timeanddate.com/time/dst/transition.html

Buckley, P., & Doyle, E. (2014). Gamification and student motivation. *Interactive Learning Environments, 24*(6), 1162–1175. doi:10.1080/10494820.2014.964263

Bueger, C., & Liebetrau, T. (2021). *Protecting hidden infrastructure: The security politics of the global submarine data cable network.* Retrieved from: tandfonline.com

Buijs, P. C., Boot, E., Shugar, A., Fung, W. L., & Bassett, A. S. (2016). Internet safety issues for adolescents and adults with intellectual disabilities. *Journal of Applied Research in Intellectual Disabilities, 30*(2), 416–418. doi:10.1111/jar.12250 PMID:26914835

Bukhori, B., Said, H., Wijaya, T., & Nor, F. M. (2019). *The effect of smartphone addiction, achievement motivation, and textbook reading intensity on students' academic achievement.* Academic Press.

Burgos Salazar, J., & Campos, P. G. (2009). Model for information security in IT. *CEUR Workshop Proceedings*, *488*, 234–253.

Burunkaya, M., & Duraklar, K. (2022). Design and Implementation of an IoT-Based Smart Classroom Incubator. *Applied Sciences (Switzerland)*, *12*(4), 2233. Advance online publication. doi:10.3390/app12042233

Business Insights: Essentials. (2010). 600 Teams Now Registered for Innovative Cybersecurity Competition. *Defense & Aerospace Business*.

Byker, E. (2014). Needing TPACK without knowing it: Integrating educational technology in social studies. *Social Studies Research & Practice*, *9*(3), 106–117. doi:10.1108/SSRP-03-2014-B0008

Byun, S., Meece, J., & Irvin, M. (2012). Rural-nonrural disparities in postsecondary educational attainment revisited. *American Educational Research Journal*, *49*(3), 412–437. doi:10.3102/0002831211416344 PMID:24285873

Cai, J., Yang, H. H., Gong, D., MacLeod, J., & Jin, Y. (2018, July). A case study to promote computational thinking: The lab rotation approach. In *International Conference on Blended Learning* (pp. 393-403). Springer. 10.1007/978-3-319-94505-7_32

Cain, J., & Piascik, P. (2015). Are serious games a good strategy for pharmacy education? *American Journal of Pharmaceutical Education*, *79*(4), 47. doi:10.5688/ajpe79447 PMID:26089556

Cairns, L. G. (2022). Learning and work: theories and developments. In M. Malloch, L. Cairns, K. Evans, & B. O'Connor (Eds.), The SAGE Handbook of Learning and Work (pp. 80–98). Sage Publishing.

Cairns, L. G., & Malloch, M. S. (2011). Theories of Work, Place and Learning: New Direction. In The SAGE Handbook of Workplace Learning. SAGE Publications.

Callaghan, T., Lueck, J., Trujillo, K., & Ferdinand, A. (2021). Rural and urban differences in COVID-19 prevention behaviors. *The Journal of Rural Health*, *37*(2), 287–295. doi:10.1111/jrh.12556 PMID:33619836

Canazza, M. R. (2018). The internet as a global public good and the role of governments and multilateral organizations in global internet governance. *Meridiano*, *47*, 19. doi:10.20889/M47e19007

Caplan, J. M., Kennedy, L. W., & Neudecker, C. H. (2020). Cholera deaths in Soho, London, 1854: Risk terrain modeling for epidemiological investigations. *PLoS One*, *15*(3), e0230725. doi:10.1371/journal.pone.0230725 PMID:32226024

Caputo, D. (2012). *Applying behavioral science to the challenges of cybersecurity*. Retrieved from: https://www.mitre.org/careers/working-at-mitre/employee-voices/applying-behavioral-science-to-the-challenges-of-cybersec
urity

Carnahan, C., Zieger, L., & Crowley, K. (2016). *Drones in education: Let your student's imaginations soar*. International Society for Technology in Education.

Carpenter, N. (2018, April 23). *8 Ivy League esports clubs are set to form the Ivy Esports Conference*. https://doteSports.com/business/news/ivy-league-eSports-conference-22992

Casero-Ripollés, A. (2012). El periodismo político en España: algunas características definitorias. In A. Casero-Ripollés (Ed.), *Periodismo político en España: concepciones, tensiones y elecciones* (pp. 19–46). Sociedad Latina de Comunicación Social.

CAST. (2011). *Universal design for learning guidelines version 2.0*. CAST.

CAST. (2018). *Universal design for learning guidelines version 2.2.* http://udlguidelines.cast.org

CAST. (2018). *Universal Design for Learning Guidelines version 2.2.* Retrieved from http://udlguidelines.cast.org

CAST. (2018). *Universal Design for Learning Guidelines version 2.2.: Provide multiple means of representation.* https://udlguidelines.cast.org/representation

Castedo, R., López, L. M., Chiquito, M., Navarro, J., Cabrera, J. D., & Ortega, M. F. (2019). Flipped classroom—Comparative case study in engineering higher education. *Computer Applications in Engineering Education, 27*(1), 206–216. doi:10.1002/cae.22069

Castro, R. (2019). Blended learning in higher education: Trends and capabilities. *Education and Information Technologies, 24*(4), 2523–2546. doi:10.100710639-019-09886-3

Catalin, C. (2020). *Personal details for the entire country of Georgia.* Retrieved from: https://www.zdnet.com/article/personal-details-for-the-entire-country-of-georgia-published-online/?fbclid=IwAR0Jp5j_NCrd w9Et4k80WGwhWW3r2l2FV6COSv7MYWTqj6Qd9YpV_50jcA8

Caton, S., & Chapman, M. (2016). The use of social media and people with intellectual disability: A systematic review and thematic analysis. *Journal of Intellectual & Developmental Disability, 41*(2), 125–139. doi:10.3109/13668250.2016.1153052

Cebrián, G., Palau, R., & Mogas, J. (2020). The smart classroom as a means to the development of ESD methodologies. *Sustainability, 12*(7), 3010. doi:10.3390u12073010

Çetin, O., Ganán, C., Altena, L., Kasama, T., Inoue, D., Tamiya, K., . . . Van Eeten, M. (2019, February). Cleaning Up the Internet of Evil Things: Real-World Evidence on ISP and Consumer Efforts to Remove Mirai. NDSS.

Chadwick, D. D. (2019). Online risk for people with intellectual disabilities. *Tizard Learning Disability Review, 24*(4), 180–187. doi:10.1108/TLDR-03-2019-0008

Chambers, D. (2019). *Assistive technology to enhance inclusive education.* Oxford Research Encyclopedia of Education. doi:10.1093/acrefore/9780190264093.013.155

Chambers, D. (2020). Assistive technology supporting inclusive education: Existing and emerging trends. In D. Chambers (Ed.), *Assistive technology to support inclusive education* (pp. 1–18). Emerald Publishing.

Chandra, S., Chang, A., Day, L., Fazlullah, A., Liu, J., McBride, L., & Weiss, D. (2020). *Closing the K–12 digital divide in the age of distance learning.* Common Sense and Boston Consulting Group. https://www.commonsensemedia.org/sites/default/files/uploads/pdfs/common_sense_media_report_final_6_29_12-42pm_web_updated.pdf

Chapman, P., Selvarajah, S., & Webster, J. (1999). Engagement in multimedia training systems. *Proceedings of the 32nd Hawaii International Conference on System Sciences.*

Chartered Institute of Personnel and Development. (2021, December 6). *PESTLE analysis.* https://www.cipd.co.uk/knowledge/strategy/organisational-development/pestle-analysis-factsheet#gref

Chassidim, H., Perentis, C., Toch, E., & Lepri, B. (2020). Between Privacy and Security: The Factors that Drive Intentions to use Cyber-Security Applications. *Behaviour & Information Technology.* Advance online publication. doi:10.1080/0144929X.2020.1781259

Chaudhary, V., Agrawal, V., & Sureka, A. (2016). *An experimental study on the learning outcome of teaching elementary level children using Lego Mindstorms EV3 robotics education kit.* https://arxiv.org/pdf/1610.09610.pdf

Chavis, S. M., Lee, K. S., & Acosta, J. D. (2008). *The Sense of Community Index (SCI) Revised: The reliability and validity of the SCI-2* [Paper presentation]. The 2nd International Community Psychology Conference, Lisbon, Portugal. http://dl.icdst.org/pdfs/files/f458f0f15016819295377e5a979b1893.pdf

Chen, D.-W., & Catrambone, R. (2014). Effects of Multimedia Interactivity on Spatial Task Learning Outcomes. *Proceedings of the Human Factors and Ergonomics Society Annual Meeting*, *58*(1), 1356–1360. doi:10.1177/1541931214581283

Cheng, H., Liu, J., Xu, T., Ren, B., Mao, J., & Zhang, W. (2020). Machine learning based low-rate DDoS attack detection for SDN enabled IoT networks. *International Journal of Sensor Networks*, *34*(1), 56–69.

Chen, Y. Y., Medi, B., Safiy, A., Shamsudin, S. S. A. I. B., De Ng, K., & Malek, K. B. A. (2021). Smartphone Usage and Psychological Well-being among Malaysian University Students. *Global Business and Management Research*, *13*(2).

Cherry, K. (2020, July 22). *Self efficacy and why believing in yourself matters.* Verywellmind. Retrieved from https://www.verywellmind.com/what-is-self-efficacy-2795954

Cherry, K. (2022, February 14). *Maslow's hierarchy of needs.* Verywellmind. Retrieved from https://www.verywellmind.com/what-is-maslows-hierarchy-of-needs-4136760

Chin, W. W., & Todd, P. A. (1995). On the Use, Usefulness, and Ease of Use of Structural Equation Modeling in MIS Research: A Note of Caution. *Management Information Systems Quarterly*, *19*(2), 237–246. doi:10.2307/249690

Chita-Tegmark, M., Gravel, J., Serpa, M., Domings, Y., & Rose, D. (2012). Using the universal design for learning framework to support culturally diverse learners. *Journal of Education*, *192*, 17–22.

Choate, K., Goldhaber, D., & Theobald, R. (2021, April). The effects of COVID-19 on teacher preparation. *Phi Delta Kappan*, *102*(7), 52–57. doi:10.1177/00317217211007340

Choi, Y. H., Liu, P., Shang, Z., Wang, H., Wang, Z., Zhang, L., Zhou, J., & Zou, Q. (2020). Using deep learning to solve computer security challenges: A survey. *Cybersecurity*, *3*(1), 15. doi:10.118642400-020-00055-5

Cho, V., & Littenberg-Tobias, J. (2016). Digital devices and teaching the whole student: Developing and validating an instrument to measure educators' attitudes and beliefs. *Educational Technology Research and Development*, *64*(4), 643–659.

CIAE. Eduinclusiva, Eduglobal. (2020). *COVID-19. Nuevos contextos, nuevas demandas y experiencia docente en Chile.* Retrieved from http://eduinclusiva.cl/wp-content/upl oads/2020/10/CIAE-COVID-VFinal-1.pdf

Cihak, D. F., Wright, R., Smith, C. C., McMahon, D., & Kraiss, K. (2015). Incorporating functional digital literacy skills as part of the curriculum for high school students with intellectual disability. *Education and Training in Autism and Developmental Disabilities*, *50*(2), 155–171. https://www.jstor.org/stable/24827532

Cisomag. (2021). Top Irish Colleges Face the Ire of Ransomware Attacks. *Cyber Security Magazine*. https://cisomag.eccouncil.org/ransomware-attack-on-two-irish-colleges/

Ciufudean C, (2014). *Cyber Security Model of Artificial Social System Man-machine.* doi:10.4018/978-1-4666-6324-4.ch031

Clark, S. E. (2021). *Nursing Faculty Experiences With Mobile Technology Use in the Classroom* [Doctoral dissertation]. Walden University.

Clark, R. C., & Mayer, R. E. (2016). *E-learning and the science of instruction: Proven guidelines for consumers*. John Wiley & Sons. doi:10.1002/9781119239086

Class, V. R. (2022). *Case Studies*. Retrieved July 20, 2022, from https://www.classvr.com/case-studies/

Clement, D. (2021). *Data Lakes and Modern Analytics for Education*. https://www.bluegranite.com/blog/data-lakes-and-modern-analytics-for-education

CNN. (2020). *Trump says 'Iran appears to be standing down following its retaliatory attacks against Iraqi bases housing US troops'*. Retrieved from: https://edition.cnn.com/2020/01/07/politics/rockets-us-airbase-iraq/index.html

Cobb, C., Sudar, S., Reiter, N., Anderson, R., Roesner, F., & Kohno, T. (2018). Computer security for data collection technologies. *Development Engineering*, *3*, 1–11. doi:10.1016/j.deveng.2017.12.002 PMID:30555887

Coble, S. (2022, April 1). *House passes better cybercrime metrics act*. Info Security Group. https://www.infosecurity-magazine.com/news/house-passes-better-cybercrime/

Cohen, J., Wong, V., Krishnamachari, A., & Berlin, R. (2020). Teacher coaching in a simulated environment. *Educational Evaluation and Policy Analysis*, *42*(2), 208–231. doi:10.3102/0162373720906217

Colclasure, B. C., Thoron, B. C., & LaRose, S. E. (2019, November 5). *Teaching Students with Disabilities: Intellectual Disabilities*. AEC599/WC261. Retrieved August 4, 2022, from https://edis.ifas.ufl.edu/publication/WC261

Computer Science Teachers Association. (2017). *CSTA K-12 computer science standards, revised 2017*. https://www.csteachers.org/page/about-csta-s-k-12-nbsp-standards

ComputerScience.org. (2022). *What is a video designer?* https://www.computerscience.org/careers/video-game-designer/

Conderman, G. (2015). Assistive technologies: A lifeline for learning. *Kappa Delta Pi*, *51*(4), 173–178.

Corwin, T. A. (1998). *Prediction of and Differences in Computer Use: Universal Adoption of Notebook Computers at Three Undergraduate Institutions* [Unpublished Doctoral Dissertation]. Iowa State University.

Cote, A. C., Can, O., Foxman, M., Harris, B. C., Jansen, J., Rahman, M. W. U., & Fickle, T. (2022). The COVID season: U.S. collegiate esports programs' material challenges and opportunities during the 2020-21 pandemic. *Games and Culture*, *0*(0), 1–22. doi:10.1177/15554120221088116

Couldry, N., & Yu, J. (2018). Deconstructing datafication's brave new world. *New Media & Society*, *20*(12), 4473–4491. doi:10.1177/1461444818775968

Council for the Accreditation of Educator Preparation. (2019, February). *2013 CAEP standards*. https://caepnet.org/~/media/Files/caep/standards/caep-standards-one-pager-0219.pdf?la=en

Council for the Accreditation of Educator Preparation. (2022). *2022 initial level standards*. https://caepnet.org/~/media/Files/caep/standards/2022-initial-standards-1-pager-final.pdf?la=en

Coupland, B. (2021, Nov. 22). Drones fly in to school curriculum. *The Vindicator*. https://www.vindy.com/news/local-news/2021/11/drones-fly-in-to-school-curriculum/

Crisp, G., Nora, A., & Taggart, A. (2009). Student characteristics, pre-college, college, and environmental factors as predictors of majoring in and earning a STEM degree: An analysis of students attending a Hispanic serving institution. *American Educational Research Journal, 46*(4), 924–942. doi:10.3102/0002831209349460

Cronbach, L. J. (1951). Coefficient Alpha and the Internal Structure of Tests. *Psychometrika, 16*(3), 297–334. doi:10.1007/BF02310555

Cui, J., Wang, M., Luo, Y., & Zhong, H. (2019). DDoS detection and defense mechanism based on cognitive-inspired computing in SDN. *Future Generation Computer Systems, 97*, 275–283.

Culbertson, S., Dimarogonas, J., Costello, K., & Lanna, S. (2019). *Crossing the Digital Divide: Applying Technology to the Global Refugee Crisis*. RAND Corporation Provides Objective Research Services and Public Policy Analysis | RAND. https://www.rand.org/content/dam/rand/pubs/research_reports/RR4300/RR4322/RAND_RR4322.pdf

Cunningham, A. (2019, August 5). Why you need a password manager: Yes, you. *The New York Times*. https://www.nytimes.com/wirecutter/blog/why-you-need-a-password-manager-yes-you/

Cunningham, L. C., & Tedesco, L. A. (2002). Mission possible: Developing effective educational partnerships. *Journal of Higher Education Outreach & Engagement, 7*(1&2), 79. https://www.boisestate.edu/servicelearning/files/2012/01/Mission-Possible-Developing-EffectiveEducation-Partnerships.pdf

Cybase. (n.d.). *9 steps to putting together a disaster recovery plan*. https://cybasetech.com/site/9-steps-building-disaster-recovery-plan/

Cyber Peace Foundation. (2019). *Cyber Safety Booklet for Children for Adolescents*. New Delhi, India; Cyber Peace Foundation. Retrieved August 5, 2022, from https://www.cbse.gov.in/cbsenew/documents/Cyber%20Safety.pdf

CyberMedia. (2020). *The coronavirus is being manipulated by hackers*. Retrieved from: https://seclab.ge/post/CoronaCovid19

Cybersecurity and Infrastructure Security Agency. (n.d.). *Guide to Industrial Control Systems (ICS) Security*. https://www.cisa.gov/cisa-tabletop-exercises-packages

D'Mello, S. K. (2017). Emotional Learning Analytics. In The Handbook of Learning Analytics. Edited (pp. 115–127). SOLAR, Society for Learning Analytics and Research. doi:10.18608/hla17.010

Dağhan, G., & Gündüz, A. Y. (2022). Research trends in educational technology journals between 2000 and 2018: A web scraping study. *Education and Information Technologies, 27*(4), 5179–5214. doi:10.100710639-021-10762-2

Dale, O., & Grut, L. (2015). Mainstream ICT can support children and adolescents with ADHD and/or autism in their everyday activities. *Studies in Health Technology and Informatics, 217*, 679–684.

Dalton, W. (2019). *What is STEM? Pearson accelerated pathways*. Retrieved from https://pearsonaccelerated.com/blog/stem

Damoukidebloba. (2020). *Information Warfare*. Retrieved from: http://damoukidebloba.ge/c/news/sainformacio_omi

Dandashly, N. A., Barbar, A., & Antoun, M. (2019). The effects of using blogs and webquests in teaching education postgraduate courses. *Global Journal of Information Technology: Emerging Technologies*, *9*(1), 12–19. doi:10.18844/gjit.v9i1.4018

Darko-Adjei, N. (2019). *The use and effect of smartphones in students' learning activities: Evidence from the University of Ghana*. Legon.

Darling-Hammond, L., Flook, L., Cook-Harvey, C., Barron, B., & Osher, D. (2020). Implications for the educational practice of the science of learning and development. *Applied Developmental Science*, *24*(2), 97–140. doi:10.1080/10888691.2018.1537791

Darling-Hammond, L., & Hyler, M. E. (2020). Preparing educators for the time of COVID… and beyond. *European Journal of Teacher Education*, *43*(4), 457–465. doi:10.1080/02619768.2020.1816961

Darvin, L. (2021, Mar 12). At colleges nationwide, esports teams dominated by men. *The ConversationEducation.* https://draweb.njcu.edu/login?url=https://draweb.njcu.edu:2073/newspapers/at-colleges-nationwide-eSports-teams-dominated/docview/2500622467/se-2

Darvin, L., Holden, J., Wells, J., & Baker, T. (2021). Breaking the glass monitor: Examining the underrepresentation of women in esports environments. *Sport Management Review*, *24*(3), 475–499. Advance online publication. doi:10.1080/14413523.2021.1891746

Darvin, L., Vooris, R., & Mahoney, T. (2020). The playing experiences of esport participants: An analysis of treatment discrimination and hostility in esport environments. *Journal of Athlete Development and Experience*, *2*(1), 3. Advance online publication. doi:10.25035/jade.02.01.03

Davis, F. D. (1986). *Technology Acceptance Model for Empirically Testing New End-user Information Systems: Theory and Results* [Unpublished Doctoral Dissertation]. Massachusetts Institute of Technology.

Davis, F. D. (1989). Perceived Usefulness, Perceived Ease of Use, and User Acceptance of Information Technology. *Management Information Systems Quarterly*, *13*(3), 318–340. doi:10.2307/249008

Davis, F. D., Bagozzi, R. P., & Warshaw, P. R. (1989). User Acceptance of Computer Technology: A Comparison of Two Theoretical Models. *Management Science*, *35*(8), 982–1003. doi:10.1287/mnsc.35.8.982

de Santana, S. J., Souza, H. A., Florentin, V. A., Paiva, R., Bittencourt, I. I., & Isotani, S. (2016, April). A quantitative analysis of the most relevant gamification elements in an online learning environment. *Proceedings of the 25th International.* 10.1145/2872518.2891074

De Vera, J. L., Andrada, M. D., Bello, A. Q., & De Vera, M. J. D. (2021, June). Teachers' competencies in educational technology integration in instructional methodologies in the new normal. *Lukad: An Online Journal of Pedagogy, 1*(1), 63–84. https://lukad.org/wp-content/uploads/2021/07/volume1_issue1_devera_et_al_June2021.pdf

Deepa, M., Reba, P., Santhanamari, G., & Susithra, N. (2021). Enriched blended learning through virtual experience in microprocessors and microcontrollers course. *Journal of Engineering Education Transformations, 34*, 642-650.

Deepa, V., Sudar, K. M., & Deepalakshmi, P. (2018, December). Detection of DDoS attack on SDN control plane using hybrid machine learning techniques. In *2018 International Conference on Smart Systems and Inventive Technology (ICSSIT)* (pp. 299-303). IEEE.

Deepa, V., Sudar, K. M., & Deepalakshmi, P. (2019, March). Design of ensemble learning methods for DDoS detection in SDN environment. In *2019 International Conference on Vision Towards Emerging Trends in Communication and Networking (ViTECoN)* (pp. 1-6). IEEE.

Delello, J. A., McWhorter, R. R., Roberts, P., Dockery, H. S., DeGiuseppe, T. & Corona, F. (2021). The rise of esports: Insights into the perceived benefits and risks for college students. *International Journal of eSports Research, 1*(1).

Deller, S., & Whitacre, B. (2019). Broadband's relationship to rural housing values. *Papers in Regional Science, 98*(5), 2135–2156. doi:10.1111/pirs.12450

Demand continues to rise for cybersecurity professionals. (2021, July 21). The college of computing and informatics. Drexel university. https://drexel.edu/cci/stories/cyber-security-job-outlook/#:~:text=The%20current%20cybersecurity%20job%20outlook,for%20those%20pursuing%20cybersecurity%20positions

Demchak, C. (2021). Achieving Systemic Resilience in a Great Systems Conflict Era. *The Cyber Defense Review, 6*(2), 51–70.

Dennis, J. M., Phinney, J. S., & Chuateco, L. I. (2005). The role of motivation, parental support, and peer support in the academic success of ethnic minority first-generation college students. *Journal of College Student Development, 46*(3), 223–236. doi:10.1353/csd.2005.0023

Deterding, S. (2012). Gamification: Designing for motivation. *Interaction, 19*(4), 14–17. doi:10.1145/2212877.2212883

Deterding, S., Dixon, D., Khaled, R., & Nacke, L. (2011, September). From game design elements to gamefulness: Defining gamification. In *Proceedings of the 15th International Academic MindTrek conference: Envisioning future media environments* (pp. 9–15). ACM. 10.1145/2181037.2181040

Dewey, J. (1928). Body and mind. *Bulletin of the New York Academy of Medicine, 4*(1), 3–19. https://www.ncbi.nlm.nih.gov/pmc/articles/PMC2393849/pdf/ bullnyacadmed00900-0005.pdf PMID:19311595

DHS. (2014). *A glossary of common cybersecurity terminology.* National Initiative for Cybersecurity Careers and Studies: Department of Homeland Security. http://niccs.uscert.gov/glossary

Dichev, C., & Dicheva, D. (2017). Gamifying education: What is known, what is believed and what remains uncertain: A critical review. *International Journal of Educational Technology in Higher Education, 14*(1), 9. doi:10.118641239-017-0042-5

DictionaryC. (n.d.). https://dictionary.cambridge.org/us/dictionary/english/sport

DiFrancisco-Donoghue, J., Jenny, S. E., Douris, P. C., Ahmad, S., Yuen, K., Hassan, T., Gan, H., Abraham, K., & Sousa, A. (2021). Breaking up prolonged sitting with a 6 min walk improves executive function in women and men esports players: A randomised trial. *BMJ Open Sport & Exercise Medicine, 7*(3), e001118. doi:10.1136/bmjsem-2021-001118

Diverse. (2020, August 4). Esports Enters HBCU Turf. *Diverse: Issues in Higher Education, 37*(14), 6. https://www.diverseeducation.com/sports/article/15107472/new-partnership-to-create-eSports-league-for-hbcus

Dolamore, S. (2021). Accessibility features in Zoom to improve quality in the MPA classroom. *Journal of Public Affairs Education, 27*(3), 376–379. https://doi.org/10.1080/15236803.2021.1929020

Dondi, M., Klier, J., Panier, F., & Schubert, J. (2021, June 25). *Defining the skills citizens will need in the future world of work.* https://www.mckinsey.com/industries/public-and-social-sector/our-insights/defining-the-skills-citizens-will-need-in-the-future-world-of-work

Dormehl, L. (2018, April 25). To catch an on- line predator: New A.I. scours chatrooms looking for sex offenders. *Digital Trends.* Retrieved from https://www.digitaltrends. com/cool-tech/catt-algorithm-seeks-preda- tors-online/

Dosal, A. (2020, April 7). *How to create an effective disaster recovery plan.* Compuquip. https://www.compuquip.com/blog/disaster-recovery-plan

Drahošová, M., & Balco, P. (2017). The analysis of advantages and disadvantages of use of social media in European Union. *Procedia Computer Science, 109*, 1005–1009. doi:10.1016/j.procs.2017.05.446

Drajati, N. A., Rakerda, H., Sulistyawati, H., Nurkamto, J., & Ilmi, M. (2021). Investigating the adoption of TPACK-21CL by English pre-service teachers in a COVID-19 teaching practicum. *Indonesian Journal of Applied Linguistics, 11*(1), 124–133. doi:10.17509/ijal.v11i1.34625

Dridi, L., & Zhani, M. F. (2016). SDN-guard: DoS attacks mitigation in SDN networks. *5th IEEE International Conference on Cloud Networking (Cloudnet),* 212-217.

Drone Racing League. (2022) https://thedroneracingleague.com/about-drl/

Duffy, C. (2022, January 17). *Here's how US lawmakers could finally reign in Facebook.* CNN Business. Retrieved from https://www.cnn.com/2022/01/17/tech/meta-facebook-regulation/index.html

Dunn, T. J., & Kennedy, M. (2019). Technology enhanced learning in higher education; motivations, engagement and academic achievement. *Computers & Education, 137*, 104–113. doi:10.1016/j.compedu.2019.04.004

Duolingo. (n.d.). *Learn a language for free. Forever.* https://www.duolingo.com/

Dweck, C. S. (2006). *Mindset: The new psychology of success.* Random House Digital, Inc.

Dwikoranto, D., Setiani, R., & Tresnaningsih, S. (2021, December). Effectiveness of Mobile Learning to Increase Collaborative Ability and Science Process Skills of Students. In *International Joint Conference on Science and Engineering 2021 (IJCSE 2021)* (pp. 441-446). Atlantis Press.

Dwikoranto, D., Setiani, R., Prahani, B. K., & Mubarok, H. (2020). Mobile learning to improve student collaborative skills: An alternative to online learning in the era of Covid-19 pandemic. *Jurnal Penelitian Dan Pengkajian Ilmu Pendidikan. E-Saintika, 4*(3), 259–271.

Dykstra, R., Koutakis, P., & Hanson, N. (2021). Relationship between physical fitness variables and reaction time in esports gamers. *International Journal of eSports Research, 1*(1), 1–14. doi:10.4018/IJER.288540

Dziuban, C., Graham, C. R., Moskal, P. D., Norberg, A., & Sicilia, N. (2018). Blended learning: The new normal and emerging technologies. *International Journal Of Educational Technology İn Higher Education, 15*(1), 1–16. doi:10.118641239-017-0087-5

Ebner, M. (2022, Apr 18). *2022 EDUCAUSE Horizon Report | Teaching and Learning Edition.* https://library.educause.edu/-/media/files/library/2022/4/2022hrteachinglearning.pdf

ECPAT, INTERPOL, & UNICEF. (2022). *Disrupting Harm in South Africa: Evidence on Online Child Sexual Exploitation and Abuse*. Global Partnership to End Violence against Children. Retrieved November 27, from https://www.unicef.org/

Edison Research. (2019a). *The podcast consumer*. Available at: www.edisonresearch.com/wp-content/uploads/2019/04/Edison-Research-Podcast-Consumer-2019.pdf

Educar, E. (2020). Situación de docentes y educadores en contexto de pandemia. *Reporte de Resultados*. Retrieved from https://eligeeducar.cl/content/uploads/2020/07/ Resultados_EncuestaEEcovid_SitioWeb_mi.pdf

Educause. (2009). *Seven things you should know about... VoiceThread*. https://voicethread.com/resources/site/docs/ELI_VoiceThread.pdf

Educause. (2017). *Toolkit for New CISOs*. Educause. https://www.educause.edu/focus-areas-and-initiatives/policy-and-security/cybersecurity-program/resources/information-security-guide/career-and-workforce-development/toolkit-for-new-cisos

Educause. (n.d.a). *Business continuity and disaster recovery*. https://www.educause.edu/focus-areas-and-initiatives/policy-and-security/cybersecurity-program/resources/information-security-guide/business-continuity-and-disaster-recovery

Educause. (n.d.b). *Incidence management and response*. https://www.educause.edu/focus-areas-and-initiatives/policy-and-security/cybersecurity-program/resources/information-security-guide/incident-management-and-response

Educause. (n.d.c). *Vendor and third-party management*. https://www.educause.edu/focus-areas-and-initiatives/policy-and-security/cybersecurity-program/resources/information-security-guide/vendor-and-thirdparty-management

Edwards, L. (2022, May 23). *What is Flipgrid and how does it work for teachers and students? Tips and tricks*. https://www.techlearning.com/how-to/what-is-flipgrid-and-how-does-it-work-for-teachers-and-students

Egencia. (2021, Nov 22). *What is risk management and why is it important?* https://www.egencia.com/en/business-traveler-risk-management-process-importance

Eguchi, A. (2014, July). Robotics as a learning tool for educational transformation. In *Proceedings of the 4th International Workshop Teaching Robotics, Teaching With Robotics, 5th International Conference Robotics in Education* (pp. 27–34). https://www.terecop.eu/TRTWR-RIE2014/files/00_WFr1/00_WFr1_04.pdf

Ejimonye, J. C., & Eneogu, N. D. (2019). Educational Use And Misuse Of Smartphones Among Economics Students In Tertiary Institutions In Enugu State, Nigeria. *ADECT 2019 Proceedings*.

Eklund, G. (2018). Master's thesis as part of research-based teacher education: A Finnish case. *Journal of Teacher Education and Educators, 8*(1), 5–20. doi:10.23865/up.v13.1973

Ellis, L. (2019). Artificial Intelligence for Precision Education in Radiology – experiences in radiology teaching from a UK foundation doctor. *The British Journal of Radiology, 92*(1104), 20190779. doi:10.1259/bjr.20190779 PMID:31646896

Elnour, F. F., Himeur, Y., Petri, I., Rezgui, Y., Meskin, N., & Ahmad, A. M. (2022). Performance and energy optimization of building automation and management systems: Towards smart sustainable carbon-neutral sports facilities. *Renewable & Sustainable Energy Reviews, 162*, 112401. doi:10.1016/j.rser.2022.112401

Eng, J. (2021, October 8). 70% of kids in sports quit by their teens – here's how (and why) to keep them in the game. *Parents Together*. https://parents-together.org/70-percent-of-kids-in-sports-quit-by-their-teens-heres-how-and-why-to-keep-them-in-the-game /

Erenli, K. (2013). The impact of gamification-recommending education scenarios. *International Journal of Emerging Technologies in Learning, 8*(S1), 15–21e. doi:10.3991/ijet.v8iS1.2320

Estrada, M., Burnett, M., Campbell, A. G., Campbell, P. B., Denetclaw, W. F., Gutiérrez, C. G., Hurtado, S., John, G. H., Matsui, J., McGee, R., Okpodu, C. M., Robinson, T. J., Summers, M. F., Werner-Wasburne, M., & Zavala, M. (2016). Improving underrepresented minority student persistence in STEM. *CBE Life Sciences Education, 12*(3), es5. doi:10.1187/cbe.16-01-0038 PMID:27543633

European Commission. (2022). *A European Strategy for a Better Internet for Kids*. Retrieved Nov. 25, 2022, from https:// digital-strategy.ec.europa.eu/ en/policies/strategy-better-internet-kids

Evmenova, A. S., & King-Sears, M. E. (2013). Technology and literacy for students with disabilities. In J. Whittingham, S. Huggman, W. Rickman, & C. Wiedmaier (Eds.), Technological tools for the literacy classroom (pp. 83-104). IGI Global.

Evmenova, A. (2020). Implementation of assistive technology in inclusive classrooms. In D. Chambers (Ed.), *Assistive technology to support inclusive education* (pp. 177–194). Emerald Publishing.

Ewing, L.-A. (2021). Mentoring novice teachers. *Mentoring & Tutoring, 29*(1), 50–69. doi:10.1080/13611267.2021.1899585

Exley, T. (2021, June 24). *Esports applications in multicultural issues*. https://www.varsityesportsfoundation.org/blog-list/2021/6/24/esports-applications-in-multicultural-issues

Fargana, N., & Abdullayeva, J. (2020). Deep Learning in Cybersecurity: Challenges and Approaches. *International Journal of Cyber Warfare & Terrorism, 10*(2), 82–104. doi:10.4018/IJCWT.2020040105

Farry, M. (2021, July 6). *An old problem in the new normal: The digital divide*. https://www.newamerica.org/the-thread/an-old-problem-in-the-new-normal-the-digital-divide/

Fatkin, N. (2021). *University of Portsmouth Beefs up its Security After 'Cyber Incident' as Campus Reopens*. The News. https://www.portsmouth.co.uk/education/university-of-portsmouth-beefsup-it-security-after-cyber-incident-as-campus-reopens-3207773

Faughnan, S. A. (2021, February 5) Competitive gaming: Now a varsity sport in Barnegat. *Tap Into Barnegat/Waretown*. https://www.tapinto.net/towns/barnegat-slash-waretown/sections/education/articles/competitive-gaming-now-a-varsity-sport-in-barnegat

Fauziah, R. N., & Sulisworo, D. (2021). The Development of Applications using Augmented Reality Technology as the Teaching Media of Special Mirror Lights. *Jurnal Pendidikan Fisika, 9*(2), 117–124.

Fawareh, H. M. A., & Jusoh, S. (2017). The Use and Effects of Smartphones in Higher Education. *IJIM*, (11), 6.

Federal Communications Commission. (2020, April 28). *Children's Internet Protection Act*. Retrieved August 1, 2022, from https://www.fcc.gov/consumers/guides/childrens-internet-protection-act

Federal Trade Commission. (1998). *Children's Online Privacy Protection Act of 1998 15 U.S.C. 6501-6506 Children's Privacy (16 CFR Part 312)*. ftc.gov/legal- ibrary/browse/statutes/childrens-online-privacy-protection-act

Fefer, R., & Archick, K. (2020). *EU Data Protection Rules and U.S. Implications*. Congressional Research Service (CRS). https://bit.ly/3Pwcddp

Fenton, W. (2018, January 12). *The best (LMS) learning management systems*. https://www.pcmag.com/picks/the-best-lms-learning-management-systems

Ferguson, C. J. (2007). The good, the bad and the ugly: A meta-analytic review of positive and negative effects of violent video games. *The Psychiatric Quarterly*, *78*(4), 309–316. doi:10.100711126-007-9056-9 PMID:17914672

Ferguson, C. J., & Wang, J. C. K. (2019). Aggressive video games are not a risk factor for future aggression in youth: A longitudinal study. *Journal of Youth and Adolescence*, *48*(8), 1439–1451. doi:10.100710964-019-01069-0 PMID:31273603

Fester, J., & Starkey, E. (2022, March 11). *Three reasons why PBL is an effective solution for teachers*. Edutopia. Retrieved from https://www.edutopia.org/article/3-reasons-why-pbl-effective-option-teachers

Figg, C., & Jaipal, K. (2009). Unpacking TPACK: TPK characteristics supporting successful implementation. In I. Gibson, R. Weber, K. McFerrin, R. Carlsen, & D. Willis (Eds.), *Proceedings of SITE 2009–Society for Information Technology & Teacher Education International Conference* (pp. 4069–4073). Association for the Advancement of Computing in Education (AACE).

Finn, J. D. (1960). A new theory for instructional technology. *Audio Visual Communication Review, 8*(5), 84-94. https://www.jstor.org/stable/30216956

Fisher, R., Perényi, Á., & Birdthistle, N. (2021). The positive relationship between flipped and blended learning and student engagement, performance and satisfaction. *Active Learning in Higher Education*, *22*(2), 97–113. doi:10.1177/1469787418801702

Fiskaali, A., Lieberoth, A., & Spindler, H. (2020). Exploring institutionalised esport in high school: A mixed methods study of well-being. *Academic Conferences International Limited*. https://draweb.njcu.edu:2072/10.34190/GBL.20.0

Fletcher, A. (2020, January). Esports and the color line: Labor, skill and the exclusion of black players. *Proceedings of the 53rd Hawaii International Conference on System Sciences*. 10.24251/HICSS.2020.325

Florentine, S. (2015). Women in tech: Why esports are a win for diversity. *Cio*. https://draweb.njcu.edu/login

Flynn, D. T. (2016). STEM field persistence: The impact of engagement on postsecondary STEM persistence for underrepresented minority students. *Journal of Educational Issues*, *2*(1), 185–214. doi:10.5296/jei.v2i1.9245

FNAE. (2020). *Guidelines for primary education*. Opetushallitus. https://www.oph.fi/fi/koulutusja-tutkinnot/opetustoimi-ja-koronavirus

For.Ge. (2013). *We know your names, addresses, and relatives and we will come to Georgia soon! We are seeking revenge!* Retrieved from: https://for.ge/view/23153/jihadi-Cven-viciT-Tqveni-saxelebi-misamarTebi-naTesavebi-da-male-saqarTveloSi-CamovalT-Cven-Su rs-viZiebT.html-ლან

Fosse, T. H., Buch, R., Säfvenbom, R., & Martinussen, M. (2016). *The impact of personality and self-efficacy on academic and military performance: The mediating role of self-efficacy.* Academic Press.

Fouad, N. S. (2021). Securing higher education against cyberthreats: From an institutional risk to a national policy challenge. *Journal of Cyber Policy*, *6*(2), 137–154. doi:10.1080/23738871.2021.1973526

Four things you can do to keep yourself cybersafe. (n.d.). Cybersecurity and Infrastructure Security Agency (CISA). https://www.cisa.gov/4-things-you-can-do-keep-yourself-cyber-safe

France 24. (2021, January 27). Haut-Commissariat pour les Refugies, Camp de Gado. *Violences en Cengtrafrique: alerte a la frontiere camerounaise.* https://youtu.be/fSa2GDXJ_jU

Francisco, M. P. B., Hartman, M., & Wang, Y. (2020). Inclusion and special education. *Education in Science*, *10*(9). https://doi.org/10.3390/edusci10090238

Francis, K., & Davis, B. (2018). Coding robots as a source of instantiations for arithmetic. digital experiences in mathematics education. *Digital Experiences in Mathematics Education*, *4*(2-3), 71–86. doi:10.100740751-018-0042-7

Frankenfield, J. (2022). *EdTech.* Retrieved on November, 9, 2022 from https://www.investopedia.com/terms/e/edtech.asp

Freeman, A., Becker, S. A., & Cummins, M. (2017). *NMC/CoSN horizon report: 2017 K.* The New Media Consortium.

French, S. (2022, February 19). *DRL viewership doubled in 2021-22 season, drone racing giant reports.* https://www.thedronegirl.com/2022/02/22/drl-viewership-doubled-2022/

Friedman, S. (2008). *Roles, responsibilities, and resources: best practices in managing people.* Paper presented at PMI® Global Congress 2008—North America, Denver, CO. Newtown Square, PA: Project Management Institute.

Friend, M., Cook, L., Hurley-Chamberlain, D., & Shamberger, C. (2010). Co-teaching: An illustration of the complexity of collaboration in special education. *Journal of Educational & Psychological Consultation*, *20*(1), 9–27.

Fuad, M., Ariyani, F., Suyanto, E., & Shidiq, A. S. (2020). Exploring teachers' TPCK: Are Indonesian language teachers ready for online learning during the COVID-19 outbreak? *Universal Journal of Educational Research*, *8*(11B), 6091–6102. doi:10.13189/ujer.2020.082245

Funk, C., & Parker, K. (2018, January 9). *Diversity in the STEM workforce varies widely across jobs.* https://www.pewsocialtrends.org/2018/01/09/diversity-in-the-stem-workforce-varies-widely-across-jobs/

Galvis, Á. H. (2018). Supporting decision-making processes on blended learning in higher education: Literature and good practices review. *International Journal of Educational Technology in Higher Education*, *15*(1), 1–38. doi:10.118641239-018-0106-1

Gama, L. (2021, January 4). *Study finds 98 per cent of young Americans use social media monthly.* https://dagamawebstudio.com/study-finds-98-per-cent-of-young-americans-use-social-media-monthly/

Gandhi, R. D., & Patel, D. S. (2018). Virtual reality - Opportunities and Challenges. *International Journal for Research in Applied Science and Engineering Technology, 5*(1), 482-489. www.irjet.net

García-Tudela, P., Prendes, P., & Solano-Fernández, I. M. (2021). Smart Learning Environments: A Basic Research Towards the Definition of a Practical Model. *Smart Learning Environments, 8*(1), 9. Advance online publication. doi:10.118640561-021-00155-w

Garden State Esports. (2022). https://gsesports.org/about/

Ge, O. (2019). *How We Defeated Cyber Assault and Propaganda in 2008.* Retrieved from: https://on.ge/

General Data Protection Regulation. (2016). *European Parliament.* https://bit.ly/2Ln3kBr

Georgian Public Television. (2020a). *Iran has declared the US military as a terrorist organization.* Retrieved from: https://1tv.ge/news/iranma-ashsh-is-samkhedro-dzalebi-terori stul-organizaciad-gamoackhada/

Georgian Public Television. (2020b). *A new confrontation between USA and Iran.* Retrieved from: https://1tv.ge/news/ashsh-is-usafrtkhoebis-uwyeba-iranis-mkh ridan-shesadzloa-ashsh-ze-%E2%80%8Bkibertavdaskhma-gankhorci eldes/

Georgian State Security Service. (2019). *The number and potential supporters of Daesh living in Georgia have decreased.* Retrieved from: https://imedinews.ge/ge/samartali/100997/susi-saqartveloshi-mtskhovreb-daeshis-shesadzlo-mkhardamcherta-raodenoba-da-gav lena-shemtsirda

Georgian State Security Service. (2020). *Combating Terrorism.* Retrieved from: https://ssg.gov.ge/page/counter-terrorism

Giakoni-Ramírez, F., Merellano-Navarro, E., & Duclos-Bastías, D. (2022). Professional esports players: Motivation and physical activity levels. *International Journal of Environmental Research and Public Health, 19*(4), 2256. doi:10.3390/ijerph19042256 PMID:35206445

Gikas, J., & Grant, M. M. (2013). Mobile computing devices in higher education: Student perspectives on learning with cellphones, smartphones & social media. *The Internet and Higher Education, 19*, 18–26. doi:10.1016/j.iheduc.2013.06.002

Gilliam, M., Jagoda, P., Fabiyi, C., Lyman, P., Wilson, C., Hill, B., & Bouris, A. (2017). Alternate reality games as an informal learning tool for generating STEM engagement among underrepresented youth: A qualitative evaluation of the source. *Journal of Science Education and Technology, 26*(3), 295–308. doi:10.100710956-016-9679-4

Giotis, K., Argyropoulos, C., Androulidakis, G., Kalogeras, D., & Maglaris, V. (2014). Combining OpenFlow and sFlow for an effective and scalable anomaly detection and mitigation mechanism on SDN environments. *Computer Networks, 62*, 122–136.

Glazer, E., Hannafin, M. J., & Song, L. (2005). Promoting technology integration through collaborative apprenticeship. *Educational Technology Research and Development, 53*(4), 57–67. doi:10.1007/BF02504685

Goldhaber, D., Krieg, J., Naito, N., & Theobald, R. (2020). Making the most of student teaching: The importance of mentors and scope for change. *Education Finance and Policy, 15*(3), 581–591. doi:10.1162/edfp_a_00305

Gotsiridze, A. (2019). *Cyber-Dimension of the 2008 Georgia-Russia War.* Retrieved from: https://www.gfsis.org/ge/blog/view/970

Gough, C. (2019, October 15). *Topic: Mobile gaming.* https://www.statista.com/topics/1906/mobile-gaming/

Government of Rwanda. (2020). *An Architecture for the Integrated Education Management Information System, Towards the Integration of the EMIS in Rwanda.* Report.

Graham, C. R. (2013). Emerging practice and research in blended learning. Handbook of Distance Education, 3, 333-350. doi:10.4324/9780203803738.ch21

Graham, C. R. (2006). Blended learning systems: Definition, current trends and future directions. In C. J. Bonk & C. R. Graham (Eds.), *The handbook of blended learning: Global perspectives, local designs* (pp. 3–21). Pfeiffer.

Graham, C. R. (2009). Blended learning models. In *Encyclopedia of Information Science and Technology* (2nd ed., pp. 375–382). IGI Global. doi:10.4018/978-1-60566-026-4.ch063

Graham, C. R., Woodfield, W., & Harrison, J. B. (2013). A framework for institutional adoption and implementation of blended learning in higher education. *The Internet and Higher Education, 18*(7), 4–14. doi:10.1016/j.iheduc.2012.09.003

Graham, M. J., Frederick, J., Byars-Winston, A., Hunter, A. B., & Handelsman, J. (2013). Increasing persistence of college students in STEM. *Science, 341*(6153), 1455–1456. doi:10.1126cience.1240487 PMID:24072909

Greene, C. (2022, June 3). *Digital accessibility's intersection with universal design for learning.* https://ctl.jhsph.edu/blog/posts/accessibility-intersection-with-UDL/

Gromik, N., & Litz, D. (2021). Study Benefits of Smartphones: Perceptions of Female Emirati Pre-Service Teacher Undergraduates. *Education Sciences, 11*(12), 817. doi:10.3390/educsci11120817

Gross, B., & Opalka, A. (2020). *Too many schools leave learning to chance during the pandemic.* Center on Reinventing Public Education. https://www.crpe.org/sites/default/files/final_national_sample_brief_2020.pdf

Gross, O. (2015). Cyber Responsibility to Protect: Legal Obligations of States Directly Affected by Cyber-Incidents. *Cornell Int'l LJ, 48*, 481.

Grover, S. (2018, February 25). *The 5th "C" of 21st century skills? Try computational thinking (not coding).* https://www.edsurge.com/news/2018-02-25-the-5th-c-of-21st-century-skills-try-computational-thinking-not-coding?

Grover, S., & Pea, R. (2013). Computational thinking in K–12: A review of the state of the field. *Educational Researcher, 42*(1), 38–43. doi:10.3102/0013189X12463051

Grynova, M., & Kalinichenko, I. (2018). Trends in inclusive education in the USA and Canada. *Comparative Professional Pedagogy, 8*(2), 28–34.

Gunes, B., Kayisoglu, G., & Bolat, P. (2021). Cyber security risk assessment for seaports: A case study of a container port. *Computers & Security, 103*, 102196. doi:10.1016/j.cose.2021.102196

Gunnell, M. (2020, Apr 10). *What is Zoombombing, and how can you stop it?* https://www.howtogeek.com/667183/what-is-zoombombing-and-how-can-you-stop-it/

Guntur, M. I. S., & Setyaningrum, W. (2021). The Effectiveness of Augmented Reality in Learning Vector to Improve Students' Spatial and Problem-Solving Skills. *International Journal of Interactive Mobile Technologies, 15*(5), 159. doi:10.3991/ijim.v15i05.19037

Guthrie, G. (2020, Nov 3). *Qualitative risk analysis vs quantitative risk analysis: What's the difference?* https://backlog.com/blog/qualitative-risk-analysis-vs-quantitative-risk-analysis-whats-difference/

Haber, J. (2014). MOOCs. The MIT Press.

Hadarics, K., Leitold, F., & Arrott, A. (2017). Distributed vulnerability assessment applied to measuring citizen cyberhealth and securing online public services. *Central and Eastern European eDem and eGov Days, 325*, 137-144.

Háhn, J., & Radke, K. (2020). Combining expertise from linguistics and tourism: a tale of two cities. In F. Helm & A. Beaven (Eds.), *Designing and implementing virtual exchange – a collection of case studies* (pp. 11–22). doi:10.14705/rpnet.2020.45.1111

Hamari, J., Koivisto, J., & Sarsa, H. (2014, January). *Does gamification work? A literature review of empirical studies on gamification* [Paper presentation]. The 47th Hawaii International Conference on System Sciences (HICSS). 10.1109/HICSS.2014.377

Hamari, J., & Sjöblom, M. (2017). What is esports and why do people watch it? *Internet Research, 27*(2), 211–232. doi:10.1108/IntR-04-2016-0085

Han, Z., & Xu, A. (2021). Ecological evolution path of smart education platform based on deep learning and image detection. *Microprocessors and Microsystems, 80*, 103343. doi:10.1016/j.micpro.2020.103343

Hao, Y. (2016). Exploring undergraduates' perspectives and flipped learning readiness in their flipped classrooms. *Computers in Human Behavior, 59*, 82–92. doi:10.1016/j.chb.2016.01.032

Hariadi, B., Sunarto, M. J., Sagirani, T., Amelia, T., Lemantara, J., Prahani, B. K., & Jatmiko, B. (2021). Higher Order Thinking Skills for Improved Learning Outcomes Among Indonesian Students: A Blended Web Mobile Learning (BWML) Model. *International Journal of Interactive Mobile Technologies, 15*(7), 4. doi:10.3991/ijim.v15i07.17909

Harris, A., & de Bruin, L. R. (2018). Secondary school creativity, teacher practice and STEAM education: An international study. *Journal of Educational Change, 19*(2), 153–179. https://doi.org/10.1007/s10833-017-9311-2

Harwell, D. (2020). Mass school closures in the wake of the coronavirus are driving a new wave. *Washington Post*. https://www.washingtonpost.com/technology/2020/04/01/online-proctoring-college-exams-coronavirus/

Hase, S., & Blaschke, L. (2022). Heutagogy, Work and Lifelong Learning. In M. Malloch, L. Cairns, K. Evans, & B. O'Connor (Ed.), The SAGE Handbook of Learning and Work (pp. 80–98). Sage Publishing.

Hase, S., & Blaschke, L. M. (2021). Heutagogy and Work. In S. Hase & L. M. Blaschke (Eds.), *Unleashing the Power of Learner Agency*. EdTech Books. https://edtechbooks.org/up/work

Hashey, A. I., & Stahl, S. (2014). Making online learning accessible for students with disabilities. *Teaching Exceptional Children, 46*(5), 70–78.

Haverinen-Shaughnessy, U., & Shaughnessy, R. J. (2015). Effects of classroom ventilation rate and temperature on students' test scores. *PLoS One, 10*(8), 1–14. doi:10.1371/journal.pone.0136165 PMID:26317643

Hayat, F., Ahmad, D. S., & Ullah, M. K. (2021). Impact of Mobile Phone Use on Students' Moral and Learning Behaviour at Higher Secondary School Level. *International Research Journal of Education and Innovation, 2*(2), 356–368. doi:10.53575/irjei.36-v2.2(21)356-368

Hayday, & Collison, H. (2020). Exploring the contested notion of social inclusion and gender inclusivity within esport spaces. *Social Inclusion, 8*(3), 197–208. doi:10.17645/si.v8i3.2755

Hayes, H. B. (2013, April 2). *How to help teachers integrate assistive technology into the classroom*. EdTech Magazine. https://edtechmagazine.com/k12/article/2013/04/how-help-teachers-integrate-assistive-technology-classroom

Hazan, B., Zhang, W., Olcum, E., Bergdoll, R., Grandoit, E., Mandelbaum, F., Wilson-Doenges, G., & Rabin, L. A. (2018). Gamification of an undergraduate psychology statistics lab: Benefits to perceived competence. *Statistics Education Research Journal, 17*(2), 255–265. doi:10.52041erj.v17i2.169

Heilporn, G., Lakhal, S., & Bélisle, M. (2021). An examination of teachers' strategies to foster student engagement in blended learning in higher education. *International Journal of Educational Technology in Higher Education, 18*(1), 1–25. doi:10.118641239-021-00260-3 PMID:34805484

Henderson, P. B., Cortina, T. J., Wing, J. M., & Hazzan, O. (2007, March). Computational thinking. *ACM SIGCSE Bulletin, 39*(1), 195–196. doi:10.1145/1227310.1227378

Hendrix, M., Al-Sherbaz, A., & Victoria, B. (2016). Game based cyber security training: Are serious games suitable for cyber security training? *International Journal of Serious Games, 3*(1), 53–61. doi:10.17083/ijsg.v3i1.107

Hernández Sampieri, R., & Mendoza Torres, C. P. (2018). *The Quantitative, Qualitative and Mixed Routes Research Methodology*. McGraw-Hill Interam.

Herr, D. J. C., Akbar, B., Brummet, J., Flores, S., Gordon, A., Gray, B., & Murday, J. (2019, August). Convergence education- an international perspective. *Journal of Nanoparticle Research, 2019*(21), 229. https://doi.org/10.1007/s11051-019-4638-7

Hilbert, J. (2019, April 9). *Gaming & gender: How inclusive are esports?* https://www.sportsintegrityinitiative.com/gaming-gender-how-inclusive-are-eSports/

Hiles, A. (2007). *The Definitive Handbook of Business Continuity Management*. John Wiley and Sons Ltd.

Hill, J. (2021). Pre-service teacher experiences during COVID 19: Exploring the uncertainties between clinical practice and distance learning. *Journal of Practical Studies in Education, 2*(2), 1–13. doi:10.46809/jpse.v2i2.18

Hoffer, M., & Grandgenett, N. (2012). TPACK development in teacher education: A longitudinal study of preservice teachers in a secondary M.A.Ed. program. *Journal of Research on Technology in Education, 45*(1), 83–106. doi:10.1080/15391523.2012.10782598

Hofstede, G. (n.d.). *National culture*. https://hi.hofstede-insights.com/national-culture

Holden, J. T., Edelman, M., & Baker, T. A. (2020) A short treatise on esports and the law: How America regulates its next national pastime. *University of Illinois Law Review*. https://www.illinoislawreview.org/wp-content/uploads/2020/04/Holden.pdf

Holmes, E. N. (2022). *Children and the Internet: Legal Considerations in Restricting Access to Content*. Congressional Research Service. Retrieved July 17, 2022, from https://crsreports.congress.gov/product/pdf/R/R47049

Holmes, K., & Prieto-Rodriguez, E. (2018). Student and staff perceptions of a learning management system for blended learning in teacher education. *Australian Journal of Teacher Education (Online), 43*(3), 21–34. doi:10.14221/ajte.2018v43n3.2

Holmquist, C., Gable, R. K., & Billups, F. D. (2013). The relationship between self-efficacy and persistence in adult remedial education. *NERA Conference Proceedings 2013*. https://opencommons.uconn.edu/nera_2013/17

Hoque, N., Bhattacharyya, D. K., & Kalita, J. K. (2016). FFSc: A novel measure for low-rate and high-rate DDoS attack detection using multivariate data analysis. *Security and Communication Networks*, *9*(13), 2032–2041.

Horn, M. B., & Staker, H. (2017). *Blended: Using disruptive innovation to improve schools*. John Wiley & Sons.

Horrigan, J. (2020). *Census Pulse data shows some growth in computer access for students, but not much for internet availability at home*. Benton Institute for Broadband & Society. https://www.benton.org/blog/digital-tools-learning

Hovey, K. A., Lohmann, M. J., & Gauvreau, A. N. (2021). Enhancing learning for all students: Using a UDL framework to create expert learners. In A. M. Quinzio-Zafran & E. A. Wilkins (Eds.), *The New Teacher's Guide to Overcoming Common Challenges: Curated Advice from Award-winning Teachers*. Routledge.

Hrastinski, S. (2019). What do we mean by blended learning? *TechTrends*, *63*(5), 564–569. doi:10.100711528-019-00375-5

Hu, C., & Fyfe, V. (2010). Impact of a new curriculum on pre-service teachers' technical, pedagogical and content knowledge (TPACK) [Paper Presentation]. In *Proceedings ASCILITE 2010* (pp. 184–189). https://www.ascilite.org/conferences/sydney10/procs/Chun_Hu-concise.pdf

Huang, K., & Pearlson, K. (2019, January). For what technology can't fix: Building a model of organizational cybersecurity culture. *Proceedings of the 52nd Hawaii International Conference on System Sciences*. 10.24251/HICSS.2019.769

Huang, K.-Y. (2009). Challenges in Human-Computer Interaction Design for Mobile Devices. *Proceedings of the World Congress on Engineering and Computer Science*.

Huawei. (2018). *Smart Education Scenarios*. Huawei Technologies Co., Ltd.

Hunter-Doniger, T. (2018). Art infusion: Ideal conditions for STEAM. *Art Education*, *2*(71), 22–27.

Hunt, T., Carter, R., Zhang, L., & Yang, S. (2020). Micro-credentials: The potential of personalized professional development. *Development and Learning in Organizations*, *34*(2), 33–35. doi:10.1108/DLO-09-2019-0215

Huspi. (2021, October 19). *Great business benefits of XR for tourism businesses*. https://huspi.com/blog-open/great-business-benefits-of-xr-for-tourism-industry/

Hutchison, A., Nadolny, L., & Estapa, A. (2016). Using coding apps to support literacy instruction and develop coding literacy. *The Reading Teacher*, *69*(5), 493–503. doi:10.1002/trtr.1440

Iagorashvili, I. (2019a). *Russia's 2 Myths About the Baltic States*. Retrieved from https://www.mythdetector.ge/ka/myth/rusetis-2-miti-baltiispiretis-kveqnebis-shesakheb

Iagorashvili, I. (2019b). *Maria Zakharova denies the occupation of Estonia by the USSR*. Retrieved from: https://www.mythdetector.ge/ka/myth/maria-zakharova-ssrk-mier-estonetis-okupatsias-uarqops

Ibanez, M. B., Di-Serio, A., & Delgado-Kloos, C. (2014). Gamification for engaging computer science students in learning activities: A case study. *IEEE Transactions on Learning Technologies*, *7*(3), 291–301. doi:10.1109/TLT.2014.2329293

IDFI. (2016). *Kremlin Information War Against Georgia: The Necessity of State Policy to Combat Propaganda.* Retrieved from: https://idfi.ge/ge/informational-war-of-kremlin-against-georgia-the-necessity-of-having-state-policy-against-propaganda

Ifeanyi, I. P., & Chukwuere, J. E. (2018). The impact of using smartphones on the academic performance of undergraduate students. *Knowledge Management & E-Learning, 10*(3), 290–308.

Imedi News. (2020a). *American Militaries killed Iranian General.* Retrieved from: https://imedinews.ge/ge/msoflio/124873/amerikelma-samkhedroebma-iraneli-generali-kasem-suleimani-mokles

Imedia News. (2020b). *Rouhani replies to Trump's Announcements.* Retrieved from: https://imedinews.ge/ge/msoflio/125067/rouhani-52-iranuli-obieqtis-shesakheb-trampis-gantskhadebas-pasukhobs

Impact, A. (2017). *Cyber Quest 2017.* Retrieved from: https://www.actionimpact.com/blog/2017/7/25/cyber-quest-2017-inspiring-the-next-generation-of-cyber-warriors-89mgj

Imwa, M., & Cabral, P. B. (2022). The Potential of Using Smartphones in Teaching and Learning in Secondary School Education: A Literature Review Study-Time to Embrace the Mobile Devices in Classrooms. *Impact of Digital Transformation in Teacher Training Models*, 211-228.

Individuals with Disabilities Education Act (IDEA). Section 300.8 (c)(6) (2017). Retrieved July 10, 2022, from http://sites.edu/gov.idea/regs/b/a/300.8/c/6

Individuals with Disabilities Education Act, 20 U.S.C. § 1400 (2004).

Inocencio, F. (2018, December 13-16). *Using gamification in education: A systematic literature review* [Paper presentation]. *Thirty Ninth International Conference on Information Systems*, San Francisco, CA, United States.

Institute of International Education, Inc. (n.d.). *U.S. Study Abroad.* https://opendoorsdata.org/annual-release/u-s-study-abroad/

International Research & Exchanges Board. (n.d.a). *About Us.* https://www.irex.org/about-us

International Research & Exchanges Board. (n.d.b). *Global solutions sustainability challenge.* https://www.irex.org/project/global-solutions

International Society for Technology in Education. (2022). *ISTE standards: Educators.* https://www.iste.org/standards/iste-standards-for-teachers

Iqbal, K. M., Khalid, F., & Barykin, S. Y. (2021). Hybrid Workplace: The Future of Work. In B. Khan, M. Kuofie, & S. Suman (Eds.), *Handbook of Research on Future Opportunities for Technology Management Education* (pp. 28–48). IGI Global. doi:10.4018/978-1-7998-8327-2.ch003

Iqbal, S., & Ahmed Bhatti, Z. (2015). An investigation of university student readiness towards m-learning using technology acceptance model. *International Review of Research in Open and Distributed Learning, 16*(4), 83–103. doi:10.19173/irrodl.v16i4.2351

Islabudeen, M., & Kavitha Devi, M. K. (2020). *A Smart Approach for Intrusion Detection and Prevention System in Mobile Ad Hoc Networks against Security Attacks, Wireless Personal Communications.* Springer. doi:10.100711277-019-07022-5

Ismail, I., Bokhare, S. F., Azizan, S. N., & Azman, N. (2013). Teaching via mobile phone: A case study on Malaysian teachers' technology acceptance and readiness. *Journal of Educators Online*, *2*(1). Advance online publication. doi:10.9743/JEO.2013.1.3

Ismaili, J., & Ibrahimi, E. H. O. (2017). Mobile learning as alternative to assistive technology devices for special needs students. *Education and Information Technologies*, *22*(3), 883–899.

Israel, M., Jeong, G., Ray, M., & Lash, T. (2020). Teaching elementary computer science through universal design for learning. In *Proceedings of the 51st ACM Technical Symposium on Computer Science Education* (pp. 1220-1226). ACM.

Israel, M., Marino, M. T., Yan, W., & Samuels, J. H. (2021). Using technology to support effective inclusive elementary schools. In *Handbook of Effective Inclusive Elementary Schools* (pp. 483–506). Routledge.

Jackson, T. (2021, Dec 15). *Examining the shared governance model in higher education*. Convene. https://www.azeusconvene.com/articles/examining-the-shared-governance-model-in-higher-education

Jang, S. J., & Chen, K. C. (2010). From PCK to TPACK: Developing a transformative model for pre-service science teachers. *Journal of Science Education and Technology*, *19*(6), 553–564. doi:10.100710956-010-9222-y

Jatmiko, B., Hariyono, E., Lestari, N. A., & Prahani, B. K. (2021). MobLen Model for Enhancing Scientific Creativity of Physics Students: An Alternative in the Covid-19 Pandemic. *Journal of Physics: Conference Series*, *1805*(1), 012006. doi:10.1088/1742-6596/1805/1/012006

Jawawi, D., Jamal, N., Abdul Halim, S., Sa'adon, N., Mamat, R., Isa, M., Mohamad, R., & Abdull Hamed, H. (2022). Nurturing secondary school student computational thinking through educational robotics. *International Journal of Emerging Technologies in Learning*, *17*(3), 117–128. https://www.learntechlib.org/p/220514/. doi:10.3991/ijet.v17i03.27311

Jenny, S. E., Keiper, M. C., Taylor, B. J., Williams, D. P., Gawrysiak, J., Manning, R. D., & Tutka, P. M. (2018). Esports venues: A new sport business opportunity. *Journal of Applied Sport Management*, *10*(1), 34–49. Advance online publication. doi:10.18666/JASM-2018-V10-I1-8469

Jiadze, N. (2022). *Georgian cybersecurity policy and International challenges*. Georgian Technical University.

Jiang, J., Wang, D., Liu, Y., Xu, Y., & Liu, J. (2018). A study on pupils' learning performance and thermal comfort of primary schools in China. *Building and Environment, 134*(November), 102-113. doi:10.1016/j.buildenv.2018.02.036

Jilbilian, I., & Canales, K. (2021, April 15). The US is readying sanctions against Russia over the SolarWinds cyberattack. *Business Insider*. https://www.businessinsider.com/solarwinds-hack-explained-government-agencies-cyber-security-2020-12

Jiménez, J. L., & Kressner, Ia. (2021). Building empathy through a comparative study of popular cultures in Caracas, Venezuela, and Albany, United States. In Virtual exchange: towards digital equity in internationalisation (pp. 113-127). Research-publishing.net. doi:10.14705/rpnet.2021.53.1294

Jimenez, R., & O'Neill, V. (2022). Strategies to Maximize Asynchronous Learning. In *Handbook of Research on Managing and Designing Online Courses in Synchronous and Asynchronous Environments* (pp. 499–521). IGI Global. doi:10.4018/978-1-7998-8701-0.ch025

Joint Task Force. (2018). *SP 800-37 Rev. 2: Risk Management Framework for Information Systems and Organizations: A System Life Cycle Approach for Security and Privacy*. U.S. Department of Commerce. https://csrc.nist.gov/publications/detail/sp/800-37/rev-2/final

Jones, K. A., & Sharma, R. S. (2019). An experiment in blended learning: Higher education without lectures? *International Journal of Digital Enterprise Technology, 1*(3), 241–275. doi:10.1504/IJDET.2019.097846

José, B., & Montealegre, R. (2016). *Measurement of Cybersecurity Maturity in Colombian MSMEs*. https://www.mckinsey.com/capabilities/risk-and-resilience/our-insights/organizational-cyber-maturity-a-survey-of-industries

Juliza, J., & Jemmy, M. R. (2018). Cyber-Physical System (CPS): State of the Art. *Int. Conf. on Computing, Electronics and Electrical Engineering (ICE Cube).*

Jung, L. A. (2021). Lesson planning with universal design for learning: Intentionally using UDL principles upfront means making fewer adaptations later— and reaching more students. *Educational Leadership, 78*(9), 38–43.

Kacetl, J., & Semradova, I. (2020). Reflection on blended learning and e-learning–case study. *Procedia Computer Science, 176*, 1322–1327. doi:10.1016/j.procs.2020.09.141

Kafai, Y. B., & Resnick, M. (1996). *Constructionism in practice: Designing, thinking, and learning in a digital world.* Erlbaum.

Kaku, M. (2013). A scientist predicts the future. *New York Times*. https://www.nytimes.com/2013/11/28/opinion/kaku-a-scientist-predicts-the-future.html

Kandilov, A., Kandilov, I., Liu, X., & Renkow, M. (2017). The impact of broadband on US agriculture: An evaluation of the USDA broadband loan program. *Applied Economic Perspectives and Policy, 39*(4), 635–661. doi:10.1093/aepp/ppx022

Kane, D., & Spradley, B.D. (2017, May 11). Recognizing esports as a sport. *The Sport Journal*. thesportjournal.org / article/recognizing-eSports-as-a-sport/

Kapp, K. M. (2012). *The gamification of learning and instruction*. Wiley.

Kärkkäinen, A. (2013). *A Cyber Security Architecture for Military Networks Using a Cognitive Network Approach* [Ph.D. Thesis]. NDU Course Library.

Kartal, T., & Dilek, I. (2021). Preservice science teachers' TPACK development in a technology-enhanced science teaching method course. *Journal of Education in Science, Environment and Health, 7*(4), 339–353. doi:10.21891/jeseh.994458

Kartimi, K., Gloria, R. Y., & Anugrah, I. R. (2021). Chemistry online distance learning during the COVID-10 outbreak: Do TPACK and teachers' attitude matter? *Indonesian Journal of Science Education, 10*(2), 228–240. doi:10.15294/jpii.v10i2.28468

Kashif, M., Rehman, A. U., Javed, M. K., & Javaid, D. (2020). *Smartphone: A Big Threat for Student's Education. Irish Interdisciplinary Journal of Science & Research.*

Kauweloa, N. S. (2021). The emergence of college esports in North America. In Y. J. Kal (Ed.), *Global esports: Transformation of Cultural Perceptions of Competitive Gaming*. Bloomsbury Academic. doi:10.5040/9781501368745.0022

Kauweloa, N., & Winter, J. (2019). Taking college esports seriously. *Loading, 12*(20), 35–50. doi:10.7202/1065896ar

Kearney, M., Maher, D., & Pham, L. (2019). Investigating pre-service teachers' informally-developed online professional learning networks. *Australasian Journal of Educational Technology, 36*(1), 21–36. doi:10.14742/ajet.4766

Kee, C. L., & Samsudin, Z. (2014). Mobile devices: Toys or learning tools for the 21st century teenagers? *The Turkish Online Journal of Educational Technology, 13*(3), 107–122.

Kegley, C., & Raymond, W. (2021). Realism in the Age of Cyber Warfare. *Ethics & International Affairs.*

Keis, O., Helbig, H., Streb, J., & Hille, K. (2014). Influence of blue-enriched classroom lighting on students' cognitive performance. *Trends in Neuroscience and Education, 3*(3-4), 86–92. doi:10.1016/j.tine.2014.09.001

Kenton, W. (2022, June 28). *Business Continuity Planning.* Investopedia. https://www.investopedia.com/terms/b/business-continuity-planning.asp

Keržič, D., Tomaževič, N., Aristovnik, A., & Umek, L. (2019). Exploring critical factors of the perceived usefulness of blended learning for higher education students. *PLoS One, 14*(11), e0223767. doi:10.1371/journal.pone.0223767 PMID:31751345

Ketheeswaran, L. K., & Mukunthan, T. (2016). Smart Phones for Learning Purposes by Students Who Follows 'Diploma in Commonwealth Youth Development Programmes' in the Colombo And Batticaloa Centres of the Open University of Sri. *IOSR Journal of Humanities and Social Science, 21*(5). Retrieved from http://www.jmest.org/wp-content/uploads/JMESTN42350643.pdf

Kezar, A., & Holcombe, E. (2017). *Creating a unified community of support: Increasing success for underrepresented students in STEM.* A final report on the CSU STEM Collaboratives Project. Pullias Center for Higher Education. https://pullias.usc.edu/download/creating-a-unified-community-of-support-increasing-success-for-underrepresented-students-in-stem/

Khalid, F. (2017). Understanding university students' use of Facebook for collaborative learning. *International Journal of Information and Education Technology (IJIET), 7*(8), 595–600. doi:10.18178/ijiet.2017.7.8.938

Khalil, M. K., Abdel Meguid, E. M., & Elkhider, I. A. (2018). Teaching of anatomical sciences: A blended learning approach. *Clinical Anatomy (New York, N.Y.), 31*(3), 323–329. doi:10.1002/ca.23052 PMID:29352730

Kibona, L., & Mgaya, G. (2015). Smartphones' Effects on Academic Performance of Higher Learning Students: A Case of Ruaha Catholic University – Iringa, Tanzania. *Journal of Multidisciplinary Engineering Science and Technology, 2*(4). http://www.jmest.org/wp- content/uploads/JMESTN42350643.pdf

Kids Online Safety Act. S.3663 - 117th Congress. (2022). Retrieved July 10, 2022, from https://www.congress.gov/bill/117th-congress/senate-bill/3663/text

Kim, B. H., & Oh, S. Y. (2014). A Study on the SMART Education System Based on Cloud and N-screen. *Journal of the Korea Academia-Industrial Cooperation Society, 15*(1), 137–143. doi:10.5762/KAIS.2014.15.1.137

Kime, C. (2021, Dec 9). *How to create an incident response plan.* https://www.esecurityplanet.com/networks/incident-response-how-to-prepare-for-attacks-and-breaches/

Kim, J. Y., & Fienup, D. M. (2022). Increasing access to online learning for students with disabilities during the COVID-19 pandemic. *The Journal of Special Education, 55*(4), 213–221. https://doi.org/10.1177/0022466921998067

Kim, S., Raza, M., & Seidman, E. (2019). Improving 21st-century teaching skills: The key to effective 21st-century learners. *Research in Comparative and International Education, 14*(1), 99–117. doi:10.1177/1745499919829214

Kim, Y., & Orazem, P. (2017). Broadband internet and new firm location decisions in rural areas. *American Journal of Agricultural Economics, 99*(1), 285–302. doi:10.1093/ajae/aaw082

Kindzeka, M. (2017, October) *Many More Refugees Flee CAR Violence to Cameroon*. https://www.voanews.com/africa/many-more-refugees-flee-car-violence-cameroon

Kingsberry, J. (2022, June 28). *Gen Z is influencing the abortion debate - from TikTok*. The Washington Post. https://www.washingtonpost.com/nation/interactive/2022/gen-z-tiktok-abortion-debate/

King-Sears, M. E., & Evmenova, A. S. (2007). Premises, principles, and processes for integrating technology into instruction. *Teaching Exceptional Children, 40*(1), 6–14.

KirkpatrickPrice. (2021, Mar 15). *The 5 components of risk management*. https://kirkpatrickprice.com/blog/5-components-risk-management/

Kiryakova, G., Angelova, N., & Yordanova, L. (2014). Gamification in education. *Proceedings of 9th International Balkan Education and Science Conference.*

Kivijärvi, M., & Katila, S. (2022). Becoming a gamer: Performative construction of gendered gamer identities. *Games and Culture, 17*(3), 461–481. doi:10.1177/15554120211042260

Kizilcec, R. F., Pérez-Sanagustín, M., & Maldonado, J. J. (2017). Self-regulated learning strategies predict learner behavior and goal attainment in Massive Open Online Courses. *Computers & Education, 104*, 18–33. doi:10.1016/j.compedu.2016.10.001

Klein, A. (2021, April 20). *During COVID-19, schools have made a mad dash to 1-to-1 computing. What happens next?* EdWeek. https://www.edweek.org/technology/during-covid-19-schools-have-made-a-mad-dash-to-1-to-1-computing-what-happens-next/2021/04

Kocaman, E. (2021). *Ofis Binalarında Kullanıcıların Demografik Karakteristiklerinin İç Ortam Isıl Konfor Memnuniyetine Etkilerinin Analiz Edilmesi* [Unpublished master's thesis]. University of Ege, Izmir, Türkiye.

Koehler, M., & Mishra, P. (2009). What is technological pedagogical content knowledge? *Contemporary Issues in Technology & Teacher Education, 9*(1), 60–70. https://citejournal.org/volume-9/issue-1-09/general/what-is-technological-pedagogicalcontent-knowledge/

Koenig, R. (2022, June 1). *With money from Facebook, 10 colleges turn their campuses into "metaversities."* https://www.edsurge.com/news/2022-06-01-with-money-from-facebook-10-colleges-turn-their-campuses-into-metaversities

Koh, K. H., Repenning, A., Nickerson, H., Endo, Y., & Motter, P. (2013, March). Will it stick? Exploring the sustainability of computational thinking education through game design. In *SIGCES '13: Proceeding of the 44th ACM technical symposium on computer science education* (pp. 597–602). 10.1145/2445196.2445372

Kohnke, L., & Moorhouse, B. L. (2021). Adopting HyFlex in higher education in response to COVID-19: Students' perspectives. *Open Learning: The Journal of Open, Distance and e-Learning, 36*(3), 231-244. doi:10.1080/02680513.2021.1906641

Kolb, D. A. (1984). *Experiential learning: Experience as the source of learning and development*. FT Press.

Kolb, D. A. (1984). *Experiential Learning: Experience as the Source of Learning and Development*. Prentice Hall. http://academic.regis.edu/ed205/Kolb.pdf

Komalavalli, K., Hemalatha, R., & Dhanalakshmi, S. (2020). A Survey of Artificial Intelligence in Smart Phones and Its Applications among the Students of Higher Education in and around Chennai City. *Shanlax International Journal of Education, 8*(3), 89–95. doi:10.34293/education.v8i3.2379

Kordaki, M., & Kakavas, P. (2017, July). *Digital storytelling as an effective framework for the development of computational thinking skills* [Paper presentation]. *The International Conference on Education and New Learning Technologies*, Barcelona, Spain. 10.21125/edulearn.2017.2435

Korkmaz, Ö. (2016). The effect of Scratch- and LEGO Mindstorms EV3-based programming activities on academic achievement, problem-solving skills, and logical mathematical thinking skills of students. *Malaysian Online Journal of Educational Sciences, 4*(3), 73–88. https://files.eric.ed.gov/fulltext/EJ1106444.pdf

Korte, M. (2020, June 22). The impact of the digital revolution on human brain and behavior: Where do we stand? *Dialogues in Clinical Neuroscience, 22*(2). https://www.ncbi.nlm.nih.gov/pmc/articles/PMC7366944/

Kozleski, E. B. (2020). *NEPC review: Special education and distance learning: Supporting students through the pandemic (ExcelinEd, June 2020)*. National Education Policy Center. https://nepc.colorado.edu/thinktank/special-education-pandemic

Kreculj, Kovacevic, Krulj, & Dihovicni. (2021). The IoT in Education and Teaching. *XXVII Skup Trendovi Razvoja: "On-Line Nastava Na Univerzitetima"*, 6433, 407-410.

Krotidou, D., Teokleous, N., & Zahariadou, A. (2012). Exploring parents' and children's awareness on internet threats in relation to internet safety. *Campus-Wide Information Systems, 29*(3), 133–143. doi:10.1108/10650741211243157

Kuchynka, S., Findley-Van Nostrand, D., & Pollenz, R. S. (2019). Evaluating psychosocial mechanisms underlying STEM persistence in undergraduates: Scalability and longitudinal analysis of three cohorts from a six-day pre-college engagement STEM academy program. *CBE Life Sciences Education, 18*(3), ar41. doi:10.1187/cbe.19-01-0028 PMID:31441721

Kumar, V. (2017, March 26). *Big data facts*. https://analyticsweek.com/content/big-data-facts/

Kuprashvili, H. (2022). *National Security of Georgia*. Universal.

Kupreishvili, T. (2020). *Everything we know about the Ukrainian plane crash*. Retrieved from: netgazeti.ge: https://netgazeti.ge/news/418935/

Kurt, S. (2015). *Educational Technology: An Overview, Teaching & Learning*. https://educationaltechnology.net/educational-technology-an-overview/

Kuss, D. J., Kristensen, A. M., Williams, A. J., & Lopez-Fernandez, O. (2022). To be or not to be a female gamer: A qualitative exploration of female gamer identity. *International Journal of Environmental Research and Public Health, 19*(3), 1169. Advance online publication. doi:10.3390/ijerph19031169 PMID:35162194

Kwet, M., & Prinsloo, P. (2020). The 'smart' classroom: A new frontier in the age of the smart university. *Teaching in Higher Education, 25*(4), 510–526. doi:10.1080/13562517.2020.1734922

L'Amoreaux, C. (2019, February 1). *Who is Seymour Papert (and why does it matter)?* https://www.claudialamoreaux.com/who-is-seymour-papert-and-why-does-it-matter/

Labs, C. (2021). *Artificial Intelligence in Cybersecurity: AI Cyberattacks, Securing Your Ecosystem with AI, and More.* https://www.xcubelabs.com/blog/artificial-intelligence-in-cybersecurity-ai-cyberattacks-securing-your-ecosystem-with-ai-and-more/

Lai, C. L., & Hwang, G. J. (2016). A self-regulated flipped classroom approach to improving students' learning performance in a mathematics course. *Computers & Education, 100*, 126–140. doi:10.1016/j.compedu.2016.05.006

Laković, L., Ognjanović, I., Šendelj, R., & Injac, O. (2021). Semantically enhanced cyber security model for industry 4.0: methodological framework. *25th Int. Conf. on Information Technology (IT)*, 1-4. 10.1109/IT51528.2021.9390120

Land, M. H. (2013). Full STEAM ahead: The benefits of integrating the arts into STEM. *Procedia Computer Science, 20.* doi:10.1016/j.procs.2013.09.317

Landers, R. N. (2015). Developing a theory of gamified learning: Linking serious games and gamification of learning. *Simulation & Gaming, 45*(6), 752–768. doi:10.1177/1046878114563660

Landers, R. N., Bauer, K. N., Callan, R. C., & Armstrong, M. B. (2015). Psychological theory and the gamification of learning. In T. Reiners & L. Wood (Eds.), *Gamification in education and business* (pp. 165–186). Springer. doi:10.1007/978-3-319-10208-5_9

Landers, R. N., & Landers, A. K. (2015). An empirical test of the theory of gamified learning: The effect of leaderboards on time-on-task and academic performance. *Simulation & Gaming, 45*(6), 769–785. doi:10.1177/1046878114563662

Langendahl, P. A., Cook, M., & Mark-Herbert, C. (2016). *Gamification in higher education: Toward a pedagogy to engage and motivate*. Department of Economics, Swedish University of Agricultural Sciences.

Latchoumi, Reddy, & Balamurugan. (2020). Applied Machine Learning Predictive Analytics to SQL Injection Attack Detection and Prevention. *European Journal of Molecular & Clinical Medicine, 7*(2), 3543–3553.

Lauber, K., McGee, D., & Gilmore, A. B. (2021). Commercial use of evidence in public health policy: A critical assessment of food industry submissions to global-level consultations on non-communicable disease prevention. *BMJ Global Health, 6*(8), e006176. doi:10.1136/bmjgh-2021-006176 PMID:34426403

Lave, J., & Wenger, E. (1991). *Situated learning: Legitimate peripheral participation.* Cambridge University Press. doi:10.1017/CBO9780511815355

Lawson, A. P., & Mayer, R. E. (2021). Benefits of Writing an Explanation During Pauses in Multimedia Lessons. *Educational Psychology Review, 33*(4), 1859–1885. doi:10.100710648-021-09594-w PMID:33776377

Lazarus, S. (2017, May). *The Cultural Iceberg and Communication.* www.emiworld.org/emi-tech/cultural-iceberg-communication

Ledger, S., & Fuqua, M. (2021). Disruption, diversity, and dynamic developments in rural education during COVID-19. *Australian and International Journal of Rural Education, 31*(1), 1–7. doi:10.47381/aijre.v31i1.297

Lee, I., Martin, F., & Apone, K. (2014). Integrating computational thinking across the K–8 curriculum. *ACM Inroads, 5*(4), 64–71. doi:10.1145/2684721.2684736

Lee, J. J., & Hammer, J. (2011). Gamification in education: What, how, why bother? *Academic Exchange Quarterly, 15*(2), 146. https://mybrainware.com/wp-content/uploads/2017/11/Gamification_in_Education_What_How_Why.pdf

Lee, J., Cho, B., Kim, Y., & Noh, J. (2015). *Smartphone addiction in university students and its implication for learning. Emerging Issues in Smart Learning*. Springer-Verlag. doi:10.1007/978-3-662-44188-6_40

Lee, M. C., Mui, K. W., Wong, L. T., Chan, W. Y., Lee, E. W. M., & Cheung, C. T. (2012). Student learning performance and indoor environmental quality (IEQ) in air-conditioned university teaching rooms. *Building and Environment*, *49*(1), 238–244. doi:10.1016/j.buildenv.2011.10.001

Lee, Y. H., Dunbar, N., Kornelson, K., Wilson, S. N., Ralston, R., Savic, M., Stewart, S., Lennox, E., Thompson, W., & Elizondo, J. (2016). Digital game-based learning for undergraduate calculus education: Immersion, calculation, and conceptual understanding. *International Journal of Gaming and Computer-Mediated Simulations*, *8*(1), 13–27. doi:10.4018/IJGCMS.2016010102

Leigh, D. (2015, Oct 29). *Cybersecurity risk management*. Educause. https://er.educause.edu/blogs/2015/10/cybersecurity-risk-management

Lei, J. (2009). Digital natives as preservice teachers: What technology preparation is needed? *Journal of Computing in Teacher Education*, *25*(3), 87–97. https://files.eric.ed.gov/fulltext/EJ835233.pdf

Lemley, M. A. (2017). Rationalizing internet safe harbors. In *Copyright Law* (pp. 291–309). Routledge. doi:10.4324/9781315095400-9

Lewin, C., Niederhauser, D., Johnson, Q., Saito, T., Sakamoto, A., & Sherman, R. (2021). Safe and responsible internet use in a connected world: Promoting cyber-wellness. *Canadian Journal of Learning and Technology*, *47*(4). https://doi.org/10.21432/cjlt28069

Lewis, D. (2016). *The History of Training and Development (Infographic)*. https://www.allencomm.com/blog/2016/04/history-training-development-infographic/

Lewis, C. L. (2015). Preservice teachers' ability to identify technology standards: Does curriculum matter? *Contemporary Issues in Technology & Teacher Education*, *15*(2), 235–254. https://citejournal.org/volume-15/issue-2-15/current-practice/preservice-teachers-ability-to-identify-technology-standards-does-curriculum-matter/

Liao, C. (2016). From interdisciplinary to transdisciplinary: An arts-integrated approach to STEAM education. *Art Education*. Retrieved from https://draweb.njcu.edu:2068

Liao, S. (2021, April 7). Asian esports players, staffers speak out on "unspeakable" racism, harassment in America. *The Washington Post*. link.gale.com/apps/doc/A657697127/AONE?u=rocklandcc&sid=bookmark-AONE&xid=33fdae9a

Liao, S. (2021, August 30). China restricts young people to playing video games three hours a week. *Washington Post*. https://link.gale.com/apps/doc/A673700847/AONE?u=rocklandcc&sid=bookmark-AONE&xid=0aca8a9a

Li, B. P., Kong, S. C., & Chen, G. (2015). A Study on the Development of the Smart Classroom Scale. In G. Chen, V. Kumar, V. Kinshuk, R. Huang, & S. Kong (Eds.), *Emerging Issues in Smart Learning*. Lecture Notes in Educational Technology. Springer. doi:10.1007/978-3-662-44188-6_6

Li, B., Kong, S. C., & Chen, G. (2015). Development and validation of the smart classroom inventory. *Smart Learning Environments*, *2*(1), 3. Advance online publication. doi:10.118640561-015-0012-0

Li, C., Wu, Y., Yuan, X., Sun, Z., Wang, W., Li, X., & Gong, L. (2018). Detection and defense of DDoS attack–based on deep learning in OpenFlow-based SDN. *International Journal of Communication Systems, 31*(5), 1–14.

Liem, M. (n.d.). *Risk in modern society.* Coursera. https://www.coursera.org/learn/risk-in-modern-society

Li, G., Sharma, P., Pan, L., Rajasegarar, S., Karmakar, C., & Patterson, N. (2021). Deep Learning Algorithms for Cyber Security Applications: A Survey. *Journal of Computer Security, 29*(5), 447–471. doi:10.3233/JCS-200095

Lightspeed Systems. (2022). *Create Engaging Learning Environments Anywhere.* Retrieved July 20, 2022, from https://www.lightspeedsystems.com/solutions/lightspeed-classroom-management

Limba, Plėta, Agafonov, & Damkus. (2017). Cyber Security Management Model for Critical Infrastructure. *International Journal Entrepreneurship and Sustainability Issues, 4*(4), 559-577. Doi:10.9770/jesi.2017.4.4

Lin, V. (2015). *Computational thinking and technology toys* [Unpublished undergraduate thesis]. Wellesley College. https://repository.wellesley.edu/thesiscollection/307

Lin, T., Capecci, D. E., Ellis, D. M., Rocha, H. A., Dommaraju, S., Oliveira, D. S., & Ebner, N. C. (2019). Susceptibility to spear-phishing emails: Effects of internet user demographics and email content. *ACM Transactions on Computer-Human Interaction, 26*(5), 1–28. doi:10.1145/3336141 PMID:32508486

Li, R. (2016). *Good luck, have fun: The rise of esports.* Skyhorse Publishing.

Liu, Z., Geng, L., & Xu, Y. (2020, January). Design of Monitoring System for Classroom Environment Parameter Based on Wireless Communication. In *2020 International Conference on Intelligent Transportation, Big Data & Smart City (ICITBS)* (pp. 502-505). IEEE. 10.1109/ICITBS49701.2020.00109

Li, Y., Yang, H. H., & MacLeod, J. (2019). Preferences toward the constructivist smart classroom learning environment: Examining preservice teachers' connectedness. *Interactive Learning Environments, 27*(3), 349–362. doi:10.1080/10494820.2018.1474232

Logo Foundation. (n.d.). *Logo resources: Archive.* https://el.media.mit.edu/logo-foundation/ resources/archive.html

Lopez-Garrido, G. (2020, August 9). *Self-efficacy theory.* Simply Psychology. Retrieved from https://www.simplypsychology.org/self-efficacy.html

LoPiccaloK. (2020). Impact of broadband penetration on US farm productivity. SSRN. doi:10.2139/ssrn.3749647

Lorenzo, N., Gallon, R., Palau, R., & Mogas, J. (2021). New Objectives for Smart Classrooms from Industry 4.0. *Technology. Knowledge and Learning, 26*(4), 719–731. doi:10.100710758-021-09527-0

Lu, K., Yang, H. H., Shi, Y., & Wang, X. (2021). *Examining the key influencing factors on college students' higher-order thinking skills in the smart classroom.* Academic Press.

Lu, G., Xie, K., & Liu, Q. (2022). What influences student situational engagement in smart classrooms: Perception of the learning environment and students' motivation. *British Journal of Educational Technology, 53*(6), 1–23. doi:10.1111/bjet.13204

Lui-Abel, A. (2011). Identifying and classifying corporate universities in the United States. In M. Malloch, L. Cairns, & K. Evans (Eds.), The SAGE handbook of workplace learning (pp. 407-419). SAGE Publications Ltd. doi:10.4135/9781446200940.n30

Luongo, C. (2020, September 17). *Colleagiate StarLeague, World Gaming Network acquired by Playfly Sports.* https://eSportsinsider.com/2020/09/collegiate-starleague-playfly-sports/

Lutfi, A., & Hidayah, R. (2021). *Gamification for Science Learning Media Challenges of Teacher and Expectations of Students.* Academic Press.

Lu, Y., & Wang, M. (2016). An easy defense mechanism against botnet-based DDoS flooding attacks originating in a SDN environment using sFlow. *Proceedings of the 11th International Conference on Future Internet Technologies*, 14-20.

Machajewski, S. T. (2017). *Application of gamification in a college STEM introductory course: A case study* [Doctoral dissertation]. Northcentral University. doi:10.13140/RG.2.2.27751.34728

Madden, D., Liu, Y., Yu, H., Sonbudak, M. F., Troiano, G. M., & Harteveld, C. (2021). Why are you playing games? You are a girl! Exploring gender biases in esports. *CHI '21: Proceeding of the 2021 CHI Conference on Human Factors in Computing Systems.* 10.1145/3411764.3445248

Madumere, C. P., Ekwelem, V. O., & Anike, C. J. (2020). Social media and smart phone usage among students in Nigeria: The implications to their academic activities. *Library Philosophy & Practice.*

Mahasuweerachai, P., Whitacre, B., & Shideler, D. (2010). Does broadband access impact migration in America? Examining differences between rural and urban areas. *The Review of Regional Studies*, *40*(1), 5–26. doi:10.52324/001c.8158

Maisaia, V. (2017). *Specifics of Information-Propaganda / Cyber-Virtual War of the Islamic Caliphate - The Concept of "Soft Power".* Retrieved from: http://geotimes.com.ge/blogi/?m=82&post_id=18&lng=geo

Ma, L., & Lee, C. S. (2021). Evaluating the effectiveness of blended learning using the ARCS model. *Journal of Computer Assisted Learning*, *37*(5), 1397–1408. doi:10.1111/jcal.12579

Malik, A. R., & Asnur, M. N. A. (2019). Using Social Media As A Learning Media Of Foreign Language Students In Higher Education. *Bahtera: Jurnal Pendidikan Bahasa Dan Sastra*, *18*(2), 166–175.

Mallampalli, M. S., Anumula, V., & Akkara, S. (2019, October). Enhancing Second Language Listening Skills Through Smartphones: A Case Study. In *Interactive Mobile Communication, Technologies and Learning* (pp. 347–356). Springer.

Mamuka, G. (2017). *Bitcoin, the future currency – Crypto Currency.* Retrieved from: https://financer.com/ge/kriptovaluta-bitcoin/

Maranga, M. J., & Nelson, M. (2019). Emerging Issues in Cyber Security for Institutions of Higher Education. *Int. J of Computer Science and Network*, *8*(4), 371–379.

Marczewski, A. (2013). *Gamification: A simple introduction.* Andrzej Marczewski.

Margulieux, L. E., McCracken, W. M., & Catrambone, R. (2016). A taxonomy to define courses that mix face-to-face and online learning. *Educational Research Review*, *19*, 104–118. doi:10.1016/j.edurev.2016.07.001

Marr, B. (2020). *The 5 biggest cybersecurity trends in 2020 everyone should know about.* Forbes. https://bit.ly/3b5w8kq

Marsick, V., Fichter, R., & Watkins, K. (2022). From work-based learning to learning based-work: exploring the changing relationship between learning and work. In M. Malloch, L. Cairns, K. Evans, & B. O'Connor (Eds.), The SAGE Handbook of Learning and Work (pp. 80–98). Sage Publishing. doi:10.4135/9781529757217.n12

Martin, S. (2016). *A descriptive and explorative case study of a scratch programming experience involving the creation of a lunar simulation/model with grade six learners* [Unpublished master's thesis]. University of Calgary. doi:10.11575/PRISM/24707

Martin, B. (2015). Successful implementation of TPACK in teacher preparation programs. *International Journal on Integrating Technology in Education, 4*(1), 17–26. doi:10.5121/ijite.2015.4102

Martín-García, A. V., Martínez-Abad, F., & Reyes-González, D. (2019). TAM and stages of adoption of blended learning in higher education by application of data mining techniques. *British Journal of Educational Technology, 50*(5), 2484–2500. doi:10.1111/bjet.12831

Martín-Lucas, J., Torrijos-Fincias, P., Serrate-González, S., & del Dujo, Á. G. (2021). Teaching use intention and self-perception of bLearning in higher education1 Intención de uso y autopercepción docente del bLearning en educación superior. *Review of Education, 391*, 199–224.

Marywood University. (2021, Aug 7). *Professional continuing education esports certification. Targeted News Service.* https://draweb.njcu.edu/login?url=https://draweb.njcu.edu:2073/wire-feeds/marywood-university-professional-continuing/docview/2559052490/se-2?accountid=12793

Masadeh, T. S. Y. (2021). Smartphone Use In Learning As Perceived By University Undergraduates: Benefits And Barriers. *International Journal of Research-GRANTHAALAYAH, 9*(3), 56–65. doi:10.29121/granthaalayah.v9.i3.2021.3764

Masiu, M. T., & Chukwuere, J. E. (2018). The Effect of Smartphones on Students' Academic Life: A Perceptive from a South African University. *International Conference on Business and Management Dynamics ICBM-2018.*

Maslow, A. H. (1981). *Motivation and personality.* Harper and Row.

Matthews, P. (1999). Workplace learning: Developing an Holistic Model. *The Learning Organization, 6*(1), 18–29. https://citeseerx.ist.psu.edu/viewdoc/download?doi=10.1.1.990.9914&rep=rep1&type=pdf

Mayer, R. (2001). Multimedia learning and games. *Computer Games and Instruction., 41*, 281–305. doi:10.1017/CBO9781139164603

Mayer, R. C. (2021). *Multimedia Learning* (3rd ed.). Cambridge University Press.

Mayer, R. E. (2014). The cognitive theory of multimedia learning. In R. E. Mayer (Ed.), *The Cambridge handbook of multimedia learning* (2nd ed., pp. 43–71). Cambridge University Press., doi:10.1017/CBO9781139547369.005

Mazzarol, T., & Soutar, G. N. (2012). Revisiting the global market for higher education. *Asia Pacific Journal of Marketing and Logistics, 24*(5), 717–737. doi:10.1108/13555851211278079

McCutcheon, K., O'Halloran, P., & Lohan, M. (2018). Online learning versus blended learning of clinical supervisee skills with pre-registration nursing students: A randomised controlled trial. *International Journal of Nursing Studies, 82*, 30–39. doi:10.1016/j.ijnurstu.2018.02.005 PMID:29574394

McGonigal, J. (2011b, January 22). Be a gamer, save the world. *The Wall Street Journal.* https://myweb.uiowa.edu/dlgould/lifeclas/docs/Be%20a%20Gamer,%20Save%20the%20World%20(1.22.11)docx.pdf

McGonigal, J. (2011a). *Reality is broken: Why games make us better and how they can change the world.* Penguin Press.

McGuire-Schwartz, M., & Arndt, J. (2007). Transforming universal design for learning in early childhood teacher education from college classroom to early childhood classroom. *Journal of Early Childhood Teacher Education, 28*(2), 127–139.

McKenzie, L. (2021). Global Higher Ed Collaboration to Share Cyberthreat Intelligence. *Inside Higher Ed*. https://www.insidehighered.com/quicktakes/2021/05/26/global-higher-ed-collaboration-share-cyberthreat-intelligence

McLaughlin, C. (2008). Emotional well-being and its relationship to schools and classrooms: A critical reflection. *British Journal of Guidance & Counselling, 36*(4), 353–366. https://draweb.njcu.edu:2085/10.1080/03069880802364486

McLeod, S. A. (2018, June 6). *Jean Piaget's theory of cognitive development*. https://www.simplypsychology.org/piaget.html

McMahon, D., & Walker, Z. (2014). Universal design for learning features and tools on iPads and iPhones. *Journal of Special Education Technology*, *29*(2), 39–49.

McMillan, D. W., & Chavis, D. M. (1986). Sense of community: A definition and theory. *Journal of Community Psychology, 14*(1), 6–23. doi:10.1002/1520-6629(198601)14:1<6::AID-JCOP2290140103>3.0.CO;2-I

MDSNY. (2017). *Human Error, We meet again. Are the employees the weakest link in the fight against cyber vulnerabilities?* Retrieved from: https://www.mdsny.com/human-error-we-meet-again-cyber-security-basics/

Mehdi, S. A., Khalid, J., & Khayam, S. A. (2011). Revisiting traffic anomaly detection using software defined networking. *International Workshop on Recent Advances in Intrusion Detection*, 161-180.

Meir, M. (2020, June 15). *The 2 types of risk assessment methodology*. Security Scorecard. https://securityscorecard.com/blog/types-of-risk-assessment-methodology#:~:text=There%20are%20two%20main%20types,assessment%20methodologies%3A%20quantitative%20and%20qualitative

Melcher, K. (2015). *Gamers: The rising stars of collegiate athletics*. TedXNapierville. https://www.youtube.com/watch?v=kcX11m1g3hs&t=818s

Mendoza, E. (2022, June 6). Ranked: The best-selling video game consoles of all time. *Visual Capitalist*. https://www.visualcapitalist.com/cp/ranked-the-best-selling-video-game-consoles-of-all-time/

Messina, D., & García, L. (2020). Estudio diagnóstico sobre docentes en América Latina y el Caribe. Documento de Trabajo, Santiago, United Nations Educational, Scientific and Cultural Organization (UNESCO).

Meta. (n.d.). *Our story: Enter the future of learning*. https://about.facebook.com/immersive-learning/our-story/

Meti, N., Narayan, D. G., & Baligar, V. P. (2017). Detection of distributed denial of service attacks using machine learning algorithms in software defined networks. *International Conference on Advances in Computing, Communications and Informatics (ICACCI)*, 1366-1371.

Mezirow, J. (1978). Perspective transformation. *Adult Education, 28*(2), 100–110. doi:10.1177/074171367802800202

Mezirow, J. (1991). *Transformative dimensions of adult learning*. Jossey Bass.

Mezirow, J. (1997). Transformative Learning: Theory to Practice. *New Directions for Adult and Continuing Education, 1997*(74), 5–12. doi:10.1002/ace.7401

Mezirow, J., & ... (Eds.). (2000). *Learning as transformation*. Jossey Bass.

Mfitzgerald. (2004, January 8). *Nine famous hacks*. ExtremeTech. https://www.extremetech.com/extreme/55530-nine-famous-hacks

Microsoft. (2022). *Microsoft ESports Teacher Academy (META)*. https://docs.microsoft.com/en-us/learn/paths/microsoft-eSports-teacher-academy/

Miguel-Revilla, D., Martínez-Ferreira, J. M., & Sánchez-Agustí, M. (2020). Assessing the digital competence of educators in social studies: An analysis in initial teacher training in using the TPACK-21 model. *Australasian Journal of Educational Technology*, *36*(2), 1–12. doi:10.14742/ajet.5281

Mihail-Văduva, D. (2020). The impact of a multimedia mobile application. *Proceedings of the IE 2020 International Conference*. 10.24818/ie2020.01.06

Miller, A. (2016, Jul 17). Esports just may pay for your college education. *Kitsap Sun*. https://draweb.njcu.edu/login?url=https://draweb.njcu.edu:2073/newspapers/eSports-just-may-pay-your-college-education/docview/1804581260/se-2?accountid=12793

Milligan, C., & Littlejohn, A. (2016). How health professionals regulate their learning in massive open online courses. *The Internet and Higher Education*, *31*, 113–121. doi:10.1016/j.iheduc.2016.07.005 PMID:27928198

Minecraft Education Edition. (2021, December 2). *A city-wide eSports smackdown in New York: BOTB*. https://education.minecraft.net/en-us/blog/battle-of-the-boroughs-eSports

Minecraft. (2021). *Finals: Battle of the Boroughs*. https://www.twitch.tv/videos/1057074324

Minecraft. (2022). https://education.minecraft.net/en-us/resources/stem-eSports-challenges

Mineduc. (2020). *Apoyos del Mineduc durante la pandemia COVID-19*. Ministerio de Educación de Chile. Retrieved from https://www.mineduc.cl/apoyos-del-mineduc-durante-la-pan demia-del-covid-19/

Ministry of Internal Affairs of Georgia. (2020). *Citizens received messages on behalf of the Ministry of Internal Affairs - what statement does the Ministry of Internal Affairs make*. Retrieved from: https://www.ambebi.ge/article/243012-shss-s-saxelit-mokalakebs-mesijebi-miuvidat-ra-g/

Miniwats Marketing Group. (2022). *World Internet usage and population statistics 2022 year-Q1 estimates. Internet world stats: Usage and population*. Retrieved from https://www.internetworldstats.com/stats.htm

Mishra, A., Gupta, N., & Gupta, B. B. (2021). Defense mechanisms against DDoS attack based on entropy in SDN-cloud using POX controller. *Telecommunication Systems*, 1–16.

Mishra, P., & Koehler, M. J. (2006). Technological pedagogical content knowledge: A framework for teacher knowledge. *Teachers College Record: The Voice of Scholarship in Education*, *108*(6), 1017–1054. doi:10.1111/j.1467-9620.2006.00684.x

Mishra, P., Koehler, M. J., & Kereluik, K. (2009). Looking back to the future of educational technology. *TechTrends*, *53*(5), 49.

Mohamed, A. H. (2018). Attitudes of special education teachers towards using technology in inclusive classrooms: A mixed-methods study. *Journal of Research in Special Educational Needs*, *18*(4), 278–288. https://doi.org/10.1111/1471-3802.12411

Mohammad, W. S. (2019). Work-related risk factors for Carpal Tunnel Syndrome among Majmaah University female touchscreen users. *Pakistan Journal of Medical Sciences*, *35*(5), 1221. doi:10.12669/pjms.35.5.683 PMID:31488982

Mohtar, N. M. M., Hassan, M. A., Hassan, M. S., & Osman, M. N. (2013). IOSR Journal Of Humanities and Social Science (IOSR-JHSS). *The Importance of Smartphone's Usage Among Malaysian Undergraduates*, *14*(3), 12–118.

Monzon, L. (2022, April 16). *The 5 most common security concerns for the Web 3.0 world.* https://www.itnewsafrica.com/2022/04/the-5-most-common-security-concerns-for-the-web-3-0-world/

Moon, J. (2007). The contribution of corporate social responsibility to sustainable development. *Sustainable Development*, *15*(5), 296–306. doi:10.1002d.346

Morais, T., Lopes, P., & Jordão, F. (2011). *Organizational culture and human resources' training and development: A study about the McDonald's Hamburger University.* https://repositorio-aberto.up.pt/bitstream/10216/71466/2/16005.pdf

More, C. M., & Travers, J. M. (2012). What's app with that? *Young Exceptional Children*, *16*(2), 15–32.

Moreno, D. A., & Carter, A. B. (2021, October 8). *Will the NCAA's NIL ruling impact collegiate esports?* https://sportslitigationalert.com/will-the-ncaas-nil-ruling-impact-collegiate-eSports/#:~:text=As%20noted%20above%2C%20the%20NCAA,violence%20of%20certain%20video%20games

Mosalanejas, L., Dehghani, A., & Abdolahofard, K. (2014). The students' experiences of ethics in online systems: A phenomenological study. *Turkish Online Journal of Distance Education*, *15*(4), 205–216.

Moskal, P., Dziuban, C., & Hartman, J. (2013). Blended learning: A dangerous idea? *The Internet and Higher Education*, *18*, 15–23. doi:10.1016/j.iheduc.2012.12.001

Mountrouidou, Li, & Burke. (2018). *Cybersecurity in liberal arts general education curriculum.* . doi:10.1145/3197091.3197110

Moyer-Packenham, P. S., & Bolyard, J. J. (2016). Revisiting the definition of a virtual manipulative. In P. S. Moyer-Packenham (Ed.), *International Perspectives on Teaching and Learning Mathematics with Virtual Manipulatives* (pp. 3–23). Springer.

Mueller, J., McConnell, K., Burow, P., Pofahl, K., Merdjanoff, A., & Farrell, J. (2021). Impacts of the COVID-19 pandemic on rural America. *Proceedings of the National Academy of Sciences of the United States of America*, *118*(1). Advance online publication. doi:10.1073/pnas.2019378118 PMID:33328335

Mueller, M., Schmidt, A., & Kuerbis, B. (2013). Internet security and networked governance in international relations. *International Studies Review*, *15*(1), 86–104. doi:10.1111/misr.12024

Müller, C., & Mildenberger, T. (2021). Facilitating flexible learning by replacing classroom time with an online learning environment: A systematic review of blended learning in higher education. *Educational Research Review*, *34*, 100394. doi:10.1016/j.edurev.2021.100394

Murad, R., Hussin, S., Yaacob, M. H., & Ahmad, A. (2019). Mobile Service Delivery Mechanism in Smart Education: Conceptual Framework. *International Journal of Academic Research in Business & Social Sciences*, *9*(2), 1242–1253. doi:10.6007/IJARBSS/v9-i2/5948

Muthamil Sudar, K., & Deepalakshmi, P. (2020). A two level security mechanism to detect a DDoS flooding attack in software-defined networks using entropy-based and C4. 5 technique. *Journal of High Speed Networks*, *26*(1), 55–76. doi:10.3233/JHS-200630

Muthamil Sudar, K., & Deepalakshmi, P. (2021). An intelligent flow-based and signature-based IDS for SDNs using ensemble feature selection and a multi-layer machine learning-based classifier. *Journal of Intelligent & Fuzzy Systems*, *40*(3), 4237–4256.

Myvideo.ge. (2013). *Al Qaeda threatens Georgian jihad against Georgian troops in Afghanistan*. Retrieved from: https://www.myvideo.ge/v/2058973

NACE. (2022). *What is NACE?* https://naceSports.org/about/

Natalia, C., & Tomaradze, G. (2014). *Virtual/cryptocurrency and its features Regulation of virtual currencies (on the example bitcoin)*. Retrieved from: https://www.nbg.gov.ge/uploads/journal/2014/2014_3/4.pdf

National Academies of Sciences, Engineering, and Medicine. (2018). *Indicators for monitoring undergraduate STEM education*. National Academies Press.

National Association of Colleges and Employers. (2021, March). *Career Readiness: Competencies for a Career-Ready Workforce*. readiness-competencies-revised-apr-2021.pdf

National Center of Educational Statistics. (2021). *Students with Disabilities*. Retrieved July 15, 2022, from https://nces.ed.gov/programs/coe/indicator/cgg

National Center on Accessible Educational Materials. (n.d.). *AEM basics*. http://aem.cast.org/about/aem-basics.html#.W3G3bS2ZNok

National Student Clearinghouse Research Center. (2015, April 22). *Persistence & retention–2015*. https://nscresearchcenter.org/snapshotreport-persistenceretention18/

NCSA. (2022). *Esports scholarships*. https://www.ncsasports.org/college-eSports-scholarships

Neilsen, L. (2019). *Esports, the down & dirty stats for educators – live from #ISTE19*. https://www.techlearning.com/news/eSports-the-down-and-dirty-stats-for-educators-live-from-iste19

Nelius, J. (2019). Excerpt: What it's like to go to college on an esports scholarship: Balancing practice and matches with academics, combating toxicity, and explaining esports to parents and professors. *TWICE: This Week in Consumer Electronics*, *34*(17), 16–17.

Nepo, K. (2017). The use of technology to improve education. *Child and Youth Care Forum*, *46*(2), 207–221.

New Jersey Division of Consumer Affairs. (2022). *Cyber Safety for Middle Schoolers: Activity and Quiz Book*. New Jersey Division of Consumer Affairs.

Newman. (2020). *Coronavirus Sets the Stage for Hacking Mayhem*. Retrieved from: https://www.wired.com/story/coronavirus-cyberattacks-ransomware-phishing/

NewsnReleases. (2022, April 7). *Engage XR partners with victory XR to launch 10 Meta funded metaversities*. https://newsnreleases.com/2022/04/07/engage-xr-partners-with-victory-xr-to-launch-10-meta-funded-metaversities/

newzoo.com. (2022). *Top Countries/Markets by Smartphone Penetration & Users*. Newzoo. https://newzoo.com/insights/rankings/top-countries-by-smartphone-penetration-and-users

Ng, S. F., Azlan, M. A. K., Kamal, A. N. A., & Manion, A. (2020). A quasi-experiment on using guided mobile learning interventions in ESL classrooms: Time use and academic performance. *Education and Information Technologies*, *25*(6), 4699–4719.

Nguyen, G. N. H., & Bower, M. (2018). Novice teacher technology-enhanced learning design practices: The case of the silent pedagogy. *British Journal of Educational Technology*, *49*(6), 1027–1043. doi:10.1111/bjet.12681

Nicholl, B., Flutter, J., Hosking, I., & Clarkson, P. (2013). Transforming practice in design and technology: Evidence from a classroom-based research study of students' responses to an intervention on inclusive design. *Curriculum Journal*, *24*(1), 86–102. https://doi.org/10.1080/09585176.2012.744696

Nickerson, C. (2021, December 15). *Rational choice theory*. Simply Psychology. Retrieved from https://www.simplypsychology.org/rational-choice-theory.html

Nicola, T., Gable, A., & Ash, J. (2020). *The Response of rural districts to the COVID-19 pandemic*. National Center for Rural Education Research Networks. https://cepr.harvard.edu/files/cepr/files/ncrern_report.pdf

Nicola, M., O'Neill, N., Sohrabi, C., Khan, M., Agha, M., & Agha, R. (2020). Evidence based management guideline for the COVID-19 pandemic-Review article. *International Journal of Surgery*, *77*, 206–216. doi:10.1016/j.ijsu.2020.04.001 PMID:32289472

Nicoletti, M. D. C., & Suemasu, E. (2021). Thoughts on computational thinking. *Academia Letters. Article, 1045*. Advance online publication. doi:10.20935/AL1045.5

Niemeyer, D. (2003). *Hard facts on smart classroom design: Ideas, guidelines, and layouts*. Scarecrow Press.

Nieves, K. (2021). Building inclusive learning environments with 1:1 devices. *Journal of Special Education Technology*, *36*(1), 54–59.

Nifakos, S., Chandramouli, K., Nikolaou, C. K., Papachristou, P., Koch, S., Panaousis, E., & Bonacina, S. (2021). Influence of human factors on cyber security within healthcare organisations: A systematic review. *Sensors (Basel)*, *21*(15), 5119. doi:10.339021155119 PMID:34372354

NJCAAE. (2022). *National Junior College Athletic Association Esports*. https://www.generationesports.com/njcaae

Nordström, T., Nilsson, S., Gustafson, S., & Svensson, I. (2018). Assistive technology applications for students with reading difficulties: Special education teachers' experiences and perceptions. *Disability and Rehabilitation*, *14*(8), 798–808. https://doi.org/10.1080/17483107.2018.1499142

Norries, C., Hossain, A., & Soloway, E. (2011). Using smartphones as essential tools for learning: A call to place schools on the right side of the 21st century. *Educational Technology*, *51*(3), 18–25.

Novak, J., & Watts, R. (2022, July 5). *Webex vs. Zoom: Which is best for your team?* Forbes. https://www.forbes.com/advisor/business/software/zoom-vs-webex/#:~:text=Both%20Webex%20and%20Zoom%20offer%20feature-rich%2C%20stable%20video%20conferencing,types%20of%20video%20conference%20users

Ntemngwa, C., & Oliver, J. S. (2018). The implementation of integrated science technology, engineering, and mathematics (STEM) instruction using robotics in the middle school science classroom. *International Journal of Education in Mathematics, Science and Technology, 6*(1), 12–40. http://dergipark.ulakbim.gov.tr/ijemst/article/view/5000195373/5000183562 doi:10.18404/ijemst.380617

Nunnally, J. C., & Bernstein, I. H. (1994). *Psychometric Theory*. McGraw-Hill.

Nye, J. (2017). Soft power: The origins and political progress of a concept. *Palgrave Communications, 3*(1), 17008. Advance online publication. doi:10.1057/palcomms.2017.8

O'Connor, B., & Lynch, D. (2011). Partnerships between and among education and the public and private sectors. In M. Malloch, L. Cairns, & K. Evans (Eds.), The SAGE handbook of workplace learning (pp. 407-419). SAGE Publications Ltd. doi:10.4135/9781446200940.n31

O'Dowd, R. (2018). From telecollaboration to virtual exchange: State-of-the-art and the role of UNICollaboration in moving forward. *Journal of Virtual Exchange, 1*, 1–23. doi:10.14705/rpnet.2018.jve.1

OECD. (2019). *Going Digital: Shaping Policies, Improving Lives*. OECD Publishing. doi:10.1787/9789264312012-

Ofgang, E. (2020). How to build an inclusive esports community: BX Start is focused on building an inclusive esports community from the ground up. *Tech & Learning*, 29. https://link.gale.com/apps/doc/A640002289/AONE?u=rocklandcc&sid=bookmark-AONE&xid=853ea267

Okaz, A. A. (2015). Integrating blended learning in higher education. *Procedia: Social and Behavioral Sciences, 186*, 600–603. doi:10.1016/j.sbspro.2015.04.086

Ok, M. W., & Rao, K. (2019). Digital tools for the inclusive classroom: Google Chrome as assistive and instructional technology. *Journal of Special Education Technology, 34*(3), 204–211. https://doi.org/10.1177%2F0162643419841546

Okolo, C. M., & Diedrich, J. (2014). Twenty-five years later: How is technology used in the education of students with disabilities? Results from a statewide study. *Journal of Special Education Technology, 29*(1), 1–20.

Olympic Council of Asia. (2022). *Press Release*. https://ocasia.org/news/3217-oca-press-release-oca-announces-new-dates-for-the-19th-asian-games-hangzhou.html

Omar, P. U. (2020). Smartphone usage among students at politeknik ungku omar. Jurnal Kejuruteraan, Teknologi dan Sains Sosial, 3(1).

Organization for Economic Cooperation and Development. (2006). *The new rural paradigm: Policies and governance*. https://www.oecd.org/cfe/regionaldevelopment/thenewruralparadigmpoliciesandgovernance.htm

Organization for Economic Cooperation and Development. (2019). *OECD Regional outlook 2019: Leveraging megatrends for cities and rural areas*. Organization for Economic Co-operation and Development. doi:10.1787/9789264312838-

Ortiz Rojas, M. E., Chiluiza, K., & Valcke, M. (2016). *Gamification in higher education and stem: A systematic review of literature* [Paper presentation]. *8th International Conference on Education and New Learning Technologies: EDULEARN 16*, Barcelona, Spain. 10.21125/edulearn.2016.0422

Ortiz, A. M., Bos, B., & Smith, S. (2015). The power of educational robotics as an integrated STEM learning experience in teacher preparation programs. *Journal of College Science Teaching, 44*(5), 42–47. doi:10.2505/4/jcst15_044_05_42

Osgood, R. L. (2005). *The history of inclusion in the United States*. Gallaudet University Press.

Osiurak, F., Navarro, J., & Reynaud, E. (2018, March 7). How our cognition shapes and is shaped by technology: A common framework for understanding human tool-use interactions in the past, present, and future. *Frontiers in Psychology*. Advance online publication. doi:10.3389/fpsyg.2018.00293

Ottenbreit-Leftwich, A., & Yadav, A. (2021). *Computational thinking in preK-5: Empirical evidence for integration and future directions.* ACM and the Robin Hood Learning + Technology Fund. https://www.acm.org/binaries/content/assets/education/ct_prek-5_web.pdf

Owuor, J., Larkan, F., Kayabu, B., Fitzgerald, G., Sheaf, G., Dinsmore, J., ... MacLachlan, M. (2018). Does assistive technology contribute to social inclusion for people with intellectual disability? A systematic review protocol. *BMJ Open*, *8*(2), e017533.

Özdemir, İ. H., Ateş Çobanoğlu, A., & Sarsar, F. (2021). Blended Learning Adaptation in Higher Education. In Technology Readings in Education 2021 (pp. 639-649). Pegem Academy Publications.

Palanivel K (2020). Emerging Technologies to Smart Education. *International Journal of Computer Trends and Technology, 68*(2), 5-16. doi:10.14445/22312803/IJCTT-V68I2P102

Palanivel, K., & Chiralekha, T. (2018). Big Data Reference Architecture for E-Learning Analytical Systems. *International Journal on Recent and Innovation Trends in Computing and Communication*, *6*(1), 55–67. doi:10.17762/ijritcc.v6i1.1381

Pallavi, K. (n.d.). *Risk: Meaning, concept and characteristics*. https://www.yourarticlelibrary.com/business/risk-management/risk-meaningconcept-and-characteristics/89506

Pallavi, K. (n.d.). *The history of risk.* https://www.youtube.com/watch?v=96_I4wEoTjM

Palmer, A. E. (2021, October 8). *Can community college students study abroad?* https://www.gooverseas.com/blog/can-community-college-students-study-abroad

Panettieri, J. (2021, June 7). *Colonial Pipeline cyberattack: Timeline and ransomeware recovery details.* MSSP Alert. https://www.msspalert.com/cybersecurity-breaches-and-attacks/ransomware/colonial-pipeline-investigation/

Papert, S. (1980). *Mindstorms: Children, computers, and powerful ideas* (1st ed.). Basic Books.

Papert, S. (1996). An exploration in the space of mathematics educations. *International Journal of Computers for Mathematical Learning*, *1*(1), 95–123. doi:10.1007/BF00191473

Papert, S. (2000). What's the big idea? Toward a pedagogy of idea power. *IBM Systems Journal*, *29*(3 & 4), 720–729. doi:10.1147j.393.0720

Parette, H. P., Peterson-Karlan, G. R., & Wojcik, B. W. (2005). The state of assistive technology services nationally and implications for future development. *Assistive Technology Outcomes and Benefits*, *2*(1), 13–24.

Parker, K. (2021). College identifies a game-changer for students with disabilities. *The Times EducationalSupplement.* https://draweb.njcu.edu/login?url=https://draweb.njcu.edu:2073/trade-journals/college-identifies-game-changer-students-with/docview/2553440846/se-2?accountid=12793

Parker, K., & Igielnik, R. (2020, May 14). *On the cusp of adulthood and facing an uncertain future: What we know about Gen Z so far.* https://www.pewresearch.org/social-trends/2020/05/14/on-the-cusp-of-adulthood-and-facing-an-uncertain-future-what-we-know-about-gen-z-so-far-2/

Parker, K., & Igielnik, R. (2022, April 1). *On the cusp of adulthood and facing an uncertain future: What we know about gen Z so far.* Pew Research Center's Social & Demographic Trends Project. Retrieved July 19, 2022, from https://www.pewresearch.org/social-trends/2020/05/14/on-the-cusp-of-adulthood-and-facing-an-uncertain-future-what-we-know-about-gen-z-so-far-2/

Patton, M. Q. (2015). Qualitative research & evaluation methods: Integrating theory and practice. *Sage (Atlanta, Ga.).*

Paxful. (2020). *What Happens When All the Bitcoin in the World Has Been Mined?* Retrieved from: https://paxful.com/blog/what-happens-when-all-21-million-bitcoins-mined/

Pelletier, K., Brown, M., Brooks, D. C., McCormack, M., Reeves, J., & Arbino, N. (2021). *EDUCAUSE Horizon Report, Teaching and Learning Edition.* EDUCAUSE. https://library.educause.edu/-/media/files/library/2021/4/2021hrteachinglearning.pdf?la=en&hash=C9DEC12398593F297CC634409DFF4B8C5A60B36E

Peng, C., Stackpole, B., Richards, D., Schwartz, D., Weeden, C., Fogle, C., Walrond, V., Johnson, D., Marcovecchio, J., & Brown, C. (2020). Visualization for spectators in cybersecurity. *2020 IEEE Conference on Visualization for Cyber Security (VizSec).* 10.1109/VizSec51108.2020.00009

Pérez-Díaz, J. A., Valdovinos, I. A., Choo, K. K. R., & Zhu, D. (2020). A flexible SDN-based architecture for identifying and mitigating low-rate DDoS attacks using machine learning. *IEEE Access: Practical Innovations, Open Solutions, 8,* 155859–155872.

Pernik, P. (2022). *Drivers of Change Impacting Cyberspace in 2030 Cyberspace Strategic Outlook 2030: Horizon Scanning and Analysis 2022.* NATO CCDCOE Publications.

Perrin, A. (2018, September 17). *5 facts about Americans and video games.* https://www.pewresearch.org/fact-tank/2018/09/17/5-facts-about-americans-and-video-games/

Peterson, D. (2016). Edtech and Student Privacy: California Law as a Model. *Berkeley Technology Law Journal, 31*(2), 961–996.

Peterson-Karlan, G. R. (2015). Assistive Technology Instruction within a Continuously Evolving Technology Environment. *Quarterly Review of Distance Education, 16*(2).

Petrin, R. A., Schafft, K. A., & Meece, J. L. (2014). Educational sorting and residential aspirations among rural high school students: What are the contributions of schools and educators to rural brain drain? *American Educational Research Journal, 51*(2), 294–326. doi:10.3102/0002831214527493

Pew Research Center. (2022). Majority of workers who quit a job in 2021 cite low pay, no opportunities for advancement, feeling disrespected. *Pew Research Center Newsletter.* https://www.pewresearch.org/fact-tank/2022/03/09/majority-of-workers-who-quit-a-job-in-2021-cite-low-pay-no-opportunities-for-advancement-feeling-disrespected/

Pew Research. (2019, June 12). *Demographics of mobile device ownership and adoption in the United States.* https://www.pewresearch.org/internet/fact-sheet/mobile/

Phoong, S. Y., Phoong, S. W., Moghavvemi, S., & Sulaiman, A. (2019). Effect of smart classroom on student achievement at higher education. *Journal of Educational Technology Systems, 48*(2), 291–304. doi:10.1177/0047239519870721

Piaget, J. (1954). *The construction of reality in the child.* Basic Books. doi:10.1037/11168-000

Picciano, A. G. (2021). Theories and frameworks for online education: Seeking an integrated model. In *A Guide to Administering Distance Learning* (pp. 79–103). Brill.

Pink, D. H. (2009). *Drive: The surprising truth about what motivates us.* Penguin.

Play, V. S. (2022). *High school eSports.* https://www.playvs.com/high-school

Playfly ESports. (2022). *NACE StarLeague.* https://playflyeSports.com/new-competitive-structure/

Popovici, D.-V., & Buică-Belciu, C. (2013). Self-concept pattern in adolescent students with intellectual disability. *Procedia: Social and Behavioral Sciences, 78,* 516–520. https://doi.org/10.1016/j.sbspro.2013.04.342

Porter, W. W., & Graham, C. R. (2016). Institutional drivers and barriers to faculty adoption of blended learning in higher education. *British Journal of Educational Technology, 47*(4), 748–762. doi:10.1111/bjet.12269

Porter, W. W., Graham, C. R., Bodily, R. G., & Sandberg, D. S. (2016). A qualitative analysis of institutional drivers and barriers to blended learning adoption in higher education. *The internet and Higher education, 28,* 17–27. doi:10.1016/j.iheduc.2015.08.003

Porter, W. W., Graham, C. R., Spring, K. A., & Welch, K. R. (2014). Blended learning in higher education: Institutional adoption and implementation. *Computers & Education, 75,* 185–195. doi:10.1016/j.compedu.2014.02.011

Potluri, Mangla, & Satpathy. (2020). Detection and Prevention Mechanisms for DDoS Attack in Cloud Computing Environment. *11th ICCCNT, IEEE Explore, 49239.*

Pougaza, S. (2008). *Essay on Transformational Growth in the Central African Republic from its independence to the present time.* Published by Academia.

Powell Sears, K. (2022, July 14). *Five ways online learning benefited some students.* https://www.insidehighered.com/views/2022/07/14/five-ways-online-learning-benefited-some-students-opinion

Pozo-Rico, T., Gilar-Corbí, R., Izquierdo, A., & Castejón, J.-L. (2020). Teacher training can make a difference: Tools to overcome the impact of COVID-19 on primacy schools. An experimental study. *International Journal of Environmental Research and Public Health, 17*(22), 8633. doi:10.3390/ijerph17228633 PMID:33233750

Previtali, P., & Scarozza, D. (2019). Blended learning adoption: A case study of one of the oldest universities in Europe. *International Journal of Educational Management, 33*(5), 990–998. doi:10.1108/IJEM-07-2018-0197

Pullen, D. J-F., Swabey, K., Abadooz, M., & Sing, T. (2015). Malaysian university students' use of mobile phones for study. *Australian Educational Computing, 30*(1). Retrieved from http://journal.acce.edu.au/index.php/AEC/article/view/55

PWC. (n.d.). *Mapping and managing cyber risks from third parties and beyond.* https://www.pwc.com/us/en/services/consulting/cybersecurity-risk-regulatory/library/third-party-risks.html

Québec. (2022). *Air quality in schools*. Retrieved July 20, 2022, from https://www.quebec.ca/en/education/preschool-elementary-and-secondary-schools/air-quality-schools

Quick, C., Ryndak, D., & Taub, D. (2017). Research and evidence-based practices to promote membership and learning in general education for students with extensive support needs. *Inclusion, 5*(2), 94–109.

Rabah, J., Cassidy, R., & Beauchemin, R. (2018, November). *Gamification in education: Real benefits or edutainment* [Paper presentation]. 17th European Conference on e-Learning, Athens, Greece. 10.13140/RG.2.2.28673.56162

Rahmadi, F. (2020). *WhatsApp Group for Teaching and Learning in Indonesian Higher Education: What's Up?* Academic Press.

Ramachandran, V. (2021, February 23). *Stanford researchers identify four causes for "Zoom fatigue" and their simple fixes*. https://news.stanford.edu/2021/02/23/four-causes-zoom-fatigue-solutions/

Rao, V. (2019). Blended Learning: A New Hybrid Teaching Methodology. *Online Submission, 3*(13).

Rao, K., Torres, C., & Smith, S. J. (2021). Digital tools and UDL-based instructional strategies to support students with disabilities online. *Journal of Special Education Technology, 36*(2), 105–112.

Ratten, V. (2015). A cross-cultural comparison of online behavioral advertising knowledge, online privacy concerns and social networking using the technology acceptance model and social cognitive theory,||. *Journal of Science & Technology Policy Management, 6*(1), 25–36. doi:10.1108/JSTPM-06-2014-0029

Raupp, A. B. (2020, April 16). *Esports and STEM education: A 2020 perspective*. Forbes. https://www.forbes.com/sites/forbestechcouncil/2020/04/16/esports-and-stem-education-a-2020-perspective/?sh=7c84fb9c4eae

Ray, S. 2021. *What is a risk register & how to create one*. ProjectManager. https://www.projectmanager.com/blog/guide-using-risk-register

Ray, S., & Srivastava, S. (2020). Virtualization of science education: A lesson from the COVID-19 pandemic. *Journal of Proteins and Proteomics, 11*(2), 77–80. doi:10.100742485-020-00038-7 PMID:33132627

Ready. (n.d.). *Business impact analysis*. https://www.ready.gov/business-impact-analysis

Reciprocity. (2021, Oct 25). *Incident response -vs- disaster recovery*. https://reciprocity.com/blog/incident-response-plan-vs-disaster-recovery-plan/

Reimers, F., & Chung. (2016). *Teaching and learning for the twenty-first century: Educational goals, policies, and curricula from six nations*. Harvard University Press.

Reimers, F., & Schleicher, A. (2020). *Schooling Disrupted. In Schooling Rethought. How the COVID19 pandemic is changing education*. OECD.

Reitenbach, G. (2015). From STEM to STEAM education. *Power, 159*(6), 6–6.

Remus, V., Cosmin, P., & Mihai, K. (2018). Study on technology as support for the activity of physical education and sport teachers in the primary and secondary education system of Cluj-Napoca. *Studia Universitatis Babes-Bolyai, Educatio Artis Gymnasticae, 63*(4).

REN-ISAC. (2021). Retrieved from https://www.ren-isac.net/about/index.html

Rennick, J. (2015). Learning that Makes a Difference: Pedagogy and Practice for Learning Abroad. *Teaching & Learning Inquiry: The ISSOTL Journal*, *3*(2), 71–88. doi:10.20343/teachlearninqu.3.2.71

Renz, A., & Hilbig, R. (2020). Prerequisites for artificial intelligence in further education: Identification of drivers, barriers, and business models of educational technology companies. *International Journal of Educational Technology in Higher Education*, *17*(1), 14. doi:10.118641239-020-00193-3

Resnick, M. (2018, September 16). *Computational fluency.* https://medium.com/@mres/computational-fluency-776143c8d725

Resnick, M., & Robinson, K. (2017). *Lifelong kindergarten: Cultivating creativity through projects, passion, peers, and play*. The MIT Press. doi:10.7551/mitpress/11017.001.0001

Rice, M., & Ortiz, K. (2021). Evaluating digital instructional materials for K-12 online and blended learning. *TechTrends*, *65*(6), 977–992. https://doi.org/10.1007/s11528-021-00671-z

Richey, R. C., Silber, K. H., & Ely, D. P. (2008). Reflections on the 2008 AECT definitions of the field. *TechTrends*, *52*(1), 24–25. doi:10.100711528-008-0108-2

Rind, A. A., Asad, M. M., Marri, S. A., Sherwani, F., & Rehman, F. U. (2022, December 6). How Integration of information and communication technologies impact academic achievement? An empirical study on Sindh education foundation. *Journal of Applied Research in Higher Education*, *14*(4), 1761–1772. doi:10.1108/JARHE-05-2021-0177

Rio, A. (2018). *The future of the corporate university.* Chief Learning Officer. https://www.chieflearningofficer.com/2018/05/03/future-corpo rate-university/

Riser-Kositsky, M., & Peele, H. (2021, July 30). Statistics on school sports: How many students play sports? Which sports do they play? *Education Week.* https://www.edweek.org/leadership/statistics-on-school-sport s-how-many-students-play-sports-which-sports-do-they-play/20 21/07

Robelen, E. (2011, December 7). STEAM Experts make case for adding the arts to STEM. *Education Week*, *1*(6).

Robledo, K., & Atarama, T. (2016). Periodismo político transmedia. Estrategias para el desarrollo de la profesión en el actual ecosistema mediático. *Correspondencias & Análisis*, (6), 31–45. doi:10.24265/cian.2016.n6.02

Rogstad. (2021). Gender in eSports research: a literature review. *European Journal for Sport and Society*, 1–19. doi:1 0.1080/16138171.2021.1930941

Rosa's Law. 74 FR 55947, Oct. 29, 2009, as amended at 82 FR 31913, July 11, 2017. https://www.govregs.com/regulations/expand/title34_chapterVI _part668_subpart_section668.231

Rosenberg, L. (2022, May 20). *VR vs. AR vs. Mr vs. XR: What's the difference?* Big Think. https://bigthink.com/the-future/vr-ar-mr-xr-metaverse/

Rosenfeld, M. (2013). Rethinking the boundaries between public law and private law for the twenty-first century: An introduction. *International Journal of Constitutional Law*, *11*(1), 125–128. https://bit.ly/3RXOB2Z. doi:10.1093/icon/mos053

Rosenthal, M. (2022, January 12. Must-know phishing statistics: Updated 2022. *Tessian*. https://www.tessian.com/blog/phishing-statistics-2020/

Rosmansyah, Y., Putro, B. L., Putri, A., Utomo, N. B., & Suhardi. (2022, January 4). Simple Model of Smart Learning Environment. *Interactive Learning Environments*, 1–22. Advance online publication. doi:10.1080/10494820.2021.2020295

Rosowsky, D., & Hallman, K. (2020, May 26). *Communicating culture in a distributed world.* Inside Higher Ed. https://www.insidehighered.com/views/2020/05/26/importance-culture-binding-higher-ed-institution-together-during-crises-pandemic

Rothwell, G., & Shaffer, M. (2019). eSports in K-12 and Post-Secondary Schools. *Education Sciences*, *9*(2), 105. doi:10.3390/educsci9020105

Routine activity theory: Crime prevention. (2011). New South Wales department of attorney general and justice. Retrieved from https://www.crimeprevention.nsw.gov.au/Documents/routine_activity_factsheet_nov2014.pdf

RSM. (2020). *Impact of the GDPR on Cyber Security Outcomes*. https://assets.publishing.service.gov.uk/government/uploads/system/uploads/attachment_data/file/906691/Impact_of_GDPR_on_cyber_security_outcomes.pdf

Runathong, W., Wongthai, W., & Panithansuwan, S. (2017). A System for Classroom Environment Monitoring Using the Internet of Things and Cloud Computing. In K. Kim & N. Joukov (Eds.), *Information Science and Applications (ICISA 2017)* (Vol. 424). Lecture Notes in Electrical Engineering, Springer. doi:10.1007/978-981-10-4154-9_84

Ruvalcaba, O., Shulze, J., Kim, A., Berzenski, S. R., & Otten, M. P. (2018). Women's experiences in eSports: Gendered differences in Peer and Spectator Feedback during competitive video game play. *Journal of Sport and Social Issues*, *42*(4), 295–311. doi:10.1177/0193723518773287

Ryan. (2017, February). Tinkering about thinking about Seymour. *Exploratorium*. https://www.exploratorium.edu/tinkering/blog/24?page=56

Sabillón, R. (2019). Audits in Cybersecurity: A Model of General Application for Companies and Nations. *RISTI - Rev. Ibérica Sist. e Tecnol. Information (Basel)*, (32), 33–48. doi:10.17013/risti.32.33-48

Sadykova, G., & Meskill, C. (2019). Interculturality in online learning: Instructor and student accommodations. *Online Learning, 23*(1), 5-21. https://bit.ly/3zsa5xK doi:10.24059/olj.v23i1.1418

Sahoo, K. S., Puthal, D., Tiwary, M., Rodrigues, J. J., Sahoo, B., & Dash, R. (2018). An early detection of low rate DDoS attack to SDN based data center networks using information distance metrics. *Future Generation Computer Systems*, *89*, 685–697.

Saini, M. K., & Goel, N. (2019). How smart are smart classrooms? A review of smart classroom technologies. *ACM Computing Surveys*, *52*(6), 1–28. Advance online publication. doi:10.1145/3365757

SAl Miaraj, A. A., & Bhat, I. B. (2021). Prevalence of Text Neck Syndrome and Its Association with Mobile Phone Usage Among University Academic Staff. *Int J Phys Med Rehabil, 9*, 10.

Sala, E., & Rantala, L. (2016). Acoustics and activity noise in school classrooms in Finland. *Applied Acoustics*, *114*, 252–259. doi:10.1016/j.apacoust.2016.08.009

Salehudin, M., Hamid, A., Zakaria, Z., Rorimpandey, W., & Yunus, M. (2020). *Instagram user experience in learning graphic design*. Academic Press.

Salomon, J. M. (2022). *Public-Private Partnerships and Collective Cyber Defence. 2022 NATO CCDCOE Publications.* Tallinn CCDCOE.

Salter, N. (2019, February 27). *The importance of minority leader representation.* Ohio State University Fisher College of Business. https://fisher.osu.edu/blogs/leadreadtoday/blog/the-importance-of-minority-leader-representation

Sánchez-Gómez, M. C., Martín-García, A. V., & Mena, J. (2020). Blended learning in tertiary education: Teachers' beliefs according to the technology acceptance model. *International Journal of Learning Technology, 15*(4), 341–359. doi:10.1504/IJLT.2020.113883

Sánchez, J., Mallorquí, A., Briones, A., Zaballos, A., & Corral, G. (2020). An integral pedagogical strategy for teaching and learning IoT cybersecurity. *Sensors (Basel), 20*(14), 3970. doi:10.339020143970 PMID:32708876

Sandanayake, T. C. (2019). Promoting open educational resources-based blended learning. *International Journal of Educational Technology in Higher Education, 16*(1), 1–16. doi:10.118641239-019-0133-6

Sang-Hun. (2021, Jun 19). Inside the 'deadly serious' world of esports in South Korea. *New York Times.* https://draweb.njcu.edu/login?url=https://draweb.njcu.edu:2073/newspapers/inside-deadly-serious-world-eSports-south-korea/docview/2542803244/se-2?accountid=12793

Santhosh Raj, P., & Silambarasan, G. (2017). Role of Data Mining in Cyber Security. *International Journal of Engineering Science and Computing, 4*(4), 13932–13935.

Santoso, L. W., & Yulia. (2017). Data Warehouse with Big Data Technology for Higher Education. *Procedia Computer Science, 124*, 93–99. doi:10.1016/j.procs.2017.12.134

Sarbu, I., & Pacurar, C. (2015). Experimental and numerical research to assess indoor environment quality and schoolwork performance in university classrooms. *Building and Environment, 93*(P2), 141–154. doi:10.1016/j.buildenv.2015.06.022

Sarfoah, E. (2017). *Smartphone use for learning: A study on University of Ghana students* [Unpublished MPhil Thesis]. Department of Communication Studies, University of Ghana.

Sarker, I. H. (2021). Deep Cybersecurity: A Comprehensive Overview from Neural Network and Deep Learning Perspective, SN. *Computer Science, 2*(3), 154. doi:10.100742979-021-00535-6

Satoshi, N. (2020). *Bitcoin: A Peer-to-Peer Electronic Cash System.* Retrieved from: https://bitcoin.org/bitcoin.pdf

Satsangi, R., Miller, B., & Savage, M. N. (2019). Helping teachers make informed decisions when selecting assistive technology for secondary students with disabilities. *Preventing School Failure, 63*(2), 97–104.

Save the Children. (2021). *2020 report, Stop the War on Children: Gender Matters.* https://www.savethechildren.org/us/charity-stories/10-worst-conflict-affected-countries-to-be-a-child

Scaradozzi, D., Sorbi, L., Pedale, A., Valzano, M., & Vergine, C. (2015). Teaching robotics at the primary school: An innovative approach. *Procedia: Social and Behavioral Sciences, 174*, 3838–3846. doi:10.1016/j.sbspro.2015.01.1122

Šćepanović, S., Žarić, N. A. Đ. A., & Matijević, T. (2015, September 24–25). *Gamification in higher education learning: State of the art, challenges, and opportunities* [Paper presentation]. In the Sixth International Conference on e-Learning (eLearning-2015), Belgrade, Serbia.

Schaaf, M. J. (2018). Editorial: Technology adoption, acceptance, satisfaction, and benefit: Integrating various assistive technology outcomes. *Special Education Technology, 33*(3), 171–181. doi:10.1177/0162643417753561

Scherer, M. J., Jutai, J., Fuhrer, M., Demers, L., & Deruyter, F. (2007). A framework for modeling the selection of assistive technology devices (ATDs). *Disability and Rehabilitation. Assistive Technology, 2*(1), 1–8. doi:10.1080/17483100600845414

Schnackner, B. (2021, November 3). *You think it's not a college sport? Buckle up as eSports is not a degree pursuit, too.* https://phys.org/news/2021-11-college-sport-buckle-eSports-degree.html

School of Education. L. U. of M. (2022, December 13). *What is Educational Technology—School of Education—Loyola Maryland.* https://www.loyola.edu/school-education/blog/2021/what-is-educational-technology

Schwartz, J. (2020). *The cyber-security problem schools and ed. tech need to face.* Education Week. https://www.edweek.org/technology/opinion-the-cyber-security-problem-schools-and-ed-tech-need-to-face/2020/01

Selwyn, N. (2020a). *After COVID-19: The longer-term impacts of the coronavirus crisis on education.* Monash University. https://educationfutures.monash.edu/all%2D%2D-present/after-covid-19

Selwyn, N., Hillman, T., Eynon, R., Ferreira, G., Knox, J., Macgilchrist, F., & Sancho-Gil, J. M. (2020b). What's next for Ed-Tech? Critical hopes and concerns for the 2020s. *Learning, Media and Technology, 45*(1), 1–6. doi:10.1080/17439884.2020.1694945

Semarayasa, I. K., Soegiyanto, K. S., Rahayu, S., & Hidayah, T. (2018, September). Impact of smartphones on the achievement of sepak takraw learners. In *International Conference on Science and Education and Technology 2018 (ISET 2018)* (pp. 237-240). Atlantis Press.

Shah, R., & Lopes Cardozo, M. (2015). Chapter 11: The politics of education in emergencies and conflicts. In T. McCowan & E. Unterhalter (Eds.), *Education and international development: An introduction* (pp. 181-200). Bloomsbury. https://www.africanstorybook.org/

Shaheen, N. L., & Lazar, J. (2017). K-12 technology accessibility: The message from state governments. *Journal of Special Education Technology, 33*(2), 83–97.

Shakoor, F., Fakhar, A., & Abbas, J. (2021). Impact of smartphones usage on the learning behaviour and academic performance of students: Empirical evidence from Pakistan. *Int. J. Acad. Res. Bus. Soc. Sci, 11*, 862–881.

Shamburg, C. (2020). Cases of successful independent educationally oriented podcasters. *E-Learning and Digital Media, 17*(6), 505–520. doi:10.1177/2042753020946281

Shapiro, J. (2018, January 8). *The sexual assault epidemic no one talks about.* NPR. Retrieved August 18, 2022, from https://www.npr.org/2018/01/08/570224090/the-sexual-assault-epidemic-no-one-talks-about

Shen, C. W., Wu, Y. C. J., & Lee, T. C. (2014). Developing a NFC-equipped smart classroom: Effects on attitudes toward computer science. *Computers in Human Behavior, 30*, 731–738. doi:10.1016/j.chb.2013.09.002

Shin, M., Bryant, D. P., Bryant, B. R., McKenna, J. W., Hou, F., & Ok, M. W. (2017). Virtual manipulatives: Tools for teaching mathematics to students with learning disabilities. *Intervention in School and Clinic, 52*, 148–153.

Showers, B., & Joyce, B. (1996). The evolution of peer coaching. *Educational Leadership, 53*(6), 12–16. https://www.ascd.org/el/articles/the-evolution-of-peer-coaching

Shree, A., & Shukla, P. C. (2016). Intellectual disability: Definition, classification, causes and characteristics. *Learning Community-An International Journal of Educational and Social Development, 7*(1), 9. doi:10.5958/2231-458x.2016.00002.6

Shute, V., Sun, C., & Asbell-Clarke, J. (2017). Demystifying computational thinking. *Educational Research Review, 22*, 1–18. doi:10.1016/j.edurev.2017.09.003

Shyyan, V. V., Thurlow, M. L., Larson, E. D., Christensen, L. L., & Lazarus, S. S. (2016). *White paper on common accessibility language for states and assessment vendors.* University of Minnesota, Data Informed Accessibility–Making Optimal Needs-Based Decisions (DIAMOND). https://nceo.umn.edu/docs/OnlinePubs/DIAMONDWhitePaper.pdf

Siemens, G. [@gsiemens]. (2020). *Research pundits. A Google scholar search of prominent voices quickly reveals those who have earned the right to provide guidance* [tweet]. Retrieved from https://twitter.com/gsiemens/status/1246920826282110976

Silva, E. (2009). Measuring skills for 21st century learning. *Phi Delta Kappan, 90*(9), 630-634. doi:10.1177/003172170909000905

Singar & Akhilesh. (2020). Role of Cyber-Security in Higher Education. In Smart Technologies: Scope and Applications (pp. 249–264). Singapore: Springer.

Singh, J., Steele, K., & Singh, L. (2021). Combining the best of online and face-to-face learning: Hybrid and blended learning approach for COVID-19, post vaccine, & post-pandemic world. *Journal of Educational Technology Systems, 50*(2), 140–171. doi:10.1177/00472395211047865

Siu, K., & Lam, M. (2012). Public computer assisted learning facilitates for children with visual impairment: Universal design for inclusive learning. *Early Childhood Education Journal, 40*, 295–303.

SmithBarrow, D. (2020, September 18). HBCUs entering the game: Black colleges join the esports bandwagon*: Washington Post.*

Soegoto, E. S., & Rinaldy, M. F. (2020). Smart Campus with A Learning Management System. *IOP Conf. Ser.: Mater. Sci. Eng., 879.*

Soegoto, H. (2019). Smartphone usage among college students. *Journal of Research in Engineering and Technology, 14*(3), 1248–1259.

So, H. J., & Bonk, C. J. (2010). Examining the roles of blended learning approaches in computer-supported collaborative learning (CSCL) environments: A Delphi study. *Journal of Educational Technology & Society, 13*(3), 189–200.

Soldner, M., Rowan-Kenyon, H., Inkelas, K. K., Garvey, J., & Robbins, C. (2012). Supporting students' intentions to persist in STEM disciplines: The role of living-learning programs among other social-cognitive factors. *The Journal of Higher Education, 83*(3), 311–336. doi:10.1353/jhe.2012.0017

Sonawat, R. (2021). *EdTech in Higher Education: Digital Equity & Cybersecurity are Concern Areas.* https://www.expresscomputer.in/news/edtech-in-higher-education-digital-equity-cybersecurity-are-concern-areas/74792/

Sosanya, V. (2022). *Beyond Cyber Security Tools: The Increasing Roles Of Human Factors And Cyber Insurance In The Survival of Social Media Organisations.* https://www.researchgate.net/profile/Olutunji-Sosanya

Sparks, S. D. (2022). Students Are Behaving Badly in Class. Excessive Screen Time Might Be to Blame. *Education Week, 41*(30). https://draweb.njcu.edu/login?url=https://draweb.njcu.edu:2073/trade-journals/students-are-behaving-badly-class-excessive/docview/2651398638/se-2?accountid=12793

Spătărelu, E. M. (2020). Beginner teacher in the recent research: A review of literature. *Journal of Education Studies, 2*(2), 107–122.

Spector, J. M. (2015). *Foundations of educational technology: Integrative approaches and interdisciplinary perspectives.* Routledge. doi:10.4324/9781315764269

St. Amour, M. (2020). Privacy and the online pivot. *Inside Higher Ed.* https://www.insidehighered.com/news/2020/03/25/pivot-online-raises-concerns-ferpa-surveillance

Staake, J. (2021, January 22). *Padlet for teachers: The best tips, tricks, and ideas for your classroom.* https://www.weareteachers.com/padlet-for-teachers/

Stachowiak, B. (2019, January 15). *How to get students engaging with each other in online and blended classes.* https://teachinginhighered.com/2019/01/15/how-to-get-students-engaging-with-each-other-in-online-or-blended-classes/

Stahlke, S., Robb, J. & Mirza-Babaei, P. (2018) The fall of the fourth wall: Designing and evaluating interactive spectator experiences. *International Journal of Gaming and Computer-Mediated Simulations, 10*(1).

Statman, M. (2010). *The cultures of risk tolerance.* SSRN Electronic Journal. https://papers.ssrn.com/sol3/papers.cfm?abstract_id=1647086 doi:10.2139/ssrn.1647086

Stefanini. (2021). *The New Role of Artificial Intelligence in Cybersecurity: How Can It Protect Your Business?* https://stefanini.com/en/trends/news/role-of-artificial-intelligence-in-cybersecurity-to-protect-busi

Stevens Initiative. (2022, January 8). https://www.stevensinitiative.org/

Stewart, M., & Price, H. (2022). Getting in the eGame: ESports Streaming Gives the University of Kentucky a New Way to Grow Revenue and Recruit Students. *Planning for Higher Education, 50*(2), 26–35. https://draweb.njcu.edu/login?url=https://draweb.njcu.edu:2073/scholarly-journals/getting-egame-eSports-streaming-gives-university/docview/2651853366/se-2?accountid=12793

Stoffregen, J. D., Pawlowski, J. M., Ras, E., Tobias, E., Šćepanović, S., Fitzpatrick, D., ... Friedrich, H. (2016). Barriers to open e-learning in public administrations: A comparative case study of the European countries Luxembourg, Germany, Montenegro and Ireland. *Technological Forecasting and Social Change, 111*, 198–208. doi:10.1016/j.techfore.2016.06.030

StopBullying.gov. (2022). *What is cyberbullying.* Retrieved July 16, 2022, from https://www.stopbullying.gov/cyberbullying/what-is-it

Stouffer, K., Lightman, S., Pillitteri, V., Abrams, M., & Hahn, A. (2015). *SP 800-82 Rev. 2: Guide to Industrial Control Systems.* U.S. Department of Commerce, Washington, D.C. NIST Series SP 800-82 Rev. 2. Supersedes: SP 800-82 Rev. 1 (05/14/2013). https://csrc.nist.gov/publications/detail/sp/800-82/rev-2/final

Strelan, P., Osborn, A., & Palmer, E. (2020). The flipped classroom: A meta-analysis of effects on student performance across disciplines and education levels. *Educational Research Review*, *30*, 100314. doi:10.1016/j.edurev.2020.100314

Suartama, I. K., Setyosari, P., & Ulfa, S. (2019). Development of an instructional design model for mobile blended learning in higher education. *International Journal of Emerging Technologies in Learning*, *14*(16), 4. doi:10.3991/ijet.v14i16.10633

Sudar, K. M., Deepalakshmi, P., & Singh, A. (2022). TFAD: TCP flooding attack detection in software-defined networking using proxy-based and machine learning-based mechanisms. *Cluster Comput.* doi:10.1007/s10586-022-03666-4

Sudar, K. M., Beulah, M., Deepalakshmi, P., Nagaraj, P., & Chinnasamy, P. (2021, January). Detection of Distributed Denial of Service Attacks in SDN using Machine learning techniques. In *2021 International Conference on Computer Communication and Informatics (ICCCI)* (pp. 1-5). IEEE.

Sudar, K. M., & Deepalakshmi, P. (2020). Comparative study on IDS using machine learning approaches for software defined networks. *International Journal of Intelligent Enterprise*, *7*(1-3), 15–27.

Sudar, K. M., & Deepalakshmi, P. (2022). Flow-Based Detection and Mitigation of Low-Rate DDOS Attack in SDN Environment Using Machine Learning Techniques. In *IoT and Analytics for Sensor Networks* (pp. 193–205). Springer. doi:10.1007/978-981-16-2919-8_18

Sudar, K. M., Deepalakshmi, P., Nagaraj, P., & Muneeswaran, V. (2020, November). Analysis of Cyberattacks and its Detection Mechanisms. In *2020 Fifth International Conference on Research in Computational Intelligence and Communication Networks (ICRCICN)* (pp. 12-16). IEEE.

Sudar, K. M., Deepalakshmi, P., Ponmozhi, K., & Nagaraj, P. (2019, December). Analysis of Security Threats and Countermeasures for various Biometric Techniques. In *2019 IEEE International Conference on Clean Energy and Energy Efficient Electronics Circuit for Sustainable Development (INCCES)* (pp. 1-6). IEEE. 10.1109/INCCES47820.2019.9167745

Suleman, Q., & Hussain, I. (2014). Effects of classroom physical environment on the academic achievement scores of secondary school students in kohat division, Pakistan. *International Journal of Learning & Development*, *4*(1), 71–82. doi:10.5296/ijld.v4i1.5174

Sulistyorini, E., & Widodo, P. (2022). The Utilization of the Deutsche Welle Learning Application in Teaching German Vocabulary. *International Journal of Linguistics, Literature and Translation*, *5*(1), 110–116.

SUNY COIL Center. (n.d.). *Welcome.* https://coil.suny.edu./

Superintendencia de la Educación. (2020). *Superintendencia de educación flexibiliza uso de la SEP para implementar estrategias de seguridad sanitaria por COVID-19.* Retrieved from https://www.supereduc.cl/prensa/superintendencia-de-educacion-flexibiliza-uso-de-la-seppara-implementar-estrategias-de-seguridad-sanitaria-por-covid-19/

Suryanti, S., Widodo, W., & Yermiandhoko, Y. (2021). *Gadget-Based Interactive Multimedia on Socio-Scientific Issues to Improve Elementary Students' Science Literacy.* Academic Press.

Swenson, S., & Ryder, R. E. (2016). *Dear colleague: Virtual schools.* Department of Education, Office of Special Education and Rehabilitative Services. https://www2.ed.gov/policy/speced/guid/idea/memosdcltrs/dcl–virtual-schools–08-05-2016.pdf

Synopsys Cybersecurity Research Center. (2020). *Peril in a Pandemic: Mobile Security.* https://www.synopsys.com/software-integrity/resources/analyst-reports/mobile-application- security-covid.html

Szajna, B. (1996). Empirical Evaluation of the Revised Technology Acceptance Model. *Management Science*, *42*(1), 85–92.

Ta'amneh, M. A. A. (2021). The Use of Smartphones in Learning English Language Skills: A Study of University Students' Perspectives. *International Journal of Applied Linguistics and English Literature*, *10*(1), 1–8.

Tagoe, M., & Abakah, E. (2014). Determining distance education students' readiness for mobile learning at University of Ghana using the Theory of Planned Behavior. *International Journal of Education and Development Using Information and Communication Technology*, *10*(1), 91.

Talbot, J. (2021, Feb 14). *Example of a risk management policy*. https://www.juliantalbot.com/post/example-of-a-risk-management-policy

Tan, J., & Sockalingam, N. (2015). *Gamification to engage students in higher education* [Working paper]. https://ink.library.smu.edu.sg/lkcsb_research/4740

Tang, H. (2021). Person-centered analysis of self-regulated learner profiles in MOOCs: A cultural perspective. *Educational Technology Research and Development*, *69*(2), 1247–1269. doi:10.100711423-021-09939-w

Tang, T., Cooper, R., & Kucek, J. (2021). Gendered ESports: Predicting Why Men and Women Play and Watch ESports Games. *Journal of Broadcasting & Electronic Media*, *65*(3), 336–356. doi:10.1080/08838151.2021.1958815

Tawalbeh, L. A., Muheidat, F., Tawalbeh, M., & Quwaider, M. (2020). IoT Privacy and security: Challenges and solutions. *Applied Sciences (Basel, Switzerland)*, *10*(12), 4102. doi:10.3390/app10124102

Taxi, D. (2022). *Drone taxi Dubai*. https://taxi-dubai.ae/drone-taxi-dubai/

Tayebinik, M., & Putch, N. (2012). Blended and e-learning. *IMACST*, *3*(1), 103–110.

Taylor, N. (2020, September 9). As collegiate eSports become more professional, women are being left out. *MedicalXpress*. https://medicalxpress.com/news/2020-09-collegiate-eSports-professional-women-left.html

Taylor, F. W. (1911). *The Principles of Scientific Management*. Harper and Brothers.

Taylor, N., & Stout, B. (2020). Gender and the two-tiered system of collegiate esports. *Critical Studies in Media Communication*, *37*(5), 451–465. doi:10.1080/15295036.2020.1813901

TDI. (2018). *Violence in the Name of Religion and the Importance of Interpretation*. Retrieved from: https://www.tdi.ge/ge/page/zaladoba-religiis-saxelit-da-interpretaciis-mnishvneloba

Teich, A. G. (2019). *Repurposing school libraries as vibrant hubs and centers of change*. https://www.techlearning.com/resources/repurposing-school-libraries-as-vibrant-hubs-and-centers-of-change

Terminalfour. (n.d.). *The Metaverse – The future of higher education*. https://www.terminalfour.com/blog/posts/the-metaverse---the-future-of-higher-education.html

Tether, B. S., & Tajar, A. (2008). Beyond industry–university links: Sourcing knowledge for innovation from consultants, private research organisations and the public science base. *Research Policy*, *37*(6-7), 1079–1095. doi:10.1016/j.respol.2008.04.003

Thakur, M. (2022). *Risk categories*. Wallstreet Mojo. https://www.wallstreetmojo.com/risk-categories/

Thales Group. (2021, May). *Beyond GDPR: Data Protection Around The World.* Thales Group. Retrieved July 1, 2022, from https://bit.ly/3BeU6o7

The Ohio State University. (2018, October 3). *The Ohio State University launches first-of-its-kind comprehensive esports program.* https://news.osu.edu/the-ohio-state-university-launches-first-of-its-kind-comprehensive-eSports-program/

The Ohio State University. (2019, September 11). *Ohio State eSports arena ready for play.* https://news.osu.edu/ohio-state-eSports-arena-open-and-ready-for-play/

The Washington Post. (2020). *The Pentagon has acknowledged that in the event of a Russian invasion, it will not be able to defend the Baltic states and Poland.* Retrieved from: https://imedinews.ge/ge/msoflio/67383/pentagonma-agiara-rom-rusetis-shechris-shemtkhvevashi-baltiispiretis-qveknebis-da-polonetis-datsvas-ver-moastsrebs

The World Bank Group. (2018). *Country Profile. Central African Republic.* worldbank.org

The World Bank Group. (2021, March 19). *DataBank World Development Indicators (WDI). Central African Republic.* https://databank.worldbank.org/reports.aspx?source=2&country=CAF#

Thier, M., Longhurst, J., Grant, P., & Hocking, J. (2021). Research deserts: A systematic mapping review of US rural education definitions and geographies. *Journal of Research in Rural Education, 37*(2). Advance online publication. doi:10.26209/jrre3702

Thiry, H. (2017). Undergraduate degree: Increasing Latino retention and completion. *Underrepresented Minorities in STEM Fields*, 66. https://par.nsf.gov/servlets/purl/10049620#page=68

Thomas, A. D. (2021). *The Use of Smartphones by K-12 School Administrators: A Gratification Study* [Doctoral dissertation]. Tennessee State University.

Thomas, C. N., Peeples, K. N., Kennedy, M. J., & Decker, M. (2019). Riding the special education technology wave: Policy, obstacles, recommendations, actionable ideas, and resources. *Intervention in School and Clinic, 54*(5), 295–303.

Thompson Reuters. (2022). *Cybercrimes.* Findlaw. https://www.findlaw.com/criminal/criminal-charges/cyber-crimes.html

Thompson, S. (2020). *Wi-Fi equipped school buses to prepare students for homeschooling.* School Bus Fleet. https://www.schoolbusfleet.com/10112966/wi-fi-equipped-school-buses-to-prepare-students-for-rhomeschooling

Timberg & Romm. (2020). *Hackers are seizing on coronavirus fears to steal data, researchers and U.S. regulators warn.* Retrieved from: https://www.washingtonpost.com/technology/2020/03/12/hackers-are-using-coronavirus-fears-target-people-looking-information-infection-maps/

Tingle, C. (2022). More research is needed on prevalence, incidence of injuries in eSports athletes. *Orthopedics Today, 42*(1), 10-12. https://draweb.njcu.edu/login?url=https://www.proquest.com/trade-journals/more-research-is-needed-on-prevalence-incidence/docview/2630948183/se-2?accountid=12793

Tissenbaum, M., & Slotta, J. D. (2019). Developing a smart classroom infrastructure to support real-time student collaboration and inquiry: A 4-year design study. *Instructional Science*, *47*(4), 423–462. doi:10.100711251-019-09486-1

Toklu, S. İ. N. A. N., & Şimşek, M. (2018). Two-layer approach for mixed high-rate and low-rate distributed denial of service (DDoS) attack detection and filtering. *Arabian Journal for Science and Engineering*, *43*(12), 7923–793.

Topal. (2022). *Cybersecurity in Higher Education: Problems and Solutions*. https://www.toptal.com/insights/innovation/cybersecurity-in-higher-education

Toperesu, B. (2020). *The impact of smartphone use on student learning experience in higher education in South Africa* [Master's thesis]. Faculty of Commerce.

Tortorella, G. L., Narayanamurthy, G., & Cauchick-Miguel, P. A. (2021). Operations Management teaching practices and information technologies adoption in emerging economies during COVID-19 outbreak. *Technological Forecasting and Social Change*, *171*, 120996.

Toyama, K. (2015, October 29). The looming gamification of higher ed. *The Chronicle of Higher Education*. https://www.chronicle.com/article/the-looming-gamification-of-higher-ed/

Treiblmaier, H., Putz, L. M., & Lowry, P. B. (2018). Setting a definition, context, and theory-based research agenda for the gamification of non-gaming applications. *Association for Information Systems Transactions on Human-Computer Interaction*, *10*(3), 129–163. doi:10.17705/1thci.00107

Trim, P. R. J., & Lee, Y. I. (2021). The Global Cyber Security Model: Counteracting Cyber Attacks through a Resilient Partnership Arrangement. *Big Data Cogn. Comput.*, *5*(3), 32. doi:10.3390/bdcc5030032

Trubina, I. I., Shutikova, M. I., Braines, A. A., Dzamykhov, A. K., & Dzamykhova, M. T. (2019). Monitoring The Assessment of Student Educational Performance: Information Aspects. In Education Environment for the Information Age, Vol 69. European Proceedings of Social and Behavioural Sciences (pp. 932-938). Future Academy. doi:10.15405/epsbs.2019.09.02.104

Truitt, A. A., & Ku, H. Y. (2018). A case study of third grade students' perceptions of the station rotation blended learning model in the United States. *Educational Media International*, *55*(2), 153–169. doi:10.1080/09523987.2018.1484042

Trump,D.(2020).*NATOshouldalsocovertheMiddleEastandcallthenewalliance"NATO+MiddleEast"-whatawonderfulname, I guess the names well.* Retrieved from: interpressnews.ge: https://www.interpressnews.ge/ka/article/580527-donald-tramp i-nato-m-axlo-agmosavletic-unda-moicvas-da-axal-alianss-dava rkvat-natoaxlo-agmosavleti-ra-mshvenieri-saxelcodebaa-saxele bs-kargad-vigoneb/

Trust, T., & Whalen, J. (2020). Should teachers be trained in emergency remote teaching? Lessons learned from the COVID-19 pandemic. *Journal of Technology and Teacher Education*, *28*(2), 189–199.

Tsiptse, O. (2021). *Protection of Personal Data in the Era of COVID-19*. http://hdl.handle.net/11544/29755

Tulchinsky, T. H. (2018). John Snow, Cholera, the broad street pump; waterborne diseases then and now. *Case Studies in Public Health*, 77.

Tuncay, N. (2016). Smartphones as tools for distance education. *Journal Of Educational And Instructional Studies in the World.*, *6*(2), 2146–7463.

U.S. Bureau of Labor Statistics. (2022, April 18). *Occupational outlook handbook.* U.S. Bureau of Labor Statistics. https://www.bls.gov/ooh/computer-and-information-technology/information-security-analysts.htm

UKEssays. (2018). *Applying Criminological Theories to Cyber Crime.* Retrieved from https://www.ukessays.com/essays/criminology/explaining-cyber crime-using.php?vref=1

UN Refugee Agency. (2020, April 6). How to ensure everyone can continue learning amid the coronavirus situation. In *Connected education: resources, considerations & guidance.* UNHCR. https://www.unhcr.org/en-us/5e787bea

UNCHR. (2021a, January 19). *Central Africans Fleeing post-election insecurity cross into Cameroon. Since December, nearly 5,000 Central Africans have crossed into Cameroon.* https://www.youtube.com/watch?v=KNQBNCFjVtI

UNCHR. (2021b, January 30). *Central African Republic situation.* Author.

UNESCO. (1994). *Final report: World conference on special needs education: Access and quality.* UNESCO.

UNESCO. (2017). *Education for Sustainable Development Goals Learning Objectives.* https://unesdoc.unesco.org/ark:/48223/pf0000247444

UNHCR. (n.d.). *The UN Refugee Agency (2001-2021). Refugee Data Finder.* https://www.unhcr.org/refugstatistics/download/?url=LwOoL9

UNICEF. (2021). *Seen, counted, included: Using data to shed light on the well-being of children with disabilities.* UNICEF.

United Nations. (2020). *COVID-19 could lead to millions of unintended pregnancies, new UN-backed data reveals.* https://news.un.org/en/story/2020/04/1062742

United Nations. (2022). *Do you know all 17 SDGs?* https://sdgs.un.org/goals

United Nations. (n.d.). *The 17 Goals.* United Nations Department of Economic and Social Affairs: Sustainable Development. https://sdgs.un.org/goals

United States Department of Education, National Center for Education Statistics. (2019). *Digest of education statistics, 2018 (NCES 2020-009).* nces.ed.gov/fastfacts/display.asp?id=59

United States Department of Education. (2022). *IDEA section 618 data products.* Retrieved July 10, 2022, from https://data.ed.gov/dataset/idea-section-618-data-products

United States Department of Health & Human Services. (2020, April 23). *Safety for Kids Activity Book - National Institutes of Health.* NIH Provides Cyber Safety Resources for Children and Families. Retrieved August 3, 2022, from https://www.cit.nih.gov/sites/default/files/NIH-Cyber-Safety-for-Kids-Activity-Book.pdf

United States Digital Literacy. (2016). *Web 2.0 to Social 3.0.* US Digital Literacy. Retrieved August 13, 2022, from http://digitalliteracy.us/web-2-0-to-social-3-0/

University of Hertfordshire. (2021). *Important Information – Mobile Application Cyber Attack.* https://www.herts.ac.uk/study/service-update

University of North Dakota. (n.d.). *7 types of cyber security threats.* https://onlinedegrees.und.edu/blog/types-of-cyber-security-threats/

University of San Diego. (2022). *Virtual/hybrid/HYFLEX classroom technology setup*. https://www.sandiego.edu/its/support/classrooms/hybrid-classroom-technology.php

Valiante, G. (n.d.). *Self-efficacy: The exercise of control: An outline composed by Gio Valiante*. Emory University. Retrieved from https://www.uky.edu/~eushe2/Pajares/effbook3.html

Valk, J., Rashid, A., & Elder, L. (2010). Using mobile phones to improve educational outcomes: An analysis of evidence from Asia. *The International Review of Research in Open and Distributed Learning*, *11*(1), 117–140. https://www.irrodl.org/index.php/irrodl/article/view/794/1507

Valtonen, T., Sointu, E., Kukkonen, J., Kontkanen, S., Lambert, M. C., & Mäkitalo-Siegl, K. (2017). TPACK updated to measure pre-service teachers' twenty-first century skills. *Australasian Journal of Educational Technology*, *33*(3), 15–31. doi:10.14742/ajet.3518

Van der Ham, J. (2021). Toward a better understanding of "cybersecurity". *Digital Threats.*, *2*(3), 1–3. doi:10.1145/3442445

Van Gieson, L. (2018, January 31). *My top 5 (Free-ish) cool tools that integrate into Canvas*. https://wp.wpi.edu/atc-ttl/2018/01/31/my-top-5-free-ish-cool-tools-that-integrate-into-canvas/

VanLone, J., Pansé-Barone, C., & Long, K. (2021). Teacher preparation and the COVID-19 disruption: Understanding the impact and implications for novice teachers. *International Journal of Educational Research Open*, *3*, 100120. Advance online publication. doi:10.1016/j.ijedro.2021.100120 PMID:35059675

Vanyi, J. (2018). *The impact of a gamified orientation on predominantly underrepresented minority, undergraduate student success and retention in a STEM academy program* (Publication No. 10937459) [Doctoral dissertation, New Jersey City University]. ProQuest Dissertations and Theses.

Varona Taborda, M. A., Montano Collazos, F. A., Escobar Marulanda, C. A., & Márceles Villalba, K. (2021). Dynamic Cybersecurity Model based on ISO standards for Higher Education Institutions in Colombia. *Revista Ingeniería Solidaria*, *17*(3), 1–21. Advance online publication. doi:10.16925/2357-6014.2021.03.05

Veerendra, U. U., Ravitheja, B., & Veeresh, K. (2017). Data Mining for Security Applications, International *Journal of Core Engineering & Management,* 38-44.

Venkat, R. (2021, September 9). *Asian Games 2022: ESports to make debut; FIFA, PUBG, Dota 2 among eight medal events*. https://olympics.com/en/news/fifa-pubg-dota-2-eSports-medal-events-asian-games-2022

Venkatesh, V., & Davis, F. D. (2000). A Theoretical Extension of the Technology Acceptance Model: Four Longitudinal Field Studies. *Management Science*, *46*(2), 186–204.

Venugopal, Shenoy, Kumar, Pushpa, Venkatesh, Sunil, & Roopa. (2020). A Systematic Study and Comprehensive Comparison of Online Teaching and Learning (OTL) Apps for Measuring the Quality of User Experience. *International Journal of Scientific Research*, *9*(7), 864–890.

Verry, J. (2016, Dec 22). *Risk tolerance: To avoid, transfer, mitigate or accept — that is the question!* https://www.pivotpointsecurity.com/blog/risk-tolerance-in-business/

Vygotsky, L. S. (1980). *Mind in society: The development of higher psychological processes*. Harvard University Press. doi:10.2307/j.ctvjf9vz4

Wainganker, R., & Vaidya, D. (n.d.). *Risk transfer*. Wallstreet Mojo. https://www.wallstreetmojo.com/risk-transfer/

Walker, Z., McMahon, D., & Rosenblatt, K. (2017). Beyond Pokémon: Augmented reality is a universal design for learning tool. *SAGE Open*, (October-December), 1–8.

Wallace, P. R. (1998). *Diffusion of Internet Adoption: A Study of the Relationship between Innovativeness, the Attitude of Teachers toward Using the Internet, and Internet Use* [Unpublished Doctoral Dissertation]. University of Tennessee, Knoxville, TN, United States.

Walsh, B., & Dalton, B. (2021). Build a better book: Enriched literacy-project-based learning for multilingual students. *Journal of Adolescent & Adult Literacy*, *65*(4), 361–365.

Walton, D. R., Lower-Hoppe, L. M., & Horger, M. (2020). Do eSports classify as intercollegiate sport? Legal analysis of Title IX. *Journal of Issues in Intercollegiate Athletics*, *2020*(13), 94–118.

Wang, T., Zhang, T., & Lovell, B. (2021). Faces a la carte: Text-to-face generation via attribute disentanglement. In *Proceedings of the IEEE/CVF Winter Conference on Applications of Computer Vision* (pp. 3380-3388). 10.1109/WACV48630.2021.00342

Warren County Community College. (2022). *Warren Unmanned Systems Technology programs*. https://www.warren.edu/drones/

Web Accessibility Initiative (WAI). (2022). *Home*. Initiative (WAI). Retrieved August 10, 2022, from https://www.w3.org/WAI/

Weintrop, D., Beheshti, E., Horn, M., Orton, K., Jona, K., Trouille, L., & Wilensky, U. (2016). Defining computational thinking for mathematics and science classrooms. *Journal of Science Education and Technology*, *25*(1), 127–147. doi:10.100710956-015-9581-5

Wenger-Trayner, E., & Wenger-Trayner, B. (2015). Learning in a landscape of practice: a framework. In E. Wenger-Trayner, M. Fenton-O'Creevy, S. Hutchinson, C. Kubiak, & B. Wenger-Trayner (Eds.), *Learning in landscapes of practice* (pp. 51–78). Routledge.

Werner, S., & Shpigelman, C.-N. (2019). Information and communication technologies: Where are persons with intellectual disabilities? *Israel Journal of Health Policy Research*, *8*(1). https://doi.org/10.1186/s13584-018-0282-4

West Virginia University. (2021, October 21). Game on: WVU prepping launch of eSports minor alongside development of new eSports team, top player already representing the gold and blue. *WVU Today*. https://wvutoday.wvu.edu/stories/2021/10/21/game-on-wvu-prepping-launch-of-eSports-minor-alongside-development-of-new-eSports-team-top-player-already-representing-the-gold-and-blue

West, C., & Fitzgerald, F. S. (2013). *The Great Gatsby*. Oxford University Press.

What we investigate: The cyber threat. (2022). Federal Bureau of Investigation. https://www.fbi.gov/investigate/cyber

Whitacre, B. E. (2021). COVID-19 and rural broadband. *Choices*, *36*(3), 1–10. doi:10.2139srn.3898548

Whitacre, B., Gallardo, R., & Strover, S. (2014). Does rural broadband impact jobs and income? Evidence from spatial and first-differenced regressions. *The Annals of Regional Science*, *53*(3), 649–670. doi:10.100700168-014-0637-x

Whitacre, B., & Manlove, J. (2016). Broadband and civic engagement in rural areas: What matters? *Community Development (Columbus, Ohio), 47*(5), 700–717. doi:10.1080/15575330.2016.1212910

White, K., & Banda, M. (2016). The role of civil society in pandemic preparedness. In *Innovation in Global Health Governance* (pp. 123–146). Routledge.

Whittaker, J. A., & Montgomery, B. L. (2012). Cultivating diversity and competency in STEM: Challenges and remedies for removing virtual barriers to constructing diverse higher education communities of success. *Journal of Undergraduate Neuroscience Education, 11*(1), A44. https://www.ncbi.nlm.nih.gov/pmc/ articles/PMC3592737/ PMID:23493445

Whitworth, S. (2022, April 22). *When was Minecraft: Education Edition launched? Exploring the history behind the game.* https://www.sportskeeda.com/minecraft/when-minecraft-education-edition-launched-exploring-history-behind-game

Wikipedia. (n.d.a). *Learning Analytics.* https://en.wikipedia.org/wiki/Learning_analytics

Wikipedia. (n.d.b). *Learning Management Systems.* https://en.wikipedia.org/wiki/Learning_management_system

Wilbanks, L. R. (2016). *Cyber Security Requirements for Institutions of Higher Education.* https://fsaconferences.ed.gov/conferences/library/2016/NASFAA/2016NASFAACybersecurityRequirementsforIHEs.pdf

Wiley Online Library. (2019). *Reevaluating the initial impact of John Broadus Watson on American psychology: The necessity of comparative parameters.* Retrieved from: https://onlinelibrary.wiley.com/doi/full/10.1002/jhbs.21962

Williams, R. (2021, December 21). Drone Racing League & Draganfly go back to school. *Boardroom.* https://boardroom.tv/drone-racing-league-draganfly-stem-program/

Williams, M. K., Foulger, T. S., & Wetzel, K. (2009). Preparing preservice teachers for 21st century classrooms: Transforming attitudes and behaviors about technology. *Journal of Technology and Teacher Education, 17*(3), 393–418.

Wilner, A. S., Luce, H., Ouellet, E., Williams, O., & Costa, N. (2021). From public health to cyber hygiene: Cybersecurity and Canada's healthcare sector. *International Journal (Toronto, Ont.), 76*(4), 522–543. doi:10.1177/00207020211067946

Wing, J. M. (2008). Computational thinking and thinking about computing. *Philosophical Transactions of the Royal Society A: Mathematical, physical, and engineering sciences, 366*(1881), 3717–3725. doi:10.1098/rsta.2008.0118

Wing, J. M. (2006). Computational thinking. *Communications of the ACM, 49*(3), 33–35. doi:10.1145/1118178.1118215

Wing, J. M. (2017). Computational thinking's influence on research and education for all. *Italian Journal of Educational Technology, 25*(2), 7–14. doi:10.17471/2499-4324/922

Winters, M. (2022). *How sports marketing and athlete branding influence public consumption.* https://digitalcommons.usf.edu/cgi/viewcontent.cgi?filename=1&article=1669&context=usf_ourconference&type=additional

Wipawasombat, M. O. (2021). *Characteristics of smartphone to support online study during COVID-19 situation* [Doctoral dissertation]. Thammasat University.

Witherspoon, E. B., Hugashi, R., Schunn, C., Baehr, E., & Shoop, R. (2017). Developing computational thinking through a virtual robotics programming curriculum. *ACM Transactions on Computing Education, 18*(1), 1–20. doi:10.1145/3104982

Wlodkowski, R. J., & Ginsberg, M. B. (1995, September 1). A framework for culturally responsive teaching. *Educational Leadership, 53*(1). https://www.ascd.org/el/articles/a-framework-for-culturally-responsive-teaching

Wolpert-Gawron, H. (2015, August 13). *What the heck is project based learing?* Edutopia. https://www.edutopia.org/blog/what-heck-project-based-learning-heather-wolpert-gawron

World Health Organization. (2019). Department of Noncommunicable Diseases and Mental Health: Our goal is to build a better, healthier future for people in the Region (No. WHO-EM/NMH/001/E). World Health Organization. Regional Office for the Eastern Mediterranean.

Wray, S. (2020, August 27). *Flying taxi trials in cities set to expand.* https://cities-today.com/cities-progress-flying-taxi-plans/

Wright, D. (2020, Nov 24). *Selecting a risk management framework for your organization.* https://www.pluralsight.com/guides/selecting-a-risk-management-framework-for-your-organization

Wright, S. (2020, October 22). Black woman launches collegiate esports & gaming company: GameStop, Intel and Nacon Gaming agree to support. *Washington Informer, 56*(1), 34.

Xingjie, Y., & Huaqun, G. (2019). A Survey on IIoT Securit. *IEEE VTS Asia Pacific Wireless Communications Symposium (APWCS)*, Singapore.

Xingshu, C., Qiang, H., Yitong, W., Long, G., & Yi, Z. (2019). Research on low-rate DDoS attack of SDN network in cloud environment. *Journal of Communication, 40*(6), 210.

Yan, L., Yiqun, Z., & Tengfei, L. (2017). Design of environmental monitoring system for intelligent classroom. *Electron Technology, 46*(05), 38–41.

Yeleswarapu, P. (2021). *Cybersecurity and EdTech: Securing the Cyberspace for Online Education.* https://www.blusapphire.com/blog/cybersecurity-in-edtech

Younes, S. S., Alharbi, A. H., & Aboeldahab, M. M. (2021). Measuring the impact of an AI-enabled mobile application for university students. *Mobile Information Systems.*

Young, A. (2022, Feb 3). Online sports games like FIFA and F1 help children develop key skills. *Express.* https://draweb.njcu.edu/login?url=https://draweb.njcu.edu:2073/newspapers/online-sports-games-like-fifa-f1-help-children/docview/2625126097/se-2?accountid=12793

Young. (2017). *'Precision Education' Hopes to Apply Big Data to Lift Diverse Student Groups.* Digital Learning in Higher Ed. https://www.edsurge.com/news/topics/digital-learning-in-higher-ed

Yuen, A. H. K. (2010). Blended learning in Higher Education: An Exploration of Teaching Approaches. *Proceedings of the 18th International Conference on Computers in Education.*

Yulkifli, Y., Yohandri, Y., & Azis, H. (2022). Development of physics e-module based on integrated project-based learning model with Ethno-STEM approach on smartphones for senior high school students. *Momentum: Physics Education Journal*, 93–103.

Yusuf Güven, Y., Gülgün, S., Manav, C., Bakır, B., & Zeynep Gürkaş Aydın, G. (2022). Multiple Classifications of Cyberattacks using Machine Learning. *Electrica.*, *22*(2), 313–320. doi:10.54614/electrica.2022.22031

Zabala, J. (1995). *The SETT framework: Critical areas to consider when making informed assistive technology decisions* (ERIC Document Reproduction Service No. ED381962). Region IV Education Service Center. https://eric.ed.gov/?id=ED381962

Zabala, J., Bowser, G., & Korsten, J. (2005). SETT and ReSETT: Concepts for AT implementation. *Closing the Gap*, *23*(5), 1–4.

Zaki, M. (2019). *The relationship between segmentation and question location within mobile video platforms for enhancing the ability of recall.* Academic Press.

Zaman, H. (2013). *Is the Taliban threatening Georgia with revenge? A shocking video from YouTube.* Retrieved from: https://www.palitravideo.ge/garthoba/skhvadaskhva/32044-gaiziare-bedniereba-erthi-qilidan-sayvareli-sasmeli-akhali-shefuthvith.html?start=140&fullComments

Zhang-Kennedy, L., & Chiasson, S. (2020) A Systematic Review of Multimedia Tools for Cybersecurity Awareness and Education. *ACM Comput. Surv.*, *54*(1). doi:10.1145/3427920

Zhao, J. (2022, Mar 31). *How to create a cybersecurity incident response plan.* https://hyperproof.io/resource/cybersecurity-incident-response-plan/

Zhijun, W., Qing, X., Jingjie, W., Meng, Y., & Liang, L. (2020). Low-rate DDoS attack detection based on factorization machine in software defined network. *IEEE Access: Practical Innovations, Open Solutions*, *8*, 7404–17418.

Zitter, L. (2020, August 7). How VR and AR can be used to support students with special needs. *TechLearningMagazine*. Retrieved July 17, 2022, from https://www.techlearning.com/how-to/how-vr-and-ar-can-be-used-to-support-students-with-special-needs

About the Contributors

Remberto Jimenez is an educator at New Jersey City University's Department of Educational Technology. He is also the Director of Learning and Development for an advertising/media firm in New York City. Dr. Jimenez graduated with his Ed.D. in the Educational Technology Leadership program at New Jersey City University. He has earned a Bachelor of Arts in Mathematics from New Jersey City University, a Master of Art, and a Post Master's Certificate in Educational Communications and Technology from New York University. Dr. Jimenez's research interests include Educational Technology, Active Learning, Distance Learning, instructional design, workplace learning, and Student Retention and Persistence.

Veronica E. O'Neill is an educator at New Jersey City University's School of Business. Dr. O'Neill graduated with her Ed.D. in the Educational Technology Leadership program at New Jersey City University. She has earned a Bachelor of Arts in Biology/Sociology from the College of the Holy Cross, an MBA in Accounting from Fairleigh Dickinson University, and a Master of Science in Organizational Leadership from Regis University. Dr. O'Neill's research interests include Educational Technology, Active Learning, Distance Learning, and Student Retention and Persistence. Prior to becoming an educator, she had a 26 year career in a major Wall Street firm.

* * *

Guy Albertini is the Associate Vice President and Chief Information Security Officer for Rutgers, the State University of New Jersey. He has over 35 years of experience in Information Technology, Information Security, Systems and Network Engineering, and Project Management. Guy's mission is to assist organizations in meeting their strategic goals with minimal cyber risk and firmly believes that security is a business enabler. In addition to Higher Education, Guy worked in Healthcare, Pharmaceutical, Manufacturing, and corporate settings. He is also the President of G-Sharp Security, holds a Master's in Information Security, a CISSP, GCIA, and ITIL. He's a member of InfraGard, ISSA and serves as an Auxiliarist for the U.S. Marine Corps Cyber Auxiliary program.

Özge Andiç-Çakir is Associate Professor at the Department of Civil Engineering of Ege University has been. She got her Bachelor's, Master's and Ph.D. degrees at Ege University and worked at TU Delft, Netherlands as Turkish Council of Higher Education research fellow following her studies. She has coordinated several R&D projects in engineering materials and in engineering education. She has been teaching testing and analysis of civil engineering materials and concrete technology. She is currently an active member of multidisciplinary research team called "Biodesign Team Turkey" since 2016. () Until now, she has actively involved in 53 projects and published 82 papers and prepared 7 book chapters/reports.

Joanna Antoniou graduated from NJCU with a Doctorate in Educational Technology Leadership in May 2021. She has been serving the students of Passaic Public Schools since 2004 and currently serves as the Supervisor of Educational Technology. She has been in the educational technology field for over 10 years, bringing in one of the first largest one-to-one Chromebook initiatives in NJ to the Passaic school district. She was also the recipient of the ISTE Making IT Happen award in 2020.

Alev Ateş-Çobanoğlu is an Associate Professor of Computer Education and Instructional Technology (CEIT) program of Faculty of Education, Ege University. She received her M.Sc in the Dokuz Eylul University in 2005. She had worked as an Information and Communication Technology (ICT) teacher at a high school of Ministry of National Education (MoNE) for three years. She received her PhD in Curriculum and Instruction from Ege University in 2013. Her academic interests are blended learning, ICT integration in education, instructional technology and instructional design.

Gulben Calis received her Bachelor of Science degree in Civil Engineering from Istanbul Technical University, Türkiye. She continued her studies at the Department of Civil Engineering at Ege University, Türkiye, where she obtained her MS and PhD in 2004 and 2009, respectively. She worked as a postdoctoral researcher at the University of Southern California between 2010 and 2012. In 2013, she joined Ege University, Türkiye as an Assistant Professor of Civil Engineering. She was promoted to Associate Professor in 2018 and is appointed Head of Construction Management Division at the Department of Civil Engineering in January 2018. Dr. Calis's research focuses on the data acquisition and big data analysis for intelligent and interactive built environments as well as prediction models, alert and decision-making tools to improve human-building interaction, built-environment efficiency, sustainability, and maintainability. In addition, she works on risk management and resilience of unexpected events and disasters. She is advising several Ph.D. students, several masters and undergraduate students in the "Intelligent Built Environments" focus area. Dr. Çalış authored and co-authored over 100 papers in peer-reviewed journals and conferences. She serves as an reviewer for several journals including Elsevier's Automation in Construction and Energy and Buildings; ASCE's Journal of Computing in Civil Engineering and Journal of Management in Engineering. She is involved in several research projects funded under the EU Framework including Horizon 2020 and COST. She is the representative of EGE University at the European Energy Research Alliance (EERA) and the selected member of Human-Data Interaction (HDI) committee of the European Council on Computing in Construction (EC3). Dr. Calis works as an external expert for several organizations and councils including the Scientific and Technological Research Council of Türkiye (TÜBİTAK), Nordic Energy Research and the European Commission.

Beril Ceylan has been working at the department of Computer Education and Instructional Technology on Education Faculty at Ege University since 2005. She had her Ph.D. degree in 2015. She is interested in technology integration, educational material design, and instructional design. She has many book chapters, articles, and presentations.

Karen Cotter has been involved in education for over 25 years both teaching and conducting workshops on STEM/STEAM-related topics in grades 6 -16. She is currently working as an adjunct professor and consultant in Educational Technology and Course Instructional Design. Additionally, Dr. Cotter is also working to incorporate social-emotional learning into her work as it relates to STEM practices. Not only is she enthusiastic about sharing new and innovative ways to help students actively engage in coursework but her incorporation of technology has been a mainstay. Her love of sharing student-centered strategies focuses on nurturing 21st-century skills (collaboration, creativity, communication, and problem-solving) that include both technology and hands-on approaches. This led to her doctoral research which sought to understand how the use of gamification in a STEM Bridge program may impact a sense of community among underrepresented students. To support faculty in creating more active learning environments in their classes, she recently completed the Applying the Quality Matters Rubric workshop. Karen has presented at numerous conferences: ISTE, NJSAL, ASHIE, HACU, ISSOTL, Montgomery Community College Technology, and Learning Conference, and the New Jersey State Science convention. She has conducted multiple Project-based workshops, new-teacher training seminars, and has worked with faculty to design lessons that focus on student-centered learning using innovative practices infused with Educational Technology. She is a CODiE and International Serious Play judge and also serves on the NJCU College of Education Advisory Board. Karen holds a doctorate in Educational Technology Leadership from New Jersey City University, a Master of Arts degree in Elementary Science Education from Farleigh Dickinson University, and a Bachelor of Science in Nursing from East Carolina University as well as a School Nurse Certificate in School Nursing from Caldwell University.

Orhan Dagdeviren received the B.Sc. and M.Sc. degrees in computer engineering from Izmir Institute of Technology, Izmir, Turkey, in 2004 and 2006, respectively, and the Ph.D. degree from the International Computer Institute, Ege University, Izmir, in 2010. He is a professor in computer engineering department in Ege University. His interests lie in the distributed computing, applied graph theory, and computer networking areas.

Swathi Mirthika G. L. has completed her Masters in Information Technology at Vel Tech Multi Tech Dr.RR Dr.SR Engineering College (2013) and completed her B.Tech Information Technology at Sasurie College of Engineering (2010). She has teaching experience of 3.5 years. Presented papers in various conferences and published papers in journals. Currently doing her Ph.d (Research) under SRM Institute of Science and Technology as full time scholar. Active researcher in Medical Recommendations, Knowledge Graph, Deep Learning, etc.

Stephen Harmon serves as the executive director of the Center for 21st Century Universities (C21U), associate dean of research in Georgia Tech Professional Education (GTPE) and as a professor at the Georgia Tech College of Design. At GTPE and C21U, he leads the invention, prototyping, and validation efforts associated with educational innovation in higher education. His previous position was professor and chair of the Learning Technologies Division in the College of Education and Human Development at Georgia State University. He earned a masters and doctorate in instructional technology, with a cognate in global policy studies, from the University of Georgia. Dr. Harmon's research centers on educational uses of emerging technologies and has, for the last few years, focused on eLearning, particularly with respect to synchronous, online learning environments. He is a past president of the Association of Educational

Communications and Technology, an international professional association of thousands of educators and others whose activities are directed toward improving instruction through technology.

Patricia Holzman has been an educator and technology coordinator for over 35 years specializing in providing educational services for students with multiple disabilities.

José Luis Jiménez is Project Coordinator VE/COIL. Researcher in virtual exchange topics, a specialist in curriculum design, and a university professor with more than 35 years of international experience. Research areas: Online collaborative learning, journalism, and democratic processes, human rights, complex systems, and the environment, sustainable development, and human ecology. Ph.D. Candidate in Comparative Studies at Florida Atlantic University. In 1993 he was honored with a scholarship from the Organization of American States to do his Master of Arts at The American University, Washington D.C.

K. Suresh Joesph received his Bachelor Degree in Computer Science & Engineering from Bharathiar University and a Master Degree in Computer Science & Engineering from the University of Madras during 1999 and 2003 respectively. He received his Doctoral Degree in Computer Science & Engineering from Anna University in 2013. Presently he is working as an Associate Professor in the Department of Computer Science, Pondicherry University. His areas of research interest include Services Computing and Image Processing. He is having more than 50 research publications in reputed and Peer-reviewed journals.

Abinaya K. completed B.E. from Avinashilingam University, M.Tech from K. Ramakrishnan College of Technology and pursuing PhD under SRM University. Her area of Research is Deep Learning, and has teaching experience of 3 years. Published papers in National and International journals.

Mehmet Emin Kaval graduated from Ege University School of Dentistry in 2004 and began his doctorate education in the Department of Endodontics of the same faculty. He completed his PhD degree in Health Science Institution of Ege University in 2010. He received the title of Associate Professor in 2017 and is currently continuing his clinical and academic career in the Department of Endodontics at Ege University, School of Dentistry. He is a member of the Turkish Dental Association, the Turkish Endodontic Society, and the European Society of Endodontology. His research interests are endodontic surgery, root canal preparation techniques, endodontic retreatment and electronic apex locators. He is the section editor of the Journal of Ege University School of Dentistry and board member of various international peer-reviewed journals.

Rita Komalasari is a lecturer at Yarsi University. Her current work is focused on the relationship between cybersecurity and public health.

Palanivel Kuppusamy received his Bachelor of Engineering in Computer Science & Engineering and Master of Technology in Computer Science & Engineering from Bharathiar University, Coimbatore, India, and Pondicherry University, Puducherry, India, in 1994 and1998 respectively. Presently he is working as a Systems Analyst in the Computer Centre of Pondicherry University, India. His field of interest is Software architecture, emerging technology, computer networks, and software architecture. He has more than two decades of experience in the field of computer applications, teaching and Research in Pondicherry University.

Amir Manzoor holds a PhD in Management Sciences. He is a graduate of NED University, Pakistan, Lahore University of Management Sciences (LUMS), Pakistan and Bangor University, United Kingdom. He has more than 20 years of diverse professional and teaching experience working at many renowned national and internal organizations and higher education institutions. His research interests include E-commerce, Strategic Management, Enterprise Resource Planning (ERP), Project Management, Supply Chain Management, Data Analysis, and Technology applications.

Cari Marks is an educator in Virginia.

Peter McAliney, PhD, is currently Director of Professional and Executive Education at Rutgers University. Since beginning his career in Management Information Systems on Wall Street, he has held leadership positions in the private sector and management consulting. These combined perspectives are now focused on developing programs that can support 21st century careers for professionals and rising executives. His credibility as an academic, as someone who has worked with C-level executives in a variety of industries, and one who has designed programs employed as part of workforce development initiatives can facilitate the organizational change brought about by increased human-computer interaction in the workplace, the emerging nature of organizations that address structural changes in the economy, and the importance for individuals of developing lifelong learning plans to address the increased rate of change that characterizes today's work environment. Peter received his PhD in higher education and workplace learning from NYU Steinhardt.

Kathryn Nieves Licwinko, Ed.D., is dedicated to using technology to support all learners in the classroom. She is currently a Teacher/Coordinator of Educational Technology Integration for the Wayne Township Public School District. Previously, she was a middle school special education teacher. Kathryn has presented nationally about special education, assistive technology, accessibility in curriculum design, online learning, blended learning, professional development, and supportive learning frameworks. Her writing and research have been featured in the Journal of Special Education Technology, Google Transformation Center, and Edutopia. Kathryn is a Google Certified Innovator and Trainer and is the founder of the platform Assembling Inclusion, which centers on making society more inclusive for all learners.

İbrahim H. Özdemir is an M.A. student in the Department of Computer Education and Instructional Technology at Ege University, Turkey. He is currently working at Kuika Software as an Educational Specialist. His research interests are instructional technology, cognitive, cognitive load, blended learning, and motivation in learning.

Nagaraj P. holds a Ph.D. degree in Computer Science and Engineering and has vast research experience in the discipline of Data Science and Analytics, Computational Intelligence. He has over 13 years of Teaching and Research Experience. He serves as a Guest editor for Frontiers in Artificial Intelligence, a peer-reviewed journal published by Frontiers Media S.A. As an author has published several articles in reputed journals like International Journal of Imaging Systems and Technology (IMA), Diabetes, Metabolic Syndrome and Obesity: Targets and Therapy, International Journal of Healthcare Information

Systems and Informatics (IJHISI), IEEE Access, and also several works as Book Chapters in Lecture Notes on Data Engineering and Communications Technologies, Studies in Computational Intelligence, Communications in Computer and Information Science, Lecture Notes in Networks and Systems, Advances in Intelligent Systems and Computing published by Springer and also works on Elsevier Book entitled Cognitive and Soft Computing Techniques for the Analysis of Healthcare Data. He has published more papers at IEEE Conference. The majority of the articles published were based on the application of health care data analytics, health for engineering applications, Diabetes Healthcare Management, Optimization Techniques, Networks, and Security, etc., He has participated in various events like webinars, workshops, and conferences and had been Resource Person in various seminars, Faculty Development Program, and workshop. He also serves as a journal reviewer in top listed Journals like IEEE Access, Applied Soft Computing, etc.

Sedar Fred Pougaza has been a professor of Economics, Finance, Business Statistics, at New Jersey City University since 2017 and at Stockton University since 2021. Professor Pougaza has taught United States university – level courses Money and Banking, Macroeconomics, Microeconomics, and credit selected studies for summer 2019 in Shanghai, China. He pursued doctoral studies in Economics at The New School University (The New School for Social Research) in New York. He earned the Master's degree in Economics from New School University in New York and Master's degree in Economics from Université de Cocody-Abidjan (now known as Université Félix Houphouët-Boigny, Abidjan, Ivory Coast). He is also completing doctorate in Educational Technology Leadership in the Department of Educational Technology at New Jersey City University, New Jersey, United States. He is fluent in French, Sango, and English. He also has some knowledge of Spanish. He likes jogging, exercising, volunteering, traveling, riding a bicycle, reading, writing, singing, watching documentaries, playing sports, and exploring the nature.

Shannon Ramsaywak is a Principal at Nathanial Rand, Inc. (NRC) leading their cybersecurity practice. With over 21 years of industry experience, Ramsaywak began as a network engineer connecting trading floors to the New York Stock Exchange, then as a system administrator building and maintaining critical systems for one of the world's largest transportation systems, the New York State Metropolitan Transportation Agency (MTA). Ramsaywak assumed the lead security role in a fledgling cybersecurity program in 2005 at the MTA Long Island Rail Road, Co., and over the next 10 years, as their Chief Information Security Officer (CISO), grew the entire security program into an enterprise leading model protecting the lives of the daily commuters within the NYC metro area. Other cybersecurity initiatives he has led include his work at KIND Snacks, LLC as their inaugural CISO and Chief Technology Officer (CTO) and as Corporate CISO for the Global Enterprise Division at NBCUniversal overseeing its global corporate cybersecurity practice.

Catherine Roche is a full-time faculty member in the Business Department at SUNY Rockland Community College. In 2013 she was awarded the SUNY Chancellor's Award for Excellence in Teaching. She is a former Business Department and Business Division/Professional Studies Chair. She has served as the campus COIL Coordinator since 2014 and has been involved in virtual exchange collaborations with Morocco, the Netherlands, Iraq, Colombia, and Jordan. She is an advocate for online and experiential learning and has served as a mentor for business honors students. She has co-authored three publications and has presented at numerous national and international conferences.

Fırat Sarsar is an Associate Professor at Ege University, Department of Computer Education and Instructional Technology in Turkey. He earned his BA and MS degrees in the Department of Computer Education and Instructional Technology in Turkey. Dr. Sarsar graduated from Georgia State University in USA with his Ph.D. in Instructional Technology as a Fulbright scholar in 2014. His PhD was fully funded by Fulbright Scholarship. He was in many project related to technology integration and teacher education. He holds the Association for Educational Communications and Technology (AECT) Cochran Intern Award in 2013 which is given for recognition of young leaders of the field. Currently, He teaches "Social Media and Web2.0 tools in Education", "Internet for Educator", Technology Integration in Education" and "e-Learning Design" courses in undergrad and graduate levels in Ege University. His research interests are motivation, online learning, mobile technologies, e-learning and online feedback strategies. He is currently the Director of Distance Learning Application and Research Center and also Vice-Director of Ege University Continuing Education Center.

Christopher Shamburg is Professor of Educational Technology and the Coordinator of the Ed.D. in Educational Technology Leadership at New Jersey City University.

Nicole Simon, PhD, teaches General Science Studies courses in the Math Department at Nassau Community College. She holds a doctorate in Educational Technology Management and Instructional Design. Her research has focused on the uses of technology within the scientific disciplines and the use of virtual experimentation in laboratory settings.

B. Sivakumar is an Associate Professor at SRM Institute of Science and Technology, who has expansive teaching experience of around 19 years of computer science and engineering at various reputed institutions. Most of his research interest is based on Artificial Intelligence and Deep Learning. He is an active member in various research societies related to AI and Deep Learning. He is having affable contact with active researchers in and around the country. His recent research work is based on fusion-based image forgery detection using AI, weather forecast prediction for solar radiation, automatic cardio ailment for identification and prevention, cardiovascular disease identification, and so on. In the last fifteen years, he has played a pivotal role in various technical symposiums and project Expo. He is serving as a reviewer of many reputed Journals and reviewed quality papers of peer researchers in unbiased manner. He has also completed one AICTE-funded project and also actively working on filing new patents. Currently, he is working on a funded project on controller design for smart industry automation. He is also working on various international project funding agencies' proposals to boost his research findings. Apart from this he continues his career as a passionate Professor and stay updated with the trends of IT industry and looks forward to incorporate it into inter disciplinary research and also taking an active part in Industry-Academia collaborations on the academics and research front.

Dana Smerda-Mason began her teaching career with the Bayonne Board of Education as a high school band teacher, and after eight years became a technology teacher at Henry E. Harris Community School, for a total of 17 years of service in the district. She is now an adjunct professor at New Jersey City University. Dr. Mason holds a Bachelor of Music in Music Performance from New York University, a Master of Arts in Educational Technology from New Jersey City University, where she also earned her Doctorate in Educational Technology Leadership. Dr. Mason became passionate about STEAM education after being accepted to the Honeywell Educators at Space Academy program where she earned a scholarship to attend this program at the NASA training center in Huntsville, AL. There she completed aspects of astronaut training and STEAM education. The following year she was accepted to the NASA Advanced Educator Training where she earned the Commander's Cup Award for teamwork and leadership. She also earned a grant through the Honeywell Institute for Ecosystems Education, where her Ecology Club earned a bronze and silver distinction in watershed and waste management categories through New Jersey Audubon. As the Media and Communications Chair of the Bayonne Water Guardians, Dr. Mason continues to support the program with community outreach efforts. Dr. Mason an adjunct professor in the Educational Technology Department at New Jersey City University, where she completed her doctoral studies. Her dissertation focused on concerns and solutions in STEAM education professional development, and she has been presenting results associated with this research at a variety of conferences in New Jersey as well as at the Space Exploration Educators Conference at the NASA Space Center in Houston, TX. In 2020 she was interviewed for the podcast Taking CTRL in STEM and Ed Tech, as a successful female in the field. She has also had her research featured in two publications, and was selected to teach STEAM education to middle school students in Shenzhen, China in 2019. Recently, she became the lead educator and board member of We are GUTSY, Inc., a non-profit organization that works with teachers in Guyana to integrate social and emotional learning and character education to their curriculum. Dr. Mason also serves as a board member for the North East Digital Learning Association (NEDLA), developing educational programming.

Ruba Soundar Kathavarayan received the A.M.I.E., degree in Computer Science and Engineering from The Institution of Engineers (India) in 2000. He received the M.E., and Ph.D., degrees in Computer Science and Engineering from Anna University, Chennai in the year 2004 and 2010 respectively. Currently he is an Associate Professor in Computer Science and Engineering Department of Mepco Schlenk Engineering College, Sivakasi, Tamil Nadu, India. He has authored / coauthored over 120 research articles in various Journals and Conferences in the areas of Cloud Computing, Image Processing, Wireless and Wired Networking.

Muthamil Sudar K. is working as an Assistant Professor in the Department of Computer Science and Engineering, Mepco Schlenk Engineering College, Sivakasi, Tamil Nādu. He has 6 years of teaching and research experience. His research interest includes Network Security, Software Defined Networking, and Machine learning techniques

Patricia E. Szobonya is Associate Professor and Program Director of the Legal Studies, Paralegal Studies, Criminal Justice, and Corporate Homeland Security programs at Rockland Community College. She is a graduate of New York Law School and licensed to practice law in New York and New Jersey. She also teaches in the Legal Studies, Criminal Justice, Business and Multi-Cultural Studies disciplines. She has participated in academic international virtual collaborations with Universities in Morocco, China, Mexico and Columbia. She co-authored a book chapter in Virtual exchange: towards digital equity in internationalisation, a collection of short papers on virtual international exchange.

Wendy Thompson has been an educator for over 30 years specializing in providing educational services for students with multiple disabilities.

Deepa V. completed her B.Tech Information Technology at PET Engineering College (2015) and She completed her Masters in Computer Science and Engineering at Kalasalingam Academy of Research and Education (2019). Presented papers in various conferences and published papers in journals. Currently doing her Ph.D. (Research) under SRM Institute of Science and Technology, Kattankulathur as full time scholar. Active researcher in SDN, Satellite Communication, and Networking Technologies.

Muneeswaran Vasudevan holds a Ph.D degree in Electronics and Communication Engineering and have vast research experience in discipline of Swarm Intelligence, Image/Signal Processing. He serves as a Guest editor for Applied Soft Computing, a peer reviewed journal published by Elsevier. As an author has published several articles in reputed journals Journal of Supercomputing, IEEE Access, Cognitive Systems Research and also several works as Book Chapters in Lecture notes in Computer Science, Advances in Intelligent Systems and Computing, Lecture Notes in Electrical Engineering and Smart Innovation, Systems and Technologies published by Springer. Majority of the articles published was based on the application of swarm intelligence for engineering applications viz., Medical Image Segmentation, optimization of Neural Networks etc., On his credit, there are several awards including Publons Peer Review Awards 2018 for placing in the top 1% of reviewers in Computer Science. At present he is working on projects related to Brain tumor segmentation using swarm intelligence techniques and Key areas in Medical Image Segmentation.

Index

D

E

F

G

H

I

J

K

L

M

N

O

P

Q

R

S

T

U

V

W